Praise for Gary J. Bass's

The Blood Telegram

Winner of the Society for Historians of American Foreign
Relations' Robert H. Ferrell Book Prize
Winner of the Ramnath Goenka Award in India

"Amazing. . . . Nixon and Kissinger spent the decades after leaving office burnishing their images as great statesmen. This book goes a long way in showing just how undeserved those reputations are."   —Dexter Filkins,
The New York Times Book Review

"Bass has defeated the attempted cover-up through laborious culling of relevant sections of the Nixon White House tapes, declassified State Department documents and interviews with former officials. . . . After reading Bass's account of this shameful episode, one has to . . . conclude that where the Bengalis were concerned, Kissinger and Nixon simply did not give a damn."   —Neil Sheehan, *The Washington Post*

"Bass takes us inside the Oval Office to reveal the scandalous role America played in the 1971 slaughter in what is now Bangladesh. Largely unknown here, the story combines the human tragedy of Darfur, the superpower geopolitics of the Cuban missile crisis and the illegal shenanigans of Iran-contra. . . . [A] harrowing tale."   —Peter Baker,
The New York Times (Favorite Book of the Year)

"Indispensable. . . . Steeped in the forensic skills of a professional academic historian, [Bass] possesses the imaginative energies of a classical moralist, and he tells the story of the choices and the decisions that led to the slaughter in Bengal . . . appropriately as a moral saga."
—Suni'

"Absorbing. . . . Bass draws up a s
Kissinger."   —Pa

"A helpful reminder of Nixon's true character. In *The Blood Telegram*, Bass expertly recounts the stunning indifference of Nixon and . . . Kissinger to the reports from U.S. diplomats of Pakistani genocide. . . . Vivid, often disquieting detail from Oval Office tapes unearthed by Bass. . . . Bass has performed an essential function." —*The Guardian* (London)

"Excellent. . . . The best book I read this year was Gary Bass's *The Blood Telegram*. . . . Superb reporting and excellent analysis." —Isaac Chotiner, *The New Republic* (Best Books of the Year)

"Stellar. . . . Astonishing. . . . A meticulously researched and searing indictment." —*Foreign Policy*

"[A] superb book. . . . Bass deploys White House recordings, including several new transcripts, to excellent effect. . . . Astonishing. . . . A morally serious book that nevertheless reads like a first-rate novel." —*The Times Literary Supplement* (London)

"It was a non-subject for scholars, a no man's land for knowledge . . . [u]ntil the arrival of a memorable book by Princeton professor Gary Bass. . . . While doing justice to the victims, also, for the first time, draws out for us its lessons. . . . The book is also a tribute to politics in its true sense. . . . I do want readers to be aware of the appearance of Gary Bass's book, which I hope will be widely read (and translated into French!). . . . Required reading." —Bernard-Henri Lévy, *Le Point*

"The definitive account. . . . Nuanced yet unflinching. . . . Fascinating and truly frightening." —*The Daily Beast*

"Blistering. . . . [A] must-read." —*The New York Post*

"Gripping, thoroughly researched, concisely organized, and engagingly written. . . . Impressive." —Harold H. Saunders, *Foreign Affairs*

"A searing indictment. . . . Shocking. . . . A deeply cautionary tale." —*The Globe and Mail* (Toronto)

"A vital contribution. . . . Meticulous scholarship. . . . An extraordinary grasp of the internal politics of [India]. . . . Important."
—Sumit Ganguly, *International Security*

"Gripping and excruciating. . . . A powerful reminder of the frailty of international law in international crises. . . . A must-read. . . . Remarkable." —*European Journal of International Law* (Best Books of the Year)

"Fascinating. . . . [A] rich book, constantly shifting between Washington, New Delhi and Islamabad, all corners of the narrative expertly covered by the author. . . . Bass's skill in unraveling the complex strands . . . is admirable."
—Michael Young, *The National* (Abu Dhabi)

"Amazing. . . . Bass exhumes the tragic, relatively unknown story." —*The Japan Times*

"It has been a long time since I have read a book that has spoken as powerfully to me as *The Blood Telegram*. The relevancy and power of this book stems from the basic moral dilemmas that it addresses on practically every page. Every person planning to join the United States Foreign Service, or already serving should read this book." —Jon P. Dorschner, *American Diplomacy*

"Harrowing. . . . A damning portrait. . . . Tremendously lucid. . . . Bass holds these leaders to a much-needed reckoning. A deeply incisive lesson for today's leaders and electorate."
—*Kirkus Reviews*, starred review (Best Books of the Year)

"With urgent, cinematic immediacy, Gary Bass reconstructs a critical—and, to this day, profoundly consequential—chapter of Cold War history defined by appalling American complicity in genocidal atrocity and terrifyingly high-stakes superpower brinkmanship. It is a story of immense scope, vividly populated by figures of enduring fascination and ripe with implications for the ongoing struggle to strike a more honorable balance between wartime realpolitik and our ideals of common humanity." —Philip Gourevitch, author of *We Wish to Inform You That Tomorrow We Will Be Killed with Our Families*

"The book sets the record straight of a disgraceful period in U.S. foreign policy. . . . Brutal detail. . . . Nixon stands disgraced over Watergate but his willful role in the genocide in East Pakistan had not till now received the full historical attention it deserved."   —*The Times of India*

"Vivid. . . . Never fails to hold the reader's attention. . . . A thoroughly researched and damning indictment. . . . Bass demolishes Kissinger's defense. . . . Deeply perceptive."
                                                        —*Outlook India*

"A scathing indictment. . . . Bass . . . dismantles the smug aura of success that has generally been attached to the Kissinger-Nixon era. . . . The book combines a racy narrative with meticulous research and excellent academic rigor. . . . Bass offers a fresh perspective."   —*The Hindu*

"Gripping. His material is so rich and his research so detailed that it is difficult to put down the book. . . . Bass has accomplished something truly remarkable."   —*The Asian Age*

"[A] gripping, if sordid, story. . . . A startling revelation."
                                                        —*Tehelka*

"Most admirable and thorough. . . . An accomplished scholar of human rights, Bass draws on a mass of documents and tapes to shed light. . . . Bass's cumulative indictment of Nixon and Kissinger is formidable. . . . A wealth of detail and range of insights in this fine book."
                                            —*The Telegraph* (Calcutta)

"A monumental account."   —*Economic & Political Weekly*

"Very important. . . . Painstaking. . . . Valuable. . . . A close view into the inner mind of power."   —*Himal Southasian*

"An absorbing book. . . . A fine portrayal. . . . A damning indictment. . . . Remarkable. . . . A precious contribution."
                                                —*The Daily Star* (Dhaka)

"The best single account. . . . A justly lauded work. . . . A uniquely fascinating glimpse into the operation of power at the highest levels. . . . Will certainly stand the test of time. . . . Holds invaluable truths and lessons for future generations."
—*The Dhaka Tribune*

"Eminently readable and exhaustively researched. . . . Gripping. . . . The book is peerless in the sheer quality and quantity of sources it uses. . . . An unmatched account."
—*Dawn* (Karachi)

"Gripping. . . . A chilling and bare-knuckle account. . . . A scalding view. . . . The book spares no players."
—*The News International* (Pakistan)

"Fascinating insights. . . . Unique. . . . The book is a powerful indictment of Nixon and Kissinger."
—*The Friday Times* (Lahore)

Gary J. Bass

The Blood Telegram

Gary J. Bass is the author of *Freedom's Battle: The Origins of Humanitarian Intervention* and *Stay the Hand of Vengeance: The Politics of War Crimes Tribunals*. He is a professor of politics and international affairs at Princeton University. A former reporter for *The Economist*, he often writes for *The New York Times* and has also written for *The New Yorker*, *The Washington Post*, the *Los Angeles Times*, *The Boston Globe*, *The New Republic*, *Foreign Affairs*, *Foreign Policy*, *Slate*, and other publications.

ALSO BY GARY J. BASS

Freedom's Battle: The Origins of Humanitarian Intervention

Stay the Hand of Vengeance: The Politics of War Crimes Tribunals

The Blood Telegram

The Blood Telegram

• • •

Nixon, Kissinger,
and a Forgotten Genocide

• • •

Gary J. Bass

Vintage Books
A Division of Random House LLC
New York

FIRST VINTAGE BOOKS EDITION, JULY 2014

The Library of Congress has cataloged the Knopf edition as follows:
Bass, Gary Jonathan.
The Blood telegram : Nixon, Kissinger, and a forgotten genocide / by
Gary J. Bass.—First Edition.
pages cm
Includes bibliographical references and index.
1. United States—Foreign relations—1969–1974.
2. Bangladesh—History—Revolution, 1971—Atrocities.
3. Genocide—Bangladesh.
4. Nixon, Richard M. (Richard Milhous), 1913–1994.
5. Kissinger, Henry, 1923–
6. United States—Foreign relations—South Asia.
7. South Asia—Foreign relations—United States. I. Title.
E855.B34   2013
327.73054090'47—dc23   2013014788

Vintage Trade Paperback ISBN: 978-0-307-74462-3
eBook ISBN: 978-0-385-35047-1

Book design by Betty Lew
Map by Mapping Specialists

www.vintagebooks.com

Printed in the United States of America

For K.G.B.

[T]he bloody massacre in Bangladesh caused Allende to be forgotten, the din of war in the Sinai Desert drowned out the groans of Bangladesh, . . . and so on, and on and on, until everyone has completely forgotten everything.

—MILAN KUNDERA, *The Book of Laughter and Forgetting*

Contents

Preface

Archer Blood, the United States' consul general in Dacca, was a gentlemanly diplomat raised in Virginia, a World War II navy veteran in the upswing of a promising Foreign Service career after several tours overseas. He was earnest and precise, known to some of his more unruly subordinates at the U.S. consulate as a good, conventional man.

He had come to like his posting to this impoverished, green, and swampy land. But outside of the consulate's grimy offices, in the steamy heat, the city was dying. Night after night, Blood heard the gunshots. On the night of March 25, 1971, the Pakistan army had begun a relentless crackdown on Bengalis, all across what was then East Pakistan and is today an independent Bangladesh. Untold thousands of people were shot, bombed, or burned to death in Dacca alone. Blood had spent that grim night on the roof of his official residence, watching as tracer bullets lit up the sky, listening to clattering machine guns and thumping tank guns. There were fires across the ramshackle city. He knew the people in the deathly darkness below. He liked them. Many of the civilians facing the bullets were professional colleagues; some were his friends.

It was, Blood and his staffers thought, their job to relay as much of this as they possibly could back to Washington. Witnessing one of the worst atrocities of the Cold War, Blood's consulate documented in horrific detail the slaughter of Bengali civilians: an area the size of two dozen city blocks that had been razed by gunfire; two newspaper office buildings in ruins; thatch-roofed villages in flames; specific targeting of the Bengalis' Hindu minority.

The U.S. consulate gave detailed accounts of the killings at Dacca University, ordinarily a leafy, handsome enclave. At the wrecked campus, professors had been hauled from their homes to be gunned down.

The provost of the Hindu dormitory, a respected scholar of English, was dragged out of his residence and shot in the neck. Blood listed six other faculty members "reliably reported killed by troops," with several more possibly dead. One American who had visited the campus said that students had been "mowed down" in their rooms or as they fled, with a residence hall in flames and youths being machine-gunned.[1]

"At least two mass graves on campus," Blood cabled. "Stench terrible." There were 148 corpses in one of these mass graves, according to the workmen forced to dig them. An official in the Dacca consulate estimated that at least five hundred students had been killed in the first two days of the crackdown, almost none of them fighting back. Blood reckoned that the rumored toll of a thousand dead at the university was "exaggerated, although nothing these days is inconceivable." After the massacre, he reported that an American eyewitness had seen an empty army truck arriving to get rid of a "tightly packed pile of approximately twenty five corpses," the last of many such batches of human remains.[2]

THIS WAS, BLOOD KNEW, THE LAST THING HIS SUPERIORS IN WASHINGton wanted to hear. Pakistan was an ally—a military dictatorship, but fiercely anticommunist. Blood detailed how Pakistan was using U.S. weapons—tanks, jet fighters, gigantic troop transport airplanes, jeeps, guns, ammunition—to crush the Bengalis. In one of the awkward alignments of the Cold War, President Richard Nixon had lined up the democratic United States with this authoritarian government, while the despots in the Soviet Union found themselves standing behind democratic India.

Nixon and Henry Kissinger, the brilliant White House national security advisor, were driven not just by such Cold War calculations, but a starkly personal and emotional dislike of India and Indians. Nixon enjoyed his friendship with Pakistan's military dictator, General Agha Muhammad Yahya Khan, known as Yahya, who was helping to set up the top secret opening to China. The White House did not want to be seen as doing anything that might hint at the breakup of Pakistan—no matter what was happening to civilians in the east wing of Pakistan.

The onslaught would continue for months. The Dacca consulate stubbornly kept up its reporting. But, Blood later recalled, his cables were met with "a deafening silence." He was not allowed to protest to the Pakistani authorities. He ratcheted up his dispatches, sending in a blistering cable tagged "Selective Genocide," urging his bosses to speak out against the atrocities being committed by the Pakistani military. The White House staff passed this up to Kissinger, who paid no heed. Then on April 6, two weeks into the slaughter, Blood and almost his entire consulate sent in a telegram formally declaring their "strong dissent"—a total repudiation of the policy that they were there to carry out. That cable—perhaps the most radical rejection of U.S. policy ever sent by its diplomats—blasted the United States for silence in the face of atrocities, for not denouncing the quashing of democracy, for showing "moral bankruptcy" in the face of what they bluntly called genocide.[3]

THIS BOOK IS ABOUT HOW TWO OF THE WORLD'S GREAT DEMOCRACIES—the United States and India—faced up to one of the most terrible humanitarian crises of the twentieth century. The slaughter in what is now Bangladesh stands as one of the cardinal moral challenges of recent history, although today it is far more familiar to South Asians than to Americans. It had a monumental impact on India, Pakistan, and Bangladesh—almost a sixth of humanity in 1971. In the dark annals of modern cruelty, it ranks as bloodier than Bosnia and by some accounts in the same rough league as Rwanda. It was a defining moment for both the United States and India, where their humane principles were put to the test.[4]

For the United States, as Archer Blood understood, a small number of atrocities are so awful that they stand outside of the normal day-to-day flow of diplomacy: the Armenian genocide, the Holocaust, Cambodia, Bosnia, Rwanda. When we think of U.S. leaders failing the test of decency in such moments, we usually think of uncaring disengagement: Franklin Roosevelt fighting World War II without taking serious steps to try to rescue Jews from the Nazi dragnet, or Bill Clinton standing idly by during the Rwandan genocide.[5]

But Pakistan's slaughter of its Bengalis in 1971 is starkly different. Here the United States was allied with the killers. The White House was actively and knowingly *supporting* a murderous regime at many of the most crucial moments. There was no question about whether the United States should intervene; it was already intervening on behalf of a military dictatorship decimating its own people.

This stands as one of the worst moments of moral blindness in

U.S. foreign policy. Pakistan's crackdown on the Bengalis was not routine or small-scale killing, not something that could be dismissed as business as usual, but a colossal and systematic onslaught. Midway through the bloodshed, both the Central Intelligence Agency and the State Department conservatively estimated that about two hundred thousand people had lost their lives. Many more would perish, cut down by Pakistani forces or dying in droves in miserable refugee camps. "The story of East Bengal will surely be written as one of the greatest nightmares of modern times," declared Edward Kennedy, who led the outcry in the Senate. But in the depths of the Cold War, Nixon and Kissinger were unyielding in their support for Pakistan, making possible horrific crimes against humanity—plausibly even a genocide—in that country's eastern wing.[6]

The ongoing Bengali slaughter led within a few months to a major war between Pakistan and India. In that time, the White House had every opportunity to grasp how bad these atrocities were. There were sober misgivings voiced in the White House, and thunderous protests from the State Department and its emissaries in Delhi and Dacca, with Archer Blood the loudest voice of all. But throughout it all, from the outbreak of civil war to the Bengali massacres to Pakistan's crushing defeat by the Indian military, Nixon and Kissinger, unfazed by detailed knowledge of the massacres, stood stoutly behind Pakistan.

As its most important international backer, the United States had great influence over Pakistan. But at almost every turning point in the crisis, Nixon and Kissinger failed to use that leverage to avert disaster. Before the shooting started, they consciously decided not to warn Pakistan's military chiefs against using violence on their own population. They did not urge caution or impose conditions that might have discouraged the Pakistani military government from butchering its own citizenry. They did not threaten the loss of U.S. support or even sanctions if Pakistan took the wrong course. They allowed the army to sweep aside the results of Pakistan's first truly free and fair democratic election, without even suggesting that the military strongmen try to work out a power-sharing deal with the Bengali leadership that had won the vote. They did not ask that Pakistan refrain from using U.S. weaponry to slaughter civilians, even though that could have impeded the military's rampage, and might have deterred the army. There was no public condemnation—nor even a private threat of it—from the president, the secretary of state, or other senior officials. The administration almost entirely contented itself with making gentle, token suggestions behind closed doors that Pakistan might lessen its brutality—and even that only after, months into the violence, it became clear that India was on the brink of attacking Pakistan.

This might give the impression of passivity, of a foreign policy on autopilot. Not so. Nixon and Kissinger actually drove their South Asia policies with gusto and impressive creativity—but only when silencing dissenters in the ranks, like Blood, or pursuing their hostility toward India. They found no appeal in India, neither out of ideological admiration for India's flawed but functioning democracy, nor from a geopolitical appreciation of the sheer size and importance of the Indian colossus. Instead, they denounced Indians individually and collectively, with an astonishingly personal and crude stream of vitriol. Alone in the Oval Office, these famous practitioners of dispassionate realpolitik were all too often propelled by emotion.

The slaughter happened at the same time that Nixon and Kissinger were planning their opening to China—a famous historic achievement that has a forgotten cost. Everyone remembers Nixon and Kissinger's months of clandestine Chinese diplomacy, followed by the amazing spectacle of the presidential visit to Mao Zedong. But what has been lost is the human toll exacted for it in Bangladesh and India. Nixon and Kissinger needed a secret channel to China, which they found in the good offices of Yahya—an impeccably discreet tyrant on warm terms with both the United States and China. While the Pakistani government was crushing the Bengalis, it was also carrying covert messages back and forth from Washington to Beijing. Archer Blood sent off his dissent telegram just three months before Kissinger took his first secret trip to Beijing, flying direct from Pakistan, which sped him on his way with hospitality, an airplane, and a cloak-and-dagger cover story. Nixon and Kissinger, always sympathetic to the Pakistani junta, were not about to condemn it while it was making itself so useful. So the Bengalis became collateral damage for realigning the global balance of power. In the bargain, Nixon and Kissinger also turned their backs on India: the strategic opening to one Asian titan meant a closing to another. Indeed, one of the very first things that the United States did with its new relationship with Mao's China was to secretly ask it to mobilize troops to threaten democratic India, in defense of Pakistan. It is absolutely right that the normalization of the American relationship with China stands as an epochal event, but those who justifiably want to celebrate it should not overlook what it meant for the Bengalis and Indians.

Kissinger and his defenders often try to shift the blame to Nixon. But the record here proves that Kissinger was almost as culpable as the president. When dealing with the White House and State Department staff, Kissinger would entertain a variety of viewpoints, showing his trademark subtlety, although pressing an anti-Indian line. But when it was just him and Nixon alone, he cannily stoked the president's fury. All the sophistication vanished, replaced with a relentless drumbeat against India. Although Kissinger billed himself around Washington as a vital restraint on Nixon's dangerous moods, here it was Kissinger who spun out of control. In the most heated moments of the crisis, when Nixon lost his nerve for a superpower confrontation with the Soviet Union that at worst could have led toward nuclear war, Kissinger goaded him on.

Nixon and Kissinger bear responsibility for a significant complicity in the slaughter of the Bengalis. This overlooked episode deserves to be a defining part of their historical reputations. But although Nixon and Kissinger have hardly been neglected by history, this major incident has largely been whitewashed out of their legacy—and not by accident. Kissinger began telling demonstrable falsehoods about the administration's record just two weeks into the crisis, and has not stopped distorting since. Nixon and Kissinger, in their vigorous efforts after Watergate to rehabilitate their own respectability as foreign policy wizards, have left us a farrago of distortions, half-truths, and outright lies about their policy toward the Bengali atrocities.[7]

To this day, four decades after the massacres, the dead hand of Nixonian cover-up still prevents Americans from knowing the full record. The White House staff routinely sanitized their records of conversations, sometimes at Kissinger's specific urging. Even now, mildewed and bogus claims of national security remain in place to bleep out particularly embarrassing portions of the White House tapes. Kissinger struck a deal with the Library of Congress that, until five years after his death, blocks researchers from seeing his papers there unless they have his written permission. Even if you could get in, according to the Library of Congress, many of Kissinger's most important papers are still hidden from daylight by a thicket of high-level classifications, security clearances, and need-to-know permissions. Kissinger did not reply to two polite requests for an interview, and then, four months later, refused outright. But against Nixon and Kissinger's own misrepresentations and immortal stonewalling, there is a different story to be found in thousands of pages of recently declassified U.S. papers, in dusty Indian archives, and on unheard hours of the White House tapes—offering a more accurate, documented account of Nixon and Kissinger's secret role in backing the perpetrators of one of the worst crimes of the twentieth century.[8]

IT WAS LEFT TO INDIA, WHICH DID NOT HAVE THE OPTION OF IGNOR-ing the slaughter of the Bengalis, to stop it. The gargantuan democracy was entwined with the tragedy next door in countless ways, from its own shocked Bengali population to its bitter confrontation with Pakistan. Indira Gandhi's government was motivated by a mix of lofty principle and brutal realpolitik: demanding an end to the slaughter of a civilian population and upholding the popular will of voters in a democratic election, but also seizing a prime opportunity to humiliate and rip apart India's hated enemy.

Indira Gandhi, India's prime minister and the great Jawaharlal Nehru's daughter, would later claim she acted "first of all, for purely humanitarian reasons." India's ambassador at the United Nations declared that his country had "absolutely nothing but the purest of motives and the purest of intentions: to rescue the people of East Bengal." But there was nothing pure about the protection of human rights. Some eminent political theorists and international lawyers have pointed to India's intervention as a singular and important case of an Asian postcolonial country launching a humanitarian intervention—a kind of war more commonly associated with Western military campaigns in Bosnia, Kosovo, and Libya. But there has been no proper chronicle of India's real motives.[9]

In fact, Indira Gandhi and her top advisers were coldly calculating strategists, even if their actions served a humane cause. India put itself in a position of breathtaking hypocrisy: demanding freedom for the Bengali people in East Pakistan, while conducting its own repression of restive populations under Indian control in Kashmir, as well as lesser-known groups like the Mizos and Nagas and—with painful irony—leftist Bengalis within India's own volatile state of West Bengal. While the Indian government emotionally spoke out on behalf of the millions of Bengalis who fled into India, its officials privately worried that these exiles might be radical subversives who would fuel more unrest and revolt in India's already shaky border states, especially West Bengal. India, in other words, was driven not just by sympathy for Bengalis, but also a certain amount of fear of revolutionary Bengalis.

While Indira Gandhi's government professed its unwavering desire for peace, she almost immediately turned to aggressive options. From the early days of the Pakistani crackdown, she had the Indian military covertly prepare for a full-scale regular war against Pakistan. India secretly had its army and security forces use bases on Indian soil to support Bengali guerrillas in their fight against the Pakistani state. India devoted enormous resources to covertly sponsoring the Bengali insurgency inside East Pakistan, providing the guerrillas with arms, training, camps, and safe passage back and forth across a porous border. Indian officials, from Gandhi on down, evaded or lied with verve, denying that they were maintaining the insurgency. But in fact, as India's own secret records prove, this massive clandestine enterprise was approved at the highest levels, involving India's intelligence services, border security forces, and army.

In the event, Pakistan rashly struck the first blow of a full-scale conventional war, with a surprise air attack in December 1971 that brought fierce combat in both West and East Pakistan. But while Indians today generally remember the war as outright Pakistani aggression, India's actual path to war shows a great degree of Indian responsibility as well. India knew it had a fearsome military advantage, and Gandhi's government used that ruthlessly. According to senior Indian generals, Gandhi wanted her forces to go to war not long after the start of Pakistan's crackdown, and had to be persuaded to wait for cooler fighting weather and more time to train. While the Indian military waited for winter, the Indian-backed insurgency bled the Pakistan army, leaving it demoralized and stretched thin. India's support for the Bengali rebels led to border clashes with Pakistani troops, and, as winter approached, to several substantial Indian incursions onto Pakistani territory. It is a patriotic delusion to imagine, as some Indian nationalists do today, that Pakistan's airstrikes were unprovoked. Still, Pakistan's air attack was a final act of folly for the military dictatorship. The war, fought in just two weeks, ended with a resounding Indian victory, and created the fledgling state of Bangladesh.

THE PRESIDENT AND THE PRIME MINISTER, IN WASHINGTON AND DELHI, were united by their need to grapple with their own democratic societies. As much as Nixon and Gandhi loathed each other, they shared a common exasperation at how their policies could be thwarted by their own people—a frustration that would in time lead both of them down their own different but alarmingly antidemocratic paths. In these two great democracies, it was not just governments but also peoples who had to confront one of the worst events of their century. Americans and Indians were challenged to make policy in a way that expressed their national sense of morality, not just their strategic interests.

The United States and India are radically different societies, in everything from wealth to ethnic composition to sheer size of population; but they do share some basic similarities in their systems of democratic governance. In both, democratic leaders were goaded and prodded by rambunctious elements at home: a free press with an ingrained habit of seeking out inconvenient or embarrassing stories; opposition politicians and partisans waiting to pounce should a president or prime minister stumble; and a public whose moral sensibilities often did not align with the dictates of the state's cold calculus of strategic interest. In both of these enormous democracies, the people were more moralistic than their governments.[10]

Americans reacted with disquiet or horror. The country's far-reaching newspapers and broadcast networks reported in shocking detail about these distant atrocities; ordinary Americans recoiled at what they learned on the news; and politicians in Congress, led by Edward Kennedy, seized the opportunity to politick against the White House. Thus even this White House found itself unable to continue its unstinting support of Pakistan through arms sales, which Kissinger would have liked to escalate, because of pressure from Congress and bureaucratic maneuvering by the State Department. Nixon and Kissinger found themselves boxed in by their country's liberal and democratic system; they had to moderate their policies, much against their will. As Kissinger complained to the president, "We are the ones who have been operating against our public opinion, against our bureaucracy, at the very edge of legality."[11]

A little further than that, actually. Nixon and Kissinger responded to these legal and democratic constraints on their authority in the classic Nixonian way: by breaking the law. Knowing full well that they were acting illegally, they provided U.S. weapons to Pakistan, which was under a U.S. arms embargo—an unknown scandal that is of a piece with the overall pattern of lawlessness that culminated with Watergate. As recently declassified documents and transcripts prove, Nixon and Kissinger approved a covert supply of sophisticated U.S. fighter airplanes via Jordan and Iran—despite explicit and emphatic warnings from both the State Department and the Defense Department that such arms transfers to Pakistan were illegal under U.S. law.

(John Mitchell, the attorney general, was in the room as Nixon and Kissinger decided on this unlawful operation, but made no objections.) Kissinger, not wanting to get caught, made it clear to the president that they were both breaking the law. Nixon went ahead anyway.

Americans' sense of outrage circulated within the administration itself. The most vociferous dissenter was Archer Blood, but he had no shortage of company. The ambassador to India, a distinguished former Republican senator named Kenneth Keating, took his opposition all the way to the Oval Office, where he confronted Nixon and Kissinger to their faces over what he called genocide. The middle ranks of the State Department, stationed in Washington, Dacca, Delhi, and even parts of West Pakistan, rose up in open defiance of the policies of the president of the United States. There were even rumblings of discontent within the National Security Council at the White House itself.

Although Nixon and Kissinger frequently sparred with the State Department over all sorts of issues, here the clash was out in the open, with an unsurpassed gulf in views of policy and morality. The State Department outfoxed Nixon and Kissinger, quietly using its bureaucratic power to jam the shipment of U.S. weaponry to Pakistan. In response, Nixon and Kissinger raged against the bureaucracy and tried to fire or demote some of the most influential dissenters, foremost among them Blood and Keating. The president and his national security advisor plowed ahead with their support of Pakistan as best they could, but were impeded by the consciences and the best advice of a surprisingly large chunk of their own administration.

There was no real question of the United States going to war to stop the slaughter. In 1971, there was no American equivalent of today's debates about humanitarian intervention in places like Bosnia and Darfur. After all, the country was already fighting a major war, trapped in the quagmire of Vietnam; there was no American appetite for another Asian conflict. Thus the leading critics of the Nixon administration, like Kennedy, linked Vietnam with Pakistan: two places where the United States was standing behind illegitimate governments, at a terrible cost to those peoples, and to the good name of the United States. American dissenters like Blood and Keating, as well as outraged political rivals like Kennedy, only wanted to see American influence repurposed to support democracy and human rights. Of course, they expected that a war would put an end to the slaughter—but that would be waged by India.

In the United States today, particularly after the disasters of the Iraq war, there are many thoughtful and serious people who criticize the promotion of human rights as arrogance, neoimperialism, and worse. No doubt, there are potent reasons for caution about trying to translate human rights ideals into statecraft. But this largely forgotten crisis, unfolding far from Washington, exemplifies an alternative way of making U.S. foreign policy, one that makes no allowance for human rights. This kind of policy has shown itself in the U.S. war against terror and may well reappear in future diplomacy. For all the very real flaws of human rights politics, Nixon and Kissinger's support of a military dictatorship engaged in mass murder is a reminder of what the world can easily look like without any concern for the pain of distant strangers.[12]

THE STAKES WERE HIGH FOR INDIA'S DEMOCRACY. SUNIL KHILNANI, A farsighted India expert, argues powerfully that India is the most important experiment in democracy since the American and French revolutions: "its outcome may well turn out to be the most significant of them all, partly because of its sheer human scale, and partly because of its location, a substantial bridgehead of effervescent liberty on the Asian continent." Nobody would idealize India's flawed democracy, least of all Indians themselves: this was and is a land of heartbreaking poverty, endemic corruption, collapsing infrastructure, enduring caste fissures, arrogant bureaucratic inefficiency, and shocking social inequality. Some 350 million Indians—roughly a third of the country's population—today live below the poverty line. But this is also a country of stupendous pluralism and vitality that, against all odds, maintains a democratic system and culture, offering a way for a fractious public to make its multitudinous voices heard and a chance for the government to correct itself.[13]

Indians were overwhelmingly outraged by the atrocities in East Pakistan. In a factionalized country where popular harmony is a surpassingly rare thing, there was a remarkable consensus: Pakistan was behaving horrifically; the Bengalis were in the right; India had to act in defense of democracy and innocent lives. Almost the entire Indian political spectrum, from Hindu nationalists on the right to socialists and communists on the left, lined up behind the Bengalis. These persecuted foreigners were not Indian citizens, but they were not altogether foreign; Bengalis were a familiar part of the Indian national scene, and India's own Bengali population rallied to their brethren. Across the country, newspapers ran furious editorials condemning Pakistan and urging the Indian government to recognize Bangladesh's independence.

Dismissing the niceties of national sovereignty in the cause of saving human beings and of respecting the popular will of the Bengalis, Indians demanded a swift recognition of an independent state of Bangladesh. Of course, since the bloody days of Partition, a great many Indians hated and feared Pakistan; plenty took a kind of angry satisfaction in lambasting Pakistani leaders like Yahya and Zulfiqar Ali Bhutto for confirming all the worst things that Indians had ever said about Pakistan. But there was a moral sensibility driving Indian politics that even the gimlet-eyed officials around Indira Gandhi, and the unsentimental Gandhi herself, could not ignore. She abandoned her father Nehru's traditional anticolonial pronouncements about the sanctity of national sovereignty. Instead, the beleaguered prime minister began to compare the bloodshed in East Pakistan to the Holocaust.

Perhaps the most striking Indian policy was something that it did not do. India did not stop masses of Bengali refugees from flooding into India. Unimaginably huge numbers of Bengalis escaped into safety on Indian soil, eventually totaling as many as ten million—five times the number of people displaced in Bosnia in the 1990s. The needs of this new, desperate population were far beyond the capacities of the feeble governments of India's border states, and Indira Gandhi's government at the center. But at that overcharged moment, the Indian public would have found it hard to accept the sight of its own soldiers and border troops opening fire to keep out these desperate and terrified people. Here, at least, was something like real humanitarianism. As payment for this kindness, India found itself crushed under the unsustainable burden of one of the biggest refugee flows in world history—which galvanized the public and the government to new heights of self-righteous fury against Pakistan.

India was left alone. Despite pleas to the rest of the world, India was given only a tiny amount of money to cope with the refugees. China was bitterly hostile; the United States only somewhat less so; the Non-Aligned Movement was, in the clutch, of no help; Egypt, Saudi Arabia, and the other Arab states were fiercely pro-Pakistan; even the United Nations seemed tilted toward Pakistan. India was forced into a tighter alignment with the Soviet Union, to the delight of leftists around Gandhi, but to the dismay of other Indians. Having been shoved aside by the democratic superpower, India cozied up to the other one.

As India grows into a world power, the story of the birth of Bangladesh has never been more important. It stands as an awful but crucial case for better understanding the politics of human rights, in a world where the duty of defending the vulnerable is not something that the West arrogates for itself alone. Today, at the advent of an Asian era in world politics, the future of human rights will increasingly depend on the ideologies, institutions, and cultures of ascendant Asian great powers like China and India. Thus India's democratic response to the plight of the Bengalis marks not just a pivotal moment for the history of the subcontinent, but for how the world's biggest democracy makes its foreign policy—and what weight it gives to human rights.

For Pakistan, the crisis of 1971 is mourned as a supreme national trauma: not just the loss of one of the country's two wings and the majority of its population, but a heightening of a truncated state's dread of the much larger and stronger Indian enemy. And the bloodletting of 1971 marks an important chapter of a U.S. embrace of military dictators at their worst. Although American popular memory about Pakistan tends to start in September 2001, it was Nixon's embrace of Yahya that helped to define a U.S. relationship with Pakistan based overwhelmingly on the military, even in its most repugnant hour. Nixon and Kissinger set the stage for an ongoing decimation of Pakistan's democratic opposition, giving time and space to Islamicize the country more and more. This pattern of U.S. antidemocratic engagement— with origins going back far beyond Pervez Musharraf, Pakistan's most recent U.S.-backed military dictator—has helped convince so many Pakistanis that the United States coldly pursues its own realpolitik interests and cares nothing for them.

Bangladeshis still mourn their losses from not so long ago. This book is not—and does not purport to be—anything like a comprehensive account of these crimes against humanity. It mostly documents the American eyewitness perspective on them, which is obviously only a part of the complete record of horrors. Still, this is an important portion, because it is the true local viewpoint of the Pakistani government's superpower ally. After all, Archer Blood and the other U.S. officials reporting back to the Nixon administration knew they had every career incentive to downplay the enormity of what they saw; their stark reporting thus stands as a crucial and credible part of that wider story.

Today we still face the legacy of Nixon and Kissinger's actions. Bangladesh, traumatized by its founding ordeal, now has the eighth-largest population on earth, bigger than Russia or Japan. With India creakily becoming a great power, and with ongoing conflict in Afghanistan and Kashmir that directly affects the United States in its war against Islamist terror, it's widely understood that South Asia has never been more important to Americans. But there is a gulf between what Americans remember of the Cold War and what its victims remember of it. Indians, Pakistanis, and Bangladeshis have not forgotten 1971—although they may be surprised by the newly declassified scope of the United States' dark record.[14]

Nixon and Kissinger have put extraordinary effort into magnifying their foreign policy achievements, so that the horrors of Watergate would appear as a smallish blot on their overall record. Today, Nixon and Kissinger's biggest success in promoting themselves as foreign policy heroes has been the historical oblivion that surrounds the killing campaign in Bangladesh. It is high time for Americans to confront what Nixon and Kissinger did in those terrible days.[15]

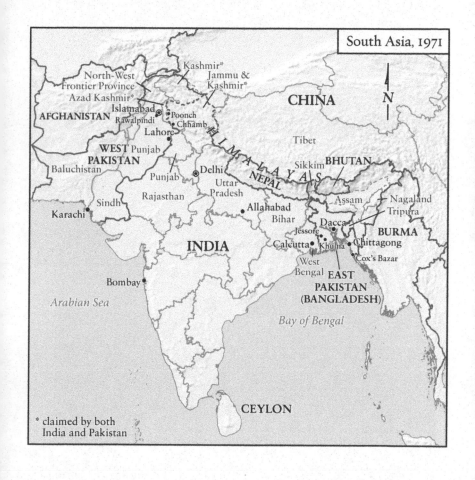

The Blood Telegram

Chapter 1

The Tilt

O N A HUSHED SATURDAY OVER THE THANKSGIVING WEEKEND IN November 1970, Richard Nixon was alone in the wooded seclusion of Camp David. Restless and keen for the new year, the president drew up a list of his aspirations, entitled "Goals for '71–'72." His list began: "1. President as moral leader—conscience of the nation."[1]

This high-minded vision did not extend as far as India. Nixon had never liked the country. "My God, South Asia is just unbelievable," he once said. "You go down there and you see it in the poverty, the hopelessness." He first visited the subcontinent in December 1953, on an Asian tour as vice president under Dwight Eisenhower. It was, by his own account, a foundational experience.[2]

Nixon was appalled by India's policy of nonalignment in the Cold War, an ostensible neutrality that seemed to him to really mean siding with the Soviet Union. Jawaharlal Nehru, India's founding prime minister, railed "obsessively and interminably" against Pakistan, to Nixon's horror: "I was convinced that his objection owed much to his personal thirst for influence, if not control, over South Asia, the Middle East, and Africa." On top of that, he and Nehru immediately disliked each other. Nixon, not much more partial to actual Brahmins than to Boston Brahmins, seemed nettled by Nehru's "softly modulated British English." He later called him "arrogant, abrasive, and suffocatingly self-righteous."[3]

Nixon's next stop was Pakistan. That went delightfully. "Pakistan is a country I would like to do everything for," he enthused when he got back to Washington. He found the Pakistanis to be staunchly anticommunist and pro-American. "The people have less complexes than the Indians," he said. "The Pakistanis are completely frank, even when it hurts." He was attracted less to the chaotic city streets than to the army's pristine cantonments. There he was impressed by the blunt generals, particularly General Muhammad Ayub Khan, who would a few years afterward stage a coup and become the first of Pakistan's military dictators. Nixon later wrote that he was haunted for the rest of his life by Ayub's lament about U.S. fickleness: "it is dangerous to be a friend of the United States."[4]

He returned to Washington as a staunch advocate of aid for Pakistan. With his support, the Eisenhower administration championed a muscular Cold War alliance with the country. The United States was seeking anti-Soviet allies across the Middle East and Asia, and newborn Pakistan intrepidly signed up as a double treaty ally of the United States, joining both the Central Treaty Organization (CENTO) and the Southeast Asia Treaty Organization (SEATO). Pakistan helpfully provided a base in Peshawar from which the Americans launched U-2 spy planes over the Soviet Union—one of which was famously shot down by the Soviets in 1960.[5]

Most important, after Nixon's visit, Eisenhower went ahead with a deal to start providing Pakistan with military aid. In 1954, the United States began supplying weapons to Pakistan, which was always seeking advantage against its Indian foe. Despite Eisenhower's reassurances that these arms were meant to ward off communists, India saw itself as the inevitable target.[6]

The Pakistan army grew strong with U.S. help. Over eleven years, by India's conservative estimate, the United States supplied Pakistan with between $1.5 billion and $2 billion worth of military equipment. India bitterly catalogued Pakistan's windfall: receiving 640 tanks, complete with modern artillery; modernizing the equipment for five army divisions; establishing three modern air bases, a naval dockyard at Karachi, and a Chittagong base. Pakistan got a submarine, a fleet tanker, and other ships. And the United States provided Pakistan with a good chunk of an air force: two squadrons of B-57 bombers, nine squadrons of F-86 Sabre jet fighters, a squadron of fighter-interceptors, thirty armed helicopters, and—crucial for a country that had to shuttle its soldiers from West Pakistan to East Pakistan—a squadron of colossal C-130 troop transport planes.[7]

Indians, still aggrieved by the fresh horrors of Partition, were infuriated. Nehru fumed, "Pakistan becomes practically a colony of the United States." To offset not just Pakistan but also the menace of China, India bought large quantities of Soviet weaponry. The United States and India sparred with each other, as insult followed insult on both sides. It only somewhat lessened the blow when Eisenhower, fearing that poverty bred radicalism, started providing substantial economic aid to India.[8]

John Kennedy, as president, did what he could to mend fences. Viewing India as an exemplar of noncommunist democracy and development, he boosted economic aid. When China went to war against India in 1962, with the Indian armed forces faltering, Nehru directly asked Kennedy for military help on a massive scale. Kennedy did not give Nehru everything he wanted, but he provided automatic weapons and ammunition and sent C-130s to move Indian troops. The military assistance continued after India's humiliating defeat in the China war, reinforcing India's mountain divisions with mortars, guns, and grenades to ward off Chinese troops in the Himalayas. This too was welcome, although India's defense ministry called it "very limited aid"—still much less than what Pakistan had gotten.[9]

When Pakistan attacked India in 1965, in an explosion of the Kashmir dispute, the United States was in the awkward position of providing arms to both sides. Lyndon Johnson's administration pressed to bring a U.S. arms embargo crashing down on India and Pakistan, which would still formally be in place at the time of the 1971 crisis. Although the cutoff was aimed at both antagonists, it hurt Pakistan much more and left that government feeling betrayed. Nor were the Indians happy. To them, it was intolerable that the United States did not condemn Pakistan for aggression.[10]

After the war, India slowly bought small amounts of U.S. arms. But all told, at best, India had received less than a quarter of what Pakistan was getting. India also won new agricultural aid from the United States, which came with unwelcome policy demands. When the Indian government sharpened its criticism of the Vietnam War, Johnson, offended, put that aid on a short leash. Once again, the governments snarled at each other. By the time Richard Nixon became president, there was much to be done to reestablish friendship between the two great democracies.[11]

NIXON AND INDIA

"I don't like the Indians," Nixon snapped at the height of the Bengali crisis. Beyond his prejudices, he had reason piled upon reason for this distaste for India and Indians. The most basic was the Cold War: presidents of the United States since Harry Truman had been frustrated by

India's policy of nonalignment, which Nixon, much like his predecessors, viewed as Nehruvian posturing. India was on suspiciously good terms with the Soviet Union. Since the days of Kennedy and Johnson, India had been pillorying the United States for the Vietnam War, and Nixon got an ample share.[12]

Then there was realpolitik. Some Americans romanticized India's democracy, but not Nixon. He was unimpressed with the world's largest republic, believing to the end of his days that the United States should base its foreign policy on what a country did outside its borders, not on whether it treated its people decently at home. So India's domestic system made little impact on the president.[13]

Nixon was baffled and annoyed by Americans' popular sympathies for India, which he repeatedly described as a psychological disorder. He scorned a "phobia" among some Americans that "everything that India does is good, and everything Pakistan does is bad," and once told the military leader of Pakistan, "There is a psychosis in this country about India." The Americans who most liked India tended to be the ones that Nixon could not stand. India was widely seen as a State Department favorite, irritating the president. He recoiled from the country's mystical fascination to the hippie counterculture, which he despised. Henry Kissinger thought that Nixon saw Democratic "obsequiousness toward India as a prime example of liberal softheadedness."[14]

Nixon's anti-Indian leanings had been reinforced when John Kennedy took a warmly pro-India line. India seemed a cause for the Democrats. This point was once driven home by George H. W. Bush, Nixon's ambassador at the United Nations, who knew how to play up to his boss. Bush said that a friend of Kennedy's had explained that "Kennedy spent more time on India, and the mystique, I know they didn't like us, but it was a kind of a liberal mystique." That, Bush and Nixon agreed, was what they were up against.[15]

On top of that, there was a mutual loathing between Nixon and Indira Gandhi. He had not cared for Nehru, her father, either, but she had an extraordinary ability to get under his skin. Back in 1967, while Nixon was out of power and planning his way back, he had met again with Gandhi on a visit to Delhi. But when he called on the new prime minister at her house, she had seemed conspicuously bored, despite the short duration of their talk. After about twenty minutes of strained chat, she asked one of her aides, in Hindi, how much longer this was going to take. Nixon had not gotten the precise meaning, but he sure caught the tone. As president, Nixon kept up his personalized approach to foreign policy, trusting his own impressions of world leaders, visiting thirty-one countries, and holding White House summits with most of the key chiefs. For all his talk of realpolitik, he could be surprisingly individualized in his foreign policy judgments. He once said that "her father was just as bad as she is." His first visit to India as president was chilly and strained.[16]

Finally, there was friendship. Richard Nixon liked very few people, but he did like General Agha Muhammad Yahya Khan. Over and over, he privately spoke of Yahya with an uncharacteristic blend of admiration and affection.[17]

Despite all his global face time, Nixon was a solitary, awkward, reclusive man. (Kissinger, who could not bring himself to say that he was fond of the president, once famously asked, "Can you imagine what this man would have been had somebody loved him?") His only true friend was Bebe Rebozo, a Florida banker. He said that "it doesn't come natural to me to be a buddy-buddy boy." Even H. R. Haldeman, the White House chief of staff, worried that the boss was too much in his own head, once tried to find the president a friend, tracking down an oilman whom Nixon had reportedly liked in his Los Angeles days and installing him in a bogus White House job. (It didn't take.)[18]

Kissinger said that Nixon had been treated very well by Pakistan even when he was out of office, and remembered that gratefully. Nixon, who had long had a soft spot for Pakistani military officers, particularly took to Yahya. The dictator was a beefy man, with amazing spiky black eyebrows and slicked-back gray hair cut with a white streak. "I'm a soldier," he liked to say, with no patience for the wiles of politicians. Yahya had become president of Pakistan in March 1969 by pushing aside another general and imposing martial law. Kissinger once wrote, "Yahya is tough, direct, and with a good sense of humor. He talks in a very clipped way, is a splendid product of Sandhurst and affects a sort of social naivete but is probably much more complicated than this."[19]

Maybe not. Despite Nixon's affection for Yahya, the strongman had none of the U.S. president's complexity and keen intelligence, let alone his focus. Yahya drank early and often. "He starts with cognac for breakfast and continues drinking throughout the day; night often finding him in a sodden state," sniffed the rival West Pakistani politician Zulfiqar Ali Bhutto. Archer Blood disliked Yahya's "brusque, strutting way," was unmoved by his British affectations and swagger stick, and leery of the general's contempt for civilian politicians. Kissinger, who did not suffer even clever people gladly, eventually concluded that

Yahya was a moron. But the general was certainly bright enough to realize the strategic advantages of nurturing his friendship with the president of the United States.[20]

HENRY KISSINGER'S OFFICE AT THE WHITE HOUSE WAS A THRILLING PLACE to work. "The power was there, he was gathering it up," says Samuel Hoskinson, who served there as Kissinger's junior official for South Asia. "You felt like you were at the political center of the universe. He and the president, that was where the decisions were made."

Kissinger, just forty-eight years old in 1971, was relatively new to the world spotlight then, and growing into the role. To Nixon, his audience of one, the White House national security advisor was unctuous and ingratiating, matching presidential moods and tempers. But to his White House staff and the rest of the foreign policy machine, he was all rough edges, jealous of any rivals. "He was not the kindly gentleman that he is today," remembers Hoskinson.

The real decisions were taken in private by Nixon and Kissinger. Throughout the crisis, Kissinger would hold countless meetings in the White House Situation Room with senior government officials, but these had the feeling of theater. Kissinger was often more accommodating in group discussions, toying with ideas, yielding some ground to the collective skepticism around the Situation Room table; but when he was with Nixon alone, something much closer to his real, unvarnished views could resurface. In the Oval Office or the president's hideaway office in the Executive Office Building, Kissinger played to the only person who mattered. He would encourage or awkwardly join in Nixon's profane denunciations of the Indians. When Nixon swore, Kissinger swore too, detonating the occasional curse to keep up with the president. (Kissinger, whose own taste in profanity ran more to "balderdash" and "poppycock" than Nixon's really foul stuff, rather touchingly tended to say "goddamned," getting the grammar right.) Again and again, Kissinger would stoke Nixon's anger against the Indians, to the president's satisfaction. "Henry is my least pathological pro-India lover around here," Nixon once said proudly.[21]

Kissinger came to the White House with a brilliant mind, a profound knowledge of world history, and a firm, principled commitment to realpolitik. From his earliest writings, he had argued that foreign policy ought not to be driven by the demands of justice. That, he thought, was the road to total war. Instead, Kissinger believed that a society's principles, no matter how deep-rooted or heartfelt, had to be compromised in the name of international stability. His focus, like that of his heroes Metternich and Castlereagh, was on the great powers. Both for him and Nixon, everything—from the Middle East to Latin America to the Indian subcontinent, and even the crucial challenge of getting the United States out of Vietnam—relied on the core realpolitik task of building a Cold War balance of power.[22]

He became the essential man in the making of American foreign policy, second only to the president. "Nixon wanted to control foreign policy," says Hoskinson, "and he had his wizard from Harvard to help him." In these early days, Nixon was dazzled by Kissinger's ability to put foreign policy in "the framework of philosophy. You've got to talk philosophy, you've got to be a great mosaic and you put in the pieces. State is not thinking in mosaic terms. The communists do. The Chinese do. The Russians do. We must."[23]

As the White House national security advisor, Kissinger was locked in nonstop bureaucratic combat with the ineffectual secretary of state, William Rogers. But it was never a halfway equal contest. Kissinger was vastly more important to the president, seen as something close to acceptably loyal, although a prima donna. Haldeman, who had to keep the staff functioning, exasperatedly wrote that "the two of them just stay on a collision course." The president had to conduct an epic smoothing of ruffled feathers, which took its toll on him. Nixon and Haldeman agonized over the "whole Rogers-K problem," with Nixon repeatedly telling Haldeman that "the price that he [Nixon] has to pay to K in terms of emotional drain on himself is very great." Again and again, Kissinger threatened to resign, reassured every time of his indispensability. In time, all the grandstanding and bigthinking wore Nixon out. The president once wearily told Haldeman, "Henry talks an awful lot."[24]

Kissinger concentrated power in the White House, sidelining the rest of the government. He had long held a profound disdain for the bureaucracy, going well beyond the standard Washington complaints about sclerotic inefficiency. The parochial experts could not see the big picture as great statesmen did. He skirmished daily with the State Department. Zhou Enlai once told him, "You don't like bureaucracy." Kissinger retorted, "Yes, and it's mutual; the bureaucracy doesn't like me."[25]

In this antipathy, he matched up neatly with the president. To Nixon, the lower echelons of government seemed stacked with northeastern elites who had never accepted him. He once told his cabinet, "Down in the government are a bunch of sons of bitches. . . . We've checked and found that 96 percent of the bureaucracy are against us; they're bastards who are here to screw us." The president's suspicion included Kissinger's own team at the White House, which had no shortage of northeasterners with fancy degrees. Soon before the Bangladesh crisis broke, he instructed Haldeman and Kissinger's own deputy national security advisor, Alexander Haig Jr., to "make sure that Henry examines his staff very closely and is really set to kick out any potential traitors and not let any others in."[26]

Kissinger's singular grip on White House power was the stuff of legend among the diplomatic corps posted to Washington. The Indians were well aware of Kissinger's outsized influence in the making of foreign policy—not least because he worked hard to let them know it. India's ambassador in Washington explained to his foreign ministry all about Kissinger's dominance in making foreign policy, while wryly warning that Kissinger's self-promotion was so pervasive that it rendered his words untrustworthy. The Indian ambassador reported cattily, "Kissinger, on his part, never misses an opportunity to emphasize and underscore his own importance." Once, after a Washington dinner, "while we were talking, he was called to the telephone five times and while others were only surmising that the calls were from the President, he himself made remarks which were intended to confirm that suspicion."[27]

KISSINGER, FOR ALL HIS BRILLIANCE, KNEW A LOT MORE ABOUT METternich's Austria than he did about modern South Asia. (He once said, "I would not recognize Pushtoon agitation if it hit me in the face.") His preoccupations at this time were the Vietnam War and the opening to China, not India and Pakistan. He relied on his own small, skillful staff at the White House's National Security Council.[28]

The White House's real expert on South Asia was Samuel Hoskinson, a burly, forceful man from Chicago, with a blunt way of speaking and a ready, gap-toothed smile. He had been working as a CIA analyst on the subcontinent, until a drinking buddy of his, Alexander Haig, became Kissinger's deputy and offered him a South Asia job. Hoskinson, in his late thirties, snapped up the precious opportunity to work at the White House. It was by far the most important post of his life. "Henry is in the genius category, as a diplomatist, as a historian," he says with undiluted admiration.

Kissinger hired his own staff with an eye for the very best talent, not for right-wing ideology. At the same time, he was an impossible person to work for. "I keep them in a state of exhaustion," he once joked. Hoskinson says, "He could be totally unreasonable." He would berate the staff, sometimes yelling at them. "He traumatized you sometimes. You're a young guy and you get smacked around so much." Hoskinson would go to Haig for reassurance. "I said, 'He doesn't like anything I do.' Haig said, 'That means he loves you.' Everyone on that staff had a tempestuous relationship with Henry." He remembers, "He could be quite volatile. You always had to weigh how things were going to go with Henry." Still, he says, "It led to great respect by the staff. There were a few who dropped by the wayside, who couldn't take the whippings. It was the highlight of my career."[29]

Winston Lord, a young staffer who became Kissinger's special assistant, could take the whippings. He found Kissinger inspiring. "It was terrific," Lord enthuses. "Whatever one's view of Henry on policy or ideology, even his greatest critics have to admit the guy is brilliant." Lord relished Kissinger's intelligence and learned from their discussions of world history and the international scene. He remembers, "He stretched you. He demanded excellence, not to mention hard work." Lord continues, "He pushed his staff very hard. Having a sense of a person's particular qualities. He obviously could drive you crazy at times, and I told him that. At a young age, you saw how hard *he* was working, what the stakes involved."

Kissinger's other official dealing with South Asia was Harold Saunders, who outranked Hoskinson. Saunders was not the type to complain; a cordial and kindly man with a blue-blooded manner, he had a PhD from Yale and a tweedy air to match. He had first joined the National Security Council under Lyndon Johnson, but quickly became a close aide to Kissinger, sticking with him for some eight years. He would go on to be a key player in Kissinger's shuttle diplomacy between Arabs and Israelis, to work on the Camp David accords between Israel and Egypt, and to serve as assistant secretary of state—one of the most distinguished American peacemakers in the Middle East. Saunders still greatly admires Kissinger and speaks with amused fondness about him. For Saunders, like Hoskinson, working for Kissinger was a formative experience, although not always an easy one for someone who would build his subsequent career around dialogue and mediation.

All these White House staffers understood well which way the president and his national security advisor leaned. For Indira Gandhi, Hoskinson says, "There was respect, but a kind of visceral dislike." He explains, "Some of this was a traditional Republican reaction to India and Indians. And of course, this is the Cold War era, and her left-wing approach to things, her socialist approach, her dalliance with the Russians, made them very, very suspicious of them. Everything was viewed through the prism of relationships with Russia, and more with China too in that case." He says, "She was just a steely personality. A real force to be dealt with."

Kissinger was somewhat less bluntly hostile to India than Nixon. While he scorned nonalignment, he got along chummily with L. K. Jha, India's urbane ambassador in Washington, and was less fueled by bigotry than the president. Still, Kissinger took insult easily and nurtured a growing list of his own grudges, and he understood the uses of stoking Nixon's prejudices for the purposes of making foreign policy.[30]

Yahya was far more to Kissinger's taste. Kissinger once said that he had "pretty good relations with Yahya," although without Nixon's full embrace. "They liked him," says Hoskinson. "He was a soldier. He had style. He was kind of a jaunty guy." Hoskinson admits that Yahya was not the brightest person, but says that for Nixon and Kissinger, "He was a man's man. He wasn't some woman running a country."[31]

YAHYA GOT A REWARD FOR HIS EFFORTS IN LATE OCTOBER 1970, WHEN he met Nixon in the Oval Office at the White House. In their last meeting before the crisis erupted, Nixon began to sell weapons to Yahya again, in what was officially billed as a one-time exception to the U.S. arms embargo imposed on both India and Pakistan back in 1965. It was the kind of exception that demolishes the rule.

That embargo had already been eroding under Johnson, but Yahya now secured a moderately big haul—a harbinger of much larger ones likely to come. The promised weapons included six F-104 fighter planes, seven B-57 bombers, and three hundred armored personnel carriers, although they would take some time to be delivered.[32]

India took it badly. Indira Gandhi would bitterly complain that this resumption of U.S. arms supplies to Pakistan increased the threat to her country. General Sam Manekshaw, chief of the Indian army staff, argued that the U.S. and Chinese supply of weaponry allowed Pakistan to take a belligerent stance against India.[33]

In the Oval Office that day, it was as friendly a meeting as two heads of state ever have, particularly when one of them was Richard Nixon. Yahya was special. Even Kissinger seemed impressed with his toughness and Sandhurst style. The two presidents spoke chummily of military and economic aid. Nixon pledged to support Pakistan despite "strong feeling in this country favoring India." He promised that "we will keep our word with Pakistan however; we will work with you; we will try to be as helpful as we can."

Yahya was grateful. He replied, "We appreciate this; our friendship is not new. We were surrounded by enemies when we became friends. We are no longer surrounded by enemies but still we remain friends. We are a sentimental people and we will never do anything to embarrass you."[34]

Chapter 2

Cyclone Pakistan

ARCHER BLOOD, THE RANKING DIPLOMAT OF THE UNITED STATES in East Pakistan, was a patriot and a career man. "From the first time he realized there was such a thing as the Foreign Service, he was keenly interested in it," remembers his widow, Margaret Millward Blood. "He had always looked at the world, and thought that everything had meaning."

A sincere and rather bookish man from Virginia, Blood was tall and solidly handsome, with kindly eyes and an athlete's frame, wearing his dark hair slicked back. Although courteous and well mannered, he confessed to having a turbulent private side, alternating "between my personal Scylla of bright expectation and Charybdis of black despair." He kept that to himself.[1]

His wife, a vivacious and gracious graphic artist from New York, who is vibrant at eighty-seven years old, recalls, "He was an exact person. He could become interested in anything, but he wanted to know the exact facts." He seemed never to sit down without having a book in hand. She was struck by how disciplined he was when reading. Once, on their honeymoon in Greece, she misquoted a line from a magazine, and he calmly supplied the exact wording, asking her to be careful about such things.

Blood was no rebel. Amid the hippies and burnouts of the 1960s and early 1970s, he was unreservedly square. In the Vietnam era, a group of American officials formed an organization called Foreign Service Officers Against the War, wearing protest badges, sometimes inside their jackets. Not Blood. His most radical affectation was, in the torrid tropical heat of Dacca (today known as Dhaka), to sometimes shed his dark business suit for a short-sleeved white shirt.

In World War II, he served as a supply officer in the U.S. Navy, posted to frigid Alaska to ward off a Japanese onslaught that never came. With the unassuming dedication of the World War II generation, he chose public service. "He was of course a patriot," says his wife, who goes by Meg Blood. "In those days everyone was geared to the war. The whole world was very, very patriotic, and very anxious to serve."[2]

Blood joined the Foreign Service in 1947, part of an entering class made up entirely of white men. He clambered his way up, working relentlessly hard, taking extra duty. His first posting was in Thessaloniki, Greece, during the civil war. He married Meg there. The young couple's next stop was Munich, in 1949, still shattered in the immediate aftermath of World War II. His wife remembers seeing "whole cities spilled into the street in brick form." Working in a displaced persons camp, Archer Blood took satisfaction in issuing huge numbers of U.S. visas to Hungarians, ethnic Germans from eastern Europe, many Poles, and even more Jews. He served briefly in Algiers and Bonn, and put in some desk time in Washington, but his career was in the doldrums, and he wanted more challenging political work. In West Germany, a fellow diplomat, asked what his ultimate wish was, replied that he only wanted to be a consul general. Blood was baffled. "I can't imagine not wanting to be an ambassador," he told his wife. "It's the top."

He grimly rode out the McCarthy era from Bonn, watching with contempt as "McCarthy's hatchet men" investigated the Foreign Service, driving many good officials out and cowing others into quietude. Blood was not inclined to resign in showy protest, but he rankled at the witch hunts. He believed in independent judgment in the Foreign Service. He remembered that anyone who had served in China was automatically under suspicion, and that careers were ended with accusations of homosexuality. It was, he later growled, "just so obnoxious." China, soon after its communist revolution, was still a taboo subject at the State Department. One young diplomat in Bonn had worked in China, and Blood was questioned about him. The security officials asked if this young China hand read the *New York Times*. "The *New York Times* was considered by the security people as a leftist newspaper. And I was young enough to say, 'Yes, I hope to hell he does.'"[3]

TWO WEEKS AFTER JOINING THE FOREIGN SERVICE, BLOOD HAD WATCHED as the flags of newborn India and Pakistan were hoisted above their Washington embassies. Steeped in British stories of the Raj, he had always been fascinated with South Asia. In 1960, he was offered a choice of postings in Madras, in India, or Dacca, in East Pakistan. He chose Dacca out of ambition: he would have more freedom there, far removed from the oversight of the U.S. embassy, and there would be more political turmoil for him to cover.

Blood arrived on the subcontinent in June 1960, as a political officer and deputy principal officer at the Dacca consulate that he would later run. His wife's first impression, as their plane neared Dacca, was that their new home would be underwater. "It was an ocean," Meg Blood says. They did not know if there would be enough land to put down an airplane. "Green and flowering," she remembers, "but definitely a land of water." For Archer Blood, as he wrote later, "there was a magical quality to this ubiquitous water, which heightened the green of the rice paddies and the purple of the water hyacinths and furnished a shimmering mirror for the famed golden sun of Bengal."[4]

Their first exposure was a shock. Driving in from the airport, with the car windows down in the swampy heat, Meg Blood was horrified to find herself face-to-face with a woman beggar with no nose. Their driver explained that the woman had probably been accused of adultery, and her husband had had her nose cut off. The car was surrounded by beggars. They saw disfigured children asking for coins. The water pump at their house turned out to be a twelve-year-old boy.

There had been a young American diplomat who arrived in Dacca, took one look around, and announced his resignation. But the Blood family—with three children in tow—settled in and learned to love their hardship post. "Our lives were delightful," says Meg Blood. The social scene was relaxed, and they made fast friends both among Bengalis and West Pakistanis. "We spent our evenings discussing tigers," remembers Meg Blood merrily. The tales grew tall. "There were a great many tigers, and they were causing trouble. They lost about ten people a month to the tigers."[5]

Unafraid of tigers was an inquisitive little boy who lived one door down from the Bloods. Shahudul Haque, eleven years old, soon befriended the three American children. He taught them cricket; they wowed him with Cokes and peanut butter and jelly sandwiches. While most of the foreigners and diplomats living in their peaceful tree-lined neighborhood kept to themselves, the Bloods welcomed the Bengali child into their home for homework sessions and slumber parties, chatting with him, as curious about his life as he was about theirs. Haque fondly remembers how good these friendly Americans were at intermingling.

Archer Blood was soothed by the pounding tropical rain on his roof. He loved to trek around the most remote hinterlands, eating humble chicken curry, finding serenity in long trips by rickety train or river steamer. He liked to be out on a tumbledown steamer, meandering down a tributary of the Ganges, watching hundreds of multicolored country boats speckling a river so vast that he could not see either bank. "I was never really in a hurry to get anywhere," he later recalled.

Not so at work. Eager for promotion, he threw himself into his duties. Although many Bengalis complained that the Americans were helping West Pakistan exploit East Pakistan, he took pride in the American economic development efforts, like the opening of the renowned Pakistan SEATO Cholera Laboratory, mostly funded and staffed by Americans. When the first young Peace Corps volunteers arrived, he was heartened by their brash vitality. And he enjoyed easy relationships with Bengalis and West Pakistanis alike, once being whirled around at a boisterous dance party by General Muhammad Ayub Khan, then the military dictator of Pakistan.[6]

Blood's work as a political officer was, he later remembered, largely about relaying the grievances of Bengalis who felt abused by West Pakistan. "This annoyed Washington because Washington liked to believe that Pakistan was a stable, united country," he said later. Still, he thoroughly enjoyed the tour of duty. He remembered, "The atmosphere, despite the grumblings of the Bengalis, was one of progress and hope." He left in June 1962, hoping one day to return.[7]

BLOOD GOT HIS CHANCE SOONER THAN HE EXPECTED, WHEN HE WAS promoted into the senior echelons of the Foreign Service. He relished his first major posting as a deputy chief of mission in Afghanistan, where he loved roaming around places like Mazar-e Sharif and Qunduz, and was surprised to find that the U.S. embassy staff was on friendly terms with the Soviets. He hoped to do the same job in Ethiopia, but was instead shunted back to Greece.

Here, for the first time, he found a posting that he hated. Greece was languishing under a military junta supported by the CIA. Blood, along with most of the political wing of the embassy in Athens, found it painful to watch the generals stifle the Greek people. Keen for elections, he worried that the Greek public would enduringly resent U.S. support of the junta.

But the U.S. embassy was bitterly split. The rival American camps, for and against the military rulers, were openly hostile. He had never been at an embassy where he could not speak bluntly about the local government. He recalled later that "if you said anything mistaken as critical about members of the junta, the C.I.A. would explode in anger." Blood's rivals tried to brand him as a troublemaker. When a new ambassador arrived, who argued that providing U.S. weaponry to the Greek junta would somehow return Greece to democracy, Blood hit the roof: "These people will never bring back Greece to democracy. And this is a lie."

The State Department, knowing how despondent Blood was in toxic Athens, came to him with welcome news: there was an opening in Dacca. He grabbed it immediately, bolting Athens in March 1970. Back in Washington, with a little pomp, he placed his hand on a Bible and was sworn in as the consul general of the United States in Dacca. He eagerly flew off to command his first post.[8]

THE U.S. CONSULATE IN DACCA WAS A YOUTHFUL, BOISTEROUS PLACE. Despite the dingy, mildewed offices in their Adamjee Court building, the place hummed with energy. Blood, who was forty-eight at the time—the same age as Henry Kissinger—ranked as the elder statesman of the outpost, but most of his staff was much younger. Their work was exhilarating.[9]

Long before Bangladesh was written off by Kissinger and others as a "basket case," it was known as a terrific place for development work. Some of the best poverty-fighting economists and experts flocked there for cutting-edge work on how to boost crop yields and resist cholera. In the city of Comilla, they worked with Akhtar Hameed Khan, whose pathbreaking work on agricultural cooperatives and microfinance would help pave the way for the Bangladeshi economist Muhammad Yunus and Grameen Bank, winners of the Nobel Peace Prize in 2006 for their own microcredit efforts. Blood's officials were proud of their professionalism and commitment.[10]

Dacca was not everyone's idea of a plum posting, but for scrappy, ambitious juveniles, it was a rush. "This was not your tea-and-crumpets European assignment," remembers Scott Butcher, Blood's junior political officer. "This was a difficult part of the developing world." After a relatively quiet stint in Burma, he had gotten word of his posting on April Fool's Day and at first thought it was a joke. "If you're a political officer, you're something of an ambulance chaser in terms of crisis reporting," he says. "I got that in spades." While he was on home leave before shipping out for East Pakistan, his predecessor in Dacca, a grizzled former U.S. Army officer, told him to brace himself. When Butcher asked him to sum up the place in a few words, he replied, "Pestilential hole."

There was considerable ridicule about all the sanguinary names at the post, heightened by a deputy political officer with the unfortunate name of Andrew Killgore. "Archer Blood, of all the names," says Samuel Hoskinson with a laugh. Scott Butcher remembers drily that cables "would be drafted by Butcher, approved by Killgore, and signed by Blood. The anti-Americans thought, 'Things bode ill.'"

Eric Griffel, the chief of the U.S. Agency for International Development team in Dacca, was happy there too. "I had begun to like Dacca, strangely enough," he recalls. He came from a Polish Jewish family; his parents had fled from Krakow to London just before World War II, and then he had moved to the United States at age seventeen to go to UCLA. Griffel is round-faced and cherubic, belying his brisk, efficient manner. He speaks with a slight Polish accent, in clipped, blunt sentences. He was a rebellious and unflappable man. (The more buttoned-down Blood found him a little abrasive, but also "a pillar of strength.") Griffel had always been curious about the subcontinent, and East Pakistan was a place with terrible poverty, and he felt needed there.[11]

Blood's youthful staff liked the boss. He was dynamic and relatively young. "He and his wife were a very dashing couple, with bright prospects," recalls Butcher, who greatly respected Blood. "He was clearly someone who was going on to much higher positions in the State Department." Griffel remembers, "One would have thought he was completely conventional." (Griffel is nobody's idea of conventional.) "He was a very nice, easygoing, conventional Foreign Service officer. Able, did his job well, hardworking. He was always there. There was no golf playing, this sort of thing." He says, "He was patriotic, very much so, but he didn't wear it ostentatiously." He sums the man up: "A very plain, good American civil servant."

Dacca was a great place for adventuring American reporters too. Sydney Schanberg, the *New York Times* reporter covering the Indian subcontinent, had wound up there by accident. With piercing eyes and a tidy beard, he is intense and indignant, fiercely moralistic, holding a deep affection for the peoples he has covered in his long career as a reporter. After graduating from Harvard and spending two years in the U.S. Army, he started out as a copy boy at the *New York Times,* and wound up staying for twenty-six years. As a cub reporter, his fondest hope was to go to Africa, where he could roam and report widely.

Instead, the *Times* foreign desk offered him the exact opposite: Poland, in the Soviet deep freeze. But by a stroke of luck, the job of Delhi bureau chief came vacant, and Schanberg, in his late thirties, grabbed the chance. He is famous for covering the murderous fall of Cambodia to the Khmer Rouge in 1975—a nightmarish experience that was turned into a movie, *The Killing Fields*—but by then he would have already seen plenty of that kind of horror in East Pakistan.[12]

DEMOCRACY IN PAKISTAN

Pakistan was in those days a country divided. The British, leaving India, had decided to create a single Muslim state in the subcontinent. To do so, they had to lump together Punjabis, Pashtuns, Baluchis, and Sindhis in the northwest with Bengalis far away in the east. Out of the bloody chaos of Partition, Pakistan was born as a cartographic oddity: a unitary state whose two territories did not connect. West Pakistan was separated from East Pakistan by a thousand miles of India—a gigantic enemy with bitter memories of the displacement of millions of people in Partition in 1947, not long earlier. A senior Indian diplomat execrated the British for leaving behind "this geographical monstrosity." People joked that only three things kept Pakistan united: Islam, the English language, and Pakistan International Airlines—and PIA was the strongest.[13]

Scott Butcher, new to the region, was surprised by the strangeness of this bifurcated nation. His first stop was in West Pakistan, to check in with the embassy in Islamabad and the consulates in Karachi and Lahore. It was hot beyond belief, like stepping into a furnace. It was 111 degrees in Lahore, he remembers, and they said it was a cool spell. Everything seemed to him brown, sandy, parched, and dry. Then he flew on to Dacca, the capital of East Pakistan, terrain roughly the size of Florida. It was completely different. "It was so emerald green it almost hurt your eyes," he says. It was also unbearably hot, in the heat of June 1969, but swampy and moistly tropical. Another official in the Dacca consulate remembers "wonderful rice paddy fields, rivers with fantastic dhows with tattered sails. Everything was so flat you could see what looked like boats sailing through rice paddy fields. They were actually miles away."

The differences were more than geographic. The central government, the main military institutions, and the established bureaucracy were based in West Pakistan, far from the concerns of the Bengalis. West Pakistanis spoke many languages, the commonest being Urdu, while in East Pakistan almost everyone spoke Bengali. The whole country was dominated by Punjabi elites in West Pakistan, to the resentment of Bengalis in East Pakistan. The Bengalis were mostly Muslim, but in an officially Islamic nation, there was some suspicion of the sizable Bengali Hindu minority. While West Pakistan nursed grudges against India, the Bengalis in East Pakistan took little interest in that feud.[14]

Many Bengalis had started off as loyal Pakistani citizens, but they came to think that they were worse off economically than their fellow citizens in West Pakistan, and found their own ethnic traditions unwelcome. West Pakistan's military elite scorned the "Bingos" as weak and unmartial. Bengali nationalists grumbled that they had replaced British colonialism with West Pakistani colonialism.[15]

IT WOULD HAVE BEEN HARD TO MAKE A UNITED PAKISTAN FUNCTION even if it had the best government in the world. It did not. The country had to withstand civilian leaders who high-handedly tried to mandate Urdu as the national language, infuriating Bengalis; and then, even worse, was the imposition of martial law in 1958. Since the British had tended to favor Punjabis as their chosen warriors, there were few Bengalis in Pakistan's military. The generals stifled the country, banning political parties and making it impossible for Bengalis to voice their grievances as they had loudly done before.[16]

Democracy was always going to be a terrible challenge for a country that was literally split in two. There were plenty of enthusiasts for democracy in both wings of the country, but they faced tough basic demographic facts: East Pakistan, with about seventy-five million people, was more populous than West Pakistan, which had a population of some sixty-one million. The east demanded its proper democratic representation; the west feared losing its grip; and so constitutional negotiations deadlocked. When Bengalis called for ending martial law and holding elections, they also hoped to turn their numbers into political clout.[17]

By the time Yahya seized power in March 1969, East Pakistan was in almost constant turmoil, with Bengali street protesters facing off against the army. When Archer Blood returned to Dacca, he found a much darker mood among his old Bengali acquaintances, including Shahudul Haque, now a restless young nationalist. The old economic resentments had simmered for too long, and after a ruinous war with India in 1965, many Bengalis were sour about being asked to take risks for the remote cause of Kashmir.[18]

Yahya was not just Pakistan's president, but also its foreign minister, defense minister, and chief martial law administrator. Still, he was far from the most antidemocratic general to rule Pakistan. Soon after taking office, he began working to end martial law and yield power to a new elected government, and then announced historic new elections. Blood and many of his staffers were impressed, but this democratic turn elicited no particular enthusiasm from Yahya's friend in the White House. "I hope you keep a strong Presidency as in France," Richard Nixon told him. Yahya agreed: "Without it Pakistan would disintegrate."[19]

The elections across the country were, after a postponement, finally set for December 7, 1970. Throughout Pakistan, a remarkably boisterous campaign went into full swing. As the balloting approached, Yahya was relaxed and expansive. "I think they miscalculated the way it would go," says Samuel Hoskinson, the White House aide. "That West Pakistani elite were quite capable of deluding themselves as well. They weren't close enough to it. Or they had faulty information from their own people—sugarcoating bad news for the bosses. I don't think they had a good appreciation of that situation."[20]

THEN A CATACLYSM STRUCK. ON NOVEMBER 13, NOT LONG AFTER YAHYA'S visit to Washington to win U.S. arms, a massive cyclone devastated East Pakistan.

The gales shrieked to 150 miles an hour, followed by a monstrous tidal wave over twenty feet high. "There are still thousands of bodies of cattle and hundred of bodies of people strewn on beaches and countryside," Blood's consulate reported over a week later, with an official in a low-flying helicopter staring in horror at the devastation below. "[D]ead and alive cattle and dead and alive humans all mixed in one area." Scott Butcher heard stories of bodies thrown thirty feet into the trees, and of corpses found sixty miles out at sea. By the estimation of U.S. humanitarian agencies, at least 230,000 people died—fully 15 percent of the population of the areas hit by the storm. The State Department put the death toll even higher, at half a million, many of them drowned. One U.S. colonel with four years of battle experience in Vietnam said that it was worse than anything he had seen there.[21]

"There was nothing to see after that water went through," recalls

Meg Blood, who went out to deliver emergency supplies. "People were up in trees holding their children, and the trees were swept clean away. There was nothing to see. The homes were mostly thatch, on the water, and they were the first to go, to be swept away." Approaching the stricken zone in a helicopter, she had the image of a huge chocolate pudding dotted with raisins. As she got closer, she realized with horror that the dots were actually human corpses.

After the natural disaster came the man-made disaster: the central Pakistani government's feeble response. Fully 90 percent of the area's inhabitants needed relief aid. A few days after the cyclone struck, Sydney Schanberg of the *New York Times* went down to an island in East Pakistan that had been razed by the storm. He heard stories of a baby torn from its mother's arms. But Schanberg was appalled by the Pakistani government's lassitude about delivering aid. Eric Griffel, the development officer who ran the large U.S. relief effort, says, "The West Pakistani government didn't do anything, and other countries did a lot, led by our own."[22]

"It was almost as if they just didn't care," Archer Blood remembered later. The international response—from the United States, the Soviet Union, Britain, and other countries—was much more visible than Pakistan's meager effort. American and Soviet helicopters were particularly conspicuous. There was huge resentment among Bengalis, notes Griffel, who saw foreigners doing more than their own government. Griffel says, "The cyclone was the real reason for the final break."[23]

Blood and Griffel's teams worked day and night, fanning out across the stricken region. The Nixon administration gave substantial aid. U.S. government officials, privately frustrated at the Pakistani government, worried that U.S. emergency measures were getting swamped by complaints about stalled aid. One of Blood's officials in Dacca noted that three months later, nothing whatsoever was being done for the victims.[24]

The Bengalis' alienation was all but complete. Even the Nixon administration secretly admitted that Pakistan's government had flubbed it. After getting roasted in the press, Yahya belatedly flew to East Pakistan to take personal command of the disaster relief. His brief appearance did not go well. Blood remembered disgustedly that Yahya had stopped in fleetingly on the way back from a China trip. "There were still bodies floating in inland rivers, mass graves being dug with backhoes, everyone wearing masks because of the smell, throwing lime on it," says Schanberg. "And he was walking through with polished boots and a walking stick with a gold knob. These people didn't have any gold anything. We asked a couple questions, and he brushed us off with blah-blah, then went home." Schanberg asked a Pakistani army captain why the military had not come sooner. The captain explained that if they had, India would have attacked. Schanberg was stunned. "It just was totally paranoid," he says.[25]

At the White House, Kissinger warned Nixon that the deep antagonism of Bengalis for the central Pakistani government was now much worse. They worried that conspicuous U.S. emergency relief efforts could undermine Yahya's authority. The election, they knew, was just two weeks away.[26]

ON DECEMBER 7, MILLIONS OF PAKISTANIS WENT TO THE POLLS, although some of the most devastated areas of East Pakistan had to delay their voting until January. The timing could not have been worse. Bengali politicians of all stripes slammed Yahya's government for ignoring their people in their hour of need. The voting gave Bengali nationalists a chance to shout their rejection of West Pakistan.[27]

The leader of the Bengalis was Sheikh Mujib-ur-Rahman, who led a popular mainstream Bengali nationalist party called the Awami League. He was a middle-class Bengali Muslim, whose lifelong activism had cost him almost ten years in Pakistani jails, making him a hero to many Bengalis. "Mujib's very appearance suggested raw power," cabled Blood, "a power drawn from the masses and from his own strong personality." He was tall and sturdy, with rugged features and intense eyes. Blood found him serene and confident amid the turmoil, but eager for power. "On the rostrum he is a fiery orator who can mesmerize hundreds of thousands in a pouring rain," Blood wrote. "Mujib has something of a messianic complex which has been reinforced by the heady experience of mass adulation. He talks of 'my people, my land, my forests, my rivers.' It seems clear that he views himself as the personification of Bengali aspirations."[28]

Mujib had distilled Bengali nationalist grievances into "Six Points," calling for democracy, and also for autonomy for both wings of a federal country, with the central government restricted to running only foreign affairs and defense. East Pakistan would be able to engage in trade and aid talks, and even to raise its own militia. The Awami League campaigned hard on their Six Point program. Mujib went to the cyclone areas to personally supervise the Awami League's own relief efforts, and returned to Dacca to declare that the Pakistani government was guilty of murder: "They have a huge army, but it is left to British marines to bury our dead." When Blood met with Mujib, the Bengali nationalist leader predicted with preternatural confidence that he would sweep almost every seat in East Pakistan.[29]

That would not spell a Cold War defeat for the United States. The Awami League was well known as moderate and pro-American. Blood described the League as center-left, a temperate and middle-class party with no animus against the United States. Mujib liked to reminisce about his affection for Americans and his love of San Francisco.[30]

THE 1970 BALLOTING WAS A TREMENDOUS EXPERIMENT IN DEMOCracy. This was the first direct election in Pakistan's twenty-three years of independence, with all adults allowed to vote—including, for the first time, women. The people of Pakistan were to choose a Constituent Assembly, which would have the difficult job of drawing up a new constitution for the fragile country. Yahya might have tried to rig the voting, or used the cyclone as an excuse for an indefinite postponement of the elections, but he opted to allow this democratic moment.[31]

In West Pakistan, the rulers wondered whether Mujib really wanted autonomy, as he repeatedly said, or an independent state of Bangladesh—a debate that goes on to this day. Blood and the Dacca consulate thought that the Bengalis could be satisfied with autonomy. (The Indian government also believed this.) Yahya and many West Pakistani leaders, however, suspected that Mujib's Six Points would prove to be merely the first six steps toward outright secession. Late in 1970, suspicious Pakistani intelligence agencies captured Mujib in a breathtakingly frank moment. They played their tape to Yahya, who was shocked to hear Mujib declare, "My aim is to establish Bangladesh." He would "tear" Yahya's federalist framework for upcoming constitutional negotiations "into pieces as soon as the elections are over. Who could challenge me once the elections are over?" Yahya, reeling, growled to one of his top political aides, "I shall fix Mujib if he betrays me."[32]

An almost equally audacious electoral campaign took place in West Pakistan. Zulfiqar Ali Bhutto, a former foreign minister heading up the Pakistan People's Party, assembled a coalition for dramatic change, drawing on conservative rural leaders and urban radicals. Bhutto was handsome, sardonic, urbane, and rich—an unlikely background for such a volatile populist. He had earlier been thrown in jail by the military, but was now back out. Yahya may have hoped that a PPP victory would allow him to stay in power, but Bhutto had his own fierce ambitions. He championed a leftist and tough vision of Pakistan, with a strong central government and a foreign policy that stood bitterly against India. Despite his Berkeley education, he was firmly anti-American. So Nixon loathed him: "the son-of-a-bitch is a total demagogue." (Kissinger, more cautiously, described him as "Violently anti-Indian. Pro-Chinese.") Blood skewered him with a single word: "malevolent."[33]

Blood, who adored elections, was thrilled at the widespread excitement as Pakistanis got their first chance to choose their government. There were plenty of rallies and parades, with Mujib and other candidates in full cry, but relatively little violence. The major party leaders got to broadcast speeches on radio and television, in their choice of two out of three languages: English, Urdu, or Bengali. "It was raucous and colorful," Butcher says, enjoying the memory. Blood was touched when a Bengali historian explained that the grinding experience of poverty had been relieved by the campaigning: powerful people asked for your vote, gave you respect, and promised to govern with your consent. You were no longer told that you did not know what was good for you.[34]

When the big day came, U.S. officials in Dacca were pleasantly surprised: the voting was impressively legitimate, the best the country had ever seen. The soldiers and policemen at the polling stations were there only to keep the peace, and Blood saw no signs of voter intimidation. Everyone agreed that it had been free and fair. Women voted in droves. "The elections were remarkably free," says Butcher. "It was fairly unique, turning a military government to civilian authority. It was a extraordinary thing."[35]

THE AWAMI LEAGUE WON HUGELY. OUT OF 169 CONTESTED SEATS IN East Pakistan, the League took all but two, winning an outright majority in the National Assembly. Mujib stood to be prime minister of all of Pakistan. "I was not surprised that Mujibur Rahman won easily and tremendously in East Pakistan," recalls Eric Griffel. "There was tremendous Bengali pride in Mujibur."[36]

Yahya's military dictatorship got trounced. His preferred candidates did miserably in both wings of the country. Humiliated, he was ruling over people who had rejected him east and west. Meanwhile the Pakistani military—some of them more hard-line than Yahya—recoiled at the prospect of Mujib running East Pakistan, demanding autonomy and resources, and perhaps making friends with India.[37]

Bhutto had ridden a populist wave to an impressive victory in West Pakistan, but because East Pakistan was more populous, Mujib won twice as many seats. The ambitious Bhutto thus found Mujib's triumph blocking his way. While Yahya and Bhutto were cutthroat rivals—a conservative, pro-American military man pitted against a leftist, anti-American firebrand—they were driven together in the panicky days after the election by a shared hostility toward India and a fear of losing East Pakistan.[38]

Blood, worried that Mujib would overplay his hand, coolly put off congratulating him for weeks. (He would later fault an exultant Mujib for a "blind faith in 'people power.'") When an Awami League leader asked if the United States would mediate if East Pakistan declared its independence, Blood flatly refused. He wanted nothing to do with secession, and hewed to the U.S. official line: one Pakistan.[39]

Galvanized by their triumph, Mujib and the Awami League had to make good on their campaign for autonomy for the Bengalis. Showing his popular strength, Mujib called a huge rally, where he pleaded with the rapturous crowd to carry on if he was assassinated. As Yahya, Mujib, and Bhutto began negotiating about the future of the country, Blood still hoped to avoid violence. He believed that Mujib was not aiming for secession except as a desperate last resort. "My thinking was that the Awami League platform was a recipe for the dissolution of Pakistan," he said later, "but it could be a recipe for the peaceful dissolution of Pakistan."[40]

THIS WAS A MOMENT WHEN THE UNITED STATES MIGHT HAVE STOOD on principle. There had been a free and fair election, truly expressive of the will of the people. The democratic superpower could have encouraged Pakistan to deepen its democratic traditions. "We are the great democracy," says Meg Blood. "And here was a democratic game being played, as if they would pay any attention once Mujib had won. They were prepared to simply push him aside." She adds, "We, the great American nation, leaned back and said nothing."[41]

The White House took almost no interest in upholding the results of Pakistan's grand experiment in democracy. Instead, the Nixon team dreaded the loss of its Cold War ally. The State Department unhappily thought that Pakistan was likely to crack apart. Kissinger asked Nixon whether the United States should be warming up to Mujib, who was friendly to the country. But Nixon, sticking with Yahya, scrawled, "not yet" and "not any position which encourages secession."[42]

Harold Saunders, the White House senior aide for South Asia, braced Kissinger for the prospect of another partition. Expecting East Pakistan to secede, he asked Kissinger how hard the United States should work to avoid bloodshed. They were, he wrote, "witnessing the possible birth of a new nation of over 70 million people. . . . [W]e could have something to do with how this comes about—peacefully or by bloody civil war."[43]

A protracted series of negotiations between Yahya, Bhutto, and Mujib amounted to nothing. "Mujib has let me down," Yahya bitterly told one of his ministers. "I was wrong in trusting this person." On March 1, under pressure from Bhutto, Yahya indefinitely postponed the opening of the National Assembly, which had been scheduled for March 3. To the Bengalis who had decisively voted for the Awami League, this looked like outright electoral theft. Yahya, wiping away the democratic election that he had allowed, declared that Pakistan was facing its "gravest political crisis."[44]

When Blood heard the news of the postponement on the radio, he dashed up to the roof of the Adamjee Court building. "We could see Bengalis pouring out of office buildings all around that neighborhood," he remembered. "Angry as hornets." They were screaming in rage. They had believed Yahya, he thought, and now were being robbed of their democratic victory. Although the crowds stayed peaceful, many people were carrying clubs or *lathis* (long wooden staffs, a weapon of choice for police in the subcontinent). He told the State Department, "I've seen the beginning of the breakup of Pakistan."[45]

Scott Butcher, the young political officer, remembers a wave of civil disobedience, with outraged crowds in the streets and a number of clashes with the Pakistani authorities. The next day, Bengalis launched a general strike, in the storied tradition of mass mobilizations against the British Empire. This showed the generals who really ran East Pakistan. At Mujib's word, normal life came to a halt. The shops were shuttered, and neither cars nor bicycles were allowed on the streets, which instead were filled with Bengalis chatting and wandering around. Bands of youths roved the city, shouting, "*Joi Bangla!*"—victory to Bengal.[46]

Catastrophe loomed. Blood worried at incidents of arson and looting, and ugly acts of intimidation of West Pakistanis. There were some small but potentially disastrous skirmishes with the army, which was out in full force. Mujib called for disciplined and peaceful mobilization of his followers. "I thought that the situation was intolerable to the army," says Griffel. "The solemnness of the population, the mild violence, the civil disobedience, the constant strikes, the university students—I don't think that was tolerable for long."[47]

Butcher was impressed by the military's restraint, which he found remarkable: "They were being spat upon, harassed and hassled by locals, but behaving quite well under the circumstances." Yahya broadcast an angry speech to the nation on March 6, accusing the "forces of disorder" of engaging in looting, arson, and killing. Under pressure from these mass demonstrations, he announced that the new National Assembly would now open on March 25. But with the politicians still deadlocked, Yahya threatened the worst: "It is the duty of the Pakistan armed forces to insure the integrity, solidarity, and security of Pakistan, and in this they have never failed."[48]

"THE RESULT WOULD BE A BLOOD-BATH"

The only possible hope was to avoid a military crackdown. Once the shooting started, the Bengalis would be radicalized; the military's prestige would be engaged; the violence could escalate into civil war. The whole region might plunge into chaos. In the last days before Yahya fired his fateful first shots, the United States did not exert itself to prevent that doom.

There was plenty of warning. Kissinger was alerted that, according to Blood's consulate, there was almost no chance of Pakistan holding together. But Nixon put his trust in Yahya. "I feel that anything that can be done to maintain Pakistan as a viable country is extremely important," he said. "They're a good people. Strong. People like Yahya are responsible leaders." Soon after, when Kissinger mentioned there was a problem coming with the separation of East Pakistan, the president was surprised: "They want to be separated?"[49]

Kissinger might breeze past advice from Blood and the distrusted State Department, but it was much harder to ignore similar alarms from his own handpicked White House staff. Samuel Hoskinson, who knew more about South Asia than anyone else in the White House, warned of a looming civil war that Yahya's government would probably lose. He recalled the recent horrors of the attempt by the Biafrans to secede from Nigeria. He suggested that Pakistan would be better off with a confederal system, giving East Pakistan under Mujib the maximum amount of autonomy short of secession. "It was not the popular thing to say," Hoskinson remembers. "We had some concern what kind of blowback we would get from Henry, which could be pretty bad." But he says, "He didn't blow up on me. Not that time."[50]

Harold Saunders was quieter and impeccably polite, but on March 5 he warned Kissinger that the Pakistan army was probably preparing to launch a futile crackdown. There was still a last chance to avoid slaughter by leaning hard on Yahya. Saunders recommended a government report that argued for threatening to stop economic aid to Pakistan to prevent bloodshed. He emphasized the crucial decision: *"The tough question is whether to make a major effort to stop West Pakistani military intervention."*[51]

The next day, Kissinger convened one of his frequent meetings in the White House Situation Room, gathering senior officials from the State Department, Pentagon, and CIA. It was the last high-level overview of U.S. policy before Yahya began his killing spree—a final opportunity for the United States to use its considerable influence to dissuade its ally from violence. A senior State Department official warned, "The judgment of all of us is that with the number of troops available to Yahya (a total of 20,000, with 12,000 combat troops) and a hostile East Pakistan population of 75 million, the result would be a bloodbath with no hope of West Pakistan reestablishing control over East Pakistan." Another senior official warned of a possible "real bloodbath . . . comparable to the Biafra situation."

Kissinger seemed convinced at first. "I agree that force won't work," he said. But when a State Department official argued that the United States should discourage Yahya from shooting, Kissinger dug in his heels. "If I may be the devil's advocate," he asked, "why should we say anything?" He asked warily, "What would we do to discourage the use of force? Tell Yahya we don't favor it?" Kissinger said firmly, "Intervention would almost certainly be self-defeating." He invoked Nixon's friendship with Yahya: "The President will be very reluctant to do anything that Yahya could interpret as a personal affront." He was skeptical of even the gentlest U.S. warnings: "If we could go in mildly as a friend to say we think it's a bad idea, it wouldn't be so bad. But if the country is breaking up, they won't be likely to receive such a message calmly." He said, "In the highly emotional atmosphere of West Pakistan under the circumstances, I wonder whether sending the American Ambassador in to argue against moving doesn't buy us the worst of everything. Will our doing so make the slightest difference? I can't imagine that they give a damn what we think." The group, following Kissinger, settled on what a State Department official called "massive inaction."[52]

Harold Saunders remembers that "there was a principle in their minds, which could be intellectually justified, although maybe not in practical terms: we're not going to tell someone else how to run his country." This was, he adds, the same tenet used for the shah of Iran. "I think it was the wrong principle myself," he says. "I heard it articulated by Henry on a number of occasions."[53]

Kissinger's decision stuck. He seemed more influenced by warnings that many West Pakistanis suspected that the United States was plotting to split up the country. The State Department instructed Blood not to try to dissuade Yahya from shooting.[54]

ON MARCH 13, KISSINGER SENT NIXON WHAT WOULD TURN OUT TO BE his final word on Pakistan before the killing started. Kissinger made "the case for inaction."[55]

He correctly warned that Yahya and the Pakistani military seemed "determined to maintain a unified Pakistan by force if necessary." And he noted that a crackdown might not succeed: "[Mujib] Rahman has embarked on a Gandhian-type non-violent non-cooperation campaign which makes it harder to justify repression; and . . . the West Pakistanis lack the military capacity to put down a full scale revolt over a long period."

But Kissinger urged the president to do nothing. He wrote that the U.S. government's consensus—forged by him—was that "the best posture was to remain inactive and do nothing that Yahya might find objectionable." Kissinger did not want to caution Yahya against opening fire on his people, ruling out "weighing in now with Yahya in an effort to prevent the possible outbreak of a bloody civil war." It was "undesirable" to speak up, because "we could realistically have little influence on the situation and anything we might do could be resented by the West Pakistanis as unwarranted interference and jeopardize our future relations." Kissinger preferred to stick with Yahya: "it is a more defensible position to operate as if the country remains united than to take any move that would appear to encourage separation. I know you share that view."[56]

There was one consideration that, while voiced by other U.S. officials, never made it into Kissinger's note to the president: simply avoiding the loss of life. The last chance of maintaining a united Pakistan would have been warning Yahya that force—especially brutal force—would be disastrous and have consequences for Pakistan's relationship with the United States. Just two weeks after the slaughter began, Kissinger would say that if the United States had had a choice on March 25, it would have urged Yahya not to use force. He was already covering up the fact that the Nixon administration had had many opportunities to make such requests to Yahya, and had expressly chosen silence.[57]

EAST PAKISTAN TEETERED ON THE VERGE OF ANARCHY. WITH THE DAYS dwindling until the fateful March 25 deadline for opening the National Assembly, the three main Pakistani leaders kept on bargaining, but with frighteningly few signs of a political breakthrough. Bhutto insisted that his party, dominant in West Pakistan, should take a big role in any new government, and that Pakistan could not be allowed to disintegrate.[58]

Mujib, at another huge rally of half a million people—many of them carrying iron rods and bamboo sticks—held back from declaring an independent Bangladesh, but demanded that the army withdraw to its barracks and yield power to the winners of the election. "It was a vast number of people who had suddenly become political," says Meg Blood. "They had been insulted because their vote had been ignored." The Pakistani security forces found themselves overwhelmed by an uprising that roiled throughout Dacca, Chittagong, Jessore, and elsewhere. The Pakistani martial law administration admitted that 172 people had been killed in the first week of March—figures they had to put out to debunk stories among livid Bengalis that hundreds or thousands had been killed. Archer Blood found the military's statement "reasonable, almost apologetic in tone, and seemingly honest."[59]

Ominously, Pakistan flew in more and more troops, who landed from West Pakistan at the Dacca airport. The airport became an armed fort, bristling with dug-in automatic antiaircraft weapons and gun emplacements. Several times in March, Blood watched about a hundred young men debarking from a Pakistan International Airlines plane, all of them dressed alike in neat short-sleeved white shirts and chino trousers. They lined up and marched off smartly. Yahya shoved aside the moderate general who had been governor of East Pakistan, terrifying Bengalis with his replacement: Lieutenant General Tikka Khan, known widely as "the butcher of Baluchistan" for his devastating repression of an uprising in that West Pakistani province. Blood knew he was one of the most extreme hawks in the military—a killer.[60]

Blood still did not quite see the massacres coming. He was relieved that Mujib had chosen to avoid declaring independence, and predicted an "essentially static waiting game" as Bengali crowds faced off against the army. (He would later be ashamed of his assessment.) He knew that Bengali nationalists would not be cowed by a whiff of grapeshot, and could not believe that Pakistan's generals would be stupid enough to try it.[61]

Blood was anything but an Awami League partisan. He saw Mujib as principled but exasperatingly obdurate, and warned the League that Yahya and his prideful senior officers had been restrained in the face of considerable provocation. Afterward, he would disgustedly condemn Mujib for overreaching. The nationalist leader had been swept away by the spectacle of "tens of thousands of militant people, men, women and children of all classes thronged by the sheikh's house chanting slogans" about the " 'emancipation' of Bangla Desh." (The name is Bengali for "Bengal Nation.") The U.S. consul was baffled by "the mystic belief that essentially unarmed masses could triumph in test of wills with martial law government backed by professional army."[62]

Still, Blood admired the Bengali nationalist crowds. Swept up in their effusive mood, he confessed in a cable "a certain lack of objectivity. It is difficult to be completely objective in Dacca in March 1971 when, out of discretion rather than valor, our cars and residences sport black flags and we echo smiling greetings of 'Joi Bangla' as we move about the streets." He enthused, "Daily we lend our ears to the outpouring of the Bengali dream, a touching admixture of bravado, wishful thinking, idealism, animal cunning, anger, and patriotic fervor. We hear on Radio Dacca and see on Dacca TV the impressive blossoming of Bengali nationalism and we watch the pitiful attempts of students and workers to play at soldiering."

But his zest was tempered with growing dread. He came to realize how this would probably end. He hoped the army would follow logic rather than emotion. Blood, whose pragmatism outweighed his Bengali sympathies, evenhandedly hoped for a political "solution which will give something to Bhutto, something to Mujib, something to Yahya and the army, still preserve at least a vestige of the unity of Pakistan, and hopefully buy time for a cooling of passions."[63]

The best prospect would be a confederation, with Yahya as president of both wings, Bhutto as prime minister of West Pakistan, and Mujib as "prime minister of Bangla Desh (East Pakistan has become a term for geographers)." Mujib could not compromise on his promises of autonomy; his people would never accept that now. But autonomy came dangerously close to independence for Bangladesh, and Blood thought that Yahya would likely balk. He presciently wrote, "The ominous prospect of a military crackdown is much more than a possibility, but it would only delay, and ensure, the independence of Bangla Desh." Blood suggested telling Yahya that the United States wanted a political solution, but the State Department—following Kissinger's guidance—maintained its silence.[64]

DACCA BECAME A MORE MENACING PLACE FOR AMERICANS. THE CIA warned Blood that communists were trying to assassinate him. Late one night, three Urdu-speaking men in a car without a license plate drove up to the Adamjee Court building that housed the consulate, threw two handmade bombs, and fired a revolver into the air. The building shook. A few nights later, Archer and Meg Blood heard several gunshots at their house. Someone in a jeep had driven up to the consul's residence, fired three shots, and raced off. Meg Blood remembers suspicions fell on the Naxalites, the Maoist revolutionaries: "They thought it would be a nice chaotic thing to assassinate the man in charge." The Bloods found bullet holes in the veranda off their bedroom. The U.S. consulate and other American buildings in Dacca faced regular bombings with Molotov cocktails, which were nerve-jangling but so far mercifully amateurish. After two Molotov cocktails were thrown at American business offices in downtown Dacca, Archer Blood shrugged it off: "Bombing gang still active and happily still ineffective."[65]

On March 15—which Blood bookishly noted was the Ides of March—Yahya arrived in Dacca for more negotiations. It was, one of Yahya's ministers despairingly recalled, "like giving oxygen to a dying patient when the doctors have declared him a lost case." Blood suffered a moment of optimism. "Things are looking up," he reported after talks between Yahya and Mujib. The same day that he wrote that, there was a serious clash twenty miles north of Dacca, as Pakistani troops opened fire when they were stopped by a furious crowd, killing at least two civilians. Mujib privately passed along a message to Blood that these provocations made it hard to sell a peace deal to his own people. Blood, having none of it, sent to Mujib "the natural rejoinders: rise above the matter; play the statesman; surely Yahya must be as unhappy about such incidents as Mujib."[66]

Despite pressure from more militant Bengalis, Mujib continued to insist to other East Pakistani politicians that he wanted to keep Pakistan's wings together, perhaps in some kind of confederation. Bhutto, adamant about Pakistan's unity, had been sitting out the negotiations. But on March 22, he came to Dacca to join in the talks with Yahya and Mujib. Blood happened to be at the Intercontinental Hotel for a lunch, and caught a glimpse of the politician in the lobby. The hatred of the Bengalis for Bhutto was palpable; people hollered obscenities at the grim-faced man, who was flanked by bodyguards with AK-47 assault rifles. Blood later remembered Bhutto staring straight ahead, his "reptilian eyes fixed on the wall. He was in the enemy's camp and he knew it." Another eyewitness saw eight truckloads of armed troops protecting Bhutto's car. At a press conference at the Intercontinental Hotel, Bhutto announced that Yahya and Mujib had reached a general agreement that made a promising basis for future negotiations.[67]

Blood was satisfied with the prospect of a deal that gave Mujib "everything but independence and which, we believe, he could sell to people of Bangla Desh." On March 24, Blood shrugged off a plea from Mujib, who wanted U.S. pressure on Yahya to avoid a crackdown. Blood saw little evidence that Yahya was "about to take a harder line." As Yahya, Bhutto, and Mujib negotiated frenetically, Blood's disastrously incorrect evaluation was agreeable to the higher-ups at the State Department, who preferred to avoid taking sides in Pakistan's politics. But Mujib suspected that the West Pakistanis were dragging out the talks to buy time to reinforce their military.[68]

The defense attaché at the Dacca consulate, a U.S. Air Force colonel, visited two senior Pakistani officers. They were unbearably tense. One of them, a Pakistani wing commander, said that they would carry out their orders, but hoped they would not have to do the worst: "It is [a] terrible thing to shoot your own people."[69]

Chapter 3

Mrs. Gandhi

INDIRA GANDHI HAD A PERSONAL CONNECTION TO BENGAL. HER father, Jawaharlal Nehru, the great opponent of British colonialism who would become India's founding prime minister, had given her a demanding if inconsistent education. In 1934, at the age of sixteen, with her father once again stuck in a cramped British jail, Indira Nehru—who would grow up to be the first woman prime minister of India—was packed off to study in the wilds of Bengal.

She had already had a singular schooling, of a kind: enduring an uncertain, anxious, and often lonely childhood, with her aristocratic grandfather, resolute father, and sickly mother campaigning for India's freedom and paying for it with long, wretched tours in British prisons; sitting in on her father's meeting with Albert Einstein; visiting her father's dear friend and mentor Mohandas Gandhi—the revered Mahatma himself—in jail, where he would affectionately pull her ears.[1]

But Santiniketan (the Abode of Peace), in the glorious countryside of what today is West Bengal, north of Calcutta (now called Kolkata), was no common place to learn. The school there was founded by the celebrated Bengali poet and philosopher Rabindranath Tagore, who would write the national anthems for two unborn states, India and Bangladesh. The Nobel laureate meant to realize Indians' intellectual independence through learning, studying all of humanity, with a special attention to Japanese and Chinese civilization. The institution was determinedly unconventional: on arriving, Indira Nehru searched in vain for the classrooms and was startled to discover that her classes were held under the trees. "Everything is so artistic and beautiful and wild!" she wrote to Nehru. In a respite from all too much politics, she was transfixed by art and poetry. She was awed by Tagore himself, a humane prophet complete with cascading white beard and hair. Following his universalist vision, she took courses in French and English, in Hindi and Bengali.²

Nehru wanted his daughter to learn to speak some Bengali and "get to know the Bengalis a little better." Later, when Bengalis were slaughtered and West Bengal was overrun with desperate refugees, Bengalis would often say that she had a special feeling for them. She was hardly the most sentimental individual, but she was familiar with Bengal's heat and spring flowers, all the sounds and smells of the place. She had found Bengali "a very sweet & nice language," and had soon gotten good enough that Tagore suggested she take literature classes in it. There was nothing abstract for her about the people who were suffering and dying. In a cruel twist, the site of this misery in 1971 was where she had tried to escape from politics long before. "I was away from politics, noise," she once said. "It was a refuge and a new world."³

SHE GREW UP TO PLUNGE BACK INTO THE POLITICS AND THE NOISE. Her idyll in West Bengal gave way to more standard schools, in India and Britain. There are not a lot of government chiefs trained at both Santiniketan and Oxford. In 1942, she married a worldly, outgoing politician and journalist, Feroze Gandhi, taking his last name. (She was no relation to Mahatma Gandhi.) In the family tradition, she was arrested by the British after speaking to a rally in Allahabad. She languished in a dirty gray prison cell, sleeping on a concrete bed in the freezing cold. In the violence of Partition, she on two separate occasions protected presumably Muslim men being chased by Hindu mobs. And she worked in filthy refugee camps for Muslims displaced by Partition.⁴

After all that, it is hard to say what the humane lessons of Tagore might have meant to a steely, calculating politician. Her wariness of others was heightened by a miserable marriage, which ended when her husband died of a sudden heart attack at the age of forty-seven. While Jawaharlal Nehru was prime minister, she was uneasy around the courtiers and hacks crowding his grand Delhi residence, Teen Murti Bhavan. But in 1959, she threw herself into public life, becoming president of the dominant Indian National Congress, her father's political party.⁵

All grown up, Indira Gandhi was nobody's idea of a charmer. Jacqueline Kennedy, who scored rather higher in the social graces, found her "a real prune—bitter, kind of pushy, horrible woman." Even those who liked her found her remote and withdrawn. Her closest friend wrote that she had a sharp temper and nursed grudges, and was secretive and private. She worked relentlessly, with the disconcerting habit of reading papers while someone was talking to her. One of her top advisers explained sympathetically that she was constantly tense from having to contend with the man's world of Indian government (her aunt once famously called her "the only man in her cabinet"), which earned her a reputation as "aloof, secretive and haughty." K. C. Pant, then a young Indian official from a prominent political family who went on to be defense minister, and says he was on friendly terms with her, recalls, "She could be very cold. Occasionally she had to freeze somebody. She could freeze them just by looking at them. She listened, she absorbed, she didn't speak much."[6]

India was born democratic. Nehru had a bedrock devotion to freedom of thought, the verdict of the ballot box, and the independence of the courts. But Gandhi had inherited somewhat less than a full portion of her iconic father's fundamental and sophisticated commitment to democracy. She was far more willing to manipulate people, and seemed quite aware that she lacked her father's saintliness. Jaswant Singh—who has served as India's foreign minister, defense minister, and finance minister in a rival party—remembers, "All along she felt, and she often said it, that 'my father was a saint in politics. I am not.' She had not the same tolerance and acceptance of a differing viewpoint."[7]

Nehru died in 1964, leaving some people wondering if India could survive as a unified and democratic country. His daughter was given the modest job of running the ministry of information and broadcasting, but when the new prime minister, Lal Bahadur Shastri, dropped dead of a heart attack early in 1966, her name was suddenly floated for prime minister. Many of the ruling Congress party's grandees imagined that she could be easily shoved around. They were wrong. In January 1966, Indira Gandhi was sworn in as prime minister in the magnificent Rashtrapati Bhavan.[8]

SHE WAS A NOVICE, JUST FORTY-SEVEN YEARS OLD AND UNTESTED, abruptly in charge of the world's largest democracy. It was and is an impossible job. She was confronted with all of India's problems: terrible poverty, widespread illiteracy, secessionist movements, bloodyminded revolutionaries, sclerotic government. But she quickly learned on the job. She reached out to the public, while presiding over a titanic patronage machine, doling out appointments and favors to every part of the country. She dedicated herself to fighting poverty. But it was rough going as she faced years of drought, a weak economy, and riots.[9]

Gandhi struggled to keep India united. She lived in dread of communal bloodshed between Hindus and Muslims in such vital states as Gujarat, Uttar Pradesh, and Bihar. To quell violence, she reminded the state governments that the central government's security forces, including the army, were available for use, and hoped "that these would be called in in time and not after the event." [10]

The new prime minister had to face secessionist revolts far from the country's center: Nagaland, Mizoram, and of course Kashmir. And while Indians preferred to point to their success stories—where democratic federalism managed to hold the country together—the Indian state sometimes harshly used force. When in March 1966 Mizo insurgents in the hill country declared their independence from India, Gandhi's government sent in both the army and the air force—the first time that the Indian air force had been unleashed against Indian citizens. India marched troops against rebels in Nagaland too, where a peace effort fell apart, followed by brutal Naga terrorist attacks on civilians. [11]

Gandhi had been installed in office by the politicos, but in 1967 she won her first electoral mandate from the Indian public. In elections for the Lok Sabha (House of the People), the lower house of India's Parliament, her Congress party managed to hold on to a majority, but was much weakened (which had the benefit of getting rid of some of her rivals inside the party). In 1969, the party split between the leftist Gandhi and her more conservative competitors, with intense sparring among them. [12]

By then, Gandhi was already chafing against the democratic restraints on her authority, eerily foreshadowing her notorious 1975 declaration of Emergency rule—the terrible rupture in India's long history of democratic governance. When she first became prime minister, she was skeptical not just about the civil service and her own Congress party, but also about parliamentary democracy itself. She bridled at the incrementalism of the unwieldy Indian political system, with its thousands of daily compromises: "Sometimes I wish . . . we had a real revolution—like France or Russia—at the time of independence." She had a penchant for crude censorship. In some of this, she had a little more in common with Richard Nixon than either of them would have liked to admit. [13]

THE ARGUMENTATIVE INDIAN

Indira Gandhi's most important adviser by far was P. N. Haksar, the principal secretary to the prime minister. Of all the self-important mandarins in South Block, arriving each morning to have their brief-cases carried from the car up to the office by a servant striding ahead of them, he was the top. The job title is much too humble: he functioned essentially as her chief of staff and foremost foreign policy adviser. (Henry Kissinger once called him "my opposite number there, Haksar, who is probably a communist.") In terms of the Nixon administration, P. N. Haksar was something like the Indian equivalent of H. R. Haldeman and Kissinger combined. He got vastly more face time with the new prime minister than any cabinet official, and exercised tremendous influence on her.[14]

Haksar was given to daydreaming and liked to dawdle in his bed, but, as he wrote late in his life, was driven to diligent toil out of "moral obligation, or out of a sense of duty." Like Nehru, he hailed from an eminent family of Kashmiri Pandits, and strove to live up to the legacy. He inherited both a sense of perfectionism and a dread of dishonor, which was, he reflected, "probably imbibed through constantly hearing since early childhood that our family could never be bribed, bought or made to bend. Such, at any rate, was the mythology of our family. And mythologies have a way of taking hold of one's mind, just as gravity holds one's body."[15]

He studied both mathematics and history, and became a conspicuously erudite lawyer, educated at Allahabad and the London School of Economics. His background was sufficiently posh that one of his uncles, who was prime minister of Jaipur under the British Empire, always served the teatime cake iced with the colors of the Union Jack. But Haksar grew up amid political turmoil, surrounded by talk of Mahatma Gandhi and Jawaharlal Nehru's freedom struggle, with his mother telling him that the English were a nation of scoundrels. "Gandhi had appeared on our horizon," he later said. "And he grew larger every day, until he covered the entire sky." As a young man, dreaming of doing extraordinary deeds, Haksar gambled on an independent India.[16]

After Partition, which he said made him "spiritually sick," he hitched his fortunes to the Nehru family. This paid off handsomely. Haksar first met Indira Nehru Gandhi in his childhood: a tiny girl, perched on a servant's shoulder, was brought over to the Haksars' house in Nagpur, fondly announced as the only child of the great Nehru. Haksar later remembered only that "her eyes seemed to get bigger and brighter the more my mother fussed over her." Nehru himself encouraged the promising young man to join India's new foreign service, extolling his flair for political work.[17]

Haksar, with a beaky nose and bushy eyebrows, was more of a professional civil servant than a politico. His government service centered on the Ministry of External Affairs, with tours of duty in Nigeria, Austria, and Britain. His British posting particularly helped him clamber upward: Indira Gandhi was then studying at Oxford, and he got to know her. His loyalty to the family was smoothly extended to her.[18]

Where Gandhi lacked a well-considered political philosophy, Haksar was there to help provide it. He anchored her in democratic politics. His words could sometimes echo Nehru's. In the great fight against poverty, Haksar wanted to work within the existing secular democratic system. He struck liberal notes on minority rights, expansively declaring his commitment to freedom of speech, assembly, and worship for every single Indian citizen.[19]

Like Kissinger, Haksar was brainy, witty, verbose, arrogant, and abrasive. He took a long-range view—again like Kissinger—sometimes to the annoyance of those who wanted immediate policy and were less indulgent of intellectualism. He consolidated power over foreign policy in his office, pushing aside foreign ministers who came belatedly to realize who the real boss was. Haksar could be merciless to underlings, while always cultivating his relationship with the prime minister.[20]

Under Haksar, the prime minister's secretariat dominated the government. His senior colleagues found him warm and approachable, running the prime minister's team with a combination of energy and confidence, although, as one top aide noted, he "tended to pontificate." Arundhati Ghose, a diplomat who served under Haksar in Vienna and after, who would later read to an elderly Haksar as he slowly went blind, remembers him fondly. "Haksar had a very wry sense of humor. He was extremely well read, very affectionate, and very warm." She recalls his outsized influence, with all the powers of the prime minister's office, and his guiding role in India's foreign policy.[21]

According to Nehru's grand vision of nonalignment, India was to stand warily above the quarrelsome superpowers of the Cold War. But Haksar was in the thick of it—firmly committed to the Soviet side. He was staunchly leftist at home and abroad, leaning toward the Soviet Union so much that it alarmed other Indian officials. He was joined in this by some of the other leading pro-Soviet Indians who were Gandhi's closest advisers—all of them Kashmiri Brahmins like her, thus quickly dubbed the "Kashmiri Mafia." Ghose remembers that her mentor never hid his left-wing views. Although he did not impose his leftism on his subordinates, she says, "It came out in everything that he said or did."[22]

Indira Gandhi was not as pro-Soviet as Haksar, but she was already leery of the United States. On her first visit to Washington as prime minister in 1966, she got along well with Lyndon Johnson, and tried to get him to restart U.S. economic aid to India, which had been suspended during the India-Pakistan war of 1965. But they sparred over the devaluation of the rupee and, later, over the Middle East and the Vietnam War. She was stung by Johnson's attempts to use food aid for leverage and by lectures from other U.S. officials. Facing famine in 1966, she resented the slowness of U.S. food shipments. Meanwhile, Haksar pushed her further toward the Soviet Union. She sought more Soviet arms sales, helping India to build up a formidable military machine. When the Soviet Union invaded Czechoslovakia in 1968, India refused to vote for a United Nations resolution condemning the brutal crackdown on Czech liberals. Gandhi's government was grateful to the Soviet Union for help with industrialization and nurturing India's defense industry. Ghose says that largely "as a result of Haksar-sahib's influence," the government had a "distrust of the Americans. They didn't trust us, we didn't trust them."[23]

For that, the Nixon administration loathed him. Samuel Hoskinson, Kissinger's staffer for South Asia at the White House, shudders operatically at the mention of his name. "It brings back nothing but bad memories," he says. "He was an arrogant Brahmin, pretty far left, difficult to discuss anything with. He always wants the upper hand. You don't have a discussion. He fires verbal volleys." Hoskinson hated his pro-Soviet politics too. "He was quite far left. He may have been a communist." (He wasn't.) Although Hoskinson doubted it, some U.S. officials felt that "he might be controlled by the Russians, that he was actually an asset of the KGB."[24]

INDIRA GANDHI'S POWER WAS LIMITED BY HER PARTY'S STANDING IN Parliament. Frustratingly dependent on socialist and leftist parties, she was in a weak position, while her more conservative foes were maneuvering against her. She had no patience for the opposition. In December 1970, taking advantage of her popularity, she boldly chose a democratic way out: calling new general elections.[25]

The Lok Sabha was dissolved, and Indian politicians hit the hustings, from Uttar Pradesh to Gujarat to Kerala. It was the biggest election in the world. In the end, more than 151 million voters cast their ballots. She gambled her entire political future on the outcome.[26] Gandhi campaigned hard on a populist platform, dedicated to ending India's grinding poverty. When her rivals put up the Hindi slogan of *"Indira Hatao!"* (Remove Indira!), she parried with what became her famous catchphrase: *"Garibi Hatao!"* (Remove Poverty!) She spoke to some 375 meetings, barely sleeping or eating as she campaigned all across the vast country. Astonishingly, in forty-three days of electioneering, she claimed to have given speeches in front of as many as thirteen million people. She later liked to boast that she never spoke at a rally with fewer than a hundred thousand people. She hammered home her core themes: getting rid of unemployment, helping peasants and shopkeepers, whipping the much-despised civil service into line.[27]

It worked. Gandhi and her team won a massive landslide. Her party—known since the split in the Congress party as Congress (R)—seized a two-thirds majority in the Lok Sabha. Her own campaigning was crucial to this terrific sweep and she was now in an extraordinarily strong position. Her foreign minister, Sardar Swaran Singh, would later brag about "the Indira typhoon." Sydney Schanberg, the *New York Times* correspondent in Delhi, was impressed. Settling into the newspaper's bureau on Janpath, in the heart of Delhi, he had grown fond of India. "It has terrible problems, but it is a democracy," he says. "The people do like to throw the bums out when they vote."[28]

Having won the election on her antipoverty campaign, Gandhi faced high expectations at home. But the crisis in Pakistan quickly overwhelmed her government's focus on relieving India's poor. As Gandhi said, "our country was poised for rapid economic advance and a more determined attack on the age-old poverty of our people. Even as we were settling down to these new tasks, we have been engulfed by a new and gigantic problem, not of our making."[29]

WHILE GANDHI'S GOVERNMENT MIGHT HAVE BEEN TEMPTED TO GLOAT at Pakistan's troubles in governing East Bengal, the Indian government was painfully aware of its own difficulties in keeping a grip on its own state of West Bengal.

The Indian state was a hotbed of Marxist and Maoist agitation, notorious as the home of the fiery Maoist revolutionaries known as the Naxalites—named after the West Bengali village of Naxalbari, where the movement originated. Haksar despised the "cult of violence" of the

Naxalites and radicals in West Bengal. Gandhi's government, horrified by the violent and pro-Chinese Naxalites, feared an armed communist takeover of parts of the country. Gandhi and her allies struggled to get the better of both the Naxalites and the powerhouse Communist Party (Marxist). "Calcutta was flooded with Maoist literature," remembered one journalist. "Mao Tse Tung, Liu Shao Chi, Marx, Lenin. The city was Red."[30]

"From October 1969 to the middle of 1971, we broke the back of the Naxalite revolt in West Bengal," remembers Lieutenant General Jacob-Farj-Rafael Jacob, then a major general and the chief of staff of the army's Eastern Command. "Mrs. Gandhi told me to do it." People were thrown in jail on specific charges or under a notorious Preventive Detention Act. Haksar knew that there were some ten thousand young people in jail in West Bengal, and that more than a hundred thousand political workers were facing criminal charges. The West Bengal state government requested the deployment of Indian army troops to maintain order. Gandhi's central government offered large coercive forces to the West Bengal local government, including battalions of police, the Border Security Force, and almost two divisions of the Indian army.[31]

Moderate politicians feared what the communists—who had done well in the elections—might do if they were allowed to run the state, and violent mass unrest if they were not. The governor of West Bengal bleakly told Gandhi that *restoring law and order . . . may be an unpleasant duty.* The Indian ambassador in Washington admitted, "Considering that we ourselves have plenty of problems in east India, we would not wish for East Bengal to be in a disturbed state."[32]

PAKISTAN VOTES

India was thrilled by Pakistan's novel experiment in democracy. The Pakistani elections in December 1970 touched a chord in India, where democratic precepts ran deep—and where Gandhi would soon have her big electoral win.

Indians savored the drubbing the Pakistani military received at the hands of their electorate, and many educated Indians relished the voting as a repudiation of the founding ideal of Pakistan as a Muslim state, which was not enough to keep the two halves of the country from coming unglued. "Mujib's thumping victory in East Bengal was a foregone conclusion," wrote a senior Indian diplomat. "Culturally they're quite different," recalls Jagat Mehta, a former Indian foreign secretary. "It was in the seeds of time."[33]

The Indian government was heartened to hear Mujib call for friendship with India and for a peaceful resolution in Kashmir. Indians hoped that a democracy in Pakistan would prove peaceful toward them, particularly if the Awami League, warm to India, managed to form a government in Islamabad. India's foreign intelligence agency, the Research and Analysis Wing (R&AW)—created as a kind of Indian answer to the CIA—concluded that a genuinely democratic Pakistan would increasingly desist from military confrontations against India.[34]

Not everyone swooned. Haksar worried that the humiliated Pakistani military would lash out against India. "I have long been feeling a sense of uneasiness about the intentions of Pakistan," he wrote to Gandhi. The Awami League's resounding victory made Pakistan's internal problems "infinitely more difficult. Consequently, the temptation to seek solution of these problems by external adventures has become very great." He implored Gandhi to quietly convene her service chiefs of staff and defense minister to "share with them her anxieties," and have the military make "a very realistic assessment both of Pakistan's capability and our response. I have a feeling that there are many weak spots in our defence capabilities."[35]

India's spies were similarly uneasy. The R&AW answered directly to Gandhi's office, and was run by yet another Kashmiri Brahmin, R. N. Kao, who was eager to burnish his agency's reputation. It delivered a top secret alert to Gandhi's government on the impressive increase of Pakistan's military power in recent years, and warned that Pakistan might foment "violent agitation" and sabotage in Kashmir. The R&AW warned that there was a "quite real" risk that Pakistan, bolstered by Chinese support, would attack India. Like Haksar, the R&AW worried that Yahya would be tempted into "a military venture against INDIA with a view to diverting the attention of the people from the internal political problems and justifying the continuance of Martial Law."[36]

But despite this, the R&AW was confident that Mujib and Bhutto—the dominant popular forces in their respective wings—would probably cut a deal, avoiding a crisis or military crackdown. Similarly, one of Gandhi's inner circle remembered that the prime minister's secretariat, reading its reports from Dacca, thought that sort of settlement between Yahya and Mujib was in the works. He recalled that even the appointment of the brutal Lieutenant General Tikka Khan as governor of East Pakistan was seen as just for show.[37]

Haksar, however, quietly prepared for the worst. "Our requirements are extremely urgent," he wrote, alarmed at Pakistan's new offensive capabilities. With Nixon starting to sell weapons to Pakistan again, India made a huge request to the Soviet Union for bomber aircraft, tanks, armored personnel carriers, ammunition, surface-to-air missiles, and radar. Haksar nervously instructed the Indian ambassador in Moscow, "We have no repeat *no* other source of supply."[38]

INDIA'S DIPLOMATS IN DACCA MADE NO ATTEMPT TO DISGUISE THEIR sympathies. They eagerly reported the mass mobilization of the Bengalis. When Mujib spoke to a colossal rally of over a million people at the Race Course in Dacca, with the crowds singing Rabindranath Tagore's nationalist song "My Golden Bengal," the top Indian official in Dacca effused that "Bengali nationalism has gone deep into the minds of the people."[39]

As Yahya flew to Dacca for constitutional negotiations with Mujib, the Indian government watched hopefully. India's chief diplomat in Dacca worried that Mujib's call for an autonomous East Pakistan seemed to undercut Pakistan's unity. Mujib ominously warned that conspiracies in Pakistan's ruling classes were trying to thwart the democratic will of the people: "But they are playing with fire. Our people are conscious and they would resist any conspiratorial move."[40]

In private, India's diplomats heaped spiteful abuse on Bhutto, who was notoriously hostile to their country. India's enthusiasm for democracy in Pakistan did not include Bhutto's own electoral triumph; the Indian mission in Karachi sneered, "Mr. Bhutto . . . has really secured power through slogan-mongering and his not inconsiderable histrionic talents." Indian officials blamed him for stonewalling the constitutional talks. A senior Indian diplomat posted in Islamabad would later accuse Bhutto of being "directly responsible for encouraging Military action against Awami League." Bhutto, one of Gandhi's senior aides later wrote, "approved of the merciless military offensive."[41]

In the middle of these tense negotiations, India faced a spectacular act of terrorism. On January 30, in Srinagar, two young separatist Kashmiri Indians hijacked an Indian Airlines airplane to Lahore, in West Pakistan, and then blew it up in a fiery blaze. Although nobody was hurt, the furious Indian government immediately assumed the hijackers were Pakistani agents. As a tough reprisal, Gandhi's government suspended flights of Pakistani military and civilian aircraft over Indian territory, making it hard for Pakistan to keep up links between its two far-flung wings. (Yahya would accuse India of arranging the hijacking to justify this decision to ban overflights.) In West Pakistan, politicians fired off denunciations of India, and Bhutto had a friendly meeting with the hijackers; but in East Pakistan, Mujib swiftly denounced the destruction of the airplane, while Bengalis, unconcerned with competing claims in Kashmir, condemned the terrorists. This episode afforded India a tantalizing glimpse of the transformed relationship that it might have enjoyed with Pakistan under a Bengali-led government.[42]

THE R&AW'S PREDICTION OF A DEAL AMONG PAKISTAN'S LEADING POLIticians proved far too optimistic. Mujib insisted that his majority in the National Assembly entitled him to frame a new Pakistani constitution, ushering in autonomy for East Pakistan. But when Bhutto dug in his heels in early March, Indian officials noted sourly that "Mr. Bhutto took recourse to his familiar anti-Indian bogey."[43]

From Islamabad, Indian diplomats warned that hard-liners were putting increasing pressure on Yahya. An Indian official wrote that "the Armed Forces and the pre-dominately Punjabi Establishment in West Pakistan is back at its 23 year old game of not allowing East Pakistan to exercise its majority share in the country's affairs." As Bengalis protested, Indian diplomats in Dacca reported with alarm that hundreds of civilians were killed or injured, and scorned Yahya's suggestion that the "the army is above democratically elected representatives 'playing at' Constitution-making." This, Indian officials wrote, smacked of Latin American–style despotism.[44]

India's government remained wholeheartedly for Mujib. The top Indian diplomat in Dacca admiringly reported, "His constitutional method, solicitude for democratic process, discussion with west Pakistan leaders and the spirit of accommodation within the framework of his commitment are likely to create a favourable impression on President Yahya Khan and the people of west Pakistan." One of Gandhi's top advisers remembers that the prime minister's staff thought that some kind of deal had been struck.[45]

Other senior Indian officials in Delhi, however, were bracing for disaster. On March 2, over three weeks *before* Yahya launched his slaughter, Gandhi ordered her best and brightest—including Haksar and the R&AW spymaster Kao—to evaluate "giving help to Bangla Desh" and the possibility of recognizing "an independent Bangla

Desh." That, Gandhi feared, could easily prompt Pakistani retaliation in Kashmir, or a Chinese military response. The prime minister was already considering military aid to the Bengalis, who would need not just medicine and food, but a helicopter and a small airplane for "quick movement inside India around the borders of Bangla Desh," as well as "Arms and ammunition (including L[ight] M[achine] G[un]s, M[edium] M[achine] G[un]s and Mortars."[46]

India urged the United States to hold Yahya back from a crackdown. In Washington, the Indian ambassador pleaded that "nothing would be more tragic than President Yahya Kahn trying to suppress East Bengali aspirations for autonomy by force."[47]

By March 15, the Pakistani foreign office complained that India had built up its military forces in West Bengal. But Yahya showed no signs of taking on India now. In the days after the hijacking, Pakistan had massed its troops on West Pakistan's border with India, but now the R&AW and the chief of the army staff, General Sam Manekshaw, found that most of those troops had been withdrawn. Yahya had more than doubled his army strength in East Pakistan. Pakistan's military rulers seemed to be marshaling their fire for their own populace.[48]

Haksar urged Gandhi to stand firm: "we should not at this stage of developments in Pakistan say anything at all placatory, but be 'tough' within reason. This is not the time to make gestures for friendship for Pakistan. Every such gesture will bring comfort to Yahya Khan and make the position of Mujib correspondingly more difficult." Haksar ominously warned the prime minister: "2½ Divisions of Pak Army is poised to decimate East Bengal."[49]

Chapter 4

"Mute and Horrified Witnesses"

DACCA IS A TROPICAL, IMPOVERISHED, POLLUTED, AND VERDANT river city, in the middle of the great part-submerged marsh that is Bangladesh. The capital city is clamorously loud, from honking cars, radios, conversations, muezzins, and mechanical disasters. People toil in steamy heat, in acrid haze and dust, hefting stones at construction sites or holding together a small shop. The streets are crammed with rickshaws decked out in explosive color, and with rickety buses whose mangled flanks, painted only a little less gaudily beautiful than the rickshaws, bear the scars of abrupt lane changes gone bad. People drive with a headlong recklessness. They jaywalk worse. The palm trees offer shelter from an implacable sun. At night, it falls truly dark in the way of very poor cities; there is only a fraction of the garish neon and fluorescent light that illuminates the wealthier megacities of South Asia. In March, it is already sweltering.

In 1971, March 25 marked the twenty-third long day of the Bengali nationalist protests in Dacca and beyond. Archer Blood warned Washington, "Storm before the calm?"[1]

He nervously reported a worsening crisis, with the army clashing with civilians in several spots in East Pakistan. In the port city of Chittagong, thousands of Bengalis tried to prevent the unloading of a cargo ship laden with weaponry and ammunition for the Pakistani military. The army—which Blood called "restrained (but presumably increasingly irritated)"—sent in five hundred troops, and eventually opened fire on the crowds, killing at least fifteen people.[2]

Finally, with ominous swiftness, Yahya flew out of Dacca for West Pakistan, abandoning the talks once and for all. Whatever hope there had been for a political deal, it was now extinguished.

. . .

THAT NIGHT, TRYING TO BREAK THE TENSION, ARCHER AND MEG BLOOD
hosted a dinner party at their residence. It was supposed to be a morale
booster, for a mixed crowd of Americans, Bengalis, and foreign diplomats. Nobody was in the mood.

The anxious group was watching an old, downbeat Spencer Tracy
movie when the emergency telephone rang. Blood was told that students were barricading the streets against Pakistan army vehicles, and
that Yahya was gone. The Bengali guests, two High Court justices with
their wives, decided to chance running home, and vanished into the
dark. But when two American guests ventured out into the streets, they
saw a dead body, and raced back to the consul's residence. A dozen of
Blood's guests—including the Yugoslav consul—nervously camped out
there for the night, too afraid to risk going home.

From the roof, they had a view of fires and shadowy terrors all
across the city. They spent much of that night, Blood later recalled,
"watching with horror the constant flash of tracer bullets across the
dark sky and listening to the more ominous clatter of machine gun fire
and the heavy clump of tank guns."[3]

They could see explosions in the sky. "Dark, dark, dark skies,
but with flak," remembers Meg Blood. "It was not like fireworks. It
was continual. It was exploding all over the sky." The detonations
were small, but bright and loud. Some of the Bengalis who worked
for the Bloods said that they knew people in the neighborhoods that
were being set aflame, including a poor bazaar area. There were army
jeeps moving around. Some of the fires were in nearby places that were
heavily populated with extremely poor people. "They were suffering
terribly," Meg Blood says.

The Pakistani military had launched a devastating assault on the
Bengalis. Truckloads of Pakistani troops drove through the city, only
barely slowed by Bengali barricades. U.S.-supplied M-24 tanks led some
of the troop columns. Throughout Dacca, people could hear the firing
of rifles and machine guns. Windows rattled from powerful explosions
from mortars or heavy weapons. The night turned red from burning
cars and buildings. It was only near daybreak that the gunfire slowed.[4]

SYDNEY SCHANBERG OF THE *NEW YORK TIMES* WAS STUCK AT THE INTER-
continental Hotel, beside himself with frustration. On that night, he
was jolted by explosions. The army corralled the foreign press. "They

kept pushing us into the hotel," he remembers. They ended up watching from the tenth floor of the Intercontinental Hotel. They could see flames from Dacca University, which was a mile and a half away, where, Schanberg says, the army seemed to be shooting artillery. The trapped reporters watched a Pakistani soldier on a jeep that had a mounted machine gun—equipment probably provided by the United States. He recalls, "They started shooting at students coming from the university, up the road about a mile. They were singing patriotic songs in Bengali. And then the army opened up. We couldn't tell when they hit the ground if they were ducking or killed."[5]

The soldiers turned on the Bengali media. "They headed for a newspaper," Schanberg remembers, "and then people were jumping out of the windows to get away from that. There wasn't any paper that wasn't supporting Mujib." As Blood's consulate reported, the Pakistani authorities violently targeted the local press, starting with pro–Awami League local newspapers like *The People* and *Ittefaq*. According to a survivor, tanks opened fire on *Ittefaq*'s building without warning. The newsprint would still be burning two days later, with a charred corpse lying outside.[6]

The army aimed to cow the foreign reporters into silence rather than kill them. Schanberg and the other captive journalists could only manage fragmentary reporting. On March 26, Pakistani troops stormed into the Intercontinental Hotel. An officer warned, "Anyone who leaves the hotel will be shot." The soldiers tore down a Bangladesh flag and burned it. Schanberg remembers being herded up with the other journalists. With their guns on showy display, the soldiers packed the foreign correspondents onto planes for Karachi. When a stubborn reporter tried to sneak out of the hotel, a Pakistani soldier stopped him. "I have killed my countryman," the soldier said. "Why shouldn't I kill you?"[7]

There were only a few foreign correspondents who managed to dodge the Pakistani dragnet, including a reporter and a photographer from the Associated Press. The London *Daily Telegraph*'s reporter hid on the roof of the Intercontinental Hotel, toured the city's devastation, and flew out two days later for West Pakistan; he evaded two strip searches by hiding his notes in his socks. Archer Blood later said that he sheltered one reporter who snuck across the border: "We hid him in our house so they could keep reporting."[8]

Along the road to the airport, Schanberg saw burned huts and houses. "We didn't see any bodies," he recalls. "They had probably

done something about that. It was clear they had killed a lot of people." They were flown first to Ceylon (Sri Lanka today), where he tried
to sneak off, and was caught in the airport by a Pakistani officer pointing a gun at him. "I wasn't ready to die," says Schanberg, "so I got
back on the plane." In Karachi, the Pakistanis tried to seize Schanberg's
notebooks, but he held on to them. He wrote up some of what he had
seen for the *New York Times*—"a surprise attack with tanks, artillery
and heavy machine guns against a virtually unarmed population"—
but had to file his reporting from the safety of Delhi.[9]

SCOTT BUTCHER, BLOOD'S YOUNG POLITICAL OFFICER, WAS SPENDING
a quiet night with his wife at their lakeside home in a comfortable
neighborhood not far from where Mujib lived—a certain target for the
Pakistan army. Late at night on March 25, he got an ominous telephone
call from a grim Schanberg, whom he knew from the latter's coverage
of the cyclone. The reporter, held by the army at the Intercontinental
Hotel, tried to sneak out a bulletin. The military was tearing down
Bangladeshi flags at the hotel; Yahya had fled; something was going
on. Butcher tried but failed to get the word out. When Butcher called
another consulate staffer, that official said he had a wounded person
at his house.

Butcher heard a gunshot or two. There was clanging and banging
outside. He ventured out to find local youths from the Awami League,
hastily trying to build a barricade to protect Mujib, when the army
came. This was going to be a major clash. Butcher had an instant of
odd clarity: he was going to need all the sleep he could get. So he and
his wife went directly to bed. Somehow they managed to fall into an
uneasy slumber.

The army came on foot. Hushed, silent in the warm night, they
crept past the makeshift barricades. Butcher and his wife did not hear
them. "All of a sudden—machine-gun fire, right outside our bedroom
window," he remembers. "I went flying off our bed." He hit the car-
pet, telling his wife to get down on the floor. They crawled into their
infant daughter's bedroom to get her. Hearing what sounded like heavy
weapons, they stayed away from the windows, afraid of getting caught
in the crossfire.

Butcher tried to phone out, but the line made a strange noise and
went dead. He felt a wave of frustration: he was a political officer, used
to walking around the city during strikes and demonstrations, but now
he could not get out. After a while, he made his way up to the roof. He

saw flames all over. The city was burning. "We could hear rhythmic firing which sounded like executions," he says. "One time a jeep with machine guns went roaring down our street. We could hear them firing off some rounds."

The army imposed a severe curfew. Anyone defying it would be shot. In a radio address on March 26, Yahya denounced Mujib and the Awami League as treasonous enemies of Pakistan. The army, he said, would hold the country together. Zulfiqar Ali Bhutto, returning to Karachi, supported the crackdown, declaring, "By the grace of God Pakistan has at last been saved." Mujib was arrested and the Awami League banned, along with all political activity. In Dacca, the main radio station broke off its sitar music to broadcast stern martial law orders: no uncensored news, speeches, or posters; no guns, axes, knives, or *lathis;* no strikes or gatherings of five or more. As a Pakistani lieutenant colonel later noted, any Bengali alleged to be a rebel or Awami Leaguer was "sent to Bangladesh"—the euphemistic "code name for death without trial."[10]

On the morning of March 27, Butcher finally went outside. He wanted to know what had happened to the man who had won the recent Pakistani elections. He saw shot-up vehicles outside Mujib's house. The residence seemed empty, except for a few guards. The Bangladesh flag was gone. The Pakistan flag was flying.

THE DEAD

It would be two days before anyone from the U.S. consulate could venture out. Butcher had a diplomatic vehicle, with the protection of consular license plates, which finally got him to the office. The Americans drove through a charred and terrified city. They could hear gunfire. The shops were closed and the traffic was stopped. There were thousands of Bengalis trying to get out of Dacca. "We were just sort of awestruck by the extent of the damage," says one U.S. official.[11]

The Americans knew many of the people being hounded or killed. "Arch made some very close friends there," says Meg Blood. "A number of them were executed at their front doors. He lost friends. One was a Hindu gentleman who had been very generous about invitations to go out on the river and study the life that teems on the rivers."

In Old Dacca, an area the size of two-dozen city blocks had been razed by gunfire. Pakistani soldiers had reportedly destroyed a Bengali police barracks, pounding it with heavy weapons and killing many, and had stormed Dacca University, whose leafy, shaded campus is ordinarily a relatively quiet sanctuary from the city's tumult. Many students and professors had backed the Awami League. Iqbal Hall had evidently been blasted by mortar fire. The inside of the hall, which had been rumored to be a weapons stockpile for the Bengali nationalists, was scorched; a corpse lay nearby. (An American witness later reported that a few students in Iqbal Hall had been armed, which enraged the troops, although a Pakistan army brigadier testified that his fellow soldiers faced no resistance and acted out of "revenge and anger.") Some of the worst killing of civilians, according to students, took place at Jagannath Hall, the Hindu dormitory.[12]

"I saw bodies rotting in the fields," says Scott Butcher. "I saw a decomposing body left in a main street, obviously left there as an example." He remembers the consulate's public safety officer, a hardbitten cop, with tears streaming down his face; the Bengalis he had worked with had all been killed. When a colleague said he had seen lots of bodies stacked up in a park, and asked Butcher if he wanted to come see them, Butcher said, "I've seen enough bodies."

Blood, Butcher, and their team grimly got down to work, gathering reliable information from as many sources as they could find. Stymied by the curfew, without functioning telephones, they managed to check in with aid workers, people from the Pakistan SEATO Cholera Laboratory, professors, missionaries, and others. Discounting what they heard from Awami League partisans, the U.S. diplomats instead secured dependable eyewitness reports, many from trusted Americans. These people had seen dead bodies and burning shantytowns. One American who worked at the posh Dacca Club's golf course saw a dozen corpses. There were, Butcher remembers, "lots of stories of atrocities, of heavy-handed military action."[13]

Butcher pressed farther out, trying to find out everything he could. It was hard to make sense of the chaos. In one village, he found a makeshift hospital, with people lying on cots with horrific, festering slash wounds. When he came across bodies rotting in grassland, he remembers, "I don't know if they were Hindus, Bengalis, or Biharis." Once, driving into Old Dacca, "We saw one man chasing another man with a cleaver. My friend saw the man get whacked in the head with the cleaver." He had no idea who was who. In some cases, the consulate's reporting on specific events may have been incomplete or wrong. Still, he says, the overall pattern was unambiguous: "It was very clear there was an excessively brutal putdown of this autonomy movement." He says that "this military that was so restrained when they were being provoked, once they were unleashed, they were unleashed with a vengeance."

Eric Griffel, the chief U.S. development officer, saw the army, unprovoked, open fire on children and fishermen, although somehow no one was hit. He remembers hearing shooting. He heard terrible rumors, "most of them true, actually." Later, when the U.S. officials were able to meet with the army, who told them that everything was perfectly normal, Griffel's impression was that they believed this would soon be over. "The Bengalis were cowardly," he says, describing the military's attitude. "It was sort of the view of the man on the horse for the shopkeeper."[14]

BLOOD AND HIS TEAM FOUND THEMSELVES ALMOST COMPLETELY ISO-lated. They were a thousand miles away from their home embassy in Islamabad, with nobody from there allowed to come check up on them for several weeks. The mail was late and erratic. The telephones were still down. The Pakistani government needed to conceal, as much as possible, the atrocities from the outside world.[15]

The consulate's only line out was a secret wireless transmitter, unauthorized by the Pakistani authorities. Unbeknownst to Yahya's government, Blood could still send cables to the State Department. This was thanks to two American officials who had braved the streets on the first night of the crackdown, making it to the consulate despite being shot at several times by Pakistani troops. The U.S. embassy in Islamabad tried to conceal these illicit telecommunications, which risked the army's fury. Even so, Blood allowed some local Bengalis to send and receive messages, to help friends in a moment of dire need.[16]

A few days into the slaughter, a State Department spokesman slipped up and mentioned information coming from the Dacca consulate about Pakistani troops firing and using tanks in the city. The U.S. ambassador to Pakistan exploded at this "dullard, thoughtless" mistake, "a stupid and colossal blunder." He wrote that "our secret transmitter in Dacca has been compromised unless we assumed total stupidity on the part of Pak intelligence. If Dacca is forced off the air and if the situation there worsens, our personnel are going to be subjected to added jeopardy."[17]

The Pakistani press blasted Blood. Pakistan's foreign ministry complained that Blood's cables were being cited publicly by Voice of America radio. In response, the U.S. government agreed to cover up the Dacca consulate's reporting on the atrocities. The U.S. embassy in Islamabad assured Yahya's government that it would henceforth keep Blood's information to itself, and demanded that no U.S. officials in Dacca be quoted describing the atrocities. Blood nervously agreed, but warned that the real story would inevitably get out. The Voice of America gave priority to Pakistan's rosy official version of events, often absurdly so. Henry Kissinger, muting Blood, asked his staff, "Are we going to keep VOA quiet about reports coming from our Consul?"[18]

"SELECTIVE GENOCIDE"

Yahya had a green light for his killing campaign. At the White House, Richard Nixon and Henry Kissinger knew that a fierce assault was starting, but made no move to stop or slow it.

On March 26, Kissinger told Nixon that the Pakistan army had moved in. Passing along the Islamabad embassy's assessment that the military could not endure over the long haul, he asked the president to consider asking Yahya to stop the bloodshed. This would win Bengali appreciation and ward off the domestic political risk that the killings "could arouse emotions like those surrounding Biafra over time."[19]

It was a jolting analogy. Biafra, an oil-rich region of Nigeria that tried to secede in 1967, had faced a devastating military crackdown and blockade from the central Nigerian government. Despite gruesome press stories and images of starving Biafran civilians, Lyndon Johnson's administration had stood against breaking up Nigeria, and had given only a modest amount of humanitarian aid as a sop to popular outrage. (Johnson said, "Just get those nigger babies off my TV set.") In the end, in 1970, the Nigerian government crushed the resistance and held on to Biafra, at a horrific human cost. Although Nixon had done little more than Johnson, he was privately shocked at the ethnic toll in Biafra: "The Ibos got decimated, finished." Now Kissinger—invoking Biafra on the first day of Pakistan's crackdown, at the prompting of his aide Samuel Hoskinson—was under no illusions about how ugly Yahya's crackdown would be.[20]

In a Situation Room meeting, Kissinger said that he had talked to Nixon: "His inclination is the same as everybody else's. He doesn't want to do anything. He doesn't want to be in the position where he can be accused of having encouraged the split-up of Pakistan. He does not favor a very active policy. This probably means that we would not undertake to warn Yahya against a civil war." State Department officials pointed out that there was already considerable anti-American suspicion in West Pakistan that the United States was secretly plotting to break up Pakistan—even though the United States was in fact secretly plotting just the opposite. The group agreed not to do anything to minimize the carnage or ask Yahya to call off or restrain his troops.[21]

There was a consensus—spanning Kissinger's staff, the State Department, and U.S. military intelligence—that Yahya could never win his civil war. Despite this, nobody wanted to caution him to back off. The State Department correctly predicted that the Pakistan army might be able to hold Dacca, but the overwhelmingly popular Bengali nationalists would seize the countryside. Conferring with these U.S. officials, Kissinger appeared to grasp the inevitability of an independent Bangladesh emerging at the end of the civil war.[22]

But Kissinger took the opposite line when he was speaking to the president alone. A day later, he told him that "it looks at the moment as if Yahya has gotten control." Nixon was surprised: "Really? How?" Kissinger told the president, "The Bengalis aren't very good fighters I guess."[23]

BLOOD'S GORY REPORTING GOT NO RESPONSE FROM WASHINGTON. AT first, he figured that his superiors were unhappy to hear damning accounts of the Pakistan army's actions. Then it began to dawn on him and his staff that maybe their bosses simply did not believe them.

Scott Butcher was baffled at the studious silence from Washington. "We're sending in all these spot reports on incidents, and not getting any particular reaction," he remembers. "Arch is engaging at the higher policy level, and still not getting any reaction." Butcher says, "We thought it was just a silence benefiting the authorities."

"March 1971 was the most horrible month of my life," Blood later wrote. He remembered the anger of his consulate, mixed with fluctuating hope and despair. Meg Blood recalls that her husband's frustration was beginning to show: "He was expecting a reaction that he wasn't getting."[24]

In response, Archer Blood decided not to soft-pedal his reports. Instead, he sent in even tougher cables. The army, he wrote, had acted "often with ruthless brutality." A consulate staffer had witnessed "heavy firing of automatic weapons by troops," much of it "seemingly at random."[25]

The next day, Blood reported an army attempt to round up all Awami League leaders, including parliamentarians and students.

There was still gunfire and explosions, although less intense than on the first nights of the crackdown. Despite daunting army checkpoints, a steady flow of people hastily fled the city, mostly from the Bengali Hindu minority but also "panic-stricken Muslims." Blood had heard of "large-scaled looting, pillaging and murder . . . against Hindus and Bengalis." The city was awash in stories of atrocities. One Bengali who worked with the consulate tearfully told Blood how the army had burst into his home to search for weapons, and had fatally bayoneted his seventeen-year-old sister when she tried to protect him.[26]

ON MARCH 28, BLOOD REACHED A BREAKING POINT. HE WAS OVER-whelmed with frustration and anger. "For three days we had been flooding Islamabad and Washington with graphic reports of a vicious military action, only to be answered with a deafening silence," he later recalled. "I was suddenly tired of shouting into the dark and I decided to ratchet the intensity of our reporting up a notch."[27]

Thus Blood sent a furious cable with a jolting subject line: "Selective Genocide." He was not a lawyer, but the use of the word "genocide" was meant to shock, to slice through the anodyne bureaucratic niceties of State Department cables.[28]

Blood held nothing back: "Here in Dacca we are mute and horrified witnesses to a reign of terror by the Pak military." (Within the U.S. government, Blood had hardly been mute, but he could not protest to Pakistani officials.) He warned of evidence that the military authorities were "systematically eliminating" Awami League supporters "by seeking them out in their homes and shooting them down." He recounted the killing of politicians, professors, and students. The streets were flooded with Hindus and others trying desperately to get out of Dacca. This assault, he wrote, could not be justified by military necessity: "There is no r[e]p[ea]t no resistance being offered in Dacca to military."[29]

Although he was low in the hierarchy of decision making, Blood proposed reversing Nixon and Kissinger's policy of acquiescent silence. He saw no point in covering up the bloodshed, or in denying that the Dacca consulate was relaying detailed accounts of the slaughter—even though he knew that that would expose the consulate, and would presumably result in Pakistan expelling him from the country. "Full horror of Pak military atrocities will come to light sooner or later," he wrote. Instead of pretending to believe Pakistan's falsehoods, he wrote, "We should be expressing our shock, at least privately to G[overnment] O[f]

P[akistan], at this wave of terror directed against their own country-
men by Pak military."[30]

BLOOD AND SOME OF THE OTHER AMERICANS HAD BEEN HIDING BEN-
galis from the Pakistan army. In this cable, he now admitted this to his
superiors: "Many Bengalis have sought refuge in homes of Americans,
most of whom are extending shelter."[31]

He later wrote that "virtually all Americans in Dacca, official and
unofficial, had terrified Muslim and Hindu Bengalis hiding in their servant quarters. As far as I know, these refugees were poor and apolitical.
My own servants were sheltering a number." He admired his servants'
compassion and was not about to stop them. Blood later said:

> We were also harboring, all of us were harboring, Bengalis,
> mostly Hindu Bengalis, who were trying to flee mostly by tak-
> ing refuge with our own servants. Our servants would give them
> refuge. All of us were doing this. I had a message from Washing-
> ton saying that they had heard we were doing this and to knock
> it off. I told them we were doing it and would continue to do
> it. We could not turn these people away. They were not politi-
> cal refugees. They were just poor, very low-class people, mostly
> Hindus, who were very much afraid that they would be killed
> solely because they were Hindu.

Meg Blood knew that her diplomatic residence was supposed to be
immune to the army. She remembers that the servants' quarters were
behind the main houses, behind the gardens, meaning that they could
give shelter without being conspicuous. "They didn't stay too long,"
she says. "They would go on to their own families. They would go over
the walls, into neighbors' servants' quarters, and were sheltered that
way as they kept out of sight."[32]

Before the crackdown, there had been a friendly group of Bengali
policemen camped out in tents in the Bloods' front yard. On the bloody
night of March 25, they realized that armed Bengalis would be shot
on sight, so they buried their rifles in the Bloods' lawn, ditched their
uniforms, and blended in with the servants. They later escaped. One
corporal later turned up at the Bloods' house, asking Archer Blood to
drive him in to the military authorities and vouch for him as trustworthy. Blood anxiously did so, and believed that the policeman was not
harmed.[33]

Not everyone protected Bengalis. Butcher, who as a political officer was already under Pakistani scrutiny, did not, although he heard about other Americans who did. He remembers a young professor's wife coming to his house. "She prostrated herself at my wife's feet and said, 'You must help us, you must help us.' It was pretty unnerving."

Eric Griffel recalls that some Americans sheltered Bengalis knowingly, but says that he did so without being aware of it. "You never really knew who lived in your quarters," he says. "I did find out that there were some relatives of some of my servants who hid out. Muslims. I wasn't surprised when I did find out." The West Pakistanis, he says, were already "angry at the local Americans, because their attitude was perfectly obvious. Private citizens, journalists, missionaries— pretty well all of them were sympathetic to the Bengalis."

Desaix Myers, a young development officer working for Griffel, was single then and had a four-bedroom apartment in a pleasant neighborhood. "I had a couple in my house," he says. He put up curtains to hide these Bengalis from view. Some of them were students at Dacca University, friends of his, who asked if they could stay there after the army stormed the campus. His cook moved in his whole family. "There must have been six or seven in the servants' quarters," Myers says. "Everyone was a little worried. We didn't know what was going to happen." Was he afraid that the Pakistan army might be angry at him? "We were young and invincible."

TO BLOOD'S SURPRISE AND RELIEF, HIS SHOCKING "SELECTIVE GENOcide" cable won a prompt endorsement from Kenneth Keating, the U.S. ambassador in Delhi.[34]

Keating was not someone who could be easily dismissed. He was a formidable political figure in his own right: a former Republican senator from New York. In his early seventies, he had a weathered handsomeness, with bright blue eyes, bushy gray eyebrows, and a full shock of elder-statesman white hair; he had served in both World Wars, leaving the army as a brigadier general, with a military bearing to match. During the Cuban Missile Crisis, he had amazed all of Washington by mysteriously managing to find out about the Soviet missiles placed in Cuba six days before John Kennedy did—and announced it from the Senate floor, to the president's humiliation and rage. (Kennedy had despondently said, "Ken Keating will probably be the next President of the United States.") But the Kennedys had gotten their own back when Robert Kennedy swept into New York and knocked Keating out of his Senate seat. In consolation, Nixon appointed him ambassador to India. Sydney Schanberg remembers him as an old-fashioned conservative, a moderate Rockefeller Republican. Schanberg liked him: "He was very undiplomatic."[35]

As the shooting started, Keating was near the end of his career and his life, unafraid to speak his mind. In Delhi, he absorbed the outrage of Indians there. Major General Jacob-Farj-Rafael Jacob of the Indian army recalls, "Keating agreed with me entirely." The general remembers Keating turning red when asked why the United States was supporting Pakistan despite the atrocities. Thus Keating became an outspoken advocate for both India and the Bengalis, repeatedly lending his own gravitas and respectability to the Dacca consulate's dissenters. "Bless him," says Meg Blood. "He was strongly for us."[36]

When Keating saw Blood's cable, he immediately backed it, firing off an equally furious cable of his own with the same jarring subject line of "Selective Genocide." He wrote, "Am deeply shocked at massacre by Pakistani military in East Pakistan, appalled at possibility these atrocities are being committed with American equipment, and greatly concerned at United States vulnerability to damaging allegations of associations with reign of military terror." The ambassador—making a complete break with U.S. policy—urged his own government to "promptly, publicly and prominently deplore this brutality," to "privately lay it on line" with the Pakistani government, and to unilaterally suspend all military supplies to Pakistan. He urged swift action now, before the "inevitable and imminent emergence of horrible truths and prior to communist initiatives to exploit situation. This is [a] time when principles make [the] best politics."[37]

Keating made sure that news of the killings would get out. "He would drop me information from time to time," remembers Schanberg. "Stuff that I would have no way of knowing." Schanberg, returning to Delhi after being thrown out of Dacca, had emotionally told Keating in detail about what he had witnessed. Keating now fed to Schanberg a story for the New York Times recounting a "massacre." Schanberg says, "Keating was really mad. That's why he was giving stuff out." The article angered the Pakistani government and U.S. officials, but Keating unrepentantly took full responsibility for the leak. He defiantly told the State Department, "I know of no word in the English language other than massacre which better describes the wanton slaughter of thousands of defenseless men, women and children."[38]

Keating also tried to appeal to Nixon's and Kissinger's pragmatism.

If Pakistan fell apart, as seemed likely, the United States would want to be on decent terms with a new Bangladesh; if Pakistan somehow held together through sheer brutality, it would be shaky and weak, with far less "geopolitical importance" than India. But he was muzzled by the State Department, not even allowed to offer a wan public expression of sympathy for the Bengali victims.[39]

KEATING WAS NOT THE ONLY AMBASSADOR WHO SEEMED TO HAVE GONE local. The U.S. ambassador to Pakistan, Joseph Farland, proved to be a vehement supporter of Yahya's government.

Farland had almost flawless conservative credentials: a Republican lawyer from West Virginia who had served at the FBI and then as ambassador to the Dominican Republic and Panama. (One flaw: attending four Communist Party meetings while in college.) He did not enjoy living in South Asia and had little curiosity about the region. Once, he crudely explained to Nixon and Kissinger that "this problem goes back to about the year AD 712, when the Muslims first invaded the Sind. There's been no peace on the subcontinent since that time because the Hindus and the Muslims have nothing in common whatsoever. Every point of their lives is diametrically opposed—economic, political, social, emotional, despite their beliefs. One prays to idols, the other prays to one God. One worships the cow; the other eats it. Simple as that." (Nixon had his usual Pavlovian reaction to the mention of India: "Miserable damn place.")[40]

"He was almost a caricature, I thought," remembers Eric Griffel, the insubordinate development chief in Dacca. "Wealthy West Virginia lawyer, bright enough, complete lack of knowledge about the subcontinent, and not interested in world politics." Farland once visited one of Griffel's development projects, a dry dock called Roosevelt Jetty. "Roosevelt Jetty?" asked the Republican ambassador. "Theodore," Griffel quickly replied.

Farland was Blood's immediate superior, even though the Islamabad embassy was a thousand miles away from Blood's consulate in Dacca. Blood was wary of Farland's chummy ties with Yahya, who often drank with him or took him on shooting excursions. Blood thought that the relationship between his consulate and Farland's remote embassy was wretched.[41]

The official view from Pakistan's military rulers was simple: the atrocity stories were fabrications, and Pakistani unity would be restored in a matter of days or weeks. As Yahya wrote to Nixon, East

Pakistan "was well under control and normal life is being restored." There was no mention of the violence in the press, which was censored under martial law.[42] Still, the Islamabad embassy did not really believe that this violence would succeed. Even Farland deplored "the brutal, ruthless and excessive use of force by Pak military." The Bengalis, he wrote, would not "accept rule by bullet." But unlike Blood and Keating, he stuck to U.S. policy. After reading Keating's cable about "Selective Genocide," Farland frostily informed him, "Intervention by one country in the internal affairs of another tends to be frowned upon."[43]

Throughout West Pakistan, many other U.S. officials were outraged at the atrocities. From Lahore, the U.S. consul cabled a report that there was a "veritable bloodbath taking place in East Pakistan with literally thousands already slain." There was enough protest among U.S. officials across Pakistan that Farland had to warn his staffers in Karachi, Lahore, and Dacca to "not r[e]p[ea]t not voice opinions or pass judgments on the army intervention in East Pakistan." U.S. diplomats should instead affect "an unemotional, professional attitude." Farland squelched their humane instincts: "Regardless of our personal feelings, what has happened is strictly an internal affair of Pakistan's about which we, as representatives of the US G[overnment], have no comment." He invoked diplomatic duty: "Since we are not only human beings but also government servants, however, righteous indignation is not itself an adequate basis for our reaction."[44]

Trying to muzzle Blood, Farland granted that his Dacca officials were having "a most difficult and personally trying time," but reminded him to ensure that his officers maintain the "discretion" expected of U.S. diplomats. Blood and his team bristled. "In a country wherein our primary interests [are] defined as humanitarian rather than strategic, moral principles indeed are relevant to issue," he retorted to Farland. "Horror and flouting of democratic norms we have reported is objective reality and not emotionally contrived."[45]

AT THE WHITE HOUSE, BLOOD'S ANGUISHED "SELECTIVE GENOCIDE" message jolted Kissinger's expert on South Asia, Samuel Hoskinson. Kissinger himself was reading the cable traffic, sometimes quite closely, but if he had somehow missed it, Hoskinson promptly alerted his boss: "Having beaten down the initial surge of resistance, the army now appears to have embarked on a reign of terror"—here he repeated Blood's phrase—"aimed at eliminating the core of future resistance."

Hoskinson put Blood's call for new policies directly to Kissinger: "Is the present U.S. posture of simply ignoring the atrocities in East Pakistan still advisable or should we now be expressing our shock at least privately to the West Pakistanis?" Hoskinson explained that Blood wanted to complain to Yahya's regime, and backed up Blood: "The full horror of what is going on will come to light sooner or later." And ongoing U.S. aid to Pakistan could be seen as a "callous" endorsement of Pakistan's actions.[46]

But Nixon shrugged off the accumulating alarms from Blood, Keating, and Hoskinson. When Kissinger brought up the slaughter in East Pakistan, Nixon refused to say anything against it: "I wouldn't put out a statement praising it, but we're not going to condemn it either."[47]

"I DIDN'T LIKE SHOOTING STARVING BIAFRANS EITHER"

Rather than being appalled by the ferocity of the crackdown, Kissinger—when speaking only to Nixon—was impressed. He thought it could work.[48]

This, remembers Hoskinson, was "a bit of wishful thinking, combined with a lack of knowledge of the Bengali drive for nationhood. Plus tough talking from the West Paks: 'We can handle this. We're supplied by you, we'll put this down, not to worry.'"

On March 29, Kissinger told Nixon, "Apparently Yahya has got control of East Pakistan." "Good," said the president. "There're sometimes the use of power is . . ." Kissinger completed the thought: "The use of power against seeming odds pays off. Cause all the experts were saying that 30,000 people can't get control of 75 million. Well, this may still turn out to be true but as of this moment it seems to be quiet."

Nixon turned philosophical, pondering the uses of repression: "Well maybe things have changed. But hell, when you look over the history of nations 30,000 well-disciplined people can take 75 million any time. Look what the Spanish did when they came in and took the Incas and all the rest. Look what the British did when they took India." "That's right," Kissinger concurred.

Far from Dacca, Nixon and Kissinger hovered comfortably at the level of academic conceptions. "But anyway I wish him well," Nixon continued about Yahya. "I mean it's better not to have it [Pakistan] come apart than to have to come apart." He said, "The real question is whether anybody can run the god-damn place." Kissinger, sympathizing with Yahya's difficulties, said, "That's right and of course the Bengalis have been extremely difficult to govern throughout their history."[49]

Kissinger's hope that the Bengalis could be pounded into submission lingered for several weeks. Pakistani military officers assured the chairman of the Joint Chiefs of Staff that they could prevail. "All our experts in the Pentagon and elsewhere were dead sure that West Pakistani military forces could not overpower the people of East Bengal," Kissinger told the Indian ambassador in Washington, "but it seems they have done so. What options do we now have? We must be Machiavellian and accept what looks like a *fait accompli*—don't you think?"[50]

SAMUEL HOSKINSON, KISSINGER'S STAFFER, REMEMBERS THAT BLOOD'S cables got no leverage in the White House—even though the CIA chief in Dacca admired Blood's coolness in terrible circumstances, and Hoskinson's friends in the Foreign Service held Blood in high regard as a reporter. Hoskinson says, "We'd call them to the attention of Henry and Haig. It didn't seem to get a lot of response in policy terms." He notes about Blood, "He was regarded as being squishy. Maybe a little bit too enamored with the Bengalis and their leadership, a little softheaded on this stuff."[51]

Blood, he recalls, was "worrying about the plight of the Bengalis, which they didn't give much credence to. Human rights didn't really count for much. . . . You don't get down and wallow around in this stuff. We've got American interests on the line there. That's the mindset." He says, "In retrospect I think he had it about right. But he didn't have the credibility. There was always the tendency to believe more what was coming from Islamabad. . . . And we got this bleeding heart out there in Dacca."

Hoskinson remembers, "There was a disconnect between the bureaucracy, even the NSC staff, and the thinking of Kissinger and the president." Trying again, he urged Kissinger to reconsider his refusal to criticize Yahya despite Blood's reports of "widespread atrocities by the West Pakistani military." Hoskinson and another White House aide pointed out that both Blood and Keating wanted the United States to distance itself from the killings, with Keating warning about the risk of the United States being associated with "a reign of military terror."[52]

But Kissinger only paid enough attention to Blood's cables to mock him for cowardice. "That Consul in Dacca doesn't have the strongest nerves," Kissinger told Nixon. "Neither does Keating," said the president. "They are all in the middle of it; it's just like Biafra. The main thing to do is to keep cool and not do anything. There's nothing in it for us either way." Nixon said, "What do they think we are going to do but help the Indians?" Kissinger agreed: "It would infuriate the West Pakistanis; it wouldn't gain anything with the East Pakistanis, who wouldn't know about it anyway and the Indians are not noted for their gratitude."[53]

Despite the United States' considerable influence on Yahya, Kissinger said, "In Pakistan it continues, but there isn't a whole lot we can do about it." He assured Nixon that they were not pressuring Pakistan. The president said that "we should just stay out—like in Biafra, what the hell can we do?" (Neither of them noticed that the United States was actually thoroughly involved, taking Pakistan's side.) "Good point," Kissinger replied. Nixon said, "I don't like it, but I didn't like shooting starving Biafrans either."[54]

HOSKINSON WANTED TO CALL A MEETING TO CONSIDER BLOOD'S AND Keating's anguished cables, but Kissinger ignored that. In a Situation Room meeting, the dissenters were laughed out of the policy debate. Someone passed along a joke from William Rogers, the secretary of state, that India might be the first to recognize an independent Bangladesh "unless Ambassador Keating beats them to the punch."

A State Department official still insisted that Yahya could not win, and warned of "a sort of Biafra situation" as the news got out. But Kissinger, informed that Dacca was quiet and that Chittagong had been smashed, wondered if rural Bengali nationalists would really resist if the cities were under Pakistani control. He asked if Yahya's crackdown might succeed after all: "Can 30,000 troops do anything against 75 million people?" A general warned that it could be "very bloody," but a CIA official opined that the Bengalis "are not fighters."

At the end of the meeting, Kissinger looped back to the reports of a massacre at Dacca University. "Did they kill Professor Razak?" he asked. "He was one of my students." A CIA official replied, "I think so. They killed a lot of people at the university." Here was a moment when the abstractions of high policy and impersonal numbers—thirty thousand troops, seventy-five million people—might have melted away, replaced with the individual human face of a pupil from more innocent days. Henry Kissinger, seemingly referring to past Muslim rulers of India, replied, "They didn't dominate 400 million Indians all those years by being gentle."[55]

Chapter 5

The Blood Telegram

BOTH RICHARD NIXON AND ARCHER BLOOD WERE KEENLY AWARE of a disquieting fact: Pakistan's military, now at war with its own people, had been heavily armed by the United States.

The ongoing assault required a formidable amount of military resources, including perhaps four Pakistan army divisions equipped with armor, as well as the Pakistan Air Force. In this, Pakistan was relying on lots of U.S. weaponry and equipment—everything from ammunition and the spare parts that keep armed forces operating, to major items like tanks and the massive C-130 transport airplanes that shuttled soldiers from West Pakistan to East Pakistan.[1]

As the crackdown began, Bengalis begged U.S. diplomats not to allow American-supplied weapons to be used for "mass murder." The Nixon administration made no move against Pakistan's use of U.S. weaponry; instead, the State Department, ducking embarrassing press questions, tried to avoid headlines about U.S. small arms and aircraft dealing out death in Pakistan.[2]

Soon before the shooting started, Kissinger had sat in a Situation Room meeting where senior U.S. officials were informed about Pakistan's evident use of C-130s to reinforce its troops in East Pakistan. Once the killing began, Blood's officials snooping around the Dacca airport could see those planes in operation. They witnessed frequent flights bringing in Pakistani troops, with one C-130 seemingly constantly coming and going from Dacca.[3]

Blood's team also saw the Pakistan Air Force using F-86 Sabres, U.S. jet fighters famed for their performance in the Korean War. Blood reported daily sorties flown by an F-86 squadron at Dacca's heavily fortified airfield, in flights of two or four. Two F-86s were seen taking off from Dacca to crush Bengali resistance in a nearby town. Another time, a *Hindustan Times* reporter in East Pakistan got a terrifyingly close view as two F-86s bombed and strafed all around him. And according to two eyewitnesses, in one rebel-controlled town, F-86s fired rockets and machine guns at the market area, the main mosque, and a local college, with many casualties.[4]

U.S. weaponry was equally noticeable on the ground. On the first day of the killing, one of Blood's officials had seen three U.S.-made M-24 Chaffee light tanks rolling through the streets of Dacca, one of which fired off a machine-gun burst. In the next ten days, many of Blood's staffers saw what appeared to be U.S. jeeps bearing U.S. .50-caliber machine guns, sometimes opening fire as they patrolled the city. Blood later noted at least eight M-24 tanks deployed around Dacca. In Chittagong, not long after, a U.S. official would see three of the tanks, evidently getting ready to fight Bengali rebels. British military officials also saw M-24s and F-86s in action in Dacca and Chittagong, as well as jeeps.[5]

This was known at the highest levels. As Harold Saunders and Samuel Hoskinson, Kissinger's staff at the White House, informed him, "There is evidence that U.S.-supplied equipment is being utilized extensively, including planes (F-86s and C-130s), tanks and light arms." Kenneth Keating, the ambassador to India, urged cutting off the U.S. arms supply to Pakistan. He was appalled to find there were ongoing negotiations about new U.S. supplies of aircraft and armored personnel carriers to Pakistan despite "clear and growing evidence of West Pakistani military massacres."[6]

Nixon always understood that such weapons could be used for domestic repression; he had recently told another brutal anticommunist strongman, Suharto of Indonesia, that "sufficient military strength is essential also for internal security." The Nixon administration never asked Pakistan to avoid using U.S. arms and supplies against Bengali civilians. As a U.S. diplomat acknowledged to Pakistan, their arms deals did not forbid using U.S. weapons for "internal security purposes"—something that Pakistan could only take as a green light.[7]

VOICE OF AMERICA

Dacca grew dangerous for the roughly five hundred American citizens there. Blood was startled into ordering an evacuation by "berserk, antiforeign action by Pak military." He later told the State Department that it was "a minor miracle that no American was killed or injured by trigger-happy Pak troops fresh from killing and looting." Blood had his own family to worry about. Meg Blood did not feel safe in their official residence. "We had had shots into the house," she recalls.[8]

Pakistan provided a daily commercial Pakistan International Airlines flight loaded up with Americans, bound for safety in Tehran or Bangkok. Yahya later reminded Nixon about this, implying that the United States owed him. Joseph Farland, the ambassador in Islamabad, admonished Blood to make sure that his evacuated staffers kept their mouths shut around the press.[9]

For the departing Americans, many of whom had lost Bengali friends and were almost all horrified by the crackdown, their exit from Dacca was a shocking moment. Each day, between three and ten PIA airplanes, under the aegis of the Pakistan Air Force, landed in Dacca from West Pakistan, loaded with fresh troops in civilian clothes, who marched into an adjacent hangar to change into military uniforms. Then the Americans, after watching the soldiers debark, were ushered onto one of the same planes. They realized they were paying for some of the cost of reinforcing the Pakistan army. Blood cabled, "To many Americans, whose close friends had been killed, were missing, or in hiding, this situation made it impossible to leave East Pakistan with even the semblance of self-respect."[10]

One of the grief-stricken evacuees was Meg Blood, with their little boy, who took the last flight out, packed onto a PIA plane bound first for Karachi and then Tehran. "It was a strange time in life," she remembers with quiet outrage. "When Arch decided that the entire American community should leave, and they accepted from the Pakistanis who were behind all of this, the airplanes came complete with men dressed in mufti, who marched off as little brigades, before they turned the so-called rescue planes to us to fly out."[11]

BLOOD WAS LEFT ALONE, HOWLING INTO THE WIND. "THE SILENCE FROM Washington was deafening," he remembered later, "suggesting to us that less credence was being given to our reporting than to the Pakistani claims that little more was involved than a police action to round up some 'miscreants' led astray by India."[12]

Blood would always have preferred a united Pakistan, but these atrocities had doomed that. He cabled with disgust, "A reign of terror began and thousands were slaughtered, innocent along with allegedly guilty. And all in the name of preserving the unity of the country." Those Bengali moderates who wanted to remain within Pakistan were now discredited by the "continuing orgy of violence," which had "terrorized populace today but radicalized political leaderships for tomorrow." Bengalis would turn to guerrilla warfare to win total independence from West Pakistan. The military, he wrote, had destroyed the country: "guardians of nation's honor and integrity have struck the sharpest blow conceivable against the raison d'etre of Pakistan."[13]

Many sorrowful Pakistanis agreed. One of Yahya's ministers went to East Pakistan to see the devastation himself. "I went to Dacca," he later wrote, "and it was the worst experience of my life. Everywhere I went, I heard the same story: one person had lost a son; another a husband; many villages were burnt." To no avail, he confronted Yahya over "the Army's atrocities." Lieutenant General A. A. K. Niazi, who soon became the military commander in East Pakistan, would later frankly write of "the killing of civilians and a scorched-earth policy," condemning "a display of stark cruelty, more merciless than the massacres . . . by Changez [Genghis] Khan . . . or at Jallianwala Bagh by the British General Dyer."[14]

As a secret Pakistani postwar judicial commission later noted, many Pakistani military officers complained about "excessive force" unrelated to any threat, as well as "wanton acts of loot, arson and rape." General Niazi admitted the "indiscriminate use of force" that "earned for the military leaders names such as, 'Changez Khan' and 'Butcher of East Pakistan.'" While blaming Bengali nationalists for cruelly provoking the Pakistan army, this judicial inquiry included the testimony of senior Pakistani officers decrying the vengeful attack on Dacca University, the execution of Bengalis by firing squads, mass sweeps in which innocent people were killed, and massacres of hundreds of people. According to a Pakistani brigadier, one general asked his soldiers, "how many Bengalis have you shot?"[15]

BLOOD REDOUBLED HIS REPORTING, RELAYING A STREAM OF "HORROR stories of varying reliability" to Washington. He reported an "atmosphere of terror" meant to cow the Bengalis into quiescence. There were ongoing shootings in Dacca and the surrounding areas, with newly killed corpses being loaded onto a truck. Blood found the few East Pakistani officials who dared come to work "stunned with grief and grim in their denunciation of Pak military brutality," with one of them sobbing. American priests in Old Dacca told Blood that the Pakistan army, facing no provocation worse than putting up barricades, would set houses on fire and then shoot people as they ran out. The priests thought Hindus had been particular targets. Other Bengalis had witnessed six people gunned down in a shantytown, with the "army going after Hindus with vengeance." The army was also shooting police, who were seen as Bengali nationalist sympathizers. One policeman told a U.S. official, "Pray for us."[16]

Shahudul Haque, the young Bengali who had befriended Archer Blood's family during his first tour in Dacca, was now twenty-one years old, an engineering student, who had joined in leftist campus protests against Pakistan and briefly been arrested. On the night of March 25, he had been taken completely by surprise by the unfamiliar heavy clatter of machine guns, the tracer bullets arcing across the sky, and the red hue of burning buildings. Rushing out to Dacca University two days later, he had been jolted at the sight of dead bodies, blood, and gore. As the crackdown continued, Haque often visited Blood in the evenings, telling him stark stories about members of his family who had fled to India or joined the rebellion. The consul replied that he and his staff were trying to inform people in the United States about what was happening. "I could feel his frustration that he wasn't getting what he wanted," Haque remembers. "But he was very diplomatic. He would not give any details."

Blood's team could hear sporadic gunshots at night across the city. "Wanton acts of violence by military are continuing in Dacca," he cabled. He reported evidence of ethnic targeting, which bolstered his accusation of genocide: "Hindus undeniably special focus of army brutality." There were large fires and the sound of shots in Hindu neighborhoods. The army was rounding up remaining activists. "Atrocity tales rampant," Blood cabled, from trusted eyewitnesses. Truckloads of Bengali prisoners went into a Pakistani camp, and one of Blood's staffers then heard the continuous firing of 180 shots in half an hour.[17]

Despite the military authorities' panicked assertions that Dacca was returning to normal, the city was a ghost town, with as much as three-quarters of the population having fled. One eyewitness was stunned at the areas in Dacca burned by the army: he had seen many bombed-out towns during World War II, but the devastation here seemed far more thorough. Americans saw the Pakistan army moving into a Bengali village, bombing huts, rounding up the men, and finally taking half a dozen away. There was a heavy bombardment on Dacca's outskirts, from what Blood reckoned to be hundreds of rounds of high explosives. Another U.S. official in Dacca cabled that witnesses saw Pakistani troops using tanks, bazookas, and machine guns on two villages made up of thatched-roof huts—rumored to be hideouts for deserters from the police and army.[18]

The consulate emphasized how Hindus were targeted. One of Blood's senior staffers privately noted "evidence of selective singling out of Hindu professors for elimination, burning of Hindu settlements including 24 square block areas on edges of Old Dacca and village built around temple.... Also attack night of March 26 on Hindu dormitory at Dacca University resulting in at least 25 deaths." Although Pakistani forces had concentrated on Awami League activists, "Hindus seem [to] bear brunt of general reign of terror."[19]

Beyond Dacca, the situation looked equally grim. One of Blood's officials saw total devastation in a nearby town. Blood noted reports of the Pakistan army unleashing bombs and napalm in a town outside of Dacca, while the military launched reprisals on another nearby village. After a week of delay, the Pakistani authorities flew some of Blood's officials into the devastated city of Chittagong, which was in flames, with many residential neighborhoods burned out. Although the Pakistani military held their fire while the diplomats toured, American citizens there had witnessed "numerous incidents of cold-blooded murder of unarmed Bengalis by Pak military." The Americans in Chittagong told of a Pakistani cover-up campaign to get rid of civilian corpses before the consular officials arrived.[20]

These reporting trips were often dangerous, with the Americans dodging mortars and hearing gunfire. Desaix Myers, a brash young development official, says, "I was running around Chittagong in my white car, going up to military guys, saying, 'I've heard rumors about your guys violating women, and I know that you as a disciplined officer would not want that to get out to the international press.' We felt we had diplomatic immunity. It just didn't seem that risky at the time."

Myers wrote a desolate letter home to his friends lamenting what he had seen in a small, impoverished Hindu village in the countryside. The army had "lined up people from their houses, shot down the lines, killing close to six hundred." The people in nearby villages heard the gunfire and fled. The rice mills were burned to charcoal, the rice to ash. The handful of villagers who had returned told their stories through sobs. A tall, frail Bengali man took Myers to his scorched house: "a room with a rice ash heap and charcoaled bed stead, nothing remained to show us that his three children and wife had lived there, died there. Another old man, pan stained teeth, mucus glazed eyes, (glaucoma or tears?), whimpered the loss of his family." Some of the wounded had escaped to a Christian village, over two hours away by boat. They lay on a concrete floor. "Most have been hit in the hand, or arm; one woman with gangrene has left; a man with an abdominal wound died; a girl of eleven with a bullet hole through her frontal lobe, passing out her right temple, lies quietly, looking at her hand; she is silent but, miraculously, alive."[21]

The overall death toll was hard to calculate precisely. "The whole objective of the West Pak army apparently was and is to hit hard and terrorize population into submission," Blood wrote. Although unsure how many people had perished in Chittagong and elsewhere, he estimated that as many as six thousand had been killed in less than a week in Dacca alone.[22]

AT THE WHITE HOUSE, KISSINGER'S AIDES WERE SHAKEN BY BLOOD'S reporting. "It was a brutal crackdown," says Winston Lord, Kissinger's special assistant, who says he read some of the cables. "In retrospect, he did a pretty good reporting job," says Samuel Hoskinson, about Blood. "He was telling power in Washington what power in Washington didn't want to hear."

So, increasingly, was Hoskinson. He was shocked and saddened by the violence, which was unlike anything he had tracked before. While loyal to Kissinger and eager to please him, he was frustrated by the national security advisor's lack of response to his warnings. He recalls, "It's going over there, and there's no sign of it." He complained to Alexander Haig, Kissinger's deputy national security advisor, that nobody was listening to him. "My old friend Al Haig is advising me, be careful, be careful. He didn't want to get him too riled up."

Hoskinson says, "I began to feel a little bit more passionate about this—about the reporting we were getting from the Dacca consulate." He was mystified. "I really didn't understand why they were leaning so much toward West Pakistan." Hoskinson knew the depth of Bengali nationalism, and saw a tragedy in the making. Trusting his own regional expertise, he tried to educate Kissinger about a brewing revolution, to no avail. He says, "Why doesn't Kissinger understand? Why doesn't he understand the realities there and adjust policy accordingly? We don't understand why they don't understand what we understand."

Harold Saunders, the senior White House official on South Asia, channeled Hoskinson's emotion into a tentative approach to Kissinger, gingerly asking him to reconsider their policy. Saunders and Hoskinson used Blood's cables to put the lie to Nixon and Kissinger's hopes for a quick Pakistani military success: "the Pakistan army has failed to achieve its initial objective of cowing the Bengalis quickly with a ruthless campaign of terror."

Kissinger's staffers dared not flout a powerful boss whose viewpoint was perfectly clear. Using Blood and Keating to give them cover, the White House aides suggested that the United States use its leverage from Pakistan's dependence on U.S. military and economic aid to limit the bloodshed. After all, the country seemed doomed to break up, and the Nixon administration would face "criticism at home and abroad that we are supporting a military terror campaign against the self-determination of a group that won a majority fairly in a national election." They asked if "in Ambassador Keating's terms, whether this is a time when 'principles make the best politics.'" Kissinger ignored them.[23]

NIXON AND KISSINGER WOULD HAVE BEEN ANGRY ENOUGH IF BLOOD'S secret cables had only been read within the administration. But despite the State Department's energetic efforts to limit official access to Blood's "Selective Genocide" cable, it leaked to the press in a matter of days. Someone also fed some of Blood's cables to Senator Edward Kennedy, a Democratic rival whom Nixon particularly loathed. Based on these cables, Kennedy promptly gave a passionate speech denouncing the use of U.S. weaponry and urging the Nixon administration to stop the killing.[24]

Blood was not the type to leak, and was chagrined about the revelations. Joseph Farland, the ambassador in Pakistan, suspected that Blood was feeding classified information to Sydney Schanberg of the New York Times, although Schanberg—who says he never even met Blood—vehemently denies this.[25]

Still, any number of people at the State Department could have done it, or someone in the Dacca consulate, or many overseas posts. Kissinger became convinced that the culprit was Kenneth Keating, the troublemaking ambassador in Delhi. A little later, Kissinger told Nixon that Keating had "divulged the contents of the Blood cables" to the New York Times. (Schanberg also denies this.) Eric Griffel, the head development official, thinks it was someone in the Dacca consulate, although he refuses to say who. He says that the leaker would only have had to go into the cable room, make a copy, and send it by mail.[26]

Desaix Myers, who was a fiery critic of Nixon's policies in Vietnam, Cambodia, and Laos, says that it could have been almost anyone in the Dacca consulate. "We were trying to get the word out to the world," he remembers. While he says he did not leak the cables, he urgently wanted press coverage of the slaughter, hoping this might stop the Pakistan army. He wrote up a long letter describing the suffering of Hindu villagers and sent it around to friends back home in the United States. He asked that it be shown around discreetly, to be used as the basis for letters to Kennedy, other influential Democratic senators, and Nixon. "Anything that would get to the press with name, source attached would probably mean I'd have to leave," he wrote, "and I don't want to leave right now."[27]

"STRONG DISSENT"

After a dozen harrowing days, Blood's staffers had had enough of standard Washington procedure. Scott Butcher, the young political officer, and some other officials talked about a complete indictment of Nixon and Kissinger's policy. They wanted to send in a dissent cable: a new device in the Foreign Service, a Vietnam-sparked reform meant to encourage candor by allowing diplomats to speak out confidentially against official policy. "This was the height of the Vietnam War," says Butcher. "We're out at Camp Swampy, totally out of touch. No one is listening to us."[28]

They agreed that they wanted a fierce, uncompromising statement. Butcher wrote it up with gusto. His draft declared their "strong dissent" from a U.S. policy that seemed morally bankrupt, a policy of refusing to speak out against the crushing of democracy and the slaughter of innocents. It called the slaughter a genocide. For several days, this draft dissent cable ricocheted around the consulate. Desaix Myers, the young development officer, signed. "I don't think we had expectations that we were going to change this," he says, "so much as we had been filled with the feeling that we can at least make a statement." At the consulate, members of the Foreign Service, the Agency for International Development, and the United States Information Service all pledged their support. The dissenters rounded up other junior officials to sign on, and then worked on more senior ones like Eric Griffel. Griffel, not one to shy from a fight, tried to make the language even sharper. "I felt bad for the Bengalis," he says simply. "I liked the Bengalis."

Nobody knew if Archer Blood would sign it. "Obviously as he proved, he had a considerable backbone," remembers Griffel. "But that wasn't obvious before." Blood was clearly appalled by the killings, but he had the most to lose. Junior officials like Butcher were too lowly to face much backlash from Washington. Griffel says he was not worried about his career: his Dacca tour of duty was almost over, and anyway he took some pleasure in giving a kick to Nixon and Kissinger. Myers, who also enjoyed the prospect of aggravating Nixon, says, "I figured, take my job and shove it."

This draft would be the Foreign Service's first formal dissent cable (hundreds more would follow over the years from diplomats around the globe), and while it probably would not shift policy, it was guaranteed to enrage powerful people in Washington. "The stakes were the highest for Arch Blood," says Butcher. "He's got all the right credentials for becoming an ambassador." Blood's deputy did not want to sign at first, for fear of backing Blood into a corner, making it seem like the whole staff was in revolt. "He knew this was not a career-enhancing action," says Butcher. "This was a case of doing the right thing."[29]

Everyone in the Dacca consulate knew what they were supposed to be telling Washington. This, after all, was the era when many career-minded military and civilian U.S. officials in Saigon had been assuring their superiors that they were winning the war in Vietnam. In Vietnam, as Americans there used to say, the rule was "fuck up and move up": the system promoted the officials who chose not to make a stir, even as the evidence massed around them. But in Dacca, the bloody facts trumped. "Arch Blood is an extraordinarily professional individual," says Butcher. "Professionalism means you have objectivity. Like a journalist, you want to get your facts right. The facts were that the place was going to hell in a handbasket on the ground. . . . They had the guns and they used them."[30]

Blood weighed his decision, aware that he could wreck his career. But he knew what he had seen and he knew his duty. He joined the dissent and endorsed the cable. His staff was thrilled, and a little apprehensive too. "He said that what we were doing was not going to help in anyone's career," remembers Griffel. "That was a heroic action on his part," says Butcher. "He could have just left it as, 'I obviously cannot subscribe to these views, but I am sending it out.' He could have pulled his punches totally. But instead, he not only authorized it, but endorsed it and embellished it." Griffel says, "Blood risked everything."

Blood shared his colleagues' distress and frustration. The dissent telegram, Blood later wrote, matched his own views. And he was touched by his young staff's idealism. He did not modify Butcher's draft cable, since "nitpicking seemed almost a sacrilege in view of the earnestness and conviction of the message." Butcher, who for years proudly carried around a copy of the original cable, remembers ruefully, "Had he drafted the whole cable himself, it might have been much more sophisticated." Instead, Blood merely had the dissent cable retyped, and added some of his own commentary at the end. When Blood's deputy heard, he was freed up to sign on, hastily scrawling his name by hand, so the deputy's name went out to Washington misspelled. Almost the entire consulate stood behind the Blood telegram.[31]

ON APRIL 6, TWO WEEKS INTO THE SLAUGHTER, BLOOD TRANSMITTED his consulate's vehement dissent.

The telegram detonated in all directions, to diplomats in Washington, Islamabad, Karachi, and Lahore. The confidential cable, with the blunt subject line of "Dissent from U.S. policy toward East Pakistan," was probably the most blistering denunciation of U.S. foreign policy ever sent by its own diplomats:

> [W]ith the conviction that U.S. policy related to recent developments in East Pakistan serves neither our moral interests broadly defined nor our national interests narrowly defined, numerous officers of Am[erican] Con[sulate] Gen[eral] Dacca . . . consider it their duty to register strong dissent with fundamental aspects of this policy. Our government has failed to denounce the suppression of democracy. Our government has failed to denounce atrocities. Our government has failed to take forceful measures to protect its citizens while at the same time bending over backwards to placate the West Pak dominated government and to lessen likely and deservedly negative international public relations impact against them. Our government has evidenced what many will consider moral bankruptcy, ironically at a time when the USSR sent President Yahya a message defending democracy, condemning arrest of leader of democratically elected majority party (incidentally pro-West) and calling for end to repressive measures and bloodshed. . . . [W]e have chosen not to intervene, even morally, on the grounds that the Awami conflict, in

which unfortunately the overworked term genocide is applicable, is purely [an] internal matter of a sovereign state. Private Americans have expressed disgust. We, as professional public servants express our dissent with current policy and fervently hope that our true and lasting interests here can be defined and our policies redirected in order to salvage our nation's position as a moral leader of the free world.

This stark message was signed by twenty officials, from the consulate's diplomatic staff as well as the U.S. government's development and information programs—what Blood later called a "roll call of honor."[32]

It is as scorching a cable as could be imagined: in the drumbeat chorus of "Our government has failed"; in its impatience with national sovereignty at a time of massacre; in its blunt accusations of U.S. moral bankruptcy; and in its warning of genocide, given credence by a world-weary sense of how the term is often abused. "It seemed pretty shocking at the time," recalls Samuel Hoskinson, who read the Blood telegram—as it quickly became known—at the White House. "The word 'genocide' seems to have lost a little of its punch because it's been overused. But not then. This conjured up visions of the Holocaust, of a determined, systematic attempt to wipe out a people. That was shocking."[33]

Blood added a kicker of his own. He bore responsibility for authorizing the transmission of the cable, as every recipient knew. He agreed with the dissent with zeal. "I support the right of the above named officers to voice their dissent," Blood wrote, and gave a fulsome endorsement in a way that went far beyond a simple seal of approval: "I believe the views of these officials, who are among the finest US officials in East Pakistan, are echoed by the vast majority of the American community, both official and unofficial. I also subscribe to these views but I do not think it appropriate for me to sign their statement as long as I am principal officer at this post." This last token note of propriety—seemingly a last-ditch attempt to minimize the damage to his own career—was given no weight by anyone, neither the anguished team in Dacca nor the senior officers in Washington. More tellingly, he added his own pragmatic dissent from U.S. policy, aimed at his strategic-minded superiors back home: since the Bengali nationalists were pro-American, and would most likely win their struggle and establish an independent Bangladesh, it was "foolish" to alienate the victors with "a rigid policy of one-sided support to the likely loser."[34]

At the State Department's hulking building, the Blood telegram quickly made the rounds. Within hours, nine of the State Department's veteran specialists on South Asia wrote to the secretary of state that they associated themselves with the dissent cable and urged a shift in U.S. policy. Although Blood and his team in Dacca were unaware of their newfound support, from Dacca to Delhi to Washington, the middle ranks of the State Department were massed in protest.[35]

THE BLOOD TELEGRAM PROVOKED RAGE AT THE HIGHEST LEVELS IN Washington. "Henry was just furious about it," says Samuel Hoskinson, Kissinger's junior staffer for South Asia. "He made himself infamous as far as Henry was concerned," says Harold Saunders, Kissinger's senior aide, about Blood.

The White House staff was taken aback by Kissinger's wrath. "These people weren't crazy," remembers Saunders about the Dacca officials. "They weren't liberal bleeding hearts. They just saw a massive population being dealt with in a way that was inconsistent with values here in this country." Hoskinson says, "The big mystery for me was, why was he furious about this? Why are they so upset about this? Is it not clear that this is happening, and how do we deal with it?" He says, about Kissinger, "I remember thinking, has he lost his mind? This is not being made up out there. Everyone says this is a good team on the ground in Dacca. But he's furious. A furious Henry Kissinger in those days was not a pleasant sight. He would rant and rave a little bit about things."

He was not the only one. A livid William Rogers quickly got on the telephone with Kissinger to denounce "that goddam message from our people in Dacca." The secretary of state said, "It's miserable. They bitched about our policy and have given it lots of distribution so it will probably leak. It's inexcusable." (Blood had only classified it as confidential, the lowest level, which he later regretted as careless. It is hard to believe that was unintentional.) Kissinger said, "And it will probably get to Ted Kennedy." Rogers agreed. Kissinger said, "Somebody gives him cables. I have had him call me about them."[36]

Rogers fumed, "It's a terrible telegram. Couldn't be worse—says we failed to defend American lives and are morally bankrupt." Kissinger asked, "Blood did that?" Rogers said, "Quite a few of them signed it. You know we are doing everything we can about it. Trying to get the telegrams back as many as we can. We are going to get a message back to them." Kissinger decided to keep the Blood telegram away from

Nixon for two days, to Rogers's relief. Kissinger and Rogers accused the Bengalis of committing their own atrocities, and Kissinger doubted some of the reports of massacres of Bengalis. Rogers, still indignant, said, "To me it is outrageous they would send this."[37]

A SENIOR STATE DEPARTMENT OFFICIAL CALLED KISSINGER ABOUT THE nine State Department officials who had endorsed the Blood telegram. Kissinger told him that there was no possibility of shifting policy, and that he should get his underlings back in line.[38]

The State Department scrambled to limit the distribution of the dissent telegram, trying to prevent a leak. Kissinger later accusingly wrote that "the cables were deliberately given a low classification and hence wide circulation." Encouraged by his talk with Kissinger, Rogers sent a stern reprimand to Blood. The secretary of state, in an unusual cable he personally approved, wrote that he welcomed the "strongly held views," but insisted that this was "primarily an internal matter of the Pakistan Government," and sent along a rehash of some of the State Department spokesman's bland verbiage—nothing more than meek expressions of "concern" over lives lost and U.S. weapons used. Rogers castigated Blood for risking that the cable might leak out.[39]

Pakistan faced nothing worse than polite suggestions offered by an assistant secretary of state to its ambassador and a tepid State Department statement of "concern" and hope for a peaceful resolution. The carnage continued.[40]

GENOCIDE

Govinda Chandra Dev was an elderly philosophy professor at Dacca University and the author of several books, including one with the unthreatening title *Buddha, the Humanist*. He was a Hindu, but reminded Blood, who was friendly with him, of Santa Claus. "He was a roly-poly, gray-haired, jovial guy," recalls Scott Butcher, who knew him. "He was a very pacifistic figure, well known and well liked in American circles. He was apolitical as far as I could tell." Early in the crackdown, Dev was dragged out of his home, hauled to a field in front of the Hindu dormitory at the university, and shot dead. "There was no other reason that he was killed other than being a Hindu professor," says Butcher.[41]

This kind of deliberate ethnic targeting was the most reliable basis for the Blood telegram's accusation of genocide. But at first, Blood used the dread term more for shock value than precision. There was considerable confusion in the consulate about what exactly genocide meant, and what they meant by using the word. (Blood, no lawyer, at one point sloppily suggested that the "Webster's definition" could apply to the killing of Awami League followers.) Eric Griffel says that "probably it wasn't. Genocide implies to me a determination to kill a whole group of people. This was a determination to kill *some* people. I would differentiate it from Hitler or the Armenian massacre or even from Cambodia." This is somewhat muddled (under international law, "genocide" means persecution intended to wipe out a group in whole or in part), but the Dacca consulate was not at first clear on which victims they were talking about. Was this a genocide against the Bengalis, or against the Hindu minority among the Bengalis?[42]

"There was clear targeting of Hindus," says Scott Butcher. "You might also talk about going after Bengalis as a racial or cultural group. It was an extraordinarily brutal crackdown." At first, in his hasty cable about "selective genocide," Blood had meant a genocidal campaign against the Bengalis overall, both the Muslim majority and the Hindu minority. (This was the same way that the Indian government used the word.) "The term 'selective genocide,' you had an army crackdown on one set of people," says Butcher. "There was a racial prejudice between Punjabis and Bengalis. You'd hear snide remarks that these people are less religious, our little brown brothers." Some West Pakistanis scorned Bengalis—even the Muslim majority—as weak and debased by too much exposure to Hindus among them. As one of Yahya's own ministers noted, the junta "looked down" upon the "non-martial Bengalis" as "Muslims converted from the lower caste Hindus." In similar terms, Sydney Schanberg reported in the *New York Times* on the "depth of the racial hatred" felt by the dominant Punjabis of West Pakistan for Bengalis.[43]

But there was mounting evidence that among the Bengalis, the Hindu minority was doubly marked out for persecution. From the first few days of the crackdown, Blood had noticed this. Many of the West Pakistanis seemed to blame Bengali nationalism and secessionism on the Hindus, even though the Bengali Muslims had overwhelmingly supported the Awami League. "There was much feeling against Hindus," says Meg Blood. "It was one way they whipped up their soldiers to do such abominable things." Butcher remembers that the Hindus were "seen as making them less pure as Pakistanis."[44]

There was, Archer Blood thought, no logic to this campaign of killings and expulsions of the Hindus, who numbered about ten million—about 13 percent of East Pakistan's population. Later he would call it "criminally insane." There was no military need for it. The Hindus were not the nucleus of any armed resistance. They were unarmed and dispersed around East Pakistan. But the Hindus were tainted by purported association with India, and were outliers in a Pakistani nation defined in Muslim terms. Lieutenant General Tikka Khan, the military governor leading the repression, argued that East Pakistan faced "enslavement" by India. He said that the outlawed Awami League would have brought the "destruction of our country which had been carved out of the subcontinent as a homeland for Muslims after great sacrifices."[45]

Desaix Myers remembers, "We were aware the Hindu markets had been attacked. The villages that we visited were Hindu. We were aware that Hindus specifically were being attacked." In a letter at the time, he wrote, "The Army continues to check, lifting lungis [a kind of sarong worn by Bengalis], checking circumcision, demanding recitation of Muslim prayers. Hindus flee or are shot." He recalls that on one trip out of Dacca, "I was convinced I saw people wearing pieces of cloth identifying themselves as Hindus." Butcher says, "You heard stories of men having to pull down their *lungis*. If they were circumcised, they were let go. If they were not, they were killed. It was singling out the Hindus for especially bad treatment, burning Hindu villages, it was like a pogrom. It was ridding the province of these people."[46]

The consulate was full of dark theories about Pakistan's motivations. In his letter home, Myers argued, "The West Pakistan Army seems bent on eliminating them; their rationale, by eliminating Hindus, Pakistan purifies itself, rids itself of anti-state, anti-Pakistan, anti-Islam elements." India might absorb the refugees who fled. "Pakistan will have ridded herself of ten million undesirables," he wrote, "having used them as a scapegoat, and East Pakistan's total population will have been reduced enough to return it once again to minority position, thereby allowing continued dominance by the West."[47]

Senior Pakistani officers would later admit much of this targeting before a secret Pakistani postwar judicial inquiry. It noted that "senior officers like the COAS [chief of army staff] and CGS [chief of general staff] were often noticed jokingly asking as to how many Hindus have been killed." One lieutenant colonel testified that Lieutenant General A. A. K. Niazi, who became the chief martial law administrator in East Pakistan and head of the army's Eastern Command, "asked as to how many Hindus we had killed. In May, there was an order in writing to kill Hindus" from a brigadier. (Niazi denied ordering the extermination of the Hindus.) Another lieutenant colonel said, "There was a general feeling of hatred against Bengalis amongst the soldiers and the officers including generals. There were verbal instructions to eliminate Hindus."[48]

BLOOD WAS PARTICULARLY UNNERVED BY THE EXECUTION OF DEV. Brooding on that death, he returned to the subject of the genocidal methods of the Pakistan army, now offering to Washington a more serious case for using the chilling word.

In the countryside, Bengali nationalists were forming an armed resistance to the Pakistan army. This brought with it some atrocities carried out by Bengalis, in vicious revenge against people thought to be loyal to West Pakistan. So Blood and his staff began to reframe the fighting more as a two-sided ugly civil war than a purely one-sided genocide. Despite ongoing reports of unprovoked killing by soldiers, Blood saw the army launching a military campaign to take control of the countryside. Still, he thought, genocide was the right description for what was happening to the Hindus. So the consulate "began to focus our 'genocidal' reporting on the Hindus." The military crackdown, he cabled, "fully meets criteria of term 'genocide.'"[49]

Over and over, Blood tried to alarm his superiors in Washington. "'Genocide' applies fully to naked, calculated and widespread selection of Hindus for special treatment," he wrote. "From outset various members of American community have witnessed either burning down of Hindu villages, Hindu enclaves in Dacca and shooting of Hindus attempting [to] escape carnage, or have witnessed after-effects which [are] visible throughout Dacca today. Gunning down of Professor Dev of Dacca University philosophy department is one graphic example."[50]

He explained that the Pakistani military evidently did not "make distinctions between Indians and Pakistan Hindus, treating both as enemies." Such anti-Hindu sentiments were lingering and widespread, Blood wrote. He and his staff tenaciously kept up their reporting of anti-Hindu atrocities, telling how the Pakistan army would move into a village, ask where the Hindus lived, and then kill the Hindu men. There was little evidence, he said, of the killing of Hindu women and children. (He also pointed out that the Bengali Muslims abhorred this slaughter.) Blood and his team emphasized the "international moral obligations to condemn genocide . . . of Pakistani Hindus."⁵¹

But for all the effort that Blood put into defining and documenting genocide, the terrible term had no impact at the White House. Neither Nixon nor Kissinger ever mentioned genocide against either the Bengalis or the Hindus. If they were shocked, they kept it to themselves. Although Nixon had once decried genocide in Biafra, as a campaign issue against Lyndon Johnson in 1968, the term held little resonance for him later. After all, the Nixon administration was, like previous administrations since Harry Truman, working quietly to avoid joining the Genocide Convention. John Mitchell, Nixon's attorney general, dismissively told Kissinger, "It's good for Biafra and the Black Panthers."⁵²

THE BIHARIS

As Bengali nationalist guerrillas fought back, all the major U.S. posts— Dacca, Islamabad, and Delhi—agreed that Yahya had little chance of winning a civil war. The Bengali resistance held the countryside, and could get arms, supplies, and safe haven from India. Even the Islamabad embassy accepted that the army could not win and that the radicalized Bengalis would never again be willing citizens of Pakistan: "Bengali grievances now etched in blood." From Dacca, Blood fervently agreed, arguing that for Yahya and his generals, "power will grow out of gun barrels."⁵³

While Pakistan plunged into civil war, Kissinger looked for massacres committed by Bengalis, to generate a moral equivalence that would exonerate Yahya. It would be convenient for Nixon and Kissinger to be able to say that both sides were equally rotten. Blood—who laid the basic responsibility for the horrors squarely on the Pakistani military authorities—might have been tempted to be one-sided in his advocacy, rather than risking giving ammunition to Kissinger. But while his cables still concentrated on the slaughter of Bengalis, he worked hard to show the cruelties committed by the Bengali nationalists too. Contrary to what was being said about him in the White House, he showed himself to be more a professional than a partisan.⁵⁴

Blood reported to Washington growing signs of a "civil war in which atrocities committed on both sides," including "atrocities by Bengalis on non-Bengalis." These non-Bengalis were known as the Biharis, an

Urdu-speaking and Muslim minority, reviled by Bengali nationalists as ostensible tools of their fellow Urdu speakers in West Pakistan. (Many were originally from the nearby Indian state of Bihar and, like so many other Muslims, had come to Pakistan in the catastrophic communal dislocations of Partition.) Some Biharis supported the Awami League, believing in autonomy for East Pakistan, but many others backed West Pakistan.[55]

When the crackdown began on March 25, the Biharis were in a terrible situation, seen as a fifth column by many Bengalis. Some Biharis helped the Pakistani authorities in their repression, looting or killing Bengalis. Scott Butcher remembers, "You had atrocities committed not just by the military but by their collaborators, by Biharis." The most violent elements on both sides now had a chance to do their worst. Despite Mujib's own declarations that the Biharis should be protected, Bengali nationalists began reprisal attacks against them. British and American aid workers reported that in one town, nearly two hundred Biharis were put up against a wall and shot. The Biharis took revenge, killing some four hundred Bengalis. Blood's consulate reported with horror about "numerous atrocities" committed by Bengali nationalists against Biharis in places such as Chittagong and Khulna.[56]

While documenting with disgust the atrocities against the Biharis, the Dacca consulate tried to keep a sense of proportion. They officials saw the civil war as primarily the result of Yahya's assault on the Bengali population, not as an inchoate spasm of violence in which all sides were matched in bloodshed—even though that view would have been more congenial to Nixon and Kissinger. Instead, Blood and his staffers reckoned that some two-thirds of the dead were Bengalis. As a State Department official would later estimate, thousands of people died in violence between Bengalis and Biharis, while tens of thousands of Hindus were killed in subsequent attacks.[57]

The reprisals between Bengalis and Biharis brought back some of the worst memories of Partition. Desaix Myers remembers that the Bengali rebels did "some pretty atrocious things to Urdu speakers." Then when the Pakistan army heard about these cruelties, it took vengeance on Bengalis. Myers remembers a Bengali who had been bravely protecting some Biharis from the Bengali rebels in Chittagong. Despite that, a Pakistani major apprehended this Bengali and put him in his jeep. Myers tried to block the jeep's path with his car, but the major stuck his gun into the car and told him to move it. "He gets around the corner," says Myers. "We heard a shot within fifty yards. The story we later got was the major was enraged, he'd seen the Bengali atrocities. So he went to get this Bengali." That night, there was a mournful gathering. "Bengalis and Pakistanis were mixed together, all wailing in grief over what essentially was another Partition. They couldn't understand. They had brothers in Islamabad, they had studied in Lahore. They were bemoaning this war among one family."

"WAS IT THEREFORE NOT IMMORAL FOR HITLER TO KILL THEM?"

Back in Washington, the Blood telegram got the attention of Kissinger and the president himself. Meeting in the Oval Office—which was decorated to impress with gold sofas and chairs, elaborate sconces, and curtains in a richer shade of gold—Kissinger told Nixon, "The Dacca consulate is in open rebellion." Nixon was worried about Yahya and startled at the prospect of cutting off economic aid to Pakistan. Kissinger, sensing presidential indecision, weighed in emphatically: "Mr. President, we're going to wind up on the worst side if we start backing a rebellion there now."

Nixon pointed out that they had not backed the rebellion in Biafra. Striking a philosophical note, the president suggested that Biafra had been worse than East Pakistan, and argued that it was moral hypocrisy to rescue Bengalis when the United States had not rescued Biafrans: "I know, there are less people in Biafra. Is that the reason?" He raised another example: "look, there weren't very many Jews in Germany." Kissinger, who had been one of those German Jews, murmured in quiet assent, "That's right." Nixon asked, "was it therefore not immoral for Hitler to kill them?" Kissinger again murmured, "That's right."

Unbidden, the president of the United States was comparing his own ally and friend to Adolf Hitler. The distinction that Nixon drew between Yahya and Hitler was about the scale of their killing of their ethnic victims. (Nixon was kicking ideas around free form, but this argument actually cut against him: if it was wrong for Hitler to kill Germany's small Jewish population, it would also be wrong for Yahya to kill Pakistan's large Bengali population.) Nixon's own rough analogies for East Pakistan, unprompted by anyone, were Biafra and the Holocaust. But rather than taking stock, let alone recoiling, he instead grew angry at what he took to be hypocrisy by his critics: "It's ridiculous."

Kissinger did not dwell on the Hitler comparison. Instead, he insisted they not pressure Yahya: "Mr. President, if we get in there now, we get West Pakistan turned against us, and . . . the Bengalis are going to go left anyway. They are by nature left." Although the State Department had explained ad nauseam that the Awami League was quite pro-American, Kissinger continued, "Their moderate leadership is in jail, maybe they shouldn't have been put in jail, but that's the way it is now"—at this point, realizing that he was actually criticizing Yahya's repression, he ran out of steam and fell silent.

Nixon, fortified, said, "I think that if we get in the middle of all this, it's a hell of a mistake." Kissinger assured him, "It's a disaster. No one else is doing it." He concluded, "It's a classic situation for us to stay out of. There's nothing for us in there to take sides in this."[58]

Chapter 6

The Inferno Next Door

INDIANS WERE HORRIFIED BY THE SLAUGHTER NEXT DOOR. "FROM the high hopes of establishing a Democratic and popular system of Government," wrote a senior Indian diplomat posted in Islamabad, "Pakistan plunged into mediaeval barbarism when naked military force was used to eliminate the right of the elected majority."[1]

Indira Gandhi's government was startled. One of her close aides recalled that "we were taken by surprise when news of the sudden termination of negotiations, followed by a savage military crackdown in Dacca, started coming." Even after getting reports of bloodshed, "we continued to believe that negotiations would be resumed after a brief show of military might." It was hard for Gandhi's team to understand why Pakistan's generals would ignite a civil war, alienating their Bengalis into a permanent rupture. But Jaswant Singh, formerly a foreign minister and defense minister, remembers that Yahya "saw the problem as a bluff soldier would, purely as a law and order problem. Therefore he sent Tikka Khan. There was also an attitudinal problem. 'Oh, these are cowardly Bengalis. We need to just put a few shotgun pellets in their buttocks and they'll run away.'"[2]

Indian diplomats in Pakistan reported that the military government there was trying to eliminate Awami League supporters and engaged in "systematic terrorisation" of the young and the poor, as well as the intelligentsia. As one of Gandhi's inner circle wrote, her advisers quickly decided that this was a well-planned operation meant to "decapitate the Awami League leadership" and "cow down the Bengali population through genocide." They were appalled. P. N. Haksar, Gandhi's top aide, wrote, "Both as a democratic country and a country firmly committed to secularism as a basis for nationhood, our sympathies naturally lie with the people of East Bengal." But he hoped to keep India's public opinion under firm control. He wanted India's opposition parties to stay calm and keep their emotions from running amok.[3]

Thus Swaran Singh, the foreign minister—a thoughtful, tall, and elegant man, with a traditional Sikh turban and graying beard, dressed impeccably in Nehru-style *achkan* suits—tried to soothe an angry Lok Sabha, the powerful lower chamber of Parliament. While voicing "deep emotions," he carefully tried to avoid provoking Pakistan. This was a disaster. Singh was roasted as uncaring, and Gandhi had to explain that her government sympathized with the suffering Bengalis.[4]

The Indian press exploded with ever more emotional stories, wildly estimating as many as three hundred thousand dead in the first week of the crackdown. Respected newspapers accused Pakistan of genocide. Gandhi was slammed for inaction not just in the English press, but also in Hindi, Urdu, Bengali, and other languages all around the country.[5]

Indian politicians of all stripes launched demonstrations, demanded swift action, and denounced the government's spinelessness. Politicians from the Communist Party of India condemned Gandhi's timidity; the Samyukta Socialist Party demanded immediate recognition of Bangladesh; even Gandhi's own Congress party decried "the crime of genocide"; and a member of the right-wing Jana Sangh, a Hindu nationalist party that was the predecessor to today's powerful Bharatiya Janata Party, wanted a naval blockade of East Pakistan. Atal Bihari Vajpayee, the leader of the Jana Sangh—who would many years later become prime minister—denounced Pakistan for genocide in front of a vast crowd at a park in Bombay, and offered to be the first to volunteer to enter East Pakistan.[6]

The public uproar was at its most intense in West Bengal, where Bengalis were shocked at the killing of their fellows in neighboring East Pakistan. The newspapers ran sensationalist stories of death tolls in the tens of thousands, with furious editorials condemning Yahya and urging Gandhi to recognize an independent Bangladesh. There were general strikes and huge demonstrations in solidarity with Mujib.[7]

Gandhi had to do something. Although true mass mobilization is a rarity for a country as gigantic and impoverished as India, she faced tremendous pressure from the middle class and elites, and from Parliament. So she joined with all her rivals in Parliament in an all-party resolution of solidarity with the Bengalis. The prime minister introduced the measure herself. On March 31, both houses of India's Parliament unanimously condemned "the atrocities now being perpetrated on an unprecedented scale upon an unarmed and innocent people," and urged all governments to press Pakistan to stop immediately "the systematic decimation of people which amounts to genocide."[8]

Pakistan's government furiously lashed back at this "gross interference" in its sovereign domestic affairs, but India's Parliament and press wanted much more. As a top strategist secretly advised Haksar and other senior leaders, after this resolution "it is too late to feel compunctions about intervention."[9]

GANDHI DECLARED THAT INDIA HAD TO RESIST SUCH "INJUSTICE AND atrocities," and Indian officials in their private correspondence routinely referred to "Bangla Desh" instead of East Pakistan. But her government repeatedly batted away calls for recognizing Bangladesh as an independent state, which could easily ignite war with Pakistan. Privately, Gandhi worried that a great many Indians would take matters into their own hands.[10]

Inside and outside of government, Indians argued that Pakistan was finished. A senior Indian diplomat in Islamabad wrote that the army and the West Pakistani establishment could never win the loyalties of the East Pakistanis. The Indian diplomatic mission in Islamabad suggested that Pakistan's military had decided that liberal and secular values in Bengali culture had become "an unacceptable threat to Pakistan's Islamic ideology and to its existence." For many Indians, the bloodshed showed a profound national crack-up in Pakistan—a historic failure of the ideal of Pakistan as an Islamic nation that united Muslims in both wings of the country. Haksar argued that Pakistan's turmoil, pitting Muslim against Muslim, "clearly establishes the total inadmissibility of trying to found a nation on a religious basis."[11]

From the start, the Indian press and Parliament ripped into the United States for supporting and arming Pakistan. Vajpayee urged the U.S. government to prevent Pakistan from using its weapons against the Bengalis, while one legislator said that the U.S. arms supply made it a "partner in genocide." The U.S. consulate in Calcutta was swamped with petitions and pleas to stop arming the Pakistani military. The *Motherland,* a Jana Sangh newspaper, declared that genocide could not be seen strictly as an internal affair of Pakistan; the *Hindustan Times* asked why the United States would meddle in Soviet internal affairs to condemn the mistreatment of Soviet Jews, but stayed silent about the Bengalis; and the *Times of India* lambasted the United States for not warning Pakistan not to unleash U.S. arms against unarmed civilians. Hindi, Urdu, and Punjabi newspapers were even harsher. As the U.S. embassy in Delhi noted, the fire came from even the most pro-American publications. When the State Department claimed that it had no firsthand knowledge about Pakistani use of U.S. arms, it drew derision in the Indian press, which reported on Pakistan's use of Sabre jets and M-24 tanks.[12]

Haksar wrote to a confidant that "our entire country is seething with a feeling of revulsion" at the Pakistan army's actions. The government had to "reckon with it and deal with it, giving it some constructive direction. Prime Minister has been able to withstand the demand echoing from all the Legislatures in our land and from all our people to accord recognition to East Bangla Desh as a separate entity." But there were demands that they give "the people of Bangla Desh . . . the necessary wherewithal with which to fight the bestiality of West Pakistan army. Many of the respected leaders of the people of East Pakistan have sent us appeals for help. We are in a terrible dilemma."[13]

"VILLAGES BURN," WROTE A U.S. OFFICIAL TRAVELING IN THE RAVAGED countryside of East Pakistan. "[W]e saw some burning Friday, villagers scurrying, bundles on their heads, children with suitcases, running, away, anywhere. Those that are fortunate have made it to India. Those that are rich have made it to the US or UK. The majority remain either waiting in their village for the attack to come, or living as refugees in the homes of Muslims, Christians, or other Hindus."[14]

The refugees came on foot. Some of the luckier ones came by rickshaws, bullock carts, or country boats, streaming toward the safety of the Indian border. From the beginning, India kept its borders open to untold thousands of the dispossessed. "The flow of refugees was simply unstoppable," recalled one of Gandhi's top aides.[15]

The Indian prime minister's secretariat knew that there was sure to be a rush of refugees, likely to overwhelm the local authorities in West Bengal. But the actual scale was a shock: the lieutenant governor of Tripura, an Indian state jutting deep into East Pakistan, alerted Gandhi to "the unexpectedly large influx of refugees." As one of Gandhi's senior aides remembered, her government now really began to worry. The expulsions seemed massive and systematic.[16]

It quickly became a human tide. By mid-April, there were more people than the stunned West Bengal government could possibly handle, necessitating help from Gandhi's central government; by the end of April, Indian officials in Pakistan were estimating that nearly a million refugees had fled into India's impoverished, volatile border states of Assam, Tripura, and, above all, West Bengal. India began setting up refugee camps in West Bengal.[17]

The refugees sharply ramped up the public pressure on Gandhi. From the border states, the Indian press reported in awful detail the exiles' tales of shootings, rape, torture, and burning. There were renewed accusations of genocide, and overheated comparisons to the Holocaust.[18]

MRS. GANDHI'S SHADOW WAR

Indira Gandhi's loyalists today often blame the war entirely on Pakistan. K. C. Pant, a young minister of state for home affairs in 1971 who went on to become Indian defense minister, recalls, "There was no, as far as I know, no intention to provoke a war, or to create a situation where war became inevitable. That was not the intention at all." But in fact, Gandhi's government was planning for war from the start, and escalated toughly as the crisis wore on.

As early as April, India's government was bracing for a military confrontation. Some Indian hawks were tempted to strike while Pakistan's rulers were still in panicky disarray. Several of Gandhi's ministers demanded that the army march into East Pakistan; she was under tremendous public pressure, particularly from the Jana Sangh; and some Indian advisers were urging the government to seize this opportunity.[19]

Just over a week after Yahya's crackdown began, the top echelon of the Indian government—including Haksar and the foreign and defense ministers—received a brilliant and brutal argument for war from K. Subrahmanyam. (He also published a truncated newspaper version, which scandalized Pakistan.) As the director of the Institute for Defence Studies and Analyses, an illustrious think tank funded by the defense ministry, Subrahmanyam was well launched on a career that, over six decades in public life, would make him India's most influential strategic thinker.[20]

Subrahmanyam secretly urged the government to swiftly escalate the crisis all the way to war, establishing Indian hegemony over all of South Asia. The Bengali guerrillas, he argued, would not be able to defeat the Pakistan army, and anyway he doubted that India could avoid directly fighting Pakistan. Pakistan's "military-bureaucratic-industrialist-oligarchic" rulers, he argued, might actually prefer to spark a war with India and lose, rather than face the bigger humiliation of defeat by Bengali people power. India's armed forces, he confidently predicted, would quickly win a two-front war, capturing East Pakistan while fighting hard against West Pakistan.

The world would accept India's fait accompli, he claimed. The United States had gotten away with its interventions in Guatemala and Cuba, and the Soviet Union with its in Hungary and Czechoslovakia. Despite China's bitter rivalry with India, he doubted that China would really ride to Pakistan's rescue. With Pakistan ripped apart, India would dominate South Asia. And Subrahmanyam saw the strategic uses of moralizing: if India could make "the Bangla Desh genocide" its cause for war, then the superpowers—and even revolutionary China—would find it hard to support Pakistan.[21]

GANDHI TOOK AN EARLY DECISION FOR WAR. "I KNEW THAT THE WAR had to come in Bangladesh," she later told a friend. Major General Jacob-Farj-Rafael Jacob, the chief of staff of the army's Eastern Command, remembers getting marching orders at the beginning of April. "This was her orders," he says. "Then I get a phone call from Manekshaw"—the top officer, General Sam Manekshaw, the chief of staff of the Indian army—"telling me to move in." But India's generals balked at the unfavorable conditions for combat. Jacob recalls, "I tell him, no way. I told him that we were mountain divisions, we had very little transport, we had no bridges."[22]

The military, according to its top ranks, persuaded Gandhi to wait awhile. The rivers and swamps of East Pakistan were daunting terrain. "There were a lot of tidal rivers to cross," says Jacob. "The monsoon was about to break. If we moved in, we'd get bogged down. We need bridges and time for training. I told Manekshaw this. I sent a brief, which he read out to Mrs. Gandhi. He asked the earliest I could move, and I said the fifteenth of November. This was conveyed to Mrs. Gandhi, who was wanting us to move in immediately, and she accepted that."[23]

At the time, Manekshaw told General William Westmoreland, the U.S. Army's chief of staff, that the Indian military had sobered its hawkish civilian politicians, who were eager to strike in East Pakistan. Since then, he has recounted a detailed story of military caution similar to Jacob's. In Manekshaw's flavorsome and well-polished version—which has taken on a halfway mythological character in Indian military circles—in April, as the refugees flooded in, Gandhi angrily waved a telegram from the chief minister of one of the border states and, in front of her cabinet, asked him, "Can't you do something?" Manek-shaw replied, "What do you want me to do?" "Go into East Pakistan," she said. "This would mean war," he replied. "I know," Gandhi report-edly said. "We don't mind a war." But the general balked. "In the Bible," he claims to have said, "it is written that God said, 'Let there be light, and there was light.' You think that by saying 'Let there be war,' there can be a war? Are you ready for a war? I am not."[24]

Manekshaw says that he explained to the cabinet that the immi-nent monsoon would make ground operations impossible, and the air force could not provide support in awful weather. Two divisions were nowhere near East Pakistan. His armor was underfunded. China could strike in defense of Pakistan. So he recommended postponing the war until winter, when snow on the Himalayan mountain passes would freeze out Chinese troops. "If you still want me to go ahead, I will," he reportedly told an unhappy Gandhi. "But I guarantee you a one hun-dred per cent defeat." Jagjivan Ram, the defense minister, urged him to act. He refused. Gandhi, fuming and red-faced, dismissed the cabinet, holding Manekshaw behind. He offered his resignation. In his account, he told her, "Give me another six months and I guarantee you a hun-dred per cent success"—unusually cocksure stuff for a professional soldier speaking to a civilian commander. Gandhi put him in charge. "Thank you," he purportedly said. "I guarantee you a victory."[25]

UNTIL THE WEATHER CHANGED, INDIA HAD ANOTHER MILITARY OPTION: helping to support a Bengali insurgency against Pakistan.

Yahya's slaughter drove Bengalis to take up arms. The nucleus of the resistance was trained Bengalis serving in Pakistan's military, in units called the East Pakistan Rifles and the East Bengal Regiment, as well as police officers. Unable to stomach the crackdown, many of these Bengalis rebelled. They became early targets for Yahya's assault. As Archer Blood remembered, the Pakistan army "deliberately set out first to destroy any Bengali units in Dacca which might have a mili-tary capability," particularly the Bengali troops in the East Pakistan Rifles. "And so they just attacked their barracks and killed all of them that they could." Scott Butcher, the junior political officer in the U.S. consulate in Dacca, says that the Pakistan army swiftly turned on the Bengalis in their ranks: "a lot of the gunfire we heard were executions of some of those personnel." Some of these Bengalis reportedly killed their own West Pakistani officers and ambushed other army units.[26]

As Indian diplomats in Pakistan reported, "Heavily armed military columns with devastating fire power and air support were used against the Freedom fighters and civilians in mopping up operations in the countryside and along the border with India." The Bengali insurgents—known first as the Mukti Fouj (Liberation Brigade), and later as the Mukti Bahini (Liberation Army)—fought back with attacks on roads and bridges. Pakistan, Indian officials thought, aimed to wipe out the guerrilla resistance before the monsoon season—or to drive them into India. "We are just waiting for the monsoon," said a Bengali rebel. "We are masters of water."[27]

ONE POWERFUL INDIAN OFFICIAL, D. P. DHAR, THE AMBASSADOR IN Moscow—a confidant of Gandhi's who was well known as part of the "Kashmiri Mafia"—wanted India's paramilitary forces to arm these rebels with artillery and heavy mortars from the start. Writing to his close friend Haksar, Dhar argued that "our main and only aim should be to ensure that the marshes and the quagmires of East Bengal swallow up" Pakistan's military. He hoped that "in the not very distant future the West Pakistan elements will find their Dien Bien Pho in East Bengal. This will relieve us of the constant threat which Pakistan has always posed to our security directly and also as a willing and pliable instrument of China." He urged Haksar, *This resistance must not be allowed to collapse.*"[28]

It was not. With extraordinary swiftness and maximum secrecy, India backed the rebellion—although the army worried about how Pakistan and China might react. India, which vocally advocated national sovereignty, would be embarrassed to be caught stirring up rebellion inside Pakistan. But as early as March 29, K. F. Rustamji, the famed police officer leading India's Border Security Force, was allowed to offer limited help to the Bengali rebels. After Parliament's bold resolution against Pakistan on March 31, Rustamji claims that Indira Gandhi privately told him, "Do what you like, but don't get caught."[29]

According to Rustamji, Gandhi herself met with Bengali leaders in the first week of April, as they were establishing their guerrilla force. On April 1, as a top secret Indian memorandum shows, two senior Bengali nationalist leaders met with the Indian government, with the Indians desperately trying to keep it secret. The Bengalis ("our Friends") had plenty of manpower, but would need some "training in guerilla tactics, to prepare for a long struggle." India would provide "material assistance," likely including arms, ammunition, organizational advice, broadcast and transit facilities, and medicine. The Border Security

Force would be the main agency in charge of these operations, but the Indian army might have to get involved too.[30]

This effort embroiled the highest levels of the Indian government and army. Gandhi, gravely worried about her government's new responsibilities, created a special committee on East Pakistan and the insurgency, including Haksar, the foreign and defense ministries, and R. N. Kao, the head of the R&AW spy agency, sometimes calling in General Manekshaw. At Gandhi's command, political talks with "the leaders of the Bangla Desh movement" went through "the secret channels of the R&AW." Haksar, fretting that the R&AW's normal spy duties were getting swamped, obliquely noted that the intelligence agency was now running "the special operations which have become necessary."[31]

India worked closely with the self-declared Bangladeshi government in exile, which was allowed—despite bitter protests from Pakistan—to set itself up on Indian soil in Calcutta. There Rustamji and General Jacob coordinated their efforts with Tajuddin Ahmad, the Bangladeshi prime minister. Keeping the R&AW in the loop, Rustamji and Jacob planned camps where the Indian army would train Bengali nationalist guerrillas, cooperating with Bengali rebel commanders on tactics. According to Jacob, the Border Security Force launched an unsuccessful raid inside East Pakistan.[32]

Gandhi was fully in the loop. In mid-April, Kao told the prime minister that "the [Pakistan] Army is planning to move towards the Indian border in order to cut off the main supply routes for the Liberation Forces." And according to Haksar's notes, Gandhi was to tell opposition lawmakers that India was spending about $80 million that year on the insurgency, and that the "burden for sustaining the fight of the people of Bangla Desh" cost as much as providing for the refugees.[33]

This exile government announced on April 17 a proclamation of independence for a sovereign democratic republic of Bangladesh, accusing Pakistan of genocide. The Border Security Force set up the event just inside East Pakistan. Gandhi still held back from recognition, withstanding the public uproar in India, but her government secretly offered them "all possible help" and assisted in keeping the guerrilla war going. India asked the Bangladeshi authorities to keep a lower profile in Calcutta and, behind closed doors, urged them to make their joint strategy appear to be the plan of the provisional government.[34]

India avidly worked to keep the rebellion in the control of pro-Indian and relatively moderate Awami League nationalists, fearing Bengali extremists who were more pro-Chinese. Haksar, disheartened that Mujib and his fellow Awami League politicians had been taken by surprise by Pakistan's onslaught, now worried at the "total absence of central political direction to the struggle inside Bangla Desh." This sustained guerrilla war, Haksar thought, would require leadership from the fledgling Bangladeshi government.[35]

Rustamji was impressed with the insurgents' fighting spirit. They toasted together to "Bangla Desh." But the Bengali fighters expected India to go to war almost immediately, and were crushed when they realized that was not in the offing. The Border Security Force was frustrated too, but Rustamji says that General Manekshaw warned him that his covert activities could easily lead to war, and India was not ready for that yet.[36]

The Indians and Bengalis secretly worked hand in glove on guerrilla warfare, on everything from recruitment (Rustamji favored university graduates) to blowing up bridges (which Tajuddin Ahmad wanted to do without hesitation even if it angered locals). The Indian army suggested targeting the Pakistan army's heavy reliance on petrol. Tajuddin Ahmad asked for medical aid, credit, and radio transmitters aimed at Dacca, all the while urging India to recognize Bangladesh.[37]

THE INDIAN ARMY TOO HAD ITS ORDERS. BY HIS OWN ACCOUNT, GENeral Sam Manekshaw, the army chief of staff, decided to have the Indian army train and equip three brigades of regular Bengali troops, drawing mostly on defectors from Pakistan's East Bengal Regiment and the East Pakistan Rifles. In addition, Manekshaw wanted to train and arm about seventy-five thousand guerrillas. Manekshaw would later frankly admit to Soviet military chiefs that India had given "all possible help in the organisation, arming and training of the Freedom Fighters."[38]

On April 22, Manekshaw held a meeting about having the army take charge of the Border Security Force, which was leading India's help to the rebellion. Manekshaw and Lieutenant General Jagjit Singh Aurora, another top officer, would give directions, and the Border Security Force would work closely with the army's units. The force was secretly in touch with the East Bengal Regiment and the East Pakistan Rifles. As a top secret Border Security Force memorandum shows, Manekshaw wanted to "step up the tempo" of guerrilla operations, with a focus on "demolition by small parties."[39]

A top secret R&AW report says that "the charge of imparting training to Mukti Fouz was given to the local Army authorities early in

May." General Jacob remembers, "The government asked us to train the Mukti Bahini, so we set up camps, with the BSF [Border Security Force] at the border areas." There were, Jacob says, "two factors required to keep that insurgency going: firm bases, and lines of supply for arms, ammunition, and money. As long as those two factors obtain, that insurgency will continue."[40]

The Indians were torn between providing proper training or quickly getting fighters into combat. Jacob recalls, "I first started with eight camps. I visualized one thousand in each camp, three months' training." Manekshaw, he says, wanted more guerrillas and less training. "Manekshaw didn't agree," Jacob says. "He said I should get one hundred thousand. I said, 'How can I train one hundred thousand?' He said, 'Three weeks is enough.' I said, 'What do you think, it's a sausage machine? A young Bengali comes in and he comes out a Gurkha in three weeks?' "

INDIA DID NOT DARE PUBLICLY ADMIT WHAT IT WAS DOING. (TO THIS day, Indian officials lie about the country's sponsorship of the insurgents.) The Indian foreign ministry denounced allegations about India arming the rebels as a cynical attempt to divert the world's attention from Pakistan's "carnage and systematic genocide in East Bengal."[41]

But only fools were fooled. India's own newspapers figured it out fast. From Calcutta, it was possible for an enterprising Indian reporter to meet up with a group of Mukti Fouj commandos, join them for a firefight with a Pakistani army garrison, and return to camp with a terrific story to file. Foreign correspondents quickly got the story too. Sydney Schanberg of the *New York Times* was eager to get back into East Pakistan after being expelled by the Pakistan army. "It was forbidden," he remembers. Like other foreign reporters, he groused that they were being told by Indian authorities to stay away from the border areas. But he found a way: "I got permission to go to [Tripura] where the border patrol were training the Mukti Bahini. So I wrote that story."[42]

He spent four days touring the border and venturing across into East Pakistan. There he spoke to young rebels determined to avenge their dead families. "They have made me an orphan," one glassy-eyed guerrilla told him. "My life is unimportant now." Schanberg saw Pakistani soldiers throwing phosphorus grenades into thatch huts and setting villages ablaze, apparently to deny hiding places to the guerrillas. He reported that, at a minimum, tens of thousands of people had been systematically killed by the army. The troops had killed much of the

Bengali leadership class, including engineers, doctors, and students. He wrote, "As smoke from the thatch and bamboo huts billowed up on the outskirts of the city of Comilla, circling vultures descended on the bodies of peasants, already being picked apart by dogs and crows."[43]

Nor was the U.S. government hoodwinked by India's claims of noninvolvement. "Nobody believed it," recalls Samuel Hoskinson, the White House aide. Many American reporters, like Schanberg, talked to U.S. officials about what they had seen: Border Security Force men running training camps, and India providing weapons. The CIA informed Kissinger about what was happening. Kissinger told Nixon that India would train Bengalis for a long guerrilla war. Kenneth Keating, the U.S. ambassador to India, urged his own government to turn a blind eye to India's secret war.[44]

While Pakistan denounced India's covert activities, India offered increasingly threadbare denials. Swaran Singh, India's foreign minister, indignantly denied these reports, while less brazen diplomats preferred to dodge, neither admitting nor denying what India was obviously doing. "Pakistan is fully aware of our activities vis-a-vis East Bengal," an Indian envoy told the foreign ministry. "I shall of course deny them but . . . this will not carry conviction."[45]

BY MAY, INDIRA GANDHI AND HER TEAM WERE COVERTLY BACKING WHAT Haksar called a "total struggle for national liberation."[46]

According to top secret Indian records, the prime minister herself covertly met with a representative of the self-declared Bangladesh government. On May 6, a leader identified only as T.—probably Tajuddin Ahmad, the exile prime minister—had a night meeting with her. Haksar briefed her that this Bengali leader had talked to Lieutenant General Jagjit Singh Aurora, the general officer commanding-in-chief of the Indian army's Eastern Command, about their future plan of action. Covering his tracks, Haksar added that everything they were doing for Bangladesh was carried out at the Bangladeshi exile government's behest.[47]

Haksar had high hopes for the insurgents. He wanted a "common strategy of warfare over a comparatively prolonged period," using "guerilla tactics, with the object of keeping the West Pakistan army continuously off their balance and to, gradually, bleed them." Preparing Gandhi for a meeting with opposition legislators, he outlined a military path to victory: "If the struggle could be sustained over a period of time of 6 to 8 months, it is not unreasonable to expect that [the] sheer burden on Pakistan of carrying on this struggle will become, sooner or later, unbearable."⁴⁸

From Moscow, Dhar rather condescendingly expressed the "delighted surprise of all of us that the East Bengalis have it in them." (This echoed the widespread conceit, prevalent not just in Pakistan but in India too, that, as one Indian activist casually put it, "Bengalis are not a martial race.") Dhar candidly laid out India's awkward mix of lofty and low motives: "Apart from the laudable cause of the Bengali aspirations for freedom and a life of respect and dignity, we have to remember our national interests. What we have to plan for is not an immediate defeat of the highly trained and superior military machine of West Pakistan; we have to create the whole of East Bengal into a bottomless ditch which will suck the strength and the resources of West Pakistan."⁴⁹

But the guerrillas faced a terribly difficult fight. R. N. Kao, the R&AW spymaster, gave Gandhi a bleak appraisal. "The Pakistan Army continues to be on the offensive," he wrote, "fanning out in strength from their main bases to capture positions held by the Liberation Forces." Despite some heavy fighting, Kao warned, "the Army is slowly gaining the upper hand," especially in controlling the cities.⁵⁰

Archer Blood and his staff at the U.S. consulate in Dacca, tracking the fight in a makeshift war room, were privately dismayed to see the Pakistan army seize the main cities. The lieutenant governor of the border state of Tripura informed Gandhi that Pakistani troops were ruthlessly taking the cities and moving out into the countryside, strafing and bombing the guerrillas. The Pakistani forces' next goal was to seal the border to isolate the insurgents, but that was not feasible, so it would still be possible for "the freedom fighters to infiltrate and carry out the hit-and-run guerilla tactics which will alone 'bleed' the enemy." He implored Gandhi to "extend the maximum assistance to the Resistance Force short of direct involvement."⁵¹

Without Indian help, the Bengali guerrillas would be in even more dire straits. The Indian government was dismayed that the insurgents had been taken by surprise by Yahya's assault. Writing to Gandhi, Haksar worried that the "desperate heroic resistance" of the rebels from the East Pakistan Rifles and the East Bengal Regiment was being squandered. Trained as regular soldiers, they would all too often launch frontal assaults against the Pakistan army and thereby suffer grievous losses, when they would have been better off trying guerrilla tactics.⁵²

So there was every reason for Gandhi's government to believe that the Bengali rebels would not be able to win alone, even with Indian support, and that Indian troops would need to join their fight directly. Subrahmanyam, the strategist, had warned that rebels alone would probably be quashed. Dhar, arguing for backing the insurgents, calmly accepted the likely consequence of an Indian war with Pakistan, which he reckoned almost inevitable.[53]

The Bengali rebels had more expansive battlefield ambitions than the Indian army, and pulled India along. General Aurora, as the R&AW noted, wanted to dismantle the East Pakistan Rifles and East Bengal Regiment and train their troops—as well as the new volunteers—for guerrilla warfare. But the Bengalis drilled for both insurgency and conventional war, seeking at least five battalions. To build up this rudimentary army, the Bengalis came up with a plan of what they needed from the Indian army. Gandhi's government approved this escalation: "This scheme was approved in toto by the highest authorities in Delhi and the Army was asked to implement it."[54]

Still, Gandhi, sobered by the warnings from her senior military men, was not yet ready to send her troops to war against Pakistan. Haksar argued that India should not recognize Bangladesh, which would "raise false hopes that recognition would be followed by direct intervention of the Armed Forces of India to sustain and support such a Government." For a meeting with opposition lawmakers, Haksar briefed Gandhi to say, "We cannot, at the present stage, contemplate armed intervention at all. . . . [A]ll the sympathy and support which the Bangla Desh has been able to evoke in the world will be drowned in Indo-Pak conflict. The main thing, therefore, is not a formal recognition, but to do whatever lies within our power to sustain the struggle."[55]

Chapter 7

"Don't Squeeze Yahya"

WINSTON LORD WAS A PATRICIAN YOUNG NEW YORKER WHO had glided from the secrecy of the Skull and Bones tomb at Yale to the State Department. He would later ascend to be Ronald Reagan's ambassador to China and then an assistant secretary of state under Bill Clinton. In 1971, he held a cherished White House job as Henry Kissinger's special assistant and indispensable aide on China. Cerebral and hardworking, he became so close with his boss that on Richard Nixon's first visit to Beijing in 1972, Kissinger brought the thirty-four-year-old staffer along to take notes on the meeting with Mao Zedong himself. His image had to be cropped out of official pictures to avoid incensing William Rogers, the secretary of state, who got left out.[1]

Lord was one of the tiny clique of people who knew the single most important fact about world politics: that Nixon and Kissinger were secretly planning an opening to China. And he also knew something that nobody in the Dacca consulate could have guessed: that Yahya, while crushing the Bengalis, was also carrying messages from China to the Nixon team.

Lord, who is keenly intelligent and enduringly loyal to Kissinger, remembers their China project with a high moral purpose: "If you're talking about human rights, if you're trying to prevent nuclear war, constraining the Soviets, if you have to hold your nose with some of your allies, balancing was also a human right if it kept the world from blowing up."

But he recalls the daunting challenges in opening to China after twenty-two years of mutual isolation. He asks, "How did you get in contact with the Chinese? The only channel we had was propaganda exchanges in Geneva and Warsaw"—mostly useless recitations of talking points, he says, and too visible anyway.

Pakistan was one of many options. "Nixon and Kissinger tried several channels," says Lord. "There was a halfhearted attempt with de Gaulle in '69. They tried through Romania." The Americans could have got to Beijing through Bucharest or Paris—or some other city—instead of Islamabad. Kissinger later told Nixon that "you thought up Romania, you were the one who thought up the Polish deal, and you were the one who talked to Yahya the first time you were there in Lahore." Kissinger also made an approach through Paris, asking his old friend Jean Sainteny, a veteran French diplomat, to set up a private channel there through the Chinese ambassador to France. And Kissinger met with Nicolae Ceauşescu, Romania's brutal despot, asking him to facilitate communications with China.[2]

Yahya leaped at his chance. As early as October 1970—before the cyclone and the Pakistani elections—Nixon had personally told Yahya that it was essential for the United States to open negotiations with China, and Yahya had volunteered himself as a conduit for secret diplomacy. The Pakistani strongman, who was going to Beijing soon, pledged to explain to the Chinese that the White House would consider a clandestine meeting in Rawalpindi, or perhaps Paris. As promised, Yahya spoke personally to Zhou Enlai, China's premier, and scored impressive results: an invitation from Mao himself for the United States to send a special envoy to Beijing. According to Yahya, Zhou had praised the use of him as an intermediary, since he was a head of state and Pakistan was "a great friend of China." Kissinger considered a meeting in Rawalpindi.[3]

"The picking of channels was done by Kissinger and Nixon," Lord recalls. "We laid out a smorgasbord, and they picked Pakistan." But while the choice seems overdetermined in retrospect (Kissinger would later claim that "we had no other means of communication with Peking"), it was not at the time. Pakistan, says Lord, was not the only option acceptable to the White House.[4]

On March 25, when the slaughter started in East Pakistan, the White House was still weighing several other China options. Ceauşescu had delivered a success too, bringing back an almost identical invitation from Mao as the one from Yahya. When Nixon replied to Zhou, he sent his message through both Pakistan and Romania. A week after the Blood telegram, Nixon and Kissinger were weighing meetings with Yahya and Ceauşescu as back channels, as well as talking about letters sent through Sainteny. A few days later, Kissinger told Nixon that they now needed a direct channel to China, and considered sending a general to Warsaw to set up communications. In late April, Kissinger was still considering using Sainteny. And on April 22—almost a month into the Bengali bloodshed—Kissinger told Nixon that Ceauşescu had sent a top official to Beijing, carrying back a message for the White House.[5]

Kissinger and his team often justify the tilt toward Pakistan as vital for the opening to China. Harold Saunders, the senior White House aide, remembers Kissinger's focus on China. "China will be looking at how we'll be treating an ally," he says, explaining his boss's thinking. "That was the governing factor. I know I took a lot of flak from my State colleagues, but I couldn't tell them that. It was a very tightly held secret."

But Kissinger later wrote that he thought their Pakistan policy was "correct on the merits, above and beyond the China connection." Lord has said, "It's a huge exaggeration to say that we did this solely as a favor to the Chinese." He is skeptical about how much the China channel really mattered for the White House's backing of Pakistan, and instead frames the issue in the Cold War: "India was allegedly nonaligned, but we considered it pro-Soviet, getting Soviet weapons. So you already had an American bias toward Pakistan before the opening to China. It was geopolitical. India's on the Russian team, so we'll put Pakistan on our team. . . . To say we tilted toward Pakistan because of the opening to China is an oversimplification. We might have done that anyway."[6]

"NEEDLING, NASTY LITTLE THINGS"

On the curb of a main downtown intersection in Dacca, there lay a corpse. The dead man was a worker, barefoot, and had been lying there for hours. Nobody touched him. Nobody even dared to look at him. People simply stepped over the body. This was not out of callousness, but fear. A U.S. official in Dacca noted that "people have been shot for moving bodies." The army seemed to want as many people as possible to see the dead.[7]

The Dacca consulate's staffers kept up their stubborn daily project of feeding their superiors with bad news. This was, in the end, a more significant achievement than the sensational dissent telegram. Ignored by Washington, they became, as Archer Blood remembered later with some pride, "testy and pugnacious," often "real pains in the neck." One official in Blood's consulate wrote that most foreigners in East Pakistan "stay because there is still the faint hope that the constant reporting will finally produce more than echoes within the corridors, and because it is extremely difficult to leave fearing the future of those left behind."[8]

Blood and his team believed they had some reason to hope. Thanks to intrepid reporters who snuck into East Pakistan, newspapers and television news ran vivid stories about the killing. Throughout the first month of slaughter, the U.S. government held a loud internal debate about its South Asia policy. There was voluminous input from the State Department and the two feuding ambassadors in Delhi and Islamabad, as well as the renegade consul in Dacca—although none of them knew what Winston Lord did. Still, despite having every opportunity to hear opposite points of view, Nixon and Kissinger—the only two people who counted—did not budge.[9]

ROGERS, THE SECRETARY OF STATE, REFLECTING SOME OF THE FERMENT among his underlings, told Nixon the time had come to reevaluate U.S. policy toward Pakistan—in particular "the Pakistan Army's use of U.S.-supplied military equipment," which was embarrassing for public opinion. From Islamabad, Joseph Farland, the U.S. ambassador there, weighed in for a nonintervention policy, but added some mild disapproval of Pakistan. At most, he wanted to privately suggest to Pakistani officials that force would not work in the long run, and find bureaucratic excuses to suspend new shipments of arms and ammunition. He warned against alienating Yahya, and doubted that economic sanctions would work any better against Pakistan than they had with South Africa or Rhodesia.[10]

Jousting back, Archer Blood rejected that cringing tone. He warned that the carnage was driving moderate Bengalis into the arms of their leftist radicals, and that the Soviet Union had been more outspoken for human rights and democracy than the United States. On behalf of his whole consulate, he urged Nixon to tell Yahya of "our deep disapproval of suppression of democratic forces and widespread loss of lives and property." He argued for cutting off U.S. military and economic assistance to Pakistan, urging a new "policy which freezes aid for the time being without apologetic statements and without utterance of hopes that US is desirous of resuming aid and anxiously awaiting G[overnment] O[f] P[akistan] plans." Blood did not even trust Yahya's government to deliver food aid, acidly noting that the military authorities' "concern with food not convincingly demonstrated by continuing razing of markets."[11]

From Delhi, Kenneth Keating similarly argued that the Nixon administration should exhort Pakistan to stop its repression and voice its "displeasure at the use of American arms and materiel," which was proving hugely embarrassing. Keating wanted to stop U.S. military supply and suspend economic aid. He tried a realpolitik argument: "Pakistan is probably finished as a unified state; India is clearly the predominant actual and potential power in this area of the world." Instead of backing a weak loser, the United States should turn to a strong winner.[12]

Rather than sticking up for his contrarians in Dacca and Delhi, the secretary of state tried to shut them up. Rogers told Kissinger, "We have Ken Keating quieted down." Kissinger replied, "I appreciated that." Thus the only diplomat whose opinion counted was Farland, whom Kissinger reached out to directly, bypassing the State Department, to ask the ambassador to send him a frank assessment.[13]

Farland decried the State Department's advocacy for the Bengalis. Although admitting that Pakistan was crumbling, he still did not want to give up on it. The Pakistan army would soon wrap up its offensive and proceed to "mopping up," which would get it out of U.S. newspapers. If the United States adopted Blood's policy of leaning hard on Pakistan, Farland threatened to resign. In this private message to Kissinger, Farland slammed Blood: "Embassy has had full-scale revolt on general issue by virtually all officers in Consulate General, Dacca, coupled with forfeiture of leadership for American community there. Dacca's reporting has been tendentious to an extreme."[14]

THE ONLY REALLY CLEAR ACHIEVEMENT OF ALL THIS DEBATE WAS TO hurt Archer Blood's feelings. He was lacerated to slowly realize that his fellow diplomats in Islamabad did not believe him. Despondent, evidently trying to salvage his career, he unconvincingly suggested that everyone—in Dacca, Islamabad, and Washington—was now on "approximately [the] same wave length," and suggested that these matters were best "discussed over a drink with friends and colleagues." Since he had just told his bosses that they were morally bankrupt and complicit with genocide, they might not have been inclined to invite him over for a beer.[15]

At an awkward meeting at the Islamabad embassy, Blood, along with Eric Griffel and Scott Butcher, held his ground, but found his fellow diplomats obviously saddened by them: Blood later wrote that "their formerly respected colleagues in the East Wing had clearly gone off the deep end." When the deputy from the Islamabad embassy came to visit Dacca, downplaying the atrocities, an astonished Blood blew up at him. He hauled the visiting skeptic to Dacca University, showing him a stairwell that was heavily pockmarked with bullet holes. There was a sickly sweet reek from the bottom of the stairwell. They could make out rotting bodies. Blood's colleague's attitude had reminded him of Yahya's reported response to the cyclone: "It doesn't look so bad."[16]

While the State Department was still busily honing its various arguments, Nixon and Kissinger could hardly have cared less. Pakistan's role as a channel to China added to their unwillingness to speak up about the killings in East Pakistan. "Thank God we didn't get into the Pakistan thing," the president said. "We are smart to stay the hell out of that." "Absolutely," agreed Kissinger. "Now, State has a whole list of needling, nasty little things they want to do to West Pakistan. I don't think we should do it, Mr. President." Nixon growled, "Not a goddamn thing. I will not allow it."[17]

ARSENAL AGAINST DEMOCRACY

The most neuralgic issue was U.S. military aid to Pakistan. As Blood persistently noted, Pakistan's armed forces were using lots of U.S. arms against the Bengalis. He gave new specifics about the weapons—F-86 Sabre jet fighters, M-24 Chaffee tanks, jeeps equipped with machine guns—saying there was "no doubt" that it was happening.[18]

In early April, Kissinger's staffers, Harold Saunders and Samuel Hoskinson, explained plainly what was at stake in continuing to arm Pakistan: "the rest of the world will assume—no matter what we might say—that we support West Pakistan in its struggle against the majority civilian population in the East. If we cut off their military supply or even suspend or slow it down, the West Pakistanis and the rest of the world will view it at a minimum as a move to dissociate ourselves and at a maximum as a move to halt the war."[19]

By concentrating only on the question of what U.S. arms might now be shipped to Pakistan, the White House addressed only the smallest and newest part of the massive U.S. arsenal provided since the Eisenhower administration. Edward Kennedy's office would calculate that 80 percent of Pakistan's military equipment was from the United States, while the State Department rather fuzzily claimed that less than half of what Pakistan was currently using was American. Either way, it was a huge chunk of Pakistan's total stockpile.[20]

But throughout the bloodshed, the White House did not make any complaints that Pakistan was using its current stores of U.S. weapons against the Bengali civilian population. Of course, even when Pakistani troops were not directly using U.S. tanks or warplanes, the presence of U.S. weaponry in other parts of Pakistan had the effect of freeing Pakistani troops up to mete out violence in East Pakistan. Still, the only weapons that the White House was considering were the latest installments of U.S. military assistance.

THE WHITE HOUSE STRUGGLED TO FIGURE OUT EXACTLY HOW MUCH weaponry was due to Pakistan. Samuel Hoskinson grimaces at the memory. "There was an endless debate about what was in the pipeline and what wasn't," he says. "We could never get a grip on it. It made you crazy. When you deal with the Pentagon, you go into a world of mirrors. It was a morass. Impossible to figure out."

The details were confounding. Legally, Pakistan was still under a U.S. arms embargo, imposed after its attack on India back in 1965. But Nixon had opened up major arms shipments again in October 1970, when he had made an "exception" to the embargo, offering a big haul, hearkening back to the lavish period of U.S. weapons supply started under Dwight Eisenhower: armored personnel carriers, fighter planes, bombers, and more. None of this had been delivered yet, but Pakistan had put in a down payment for the armored personnel carriers, and was eager to get hold of the rest. Saunders calculated that Pakistan had some $44 million worth of military equipment on order from the United States, including $18 million of lethal arms, $3 million of ammunition, and $18 million of spare parts vital to keep the army and air force functioning. Kissinger somewhat more conservatively told Nixon that altogether, Pakistan was still awaiting delivery of some $34 million worth of military equipment, purchased over the past few years, although the real amount that would ship anytime soon would probably be half of that.[21]

This, Kissinger knew, would generate all the wrong kinds of headlines. The press was already in full cry over revelations that some ammunition and spare parts were still going out to Pakistan. Kissinger informed Nixon that "we have deliberately avoided" reimposing a total "formal embargo" on Pakistan. But they needed to avoid the embarrassment of major arms shipments to Pakistan at this moment. Through sheer good luck, it turned out that none of the major deliveries were scheduled during the crisis, which let the White House look less obdurate. As Kissinger told Nixon, if some spectacular U.S. weapons systems turned up in Pakistan now, "the appearance of insensitivity" would provoke the Democrats who controlled Congress to legislate their own stop to arms shipments—which would be tougher than anything that the Nixon administration could contemplate.[22]

As the White House weighed its options, it did not realize that it had already been outmaneuvered by the State Department. Soon after the shooting started on March 25, the State Department had quietly imposed an administrative hold on military equipment for Pakistan, which was ostensibly only supposed to last until the White House could make a formal decision. The chairman of the Joint Chiefs of Staff said that the Pakistani military was "very bitter about the arms supply."[23]

The result was a quiet suspension of the biggest shipments, like those three hundred armored personnel carriers and the fighter and bomber aircraft. Pakistan was still getting some U.S. supplies that were already under way. This was couched, Kissinger told Nixon, as "simple administrative sluggishness," rather than a reprimand, because "we wanted to avoid the political signal which an embargo would convey." Kissinger, evidently trying to drop a mollifying hint to Democrats, told McGeorge Bundy, the former national security advisor to John Kennedy and Lyndon Johnson, that there were a "few spare parts" on their way to Pakistan, but "nothing new is scheduled for shipment for six months or so. So we don't have to face that for a few months. We're going to drag our feet on implementing sales and drag out negotiations."[24]

Kissinger was clear that neither he nor Nixon would support stopping arms supplies to Pakistan. This was merely a temporary, informal dodge, until the press found something else to write about. Those armored personnel carriers, for instance, were not due to be delivered until May 1972, and Kissinger, while deferring a decision about them, was not about to stop the sale or return the down payment. Kissinger suggested buying time on technical grounds. The deputy secretary of defense admitted that it was possible that some armaments would show up in Pakistan: "Congress may holler and you can just blame it on the stupid Defense Department."

Some military supply would keep going. When it was pointed out that twenty-eight thousand rounds of ammunition and some bomb parts were due in July, and that Congress might object, Kissinger told a Situation Room meeting, "But we would pay a very heavy price with

Yahya if they were not delivered." He insisted that an explicit decision be taken by Nixon "before we hold up any shipments. This would be the exact opposite of his policy. He is not eager for a confrontation with Yahya." Kissinger added, "If these weapons could be used in East Pakistan, it would be different"—although in fact the United States had not asked Pakistan to stop using tanks or warplanes against Bengalis.[25]

NIXON AND KISSINGER WERE PLEASED THAT THE PAKISTAN ARMY WAS regaining control of the scorched cities. In April, as his soldiers surged forward, Yahya tried to create a new government in East Pakistan to replace the elected leaders of the outlawed Awami League. He put forward Bengalis who were committed to a united Pakistan and disparaged the Awami League—in other words, the kind of people who had lost the elections. Blood laughed at Yahya's docile group of collaborationist politicians, seen by the overwhelming majority of Bengalis as a "puppet regime."[26]

Blood understood that this was only the first phase of a long civil war. The rebels, he reported, were avoiding direct clashes with the better-armed Pakistan army, to preserve their strength for later guerrilla combat. So the real war would come during the monsoon rains, as the fighting raged on in the countryside.[27]

The most surreal debate about who would win the civil war came when Blood, on a trip to the Islamabad embassy, had a face-off with, of all people, Chuck Yeager—the famous test pilot who had been the first human to break the sound barrier. Joseph Farland had somehow managed to enlist his fellow West Virginian, now a brigadier general, as a U.S. defense representative. By his own admission, Yeager knew almost nothing about Pakistan (a "very primitive and rough country and Moslem"), but quickly became a vehement supporter of Pakistan's military.[28]

As Blood remembered, Yeager sneeringly asked him how the ill-equipped Bengalis could possibly stand up to the disciplined Pakistan army. Blood felt like snapping back, "Haven't you fellows learned anything from Vietnam?" Restraining himself, he managed a suitably professional reply—that the guerrillas would wear down and outnumber the Pakistan army, and that India could quickly crush the Pakistan army too—but suddenly felt depressed and terribly lonely.[29]

Pakistan's military advances throughout April reassured Nixon and

Kissinger that Yahya might subdue East Pakistan after all. Alexander Haig, Kissinger's deputy national security advisor—who would go on to be Ronald Reagan's secretary of state—reassured Nixon, "The fighting is about over—there is considerable stability now." Kissinger was bolstered by the CIA's deputy director, who said that the Bengali rebels were collapsing. Heartened, Kissinger questioned the prospect of a long war. He admitted that if the Bengali nationalists launched mass noncooperation campaigns and marshaled guerrilla forces, the situation could prove "very tough," but saw no evidence that they were doing that. Instead, he said, "West Pakistani superiority seems evident. I agree I used to think that 30,000 men couldn't possibly subdue 75 million, which I suppose is the Western way of looking at it"—here he omitted his private discussions with Nixon, in which he had concluded quite the opposite. "But if the 75 million don't organize and don't fight, the situation is different."[30]

YAHYA WAS EFFUSIVE IN HIS GRATITUDE TO NIXON. IN A WARM LETTER, he sympathized about the American public pressure that Nixon was withstanding, and insisted that reports of atrocities were Indian-inspired exaggerations. He was "deeply gratified" that the United States saw the crisis as "an internal affair" to be resolved by Pakistan's government.[31]

This was certainly Kissinger's view. Even relatively minor insults to Pakistan's sovereign prerogatives were too much for him. When it was suggested that Yahya promise that U.S. food aid would get to rural Bengalis, Kissinger recoiled at that "substantial challenge to the West Pakistan notion of sovereignty." He said, "It would be as though, in our civil war, the British had offered food to Lincoln on the condition that it be used to feed the people in Alabama."[32]

To others, Yahya looked a lot more like King George III than Abraham Lincoln. Keating, the ambassador to India, told a reporter that the concept of national sovereignty could be "overdone" (for which the State Department told him to shut up). And Blood and his consulate refused to accept that Yahya could do whatever he wanted within Pakistan's sovereign borders, overturning a fair election and killing his citizenry. The "extra-constitutional martial law regime of President Yahya Khan is of dubious legitimacy (how many votes did Yahya obtain?)." They heralded the "anti-colonial" Bengali struggle, comparing it to the American Revolution. "They want to participate in deciding their own destiny," Blood's team wrote. "Even our forefathers fought for similar ideals."[33]

There was another administration official with rather brighter career prospects who brought up human rights: George H. W. Bush, then the U.S. ambassador at the United Nations. The future president's mission argued that India should be allowed to criticize Pakistan's domestic human rights record at a United Nations body, because of the "tradition which we have supported that [the] human rights question transcend[s] domestic jurisdiction and should be freely debated," notably Soviet and Arab oppression of Jews. "We have never objected to the right of others to criticize domestic conditions in the US maintaining that, as a free society, our policies are fully open to scrutiny." That had the ring of principle, but Bush was not about to pick a fight with Nixon or Kissinger. Although he knew that something truly awful was happening in East Pakistan—his office had recently reported that the Indian government estimated the Bengali civilian death toll at between thirty thousand and a million, with the sober-minded Indian ambassador at the United Nations reckoning the total at roughly one hundred thousand—Bush made no effort to say anything beyond the official timid line of "concern" about the Bengalis.[34]

AT THE WHITE HOUSE, HAROLD SAUNDERS, KISSINGER'S SENIOR AIDE on South Asia, tried a somewhat louder—but still genteel—challenge to U.S. policy. Saunders remembers that he absorbed the angry complaints coming from the State Department, including those from Blood and others. "I was closely working with the people in State, who obviously were close to our people on the ground," he says. "I realize how strongly they felt. And, I thought, with good reason. I agreed with them."[35]

Saunders and Samuel Hoskinson argued that the Bengalis would almost certainly win, breaking free of a distant government in Islamabad with limited resources. The American public would recoil: a military regime was using mass killings to crush a majority that had won a fair election. Soon after, Saunders, appealing to Kissinger's strategic sensibilities, tried out a realpolitik pitch for India: "Insofar as US interests can be defined simply in terms of a balance of power among states, it would be logical—if a choice were required—for the US to align itself with the 600 million people of India and East Pakistan and to leave the 60 million of West Pakistan in relative geographical isolation." Kissinger was unmoved: "Whom are we trying to impress in East Pakistan?"[36]

On April 19, Saunders sent Kissinger a memorandum with the unusually intimate title "Pakistan—a Personal Reflection on the Choice Before Us." Challenging Kissinger's hope for Yahya's military victory, he declared that the disintegration of Pakistan was inevitable. (This was confirmed by an intelligence community analysis, which said there was little chance that the army could put down the Bengali insurgency.) Saunders wanted to coax Yahya to pull back from a ruinous civil war, gently encouraging him toward autonomy for East Pakistan. Rather than threatening to cut off aid, as Blood would, he put his trust in Pakistani goodwill: "I would not tell Yahya that he must do anything." This, he mildly wrote, would be merely *an effort to help a friend find a practical and face-saving way out of a bind.*" In a joint paper with Samuel Hoskinson, he was somewhat more direct, saying that U.S. pressure could "preserve a relationship with Yahya while making a serious effort to get him—and us—off a disastrous course."[37]

Temperate as this was, Kissinger was unswayed. Saunders remembers that his boss held fast to the principle that the United States should not tell other leaders how to run their countries: "So he didn't buy it." Saunders says that, in retrospect, "the China thought was paramount."

In a Situation Room meeting that day, Saunders had to sit silently while Kissinger resisted putting any pressure on Pakistan. Kissinger batted away proposals for cutting off military aid or development loans, which would bring "a substantial rupture of our relations with Yahya." He stood firm against confronting Yahya: "no matter what our view may be of the savagery of the West Pakistan troops, we would just be pulling India's chestnuts out of the fire if we take on West Pakistan."

Kissinger had repeatedly reminded senior officials that Nixon "does have a special feeling about Yahya." Each time that Kissinger invoked presidential authority, he emphasized how hard it would be to drive any wedge between Nixon and Yahya: "The President thinks he has a special relationship with Yahya; he would be most reluctant to take him on. This reluctance might be overcome, but we can't do it at this level." Kissinger ended the meeting by saying he would go to the president. Everyone in the Situation Room knew what that meant.[38]

ON APRIL 21, ZHOU ENLAI SENT A BREAKTHROUGH MESSAGE USING Yahya, in which the Chinese premier suggested that Kissinger, Rogers, or even Nixon himself come to Beijing. Zhou suggested that all the arrangements could "be made through the good offices of President Yahya Khan."[39]

At this point, the White House retired its other China channels. Bucharest, Warsaw, Paris—all were shut down. Kissinger had written another letter for Jean Sainteny in Paris, which was now abandoned. Saunders remembers that Kissinger thought the Romanian government was untrustworthy. The Chinese leadership did not trust any communist country, Lord notes. Nor would they rely on France, a U.S. ally.[40]

Nixon and Kissinger relished their coming triumph. This, Kissinger told the president, would end the Vietnam War this year. They left the State Department in the dark. When Nixon suggested sending George Bush to Beijing, soon after the future president had argued for India's right to speak about human rights, Kissinger was withering: "Absolutely not, he is too soft and not sophisticated enough." This was a job that Kissinger wanted for himself.[41]

Winston Lord, Kissinger's special assistant, was primarily concerned with how useful Yahya's government had been with China. But as he uncomfortably wrote to Kissinger, "We can afford neither to alienate Pakistan nor to ignore Indian sensitivities, the nasty practices of Yahya's army, and the fact that almost all observers believe that Bangla Desh will eventually become an independent entity."[42]

But Yahya won fresh appreciation from the White House. With perfect timing, his newfound role in the opening to China came precisely as the Nixon administration was firming up its policy on Pakistan. "Yahya sent you the message from Zhou Enlai," Kissinger told Nixon, "saying that it's the first time we've had a direct report from a president, through a president, to a president." This was a phrase that Nixon would savor for the rest of his days—it even, he later claimed, echoed in his mind on his last, dark night in the White House before resigning.[43]

NIXON AND KISSINGER BITTERLY REMEMBERED THE BLOOD TELEGRAM as an act of unbearable insolence. But almost nothing of the reporting and advocacy by Blood's consulate had any lasting impact on them. A month into the slaughter, the Nixon administration firmed up its Pakistan policy in the quiet of the Oval Office. Kissinger urged the president to continue support for Yahya, with only a little retreat.

Kissinger firmly believed in exercising leverage over other governments. He once told Nixon that "pressure gets you to places, or the potentiality of pressure. No one has yet done a thing for us because we needed it or because we were nice guys." But here, despite crucial U.S. diplomatic and economic support and ongoing military supply—which Kissinger called "relatively small" but "an important symbolic element"—he avoided wielding any such pressure. No doubt there were limits to U.S. influence, but Kissinger never explored them.[44]

He was coy about whether Pakistan could survive as a single country. He admitted that even if the rebels were soon crushed, East Pakistan would remain a tinderbox of "widespread discontent and hatred," but he also offered Nixon some hope: the Pakistan army would probably soon retake control of the cities, with the Bengali nationalist resistance too weak and poorly armed to prevent that now.

Kissinger recommended trying to help Yahya reach a negotiated settlement to the war. On paper, this was not the most extreme possible option (in the classic Washington trick, he had included two other sucker choices, one totally pro-Pakistan and one pro-Bengali), but on closer examination, it meant strong support for Yahya. There would be nothing like the duress that Blood wanted: "We would not withhold aid now for the sake of applying pressure." (That would only be contemplated much later, he wrote, after the West Pakistanis had been given every chance to negotiate themselves a settlement.) To the contrary, the United States would give emergency economic help, and would support assistance from the World Bank and International Monetary Fund.

Kissinger never suggested that the massacres should be a factor in U.S. policy, even as an indicator of Yahya's misjudgment or unreliability. Nor did he broach complaining to Pakistan about its use of its vast arsenal of U.S. weapons against civilians. Instead, he only considered *future* shipments of arms and military supplies, which would be a small fraction of what Pakistan already had on hand. Here, Kissinger wanted to help as much as possible without running afoul of Congress: "allowing enough shipments of non-lethal spares and equipment to continue to avoid giving Yahya the impression we are cutting off military assistance but holding shipment of more controversial items in order not to provoke the Congress to force cutting off all aid."

It was, in the end, no choice at all. Nixon dutifully initialed the option that Kissinger recommended. Lest the bureaucracy get any ideas, Kissinger had also suggested that Nixon should specify that nothing should be done to squeeze West Pakistan. Duly coached, Nixon added his own commentary, veering closer to the sucker option of total backing for Pakistan. The president scrawled, *"To all hands.*

Don't squeeze Yahya at this time." He underlined the word "Don't" three times.[45]

"THIS MANIAC IN DACCA"

Richard Nixon was not the kind of president who indulged whistle-blowers or dissenters. Although formally his administration had created the dissent channel, he had no patience for those who dared step out of line. "We never fire anybody," he once complained. "We always promote the sons of bitches that kick us in the ass. . . . When a bureaucrat deliberately thumbs his nose, we're going to get him. . . . The little boys over in State particularly, that are against us, we will do it." Another time, he told his staffers that he welcomed dissent memoranda sent directly to him, but immediately sarcastically noted that he would "be sure, once he's received it, that it's marked Top Secret so it will get out in all the newspapers."[46]

"We've got a lot of little people who love to be heroes," the president complained to his cabinet in June. He loathed someone like Daniel Ellsberg, the military analyst who leaked the Pentagon Papers to the _New York Times_. Nixon had no patience for such showy displays of conscience, as he told the cabinet: "I get a lot of advice on PR and personality and how I've got to put on my nice-guy hat and dance at the White House, so I did it, but let me make it clear that's not my nature."[47]

Kissinger worked Nixon up. "It shows you're a weakling, Mr. President," he said. "[T]hese leaks are slowly and systematically destroying us. . . . It could destroy our ability to conduct foreign policy." Nixon's fury went beyond the law. "We're up against an enemy, a conspiracy," he told H. R. Haldeman, the White House chief of staff. "They're using any means. We are going to use any means. Is that clear?" He created a team—the Plumbers—to hunt down leakers, and ordered Haldeman to have someone break into the Brookings Institution and Ellsberg's psychiatrist's office, seeking material for a smear campaign. "You can't drop it, Bob," Nixon told Haldeman. "You can't let the Jew steal that stuff and get away with it."[48]

Kissinger, with his professorial background, presented himself as someone who could handle criticism. But he hated leaks, once telling a Chinese delegation that "our bureaucracy doesn't always speak with one voice, and . . . those who don't speak with one voice usually speak to the _New York Times_." His bullying of the State Department went so far that few there dared stand up to him. "You don't have to threaten us or intimidate us," a much-vilified State Department official once snapped at him. "You will scare the hell out of so many people in this building that no one will give you the information you should hear."[49]

So the Blood telegram invited stern retaliation from the White House. The spectacular act of the dissent cable had lodged firmly in Kissinger's memory. He (garbling Blood's and Farland's postings) complained, "The Embassy in Dacca and the Consul in Islamabad are at war with each other." In a private conversation with Nixon in the Oval Office, he later denounced Blood as "this maniac in Dacca, the Consul General who is in rebellion."[50]

There was a familiar Nixonian remedy: fire Blood. "It was the kind of thing that was done in those days," says Samuel Hoskinson, Kissinger's aide at the White House. "They did remove people from posts that they didn't like. In the context of the time, it seemed quite natural."[51]

By late April, as Nixon reached his decision not to squeeze Yahya, Blood was shoved out of the Dacca consulate. The ambassador in Islamabad informed Blood that a decision had been made "at the highest level" to move him out of Dacca. He was asked to request home leave and transfer back to the State Department—in other words, unceremoniously sacked from his position as consul general in Dacca.[52]

"They were cleaning out the house of miscreants," remembers Scott Butcher, the Dacca consulate's junior political officer, sarcastically using the term that the Pakistan army leveled against Bengali nationalists. Hoskinson says, "It was almost surprising he lasted as long as he did." Since sending in the dissent cable, Blood had expected this, but, he later recalled, it "still came as a jolt." He was particularly wounded to learn that his fellow diplomats questioned his judgment. It was the low point of his career. As he put it afterward, he "hit rock bottom."[53]

At the White House, Hoskinson and Harold Saunders watched in queasy silence. Saunders says respectfully of Blood, "He took the responsibility. He paid the price." "Hal and I had the same attitude about this throughout," says Hoskinson. "It's like, this is above our pay grade. Henry makes his mind up, and out goes Blood. This is not something that you ask Henry why you did it. Maybe the president wants him out. One did not want to be perceived as being too much on Blood's side. I was always a little vulnerable in this regard."

Saunders says about Blood, "He was just an honest FSO"—Foreign Service Officer—"who had experience in this part of the world. And he thought this needed to be put at the top of the agenda." Saunders says that over eight years in power, Kissinger came to have enormous respect for the Foreign Service, but "when he came into his White House job, he had a view of them as bleeding hearts. They were certainly not the realpolitik thinkers that he would have been looking for. It was a prejudice, a bias." Saunders had no illusions about how Kissinger responded to dissenters: "I know how he felt about people who would speak up. He was not tolerant of a lot of that."[54]

After being told that he was sacked from his post, Blood managed to fire off some final reporting on the persecution of the Hindus. But he was a lame duck, and even before he left Dacca, the situation reports from East Pakistan started to come from another diplomat, Herbert Spivack—who had not signed the Blood telegram. Spivack, says Eric Griffel, the development official, was "a much more conservative character." (Major General Jacob-Farj-Rafael Jacob of the Indian army is less polite: "Spivack was a clown.") The new boss was, Griffel says, "quite a different person. Emotionally uninvolved. We were all emotionally involved." Griffel recalls, "Spivack was a much more old faithful bureaucrat. The cables became much milder. Also, everyone knew that the battle had been lost as far as the consulate was concerned."[55]

Nobody in the Dacca consulate could have guessed at the time exactly what Nixon and Kissinger were saying about them in the Oval Office. But Eric Griffel laughs out loud when told of Kissinger's description of Blood as "this maniac in Dacca." He says, "I can think of few people in the world who are less maniacal than Arch Blood. The thing about Blood that is rather remarkable is that he is very much a product of the State Department. A very loyal officer. A very conservative—not in the political sense—human being."

Scott Butcher, hearing about what was said in the Oval Office, blows up. "It's totally wrong," he says heatedly. "They cast a lot of aspersions on our professionalism. We were on the ground. Arch Blood's prognostications were absolutely right. Shame on them." Meg Blood says calmly, "We recognized at the time that they were going to do this. They were going to simply ignore the reality of who he was."

"Had Blood not done this," says Griffel, "he would have hit rock bottom in a different way. And possibly a worse way. Not for everyone, but for a man like Arch, there are worse things than losing your career. I don't like using words that don't have an accurate meaning, but he was a man of honor. In his own view, he would have lost his honor."

Chapter 8

Exodus

I T WAS BIBLICAL," REMEMBERS SYDNEY SCHANBERG, WHO REPORTED on the refugees for the *New York Times.*

Schanberg, steeped in the worst horrors of war from Vietnam and Cambodia, goes quiet at the memory of the desperate millions who fled into India. "You don't tune out," he says, "but there's a numbness. Either that or you feel like crying. There was a tremendous loss of life on those treks out." He remembers, "Their bodies have adjusted to those germs in their water, but suddenly they're drinking different water with different germs. Suddenly they've got cholera. People were dying all around us. You'd see that someone had left a body on the side of the road, wrapped in pieces of bamboo, and there'd be a vulture trying to get inside to eat the body. You would come into a schoolyard, and a mother was losing her child. He was in her lap. He coughed and coughed and then died." He pauses and composes himself. "They went through holy hell and back."

Major General Jacob-Farj-Rafael Jacob, the gruff, battle-hardened chief of staff of the Indian army's Eastern Command, went to the border to watch the refugees streaming in. "It was terrible, pathetic," he recalls. The displaced throngs inescapably called to mind nightmare memories of Partition in 1947, not so long before. "It's a terrible human agony," says Jaswant Singh, a former Indian foreign minister. "It was as if we were reliving the Partition."[1]

The mounting demands of providing food, shelter, and medical care were more than an impoverished country like India—which could not cope with the needs of millions of its own desperately poor and sick citizens—could possibly handle. By late April, with the monsoons looming, the rush of refugees became a public health disaster. India frantically built refugee camps, each one holding some forty thousand people. Indira Gandhi's government quietly tried to link these camps to the Awami League authorities, and even did some social engineering, mixing Hindus and Muslims together in the Indian secular way. While it was almost impossible to count the refugees precisely, by the middle of May, India estimated that it was sheltering almost two million souls, with about fifty thousand more arriving daily.[2]

From Tripura, a hard-hit border state, the lieutenant governor warned Gandhi of the massive scale of it: "It is clear now that the Pak Army's objective is to push across our borders as many people as possible with a view to disrupt completely life here." The Tripura government was housing exiles in camps in school buildings and haphazard temporary shelters. They could handle at best fifty thousand refugees, but already had over twice that many. The roads and railways could not bring in enough supplies. And commodities prices were soaring, with awful consequences for poor Indians.[3]

These displaced masses greatly ratcheted up the popular pressure on India's democratic government. Indian reporters raced to the borders, shocking their readership with gruesome coverage of the refugees' harrowing ordeals. From Tripura, one newspaper showed the individual faces in the human tide: desperately poor peasants selling their utensils, because it was all they had left; privileged, well-educated lawyers and architects who suddenly found themselves dodging soldiers; and a movie actress with deals inked for a dozen films who slogged through the mud for two days seeking safety, just like everyone else.[4]

At every rank, Indians seethed. Swaran Singh, the ordinarily unflappable foreign minister, indignantly told his diplomats, "Artillery, tanks, automatic weapons, mortars, aeroplanes, everything which is normally used against invading armed forces, were utilised and very large-scale killings took place; selective killings of individuals, acts of molestation and rape against the university students, girls, picking out the Awami League leaders, their supporters and later on especially concentrating on the localities in which Hindus predominated." P. N. Haksar anxiously wrote that "our people have been deeply stirred by the carnage in East Bengal. Government of India have endeavoured to contain the emotions which have been aroused in our country, but we find it increasingly difficult to do this because of the systematic effort on the part of Pakistan to force millions of people to leave their hearths and homes taking shelter in our territory."[5]

Worse, Haksar noted, the refugees would cause social tension and spark religious strife in volatile West Bengal, Assam, and Tripura.

These border states, which had absorbed waves of refugees after Partition, were already poverty-stricken and notoriously unstable, and the Indian government dreaded the fiery leftist revolutionaries and Naxalites there. Since the people's will was being stifled in East Bengal, Haksar secretly wrote that "extremist political elements will inevitably gain ground. With our own difficulties in West Bengal, the dangers of a link-up between the extremists in the two Bengals are real."[6]

THE INDIAN GOVERNMENT, FROM INDIRA GANDHI ON DOWN, WORKED hard to hide an ugly reality from its own people: by an official reckoning, as many as 90 percent of the refugees were Hindus.[7]

This skew was the inevitable consequence of Pakistani targeting of Hindus in East Pakistan—what Archer Blood and his staffers had condemned as genocide. The population of East Pakistan was only 16 or 17 percent Hindu, but this minority comprised the overwhelming bulk of the refugees. India secretly recorded that by the middle of June, there were some 5,330,000 Hindus, as against 443,000 Muslims and 150,000 from other groups. Many Indian diplomats believed that the Hindus would be too afraid ever to go back.[8]

The first wave of refugees was made up of a great many Bengali Muslims, but as early as mid-April, one of Gandhi's top officials noted, India decided that Pakistan was systematically expelling the Hindus. The Indian government privately believed, as this aide noted, that Pakistan, by "driving out Hindus in their millions," hoped to reduce the number of Bengalis so they were no longer the majority in Pakistan, and to destroy the Awami League as a political force by getting rid of "the 'wily Hindu' who was supposed to have misled simple Bengali Muslims into demanding autonomy."[9]

But the Indian government assiduously hid this stark fact from Indians. "In India we have tried to cover that up," Swaran Singh candidly told a meeting of Indian diplomats in London, "but we have no hesitation in stating the figure to foreigners." (Sydney Schanberg and John Kenneth Galbraith, the Kennedy administration's ambassador to India, separately highlighted the fact in the *New York Times*.) Singh instructed his staff to distort for their country: "We should avoid making this into an Indo-Pakistan or Hindu[-]Muslim conflict. We should point out that there are Buddhists and Christians besides the Muslims among the refugees, who had felt the brunt of repression." In a major speech, Gandhi misleadingly described refugees of "every religious persuasion—Hindu, Muslim, Buddhist and Christian."[10]

The Indian government feared that the plain truth would splinter its own country between Hindus and Muslims. India had almost seventy million Muslim citizens, and as Singh told his diplomats, the government's worst fear was vengeful sectarian confrontations. By not mentioning the Bengali Hindus, India also avoided hinting to Pakistan that it might be willing to accept them permanently. And Indian officials did not want to provide further ammunition to the irate Hindu nationalists in the Jana Sangh party. From Moscow, D. P. Dhar, India's ambassador there, decried the Pakistan army's "preplanned policy of selecting Hindus for butchery," but, fearing inflammatory politicking from "rightist reactionary Hindu chauvinist parties like Jana Sangh," he wrote, "We were doing our best not to allow this aspect of the matter to be publicised in India."[11]

Gandhi's officials freely accused Pakistan of genocide—Indian diplomats in Islamabad secretly wrote of "the holocaust in East Bengal," and Dhar blasted Pakistan's campaign of "carnage and genocide"—but not in the same way that Blood did. Rather than basing this accusation primarily on the victimization of Hindus, India tended to focus on the decimation of the Bengalis as a group. The Indian foreign ministry argued that Pakistan's generals, having lost an election because their country had too many Bengalis, were now slaughtering their way to "a wholesale reduction in the population of East Bengal" so that it would no longer comprise a majority in Pakistan.[12]

NEHRUVIANS

India, supporting this Bengali rebellion, faced an awkward ideological problem. Since Nehru's day, a core doctrine of Indian foreign policy was refusing to meddle in the internal affairs of other countries. This pervasive Nehruvian attitude was supremely protective of India's own national sovereignty, wrested from the British Empire at such a terrible cost. So how could India possibly justify intervening inside part of sovereign Pakistan?[13]

Soon after the crackdown started, Haksar—as steeped in Nehruvian thinking as anyone—wrote, "While our sympathy for the people of Bangla Desh is natural, India, as a State, has to walk warily. Pakistan is a State. It is a Member of the U.N. and, therefore, outside interference in events internal to Pakistan will not earn us either understanding or goodwill from the majority of nation-States."[14]

There was a less elevated motive: it was embarrassing for India to cheer on secession in East Pakistan while stifling it in Kashmir. India had long accused Pakistan of trying to stir up separatism among Muslims in the Indian state of Jammu and Kashmir. In the Indian-controlled part of Kashmir, as Haksar uncomfortably reminded Gandhi, it was "unlawful to preach secession." Secessionist organizations were outlawed and would not be allowed to take part in elections. So Haksar privately argued, "We have also got to be careful that we do not publicly say or do anything which will cast any shadow on the stand we have consistently taken in respect of Kashmir that we cannot allow its secession and that whatever happens there is a matter of domestic concern to India and that we shall not tolerate any outside interference." Dhar feared being "exposed to the counter charge of suppressing, by force, the people in Kashmir."[15]

With the bullets flying in East Pakistan, Indian officials found they could not hew to Nehruvian pieties. It would be impossible as a practical matter and disastrous in domestic politics. In its fury, the Indian public shrugged off the impropriety of criticizing what Pakistan did inside its own borders. The firebrand activist Jayaprakash Narayan quickly declared that "what is happening in Pakistan is surely not that country's internal matter alone." Just a few days into the slaughter, India's ambassador at the United Nations intoned, "The scale of human sufferings is such that it ceases to be a matter of the domestic concern of Pakistan alone." India brought a complaint against Pakistan's violations of human rights to a United Nations body, which Pakistan promptly denounced as outside meddling.[16]

For months, the Indian government cast about in search of a serviceable ideological justification for resisting what it called genocide. Haksar tried and failed to get Gandhi to declare, "For countries situated far away, it is natural to argue that events in East Bengal are, legally and juridically, matters pertaining to the internal affairs of Pakistan. For us in India this mood of calm detachment cannot be sustained. There is a vast revulsion of feeling in India against the atrocities which are being daily perpetrated." Narayan, going further, dismissed the whole concept of noninterference as a "fiction," since the great powers were constantly intervening in weaker countries. Unlike the coldhearted superpowers, he argued, India would be "interfering . . . in the interest of humanity, freedom, democracy and justice." "It depends on how you describe national sovereignty," says K. C. Pant, who was then a minister of state for home affairs. "National sovereignty in a country where people reject the system is different from the people's acceptance of a government and a political system."[17]

There was a possible precedent. The young Mahatma Gandhi had famously campaigned against white supremacy in South Africa; Nehru later championed that cause at the United Nations; and Indira Gandhi's government crusaded against South African apartheid. India went even further against the racist regime in Rhodesia (today Zimbabwe): promoting economic sanctions and asking Britain, the colonial power there, to take military action. "India and other nations have repeatedly urged Britain to use force against Rhodesian regime in defence of the rights of majority of Rhodesians," the strategist K. Subrahmanyam bluntly wrote in his secret report. "The U.N. has been calling for sanctions against South Africa to compel the white minority regime to give up the oppression against the majority. . . . There is no need for India to feel guilty of having interfered in the affairs of another nation." India's foreign ministry urged the United Nations to show "the same kind of concern about the actions of Yahya Khan in East Bengal as they have done about racialism and colonialism in South Africa, Portuguese colonies and Rhodesia."[18]

Whatever compunctions the Indian government had left about Pakistan's sovereignty, they cracked as the refugees poured across the border. Haksar wrote, "Even if the international community concedes to the military rulers of Pakistan the right to decimate their own people, I cannot see how that right could be extended to the throwing of unconscionable burden on us by forcible eviction of millions of Pakistani citizens." The refugee crisis afforded India a devastating riposte: what Pakistan did within its borders was having a massive impact *outside* its borders.[19]

In public, Indian officials such as Swaran Singh would impeccably speak up for sovereignty. But behind closed doors, he coached his officials to take the opposite line: "repression internally has resulted in the uprooting of six million refugees. With what stretch of the imagination is this an internal matter?" Upending the argument, he accused the United States of meddling in Pakistan's internal affairs by helping a military junta to slaughter the Bengali majority: supporting Yahya was "truly interference in the internal affairs." He instructed his diplomats, "You can use your genius for the purpose of thinking of other such arguments."[20]

INDIRA GANDHI'S LOYALISTS HAVE EMPHASIZED THE HEROIC AND LEVEL-headed leadership of her government in this crisis. Still, India's leaders were prey to the usual range of human failings: self-doubt, stress, and exhaustion.[21]

The prime minister's secretariat roiled with confusion, inundated with harebrained schemes. Some people pragmatically argued that the refugees would never go back and that India should concentrate on winning international aid for looking after them; others demanded that India let only Hindus in, shutting out Muslims; some wanted to seal the borders outright; there were even suggestions of population exchanges.[22]

Haksar, the impresario of much of the government's policy, privately despaired. He confided to Dhar, a close friend, "As far as I am capable of knowing about myself, all that I can say at this stage is that I feel, physically and mentally, stretched beyond the breaking point. I feel that I just cannot carry on." He needed "a little rest and time to think." He knew that the crisis was escalating, possibly in terrifying ways, and could not bear the responsibility: "My present assessment is that for the new phase which has begun I am not the man."[23]

For two days, Gandhi went to West Bengal, Assam, and Tripura to see the refugees herself. She and her staff were shaken. After sitting in South Block dealing with abstract statistics of refugees and rupees, they came face-to-face with real people, hearing their stories of terror. What they witnessed, as one of the prime minister's senior aides wrote later, "assaulted our moral sensibility."[24]

Gandhi was overwhelmed. She visited slapdash camps, where thousands of tents had been hastily pitched. Any functional local building had been requisitioned. People urgently needed clean water. Many of the refugees were wounded, beyond what local hospitals could handle, needing special teams of doctors and public health workers. She impatiently interrogated an Indian camp commander, who later snapped to one of her senior aides, "Sir, please tell the prime minister that even hurry takes time." By the end of the tour, when she was supposed to deliver some remarks, she was so overcome that she could barely speak. When she and her team got back to Calcutta, a senior aide later recalled, she said that "we cannot let Pakistan continue this holocaust."[25]

After this, she was determined that India could not absorb the refugees. They would have to go home. This, in turn, would require the Pakistani government to make a generous political deal with the Bengalis to end the civil war. She was scheduled to make a major speech to the Lok Sabha, and Haksar, despite his exhaustion, junked a more cautiously diplomatic draft from the foreign ministry, persuading her instead to tell Indians and the whole world exactly how grave the situation was.[26]

She did so thunderously. "Has Pakistan the right to compel at bayonet-point not hundreds, not thousands, not hundreds of thousands, but millions of its citizens to flee their homes?" she asked the lawmakers. In front of some of the same legislators whom she had just briefed about India's clandestine support for the rebels in East Pakistan, she falsely declared that "we have never tried to interfere with the internal affairs of Pakistan." Then, using Haksar's language, she inverted Pakistan's insistence on its own national sovereignty: "What was claimed to be an internal problem of Pakistan, has also become an internal problem for India. We are, therefore, entitled to ask Pakistan to desist immediately from all actions which it is taking in the name of domestic jurisdiction, and which vitally affect the peace and well-being of millions of our own citizens. Pakistan cannot be allowed to seek a solution of its political or other problems at the expense of India and on Indian soil." This became her government's core argument for why India was entitled to ask Pakistan to stop killing its own citizens and instead make peace with them.[27]

Gandhi demanded that the refugees be allowed to return in safety. She made a plea to the "conscience of the world," even though it was "unconscionably" slow to react. She warned, "this suppression of human rights, the uprooting of people, and the continued homelessness of vast numbers of human beings will threaten peace." Without foreign succor, she said, India would have to "take all measures as may be necessary"—an unsubtle threat of war.[28]

These unequivocal Indian demands, which Pakistan would surely not meet, posed the manifest prospect of war. Indian officials simply did not believe that Yahya would do anything serious to bring the refugees home. Pakistan's government, they said, was still systematically driving them out, while providing soothing speeches that the United States could use as propaganda. The foreign ministry dismissed the Pakistani government's weak proposals for finding some new civilian authorities as dictatorial puppetry. India would only be satisfied with a government formed by Mujib.

In private, Swaran Singh argued that Yahya's dictatorship had to fall. He told a meeting of his diplomats that since the refugees would never return home while Pakistan's military government was in power, "this regime must be replaced by a regime which is responsible to the people." He said flatly, "Our ultimate objective is that this military regime should give way to a regime which is truly representative of the Awami League."

Singh instructed his officials to make their threats of war implicitly, telling foreigners that India did not want to be left alone to face the storm. But he frankly told his staff to be ready for an Indian attack: "when war comes even if it is our action, we should be able to make a case that it has been forced on us." Gandhi, Haksar, and Singh stayed resolutely on their path, knowing it was inexorably leading them toward war.[29]

OF ALL THE INDIANS SPEAKING OUT FOR THE BENGALIS, THE MOST striking name to protest was Jayaprakash Narayan. He was an elder statesman of India's independence struggle against the British Empire, who had been uneasily won over to a tactical kind of nonviolence by Mahatma Gandhi. Narayan—known as J.P.—was a close friend of Jawaharlal Nehru, but his name is eternally linked to Indira Gandhi's for a more tragic reason. In 1975, Narayan would challenge her rule with a mass mobilization of his supporters, and she would in response declare her notorious Emergency, suspending India's democracy.[30]

When Yahya's onslaught began, Indira Gandhi later recalled, Narayan argued that "we should have gone to war right at the beginning." Haksar noted, "Even a pacifist like Jayaprakash and his co-workers demand recognition of Bangla Desh." (This exaggerated Narayan's commitment to nonviolence, which did reluctantly allow armed resistance in desperate cases.) According to Gandhi's closest friend, he urged Gandhi to swiftly invade East Pakistan. She listened intently but did not reply.[31]

Narayan fierily supported the Bengali guerrillas, meeting with Bengali political leaders and Mukti Bahini officers, and taking a particular interest in supplying them with arms and artillery. He demanded the defense of the "political and human rights" of the Bengalis, and decried a "holocaust" carried out by a "Hitlerian junta in power in

Islamabad." In early June, Narayan raced around the globe, from Jakarta to Moscow to Cairo, denouncing genocide to everyone from Tito to the pope to the Council on Foreign Relations. (His Burmese contact of choice was Ne Win, the vicious military dictator.) In Washington, he met with Henry Kissinger and told a senior State Department official that he remembered from his own days struggling against British colonial rule in India what it meant "to be an irreconcilable." He had accepted nothing less than independence, and neither would the leaders of Bangladesh.[32]

Still, even in this dire moment, Indira Gandhi and Jayaprakash Narayan could not get along. They squabbled with petty fury. According to her close friend, she did not want to let him become India's main voice on Bangladesh. When he held a conference in Delhi to condemn the atrocities, she had her political party avoid it. "I was shocked," he wrote to her. "Does she think she can ignore me?" he exploded, according to one account. "I have seen her as a child in frocks." When she got wind of that outburst, she froze him out. The sourness in their relations would linger for years.[33]

INDIA'S BENGALIS

Inside India, Bengalis were anything but an alien, unfamiliar people. They composed a major part of society: Bengali was one of the most commonly spoken languages in India, and its culture was celebrated. "Bangladesh was part of India less than a quarter century back," remembers Jaswant Singh, a former Indian foreign minister. "It was all one country. It was part of India. It didn't feel like a separate land. They were kith and kin."[34]

In 1947, in Partition, the British Empire had finally severed what had once been a united Bengal. After massive dislocations of populations and terrible violence, the mostly Hindu people in the west found themselves in India's state of West Bengal, and the mostly Muslim people in the east in what was known alternately as East Bengal or East Pakistan. So India's own Bengali citizens, in West Bengal and other parts of the country, were particularly horrified by what was happening to people who spoke their language and shared their customs across the border in East Pakistan.[35]

One of these Bengali Indians was Arundhati Ghose, a protégée of Haksar, who, while raised in Bombay in a prominent Bengali family, had ancestors from East Bengal. Ghose talks fast, cracks wise, chain-smokes. She would eventually rise to be ambassador to South Korea and Egypt, and would fiercely lead India's diplomatic campaign against the Comprehensive Test Ban Treaty. But in 1971 she was only an undersecretary in the Indian diplomatic service, on what she cheerfully calls the bottom rung.[36]

She remembers how proud Bengali Indians were at the Awami League's electoral triumph. They glorified Mujib, she says, overjoyed to see their fellow Bengalis standing up for their language and their rights. Then, when the shooting started, there was an intense revulsion. Bengali Indians rallied for the cause. "I'm Bengali," she says. "It was an emotional thing. We were raising funds. Delhi was full of that." Since she was a government staffer, she quickly adds, "Nothing officially. Officially I had nothing to do with it." She recalls, "Initially it was just Bengalis, and I think that's why I got swept in. But then it was just people who were against the crackdown, because they were killing civilians. You're powerless. There's nothing you can do. Raising money is all right when you're talking about Bengalis singing Bengali songs, but it's not so hot when people are being shot and burned."

Ghose remembers the strain on the government caused by seething Bengali Indians. Haksar worried that in "our own part of Bengal," there was "an impetuous demand that hundreds of thousands of volunteers be allowed to go and fight alongside the East Bengalis"—and that such pressures would only increase. "As Bengalis," wrote an eminent former Indian minister, on behalf of India's Bengal Association, "we feel all the more indignant" at "the wanton bestiality of genocide" against "our brothers and sisters of Bangla Desh." When the killing started, he urged, "The freedom fighters of Bangla Desh must be allowed the free use of our border territory for the purpose of sanctuary or for organising their liberation struggle."[37]

Some might have found this touching. Not Haksar. He loathed this kind of identity politics among Indians. Like other Congress mandarins, he insisted on putting India itself above any ethnic, regional, or national loyalties. (He overlooked that many Bengali Hindus were standing up for Bengali Muslims.) "I am reduced to a state of despair and dark forebodings about our country," wrote Haksar, who enjoyed a little melodrama. Asking the prime minister to dress down this unfortunate ex-minister personally, he loftily insisted that this Bengali Indian should "have the sensitiveness to see that what is happening in East Pakistan is a matter of national concern and that Bengalis, as Bengalis, especially those who claim to be Indians, have no special responsibility, any more than Tamilians should have a say in fashioning our relations with Ceylon or with Malaysia, or Gujaratis should have a say in how we conduct our relations with East Africa."[38]

But the pressure from West Bengali public opinion proved too intense, and in early April, Haksar proposed appointing a special officer in the foreign ministry to handle India's outraged Bengali citizens, hearing out their ideas and proposals. For the rest of the crisis, he had to accustom himself to handpicking Bengali Indians for key jobs, lauding one official as "a balanced Bengali."[39]

Ghose was one of them. Posted in Nepal when Yahya's crackdown began, she had never been to East Pakistan and knew precious little about the place. "They went through the foreign service to find everyone who spoke Bengali," she remembers. "Unfortunately they had to take the girl." They asked several men, who demurred, not wanting to risk their careers. "But I was too junior, and I thought it'd be good fun." In April or May, she was summoned and "told, not asked, that I had to go to Calcutta." Her job was to help set up a secretariat to work with the Bangladesh exile government. She arrived amid chaos and fresh hopes. "The refugees, we didn't feel that in Delhi," she says. "In Calcutta it started very much as, these are great things for Bengali culture, Bengali language, and they're willing to fight for it."

"ALL-PERVASIVE FEAR"

In June, a reporter for *Life*, among the teeming crowds in West Bengal, was struck by the thriving of the vultures: "The flesh-eaters were glossy, repulsively replete." The correspondent moved past "the corpse of a baby, the clean-picked skeleton of a young child, and then dead refugees wrapped in mats and saris and looking like parcels fallen from a speeding truck." The living were packed together, exhausted, baked by the sun. People vomited. Those who were not too far gone begged for spaces on a truck. An overworked Indian administrator felt physically ill from watching children dying. He asked, "Can we cope? The civil administration ceased to be able to cope long ago." As cholera and other diseases spread, the lucky ones made it to a hospital, carried by rickshaw or oxcart: "Hollow-eyed and only semi-conscious in the listless torpor of total exhaustion, they lay and retched. Relatives fanned the black fog of flies from their faces."[40]

It was all too easy for Schanberg to fill the pages of the *New York Times* with horror. At a railway station, he was overcome by the sight of some five thousand refugees pressed together on the concrete floor: "someone vomits, someone moans. A baby wails. An old man lies writhing on his back on the floor, delirious, dying. Emaciated, fly-covered infants thrash and roll." Filing from a border town in West Bengal, Schanberg reported the unclean sounds of the cholera epidemic: "coughing, vomiting, groaning and weeping." An emaciated seventy-year-old man had just died. His son and granddaughter sat sobbing beside the body, as flies gathered. When a young mother died of cholera, her baby continued to nurse until a doctor pulled the infant away. The husband of that dead woman, a rice farmer, cried to Schanberg that the family had fled Pakistani soldiers who burned down their house. "My wife is dead," he wailed. "Three of my children are dead. What else can happen?"[41]

To reach the relative safety of India, Bengalis endured a terrifying and grueling trek, hiking through thick jungles in the deluges of the monsoons. One reputable Indian government official, himself a Bengali, relied on his local sources to remind Haksar what the refugees were fleeing: with encouragement from the Pakistan army, volunteers deliberately killed the Hindu men. He darkly wrote that it was not hard to imagine what had happened to the women. There were some Hindu families hidden in the granaries of "kind hearted Muslims who are against these deliberate atrocities but who find themselves entirely helpless."[42]

These kinds of stories were echoed six million times—the number of refugees that India officially estimated it was now sheltering. That number was, the Indian foreign ministry claimed, unparalleled in the world's history. Gandhi's government hoped to confine them to the refugee camps, but millions slipped off into the cities and villages, finding their way into informal labor markets and sweatshops, or simply ending up as beggars.[43]

India's sympathy for the refugees had limits. Some Indian officials worried that Pakistan was planting agents among the crowds. And the Indian government was ambivalent about having to shelter Biharis. One of Gandhi's top officials accused these Urdu-speaking Muslims of being stalwart supporters of the Pakistan army and of organizing groups of fanatics to help crush the Bengalis' autonomy movement. They were now fleeing reprisals from the Bengalis, and this official did not hide his resentment at having to look after them.[44]

As the numbers of refugees mounted, Yahya himself seemed to be in denial. He assured foreign governments that normalcy had been restored and declared that there was "no slaughter going on." When a visiting U.S. diplomat told him that he had seen with his own eyes refugees streaming out of East Pakistan into India, and had heard their tales of terror and dispossession, Yahya flatly refused to believe it. Since Bengalis "look alike," outsiders might be fooled by people "claiming to be refugees."[45]

But when Yahya's government allowed a World Bank team of seasoned development specialists to tour East Pakistan, their secret report found an "all-pervasive fear." The infrastructure was devastated, largely because of army campaigns in the big cities and towns. "In all cities visited there are areas that have been razed; and in all districts visited there are villages which have simply ceased to exist." There were ongoing military strikes, which, even when targeting "Awami Leaguers, students or Hindus," frightened the whole population. There was a "trail of devastation running from Khulna to Jessore to Kushtia to Pabna, Bogra, Rangpur and Dinajpur."[46]

THIS REFUGEE POPULATION IN INDIA WAS FAR BEYOND THE CAPABILI-ties of a government that strained to lift its own citizens out of poverty. In a June survey, Indian observers were staggered by the conditions in refugee camps in the border states of Assam and Tripura. The temporary housing was "pitiable"; without sanitation, the Indians were horrified by "the stinking foul-smell"; and due to an unchecked cholera epidemic, on average thirty to forty people were dying every day. In a brief visit of a few hours in one camp, they saw several dead bodies being hauled out for cremation.[47]

India's relief work was shot through with failures. Gandhi herself complained that efforts to prevent cholera were "dragging on for far too long." There were not enough doctors; angry young men sat around idly; Hindu nationalists spread resentment of Muslims; women had to give birth without even the shelter of a tent. According to this Indian report, corrupt contractors reportedly pocketed fees for tarpaulin sheets, but never supplied them. Other contractors would not allow Bengali youths to help build up their own camps. When a cholera epidemic broke out in one camp, there was outright panic and a near-total breakdown of operations. The contractors, police, and some civilian officials abandoned their posts, leaving the refugees without rations for two weeks. "From one of these camps some 3–4 thousands evacuees returned to Bangla Desh in sheer disgust."[48]

The burden fell on some of the poorest people in India. K. C. Pant, the minister of state for home affairs whose portfolio included the eastern border, remembers, "Among the common people, there was an understanding that a lot of things are happening in East Pakistan which they found highly offensive. It was a natural kind of reaction, to people being driven out of their homes, carrying with them stories of what had happened." There was, he recalls from a visit to the border areas, lots of sympathy. Still, it would be too much to expect a purely high-minded public response. Some local officials in Assam seemed outright hostile. According to this Indian report, the impoverished Indians in the border states did not welcome the refugees. The sheer numbers instantly turned the locals into minorities in their own home villages: in Bagmara, for instance, four thousand locals were vastly outnumbered by more than seventy-two thousand refugees. "In all the places we visited the local population did not appear very favourably inclined towards the evacuees. In Meghalaya the local people were not only passively hostile but had even started an active campaign against the helpless evacuees." The Indian team heard accounts of "evacuees having been mercilessly beaten by the local people. There were case of even attempted rape."[49]

By September, India would record almost six thousand deaths from cholera alone. As the state governments reeled, they turned to Gandhi's central government for help. In Assam, state officials were convinced that the refugees—particularly the Hindus—would not return without some drastic action by Gandhi's government. The refugee crisis was driving India toward war.[50]

Chapter 9

India Alone

IN BEIJING, AMID THE RADICAL THROES OF MAO ZEDONG'S CULTURAL
Revolution, Red Guard cadres and zealous demonstrators would
sometimes besiege the Indian embassy, burning a straw effigy of Indira
Gandhi. Even as India hurtled toward war with Pakistan, it actually
dreaded its Chinese enemy far more. Mao's regime was a sworn foe of
"bourgeois" and democratic India, and had thrashed India in a major
war in 1962. Indian diplomats in Beijing anxiously argued that China
was wary of India—with its massive population, and military and economic potential—emerging as a rival great power.[1]

Indira Gandhi worried that "if Pakistan attacks us, China may
join them." China was a close partner of Pakistan, hosting Yahya on
a showy visit, selling him a considerable amount of weaponry in years
past, and maintaining tight military ties. If war came, the R&AW's
spies were sure that China would provide Pakistan with a steady
stream of military supplies. Indian intelligence was constantly working
on paramilitary plans for guerrilla warfare against a Chinese threat.[2]

The Chinese government, with its own searing experience of Western and Japanese imperialism, had a bedrock ideological commitment
to national sovereignty. It loathed secessionists in Taiwan and Tibet.
India's domestic outcry about atrocities inside East Pakistan thus
offended China, and Zhou Enlai, China's premier, vowed to support
Pakistan against "Indian expansionists," even lodging a formal protest
against India's "gross interference in internal affairs of Pakistan."[3]

Worse, the Indian government secretly worried that China was
sponsoring radical pro-Chinese factions among the East Bengalis that
would, as the civil war dragged on, undermine Mujib's mainstream
nationalists. P. N. Haksar, Gandhi's top adviser, wrote, "China, as
usual, is playing a double-faced game by giving public support to West

Pakistan and working clandestinely to increase its political influence in East Pakistan." The Indian government nervously detected some rumblings among East Pakistanis that the Awami League moderates had failed and it was time to turn to the Maoist radicals in India's West Bengal. Meanwhile, the Awami League warned that thousands of fighting Naxalites from West Bengal had crossed into East Pakistan to try to commandeer the struggle.[4]

THE SOVIET UNION SHARED INDIA'S ANXIETY ABOUT CHINA. THE TWO communist behemoths, having just fought a border war in 1969, were mortal rivals. The Soviet defense minister told the Indians, "If I were you, I would not be worried by Pakistan. You should take into account the unpredictable enemy from the North."[5]

Gandhi once showily declared that there was no need for the United States to worry about India's relationship with the Soviet Union, since India was a democracy like the United States. But in fact, with Mao venomously hostile and Richard Nixon truculent, it was not hard for pro-Soviet officials like Haksar to pull India further into the orbit of, in his words, "our Soviet friends." Fearing war, he wrote to D. P. Dhar, the ambassador in Moscow, "we shall be assuming a very heavy burden and will expose ourselves to serious risks. We cannot do this alone."[6]

Dhar led the charge. He had a sensitive face and wispy hair, and wore his neckties ostentatiously. Florid and wordy, he was stoutly pro-Soviet, writing fondly of their commissars and extolling the grayest Soviet pronouncements with enthusiasm. He was the kind of useful idiot who isn't an idiot. From Moscow, where anti-Chinese sentiment hung thick in the air, Dhar warned of "diabolical plans hatched in Peking or Rawalpindi."[7]

For months, Dhar had been toiling on what he obliquely called the "Document"—a formal friendship treaty between India and the Soviet Union. He urged the foreign ministry to sign it now, which he thought would thrill the Indian public. The Soviets—who argued that a treaty could deter both Pakistan and China from attacking India— had suggested this more than two years earlier, but India had put it on hold before Gandhi's victory in the March elections. There had been no particular urgency. The government was not eager to get pounded by conservatives in Parliament for throwing the country into the Soviet camp, and it would be a disaster for India's image as a leader of the Non-Aligned Movement. But now India had to shore up its Soviet relationship.[8]

Dhar was thrilled when, on April 3, the Soviet Union sent Yahya a stinging message, calling for an end to killing and repression and urging respect for the results of democratic elections and the principles of the Universal Declaration of Human Rights. Even as Dhar crowed, he understood that Leonid Brezhnev's regime did not generally come out swinging for human rights. The Soviets, he wrote, had to "overcome their inhibitions about so-called principles of national integrity etc." But the Soviets "have, as never before, a nice appreciation of the sheer weight of India in Asia today."[9]

Following up, Gandhi sent Dhar to press Aleksei Kosygin, the Soviet premier, for any and all kinds of help. India seems to have been hoping for Soviet approval for more aggressive action, possibly even a war. But the Soviet Union refused, pressing India to avoid war. Instead, the Soviets produced a minor masterpiece of apparatchik obfuscation, asking India to avoid escalation, leaving Haksar and Dhar crestfallen.[10]

Preparing for confrontation, India badgered the Soviet Union for more military assistance, such as Soviet T-55 battle tanks, armored personnel carriers, and artillery rounds. Haksar bluntly told Gandhi of the urgency of their defense needs. In late April, she begged Kosygin for a long list of military supplies, including bombers that could, as Dhar noted, hit targets all across Pakistan and strike deep into China. Here again, there were limits to Soviet support: they only offered some supersonic but unreliable Tu-22s, which were so unacceptable to the Indian Air Force that India rejected them. Dhar, mortified at the snub, argued that these bombers could carry "nuclear war-heads" for "nuclear warfare in the future." Nor did the Soviet Union come through in helping the refugees; while making some donations, it wound up being handily outspent by the United States.[11]

FUTILE DIPLOMACY

In dire need of foreign help, India's creaky diplomatic machinery heaved itself into action. The initial international response was minimal.[12]

George H. W. Bush, the U.S. ambassador to the United Nations, quietly told his Pakistani counterpart of U.S. humanitarian "concern"—the future president, like other U.S. diplomats, could go no further than that pallid word—and asked him to consider accepting international aid. But as Bush noted, the Pakistani government flatly rejected international relief. It was not until late May that Yahya finally agreed to let the United Nations provide humanitarian relief in East Pakistan. And the United Nations' high commissioner for refugees, Prince Sadruddin Khan, considered himself close to Yahya personally and was known among international aid officials for his warm ties with Pakistan's government. Bush wrote that Sadruddin was skeptical about the Indians' motives and suspected they were greatly exaggerating the scale of the refugee problem.[13]

In May, Gandhi sent out a global appeal for help, accusing Pakistan of "trying to solve its internal problems by cutting down the size of its population in East Bengal." She candidly admitted, "The regions which the refugees are entering are over-crowded and politically the most sensitive parts of India. The situation in these areas can very easily become explosive. The influx of refugees thus constitutes a grave security risk which no responsible government can allow to develop."[14]

India frantically blanketed the world with almost identical copies of Gandhi's letter, sent to sixty-one countries—from the superpowers to friends in the Non-Aligned Movement such as Yugoslavia and Egypt, from storied figures like Haile Selassie of Ethiopia and Julius Nyerere of Tanzania to the sordid likes of Muhammad Reza Shah Pahlavi of Iran and Muammar al-Qaddafi of Libya. Although Gandhi had been lethargic about reaching out to the Americans—even sluggish in accepting an invitation from Nixon for a Washington summit in November—Haksar instructed his ambassador in Washington that it was vital to know whether the U.S. government saw "the squeezing out of millions of its [Pakistan's] own citizens by Pakistan as legitimate." Gandhi pleaded to Nixon to use U.S. power to uphold democracy in Pakistan.[15]

Gandhi and Haksar were morose about the prospects for international help. Most of the costs, they assumed, would fall on India. The major governments were, Haksar wrote, "watching and waiting," with the United States, Britain, France, Germany, and Japan all seeing the atrocities as an internal matter for Pakistan. The Soviet Union was only a little more forthcoming. But most Western governments would not recognize Bangladesh until the rebels won territory and authority. The Bengalis would first have to win their fight on the battlefield.[16]

FOLLOWING UP ON GANDHI'S APPEAL, INDIA DISPATCHED A SMALL ARMY of ministers and diplomats to plead its case around the world, everywhere from Afghanistan to Kenya to Chile. An envoy slated for Bucharest balked at the dismal prospect, but Haksar packed him off anyway. Haksar instructed the Indian ambassador in Warsaw that "the Poles should be made to understand that there is an irrevocable break between the people of East Bengal and the people of what is now called West Pakistan."[17]

India's diplomats were fully aware of the public relations aspect of humanitarianism: "We have to launch a massive programme of assistance to the refugees and see to it that this is done in the full glare of international publicity." The Indian foreign ministry secretly helped the Bangladeshi exile government create and circulate pamphlets decrying genocide against the Bengalis, while publicly denying that it had anything to do with it. And an Indian team touring the refugee camps wanted to organize doctors, engineers, professors, and lawyers among the refugees, who could be sent to tour the world to plead their cause: "The Bangla Desh movement offers vast scope for destroying and demolishing the communal and parochial foundations of Pakistan."[18]

Swaran Singh, India's foreign minister, working himself mercilessly, berated his discouraged diplomats for substandard advocacy. India was a big country and they should throw their weight around. They should reach out not just to foreign officials, but to the press, activists, political parties, and legislatures. They should make nuisances of themselves. "We are in the right and we have always to say that our cause is just," he exhorted them. "Plug this once, twice, thrice, four times. Start from the lower rung[,] go up to the highest levels."[19]

In June, Singh made an energetic tour of foreign capitals. What India really needed was international pressure on Pakistan, but that was a faint hope. "I do not hope to achieve any spectacular results during these visits," he said glumly. He scored his only real success in Moscow, where, fulfilling Dhar's dream, the two sides returned to the drafting of a friendship treaty between India and the Soviet Union—a bulwark against Pakistan and China. The Soviet Union issued a joint statement demanding that the flow of refugees stop and that the exiles return home. In private, Kosygin urged Singh to hold off from recognizing Bangladesh, but also hawkishly said that "you and I have to act in the best way so that the struggle continues, so that it succeeds after the return of the refugees. It may take any form—guerilla activity, an open mass struggle, war." Dhar, pleased as ever with the Soviet leadership, cheered. "If we receive a response half as good in other capitals we shall have won the day."[20]

They did not. India's education minister made a catastrophic trek around Asia, striking out in capital after capital. The minister, himself a Bengali from Calcutta, reported that Japan's government agreed that an independent Bangladesh was inevitable, but dared not say so in public. Australia said it could not do much, while its foreign minister consolingly said, "You are in a hell of a jam." The Indian envoy was cheered up by a friendly welcome in Malaysia, whose government secretly agreed that this was not an internal Pakistani issue, and a Malaysian minister griped that Bhutto had "called us many funny names." But the Malaysian government said it was too fragile and unstable to take any public stance, and yielded to Indonesian pressure to back Pakistan. Thailand also privately agreed this was no internal matter of Pakistan's, but was too scared of a hostile China to say anything. The Indian minister slunk home in defeat.[21]

K. C. Pant, the minister of state for home affairs, who would go on to become defense minister, got precious little from a two-week circuit in Latin America, winning a few public statements of sympathy from Panama and Mexico, and not even that from Jamaica and Cuba. He remembers the incredulity of Mexico's president when told about Pakistan's bisected geography. "He asked someone to bring him an atlas," Pant recalls. "And he said, 'By God, it's really so.'"[22]

Things were only a little better in Europe. Willy Brandt, the West German chancellor, was the most supportive. Edward Heath, Britain's prime minister, had personally urged Yahya to stop assaults on civilians, but also vigorously pressed India to avoid escalation. From Paris, the Indian ambassador was funereal. "The problem really is of India, and the world in general is not directly affected," he wrote. "As time goes on, the world publicity media will tend to forget the tragedy in East Bengal and even if the resistance continues, it will evoke irritation—not sympathy. What we may admire as resistance will be criticized as terrorism by others. (The French were too intelligent to engage in serious resistance until German armies were broken in Russia.)"[23]

In Indonesia and elsewhere, India was stung by the betrayal of its fellows in the Non-Aligned Movement. Only Yugoslavia rallied to India, with Josip Broz Tito visiting India and issuing a heartening statement. In the Middle East in particular, India was bitterly disappointed. After all, Nehru had partnered with Gamal Abdel Nasser to form the Non-Aligned Movement; Indians and Arabs shared cruel experiences of colonialism; and India firmly sided with the Arab states warring against Israel. Haksar hoped that these commonalities would dissuade Muslim states from rallying to Pakistan's side. "The foreign policy of so-called Muslim countries is not conducted on the basis of Pavlovian complex of Islam," he wrote. "Their relations with India are not affected when Muslims are killed in India any more than they would be affected with Pakistan just because Muslims are being killed there."[24]

Saudi Arabia vehemently supported Pakistan's prerogative to take any steps to maintain its domestic stability, urging the United States to affirm that Pakistan had the right to deal with its internal problems however it saw fit. Singh sourly told Indian diplomats that Saudi Arabia and Iran would give financial assistance to Pakistan, although they were "extremely greedy" and would not give much.[25]

Egypt proved especially dismaying. The Indian ambassador in Cairo was crestfallen at Egypt's "studied indifference" throughout the crisis. He noted that Anwar al-Sadat's government was unsympathetic to India's refugee problem and seemed fixated on preventing East Pakistan's secession. The state-controlled Egyptian media gave "almost no coverage to the genocide," leaving Egyptians in the dark about the basic facts. In a United Nations council, Amr Moussa, a prominent Egyptian diplomat who later went on to be Egypt's foreign minister and the secretary-general of the Arab League, insisted on maintaining Pakistan's unity. Bad as this was, Egypt was probably the most pro-Indian country in the Arab world, with Saudi Arabia, Libya, and Kuwait all pressuring Egypt to be even more pro-Pakistan.[26]

There was one surprising minor success: Israel. India did not have diplomatic relations with the Jewish state, and Haksar and many Indian leaders were frosty toward it. But in July, Golda Meir, Israel's prime minister, secretly got an Israeli arms manufacturer to provide India with some mortars and ammunition, along with a few instructors. When Haksar pressed Israel for support, Meir promised to continue helping out.[27]

The absolute worst was China. The embassy there complained of "Peking's near pathological suspicion of Indian motives," especially by Zhou. China's state media accused India of fomenting war and preventing the refugees from returning. The Indian embassy in Beijing—whose forlorn diplomats spent their days skittishly poring over Politburo lineups, turgid government statements, and propaganda newspapers in search of dim inklings as to what Mao and his henchmen might actually be thinking—did note that China's rhetoric was somewhat less incendiary than it could have been.[28]

Even the prolix Haksar could barely bring himself to pen an appeal to China. Admitting that he was dismally late in taking a stab at this "extremely difficult exercise," he was atypically seized with self-doubt.

Haksar did not even ask China for help. Instead, he produced wavering verbiage about "international proportions" that tried to circumvent China's simple insistence that Pakistan could do whatever it wanted to crush secessionists. India's government braced itself against the inevitable slap from Zhongnanhai. Haksar noted that "we have refrained from making any statement which might even remotely irritate them."[29]

IN THE END, INDIA'S GLOBAL DIPLOMATIC ROUNDS PROVED CRUSHINGLY disappointing. Nobody was going to put serious pressure on Pakistan—the kind that might have averted a war. Most countries only offered sympathetic words or token relief aid.[30]

But India demanded more than cash. Singh believed that rich Western governments thought that India had absorbed refugees before and would do so again, if paid off by the Soviet Union or the West. He bristled. This was not about money. India could not shelter the refugees permanently. As he complained to a meeting of Indian diplomats in London, "The help that they are giving is not at all a help to me. They are helping the Pakistani nationals"—the refugees—"to live; because these Pakistani nationals are the primary responsibility of Pakistan and if you give any money to India it is not a favour to India." The exiles would have to go home, perhaps through "harsher action"—a threat of war.[31]

Anyway, the donations were, as Haksar told Gandhi, "very disappointing." India would need some $400 million to look after these refugees for half a year, and more were coming every day. By the White House's reckoning, the Indians netted merely about $20 million from the whole world, as well as roughly $12 million from the Soviet Union. Nixon said that "the European nations have talked a great deal but done very little." Frustratingly, these miserly donations usually came without plausible suggestions for getting the refugees home, but with firm exhortations to avoid military confrontation with Pakistan. India was left buckling under its burdens.[32]

"THEY'RE SUCH BASTARDS"

India's most important disappointment came from the United States. Nixon's initial impulse was not to help the refugees at all. "Someone is saying we are contemplating sending aid to help the Pakistani refugees," he said. "I hope to hell we're not."[33]

Yahya would resent such relief, but Kissinger thought some token donations were inevitable, if only to undercut press and congressional criticism of the White House's support for Pakistan. Kissinger grudgingly wrote, "Despite the possible West Pakistani reaction, I do not see how we can not go ahead with some such assistance." Still, Nixon would not sign off until being promised that the aid would bypass India and instead be funneled through international or U.S. agencies. Both Kissinger and his deputy, Alexander Haig, worried that some of the refugees were probably guerrillas, with Haig wanting to be sure that U.S. supplies were not used to help the Bengali insurgency. Once reassured, Nixon agreed to a "modest" $2.5 million of mostly food aid, which might temporarily feed some three hundred thousand refugees—a small slice of those millions.[34]

The refugee crisis drew Nixon and Kissinger's attention primarily because it could drive Gandhi to war. "Of course everyone believes that she wanted to attack," remembers Samuel Hoskinson, Kissinger's staffer. "That seemed to be her mind-set. It fit the mind-set in Washington about her." By offering some aid, the Nixon administration sought to undercut India's primary reason for war, and ease Indian domestic pressure on Gandhi. Showing his CIA background, Hoskinson says, "We do have a pretty good picture of Delhi during this period, from embassy reporting and good old human intelligence. By well-placed sources in high places, we have a pretty good perception of her and her generals. Manekshaw was a piece of work. When you marry this intel with a mind-set about her anyway, and mix in this concern about the Russians, it all is very credible and very worrisome."[35]

Hoskinson wrote to Kissinger, "Mrs. Gandhi reportedly has ordered her army to prepare a plan for a rapid take-over of East Pakistan and is said to be particularly interested in an 'Israeli-type lightening thrust' that would present the world with a fait accompli." There were exchanges of artillery and small arms fire at India's border with East Pakistan. In the Situation Room, General William Westmoreland, the U.S. Army chief of staff, briefed Kissinger that India would trounce Pakistan if war came.[36]

Kissinger stuck to a core principle: Pakistan could do whatever it wanted to its people, despite consequences spilling beyond its borders. He put India's ambassador in Washington on notice that "you can't go to war over refugees." Kissinger told Nixon that "there is absolutely no justification for it—they don't have a right to invade Pakistan no matter what Pakistan does in its territory." He then added, "Besides the killing has stopped"—which was not true, as all posts in South Asia were reporting. Nixon said, "It has quieted down."[37]

At most, Nixon and Kissinger's aid would relieve a fraction of the consequences of Pakistan's slaughter. If the Nixon administration had wanted to make major efforts, winning over the Indian public in the process, there was a limitless amount of refugee misery to be addressed. But Harold Saunders remembers, "That's not the way he [Kissinger] thought. Using a humanitarian crisis as a political way in—that was not something that he would have come to mind right away."[38]

One program gives a sense of the possibilities: an Indian request for a U.S. airlift, with four U.S. Air Force C-130 transport airplanes flying refugees from overcrowded Tripura to Assam. Hoskinson persuaded Kissinger that this could help hold India back from war, and for a month the gargantuan planes carried relief supplies and flew some twenty-three thousand Bengali refugees to Assam. This was not the same as getting the refugees back home, but it was creative and helpful—a tantalizing glimpse of what could have been done.[39]

With alarms of imminent war ringing in their ears, Nixon and Kissinger boosted U.S. aid up to a new total of $17.5 million. This was far less than the State Department wanted, although more than the Soviet Union had given. As welcome as it was, it still composed only a sliver of India's overall costs, which Kissinger's staff reckoned at more than $400 million annually—assuming that no more refugees came, which was daily shown to be wrong. Along with the relief, Nixon exhorted Gandhi not to go to war. While pleased with the fresh donation, Haksar rankled at that pressure. "The developing insurgency in Bangla Desh cannot be halted even if we wish to do so," he told Gandhi. "Consequently, these exhortations for 'maximum restraint' sound a little hollow and meaningless."[40]

In the privacy of the Oval Office, Nixon said that "if they're not going to have a famine the last thing they need is another war. Let the goddamn Indians fight a war." Kissinger agreed: "They are the most aggressive goddamn people around there." He said that they should pressure Gandhi to avoid military action, and complained that the Indians were "getting so devious now."

Nixon wanted to be sure that Pakistan would be well looked after: "But we don't say anything against Yahya?" "No, no," Kissinger assured the president. "You just say you hope the refugees will soon be able to go back to East Pakistan. He will then reply to you that's exactly what he wants. I've got it all arranged with the embassy. You can tell the Indians to pipe down, and we'll keep Yahya happy."

Nixon bitterly said, "The Indians need—what they need really is a—" Kissinger interjected, "They're such bastards." Nixon finished his thought: "A mass famine."[41]

Chapter 10

The China Channel

R ICHARD NIXON, FEELING THE STING OF BETRAYAL FROM THE LEAK-
ing of the Pentagon Papers, developed a renewed appreciation
for Yahya. Carrying the most secret of messages back and forth from
China, Yahya proved himself a thoroughgoing loyalist and flawlessly
discreet. Compared to Daniel Ellsberg or Archer Blood, the Pakistani
dictator looked pretty good.

"This is the kind of thing that the leader of a country is going to
be personally managing," remembers Winston Lord, Henry Kissinger's
special assistant at the White House. "You better have trust in that
person."

Yahya had decisively beaten out the rival options for the prized role
of go-between. Pakistan, notwithstanding Archer Blood's hectoring
cables about genocide, had distinct advantages. "Pakistan was a good
friend of both of ours, in the Cold War context," Lord says. The Chinese leadership, he recalls, would feel that they could trust Yahya. "The
case for secrecy was very strong," says Lord. "Above all, even though
we were trying to reassure each other through Pakistani channels that
Kissinger and Nixon's visits would go well, we couldn't be sure. There
was no assurance that it would work out. It was still somewhat a gam-
ble." The stakes were high: "You don't want a big public display of
an initiative that falls flat on its face." If news of the upcoming trip
got out, Lord says, then Nixon would face opposition from conservatives and pro-Taiwan advocates, while Congress tried to constrain him.
Harold Saunders, Kissinger's senior aide for South Asia, remembers
the necessity of finding a clandestine channel: "We did need someone
to keep it secret, even from State." When a White House aide suggested
trying to garner publicity for the early covert steps, Nixon barked,
"*Don't* screw it up."[1]

Kissinger might have made a cooler calculation of the strategic relationship between the United States and Pakistan, but for Nixon this trust was deeply personal, resting on his friendship with Yahya. "Nixon did do a lot of traveling as vice president," Lord says, "that's one way he got so expert on foreign policy. He remembered on his trips who was treating him nicely, back when his political career looked like it might be over. If he got a good reception, and he did from Yahya and the Pakistanis, he would certainly remember that. I don't think Kissinger had any such feelings."[2]

Ironically, it is Kissinger's own worldview that makes the strongest argument against overvaluing Yahya. To a realist thinker like him, if two states were facing a grave threat from a common foe, they would be forced together. Since the two countries' shared fundamental strategic interests would propel them into partnership, the logistical details of arranging some meetings should not matter too much. As Kissinger, while praising the U.S. and Chinese leadership, recently wrote, "That China and the United States would find a way to come together was inevitable given the necessities of the time. It would have happened sooner or later whatever the leadership in either country." But his younger self, fretting and hoping in his West Wing office, was not so confident.[3]

"HE'S A DECENT MAN"

In this uncertain landscape, Yahya was, more than ever, the essential man. Saunders reminded Kissinger that "the prospect of the Peking trip imposed limits" on criticizing Pakistan "that had nothing to do with South Asia, except that the Pakistanis were in position to exploit those limits."[4]

Those limits were on display in a remarkably warm letter from Nixon to Yahya in May. As Alexander Haig, Kissinger's deputy, candidly told Nixon, "I have toned down" the letter "to eliminate any inference of pressure from you." Thus Nixon wrote that Yahya must "be deeply disappointed not to have been able to transfer power to a civilian government according to the plan you had adopted"—as if Yahya had had no choice in the matter. Saying nothing about the slaughter, Nixon blandly voiced "our concern over the loss of life and human suffering"—even for the president, the word "concern" was the maximum extent of U.S. rhetoric. While noting the opposition among the American people and Congress to U.S. military and economic aid to Pakistan, he hoped that would fade as the civil war continued to subside. Nixon expressed solicitude for the man who had chosen carnage: "I understand the anguish you must have felt in making the difficult decisions you have faced." This was hardly the kind of thing to concentrate the minds of the generals in Rawalpindi.[5]

There were advantages to working with a dictatorship. As Saunders points out, only two Pakistanis had to be involved—Yahya and his ambassador in Washington—making it easier to dodge the U.S. agents spying on the Pakistani embassy's communications. "Keeping it out of U.S. government channels was not easy," Saunders remembers. "Having someone who could play that game was important." Yahya would personally deliver the White House's notes to the Chinese ambassador in Islamabad, bound directly for Beijing, usually arriving there a day later.[6]

With so much traffic going through the China channel, Nixon brought Joseph Farland, the loyal U.S. ambassador in Pakistan, in on the secret. The president had Farland hastily manufacture some plausible personal excuse to travel from Islamabad to meet Kissinger in Palm Springs, California, not breathing a word to anyone else. The ambassador, with no clue what he was there to do, launched into stroppy denunciations of rivals who were out to trash Pakistan: Kenneth Keating, the ambassador in Delhi, had gone "berserk," leaking the essence of Blood's reporting to Sydney Schanberg of the New York Times; the Dacca press corps were inexperienced "missionaries" who were exaggerating the amount of killing there.

But Kissinger, with far bigger fish to fry, notified the dumbfounded ambassador that for some time the White House had been sending messages through Pakistan to China. Farland would now be responsible for personally passing along to Yahya letters classified dauntingly as TOP SECRET/SENSITIVE/EXCLUSIVELY EYES ONLY. Kissinger was hoping to meet Zhou Enlai, China's premier, in Pakistan or somewhere in China that was easily reachable from Pakistan, with Yahya setting up the trip. Kissinger, comforted that Farland was "a man outside the regular Foreign Service Establishment," told him to get in touch with him if he ever got "intolerable" instructions from the State Department.[7]

A few days later, on May 10, Nixon replied to the Chinese, proposing a "preliminary secret meeting" between Kissinger and Zhou, "on Chinese soil preferably at some location within convenient flying distance from Pakistan." Nixon's own visit would follow soon after. All the details would be figured out through the Pakistani channel: *"For secrecy, it is essential that no other channel be used."*[8]

Kissinger's time horizon shrank. He said, "Yahya must be kept afloat for six more months." When told that Yahya could not hold on to East Pakistan in the long run, Kissinger said that "all we need is six months." Or maybe less: Kissinger pressed Robert McNamara, the former defense secretary who was now running the World Bank, to help keep Yahya in power by providing international economic support, saying, "We really need these guys for three months and then we will relent." Kissinger made the same pitch to John Connally, Nixon's Treasury secretary: "We really need these guys for the next three months."[9]

On May 23, Kissinger told Nixon that "that is the last thing we can afford now to have the Pakistan government overthrown, given the other things we are doing."[10]

YAHYA'S CHANNEL CAME AT A TERRIBLE COST. THE STATE DEPARTMENT estimated publicly in late June that at least two hundred thousand people had already died in East Pakistan. Not long after, in the *New York Times,* Sydney Schanberg reported that, according to his reliable diplomatic sources, the Pakistan army had killed at least two hundred thousand Bengalis.[11]

The Nixon administration had ample evidence not just of the scale of the massacres, but also of their ethnic targeting of the Hindu minority—what Blood had condemned as genocide. This was common knowledge throughout the Nixon administration. Kissinger once told the president himself, "Another stupid mistake he [Yahya] made was to expel so many Hindus from East Pakistan. It gave the Indians a great cause" for war. Kissinger, in a memorandum drafted by Saunders, alerted Nixon to the difficulty of getting Hindu refugees to return. The undersecretary of state said to Nixon, "The Hindu population has suffered strong persecution, and many have fled the country."[12]

Kissinger was repeatedly alerted about this genocide. Harold Saunders informed him about reports that the Pakistan army was "deliberately seeking out Hindus and killing them," while a senior State Department official notified him that Pakistan's policy was "getting rid of the Hindus." In a Situation Room meeting, another State Department official plainly told Kissinger, "Eighty percent of the refugees are Hindus." In the same meeting, the CIA director doubted the prospects of refugees returning to East Pakistan, no matter what Yahya said to them: "The way the Pakistanis have been beating up on the Hindus, the refugees would have to be convinced they wouldn't be shot in the head."[13]

Even Farland's embassy in Islamabad—helmed by an ambassador who saw the best in Yahya—admitted that the "army has clearly been singling out Hindus for especially harsh treatment," although he did not think that "army policy as such is to expel Hindus." He wrote, "Coupled with official anti-Hindu propaganda, army brutality has effect of spurring Hindu exodus." He noted "an emotional anti-Hindu bias" in the "thinking of West Paks." Even if Yahya's government was not "officially encouraging mass exodus, we doubt it [is] sorry Hindus are leaving. Pak military probably view Hindu departure as blessing which reduces element [they] regard as untrustworthy and subversive."[14]

None of this put much of a dent in Nixon's fondness for Yahya. "He's a decent man," Nixon said, "for him to do a difficult job trying to hold those two parts of the country separated by thousands of miles and keep them together."[15]

AS MILLIONS OF REFUGEES FLED INTO INDIA, THE NIXON ADMINISTRA-tion had ruled out using all of its major diplomatic tools: threats to withhold military or economic aid, or rumbles of public denunciation. Instead, the United States was left with nothing more than making private suggestions to Yahya.

Nixon told a senior envoy from Pakistan that Yahya was a "good friend," and empathized again with the "anguish" of the decisions that the Pakistani dictator had had to make. While warning that he was boxed in by Congress, legal restrictions, and public opinion, Nixon reassured the envoy that the United States was not going to tell Pakistan how to deal with its political problems. It was "wrong," Nixon said, "to assume that the US should go around telling other countries how to arrange their political affairs."[16]

The only stern words came not from Nixon, Kissinger, or Rogers, but merely from a friendly ambassador. Farland—in the middle of his other China business—told Yahya that he first needed "to stop the shooting and to start the rebuilding," and reminded him of the pervasive fear in East Pakistan. On May 22, after almost two months of targeted slaughter of the Hindus of East Pakistan, Farland finally gingerly raised these killings with Yahya, in a tense meeting at the President's House in Karachi. He read Yahya some sanitized sections of a recent cable from Archer Blood. This stung Yahya, who raged about Indian propaganda, pledging that this persecution definitely was not happening with his government's assent. When he cooled off, he said he would look into it.[17]

After Yahya declared a general amnesty for refugees returning home, Farland in June recommended that he emphasize that exiles of all religions—including Hindus—could come back. Yahya, still denying that Hindus were targeted, agreed. Farland warned him that this ongoing "Hindu exodus" could spark a war with India, and that the flow of refugees would not let up until the army stopped its repression of the locals, particularly the Hindus. India was predictably unimpressed: Indian diplomats in Islamabad wrote that Pakistan's real goal was eliminating the Hindus from East Pakistan and Yahya's assurance to them could not be taken seriously.[18]

Nixon wrote to Yahya, praising him for this amnesty declaration, as well as for saying that he would restore power to civilians. In his firmest warning yet, Nixon voiced "deep concern" about the risk of war, writing that it was "absolutely vital" for peace to create conditions in East Pakistan that would allow the swift return of the refugees.[19]

This uptick in U.S. private criticism had no obvious impact. Yahya, taking full advantage of his utility from the China channel, showered Nixon with beseeching mail. He urged Nixon to maintain his personal support, to help get Pakistan international aid, and to ward off India. Indira Gandhi, Yahya wrote, was "determined to exploit the presence of displaced persons in India to . . . justify military intervention in East Pakistan." But Yahya could only rather limply point to the return of thousands of refugees—nothing compared with the 154,000 fleeing *daily* in June, or the 21,000 fleeing every day in July, or the millions who had already fled.[20]

On June 28, Yahya delivered a national address, calling for refugees to return and seeking a new constitution and a new East Pakistan government. But the Awami League remained banned; any previously elected Bengalis who were deemed secessionist would be disqualified from taking their seats; the constitution would be written by carefully selected experts, rather than by the elected members of the National Assembly; and martial law would remain in place for an unspecified period of time. The State Department saw such halfhearted gestures as failures, with one senior official telling Kissinger there could be no political solution so long as the Awami League remained banned: "It's like telling Ted Kennedy not to be a Democrat." The White House staff told Kissinger that Yahya had not done what was necessary to get the refugees to return. And the U.S. embassy in Delhi angrily pointed to the ongoing flood of refugees as proof that Yahya had done nothing to restrain his army. Since U.S. support was the "mainstay" of the survival of Yahya's government, it was "indefensible" not to lean on him: "We are the key factor in all of Yahya's calculations for the immediate future."[21]

THE AMBASSADOR'S CONSCIENCE

In the next Chinese message delivered through Yahya, Zhou Enlai welcomed the prospect of Kissinger's visit. When Kissinger got this word, he was, according to H. R. Haldeman, "ecstatic."[22]

The White House was galvanized. They quickly fixed the dates of July 9 through 11, with Kissinger to fly in and out of Beijing on a Pakistani Boeing aircraft. Kissinger told Nixon that Yahya had "set up a tremendous cover operation."[23]

But Kissinger had some drearier business to handle before that momentous day. He had to personally face down a remaining dissenter, Kenneth Keating, the U.S. ambassador to India. Keating—unaware of the China channel, not knowing that his timing was terrible—made himself impossible to ignore with a trip to Washington. He was in town to sit in on meetings with Swaran Singh, the Indian foreign minister, and wanted to meet both Kissinger and Nixon privately.

Archer Blood had been easily dismissed, but it was trickier to oust a well-connected former Republican senator. It would look bad to fire the ambassador in the middle of a crisis. And Keating leaked plenty to the press while he was still working for the administration; he could have done far worse if sacked. "He's got all the credentials," remembers Samuel Hoskinson, Kissinger's staffer. "When he says it, then people have to listen to it."

Hoskinson recalls Nixon and Kissinger's anger: "We were aware that Keating was on the bad guy list. 'What's happened to Ken?'" He explains, "What really upset them is Keating is not just another ambassador. He is a man of Washington, with an independent reputation. He knows how to get the word out, he knows how to deal with the media, he has his own base of influence, he's well respected by other Republicans. This is not just Archer Blood anymore, not this guy out there in Bangladesh and a couple of Foreign Service Officers."[24]

Meeting Kissinger at the White House, Keating vented his anguish.

Kissinger, noncommittal, explained that Nixon wanted to give Yahya a few months. Kissinger said that "the President has a special feeling for President Yahya. One cannot make policy on that basis, but it is a fact of life."

Keating shot back that he recognized Nixon's "special relationship" with Yahya, but was baffled by it. He could not see why the United States should stick up for Yahya "just out of loyalty to a friend." He vehemently argued that ammunition shipments and military assistance to Pakistan should be "just out of the question now while they are still killing in East Pakistan and refugees are fleeing across the border."

Rather than merely sending toothless notes, Keating wanted U.S. economic aid to Pakistan to be conditional on an end to the killing. Echoing Blood, he reminded Kissinger that the army was concentrating on the Hindus. At first, the refugees fleeing into India had been in the same proportion as existed in the overall population of East Pakistan, but now 90 percent were Hindus.

Kissinger did not respond to most of this. He merely tried to assure the ambassador that the White House had no illusions that the Pakistani government could hold on to East Pakistan, and had no interest in its doing so. They just wanted to buy time for a gradual process.[25]

The next day, in the Oval Office, Kissinger complained to Nixon, "He's almost fanatical on this issue." Nixon resented having to meet with Keating. The president thought his man in Delhi had gone completely native: "Keating, like every Ambassador who goes over there, goes over there and gets sucked in."

Nixon asked, "Well what the hell does he think we should do about it?" When Kissinger explained—"he thinks we should cut off all military aid, all economic aid, and in effect help the Indians to push the Pakistanis out of" East Pakistan—it was more than Nixon could take: "I don't want him to come in with that kind of jackass thing with me."

Kissinger railed against the Indians: "Those sons-of-bitches, who never have lifted a finger for us, why should we get involved in the morass of East Pakistan?" He wrote off the future of Bangladesh before it had even been born: "if East Pakistan becomes independent, it is going to become a cesspool. It's going be 100 million people, they have the lowest standard of living in Asia. No resources. They're going to become a ripe field for Communist infiltration." He attempted to fathom the depths of Indian perfidy: "they're going to bring pressure on India because of West Bengal. So that the Indians in their usual idiotic way are playing for little stakes, unless they have in the back of their minds that they could turn East Pakistan into a sort of protectorate that they could control from Calcutta." Nixon had a simpler explanation: "Oh, what they had in the back of their mind was to destroy Pakistan."

The tape quality is bad, but Kissinger said, "Mr. President, actually we've got to keep Yahya, we have to keep Yahya [unclear] public executions for the next month"—evidently a call to temporarily prevent Yahya from carrying out any public killings.

Wrapping up, Nixon was emphatic that the opening to China was not his only reason for backing Pakistan: "Look, even apart from the Chinese thing, I wouldn't do that to help the Indians, the Indians are no goddamn good."[26]

ON JUNE 15, KEATING GOT HIS CHANCE TO DIRECTLY CONFRONT THE president. Waiting in the Oval Office for the showdown, the president groused to Kissinger, "Like all of our other Indian ambassadors, he's been brainwashed." He added, "Anti-Pakistan."

The brawling began immediately. As Keating entered, Nixon threw him off balance by asking, "Where are your sandals?" Decoding this mystifying gibe, the president explained, "I hope you haven't turned the Embassy over to those hippies like your predecessor." Keating—a World War I and World War II officer and former Republican senator with a fondness for seersucker suits, infrequently mistaken for a hippie—tried to regain his footing, as Nixon reminded him who was boss: "We don't normally have ambassadors in."

Despite this presidential onslaught, Keating rallied. The elderly Republican stalwart tried to show his loyalty to the White House, noting that he had repeatedly stood up to the Indians over Vietnam and other issues. But he argued that India was a strong and stable power, while Pakistan was in turmoil. "What do they want us to do?" asked Nixon, about the Indians. "Break up Pakistan?" Keating assured him they did not, but they could not stand the strain of some five million refugees. Nixon suggested, "Why don't they shoot them?"

Keating, prudently letting that pass without comment, launched into an impassioned plea. The Pakistani government had killed the Bengalis' intellectuals, arrested Mujib as a traitor, and outlawed the political party that had won all but two of the available seats. The former senator from New York explained that three million of the refugees were in Calcutta: "Calcutta is the size of New York. It'd be like dumping three million people into New York, except that Calcutta is in much worse shape than New York. Not too much, but it's worse."

In the Oval Office, the ambassador directly told the president of the United States and his national security advisor that their ally was committing genocide. The reason that the refugees kept coming, at a rate of 150,000 a day, was "because they're killing the Hindus." He explained that "in the beginning, these refugees were about in the proportion to the population—85 percent Muslim, 15 percent Hindus. Because when they started the killing it was indiscriminate. Now, having gotten control of the large centers, it is almost entirely a matter of genocide killing the Hindus."

Neither Nixon nor Kissinger said anything. With those awful words hanging in the air, Keating kept going. The Hindus would never go back, but the Muslims might if there was a political settlement and an end to the killing. He said that the Bengalis' bitterness was so great that he—as well as Joseph Farland, his counterpart in Islamabad—believed that the old Pakistan was finished. He demanded new pressure on Yahya's government. But Nixon, while pledging to be conciliatory to India, would not "allow the refugee problem to get us involved in the internal political problems. You see that's our policy too."

Nixon could not mention one of his motives: the secret China channel. Keating soothingly told Nixon, "Now, I am conscious of the special relationship that you have with Yahya. And I respect it." The president opaquely replied, "Not only just that, but there are some other major considerations." A little later, he mysteriously said that Pakistan's collapse was "not in our interest," especially now, "for reasons we can't go into. Under those circumstances, what we have to do, Ken, is to find a way to be just as generous as we can to the Indians, but also we do not want to do something that is an open breach with Yahya—an open breach, an embarrassing situation."

Nixon made a brief effort to speak nicely of the Indians. It did not go well. "Let me say this," he intoned, "I don't want to give you the wrong impression about India. There are 400 million Indians." Keating corrected him; there were actually 550 million Indians. Nixon was surprised: "I don't know why the hell anybody would reproduce in that damn country but they do." Trying to revert to kindness, he said that India had "some semblance of democracy" and that "we want them to succeed. Because there are 550 million people, we want them to do well." Then, as if overtaxed by that niceness, he added, "And they always hate us . . . internationally, we know that."[27]

WHEN THE TROUBLESOME AMBASSADOR DEPARTED, NIXON AND KIS-singer were left in the Oval Office to splutter. After Nixon's most direct, personal confrontation with one of the dissenters in his own administration, he and Kissinger were unswayed. They never mentioned the accusation of genocide, nor expressed a hint of compassion for the Hindus or the refugees. But they were furious at Keating and Blood.

"I don't know what the Christ we are up to," said Nixon as soon as the coast was clear. "The most insulting way we can—" started Kissinger, before the president cut him off. Nixon asked, "My God, does Farland, is he sending memoranda that he thinks Pakistan is finished also?" (He was.) Kissinger blasted away at Archer Blood: "Baloney. He's got this maniac in Dacca, the Consul General who is in rebellion."

Kissinger reassured the president that he had told the Indian government that "we need 3 or 4 months to work it out. We will find them some money, we will gradually move into a position to be helpful, but we've got to do it our way. Just to shut them up." Kissinger warned Nixon not to speak "in front of Keating he'll blab it all over." Nixon agreed: "Keating will go blab it over to the State Department."

Kissinger had the China channel uppermost in his mind: "Well it would be considered such an insult by Yahya that the whole deal would be off." Nixon repeated, "I don't know what the Christ he's talking about." Kissinger resolved to reduce their dependency on Yahya: "I will, when I'm talking to the Chinese, set up a separate channel so that we're not so vulnerable."

Nixon, shaken, dolefully contemplated Yahya's fall: "I don't know, Henry, it just may be that the poor son-of-a-bitch can't survive." He wondered how big the refugee problem was: "Five million? Is it that bad really or are they exaggerating?" Kissinger, echoing Nixon's comment about how Indians reproduced, applied the same unkind thought to the breeding of Bengalis: "Of course, I don't know how many of them they generate?"[28]

THE SHIPPING NEWS

The day after that Oval Office clash, Nixon and Kissinger had an opportunity to urge restraint on India. Swaran Singh was wrapping up his emergency tour of foreign capitals with a visit to Washington.

Kissinger—who later called Singh, an elegant Sikh, "that bearded character"—instructed Nixon to show him a mixture of sympathy and great firmness. Kissinger's goal was simple: "I'm just trying to keep them from attacking for 3 months." He reminded Nixon of what to say: "that you think that overt pressure on Pakistan would have a counter-productive effect, and that you are working with Yahya in your own way. It's a little duplicitous, but these bastards understand that." (Nixon took a moment to stew over his man in Delhi: "I must say I am not too damned impressed with Keating. I think he's just gone overboard.") Kissinger kept the president focused on the real point of the meeting: "We have to keep them from attacking for our own reasons."[29]

To hold back an Indian assault, the Nixon administration boosted the amount of refugee aid they would give India to $70 million. In his Oval Office meeting with Singh, the president dazzlingly turned on the charm, commiserating with India's "terrible agony" and suggesting that he could try to influence Yahya, although not "in a public, blunt way." While Singh was grateful for the $70 million, Nixon admitted that even ten times that amount would not "buy the problem away." The president conceded that this cash was not enough for six million refugees: "For how long? Not long. It'll help." Singh was so impressed that he reckoned Nixon more helpful than the State Department, and overoptimistically thought he had pledges in hand that the United States would now pressure Yahya. For once, Nixon's and Gandhi's governments savored a rare moment of harmony.[30]

It lasted for all of six days. On June 22, the White House got a rude surprise. The *New York Times* ran a front-page scoop: there was a Pakistani freighter in New York harbor, ready to sail, loaded up with U.S. military spare parts and eight aircraft. Another ship, bearing parts for armored personnel carriers, had already sailed early in May and was about to arrive in Karachi.[31]

This blindsided the Indian government in general and Swaran Singh in particular, who had returned from Washington to Delhi in good cheer, and now looked like a chump. The Indian foreign ministry was convinced that this was a policy approved at the highest levels. Humiliated, Singh went before both houses of India's freshly enraged Parliament to say that the United States should stand up for its democratic principles by stopping all shipments of arms to Pakistan so long as it kept up its atrocities and refused to deal with the Awami League. A few weeks later, he denounced the United States' supply of weapons as an "intervention on the side of the military rulers of West Pakistan against the people of Bangla Desh" and a "condonation of genocide in Bangla Desh."[32]

These shipments were the inevitable consequence of a muddled policy, born of different clashing bits of the U.S. government. On the one hand, the State Department still maintained an informal administrative hold on military supplies to Pakistan, well short of a formal embargo. Congress was waiting in the wings to legislate a new outright ban if the White House did not cool its support for Pakistan. On the other hand, Nixon and Kissinger did not want to slap Yahya in the face with an embargo. Yahya, Kissinger's staff wrote, seemed grateful that the White House had not joined in the worldwide condemnations of Pakistan by establishing such a ban. As Kissinger had recently explained in the Situation Room, Nixon wanted to proceed with spare parts for ongoing programs, but try to delay any bigger shipments for now, and figure that out later. Nixon recoiled from the "positive hostile act" of stopping the spare parts. Kissinger said, "The President is eager to avoid any break with Yahya." So rather than a simple policy of trying to halt all shipments, they were confusingly allowing whatever was left in the pipeline to go forward, waiting for that to gradually run dry over the coming months.[33]

But nobody was quite sure what really was in the pipeline. The White House scrambled to find out how many other potential unpleasant surprises might be lurking on a freighter somewhere. Samuel Hoskinson, the South Asia expert on Kissinger's staff, was the White House official in charge of figuring out what U.S. weapons might still be on their way to Pakistan. "I never felt like I could get a handle on that," he remembers miserably. "Henry was anxious and I couldn't come up with numbers. As soon as you came up with numbers, something happened. Whoops, two more ships have gone."

As Kissinger told Nixon, there were still military supplies moving toward Pakistan (anything with a valid export license that had already been turned over to Pakistani shippers or was coming to Pakistan directly from a commercial U.S. supplier). But with so many suppliers, it was hard to figure out exactly what was where. And even as the bloodshed went on, Pakistan continued to try to secure hefty military licenses for U.S. military equipment. Hoskinson had countless collisions with the Pentagon, with shifting numbers at every stage. "I don't think the Pentagon knew," he says. "I finally came to the conclusion: it's not that they're hiding this from us; *they* don't know."[34]

The White House and State Department cobbled together a rather wobbly impression of what Pakistan was due to receive: mostly spare parts for aircraft, tanks, and other military vehicles, as well as some ammunition, replacement parts for engines, communication hardware, and some small submarine components. There was $29 million worth owed to Pakistan, but about half of that was temporarily halted. That left about $15 million worth of military supplies left in the pipeline to Pakistan, which would trickle away to about $4 million by the end of August.[35]

The dollar sums of arms sales do not indicate the real value of weaponry and matériel, however, since it is often sold to friendly governments for below the market price. And while spare parts are cheap, they make a big difference in the functioning of any military—a fact well known by Alexander Haig, a veteran of wars in Korea and Vietnam, who wanted to quietly continue the sale of spare parts as if everything were normal. Harold Saunders reminded Kissinger that a supply of spares was "essential to keeping the US-equipped part of the Pakistan air force flying. As you know, the air force has been used in East Pakistan."[36]

Yahya dreaded the stopping of U.S. military shipments—for the immediate consequences and the humiliation, and because it would encourage other foreign governments to follow the Americans' example. In another context, Nixon and Kissinger would surely have seen the leverage that this afforded them: since Yahya really feared it, they could effectively threaten him with it. But they never tried to play this strong hand.[37]

These freighters were the last straw for the State Department, which asked Nixon to suspend all military shipments to Pakistan until they could screen out anything that might have an impact on the killing in East Pakistan. Kissinger flatly refused. He urged Nixon to continue their current policy, ruling out even a temporary suspension of military items outside of U.S. control. He kept open the option of releasing more military equipment after "the current flap dies down." Nixon agreed. It was worth taking the hit with Congress, Kissinger told the president, to avoid the unfriendly signal to Pakistan.[38]

DURING ALL THIS, YAHYA WAS BUSILY CONTRIVING AN ELABORATE RUSE to sneak Kissinger into China. Kissinger would go to Pakistan, fake sickness, retreat to Yahya's hill resort to recover, and then secretly fly from there to Beijing. After his meetings with the Chinese leadership, he would fly back and return to public view in Pakistan, feeling much improved. Yahya confidently notified Kissinger that "absolute fool-proof arrangements will be made by us and he need have no anxiety on this count."[39]

Farland suggested that Kissinger be disguised with a hat and sun-glasses. Winston Lord and two other White House staffers would go to Beijing, as well as two Secret Service agents, leaving Harold Saunders behind in Rawalpindi, near Islamabad, to keep up appearances. Far-land was under strict orders to prevent the U.S. embassy doctor from tending to Kissinger. To the last minute, the team fretted that its secret would slip out. Kissinger, Saunders recalls, "had to be ready to plausi-bly deny."[40]

Nixon and Kissinger were thrilled. "I've been talking to Yahya for years, a couple years now about this," reminisced Nixon. On June 28, as Haldeman recorded, the president privately said that "we're sitting at a great watershed in history, clearly the greatest since WWII. Henry interjected that he considered it to be the greatest since the Civil War." Nixon later remembered Kissinger bursting into the Lincoln Sitting Room late at night, out of breath and trembling. The two men toasted their epoch-making success with two glasses of very old brandy. Hal-deman noted, "The P obviously is really cranked up about this whole Chinese thing, and did go on and on talking about it."[41]

Kissinger's route to Beijing might have literally gone through Dacca. One early U.S. plan suggested that Kissinger "stop at Dacca for first hand look at our humanitarian interests," and then secretly fly into China. Later, as part of the evolving secret operation, Yahya offered transportation on a Pakistan International Airlines aircraft "on either Hindukush or Dacca route." As Kissinger's plane approached Dacca's fortified airport, he could have looked out his window at the smoldering city. While he waited for takeoff, he might have been able to watch the Pakistan Air Force's U.S.-made C-130s or F-86 Sabre jet fighters in action. But someone either in Washington or Islamabad had the tact to choose another route for him.[42]

Chapter 11

The East Is Red

ON JULY 6, ABOARD A U.S. AIR FORCE AIRPLANE THAT WAS BRISTLING with Secret Service and military officers, Henry Kissinger descended toward Delhi's airport. Since the presidential aircraft were all being used, Kissinger had to content himself with a modified command plane borrowed from the Tactical Air Command. The uncomfortable, hulking airplane would only grudgingly lift off runways, as Kissinger later noted: "On takeoff one had the feeling that the plane really preferred to reach its destination overland." Cruising down toward the landing strip, he was keenly aware that he was on a genuinely historic trip, quite probably the most important of his lifetime. It was not his two-day visit to India. He dutifully did the rounds in Delhi and then Islamabad, but the real point of his journey was his secret final destination: Beijing.[1]

India was a stopover for Kissinger in every possible way. In order to get to China, he needed to go through Pakistan; but in order to get to Pakistan, for balance, he had to show his face in India. His perfunctory visit there made a tidy symbol of how little that country mattered in the Nixon-Kissinger cosmology.

Harold Saunders was along for the ride. As Kissinger's senior aide for India and Pakistan, he had to be there to allay suspicions. "The India stop was for general obvious deflection reasons," he remembers. "He [Kissinger] presented himself in a normal way there. And then on to Pakistan."

Kissinger and his team landed in a downpour, which was not enough to rain out the inevitable leftist protesters. At the airport, outnumbering the police, they shouted, "Kissinger go back," "Murderer go back," while waving black flags and big banners reading "Kissinger of death go back." The Americans were hustled into cars and whisked off. The demonstrators, cheated of their intended target, let fly with tomatoes and rotten eggs at any other car that had the misfortune to be leaving the airport. Other protesters had been assembling at the U.S. embassy, massing to about 450. Scores of them now broke into the embassy compound, charging toward the main doors, to the surprise of the U.S. Marine guards. Before the mob could break open those doors, Indian police swept in and arrested them, leaving behind only a red flag planted in the embassy's lawn. The leftist crowds wrongly reckoned that Kissinger would be at the embassy, where they continued to chant slogans against him. In fact, he and his jet-lagged entourage had checked into the luxurious Ashoka Hotel—something that had evidently not occurred to the organizing cadres of the Communist Party of India.[2]

This was about as far as Kissinger could be from the teeming miseries of West Bengal and Tripura while still inside India. The Indian government asked him to come visit the refugee camps for himself. If he had served in another White House, he might have at least made a side trip to Calcutta, or perhaps have been packed off to one of the hundreds of camps in West Bengal to see U.S. dollars at work feeding the destitute. But Kissinger refused. Samuel Hoskinson, Kissinger's aide, says, "It's not really Henry's kind of thing." Kissinger was clear that, as an Indian diplomat noted, "he would *not* be able to visit any of the refugee camps."[3]

KISSINGER IN INDIA

That day, Henry Kissinger and P. N. Haksar confronted each other face-to-face. Kissinger told Haksar that "we are men of the world." In Haksar's office in South Block, the two paramount foreign policy advisers went after each other with polite but unmistakable vehemence, interrupted only by Haksar's attempts to dazzle Kissinger with wordy disquisitions.[4]

Haksar, already irate about U.S. arms sales to Pakistan, was stewing over the recent *New York Times* revelations of ongoing shipments. Kissinger blamed that on a "bureaucratic muddle," and said he had been surprised to read about it in the newspaper. To avoid such muddles, Haksar said, arms shipments should be stopped outright. Kissinger rebuffed that, saying that the arms supplies were of marginal significance and that the United States needed to maintain its leverage over Yahya. Haksar ripped into arms shipments past and present,

162 ~ The Blood Telegram

noting that the White House should not ignore the vast stocks given to Pakistan since the days of Dwight Eisenhower. When Kissinger, trying to downplay the importance of the supply, said that the Pentagon had not wanted to completely cut off "basically non-lethal" matériel, Haksar—who knew as well as his visitor did that cheap spare parts kept expensive weapons humming—shot back that he did not accept the "metaphysical concept called 'non-lethal.' "[5]

To Haksar's disbelief, Kissinger said that even if the United States "shipped all $29 million worth of military equipment, it would not make any difference in the situation. So let's stop yelling about something that does not make a difference." He snapped that "if India were going into a paroxysm over this there was no way in which the US could respond."[6]

Kissinger, trying flattery, said that Richard Nixon believed that India was the only country in the region that could be "not only a big Power, but a Power for peace and stability." Pakistan was only a small regional power—a soothing point that Haksar took to heart. For this, Haksar rewarded him with a pedantic lecture about the artificiality of Pakistan's Islamic identity: "If religion could provide a basis for creating Nation-States, Europe would probably still have the Holy Roman Empire."[7]

Haksar warned that the refugees were disrupting India's borders, emphasizing that almost 90 percent of the people fleeing East Pakistan were Hindus. This, he said, struck against the root of India's efforts to build up a secular democracy. While India could not drive the refugees out if they feared being butchered back in East Pakistan, they would return if East Pakistan got a democratic government. Kissinger, unswayed, brusquely told Haksar that "the Indians were just making a lot of noise in order to set up an invasion of East Pakistan."[8]

An exasperated Kissinger went for the jugular, suggesting that India's support for the Bengali guerrillas kept the situation inflamed. Haksar replied, "I shall be perfectly frank with you," which is how politicians in both Delhi and Washington preface a real whopper of a lie: "we have given no arms." India, he said evasively, could not seal its frontier everywhere, neglecting to mention the Indian army's and Border Security Force's many training camps, or the rebel raids being launched from Indian soil deep into East Pakistan.[9]

In Kissinger's recollection, their meeting was mostly a matter of him pacifying an excitable Haksar. He coolly recalled that he "had calmed Haksar down." He urged Haksar to lower the volume: "If the

Indians could quiet down, the US would try to work quietly over the next few months to encourage a settlement of the refugee problem." Haksar explained the Indian government's problem: "It did not want to go to war but it did not know how not to go to war."[10]

Kissinger only hinted at the real reason he was in Asia, mentioning that he wanted to rapidly improve relations with China. He reassured Haksar that the United States would not help China, India's sworn enemy, to dominate India. But then he warned Haksar that if a war broke out with Pakistan, China would react—a terrifying prospect for India. That, in turn, would drive India to seek help from the Soviet Union, and "cause complications for us in America." Haksar bristled. He said that if India found itself at war with Pakistan and facing Chinese intervention, he hoped that the United States would be sympathetic to India.[11]

Kissinger was not above swooning for the urbane, cerebral elder-statesman type, as he was about to do for Zhou Enlai. But Haksar left him cold, despite the Indian official's ostentatious efforts. After his showdown with his Indian counterpart, Kissinger saw the Indian government as unemotional but seeking a serviceable pretext for a war. Having spent less than a full day in Delhi, he did not believe there was "genuine Indian feeling against our arms aid to Pakistan." Once rid of Haksar, Kissinger concluded that "they are playing power politics with cold calculations."[12]

KISSINGER SPENT THE NEXT DAY STAGGERING FROM ONE BRUTAL MEET-ing to another. He was denounced, provoked, and prodded by Indians official and unofficial. On top of it all, patriotic Indian microbes took revenge on him. Kissinger's whole upcoming ruse in Pakistan rested on him faking a sudden upset stomach—but in India, too soon, he really did get sick. To make his cover story work, he spent his time in Delhi miserably keeping his gastrointestinal woes to himself.[13]

The Indian government's efforts at politesse were clumsy (one senior Indian diplomat reminded her colleagues to avoid mentioning the Arab-Israeli conflict because "Dr. Kissinger is a Jew"). The Indian press gleefully reported on demonstrations against him, and roasted him on the editorial pages. Members of the Lok Sabha erupted at a rumor that Pakistan would get several more ships loaded with military spares and ammunition. But what he faced in his meetings was worse.[14]

He kicked off his day with breakfast with Indian thinkers and aca-demics at the Ashoka Hotel. It went horribly. One of the Indians was especially livid: K. Subrahmanyam, the author of that April secret strategic report that urged India's top leaders to attack Pakistan to secure India's regional hegemony. Subrahmanyam, emotional and bitter, told Kissinger that he, as a refugee himself, should understand the horror of what was happening. The United States was "making the same mistake as it made with Hitler in the 1930s—trying to deal with and placate an authoritarian regime which has embarked on a major program of reducing its population." Kissinger, at the start of what was clearly going to be a very long day, tried to duck confronting him.[15]

For lunch, Kissinger had to face Haksar again for another ruined meal at the Ashoka Hotel, with fresh sparring over U.S. arms shipments to Pakistan. Later, Kissinger was shredded by the defense minister, Jagjivan Ram, a venerable politician who had been born into a downtrodden Dalit caste but enjoyed a meteoric rise under Nehru. Ram said he was under almost unbearable pressure to act against Pakistan. He had recently been at Agartala, near the East Pakistan border, where Pakistan was lobbing shells into India. "Pakistan has been sustained entirely by you," he accused. Kissinger replied, "Only partially." Ram smilingly retorted, "No, not just partially, almost entirely."[16]

There was also the embarrassing chore of mollifying Swaran Singh, who had returned from his Washington trip just in time to be sideswiped by the New York Times scoop about ongoing arms shipments to Pakistan. Kissinger, in the foreign minister's South Block office, quickly said that the White House and the top ranks of the State Department had not known that there might be shipments on their way to Pakistan—soothing, although a lie. There would be nothing more than $29 million worth on its way, he said, and, noting Nixon's personal relationship with Yahya, said that the State Department's unwelcome administrative hold on arms shipments had been a big step for the president. Singh, burning with humiliation, complained about this loophole, and said, "I would give hell to my staff if they did not give me full information." Kissinger replied, "I am raising hell." (He wasn't.) Singh said, "It passes my comprehension what your interest in maintaining such a close relationship with Pakistan is." Demanding a complete halt to arms shipments, he bluntly told Kissinger that "your giving of arms to Pakistan will provoke a war."[17]

During his disagreeable, gut-churning day, Kissinger repeatedly made a crucial commitment: he promised Indian officials that the United States would back India if China began military moves against it. In his lunch with Haksar, Kissinger hinted at upcoming "significant starts" in U.S. relations with China. He then pledged to Haksar that "under any conceivable circumstances the U.S. would back India against any Chinese pressures. In any dialogue with China, we would of course not encourage her against India."[18]

At the end of his excruciating meeting with Swaran Singh, Kissinger took him aside and vaguely sketched out the upcoming China opening. Assuring the foreign minister that this initiative was not directed against India, he said that the United States would "take the gravest view of any unprovoked Chinese aggression against India." (This obviously left open the prospect of provoked Chinese strikes on India, so Singh asked for a pledge that the United States would provide military equipment to India if China attacked. He evidently got no answer.)[19]

Later the same day, Kissinger, showing a keen interest in the prospect of Chinese movement against India, made a firm pledge to Jagjivan Ram: "we would take a very grave view of any Chinese move against India." He reassured the defense minister, "We will leave them in no doubt." Ram was delighted. Kissinger, seemingly trying to preempt Indian alarm when they learned of his China trip, said, "We have been adopting a certain attitude in order to promote tranquility and peace but if it looks as if they are going in for violence, we would take a very grave view."[20]

For the Indians, still traumatized by their humbling defeat by the People's Republic in the 1962 war, this was tremendously reassuring. But five months later, Kissinger would in fact be encouraging China to move troops to confront India.

THE CENTERPIECE OF THE DAY WAS KISSINGER'S AUDIENCE WITH INDIRA Gandhi herself. He was ushered into the prime minister's office in the majestic, domed South Block. But, much like Kissinger's other meetings in Delhi, this encounter proved heatedly contentious.[21]

Kissinger began the meeting alone with the prime minister, shutting out all their staffers for a few secretive minutes. Thus sequestered, he vaguely alerted her about upcoming "significant developments" in the U.S. relationship with China, which he said were not directed against India. He also handed her a cheerless letter from Nixon, which reminded her of U.S. humanitarian aid for the refugees but gave no ground on arms shipments.[22]

After that, Haksar, Kenneth Keating—in a seersucker suit to fight the sweltering July heat in Delhi—and Harold Saunders were allowed to troop into the prime minister's office. Kissinger showed signs of the impact of his rough visit. No longer blasé, he said he was now impressed by the intensity of Indian emotions. Still, echoing Nixon, he said the whole point of U.S. support for Pakistan was to maintain influence over Yahya to encourage the refugees to return. He agreed that it would take a political deal in Pakistan to get the refugees to return home, but admitted that "the US has no ideas at this moment."

Gandhi, pointing to almost seven million refugees by now, warned of her "emotional" public. Kissinger asked when the problem would become unmanageable. Gandhi said it was already unmanageable: "We are just holding it together by sheer will power." There were "hardly two people in Parliament who approve our policy."

Kissinger, playing for time, asked for a few more months before any extreme measures. He doubted that there was any point to cutting off economic and military aid to Pakistan: "the limited number of arms now being shipped to Pakistan makes almost no difference in the military balance." Gandhi said that whatever the practical impact of the arms shipments, they mattered greatly psychologically and politically.[23]

The prime minister sliced into Pakistan, which, she declared, based its existence on stoking hostility to India. Pakistan had long felt that it would get U.S. support no matter what it did, encouraging Pakistani "adventurism and Indophobia." She complained that Pakistan turned every issue into a clash between Hindus and Muslims: "Indophobia was clothed in the metaphysics of holy wars and the defence of Islam." If Pakistan really cared about Islam, she said cuttingly, it would consider the impact of its actions on the sixty million Muslims in India. Gandhi said that she did not want to take extreme measures, but that would depend on how the situation developed—thus leaving the option of war wide open.[24]

Kissinger had an odd way of lying even when he did not need to. He assured Gandhi that it "was the assessment of all of the US specialists in March that it was impossible that force would be used by the West Pakistani Government in East Pakistan." This was false; there was in fact at least one U.S. expert in that very room—Harold Saunders—who had warned him of an imminent crackdown early in March. Keating prudently changed the subject.[25]

Finally, Kissinger showed his charm. He said he did not want to risk the United States' fundamental relationship with five hundred million people in a strong democracy over "an essentially regional issue where America's vital national interests were not involved." And in what the Indians would soon realize was a reference to China, he promised that "America would, under no circumstances, allow any outside power to pressurize or threaten India."[26]

This line delighted his hosts. The Indian government eagerly seized on Kissinger's multiple promises of U.S. support for India against Chinese pressure, highlighting them as perhaps the most important thing that the national security advisor said in all his meetings with India's ministers.[27]

Finally, Kissinger urged Gandhi to visit Washington—a prospect that in reality filled Nixon with dread. The prime minister ended the tense meeting with a churlish reply: she smiled and said she would like to come, but "could not breathe a word of it" without having her domestic critics bludgeon her into having to say no.[28]

IT HAD BEEN A GRUELING DAY. AS KISSINGER JETTED OFF FOR ISLAM-abad and Beijing, both he and Haksar brooded on his ghastly visit.

Haksar still had no clue what Kissinger was really doing there. "Kissinger talked bravely about getting away from the past, but the past, even if buried, rules thoughts and actions from its grave." Bemused by the chaotic nature of U.S. policy, he thought that the United States wanted India to be a counterweight to China. Haksar did not realize that exactly the opposite was happening: Nixon and Kissinger were going to try to use China to balance against India.[29]

Kissinger left India sobered and alarmed. He grumbled about the viciousness of the Indian press. When he returned to Washington, he would tell Nixon that "what the Indians are really after, that became clear to me on my trip. . . . They think that . . . if they can undermine East Pakistan then in West Pakistan so many forces . . . will be turned loose that the whole Pakistan issue will disappear. The Indians and West Pakistanis they hate each other."[30]

On his way to Pakistan, Kissinger secretly wrote, "I have had full exposure to the strong Indian feelings." He ruminated on Gandhi's statement that the pressure was unbearable, and that her government was just hanging on by willpower. There was, he grimly wrote, "a growing sense of the inevitability of war or at least widespread Hindu-Muslim violence, not necessarily because anyone wants it but because in the end they fear they will not know how to avoid it"—one pithy line from Haksar that, at least, had struck home.[31]

"THE ARMY WAS DRIVING OUT THE HINDUS"

It was with palpable relief that Kissinger flew to Islamabad. For Winston Lord, the whole trip was a blur, his mind fixated on Beijing. "I was so preoccupied with where we were going secretly, and in charge of that," he remembers. On the plane, he says, he was kept busy juggling three sets of briefing books: one for people who knew nothing about the China trip; another for the few officials on the plane who knew their ultimate destination; and one "for those, like Hal Saunders, who knew that we were going to China, and had to provide cover."

The visit of Nixon's top foreign policy adviser was a gala occasion for the U.S. embassy in Islamabad, and the ambassador, Joseph Farland—the only person there who knew what Kissinger was really up to—had summoned his consuls from across the country. Archer Blood, already ousted, was not there. But one of Blood's horrified colleagues seized the chance to confront Kissinger personally.

Eric Griffel was the top development officer posted in the Dacca consulate, admired by his colleagues for leading the U.S. relief after the cyclone. Griffel, who had signed the Blood telegram, had been on a personal visit to Los Angeles, but raced around the globe to Islamabad for the opportunity to challenge Kissinger. He was spoiling for a fight. Kissinger, Griffel thought, had "a disdain for anyone on the subcontinent," and had "the Lawrence of Arabia view of the locals. If they don't ride horses, they're no good." He says, "He's impressed by Pakistani men in uniform and he doesn't like shopkeepers.[32]

"He knew of the [Dacca] consulate's position on East Pakistan," recalls Griffel, "which was quite different from his. We were allowed to state the case. He listened quite politely, and was rather charming. But he obviously had other fish to fry, since he was on the way to Peking"—something that Griffel had not known at the time. "He obviously paid no attention."

Griffel spoke up repeatedly, bluntly contradicting more compliant officials and discomfiting Kissinger whenever he could. He told Kissinger that the insurgency was local enough to survive without Indian help (the Bengalis could "run a good terror campaign"), alerted him to the Bengalis' "abiding fear and hatred of West Pakistan," and recounted a story about the "fanaticism" of a young Pakistani army officer. When Kissinger said that the United States had wanted to stay out of "another civil war in Asia," Griffel shot back that if there was a war, India would win swiftly. He warned Kissinger that the United States had limited influence, but that so long as U.S. economic aid flowed, it would be harder for the Pakistani government to realize that what they were doing was "nonsense."

Kissinger, demonstrating that the Dacca consulate's frequent warnings about genocide against the Hindus were familiar to him, asked him "why the army was driving out the Hindus." Griffel replied curtly that it was "simply an opportunity to purify East Pakistan." Farland, only a notch more pleasingly, added that the army thought that the Hindus were behind Mujib's plot. Griffel warned that more refugees might flee because of hunger, and that there were seven million Hindus still in East Pakistan who were particularly vulnerable.[33]

Griffel, who pugnaciously savors the memory of the clash, had little hope that he was going to change Kissinger's mind. "It was really something to get off my chest, maybe to soften our policy a little bit," he remembers. "I did not at that time have any hope that the policy would change." Was he worried about confronting Kissinger? "There was a risk that he'd say, 'Get this man out of there.' But A, I didn't think it would happen, and B, it wouldn't have worried me terribly." He had had enough of Dacca, he says, and the dissenters were emotional. "We were really very annoyed," he says. "We were probably not acting as coolly as we might some other time."

The other diplomats were less inclined to rough up Kissinger, but still painted a grim picture. Dennis Kux, an insightful political officer, did not think Yahya would remain in power long, doubted that there would be a political compromise, noted that the refugees—especially the Hindus—were not going back, and put the chances of war at one in three. Kissinger said that after his Delhi trip, he would give war a better chance than that. He wearily said that this was "one damn thing we didn't need."

One of the men in the room was Chuck Yeager, the test pilot who broke the sound barrier. Yeager, serving as U.S. defense representative, relished advising the awestruck officers of the Pakistan Air Force. "I was damned impressed," he wrote later. "These guys just lived and breathed flying." Yeager predicted, with uncanny accuracy, that the Pakistan army would only last about two weeks in a war against India. A militant supporter of Pakistan who had clashed with Blood, he had his own dissent with U.S. policy: there were not enough military shipments. (When war finally came, India would get its own back by pounding into oblivion Yeager's little light airplane, which was caught on the ground in a bombing raid at Islamabad's airport. Yeager would later growl, "It was the Indian way of giving Uncle Sam the finger.")[34]

KISSINGER, SETTLING IN AT THE PRESIDENT'S GUEST HOUSE IN NEARBY Rawalpindi, got a warm reception from the Pakistani government. He and top Pakistani officials commiserated about the bias of the media: it was a pleasure, he said, to see newspapers that were not reporting critically about him—not mentioning that Pakistan had a censored press.

Kissinger told his hosts that he was "really shocked by the hostility, bitterness and hawkishness of the Indians." He made no threats, exercised no leverage, and gave no proposed blueprint for a political compromise. He said that he "did not presume to advise the Pakistanis," but urged them to think hard about their dilemma. "The refugees today can be represented to the world by India as a cause of war," he said. He told a senior Pakistani official that seven million refugees was an intolerable burden for India—and the Indians thought they would win a war.[35]

Kissinger met alone with Yahya. Winston Lord was leery of him, remembering that he found the dictator "cordial, friendly, but you didn't mistake the fact that he was a tough guy. He was quite gregarious. But you had no illusions, this guy was no Thomas Jefferson." Kissinger passed along a friendly letter from Nixon praising Yahya's unsuccessful steps to get refugees to return and promising to push forward with new economic aid soon.[36]

Kissinger did not leave notes on his meeting, so all that is known is a sketch. He told the Pakistani strongman of the hawkish mood in Delhi, and coaxed him to consider appointing a new civil authority in East Pakistan to try to lure back refugees. Yahya said he would think about it.[37]

Yahya did manage to convince Kissinger that he was an idiot. "Yahya is no genius," Kissinger later told Nixon, forsaking the president's sentimental fondness for the man. Soon after his return to Washington, Kissinger said scornfully, "it is my impression that Yahya and his group would never win any prizes for high IQs or for the subtlety of their political comprehension. They are loyal, blunt soldiers, but I think they have a real intellectual problem in understanding why East Pakistan should not be part of West Pakistan." He later recalled that "fundamentally he [Yahya] was oblivious to his perils and unprepared to face necessities. He and his colleagues did not feel that India was planning war; if so, they were convinced that they would win. When I asked as tactfully as I could about the Indian advantage in numbers and equipment, Yahya and his colleagues answered with bravado about the historic superiority of Moslem fighters."[38]

At a dinner—where Kissinger started showily complaining of a stomachache—Yahya bellowed, "Everyone calls me a dictator." He went around the table asking all the guests, Pakistanis and Americans, "Am I a dictator?" Everyone tactfully said that he was not, until he came to Kissinger. "I don't know, Mr. President," replied Kissinger, "except that for a dictator you run a lousy election."[39]

TURMOIL UNDER HEAVEN

At long last the moment arrived for Kissinger to affect succumbing to a wicked case of Delhi belly, and for Yahya to pretend to gallantly tend to his ailing guest with some rest at his hill resort of Nathiagali. "Yahya was enthralled by the cops-and-robbers atmosphere of the enterprise," Kissinger later wrote. Harold Saunders was left behind in Pakistan, while his boss winged off into history. "I was the decoy," Saunders says. "I kept Henry's appointments on Friday. The press got bored. By Saturday afternoon things quieted down. I went and bought a rug. I went down to the souk." Bracing himself, Yahya handed Saunders a piece of paper with his personal telephone number to call if there was a leak back in the United States. Yahya would then phone Beijing.[40]

Although Saunders noted growing suspicions in Islamabad about Kissinger's illness, this was not for lack of trying by Yahya's government. Yahya sent out a dummy motorcade ostensibly bearing Kissinger up to Nathiagali. To cover Kissinger's forty-nine-hour absence, they planted stories in the newspapers about the comings and goings of top Pakistani officials to the indisposed American.[41]

In fact, Kissinger later recalled, he boarded a "Pakistani plane in pre-dawn obscurity." Yahya provided a PIA Boeing 707 flown by his personal pilot, who knew to beware of radio intercepts. On board, Kissinger was greeted by several top Chinese officials, who had flown in from Beijing just for the trip. The journey, he later grandly wrote, was so extraordinary that it jolted him back to childhood "when every day was a precious adventure in defining the meaning of life. That is how it was for me as the aircraft crossed the snow-capped Himalayas, thrusting toward the heavens in the roseate glow of a rising sun." (As the plane approached Chinese territory, Winston Lord was closest to the front, allowing him bragging rights as the first American official to enter China since 1949.) From a Beijing military airport, the Americans were, as Kissinger told Nixon afterward, "whisked in Chinese-built limousines, curtains drawn, through wide, clean streets, with little traffic except bicycles."[42]

Kissinger, ensconced in the graceful Diaoyutai compound, was awestruck. From Beijing, he wrote that the talks had been "the most intense, important, and far reaching of my White House experience." On his return, he would tell Nixon that he had had "the most searching, sweeping and significant discussions I have ever had in government," starting a process too large to be contained by any one metaphor: "We have laid the groundwork for you and Mao to turn a page in history." He was dazzled by Zhou Enlai's "clarity and eloquence," his "philosophic sweeps, historical analysis, tactical probing, light repartee." Kissinger ranked him with Charles de Gaulle as "the most impressive foreign statesmen I have met." In full swoon, he wrote to Nixon, "I am frank to say that this visit was a very moving experience. The historic aspects of the occasion; the warmth and dignity of the Chinese; the splendor of the Forbidden City, Chinese history and culture; the heroic stature of Chou En-lai; and the intensity and sweep of our talks combined to make an indelible impression."[43]

Kissinger never felt anything like that about India. As Winston Lord has noted, Kissinger worried about Indian militarism, but tended to give Chinese belligerence a free pass. He did no such rhapsodizing about what was, for all its flaws, the world's largest democracy. "They're never going to say they didn't like the fact that India was a democracy," says Lord, about Nixon and Kissinger. "I think they thought that it's sometimes easier to deal with dictators for decision making than with a messy democracy with all its free debate and parliament. I'm sure there's some rueful sense of, if you go with Mao and Zhou Enlai that's all you need to do. The same thing is true for Yahya, I'm sure. India is much messier."[44]

ZHOU WAS ALL ELEGANCE AND COURTESY ON THEIR FIRST DAY, BUT on the second day he threw Kissinger off balance. Kissinger was taken aback by the Chinese leadership's venomous, seething hostility to India. As Kissinger told Nixon later, he was struck by Zhou's "contempt" and "historical distrust" of India. The Chinese premier seemed obsessed with China's 1962 war against India, repeatedly blaming India as the aggressor.[45]

In one of their marathon meetings in the cavernous Great Hall of the People, Zhou icily accused India of planning aggression, and implied that India was getting clandestine U.S. support. This came as a genuine jolt to Kissinger, who was unaccustomed to being labeled a bosom friend of India. Kissinger was baffled: "Mr. Prime Minister, India doesn't get military equipment from us." Zhou retorted, "That's what I heard, but you are giving Pakistan some equipment." "Yes," said Kissinger, "but so are you."[46]

Zhou blamed the entire current crisis on India. "The so-called Government of Bangla Desh set up its headquarters in India," he said. "Isn't that subversion of the Pakistani Government?" Kissinger was confounded again: "The Prime Minister doesn't think that we are cooperating with this, does he?" Kissinger assured the Chinese premier that they were on the same page about Pakistan: "You know from President Yahya Khan the strong friendship we feel for him and his country."[47]

There was, it turned out, a government in the world that was even more strongly supportive of Yahya than the Nixon administration. This bitter Chinese animosity toward India took Kissinger's breath away—and he quickly realized that this could be useful for leverage against India. To close their historic meetings, Zhou's final words were about Pakistan: "Please tell President Yahya Khan that if India commits aggression, we will support Pakistan. You are also against that." To Kissinger, that sounded like a pledge of military support. He replied, "We will oppose that, but we cannot take military measures." "You are too far away," agreed Zhou, asking him to use the United States' "strength to persuade India." Kissinger promised to do his best. As Kissinger explained to Nixon afterward, Zhou worried "that we might not be able to do too much because we were 10,000 miles away. China, however, was much closer. Chou recalled the Chinese defeat of India in 1962 and hinted rather broadly that the same thing could happen again."[48]

For the flight back to Pakistan, the Chinese loaded up the plane with a last round of delectable Chinese food, a new English version of Mao's works, and souvenir photo albums of the trip. The stage was set for Nixon's own visit to Beijing. "You have had many barbarian invasions," Kissinger drily told the Chinese, "but I am not sure that you are prepared for this one."[49]

WITH THAT, YAHYA'S SPECIAL USEFULNESS TO THE UNITED STATES AND China expired. There were now easier ways to talk to the Chinese.

"There was quite a bit of briefing of the Chinese about what we were doing," recalls Winston Lord. "The way we communicated was through the UN mission in New York and through Paris." The White House could now send secret letters through a trusted military attaché in Paris, who would hand them over to the Chinese ambassador there. "I have come to France secretly eleven times by five different methods," Kissinger later told the Chinese ambassador in Paris. "I am going to write a detective story when I am through."[50]

But that gratitude to Yahya lingered. "Please tell President Yahya that when necessary we'll still use his channel," said Zhou. "We have a saying in China that one shouldn't break the bridge after crossing it." Kissinger courteously agreed: "We might exchange some communications through him for politeness." Zhou said that the Americans had "confidence in him, and we also respect him." Still, both sides knew that Yahya had served his purpose. "There are just some things which we don't want to say through friends, no matter how trustworthy," said Kissinger. "We'll send nothing substantive," agreed Zhou.[51]

Kissinger now argued that U.S. demonstrations of fealty to Pakistan would play well for the Chinese. Summing up for Nixon, the national security advisor wrote, "The Chinese detestation of the Indians came through loud and clear. Conversely, China's warm friendship for Pakistan as a firm and reliable friend was made very plain. The lesson that Chou may have been trying to make here was that those who stand by China and keep their word will be treated in kind." Kissinger wanted to match that. As Lord remembers, "This was the first crisis that was happening after twenty-two years where we were talking" to China. "So certainly a calculation by Nixon and Kissinger was that we had to show that we shared some of the same perspectives on this crisis, that we could be a reliable interlocutor." Saunders says, "We did not want the Chinese to see us as doing anything except supporting Pakistan."[52]

Thus even after Pakistan had outlived its utility as a back channel, it secured another continuing claim on the White House. Nixon and Kissinger's unwavering support for Pakistan's government throughout the killing would demonstrate to Mao and Zhou the reliability of the United States as an ally through thick and thin. A while after Kissinger returned from Beijing, he said, "We cannot turn on Pakistan and I think it would have disastrous consequences with China that after they gave us an airport we massacre them." (In this case, for Kissinger, "massacre" meant putting pressure on a government, not the actual massacres.) The White House did not want to let the Chinese leadership think that the United States was a fickle friend, cutting Pakistan loose for what it did to its own people. That would be a troubling prospect for Mao, whose own body counts exceeded even Yahya's, soaring into the millions.[53]

WHEN KISSINGER LANDED BACK IN ISLAMABAD, THE PAKISTANIS MAINtained the deception, driving him out of town and then back into the city, as if returning from the Nathiagali hill station. Kissinger, paying a quick thank-you call on Yahya, found him "boyishly ecstatic at having pulled off this coup"—a somewhat unfortunate phrase for a military dictator. Harold Saunders remembers his boss's excitement. "There was a feeling of real achievement," he says. "Henry was not one to show real exuberance, but he was very strongly moved." He adds, "You see the depth in which he thought about the relationship with Zhou, which translates back into how we conducted the relationship with Pakistan."[54]

At Nixon's mansion in San Clemente, California, the president waited anxiously. Nixon said that "when Henry gets back, he'll be the mystery man of the age." The president did not want to let in daylight upon magic: "the key to this whole story . . . is to create doubt and mystery. Never deny the 'stomachache' thing in Pakistan. Say it was true, but then the other things also happened." When a beaming Kissinger finally landed in San Clemente at 7 a.m. on July 13, he was greeted by the president, who took him to a celebratory breakfast. H. R. Haldeman noted, "It's pretty clear that the Chinese want it just as badly as we do." Kissinger's team was met by Alexander Haig, the deputy national security advisor, who, as Saunders recalls, "came over and warned each of us individually not to tell anyone where you'd been." He remembers, "We didn't want it to come out until Nixon announced it. Al said, 'Now I have to go explain to Secretary Rogers what happened.'"[55]

Two days later, on July 15, Nixon went on national television to astound Americans by announcing that he had accepted an invitation to visit China. People around the globe were flabbergasted at Kissinger's secret mission. From the Islamabad embassy, Joseph Farland informed Kissinger, he "had never seen so many jaws drop."[56]

Nixon gushingly told Yahya that he would "always remember with deep gratitude what you have done." Kissinger warmly wrote to Yahya, "I have so many reasons to thank you that it is difficult to know where to begin." As Nixon told the Pakistani ambassador, "it all started with my good relationship with Yahya." Years later, Nixon still deplored that the United States had not managed to be generous enough to Yahya. Haldeman wrote that he and the president "got to talking about Yahya's cooperation in this whole thing with Henry, particularly how funny it was that Yahya made such a point at the luncheon in Islamabad of making a fuss over Henry's so-called stomachache, and in effect ordering him to the mountain retreat, saying he would send his Deputy Foreign Minister to keep him company, and so on, making a big public fuss out of Henry's indisposition so it would be reported as such and give Henry the cover he was seeking."[57]

INDIRA GANDHI'S GOVERNMENT WAS LEFT SPLUTTERING. INDIANS WHO had imagined that their travails warranted Kissinger's attentions were humiliated to realize how little they really mattered. As the Indian embassy in Beijing lamented, Kissinger's move was met with "incredulity, followed by euphoria, shock or plain numbness, depending on one's political convictions." Major General Jacob-Farj-Rafael Jacob, the chief of staff of the Indian army's Eastern Command, remembers, "Kissinger arranged with Yahya Khan to meet the Chinese. After that, he felt obligated to Pakistan that they had done that." Jagat Mehta, a former Indian foreign secretary, says, "It was as much a signal to China that the U.S. can be a reliable friend, but we tended to see it as if it was a threat to India."[58]

India's diplomats in Islamabad, who had not noticed the main event as it went on under their noses, complained ineffectually that "Kissinger's dash to Peking" drew "world attention away from the Yahya regime's guilt in perpetrating one of history's biggest carnages in East Bengal." The Nixon administration had "incurred some kind of obligation to help the Yahya regime continue its rule over East Bengal by brute force, against all considerations of democracy and justice."[59]

Samuel Hoskinson, Kissinger's staffer on South Asia, had had no idea about what his boss was doing on China. This revelation, he says, explained the studied silence that his questioning of the administration's Pakistan policy had gotten from Kissinger. He suddenly realized that "the paramount thing is this approach to China. So I'm making noise out here, not getting much response one way or the other." Without the secret overtures to China, he says, Nixon and Kissinger might have taken a different stance on Pakistan. "It was a China-first policy. Everything else was secondary."

The Dacca consulate was blindsided. Archer Blood later reflected that he hoped he would have joined with the dissent telegram even if he had known. "You need to let your soldiers in the field have some idea of what the battle is for," says Scott Butcher, the junior political officer. "They could have sent a cable to Arch Blood saying, 'We hear you, but we are not able to be as assertive as we'd like.' We still would have dissented, but the decibel level would have been down a notch or two. At least we'd know it wasn't a total black hole of silence."[60]

With Nixon's own upcoming historic trip to China in the works, the president could not afford a subcontinental war in the next three or four months. "The Indians are stirring it up," he told his senior foreign policy team in mid-July at a meeting at the Western White House in San Clemente. Taking the lead, he said that it was vital that Pakistan "not be embarrassed at this point." The Indians are "a slippery, treacherous people." They "would like nothing better than to use this tragedy to destroy Pakistan." Nixon admitted that he had "a bias" here—a fact lost on nobody in the room. Kissinger, the man of the hour, agreed that the Indians seemed "bent on war. Everything they have done is an excuse for war." He called the Indians "insufferably arrogant."

Kissinger, however, now seemed to realize that it was inevitable that Pakistan would break up. Standing up to Nixon and disparaging Yahya, he said that over the long run, seventy thousand West Pakistanis could not hold down East Pakistan—finally recanting his own opinion in the fatal days of March, when it had mattered most. Nixon, still sticking up for his Pakistani friend, interrupted with the high compliment that Yahya was not a politician. Kissinger, holding his ground, replied that he had urged Yahya to deliver a generous deal on the refugees, so that India would "lose that card as an excuse for intervention." He warned that if there was a war that dragged in China, everything they had done with China "will go down the drain."[61]

On July 19, Nixon and Kissinger summoned the White House staff to the Roosevelt Room for a briefing about the president's upcoming trip to China. This momentous achievement would help to end the Vietnam War and win the Cold War itself. Nixon was somber, but Kissinger was giddy with success. "The cloak and dagger exercise in Pakistan arranging the trip was fascinating," he said. "Yahya hasn't had such fun since the last Hindu massacre!"[62]

Chapter 12

The Mukti Bahini

THIS WAS SYDNEY SCHANBERG'S FIRST WAR. THE *NEW YORK TIMES* bureau chief in Delhi would go on to cover terrifying combat in Cambodia and Vietnam, but he was green as he began reporting on Bangladesh's guerrilla warfare. "You learn a lot in a short time," he recalls grimly.

For his early education in war, he ventured out alongside the Bengali insurgents. He got permission to go to the Indian border, he says, where Indians in the Border Security Force were training the Mukti Bahini—the Liberation Army, as the Bengali rebels called themselves. The Indians said they would take him out and show him what they did. The raid still has an awful clarity for Schanberg. He went in with a squad of about ten rebels, three of whom did not even have shoes. They were creeping stealthily by a river when the insurgents spotted a unit of unsuspecting Pakistani soldiers. The Bengalis told him to crouch down and keep quiet.

"Suddenly my guys open fire," he says. "All I really remember was that they hit a man, who had been standing up. When you hit someone, the body goes up, and then comes down. That's what he did." Schanberg was overcome with horror. "I could see they were showing off for me," he recalls. "I knew they were doing it to show me that they were doing their jobs." He beseeched them, "That's enough." He finally got them to stop.[1]

He was struck by the youth of the guerrillas. "They were revved up," he says. "The ones I went in with, I don't think anyone was over twenty. They weren't child soldiers"—although there actually were some rebels as young as ten. Schanberg says, "They came from rural backgrounds, which was the most exploited of all the people in Bangladesh. They didn't speak much English. Sheikh Mujib had one hell of a following, though." He remembers how unequal the war was. The rebels could blow up bridges or power stations, but could not win their independence: "They really weren't an effective fighting group; they couldn't fight the Pakistan army."

The insurgency raged on throughout the sweltering summer. In public, Indira Gandhi dodged admitting India's supporting role. "There is a liberation struggle in Bangla Desh," she said. "What is the point of mediating with us?" When asked specifically about Indian sponsorship, the prime minister deflected: "The freedom-fighters have many resources."[2]

In fact, Gandhi's government escalated its backing for the Bengali uprising from July onward. The Indian army had direct orders to help the rebels, involving India's top generals. India secretly helped the insurgents buy weapons and ammunition. D. P. Dhar, back from his ambassadorship in Moscow and wielding great influence in the government, wrote, "All arms must be procured by us." While conceding that such clandestine arms deals were "full of profanities," he urged India to take the lead. With the help of India's foreign minister, Bengali exiles in London bought weapons in Belgium and shipped them to the guerrillas.[3]

When asked later if India had provoked the December war, Gandhi candidly said that "if you want to go way back, we helped the Mukti Bahini. So, if you consider it all as beginning with that aid and from that moment, yes—we were the ones to start it." But by sponsoring guerrilla war, India was postponing a direct clash with Pakistan. "War—open declared war—fortunately in my opinion, in the present case is not the only alternative," Dhar told his friend P. N. Haksar. "We have to use the Bengali human material and the Bengali terrain to launch a comprehensive war of liberation."[4]

ONE SMALL PART OF THIS WAR EFFORT WAS SHAHUDUL HAQUE, ARCHER Blood's young Bengali friend. "It was all very idealistic," he recalls. "I had no clue what was happening." Radicalized by the military crackdown, and emboldened by the example of friends and a cousin who had gone off to join the rebels, he packed a small rucksack and set out for the Indian border. Guided by a relative, he reached the frontier, dodging Pakistan army trucks along the way. He could hear firefights. He met up with a guerrilla guide, who walked him across to a sprawling, makeshift training camp.

The rebels would ambush small groups of Pakistani troops, try-

ing to kill them and capture their weapons. They hit Pakistani supply dumps, railways, bridges, and boats. As a makeshift report seen
by Haksar put it, "Mukti Fauz man must learn to convert night into
day and day into night." Sometimes they used animal calls to indicate
a particular battle formation. Although the insurgency's original core
of soldiers from the East Pakistan Rifles and the East Bengal Regiment could handle sophisticated weapons, the new volunteers required
lots of drilling. To fight an effective riverine campaign, the rebels—
accustomed to their homeland of marshes and waterways—needed to
be taught about camouflage and crawling, about trap pits with *punji*
stakes, how to lurk underwater while breathing through a pipe, how to
use rifles and grenades, and how to treat shock and stanch bleeding.[5]

This was a politicized insurgency, aiming to win over the peasantry.
As one senior Bangladeshi politician wrote, "I would quote Mao Tse-
tung, 'Guerillas are like fishes and the people are like water.' If water
is dried up, fish cannot survive. Already Pak army has started killing
the innocent civilians including women and children, whenever there is
any sign of guerilla activity." In pursuit of their nationalist revolution,
Bengali rebels wanted the active involvement of their whole people:
women to endure hardships, peasants to seize land, locals to torch
wooden bridges or cut telephone and electric lines. Chillingly, the guerrillas demanded unity in revolution—"Yahya Khan has not found any
quislings so far and he is not going to get any stooges from among
Bengalis"—and harshly ensured it by teaching their fighters to be "ever
vigilant of enemy agents and ruthlessly anihilate [*sic*] them. Thus, cut
away the tentacles of this monstrous octopus."[6]

THE INDIAN ARMY AND OTHER UNITS BUSILY TRAINED AND SPON-
sored the Bengali rebels, then also known as the Mukti Fouj (Liberation Brigade). Bengalis discreetly referred to the Indians as their
"Friends" or the "Friend army"—a pitiful subterfuge that could hardly
have gulled the dimmest Pakistani officer. As an Indian intelligence
agency secretly noted, "Our Army took up the training of guerillas
on an extensive scale, and established a fairly big organisation for this
purpose."[7]

India was thoroughly enmeshed in this guerrilla warfare, as shown
by a report to Gandhi's government from an Indian team touring the
border states of Assam and Tripura. (This report was fed to India's
government by the activist Jayaprakash Narayan, urging Gandhi, Haksar, and the defense minister, Jagjivan Ram, to help the cause.) Dhar

wanted to quicken India's training programs, heighten the rebels' political motivation, and instruct them in all kinds of arms and warfare. The rebel training camps, on the Indian side of the border, were either supervised by India's Border Security Force or under the direct control of the Indian army.[8]

The Border Security Force provided cover when the rebels attacked towns or Pakistan army positions. Under fire, the guerrillas relied on the force to provide support or resupply them with ammunition. (In one firefight, the Indian forces fled.) Indian officers were in direct command in many places. In some sectors, the Border Security Force even disarmed the Bengali guerrillas to prevent them from rashly attacking the Pakistan army.[9]

India's spies played a major role too. The R&AW kept up ties with Bengali forces. Another intelligence agency, the Special Service Bureau, had been set up to run underground resistance if China ever attacked India again, but was now repurposed for the Bengali insurgency. The SSB and another agency—the Directorate General of Security, which answered directly to the R&AW—ran two main training camps, specializing in advanced methods of guerrilla warfare. In strict secrecy, they drilled more than five thousand insurgents in the use of firearms and explosives, "elementary field techniques involving ambush, demolition, disruption of lines of communication etc."[10]

CAPTAIN MIHIR ROY, INDIA'S DIRECTOR OF NAVAL INTELLIGENCE, WAS glad to run India's support of the rebels' destructive naval operations. He believed in the cause. "When the genocide started," he remembers, "it was obvious that we cannot run a country with ten million refugees. We have to get them back to their homes." Roy—who would later be promoted to vice admiral—talks proudly about India's backing for the Mukti Bahini, saying it put great pressure on the Pakistani military. The Indian generals, who shared some of their Pakistani counterparts' stereotypes about Bengali cowardice, were not invariably impressed. "[General Sam] Manekshaw said, 'You Bengalis run, you don't fight.' So we had to bleed them slowly. Attack, run away, attack, run away."

Roy, who speaks Bengali, wanted to block East Pakistan's ports, so that the Pakistan army would only be able to reinforce itself by air from West Pakistan. "So we formed the frogmen," he says. "I said I wanted volunteers, those whose sisters were raped, whose mothers had been killed." He hastily trained them in India, he says, running a frogmen camp, made up mostly of well-educated university students. They were excellent swimmers and knew the terrain. "If we wanted to attack Chittagong, I took people who lived in Chittagong.

"Surprise was the most important thing," he explains. "We knew the first attack must be a major attack. We shall choose the time. It should be a moonless night. We infiltrated people into these places. They are Bengalis, so it's no problem infiltrating. At first we gave them equipment, but then you get found out." He says he had some two hundred frogmen striking all over East Pakistan.

Richard Nixon angrily said that the Indians "are blowing up the damn boats and everything." In total, Roy remembers with satisfaction, the Lloyd's of London insurance firm estimated "we had damaged one lakh"—one hundred thousand—"tons of shipping. There was no movement in the ports." Major General Jacob-Farj-Rafael Jacob, working closely with Roy, says, "We sank a lot of ships. I don't want to say more. We'll be sued by the merchant ship owners."[11]

THE REBELS, IN DESPERATION, USED CHILDREN AS SOLDIERS. THIS WAS widely known. A few months later, in a Delhi speech, Indira Gandhi would praise the bravery of "young boys of even 12 years of age who joined the Mukti Bahini." In a major speech to India's Parliament, she would say, "We hail the brave young men and boys of the Mukti Bahini for their valour and dedication."[12]

Under the eyes of the Indian army, Bengali rebels trained child soldiers as young as ten years old. Although a great many were older than that, there was no apparent effort to screen out children in camps in Assam and Tripura. Indian observers noted that "the boys are taken over by the Indian Army for special and regular military training." The Indian government planned youth training camps—including children and older youths—which started with political indoctrination and then four to six weeks of training in guerrilla warfare, after which they were sent into battle. Many of the youth camps were supervised by the Awami League and run by India's Border Security Force, with the military training given by the Indian army.[13]

The conditions in the youth camps were miserable, without adequate clean water or food. Although many young rebels arrived wearing only a *lungi,* there were no clothes or shoes provided. In one camp, Indian observers saw "young boys huddled in torrential rain without any shelter." After visiting all twenty-one youth camps in the Indian border state of Tripura, a senior Bangladeshi official "found the boys living in sub-human conditions." He claimed that some youths, rather than stay in the camps, had returned to East Pakistan—where reportedly "a good number of boys were shot at sight."[14] The Indian troops and Border Security Force men were impressed with the Bengali youths, who proved to be courageous fighters. Based in Border Security Force camps on Indian soil, the young rebels launched sorties twenty miles deep into East Pakistan. At one such camp, these Indian observers saw that a "unit of 32–40 boys, hardly 10–12 years old, was getting training in the use of hand-grenades." Two of "these boys" had infiltrated into East Pakistan, where they lobbed two hand grenades at the Pakistan army. This often meant their death. As a senior Bangladeshi politician wrote with horror, these child soldiers were being used as little more than cannon fodder: "boys trained in guerilla warfare are sent deep into the occupied zone in groups of 5 to 10 with one or two handgrenades and one or two conventional and obsolete weapons. In such circumstances, most of them cannot but fall helpless prey to the enemy."[15]

"SOMEONE HAS TO COME TO THEIR AID"

Indira Gandhi's government had at first harbored some hope that the Bengali insurgents might be able to triumph over Pakistan by themselves. She later said with a slight smile, "I was certain the revolution would succeed."[16]

By July, the Mukti Bahini claimed to have killed as many as fifteen thousand Pakistani troops, with demoralized soldiers fearing to leave their camps after dusk. The Indian mission in Islamabad noted with satisfaction that intensifying attacks had inflicted heavy casualties on the Pakistan army, disrupted transportation and the power supply, and eroded the morale of Yahya's military government. Yahya, aiming to prove that everything in East Pakistan was normal, had hoped to visit Dacca in late July, but was forced to call off the trip because of the Mukti Bahini menace. Gandhi declared publicly, "History has shown that such battles for freedom may have a setback but they are always won."[17]

But the real situation was grim. Gandhi's government worried that the Bangladeshi exile government was botching the war. Haksar wished that the Awami Leaguers would show more vision, openness, and organizational acumen. After scrutinizing plans for the insurgency, Haksar told Gandhi that they needed better and more broad-based political leadership: "the youth cannot be trained, enthused, made to accept self-annihilation unless they know they have behind them men of calibre, of integrity, of great dedication and idealism." One Bengali rebel officer complained that "no one in the Bangladesh cabinet knows anything about war." He disgustedly pointed out that Awami League politicians were seeking "absurd things like (a) vertical take-off and land (VTOL) interceptal plane; (b) Surface to air missiles (SAM); (c) Lasser beams."[18]

The Indian and Bengali military and political leaders squabbled openly. Haksar did not disguise his annoyance at the Bengali nationalists, while one Indian minister warned that "the minds of our friends are already beginning to get estranged from us." Jayaprakash Narayan, the Indian activist, warned Gandhi of "the danger of Big Brother behaviour on our part with the Bangladesh Ministers and Mukti Fauj. Superiority complex is not one of the lesser virtues of our officers." He added, "The American behaviour record in South Vietnam should be a lesson for us—do you remember the *Ugly American?*"[19]

Both Indian and Bengali leaders knew that the outgunned rebels were in serious military trouble—with the obvious implication that Indian troops would have to become more directly involved in the fight. The faltering insurgency increased the pressure on Gandhi and the Indian military to move. The rebels were badly outnumbered; many, bearing only knives and hand grenades, were reluctant to attack Pakistan army units. Even the better-armed insurgents were outmatched by Pakistan's artillery and air force. Without their own heavy artillery or antitank guns, the rebels had to retreat in the face of the superior firepower of the Pakistan army, asking the Indian army for support—and not getting enough. Narayan argued that there was no chance that ragtag guerrillas could succeed against well-trained divisions: "Someone has to come to their aid."[20]

The guerrillas, often fighting with weapons captured from Pakistan, desperately wanted more arms and ammunition from India. The rebel officers pleaded for heavy artillery, antiaircraft rounds, and antitank grenades. They needed everything: rifles, mortars, walkie-talkies, field telephone sets, maps, pocket money (to avoid temptations to corruption), medical kits, binoculars. But India seemed worried about the embarrassment that would inevitably follow when Indian weapons were captured during the fighting.[21]

For their part, Bengali rebels chafed at Indian supervision. In a devastating Bangladeshi assessment of the war, a top Awami League leader, Mijanur Rahman Choudhury, lambasted the performance of the Indian army. Choudhury, who would later go on to become prime minister of Bangladesh, wrote that "never was such a heroic force neglected so much as the Mukti Fouz."

Even with the Indian army in charge, the Bangladeshi exile government wanted more training camps and arms. The rebels, going up against Pakistani armor, got only ten rounds of ammunition a day—not enough "for amateurish hunters in the jungles." Officers waited for days to get ammunition for a raid. Senior officers lacked weapons, and everyone was short on rations, uniforms, Pakistani cash (necessary on missions inside East Pakistan), tents, soap, cigarettes, and shoes. "My heart ached when I saw our freedom fighters have to move bare-footed and in tattered clothes," Choudhury wrote. "I have seen Sector Commanders have to roam like beggars to procure medicine from various sources for their ailing men."

He bitterly complained, "We were assured that the 'Friends' promised to look after the basic necessities of our men, but the bare truth is that our men never get what they require." Choudhury, chafing at the insurgents' "absolute dependence" on the "Friend army," wrote, "Mukti Fouz must not be left to the mercy of the 'friends' alone though their assistance is most prized."[22]

At the root of this distrust was a mismatch between Indian and Bangladeshi objectives. While India—not ready for war until November—had hesitations in its sponsorship of the rebels, the Bengalis were charging forward in a full war for national independence. Many Bengalis understandably thought that India might only want to carve out a chunk of East Pakistani territory and set up a Bangladeshi government there, rather than risk invading all of East Pakistan. Step by step, the Mukti Fouj were dragging India deeper into their war. The team of Indian observers argued that the guerrillas would fare better with "proper support and cover by the Indian Army against bombing and strafing by the Pakistani Army."[23]

By the end of May, Major General Jacob-Farj-Rafael Jacob had drawn up an Indian war plan for taking East Pakistan. Lieutenant General K. K. Singh also boldly drafted military blueprints. By July, the army was quietly moving weapons, supplies, ammunition, and spare parts to the front, to be ready when the orders came. In early August, General Sam Manekshaw and his senior officers were secretly debating their invasion options and holding detailed war games. The Special Service Bureau prepared for a major war, setting up posts along the border and carrying out "counter-sabotage and counter-espionage measures."[24]

By mid-July, India's government resolved that if Pakistan could not produce a viable political settlement to get the refugees back home, India would have to gradually move to war. As Dhar, one of the government's foremost hawks, bluntly noted, if the Bengali rebels began fighting more effectively "with guarantees of sanctuary in the neighbouring territory of our country, it is quite likely that the situation may escalate into a war between Pakistan and India. Of such a possibility we need not be unduly afraid. If war comes in this manner, well, let it come and we should not avoid it."[25]

MAO, IN HIS FAMOUS HANDBOOK FOR GUERRILLA WARFARE, WROTE, "During the progress of hostilities, guerrillas gradually develop into orthodox forces." Sure enough, many Bengalis saw that as their next phase. Choudhury wanted to turn the ragged insurgents into "an organised and regular army," capable of using artillery and antiaircraft weapons, with a small air force. He wrote, "We should finally settle with the 'Friend Govt.' as to whether they will meet our total demand."[26]

The Bangladeshi exile government sought to create a regular army division around the nucleus of the old East Bengal Regiment. In July, building on the irregulars, a rudimentary army—now called the Bangla Desh Forces—set up a unified command headquarters, reporting to a commander in chief, M. A. G. Osmani. Now operating under the command of the Bangla Desh Forces, the rebels had a battle plan that makes a revealing study in how to wage an insurgency.[27]

Osmani's staff put all guerrillas under their command. The fighters were organized into cells of seven rebels and an officer, supervised by a political adviser. They hoped to be armed with pistols, rifles, cheap submachine guns, or light machine guns, as well as a few rocket launchers to blow up gunboats, bunkers, and ammunition dumps. Dressed in coarse civilian *lungis* and *kurtas,* they blended in with the locals. (This, if anyone cared, was a violation of the Geneva Conventions, which forbade combatants from faking civilian status.) Whenever possible, the guerrillas would fight near their own homes. Their commanders wanted them to launch "a series of well-planned and vigorous (daily growing in tempo) guerilla strikes over a wide area," including the "[l]iquidation of enemy agents, informers and collaborators"—a brutal task that invited the worst kind of score settling and abuses. The insurgents now aimed to destroy not just bridges and railways, but also river ports, refineries, power stations, petroleum and oil depots, and air bases. In time, this would hopefully leave the Pakistanis "bled and incapacitated," so that the rebels could turn to "[k]nocking out the last breath . . . from the enemy." The victorious irregulars would then be transitioned "from a guerilla force to a People's Army."[28]

Such bullish planning aside, the reality was chaotic. Shahudul Haque, Archer Blood's friend, was put in charge of a platoon in a training camp in Tripura. "I was very disappointed at how scratchy it all was," he remembers, although proud of the freedom fighters. "No money, no ammunition, no equipment, only dedicated soldiers to teach us." There was nothing to eat but jackfruit, which he loathes to this day. Sleeping on bamboo platforms, the guerrillas were nearly washed away by monsoon storms. After a few weeks, he got seriously ill, bleeding in his stool. With no doctors or medicine, he could only try the home remedy of coconut water, to no avail. While some of his friends went out to place bombs in Dacca or ambush Pakistani army patrols, Haque had to be taken home. In six weeks, he says, he had lost half his weight.

Another rebel remembered that they were "scared like hell," their hands shaking uncontrollably as they tried to light explosives, doing things they had only seen in war movies. Conditions were still miserable, with the fighters in dire need of mosquito repellent, waterproof sheets against the pounding monsoon rains, and antivenom serum for snakebites. At best, they got one cake of soap a month. The troops were running out of ammunition and grenades. As a major in this new Bangladeshi army wrote, there was a "dictatorship in the army command," so that "the field commanders feel very insecure. . . . A strategical plan has never been thought of. . . . [T]he war of Liberation [is] being handled like a novice and non-professional way." He dismissed Osmani, the top commander, as "a retired Colonel from the Supply Corps who miserably failed to be an infantry soldier."[29]

As the civil war escalated, so did the feud between the Bengali rebels and the Indian army. This Bangladeshi major, who had a reputation as pro-Indian, complained of widespread resentment as he and his fellow officers came to feel that "command of the Bangladesh troops was being gradually handed over under direct control of the Indian Army." Even the use of child soldiers was mismanaged: "The boys who were returned from training were not being armed. This never happened when BSF was in direct charge."[30]

The Bangladeshi commanders, who were particularly incensed at Lieutenant General Jagjit Singh Aurora, the Indian army officer in charge of the Eastern Command, took their grievances to the Indian army and the Border Security Force. They also complained to R. N. Kao, the R&AW spymaster, that Aurora's troops were not giving the support that India had earlier pledged to the rebels, despite a top-level decision from Gandhi's government. In response, Kao alerted the prime minister herself: "Nothing has so far been done about giving guerilla training to the volunteers produced by the B[angla] D[esh] Government." He warned that there was bad blood between Osmani and Aurora, and "a lot of dissatisfaction, discontentment and misgivings in the B[angla] D[esh] Army."[31]

Kao forthrightly gave Gandhi a bleak assessment. Many rebels believed, he wrote, that "the Govt of India has adopted a go-slow policy and that no efforts are being made to increase the efficiency and speed of action of the BD Army." The insurgents claimed that the Indian army was reluctant to provide enough arms. Bangladeshi commanders resented "constant interference in the administration of the BD Army," including hiring, posting, and sacking of troops. Even when getting paid, Bengalis chafed at feeling that they were on the Indian army's payroll. A senior Bangladeshi officer requested to Kao that the Indian army should not give orders to the Bangladeshi forces that contradicted ones by the Bangladeshi commander.

Kao urged Gandhi's government to act fast to patch up relations between the Indian army's Eastern Command and the Bangladeshi nationalist forces. Two Bangladeshi officers emphatically warned that if Indian support did not improve in the crucial monsoon months, the civil war would drag on, bringing misery to the people. This would help revolutionaries to supplant the Awami League, "in which case Communist China may actively take up the cause of these leftist elements."[32]

War efforts usually look like failures from the inside. Still, for Haksar and other leaders reading these reports in Delhi, it was clear that the Mukti Bahini could bleed the Pakistan army and, with covert Indian support, do terrible damage. But it would take more direct Indian intervention to drive the Pakistan army out of Bangladesh.

THE WEST BENGAL POWDER KEG

The raging civil war sent fresh droves of refugees fleeing into India. "We cannot allow their permanent settlement in India," wrote Indira

Gandhi, "but certain needs must be met while they are here." This was a disaster for the destitute border states—above all for West Bengal.[33] The state was by far the hardest hit. In July, India hosted six and a half million refugees, over five million of them in West Bengal, which contained 419 out of the 593 refugee camps in India. Over a million and a half of the refugees had spilled outside of the camps into the rest of the state. There were hordes of refugees in Calcutta itself, with thousands dug in around the city's airport. India's intelligence services reported to Gandhi that the Naxalites—the Maoist radicals—were active in the refugee camps, trying to spark revolution.[34]

These masses inevitably strained West Bengali hospitality. Arundhati Ghose, the young Indian diplomat posted to Calcutta, remembers that "then as the refugees came in, there was a beginning of sympathy, tinged with a little bit of resentment. Schools were occupied, there was no free land, they were just everywhere." The influx heightened tensions between Hindus and Muslims. While the Indian government tried to find housing for the refugees, as well as for leaders of the exile Bangladeshi government, Ghose recalls, sometimes there were "people saying we don't want to rent out our houses to these people. So we'd say, well, we are requisitioning it."

"West Bengal today is deluged with millions of victims of Pakistan's oppression," the state's chief minister wrote in June. His shaky government collapsed late in that month, and for the rest of the crisis West Bengal was placed under central rule by Gandhi's government. The fallen chief minister wrote that the refugee crisis was a gift to communist and Naxalite revolutionaries, "ever ready to exploit human misery for their own nefarious ends," and now working "upon the dejected, desolate minds of the refugees."[35]

Gandhi's government showed its most undemocratic face. Haksar panicked at "the determined onslaught of the Naxalites and the CPM"—the Communist Party (Marxist). He dreaded a fresh vote: "For the present, elections may be ruled out since the CPM will sweep the poll." But even so, remembering more enlightened principles, he knew that there would have to be elections eventually, or a Naxalite revolution. If the situation in East Pakistan did not improve, he argued, the communists would win new recruits. "If the refugees are not able to go back, the bulk of them will sooner or later be grist to CPM propaganda, so that things can only worsen."[36]

Haksar unhappily noted that the government had to "restore law and order through a firm deployment of armed forces" in West Bengal, with "a cordoning of known trouble spots and combing of villages and certain urban blocs all over the State by the army." He predicted, "There will be no economic miracle but plenty of political repression." In florid hopelessness, he wrote that "what is being enacted in West Bengal is the unfolding of a Greek tragedy. . . . All the wrong steps and all the wrong moves are being taken in a sequence of inexorability. . . . We go ahead nonetheless, caught in a pincer of fatal historicism."

While India raged against Pakistan, here it was thwarting democracy too. Haksar was too intelligent to avoid the painful parallel to Pakistan's own—and more bloody—crackdown on its Bengalis. Indira Gandhi grew notorious for her repression of the left in West Bengal. "Arrests and suppression will not diminish the ranks of the young people," Haksar wrote. "We have seen in the past that they never do." To ward off leftist revolutionary violence in West Bengal, he urged economic development, an amnesty to empty out the jails, and allowing the Communist Party (Marxist) to come to power. If not, "The alternative would be a situation closely parallel to what has developed in East Bengal. (I am purposely not bringing in Vietnam.)" To Gandhi's government, the refugees were not just fellow human beings in desperate need of succor; they were also potential revolutionaries and subversives, whose return would leave India a safer country.[37]

A LINE NOT DRAWN

The most decent decision of the Indian government was also its most costly one. India never closed its borders to keep out the Bengali refugees, although it was tempting to do so. As Edward Kennedy said, "The government of India, as it first saw this tide of human misery begin to flow across its borders, could have cordoned off its land and refused entry. But, to its everlasting credit, India chose the way of compassion."[38]

By September, India estimated it had taken in some eight million refugees, with no end in sight. This represented as much as a tenth of the overall population of East Pakistan, by the CIA's estimation. The economic and political consequences were dire. There was a desperate need for medical facilities in Tripura and Assam, where they were short of ambulances, X-ray machines, plasma, antibiotics, oxygen, splints, and bandages. In a camp of 20,000, there was just one doctor, who was only there for three hours a day. The refugee camps stank of feces and filth. There was not enough food. Children were especially vulnerable.

To its horror, the Indian government estimated that there were 1.2 million refugees under the age of two. The results were as grim as they were inevitable: refugees—particularly children—died in droves, with mortality rates as least five times worse than among other migrant populations in India. Bad as this was, Haksar feared that in the general collapse inside East Pakistan, there might be a terrible famine, driving millions more into India.[39]

In all its border states, not just West Bengal, the Indian government increasingly feared political explosions. The fragile local economies were collapsing, with sudden inflation and unemployment, rising crime, and spikes in food prices—a devastating burden for the poor. There was simmering tension between Indian citizens and the refugees. When Bengali exiles tried to find jobs, many in the local Indian population resented it. The Indian foreign ministry accused Pakistan of intentionally "fomenting tensions between Hindus and Muslims in West Bengal, between Bengali refugees and Assamese in Assam, between tribals (mostly Christians) and Bengali refugees in Meghalaya and creating a situation of near suffocation in Tripura where the number of refugees (over 1 million) is more than two thirds of the original population of 1.5 million." In Tripura in particular, this upset a delicate balance between tribal and nontribal peoples. India's government complained that leftist radicals were hard at work "spreading their gospel in areas where the refugees have come in." And as a result of the Pakistan army's onslaught against Hindus, seven million out of over eight million refugees were Hindus.[40]

So the idea of trying to seal the borders was compelling. The Indian foreign ministry secretly wrote that if the United States would not stop the exodus of refugees, then it could not fairly "oppose any action by India to push them back across the same frontier." In private, the governor of Gujarat repeatedly urged Gandhi to close the border. "I still feel strongly that we should take effective steps to check the inflow of evacuees from East Bengal," he wrote. "I think it is high time we sealed our borders, without announcing it in so many words." He emphasized the same point to her in person.[41]

But this would be a terrible task, almost certainly requiring shooting at some of the refugees, and apprehending and tracking down many others. Indian diplomats knew their country was unlikely to push out the refugees. Gandhi rebuffed the governor's suggestion, although more on practical than moral grounds. The border was some twenty-seven hundred miles long, without much in the way of natural barriers. "I told him how difficult it is for us to seal such a long border," the prime minister noted, and pointed out that even the "Americans could not seal" off the "territory through which the Viet Cong used to come."[42]

Gandhi's government kept its frontier open, hosting refugees and sheltering rebels. "India did not prevent East Bengal refugees coming in," the Indian foreign ministry noted. Sydney Schanberg of the *New York Times* recalls, "The Indians weren't going to push them out, because they were Bengalis, and they were now in West Bengal." As so many of Gandhi's decisions, this one mixed humanitarianism with a tough stance against Pakistan. "The Government of India did not stop the refugees from East Bengal from coming into India," said a top foreign ministry official, "neither do they have any intention of stopping these refugees from returning to their country to fight for their liberty."[43]

"BUT, IS GOD ON OUR SIDE?"

As India staggered under an international problem, it might seem natural to turn to the United Nations. But the Indian government was profoundly distrustful of the UN—its bureaucracy, its refugee relief operations, the General Assembly, and above all the Security Council. "I am fully convinced about the total ineffectiveness of the UN Organisation," Swaran Singh, the Indian foreign minister, privately told a meeting of his diplomats. "They talk and talk and do nothing."[44]

Gandhi's government had long seen the United Nations as hopelessly biased against India. "The 'United Nations Organisation' reflects the 'Establishment' of this World," the Indian ambassador in Paris fatalistically wrote:

India is regarded warily in the West because she is against the concept of Imperialism and because she "invented" the "Third World." India is looked on with suspicion in the "Third World" because of her (subversive) sentiments for democracy, human rights etc; the Muslim world is wrathful because of our secularism. The Communist countries regard India as insolent and potentially dangerous because we have rejected Communism as the Prime Condition for Progress. We are, of course, on the side of God. But, is God on our side?[45]

India dreaded the Security Council, where it would soon face two hostile permanent members: the United States and mainland China, which was about to displace Taiwan there. While China monotonously inveighed that "no other country has a right to interfere under any pretext" in East Pakistan, the Indian foreign ministry was busy trying to ward off any UN actions that would "interfere with the successful operations of the Mukti Bahini." After all, the Indian ambassador to France wrote with jaundiced *tiers-mondisme,* those permanent members were all guilty of "massacres of adequate dimensions. The records of Russia and America are sufficiently impressive. Besides, America, under her greatest President, fought a bloody civil war to prevent secession of the southern States. France did not do too well in Algeria but, of course, her scope was limited. She did very much better under Napoleon in Spain. The point is that there is nothing great about the Great Powers except for their capacity for destruction."⁴⁶

Nor did India have any confidence in the General Assembly, where it found few friends. The Indian ambassador in Paris caviled that the "august body" was dominated by countries "suspicious of democracy, human rights, etc. They have had long practice at suppressing them at home." Sure enough, Pakistan did well by arguing that the UN Charter guaranteed noninterference in member states. With unconcealed contempt for the General Assembly's verbosity and pomposity, Swaran Singh irately said that "the snuffing-out of all human rights, and the reign of terror, which still continues, have shocked the conscience of mankind"—which, if true, was not in evidence in the chamber.⁴⁷

"Once an issue is taken to the United Nations," wrote the Indian ambassador in Paris, "debates and propaganda become interminable— the object being to prevent the settlement of the issue. If action is our aim, then the United Nations is to be avoided." Still, India squirmed when U Thant, the secretary-general, floated bringing the crisis to the Security Council.⁴⁸

India was even more horrified when Thant proposed that observers from the United Nations High Commission for Refugees keep an eye on both sides of India's border with East Pakistan. The Indian foreign ministry did not see how a few observers could help stop the genocide of a whole ethnic group. Haksar wrote that refugees could not be expected to return to East Pakistan to be "butchered," hoping instead for a political settlement reflecting the wishes of the people in Bangladesh.⁴⁹

Nor did India trust the UN's officials to oversee this observer mission. While appreciating the assistance of the United Nations High Commission for Refugees, India's government could not stand its chief,

Prince Sadruddin Agha Khan, who was seen as a U.S. and Pakistani stooge. He sympathized with Yahya, and privately lashed out at India for aggression, as well as the "continuous squalor" of India's refugee camps. When Sadruddin was quoted saying that things in East Pakistan had returned to normal, Gandhi's government had to fight off a parliamentary call to chastise the United Nations in its entirety, with Haksar soberly pointing out that India could not condemn all its 132 member states.[50]

Most important, these observers could expose or interfere with India's covert support of the Mukti Bahini. That was certainly the White House's hope when it supported this UN proposal. A senior Indian diplomat scornfully called this plan "only a polite, surface cover for British-American scheme, to which SADRUDDIN seems to be privy," meant to win the Pakistan army time to crush East Bengal. Haksar alerted Gandhi that "some of the big Powers, specially the United States, are very keen that U.N. should be so involved largely to prevent activities of Bangla Desh freedom fighters. We are resisting these attempts." As Haksar frankly told the prime minister, "All our diplomatic efforts are directed towards ensuring that neither the Security Council nor the U.N. High Commission for Refugees become a brake on the struggle of the people of East Bengal for their democratic rights and liberties. I am saying all this to show that the so-called 'inactivity' of the U.N. as an organisation is, in many ways, not so harmful."[51]

So India turned to the Soviet Union—its only friend on the Security Council—to scuttle these proposed UN observers. Thanks to Soviet clout, the proposal for observers quietly expired.[52]

Until the outbreak of war, the Indian government would remain deeply frustrated with the United Nations. The institution dealt primarily with crises between its member states, not inside them. So India, which argued the real cause of trouble was "the continued denial of fun[d]amental human rights," could find no satisfaction there. Singh said dismissively that "everybody will say this is the usual Indo-Pakistan controversy. People get bored."[53]

DEMOCRACY IN INDIA

It might have improved Nixon's and Kissinger's view of India if they had known just how little their counterparts in Delhi were enjoying their own democratic politics. Gandhi and Haksar were exasperated at feckless partisan politicians, uppity journalists, and obstructionist bureaucrats. They sought to entrench loyalists in key positions; they harangued rivals; they were thin-skinned about public criticism. This all might have sounded vaguely familiar in the Nixon White House. Gandhi's government was galled by caustic editorializing from India's free press, which prompted her to think of ways to undercut the media. The prime minister wearily told reporters that "there is nothing that we want to hide or we can hide in the sort of society which we have in India." Gandhi, who disliked "the Jewish press" in the West, was terribly sensitive to foreign press criticism. Sydney Schanberg, who interviewed her once for the *New York Times,* remembers, "It wasn't much of an interview. She was always wary of how she was going to be quoted." His accurate *Times* coverage of India's support for the insurgents discomfited the government, with a senior Indian diplomat wondering darkly how "well-meaning correspondents like SCHANBERG could be tackled, if at all." Schanberg says, "The interesting thing about embarrassing India is that they didn't throw you out. Unlike Pakistan. But they thought about it at times."[54]

Indian reporters recounted the insurgents' fight with vivid immediacy, but also revealed India's covert support for the guerrillas. Although D. P. Dhar was scandalized that the "prying eye" of the press had uncovered these secret operations, the foreign ministry reluctantly admitted that international reporters had also dug up plenty of similar stories, making official denials sound ridiculous.[55]

To a great many Indians, their government appeared adrift, without any sense of how to respond to the catastrophe next door. Gandhi's government seemed simply punch-drunk from press criticism. After fresh disparagement from a prominent journalist, Haksar exploded that "he should not really assume that Government of India consists of cretins who do not know what is going on."[56]

In Parliament, the brickbats came from all sides. As Haksar told Gandhi, "Parliament, public opinion, Congress Party itself, C.P.I. [Communist Party of India], C.P.M. [Communist Party (Marxist)], Jan Sang—all emotionally aroused. All demanding recognition of the Bangla Desh." In both chambers, almost all parties were explosively angry about the revelations that U.S. arms shipments were still finding their way to Pakistan.[57]

On the left, the Communist Party of India was fervently for Bangladesh. Gandhi's government looked with sour suspicion at the Communist Party (Marxist), powerful in West Bengal, which, like the CPI, wanted a swift recognition of Bangladesh. As one senior official in

Gandhi's office noted, these Indian communists might link up with their comrades in East Pakistan, and help China. More extreme leftists, this official thought, wanted to use the crisis to catalyze revolution in India itself. Meanwhile on the right, the Jana Sangh, the Hindu nationalist party, pressed for a Hindu war against Pakistan's Muslims. These cries became so vehement that Haksar urged Gandhi to rebuke the hawkish party for its emotional rhetoric.[58]

The Indian public asked tough questions. Why had Gandhi's government not foiled Yahya's military buildup in East Pakistan before the start of the slaughter? Why had India not struck soon after to rescue the Bengalis? Would Bengali leftists sweep aside the pro-Indian leadership of the Awami League? Why rely so heavily on the Mukti Bahini, since guerrilla warfare alone could neither break the back of the Pakistan army nor get the refugees back home? Why not attack Pakistan right now, while its troops were still bogged down in the fight against the Mukti Bahini and while the Pakistani economy was weak?[59]

Dhar, when he wound up his tour in Moscow and returned to wield considerable power in Delhi, was astonished to hear "open talks of war being mentioned from various forums and platforms—the lobbies of the Parliament, newspaper offices, the gossipy parlours of the idle rich, the coffee houses and the tea corners. The original faith in the wisdom and competence of the policies of the Government is slowly wearing thin and except a fatalistic belief of the common man that the Prime Minister may pull out a miracle from the magic bag, early signs of despondency are broadly visible." In Parliament, he grumbled that "they suffer from discontent which has a touch of divinity about it." Some Indians thought that Gandhi had missed her best opportunity back in March, by not attacking Pakistan immediately. The government had not explained its foreign policy properly, Dhar thought, with the result that public opinion was beginning to show panic at the prospect of as many as ten million refugees staying permanently in India, while Pakistan managed to "eliminate the remanents of the inconvenient Hindu."[60]

Outside Parliament's confines, Jayaprakash Narayan demanded action: "the Prime Minister has done nothing to stop it." She had won the nationwide vote, but was facing important elections in thirteen states, which would be called for March 1972—and she did not like to lose.[61]

Gandhi still had a large majority in the Lok Sabha and a resilient personal approval rating, and could rely on the relative powerlessness of elites and an undereducated mass public that had far more urgent concerns than foreign policy. While her electoral mandate allowed her to bide her time—following General Sam Manekshaw's advice to wait for cooler weather—she still had to respond. As Gandhi had learned in two national elections, Indian politicians lived by the ballot box, and constantly had to worry about the next vote. While public expectations were high, her popularity was always preyed on by a host of domestic problems: her antipoverty pledges, unemployment, rising prices, strikes, corruption. More than half of Indians wanted to recognize Bangladesh, which would likely mean war, while just a quarter opposed doing so—the government's stated position. Arundhati Ghose, Haksar's protégée at the foreign ministry, remembers, "Haksar-sahib would have been against going to war except for the refugees and public opinion."[62]

To make matters worse, India's fractious bureaucracy was thoroughly overwhelmed by the crisis. Haksar had many of the same complaints about his subordinate officials as Kissinger did. He preferred to rely on trustworthy cronies, installing Dhar as the principal liaison with the Bangladesh exile government.[63]

Exasperated with Indian public opinion, Dhar proposed thwarting it in the most radical way. "Can we promulgate a state of Emergency?" he asked. While admitting that Indians would recoil at the "suspension" of their "Fundamental Rights," he suggested "declaring the Emergency without, for the time being, suspending the operation of Fundamental Rights." This chillingly presaged Indira Gandhi's eventual declaration of her own Emergency in 1975—the worst rupture in India's democratic tradition.[64]

Chapter 13

"The Hell with the Damn Congress"

O N MARCH 29, DAYS AFTER THE START OF YAHYA'S ONSLAUGHT, A U.S. court-martial found William Calley Jr., a U.S. Army first lieutenant, guilty of the premeditated murder of twenty-two Vietnamese civilians at the village of My Lai. For Richard Nixon, who would free Calley from the stockade to his apartment and reduce his sentence, the firestorm over the My Lai massacre was not really about morality, but an opportunity for his critics to score political points against the Vietnam War.[1]

The My Lai trial was only the latest unbearable news from Vietnam. So the massacres in East Pakistan came at a moment when many Americans had already despaired of their government's foreign policy in Asia, above all in Vietnam. The war there was the most important problem weighing on the minds of Americans, even ahead of the economy, crowding out almost all public interest in other foreign issues.[2]

Vietnam preyed constantly on Nixon's and Kissinger's thoughts. The administration was trying to withdraw troops from Vietnam without destroying U.S. credibility abroad, while still propping up a faltering government and army in South Vietnam. Despite Nixon's talk of winding down the war, the fighting seemed not just endless, but endlessly escalating: the bombing and invasion of Cambodia in 1970, and more recently U.S. military support for the South Vietnamese army's botched offensive into Laos. At home, the spring of 1971 was a time of massive demonstrations against the Vietnam War, now drawing in sizable numbers of veterans and even some active-duty soldiers. Public support for Nixon sank to some of its lowest depths, and the White House faced a rush of congressional legislation trying to stop the war.[3]

By early 1971, Nixon had begun to fear that he might not be reelected. In January, almost three-quarters of Americans wanted Congress to bring all U.S. troops home from Vietnam. And in March—as Yahya began his atrocities—more Americans disapproved of Nixon's handling of Vietnam than approved of it, while two-thirds thought that the Nixon administration was not telling the public all that it should know about the Vietnam War.[4]

The White House's critics drew a straight line from Vietnam to Bangladesh, blasting the Nixon administration for supporting brutal dictatorships in Saigon and Islamabad alike. Democratic politicians seized on the Bengali massacres as a fresh example of Nixon's amoral foreign policy, and urged the president to exercise his substantial influence on Pakistan. Of course, unlike in more recent debates about Bosnia and Darfur, no U.S. leaders were contemplating using force to save the Bengalis. Even Edward Kennedy did not float that option. With the United States painfully trying to extricate itself from Vietnam, nobody wanted more military involvement in Asia, and certainly not anything that might drag the United States into another war. As John Kenneth Galbraith donnishly put it in an appeal for the Bengalis, "Those of us who have urged a less ambitious policy in Indochina are in a poor position to ask for American remedial action elsewhere in Asia." In an anguished letter home, a U.S. official based in Dacca wrote, "It is easy to understand why, far away, tired by Vietnam, a day at the office, hassled kids, and with very little to gain, [t]he United States, the government and its citizen, would rather prevaricate, hover, postpone, abey. It is not unreasonable, irrational, or even particularly selfish; it is only tragic."[5]

This exhausted, dispirited American mood proved a boon to the White House. Nixon's political advisers expected that Americans, soured on overseas adventures, would prove apathetic about the Bengalis, so they exaggeratedly painted Kennedy and the Democrats as calling for intervention in another civil war in Asia. At the start of the Pakistan army's crackdown, Nixon told Kissinger, "The people that bitch about Vietnam bitched about it because we intervened in what they say was a civil war. . . . Now some of those same bastards . . . want us *to* intervene in Biafra. And some of those same people want us to intervene here. Both civil wars. Real civil wars." Kissinger later said that "the very people who were accusing us of being too deeply involved in Southeast Asia are accusing us of not having had enough involvement in South Asia. The one is against the communists, the other would have been against Yahya."[6]

This was, in the end, a crushingly effective argument. Despite the extensive and heartrending press coverage, the advocacy of Kennedy and others in Congress, and some public activism, the American public never really mobilized for the Bengalis. Disillusioned and enervated from Vietnam, Americans were not about to risk another Asian quagmire.

"ONE OF THE FEW STICKS THEY COULD BEAT HIM WITH"

Ordinarily the daily sufferings of the desperately poor in South Asia did not attract much attention from the U.S. press, let alone Congress. But Yahya's onslaught was the kind of spectacular event that drew notice. With so much vivid media coverage, this human catastrophe could be explained in simple terms to constituents—and blamed on the Nixon administration.[7]

The Indian government, accustomed to dealing with its own rambunctious public and Parliament, took its case directly to the American people. Indian diplomats eagerly reported that the American press had almost universally condemned Pakistan's massacres, with even the conservative *Chicago Tribune* blasting Pakistan. There was, the Indian embassy in Washington reported, widespread outrage among American academics, journalists, and officials. Indian diplomats assiduously courted Congress, cannily working over impressionable new members of Congress, and lobbying congressional staffers.[8]

Indian officials were coolly cynical about the motives of leading Democrats. While some might be genuinely interested in South Asia, an Indian diplomat secretly wrote, it was likely that most of the important pro-Indian senators, including Hubert Humphrey and Edmund Muskie, were driven by "their opposition to the President" and because they were "Presidential hopefuls." Nixon and Kissinger could have agreed with every word. The Indian diplomat concluded, "They found that this was one of the few sticks they could beat him with."[9]

Nonetheless, the Indian government, reckoning (wrongly) that Muskie was the Democratic front-runner for the 1972 presidential election, launched a charm offensive. The Indian ambassador in Washington told him that "the Presidential crown had been inherited by those who had already been to India," and shamelessly reported that Muskie's wife, who was keen to visit India, was taking "Yoga lessons from an Indian lady."[10]

Nixon was more worried about another Democratic presidential contender: Edward Kennedy, the Massachusetts senator who fast became the loudest voice in Congress decrying the atrocities in East Pakistan. Nixon, with an obsessive fear and loathing of the Kennedys that went deeper than political calculations, wanted to wiretap the senator. The White House had good reason to worry about Kennedy, who was neck and neck with Muskie as the top choice of Democrats for their presidential nominee. In a direct race, polls put Nixon ahead of Kennedy, but the challenger had plenty of time to close in on the president, and often slammed Nixon on foreign policy, including Vietnam and China. However, if he was going to run, Kennedy needed to shake off scandal: in July 1969, he claimed he made a fatal wrong turn on the tiny island of Chappaquiddick, Massachusetts, and Mary Jo Kopechne, a young worker on Robert Kennedy's campaign, had drowned in his submerged car. He had taken ten hours to report it to the police.[11]

When the killing started in East Pakistan, Kennedy quickly got hold of some of Archer Blood's cables and began giving speeches harshly denouncing Yahya's killings, Nixon's silence, and the use of U.S. arms by Pakistan. On May 3, he told the Senate that thousands or even millions of lives were at stake, "whose destruction will burden the conscience of all mankind." He complained that Blood's reports were being suppressed, and that he was being denied access to cable traffic from the Dacca consulate.[12]

The flight of millions of refugees gave Kennedy a platform: he was chairman of the Senate's subcommittee on refugees. He highlighted the ugly fact that the bulk of the exiles were Hindus, blasted the White House for "rhetoric and tokenism and paper plans" in helping the refugees, and denounced Nixon's "continued silence, and apparent indifference, over the actions of the American supplied Pakistan army." He was so vocal that he became an overnight hero among Bengalis, while Pakistan griped that his meddling in its domestic affairs was a violation of the United Nations Charter. At the White House, Kennedy's advocacy set off all possible alarms, with Kissinger and Alexander Haig darkly suspecting that he was in cahoots with the State Department. By June, as Nixon reeled from Vietnam demonstrations, a new poll showed Kennedy tied with Nixon in a presidential heat.[13]

Other senators rallied too, including some Republicans, and almost all leading Democrats. Muskie was horrified that "American tanks, planes and guns have been used to help level unprotected cities and to kill an estimated 200,000 unarmed civilians," while Walter Mondale introduced legislation to suspend military aid to Pakistan. William Fulbright, the powerful Arkansas Democrat who chaired the Senate Foreign Relations Committee, asked the administration for the Blood telegram and other Dacca cables. When the State Department refused, Fulbright and other senators publicly excoriated the Nixon administration for downplaying the atrocities.[14]

Stymied, Fulbright instead summoned Blood—just back from Dacca and sinking into despair at his desk job at the State Department— to testify before the Senate Foreign Relations Committee on June 24. Blood, defying Nixon's policy, said that the United States should speak out against the killing, suspend economic aid to Pakistan, and pressure Yahya to make a political settlement. Although seemingly trying to be circumspect, he said that the "ongoing persecution of Hindus" suggested that some of the Pakistan army wanted "a general exodus of the Hindu minority." Yahya himself was disturbed by Blood's testimony.[15]

Kennedy had Blood testify before his own subcommittee four days later. There was a raging thunderstorm that day, with lightning bolts so intense that they jolted the senators. But while Kennedy surely wanted pyrotechnics to match, Blood was still thoroughly a Foreign Service man despite it all, and he was not about to air everything in front of the barbarian Senate. Yanked back to Washington, he had not vented his wrath in the opinion pages or on the airwaves. Nor had he resigned in protest, as several of Kissinger's staffers had angrily done over the invasion of Cambodia. Blood did not mention his dissent telegram, and while he strongly hinted that he had left Dacca in unorthodox circumstances, Kennedy did not catch on.[16]

While Blood was privately pleased that someone of Kennedy's stature was taking an interest in the Bengalis, the former consul's tone was composed and professional. Blood still harbored professional ambitions, and he had a State Department boss keeping a watchful eye on him as he testified, who would pounce if he spilled any classified information. He may well have been shaken up by his sudden downfall. Still, he was under oath, and his answers were devastating. He testified of "a continued exodus" of Bengali refugees up until the day he departed Dacca. They were fleeing from any city or village that the military had struck. Most of them were Hindus, leaving because of specific persecution. Kennedy seemed a little frustrated with Blood's measured performance, but the diplomat's work provided him the basis for his own best grandstanding. The senator dramatically ripped into the senior State Department official there about U.S. weapons, forcing him to admit that Pakistan had used F-86 Sabre jet fighters and M-24 Chaffee tanks—a fact established by Blood and his team.[17]

MEANWHILE, THE PRESS TOO KEPT UP A DRUMBEAT. REPORTERS SNUCK into East Pakistan, and the refugees in India brought with them terrible tales, which Pakistan could not censor. From Calcutta, the Indian army did what it could to encourage journalists to venture across the border into East Pakistan.[18]

Bengalis were stunned to hear that some U.S. arms were still making their way to the Pakistan army. In the midst of the army's terror, these fearful people got their news by radio. "Why are you sending the army more guns?" a Bengali bitterly asked a *Washington Post* reporter.[19]

In London, the *Sunday Times* published a detailed and gruesome story by a Pakistani journalist, Anthony Mascarenhas, with the screaming headline GENOCIDE. *Newsweek* ran a horrific cover story. Village after village had been reduced to rubble, with stinking corpses. The magazine said that a quarter of a million Bengalis had died. It told of a three-year-old child and his teenage mother, both of them refugees: "They sat on ground made muddy by the steady drizzle of the summer rains. The baby's stomach was grotesquely distended, his feet swollen, his arms no thicker than a man's finger. His mother tried to coax him to eat some rice and dried fish. Finally, the baby mouthed the food feebly, wheezed—and died."[20]

Trying to blunt the impact of these terrible stories, Pakistan allowed in some foreign correspondents. Sydney Schanberg of the *New York Times,* who had been expelled from Dacca in March, jumped at the chance. He remembers the Pakistan army's contempt for Bengalis: "Even the officers in charge of these units would say, 'You can't trust these people, they're low, they lie.'" The officers gave "no denials that they had just killed them." He recalls, "You'd see places where they had marked little wooden houses as Hindus." Survivors told him that the army would "come through yelling, 'Are there any Hindus there?' When they found out there were, they would kill them." He concludes, "It was a genocide"—perhaps even a more clear case than Cambodia.[21]

In the *New York Times,* Schanberg reported, "The Pakistani Army has painted big yellow 'H's' on the Hindu shops still standing in this town." Emphasizing the targeting of Hindus, he described "the hate and terror and fear" throughout the "conquered province." Back in Dacca at last, Schanberg found the city "half-deserted," with fresh loads of troops arriving daily from West Pakistan at the airport. Terrified merchants had taken down signs in the Bengali language and put up new ones in English, because they did not know Urdu. He wrote that foreign diplomats estimated that the army had killed at least two hundred thousand Bengalis.[22]

Soon after, Schanberg says, the Pakistani authorities kicked him out for the second time. They sent an officer he knew to tell him he had to be on a plane out the next day. The reporter was glad that nobody roughed him up. When the Pakistani tried to get him to pay for the flight, he refused. Schanberg says, "So I saved my paper a one-way ticket."

BY EARLY SUMMER, THE WHITE HOUSE BELIEVED THAT IT HAD A DAUNT-ing public opinion problem. "It was very controversial on the human rights and genocide dimension," says Winston Lord, Kissinger's special assistant. "The media, Capitol Hill, the Democrats, and some Republicans joined in." He says, "On a public basis, Nixon and Kissinger couldn't and wouldn't ignore a domestic firestorm."[23]

Nixon and Kissinger self-pityingly catalogued the foes arrayed against them. Nixon said that "the American press is the same as the Indian press, follows everything they say"; Kissinger said that "the entire liberal community" is "emotionally against Yahya"; and Nixon said that "we are fought by all the Democrats," particularly Kennedy. The Indians, Kissinger said, "are already killing us in the press and lobbying with the Congress." When the Indian ambassador mentioned U.S. public opinion, Kissinger snapped, "don't threaten us with the terrible unpopularity the US will have if it does not fall in line with your policies and view-point." Kissinger had to explain to a Chinese delegation that the New York Times and other publications did not represent the administration's policy on Pakistan. While Nixon and Kissinger agreed that they had to rebut congressional and press criticism, they needed to do so without saying anything that might offend Yahya.[24]

That was uphill work. Harold Saunders, Kissinger's senior aide for South Asia, pointed out that the administration was defending killing and the squelching of democracy. When Kissinger tried to coach the Pakistani ambassador on public relations, the ambassador complained that a World Bank team described East Pakistan as resembling "Arnheim after the Nazi blitz" and "a country after a nuclear attack." Nixon and Kissinger urged their officials to reach out to the press, with Kissinger arguing that background briefings for reporters were better than congressional testimony. "That's where it counts," agreed Nixon. "The hell with the damn Congress."[25]

ARMS AND INFLUENCE

Nixon and Kissinger never reprimanded Pakistan about its use of U.S. weaponry; left to their own devices, they would almost certainly have found a way to get substantial arms supplies flowing to Pakistan. According to a report by Congress's investigative office, at the start of the crackdown on March 25, Pakistan was owed roughly $35 million worth of U.S. munitions that had not been shipped. As Kissinger's staff noted, "Our military sales to Pakistan are of paramount psychological and practical significance to the West Pakistanis." Without the deterrent effect of U.S. military supply to Pakistan, both Nixon and Kissinger believed that India would likely attack. Kissinger later suggested that "the best way to deter war would have been to continue arms deliveries to Pakistan."[26]

But Nixon and Kissinger were boxed in by the combined pressures of Congress and public opinion, and some deft maneuvering by the State Department. The department had managed to impose an informal, temporary administrative halt on shipments; this was not meant to last, but as the American public recoiled at the atrocities, it gradually sank in for Nixon and Kissinger that lifting that suspension would be disastrous.[27]

Meanwhile, Congress redoubled its demands to cut off military supply to Pakistan after the New York Times scoop about two Pakistani freighters bearing U.S. military equipment. Frank Church, an influential Democrat on the Senate Foreign Relations Committee, fervidly asked Nixon to send the Coast Guard to intercept one freighter in U.S. waters. Kennedy accused the Nixon administration of not just "silence and indifference, but a degree of complicity, which is unconscionable." But Nixon and Kissinger flatly refused to suspend all military shipments as the State Department wanted.[28]

So the Democrats struck back, introducing measures to halt military and economic aid to Pakistan until the refugees returned home. Church stormed that "the U.S. Government is aiding and abetting a terrible massacre on the part of the West Pakistan military regime." William Proxmire, a Wisconsin senator who tenaciously gave thousands of speeches from 1967 until 1986 urging U.S. ratification of the

Genocide Convention, decried "the genocide which is occurring at this very moment." And George McGovern, who would be the antiwar Democratic candidate running against Nixon in 1972, declared, "We have not learned the lesson of Vietnam if we insist on taking sides in another Asian civil war."[29]

Nixon was still, as Kissinger noted, "very reluctant" to do anything to halt arms shipments to Pakistan. Kissinger said there was only about $4 million left in the dwindling pipeline. But they now had no choice but to lie low, as Kissinger's staff unhappily pointed out. Their only hope was to write off military aid, the better to defend continuing economic aid. The decisions on arms shipments were slipping out of Nixon's and Kissinger's hands. Yet even after the killing started, U.S. military services continued to offer new sales to Pakistan, worth over $10 million. It was not until July or August that the Pentagon instructed the military services to stop making these offers. Although the numbers vary somewhat, according to Congress's investigative office, between March 25 and the end of September, Pakistan got about $3.8 million worth of U.S. munitions.[30]

If Congress was the hammer, the State Department was the anvil. Kissinger was appalled to realize that, contrary to Nixon's instructions in June, the State Department had managed to largely cut off arms supplies to Pakistan.

Kissinger fumed when a senior State Department official told him that resuming arms deliveries would be "suicide." Kissinger asked, "Do the Pakistanis know they are under the guillotine?" He heatedly rebuked State Department staff for working around the president's specific refusal to cut off military supply to Pakistan. By the middle of August, he said, "we will have done exactly what the President did not want to do in June except for $4 million"—those last remaining shipments in the pipeline.[31]

But writing privately to Nixon, an embarrassed Kissinger had to admit how their own bureaucracy had outfoxed them. Despite Kissinger's insistence that the administration should do nothing to pressure Pakistan or undercut Nixon's "special relationship with President Yahya," the State Department's tentative early hold on arms shipments had turned out to be far more potent than expected. (Although the Pakistani military was troubled by the resulting loss of weaponry, Yahya himself was relieved to avoid the humiliations of an outright embargo or U.S. condemnation.)[32]

Still, Kissinger warned the president, Congress was indignant that they had not imposed a new total arms embargo. Reluctantly cutting his losses, Kissinger wanted to try to keep up economic aid to Pakistan, which was more important but also at risk from Congress. He explained to Nixon, "We are trying to make it so it at least the economic help can be given," but "arms itself is hopeless."[33]

Nixon was appalled: "Are we for an arms embargo in Pakistan?" Kissinger gave him the public line: "In effect we have not sent any arms after April 1 except those in depots and it's down to $3–5 million outstanding." Nixon asked what they should say about future military export licenses. "Fudge it," Kissinger replied. "No license at this time." Nixon was disgruntled: "We will evaluate it as it goes along. We will have to take the heat on this." "It's not just but I know the problem," said Kissinger understandingly. Nixon angrily said, "They are doing it for reasons of screwing us up. They want Pakistan to go down and screw us up. They want a war."[34]

Pakistan, as Kissinger's aides put it, finally saw "the congressional handwriting on the wall." Kissinger repeatedly told one of Yahya's generals that he was not trying to pressure Pakistan, but broke the bad news that military shipments were endangering economic aid. When the general tried to get hold of some fifty tons of unlicensed military supplies currently sitting in New York warehouses, about $1 million of aircraft spares, Kissinger's main concern was not getting caught in the act. He said, "Much would seem to depend on how many people know or might find out about such shipments"—a line so brazen that he later had it struck from the official notes.[35]

Kissinger told the president that the problem was that there was "no military aid to Pakistan, they are not even getting economic aid. If anything will tempt the Indians to attack, it will be the complete helplessness of Pakistan." Nixon said, "After all they have done, we just aren't going to let that happen."[36]

"SICK BASTARDS"

Kissinger, in his Situation Room meetings, ripped into India, in terms only somewhat less vehement than he used when he was alone with Nixon. He warned, "The Indians should be under no illusion that if they go to war there will be unshirted hell to pay." He doubted the sincerity of India's humanitarianism: "I have my own views on the Indian attitude toward human suffering." And he said, "My impression is that the Indians have a tendency to build to hysteria from which they won't know how to escape."[37]

But the State Department revolted at this. Pushing back, one top official highlighted Pakistan's persecution of Hindus, and criticized Kissinger for behaving as if "the only way to move the Indians is with a stick." When Kissinger said that Yahya, still trying to come up with a viable plan for the refugees, "has been pretty good about the refugees," senior State Department officials gagged.[38]

Harold Saunders, the senior White House aide, bleakly told Kissinger that the Hindu refugees would probably never return. Both in India's refugee camps and inside East Pakistan, the international relief effort had fallen short and was doing little to lighten the burden. When Congress added $100 million in aid to India, Saunders did not think it enough. Something needed to be done to reduce the Bengalis' "pervasive sense of fear." Saunders asked his boss to "delicately" use some of the United States' influence before it was too late.[39]

After four months of resisting it, Kissinger was by late July openly willing to discuss pressuring Pakistan. Congress was hyperventilating; the China channel was less of a factor; and he needed to find a way to prevent Indira Gandhi from attacking Pakistan. "Both the President and I have some money in the bank" with the Pakistanis, he said. "We might get them to do something if we know what we want them to do." He told his officials that the White House was ready to press Pakistan.[40]

But after so much killing, it was hard to see what could really make a difference. Whatever faint hopes that U.S. officials had once held that Yahya would make a political accommodation in East Pakistan, they were by now thoroughly dashed. The White House and State Department staffs were unanimous that there had been no political progress.[41]

The only prospect for avoiding war was a deal between Yahya and a popular Awami League leadership, restoring enough calm in East Pakistan that refugees could come home without fear. "It seems inevitable that any political process will end with some degree of autonomy for East Bengal," Kissinger told a Situation Room meeting on July 23, finally coming around to what many of them had been unsuccessfully telling him since before the shooting started. "The Pakistanis don't have the political imagination to do this themselves."[42]

But soon after, he was skeptical about a political bargain. India, he believed, thought that such a deal meant splitting Pakistan in two.

He wanted to urge Yahya to restore some political participation to the Bengalis, but thought that India would go to war before Yahya managed to do that. It was, he told a trusted official, better to talk to Yahya "with love rather than with brutality." When he told Nixon that the State Department was "screaming for political accommodation," the president, showing no interest in asking Yahya to deal with the Bengalis, said, "We've just got to give plenty of relief, that's all."[43]

The best chance for a breakthrough would be for Yahya to negotiate autonomy with Mujib himself, the Awami League's top leader—a bold move that would impress Bengalis and give their leadership an incentive to lay down their arms. But Kissinger insisted that Yahya would not deal with Mujib. He also ruled out pressing Yahya to work with the Awami League. He resented India's belief that the only deal that would stick would include Mujib: "The Indians have a right to want to get the refugees off their territory but they have no right to insist on any particular political formula to do so." Emboldened, the State Department recommended a tough approach to Yahya, including having Nixon send him a letter asking him to make peace with the Awami League and stop destroying Hindu villages.[44]

IN THE PRIVACY OF THE OVAL OFFICE, NIXON AND KISSINGER WERE IN despair as they waited for India to smash Yahya. Nixon, told that a desperate Yahya would probably attack India, was crushed by the prospect of Pakistan's defeat. "He will commit suicide," Nixon said. Kissinger once again compared Yahya to Abraham Lincoln, whose bust sat behind Nixon's desk: "He will fight. Just as Lincoln would have fought. To him East Pakistan is part of Pakistan."

Turning fatalistic, the president said, "Inevitably it will be a bloodbath down there." He railed against India: "We warned the Indians very strongly that if they start anything—and believe me it would be a hell of a pleasure as far as I am concerned—if we just cut off every damn bit of aid we give them, at least for whatever it's worth."[45]

Kissinger fumed at his Democratic critics, pointedly telling Robert McNamara, "We think that the orgy here—people who urged us to ignore Biafra are asking us to brutalize Pakistan." He said, "The Indians are playing an absolutely ruthless game." Nixon angrily told Kissinger, "It's just *ridiculous,* those goddamn Indians. As you know, they're just as much at fault in this, frankly, as the Pakistanis in my opinion."[46]

In a Situation Room meeting, Kissinger defended the president's man. "We're not out of gas with Yahya," he said. "Yahya will be reasonable." He preferred to be gentle with Yahya, not hectoring or squeezing him. When a State Department official suggested getting the army out of running East Pakistan, Kissinger stood up for Pakistan's sovereignty: "Why is it our business to tell the Pakistanis how to run their government?" The official said that they could give advice to a friend, at which point Kissinger exploded: "What would an enemy do to Pakistan? We are already cutting off military and economic aid to them. The President has said repeatedly that we should lean toward Pakistan, but every proposal that is made goes directly counter to these instructions."[47]

Kissinger would later recall these fights as the most profound split between the White House and the State Department in Nixon's presidency, except perhaps for Cambodia. In private, Kissinger raged, "State is driving me to tears." He ripped into their senior ranks, calling one official "an idiot" and another "a maniac" and "such a whore."[48]

NIXON AND KISSINGER WANTED RETRIBUTION AGAINST THEIR UNDERlings. They fixated on Kenneth Keating, the ambassador to India who had dared to challenge the president in the Oval Office, and was still firing off angry cables. Despite his formidable connections and credentials, the former Republican senator's job was on the line. "All things being equal, I think they would have removed Keating," says Samuel Hoskinson, Kissinger's staffer at the White House.[49]

"We've got to put some kind of a leash on Keating," Nixon told Kissinger. The president recalled with satisfaction that when he had raised this with William Rogers, the secretary of state had said that Keating was senile. Nixon later said, "Keating's a traitor."[50]

Nixon told Kissinger that they should fire him. The Indians, Nixon said, were "Awful but they are getting some assistance from Keating, of course." Kissinger agreed: "A lot of assistance; he is practically their mouthpiece." He added, "He has gone native. As I told you, I saw the Indians and listened to their complaints and Keating kept interrupting and saying but you forgot to mention this or that." (This was false: in the meetings in Delhi, Keating only spoke once, to break an awkward silence in the conversation with Indira Gandhi.)[51]

Nixon said, "I think we ought to get moving on him; he is 71 years old." "Yes," replied Kissinger, "but he would do us a lot of damage now"—the inevitable congressional outrage if their old colleague was pushed out. "We should wait until things quiet down." Nixon said, "Two or 3 months and then I think we ought to do it."[52]

Keating proved too powerful to oust, but lower-ranked officials in the Dacca consulate were not so lucky. "These guys were troublesome," remembers Hoskinson.

The president was still seething at Archer Blood. When the loyal ambassador to Pakistan, Joseph Farland—treated to an Oval Office meeting with Nixon and Kissinger as a reward for his work with Yahya on the China channel—brought up Blood, Nixon exclaimed, "He's no good." Blood, Farland said, "blew the whistle on the whole thing." Nixon asked, "He's bad, isn't he?" Farland replied, "Well he's gone. He's here in the Department now."[53]

That was not all. Nixon and Kissinger heard the full extent of the reprisals taken against the dissenters in Dacca. Brian Bell, the top United States Information Service officer in Dacca, had bravely reported and wrote some of the most devastating accounts of the bloodshed, and had signed the Blood telegram. He did not scare easily: a former foreign correspondent for the *Washington Evening Star* and the Associated Press, he had briefly played professional football for the Washington Redskins and the Detroit Lions before a knee injury ended his sports career. Farland said that Bell had been "just as tendentious in his reporting" as Blood. For that, Bell had been suitably punished: "Got rid of him." "Good," said Nixon.[54]

Next was Eric Griffel, another signatory of the Blood telegram, the rebellious development officer who had confronted Kissinger on his recent visit to Pakistan. Farland told Nixon and Kissinger, "The one remaining, who is a very critical situation, this fellow Eric Griffel, who is the head of AID, he will be out in September. I wish he were out now. I don't think you could pull him out without—" Nixon finished the thought: "Repercussions." Farland agreed: "repercussions on the Hill. And my guess is that he has been instrumental in leaking some of this information."

"Sick bastards," said Nixon. "You just keep right after it on this thing."[55]

ROCK AND ROLL

George Harrison knew the uses of celebrity. The guitarist for the Beatles, who had broken up in 1970, was a soulful, confused, and tender-hearted man, but also an unexpectedly politically savvy operator.

Over the last few years, he had grown close with Ravi Shankar, the famed Indian musician. Harrison spent six weeks in India, gulping in lessons in the sitar and spirituality; sitar music popped up in classic Beatles songs like "Norwegian Wood." Now, as the number of refugees in India soared into the millions, Shankar, a Bengali, asked Harrison for help with a benefit concert.[56]

Other musicians spoke up too, such as Joan Baez, who wrote a mournful "Song of Bangladesh." But Harrison had a practical purpose in mind—to raise some money, as he later explained, but mostly to raise awareness that Bengalis "were getting killed and wiped out, and there was a lot of countries were supporting Pakistan with armaments and stuff." Since the concert was being held in New York, there was no doubt about which country in particular Harrison and his friends had in mind.

The Concert for Bangladesh was the first rock event for humanitarian relief—the precursor for shows like Live Aid in 1985, with all the attendant sincerity, vapidity, and showy self-righteousness. Harrison and his crew threw together the event at breakneck speed, choosing August 1 because it was the only date on which Madison Square Garden, in midtown Manhattan, was available. Two shows sold out fast to more than forty thousand fans.[57]

Under the spotlights, in a cream suit with a hideous orange shirt, sporting shaggy hair and a huge scraggly beard, Harrison was a fervid countercultural figure to dumbfound the generals in Rawalpindi. With rather more adrenalized benevolence than comprehension, he ardently sang, "Bangla Desh, Bangla Desh / Such a great disaster, I don't understand / But it sure looks like a mess / I've never known such distress." Harrison had hastily assembled a scruffy all-star band from his old friends, including Ringo Starr on drums and Eric Clapton on guitar, although John Lennon and Paul McCartney never showed. Shankar and other Indian musicians played sitar to general puzzlement.

Of course, the eager young crowd came mainly for the music. But many of them knew about the horrors, and Shankar explained to the audience the misery of the Bengalis. In between freewheeling sets, the musicians showed devastating films of the refugee camps, with corpses and starving children. The *Village Voice* wrote, "How glorious—to be able to launder one's conscience by laying out a few tax-deductible dollars to hear the biggies."[58]

After a series of blazing performances, Harrison had a rare surprise. "I'd like to bring out a friend of us all," he told the startled crowd, "Mr. Bob Dylan." This, the *Village Voice* raved, was the "real cortex-snapping moment." Dylan—who had been largely in seclusion since a near-fatal motorcycle accident—appeared from the darkness, slight and unmistakable, in a jean jacket, with a guitar and a harmonica. After the pandemonium subsided, he blazed through thrillingly emotional renditions of "A Hard Rain's A-Gonna Fall" and "Blowin' in the Wind." As if aiming at Nixon, he sang passionately, "How many deaths will it take till he knows / Too many people have died?"[59]

The Indian government was delighted by this unexpected windfall, scrambling to get copies of Harrison's record. For its part, Pakistan's military regime was flummoxed by the power of rock and roll. The Pakistani authorities were humorlessly wrong-footed by Harrison and his hirsute musician friends. A Pakistani official warned all Pakistani embassies about an "Anti-Pakistan gramophone record entitled 'Bangla Desh,'" which was "sung by George Harrison, a member of the Beatles' Trio" (undercounting the Beatles by one). "It contains hostile propaganda against Pakistan." This official, considering banning the song in Pakistan, ordered all of Pakistan's embassies to somehow try to prevent its broadcast worldwide.[60]

In the Oval Office, Nixon grumpily told Kissinger, "I see now the Beatles are up raising money for it. You know, it's a funny thing the way we are in this goddamn country, is, we get involved in all these screwball causes."

Kissinger asked if the aid was going to Pakistan or India: "for whom are the Beatles raising money, for the refugees in India?" (Poignantly, both men were evidently unaware that the Beatles had broken up.) Nixon replied, "The goddamn Indians." In that case, Kissinger thought that Harrison need not have bothered: "the Indian side of it is economically in good shape. We've given them $70 million, more is coming in." (In fact, India would need more than ten times that amount to provide for a year of looking after the refugees.) The problem, he said, was Gandhi's government: "no one knows how they're using the goddamn money." "You're giving it to the government?" asked Nixon, appalled. "That's a terrible mistake." Kissinger said there was no choice: "they don't let anyone in there. They permit no foreigners into the refugee areas. No foreigners at all. Their record is outrageous."

Perhaps fearing sounding soft, Kissinger quickly denounced India's calls for a political deal between Yahya and the Bengalis, wanting to "get this goddamned lecturing on political structure stopped as much as we can. Eventually there's gonna be autonomy in East Bengal, within the next two years. But not in the next six months. And the Indians are just playing a revolting, rough game." Whatever George

Harrison's hopes of raising awareness, Nixon and Kissinger were not his audience.[61]

"THE PAKISTANIS ARE A DIFFERENT BREED"

Pressed beyond endurance, Nixon and Kissinger decided to whip the wayward State Department back into line. During a Situation Room meeting in August, the president surprised his top officials by summoning them to the Oval Office to lay down the law. Nixon said beforehand with satisfaction, "It's good for them to get a little shock now and then." Taken off guard, the officials from the State Department and other agencies anxiously trooped upstairs to the Oval Office. The president glowered at them. He insisted that his administration had to follow his policy.[62]

Nixon showed far better form in this meeting than when he was sequestered with Kissinger or H. R. Haldeman. Highlighting U.S. donations for the refugees, he for once mentioned "human suffering," and said that they must "go all out—all out—on the relief side." But then he said, "Now let me be very blunt," and ripped into Kenneth Keating: "Every Ambassador who goes to India falls in love with India." (This direct presidential attack was so far out of bounds that Kissinger and Saunders censored it out of their official record of the conversation for the State Department.) Nixon told the senior State Department officials that they "have to cool off the pro-Indians in the State Department and out in South Asia." He added that fewer Americans swooned for Pakistan, "because the Pakistanis are a different breed. The Pakistanis are straightforward—and sometimes extremely stupid. The Indians are more devious, sometimes so smart that we fall for their line."[63]

Although Nixon said he "holds no brief" for what Yahya had done, the United States could not allow India to use the refugees to launch a war to tear Pakistan apart. Starting a war that way, the president said, was what he might do if he were in New Delhi. "If there is a war, I will go on national television and ask Congress to cut off all aid to India," said Nixon. "They won't get a dime."

Pakistan got far gentler treatment. Nixon, noting his good relationship with Yahya, said that they needed to maintain some leverage there, and would only make suggestions in private. "It is not our job to determine the political future of Pakistan," he said, dismissing getting involved in a political deal. "The Pakistanis have to work out their own future." He firmly stuck up for Pakistan's sovereignty, unshaken by the bloodshed there: "We will not measure our relationship with the government in terms of what it has done in East Pakistan. By that criterion, we would cut off relations with every Communist government in the world because of the slaughter that has taken place in the Communist countries."

Kissinger, fortified with presidential authority, returned to his Lincoln analogy: asking Yahya to deal with the Awami League leaders in Calcutta was "like asking Abraham Lincoln to deal with Jefferson Davis." The United States could not participate in breaking Pakistan apart. Nixon agreed: "We can't allow India to dictate the political future of East Pakistan." Kissinger reminded them that U.S. relief was not "to squeeze Yahya to set political conditions," but "to deprive the Indians of an excuse to attack."[64]

Finally the president dismissed his underlings, who trudged back downstairs to the Situation Room. Chastened, they scrambled into line. Now, as their meeting picked up after their Oval Office reprimand, when Kissinger delivered one of his familiar exhortations to the officials in the Situation Room ("I consider it intolerable that the World Bank should be setting political conditions for the resumption of assistance" to Pakistan), the group agreed heartily.[65]

Nevertheless, Kissinger remained furious at them. He berated a Situation Room meeting for moving against the president's wishes. When a State Department official mentioned drying up the pipeline of arms shipments to Pakistan, Kissinger snapped: "That's not where we stand. *You* are trying to dry up the pipeline. You are asking them to dry up the pipeline." He fumed, "The President has ruled on this 500 times." He was sick of them going beyond their instructions: "I wonder what we would do if we were instructed to use a baseball bat—go to nuclear war?"[66]

IN AUGUST, TRYING TO MUTE THE PUBLIC UPROAR, NIXON USED A PRESS conference to issue his first official statement on the Bengali massacres. As he told Kissinger beforehand, "I want to say very, very little about this. There's gonna be questions, but I don't give a damn, I'm just gonna cut 'em off, truthfully."[67]

Thus, in a brief comment to the reporters, the president rejected the idea of halting aid to Pakistan, saying instead that the "most constructive role we can play is to continue our economic assistance to West Pakistan." Nixon did not condemn the slaughter, and instead said,

"We are not going to engage in public pressure on the Government of Pakistan. That would be totally counterproductive. These are matters that we will discuss only in private channels."[68]

But Nixon had an enduring faith in the apathy of the American people. In the Oval Office, he told Haldeman that "nobody . . . gives a shit about Europe," nor Latin America, nor Africa. "They care about the Jews in Israel because they've had a war, and India-Pakistan will make the news because there ain't much else. But you know, I don't think people are all stirred up about Pakistan. Do you?" "No," said Haldeman. "I think Teddy's trying to stir them." There had been "horrible pictures" from East Pakistan, Haldeman conceded, but "You've been seeing horrible pictures of Indians and Pakistanis all your life, I mean the beggars in Delhi and all that kind of stuff." Nixon said, "Any more than they were stirred up about Biafra. You know, Biafra stirred up a few Catholics. But you know, I think Biafra stirred people up more than Pakistan, because Pakistan they're just a bunch of brown goddamn Moslems."[69]

Chapter 14

Soviet Friends

AN INDIAN ACTIVIST, SICKENED AT "BUTCHER NIXON," TOLD ANY-one who would listen that "the butcher of Vietnam has met the butcher of Bangladesh and both butchers feel cosy in each other's company." A writer for the *Times of India* declared that Yahya was "guilty of as monstrous a crime as Hitler." The campaigner Jayaprakash Narayan bitterly declared that the United States, which had once revolted against British imperial rule, "has become a major colonial power."[1]

To increasing numbers of Indians, the United States seemed more and more like an adversary. Indian strategists recoiled at U.S. backing for dictatorships in Greece, Spain, and Portugal, as well as Pakistan, while various Indian officials scathingly equated U.S. sponsorship of cruel regimes in Vietnam and Pakistan. Although the United States had been popular among Indians before, now the fraction of Indians who held good views of the country plummeted from two-thirds to one-half.[2]

Above all, Indians seethed at the continuing flow of U.S. supplies to Pakistan. The Parliament was infuriated to discover that the U.S. Commerce Department had leased two Boeing 707s to Pakistan International Airlines, which would likely be used to fly Pakistani troops into Dacca. The facts were often distorted, with untrue and inflammatory Indian press reports that the United States was directly flying troops from West Pakistan to East Pakistan, and that U.S. arms were coming to Pakistan from Vietnam.[3]

As Henry Kissinger explained to Richard Nixon, "Our military supply policy toward Pakistan has, more than any other single issue, contributed to the sharp deterioration in Indo-US relations." It was "an emotionally charged and highly symbolic public issue," with many Indians seeing "the trickle of arms we have continued to provide" as support for Yahya's oppression of the Bengalis. Indeed, the Indian foreign ministry secretly argued that no matter the size of the arms shipments, they symbolized U.S. backing for Pakistan's military crackdown, and had a psychological impact both on the Pakistani government and the Bengalis. Even the courteous foreign minister, Swaran Singh, burned once too often by Nixon and Kissinger, thundered to Parliament that the U.S. arms supply "amounts to condonation of genocide in Bangla Desh and encouragement to the continuation of the atrocities by the military rulers of Pakistan. It also amounts to an intervention on the side of the military rulers of West Pakistan against the people of Bangla Desh."[4]

From Delhi, the U.S. ambassador, Kenneth Keating, cabled a long and alarming report about deepening anti-Americanism, with the jaunty (although wrong) subject line "There's No Place to Go but Up." The Americans could no longer rely on the old assumption that Indians were unshakably fond of their country. He got massive stacks of hostile mail, berating the United States for helping to crush democracy, arming killers, and at best being a "silent spectator to genocide." Everywhere he and his staff went, they were castigated by Indians from all ranks and classes, from a top general to an elderly servant in Punjab who was scandalized to have an American in his home. The Nixon administration was enduringly alienating not just Indira Gandhi, not just pro-Soviet officials such as P. N. Haksar and D. P. Dhar, not just leftist elites and journalists, but a whole democratic society.[5]

THE INDO-SOVIET FRIENDSHIP TREATY

Indira Gandhi decided to go on a last-ditch tour of Western capitals. Haksar, while urging the prime minister to visit the West too, exhorted her to accept an invitation from Aleksei Kosygin, the Soviet premier, to a "people's welcome" in Moscow. India's relationship with the Soviet Union was thriving, with the Indian embassy in Moscow rejoicing at the "buoyant mood" there.[6]

Despite months of lobbying by Dhar, until recently India's ambassador in Moscow, Gandhi had shown no particular hurry to sign a friendship treaty with the Soviet Union. But now she faced the prospect of war with Pakistan, while the United States seemed distinctly hostile. After Kissinger's breakthrough visit to Beijing, the United States and China could line up together against India. So in early August, Dhar raced from India back to Moscow to finalize the treaty.[7]

K. C. Pant, a minister of state for home affairs, says this was a pragmatic measure, made necessary because India was preparing to go to war. In his Moscow meetings, Dhar was rhapsodic. He denounced Pakistan's "genocide on a majority" and the United States for supporting that with arms shipments. The United States and Pakistan, he said, would be infuriated by the treaty: "Great friendships do invite big jealousies."[8]

Although today many Indians remember fondly the Soviet Union's support in their time of need, the Soviet leadership was still unenthusiastic about India's rush toward war. Throughout the crisis, Leonid Brezhnev's regime was wary of war, with no stomach for the likely outcome of a dismembered Pakistan. The Soviet Union was not about to recognize Bangladesh. Clearly referring to the Mukti Bahini rebels, Kosygin uncomfortably suggested that the Indians maintain total secrecy about what was happening at their borders. Not pledging Soviet support in the event of a war, he instead urged India to strengthen its own military. Even at this climactic moment, he reiterated the "absolute need of protecting peace," and bluntly said that war was not in India's interest. On the single most important issue, the two states were at odds.[9]

Still, on August 8, Andrei Gromyko, the Soviet foreign minister, was in Delhi, ready to sign the treaty. This was, Haksar enthusiastically told Gandhi, a historic moment with the highest importance. Admitting Indian sponsorship of the Mukti Bahini, Haksar was comfortable privately telling the Soviets about "the cost of giving support to the freedom fighters." Haksar reminded the Soviets of the cruelty of Pakistan's actions and the public pressure on India's democratic government— something that Gromyko, representing a tyrannical state with an awful human rights record, might not have altogether appreciated. Above all, Haksar was pleased to have Soviet support, offsetting the risk that, "egged on by China and general support of the United States, Pakistani Military Junta might, in fact, precipitate a conflict." Both Gandhi and Haksar fully understood that a Soviet treaty "would certainly infuriate President Nixon and also the Chinese."[10]

Gandhi—flanked by Haksar and Dhar, the two ebullient architects of this Soviet deal, as well as the pro-Soviet foreign secretary, T. N. Kaul—gave Gromyko a warm welcome to Delhi. Trying to allay Soviet anxieties about Indian belligerence, she assured him that the treaty would help bring peace. But she also told Gromyko that she felt "like an island being pressurised by the rest of Indian humanity to adopt a militant line." Haksar hoped for Soviet help to prevent a war, or to help India win one. But while the Indians were obviously fishing for some kind of permission to go to war, as far as can be gleaned from the Indian documentary record, Gromyko did not give it. He praised the Indian army as "the army of a peace-loving State," and said that nobody who favored peace could dislike the treaty.[11]

Even so, Gromyko came bearing gifts. The Soviet Union's assistance with refugee relief remained quite miserly, but he offered a limited amount of weaponry: artillery, patrol ships, military helicopters. None of it would be available in time for an imminent war. In a haunting preview of a nuclearized subcontinent, Gromyko offered tons of heavy water for "the peaceful development of atomic energy."[12]

ON AUGUST 9, SWARAN SINGH AND GROMYKO SIGNED THEIR TREATY of Peace, Friendship and Cooperation. Even as these things go, it was a distinctly gaseous document, pledging "sincere friendship, good neighbourliness and comprehensive cooperation." The most crucial point was an article declaring that if either country was attacked, the other would consult to "remove such threat" and "take appropriate effective measures to ensure peace and the security of their countries." This stopped short of an actual promise of defense, but, as the Indian embassy in Moscow proudly noted, was widely seen as a "deterrent warning to both China and Pakistan."[13]

To this day, many Indians remember the Soviet treaty as a grand occasion, with a stalwart foreign friend proving its mettle in the darkest hour. Haksar wrote that "many hopes will be aroused." Indian diplomats reported that the treaty "shocked Islamabad into a sense of reality." Major General Jacob-Farj-Rafael Jacob says, "The Russians helped us a lot. I always will appreciate it. I have a lot of time for the Russians." The Soviet Union did find ways to be helpful—warning India about the perils posed by Nixon's upcoming trip to China, swiftly backing up India's complaints about Mujib being put on trial, agreeing to have Gromyko skip a visit to Pakistan—so long as it did not mean encouraging a war. But for all the hoopla, the treaty did not overcome the major disconnect between the Brezhnev and Gandhi governments: the Soviet wish that India avoid a war with Pakistan.[14]

The Indian government basked in a moment of success. Before the Bengali crisis, Indian officials could have expected domestic complaints about such a shock to nonalignment. But now, after months of parliamentary hazing about a sluggish foreign policy, this bold move gave Gandhi's government something to boast about.

Parliament quickly ratified the treaty, and even Jayaprakash Narayan, a constant burr in Gandhi's hide, welcomed it, although not without testily adding that it was high time for the government to recognize Bangladesh. Still, some in Parliament were less enthusiastic, grumbling that the treaty would limit India's independence. The Jana Sangh was leery. One rival legislator warned of the danger that India, having driven out the British, could become a kind of Soviet colony. Another Lok Sabha member warned that Hungary and Czechoslovakia had signed similar treaties before being crushed by Soviet tanks.[15]

Gandhi's government emphasized that the treaty would bolster its policy of nonalignment—as if the magical incantation of the words could obscure the plain meaning of signing a treaty with one superpower against the other one. The Nehruvian ideal of nonalignment had imagined India standing aloof from the Cold War. But this crisis had now pulled in both the superpowers, as well as China. With the White House's opening to China and now India's Soviet treaty, the Cold War enveloped the subcontinent.[16]

"THE REFUGEES WHO FLED FROM HITLER'S TYRANNY"

Long before the Soviet treaty, Nixon had been vexed at India for its chummy relationship with the Soviet Union. Now he was livid.

He menacingly said that if he were Indian, "I would be damned concerned about having my great, good friend be a Soviet, with the Chinese sitting out there and the United States a hell of a long way off." After trying to dismissively brush off the Soviet Union's "little deal," Nixon darkly suggested that the Soviets might help unleash a war in the subcontinent.[17]

Kissinger had never been particularly interested in the messy politics of Bengali nationalism, but things had shifted to his familiar Cold War chessboard. This now looked like a contest of U.S. and Soviet client states. He later wrote, "With the treaty, Moscow threw a lighted match into a powder keg." He sharply noted that the treaty's mere existence "seriously undercut" India's "cherished" principle of nonalignment. For now, he took a relatively benign view of Soviet intentions, suggesting that the Soviets were trying to deter Pakistan and restrain

India. But Soviet backing might tempt Indians to confront Pakistan, potentially sparking a war. Showing his realpolitik genius, Kissinger later said that if the Indians "move into the Russian camp it will drive the Chinese over to us."[18]

For anyone who misremembers the Cold War as a tidy contest of democracies against dictatorships, this was topsy-turvy. Rubbing it in, the Soviet ambassador in Washington wryly informed Kissinger of the irony of seeing the Soviet Union lined up with "the pillar of democracy" while the United States lined up with the Chinese. Kissinger later retorted (paraphrasing an Austrian statesman from 1848) that the Soviets "will be surprised to learn the depths of Indian ingratitude."[19]

In fact, in Delhi, P. N. Haksar was fulsome in his gratefulness. Drafting a speech for Gandhi, he raised the temperature on the Americans: "Bangla Desh constitutes a test of the professions of peoples and governments; it is a test for the conscience of every individual who cares for human liberty and dignity." He indirectly blasted the United States: "Do the seventy-five million people of Bangla Desh have the right to live? Can a majority be tyrannised by a small minority? Is it right that this minority should continue to receive arms and political comfort from other countries?"[20]

Gandhi, more tactfully, clearly saw the need for damage control. She was not as enamored of the Soviet Union as Haksar or Dhar, and had taken some cajoling to go along with this turn from nonalignment. She did not go so far as to offer a similar friendship treaty to the United States, as Kaul suggested, but on August 7—just two days before the signing of the Soviet treaty—she finally bestirred herself to accept the Nixon administration's invitation to make a state visit to Washington. She had still not replied to two letters from Nixon, one from May, the other personally handed to her by Kissinger in Delhi in July. Presidents of the United States are accustomed to getting their mail answered a little more punctually.[21]

Kissinger later reckoned that Gandhi decided to visit because of a faintly guilty conscience. "We don't want India in the Soviet camp," he said, "even though the Indians may be driving themselves there deliberately through the creation of a phony crisis." Gandhi would later send a message to Kissinger, through his guru Nelson Rockefeller, that the treaty was merely an act of expedience. When Rockefeller slammed her for the pact, asking her why she had put all her eggs in one basket, she replied that "we won't if there's another basket."[22]

India's outreach was clumsy in other ways. In another bit of questionable etiquette, the Indian ambassador, delivering Gandhi's letter to Kissinger, invited himself over to the White House on the very day of the treaty signing. Kissinger grouchily noted the awkwardness. Warning India not to be tempted into a war because of Soviet support, he sniffed at the prospect of India as a "diplomatic appendage to the Soviet Union." The Indian ambassador hastened to blame the treaty on the leftist Haksar, and assured Kissinger that Gandhi's letter was conciliatory.[23]

Kissinger found her tone moderate and a little defensive, evidently not yet ready to write off the United States. But her letter, drawn up by Haksar, was unyielding. She saw no signs of political accommodation from Yahya. India, she wrote, was "greatly embarrassed" by the recent news of fresh U.S. arms shipments to Pakistan. Since the days of Eisenhower, she protested, U.S. weapons had been used against India, and were now being unleashed against East Pakistanis whose only sin was believing in the democracy that Yahya had promised them. And in rejecting a proposal to post United Nations observers on both sides of the India-Pakistan border—which she and Haksar knew might interfere with India's covert sponsorship of the Mukti Bahini's guerrilla war—she reached shocking rhetorical heights: "Would the League of Nations Observers have succeeded in persuading the refugees who fled from Hitler's tyranny to return even whilst the pogroms against the Jews and political opponents of Nazism continued unabated?"[24]

This was hardly the first Indian use of Nazi imagery. Countless Indian officials had accused Pakistan of genocide; Jayaprakash Narayan spoke of a "Hitlerian junta" in Islamabad; and Haksar had privately written that Pakistan's propaganda was "based, as always, on the pattern set by Gobbels." But here was the prime minister of India, in a formal letter to the president of the United States, comparing a U.S. ally to Nazi Germany.[25]

INDIRA GANDHI WAS NOW PLANNING TO ORDER AN ATTACK ON PAKI-stan, according to the diaries of K. F. Rustamji, the Border Security Force head who had done so much to support the Mukti Bahini. General Sam Manekshaw and the other service chiefs knew they had to be ready for war, but did not know what Gandhi had in mind.

On this account, in late August—not long after the signing of the Soviet treaty—she went to a military headquarters in West Bengal to meet with her service chiefs and to tour some more of the refugee camps. She asked to see a nearby Mukti Bahini training camp in West

Bengal. In the drenching rain, the prime minister scrambled into a jeep with two anxious senior Border Security Force men; she proved surprisingly nimble in leaping over a ditch along their way.

She met with the rebels being trained there, and offered them some reassurances. When she returned from her extraordinary tour, she took aside a senior Border Security Force official and asked bluntly, "At this rate when do you expect to be in Dacca?" He said never, not without the Indian army. The Border Security Force could not withstand Pakistan's armor and artillery, nor its air force. They would need the Indian army and air force to counter that. Gandhi agreed. She said that she was concerned about how to withstand a Pakistan army thrust from the west. He said that that would require ground that was dry enough for tanks to operate and some cover. She agreed.

He asked when they should expect the green signal from her. The prime minister said, "Say in the third week of November."[26]

Chapter 15

Kennedy

I N TOWN AFTER TOWN IN EAST PAKISTAN, BENGALIS COULD LIST with gratitude the U.S. senators calling for cutting off aid to Pakistan. There was one name in particular that won their admiration: Ted Kennedy.[1]

Kennedy earned his hero status with fervent speeches ripping into Pakistan's repression. Jabbing at the Nixon administration's underbelly, he said that Yahya's terror had generated more refugees in less than two hundred days than the total from the entire Vietnam War. To the administration's chagrin, Kennedy managed to get two more secret cables from the Dacca consulate leaked to him, which the senator's staff obligingly photocopied and handed out to the press.[2]

When Kennedy decided he needed to go see the situation in India and Pakistan for himself, Pakistan's ambassador in Washington sounded the alarm to Henry Kissinger. "Let him go," said Kissinger. Instead, learning that two of Kennedy's aides were planning to sneak into East Pakistan, the ambassador told Kennedy that they had not applied for visas. When they did, Pakistan turned them down flat, claiming feebly that hotels and transport were unavailable. The ambassador menacingly noted that anyone slipping into Pakistan risked being shot by the army as an enemy infiltrator.[3]

For India, Kennedy's visit was a bonanza. Indian diplomats in Washington believed that he might be Richard Nixon's strongest Democratic challenger for the presidency in 1972, and immediately sought to woo a possible future president. Thus the government smoothed Kennedy's way, drawing up a list of local memorials to John Kennedy from Punjab to Kerala, lavishing attention on the two Kennedy staffers whom Pakistan had threatened to shoot, and making sure there were crowds to greet the senator. His visit, wrote a senior Indian official, would be "mercilessly but usefully full and busy."[4]

Rather than pump Kennedy with rhetoric, the Indian government chose to simply bring him to the border states and show him around. A senior Indian diplomat instructed that the senator "should be given fullest possible view of refugee problem, enabled to see as many camps as he wishes and to meet and talk with a wide cross-section of refugees so that they may form a proper first-hand idea of the tragedy and terror perpetuated in East Bengal." The foreign ministry ordered the authorities to do everything to help, noting that Kennedy wanted to witness refugees crossing the border.[5]

The White House was scandalized. Kissinger warned that the trip would be trouble, while Nixon raged, "Now I want the State Department to know that any son of a bitch that does more than give him just the minimum is going to be fired. Is that clear?" The president fumed, "Goddamn it, I took trips abroad and nobody ever helped me." Worried about his pro-Indian ambassador in Delhi, he said, "I want Keating not to fuck around, is that clear?"[6]

Kissinger—indignant that Kennedy had had the nerve to ask Pakistan to get him a visa to visit China—knew about the denial of Pakistani visas for Kennedy's staffers, but made no objection. During Kennedy's trip, at a Situation Room meeting downstairs at the White House, the CIA director said they should "get Ted Kennedy home." Kissinger wryly replied, "I'm not sure they would agree about that upstairs."[7]

THE SPIRIT OF MASSACHUSETTS

Kennedy landed in India on August 10. He was also planning to tour East Pakistan and to visit Yahya in Islamabad, but the Pakistani government suddenly canceled his visa.[8]

His visit to India was poles apart from Kissinger's, who, a month before, had seen little more than South Block offices and a swank hotel in Delhi's leafy diplomatic enclave. Setting off from Calcutta, Kennedy spent four grueling days visiting miserable refugee camps, covering the entire Indian border from West Bengal to Tripura.

His mission was to meet refugees, and he made a point of talking primarily to exiles and relief workers, not just to Indian officials. (Despite Nixon's fears, his lowest priority was the U.S. embassy, not wanting the State Department to take control of his trip.) Although

Kennedy was trailed everywhere by a crowd of Indian and American reporters, including ABC and CBS television news crews, he kept them at arm's length, ducking questions and refusing to criticize the U.S. government while abroad.[9]

Kennedy brought along seasoned American experts on development and refugee relief. One of them was Nevin Scrimshaw, a nutrition professor at MIT who had done cutting-edge work fighting malnutrition in children in Guatemala and India. Scrimshaw had a clinical familiarity with what they saw. "Edema, profound apathy, hair loss, pallor of the hair, and so forth," he recalls. "To me, what was so devastating was the scale." It was worse than anything he had seen in his long years in the field, from Panama to Egypt. He was stunned at the size of the first camp they visited, near Calcutta, where some ten thousand refugees were sheltering. "Imagine looking out on a field, hundreds of people squatting, most of them with diarrhea," he says, still appalled by the memory at the age of ninety-four. "Imagine the people politely inviting you into their tent, and while they're talking, picking up a rag in a corner, and seeing a child that's going to be dead in a few hours."[10]

The camp reeked of human shit. There was no sanitation and little access to clean water. The Indian authorities had designated a field the size of a city block as the latrine, but colossal numbers of children and adults were stricken with diarrhea, and often could not make it. Thus the ditches of muddy water between the makeshift tents, swollen by the monsoons, were fouled with excrement. The feces mixed in with the mud and water, and slopped into the overcrowded tents where people lived and ate. Against the monsoons, the refugees had only torn, leaky tents for shelter. Hundreds of people massed around the visitors, many carrying desperately malnourished children. "This was something beyond anything Kennedy had seen or imagined," says Scrimshaw. The senator was visibly overwhelmed.[11]

Like everyone, Kennedy was drenched by the downpour (although he could guiltily change into dry clothes later). In pummeling rain, he got out ahead of the Indian soldiers assigned to protect him, plunging into the crowds with scant concern for his own safety. Scrimshaw, worried that there was nobody to shield the senator, got in front of him and used his shoulders to clear a path among hundreds of people, thinking incongruously of running interference in football. They found themselves wading in two feet of water, over unfamiliar terrain, with no idea if they were about to plummet down into a submerged hole.

Eager to talk to refugees, Kennedy wandered into any part of the camps or hospitals, often leaving his Indian and American retinue behind. After a full day of touring camps in Tripura, when everyone thought he was done for the day, at 10:30 p.m. he announced that he wanted to see another camp. After that, he visited a children's hospital, returning after midnight. He forayed as close as possible to the East Pakistan border. Kennedy watched several small flatboats crammed with refugees crossing the river into Indian territory. In camps at Barast and Kalyani, he talked to hundreds of refugees. Over and over, Kennedy heard harrowing tales of terror and flight, of days or weeks spent trudging on foot to relative safety. Scrimshaw remembers that "their houses had been shelled and they were forced to go, by the Pakistani military." Many of them were Bengali professionals, with good English, crushed by their sudden change of fortunes. "I do not know why they shot me," a fifty-five-year-old Muslim railway employee told Kennedy. "I don't belong to any political party. I was just a railway clerk."[12]

In a Tripura hospital, Kennedy saw children who had been shot through the side. As night fell, he spoke to a hospitalized woman who had been shot in the gut. In total, he and his team saw hundreds of civilians, from India and East Pakistan, who had been wounded by bullets, shrapnel, or artillery fire. Although Kennedy tended not to mention it afterward, he also got to see Mukti Bahini guerrillas who were being treated for combat gunshot wounds, Scrimshaw says. Hiking along a road north of Calcutta, Kennedy heard stories of massacre from dozens of Bengali peasant farmers—a small sample of the seven thousand refugees along the banks of the river crossing to East Pakistan. There were children dying along the road as their parents pleaded for help. Many were obviously in shock, sitting in despair by the side of the road or wandering blindly. Most of them, he realized, were Hindus.

Kennedy got a heartbreaking crash course in emergency relief. He learned fast about the difficulties of burying dead children. Scrimshaw and the local doctors—many of them Bengali refugees themselves—explained that the main threats were diarrhea and respiratory diseases, which were racing through the camps. "I was so busy interpreting what he was seeing in human terms," says Scrimshaw. Kennedy "saw those conditions and he *cared*." Soon the senator could take one look at moribund children nestled in their mothers' arms and expertly point out cases of kwashiorkor and marasmus, dire conditions of malnutrition. "There's one," he said. "There's another."

Despite the efforts of the Indians, the camps were racked with despair and gloom. "The conditions in the tents, camps, makeshift

Archer Blood, the U.S. consul general in Dacca, became a staunch dissenter against White House policy. He (*left*) was at Dacca airport with his wife, Meg Blood (*center*), and a U.S. Air Force officer (*right*) on December 18, 1970.

Henry Kissinger, the brilliant White House national security advisor, exercised great influence over the president. Nixon (*left*) and Kissinger pose in the Oval Office, February 10, 1971.

East Pakistan in 1970: a street scene in Dacca (*above*),
and a group of Bengalis in the countryside (*below*).

Richard Nixon was enduringly loyal to Pakistan's military dictator, General Agha Muhammad Yahya Khan. At this Oval Office meeting, Nixon (*right*) promises fresh arms sales to Yahya (*left*), on October 25, 1970.

Indira Gandhi, India's prime minister, took a tough line against Pakistan. Here she campaigns at the Red Fort in Delhi, March 3, 1971.

Sheikh Mujib-ur-Rahman, the Bengali nationalist leader, triumphed in Pakistan's 1970 elections. He rallies his followers at a mass meeting in Dacca, beneath a Bangladeshi flag, March 7, 1971.

On March 25, 1971, Pakistan's military government began a devastating crackdown across East Pakistan. Here Bengalis flee their burning homes in the countryside.

Kenneth Keating, the U.S. ambassador to India, confronted Nixon and Kissinger directly about genocide in East Pakistan. Here he (*center*), Nixon (*left*), and Kissinger (*right*) smile for a White House photographer, despite their tense meeting in the Oval Office, June 15, 1971.

Kissinger was preoccupied with his historic opening to China, helped by Yahya. On Kissinger's first secret visit to Beijing, he (*left*) was awed by Zhou Enlai (*right*), China's premier, on July 10–11, 1971.

Millions of refugees fled to India, often winding up in desperate
conditions in overcrowded refugee camps.

Ted Kennedy (*center in white shirt*),
one of Nixon's toughest Democratic
rivals, championed the Bengali cause.
He was shocked by the suffering
of refugees in India's border states,
including in this refugee hospital in
West Bengal, August 12, 1971.

Richard Nixon and Indira Gandhi, who despised each other, during their disastrous Washington summit, on the South Lawn of the White House, November 4, 1971.

Bengali insurgents in East Pakistan train for combat against the Pakistan army, November 22, 1971.

The war for Bangladesh: Indian infantry fighting on the eastern front, December 1971.

George H. W. Bush, the future president, made the U.S.'s case against India at the United Nations.

New York Times reporter Sydney Schanberg with Indian army officers at war, December 1971.

Defeated in Dacca, Pakistan's Lieutenant General A. A. K. Niazi (*right, seated*) surrenders to India's Lieutenant General Jagjit Singh Aurora (*left, seated*), while India's Major General Jacob-Farj-Rafael Jacob (*standing, far right*) watches, on December 16, 1971—securing the new state of Bangladesh.

shelters, were horrible," says Scrimshaw. The whole state of West Bengal seemed like a huge refugee camp, with its muddy roads jammed with endless lines for inoculations or registration cards. The youngest children and the elderly had been the first to die. Again and again, Kennedy saw little ones, under the age of five, who would obviously be dead within days or hours. He saw dead children. When Kennedy asked the director of one of the refugee camps what he most urgently needed, he replied, "a crematorium."[13]

In an infinity of suffering, the horror finally overwhelmed Kennedy when it came on the smallest scale. Scrimshaw pointed out one little boy whose eye had clouded over. He would be permanently blind. He was just one of countless children so stricken. If the boy had been given a simple injection of vitamin A just a day earlier, the blindness would have been easily preventable. Scrimshaw invited the senator to peer closely into the boy's ruined eye. Kennedy could not. He turned away.

KENNEDY SEEMED THOROUGHLY TRAUMATIZED, BUT THE TRIP HAD ITS peculiar balms too. The senator, dogged by Chappaquiddick back home, was greeted everywhere by cheering crowds and enthusiastic press coverage. Along the roads, people stood waving "Welcome Kennedy" signs or placards hailing him as a friend of India. There was so much of this that it seemed stage-managed, although even the U.S. embassy did not doubt that the sentiment was genuine. Some young men chanted that the United States should stop sending arms to Pakistan. Kenneth Keating, the U.S. ambassador, cabled, "Seldom in the memory of the embassy has any foreign visitor received a more effusive welcome."[14]

Kennedy—whose family's name was revered in India—declared that his late brother John had believed that India was the real test for the future of democracy. If the democratic experiment failed in India, President Kennedy thought, then political philosophers would conclude that democracy was only for the rich. Now the refugee crisis was testing India's democracy.[15]

Kennedy got gala hospitality from the Indian government, including being flown around the east on an Indian Air Force airplane and helicopter. When he finally arrived in Delhi at the end of his trip, the foreign ministry hosted a reception with everyone from P. N. Haksar to Jayaprakash Narayan. A modest address to some legislators swiftly metamorphosed into an impromptu joint address to both packed houses of Parliament, complete with a standing ovation. Indira Gandhi invited him to accompany her to the grand Independence Day ceremony at the Red Fort, which Kennedy ducked after Keating reminded him to keep some distance from her government.[16]

In Delhi and Calcutta, the Indian government set up secret meetings for Kennedy and his staff with the Bangladeshi exile government. He received a full dose of official Indian hawkishness while doing the rounds in Delhi, where the foreign secretary vitriolically compared Pakistan to Nazi Germany.[17]

Nevin Scrimshaw remembers, "After we went back to Delhi, we knew for sure that the Indians were going to invade what is now Bangladesh. It was just so obvious." This was starkly clear to everyone on the team, he says, including Kennedy. Scrimshaw recalls, "Their stores were running out. They weren't getting the help from the U.S. and Europe that they had expected. They would have no alternative. They had no way of feeding these people."[18]

On his last day in India, Kennedy met privately with Indira Gandhi, scion to scion. She warned that she could not hold on for long. Parliament was getting out of control; communists and Naxalites were gaining strength; there was public pressure to support the Mukti Bahini; and despite India's best efforts, the refugees were still "living in appalling conditions." When Kennedy suggested handing out a basic guide to malnutrition, with instructions on using milk, Gandhi had to explain that milk was rare stuff in those parts of India. It was, the prime minister said, hard to do anything special for the refugees and not for impoverished Indians in similar need.[19]

Kennedy, trying to avoid bashing the Nixon administration from foreign soil, wanted to duck questions from reporters. But the Indian foreign ministry, not about to miss this opportunity, nimbly sent out engraved invitations to a Kennedy press conference to the whole Delhi press corps. Prolonged silence is not a natural condition for a United States senator, and when asked—as the first question—if Pakistan was committing genocide, he immediately said yes. Pledging to do everything he could to stop U.S. military and economic aid to Pakistan, he said that Nixon's policy "baffles me." And he stuck up for democratic principles, saying that it was a "travesty" that Mujib, the Awami League leader, had been put on trial in a secret military court: "the only crime that Mujib is guilty of is winning an election."[20]

WITH THAT, KENNEDY DEPARTED FOR WASHINGTON. INDIAN AND U.S. officials alike were impressed with the seriousness of his inquiry. "The dynamic fact finding Senator has come and gone," an Indian diplomat wistfully wrote.[21]

Kennedy's public acclaim was doubly impressive considering that he had landed in India the day after the signing of the Soviet treaty. Anyone who thought that the Indian public was fundamentally anti-American should have seen the ebullient throngs cheering him. Kennedy winningly suggested that India could sign another friendship treaty with the United States. As much as the White House cursed Kennedy's trip, he stole some of the Soviet Union's thunder.[22]

Indians, acclaiming Kennedy, imagined being rid of Nixon. As if Kennedy were already president, Gandhi threw him a rare lunch in his honor, a tribute usually reserved for a head of state. At the Parliament, Atal Bihari Vajpayee—himself a future prime minister—said, "I would like to ask on behalf of many Members of Parliament when Senator Kennedy is going to become the President of the United States." Kennedy laughed. "I like this kind of question."[23]

The senator's staff, exhilarated by the crowds, had the same thought. Back in Delhi, the senator took a break from the stifling August heat with a swim at the U.S. embassy's pool. Nevin Scrimshaw remembers one of his aides looking admiringly at an exceedingly fit Kennedy on the diving board. The staffer, seemingly confident that Chappaquiddick would blow over, said that Kennedy was likely to become president.

Kennedy—about as far as one could get from Chappaquiddick but still mindful of it—was not so sure. Once, while he was being driven toward a refugee camp, his convoy turned left, and soon came to a halt by the side of the road. Scrimshaw remembers that an Indian official came back to Kennedy's car and stuck his head in through the window. Kennedy asked, "Why are we stopped?" The Indian official said, "Wrong turn." Under his breath, Kennedy muttered, "Story of my life."

"AN AMERICA THAT SUPPORTS MILITARY REPRESSION"

At the White House, Kissinger worried that "when Kennedy comes back, he will blow the roof off." He was right: the senator returned to Washington, haunted by what he had seen, to deliver a jeremiad against Nixon.[24]

He had just witnessed, he told the Beltway crowd at the National Press Club, "the most appalling tide of human misery in modern times." He unsparingly told of hearing "stories of atrocities, of slaughter, of looting and burning." He was harrowed by seeing listless infants with "skin hanging loosely in folds from their tiny bones," children with "legs and feet swollen from edema and malnutrition, limp in the arms of their mothers," and, worst of all, "the corpse of the child who died just the night before." He could not forget "the look on the face of a child paralyzed from the waist down, never to walk again; or a child quivering in fear on a mat in a small tent still in shock from seeing his parents, his brothers and his sisters executed before his eyes; or the anxiety of a 10-year-old girl out foraging for something to cover the body of her baby brother who had died of cholera a few moments before our arrival."

This, he thundered, was what the United States was supporting. This misery should "particularly distress Americans, since it is our military hardware—our guns and tanks and aircraft delivered over a decade—which are contributing substantially to the suffering." While Nixon and Kissinger often privately spoke of not getting involved, Kennedy pointed out that the United States was actually intervening on Yahya's side. "You may say that we have no business getting involved—that we cannot police the world," he said. "That may be true. But the cold fact is that we already are involved in East Bengal. Our guns are involved. Our money—invested over two decades of economic assistance—is involved." He blasted the White House's fixation on maintaining leverage over Yahya: "Why, if we have the leverage to influence the government of Pakistan, must our great nation assist in this shabby and shameful enterprise?"

While the Nixon administration prided itself on giving India more aid than the rest of the world combined, that "pride is quickly dispelled by the vastly greater burden now being carried single-handedly by the government and people of India." Measured against the reality of the refugee camps, "we realize how little the outside world is really doing, and how paltry the American contribution really is." And Kennedy wanted to treat the causes, not the results—to "stop the use of U.S. arms which produce the refugees and civilian victims that we then must help support in India."

Hitting the Nixon administration where it hurt, he turned to Vietnam. There, the United States was trying to prop up a purported democracy, while "in East Bengal—less than 2000 miles from Saigon—we ignore the results of a free election only to help a group of generals suppress an electoral mandate and, in the process, to subvert all the principles for which we have sacrificed so much for so long." He declared, "Unfortunately, the face of America today in South Asia is not much different from its image over the past years in Southeast Asia. It is the image of an America that supports military repression and fuels military violence. It is the image of an America comfortably consorting with an authoritarian regime."

Radicalized by his personal experience, he demanded that Nixon himself pressure Yahya, and end all arms shipments and economic aid to "a regime that continues to violate the most basic principles of humanity. We must demonstrate to the generals of West Pakistan and to the peoples of the world that the United States has a deep and abiding revulsion of the monumental slaughter that has ravaged East Bengal." And then he concluded with famous verses from the great Bengali poet Rabindranath Tagore: "Where the mind is without fear and the head is held high; / Where knowledge is free; / Where the world has not been broken up into fragments by narrow domestic walls . . . / Into that heaven of freedom, my Father, let my country awake."[25]

Kennedy's words were greeted rapturously in India. The *Indian Express* wrote, "Like his brothers John and Robert before him, Edward Kennedy now symbolises the essential liberalism and deep humanity of the American spirit." His speech was "the voice of America's conscience."[26]

THE WHITE HOUSE, STUNG, PUT OUT WORD THAT THEY AGREED THERE should be more humanitarian aid. Nixon and Kissinger, worried about Kennedy, decided to ask Congress for more money—about $100 million of relief aid for East Pakistan for the coming fiscal year, and $150 million for the refugees in India. On top of $89 million already promised, this was a substantial sum, but dwarfed by the actual amounts that the White House estimated were really needed annually: as much as $315 million for East Pakistan, and $830 million for eight million refugees in India. (Even so, George Shultz, the White House budget director, who would be Ronald Reagan's secretary of state, objected that it was "a hell of a lot of money," and had to be steamrollered by Kissinger.)[27]

Harold Saunders, Kissinger's senior aide, called Kennedy "demagogic" and bristled at his "innuendo that the Administration is largely responsible for Yahya's policies." The United States, Saunders wrote, should concentrate on the refugees, not on winning autonomy for East Pakistan. Kennedy met with Kissinger on September 8, but there is no

White House record of what they said, except that Kennedy claimed that Mujib was probably already dead, which Kissinger found ridiculous.[28]

Saunders was put to work drafting speeches for Republican lawmakers, lambasting Kennedy as hysterical and one-sided. The White House's surrogates included Gerald Ford, the next president, then a Michigan representative, and Bob Dole, the Kansas senator who would be the Republican presidential nominee in 1996. Dole hit every White House note: lauding Nixon's refugee relief, downplaying arms shipments, and declaring that "in the name of morality" the United States must "not cut ourselves off from the only people—the Government of Pakistan—that have the capacity to change the immediate situation."[29]

From Delhi, Keating, the U.S. ambassador who had lost his Senate seat to Robert Kennedy, warned the White House that Ted Kennedy "will probably continue hammering at this until November 1972"—the presidential election. "He and his staff evidently think they have an issue." Nixon said that American public opinion had been duped by India: "there's a huge public relations campaign here. Many of our friends in the other party, and including, I must say, some of the nuts in our own party, soft-heads, have jumped on, have completely bought the Indian line. And India has a very great propaganda line."[30]

All this time, Kennedy was relentless. On the Senate floor, he repeatedly accused Pakistan of genocide. Since his trip, he said, "nearly a million more East Bengalis has found it necessary to flee inhuman conditions and truly genocidal acts of their government."[31]

Kennedy produced a bombshell for the White House. The Nixon administration had publicly declared that arms shipments to Pakistan had ended, and specifically promised that nothing had moved from Pentagon stocks. Not so. Kennedy had congressional investigators check up on whether U.S. weaponry was still getting to Pakistan; they found that more than $2 million worth of equipment had been released from the Pentagon's depots.[32]

The worst offender was the U.S. Air Force, which kept on supplying some $2.4 million worth of spares—70 percent of that lethal—to the Pakistan Air Force until July. The U.S. Army and Navy had also been releasing lethal spare parts for Pakistan. Harold Saunders and Samuel Hoskinson, Kissinger's aides, were chagrined, and skeptical that this had happened by accident. They wrote to Kissinger, "What this boils down to is that, allowing for shipment delays and expiration of licenses, probably at least half of the $3.8 million shipped to Pakistan should never have been released under the ground rules which we imposed on ourselves and made public."[33]

By now, Kennedy did not believe a word that the Nixon administration said about Pakistan. He introduced a bill authorizing $250 million to alleviate the ongoing lethal deprivation among the refugees in India, calling the administration's current efforts "inexcusably slow" and far outstripped by the actual needs. India counted 1.76 million refugee children under eight years old, and Kennedy's team—joined with Nevin Scrimshaw and a leading development expert at Princeton—calculated that at least three hundred thousand children desperately needed treatment for malnutrition. At first, they estimated, hundreds of children had been dying of hunger each day, then thousands, and now forty-three hundred daily. Without emergency relief, they argued, as many as two hundred thousand young children would have perished by the end of the year.[34]

Kennedy declared, "Nothing is more clear, or easily documented, than the systematic campaign of terror—and its genocidal consequences—launched by the Pakistan army on the night of March 25th." Invoking the Holocaust, he said that Hindus were being specifically targeted, "systematically slaughtered, and, in some places, painted with yellow patches marked 'H.'" He blamed the Nixon administration for much of this: "America's heavy support of Islamabad is nothing short of complicity in the human and political tragedy of East Bengal."[35]

Chapter 16

"We Really Slobbered over the Old Witch"

NOBODY IN THE WHITE HOUSE COULD CLAIM NOT TO KNOW THE horrors that had been visited upon East Pakistan. In a major report in September, the CIA guessed that "some 200,000 or more residents of the area have been killed," and noted that East Pakistan had experienced "one of the largest and most rapid population transfers in modern times."

The CIA had a blunt explanation for this "incredible" migration: "many if not most of the Hindus fled for fear of their lives." Lieutenant General Tikka Khan, Yahya's military governor, evidently thought he could quickly frighten the Bengalis into submission. The Pakistan army, the CIA noted, seemed to have singled out Hindus as targets.

Although the CIA refrained from crying genocide, it did insist this was an ethnic campaign, with 80 percent—or possibly even 90 percent— of the refugees being Hindus. So far, out of eight million refugees, over six million were Hindus, and many more might follow—ending perhaps only when East Pakistan had no more Hindus left. Yahya's recent efforts to curtail such attacks had been of little use in a "virulent atmosphere" where loyalists got used to persecuting the Hindu minority.[1]

Even with Archer Blood gone, the Dacca consulate warned of persecution of Hindus in the Mymensingh area, and fresh waves of Hindus fleeing to India. The locals said there was widespread rape. This was confirmed by Sydney Schanberg of the *New York Times,* who, interviewing refugees in India, found that almost all of them were Hindus, who said that they were still specifically hounded by the Pakistan army. Schanberg remembers, "There were stories about rape by the Pakistani army, and those were true. Story after story. It was quite clear this had really happened."[2]

As a respected U.S. development official reported, the Pakistan army, driven by anti-Hindu ideology, was clearing East Pakistan of Hindus. Even Major General Rao Farman Ali Khan, the senior military man ruling East Pakistan, agreed with this U.S. official's assessment that some 80 percent of the Hindus had left East Pakistan. Off the record, the Pakistani general admitted there were roughly six million refugees, and that another million and a half would eventually flee into India— roughly the number of Hindus still remaining in East Pakistan.[3]

UNLEASHING CHINA

Richard Nixon and Henry Kissinger stood firm behind Pakistan, with China on their minds. "I think we ought to toughen a little bit on Peking," Kissinger said. "If we screw Pakistan too outrageously, that really—and if a war starts there, that really could blow up everything." Nixon feared what a war might do for his upcoming visit to China.[4]

Kissinger warned the president that if China decided that the United States was trying to "split off part of Pakistan in the name of self-determination," that would be an unacceptable precedent "for Taiwan and Tibet in Peking's eyes." Nixon now wanted "a big, big, big package" of humanitarian aid to Pakistan, which, Kissinger thought, would impress China. Despite the mounting pressure from Congress, Nixon wanted China to know that he was still "standing firm for Pakistan."[5]

Thus on August 16, Kissinger went to the Chinese embassy in Paris to hammer out details for Nixon's upcoming trip to Beijing. Wanting to showcase how resolute the United States was as an ally of Pakistan, he instead found himself forced to explain the unwelcome restraints imposed on him by the U.S. democratic system, especially the press and Congress. "Indian propaganda is extremely skillful and the opposition party in the United States, which controls Congress, is completely on the side of Indian propaganda," Kissinger said. "They make it next to impossible to continue military supplies to Pakistan." He asked China, which was unconstrained by the hassles of a democratic legislature, to pick up the slack. Still, he said, the United States would not let India "humiliate Pakistan." While asking China to encourage Pakistan to defuse India's pretext for war by getting refugees home, Kissinger pledged to make no public statements that could embarrass Pakistan's government.[6]

238 ~ The Blood Telegram

Using a line from Samuel Hoskinson, Kissinger once wrote to Nixon, "Above all we must avoid being forced to choose between our policy toward the government of 700 million Chinese and over 600 million Indians and Bengalis." But the White House had clearly chosen. Later, when facing criticism that they were sacrificing India for China, Nixon was incredulous. "Sacrificing India? For Christ sakes." Kissinger said, "Mr. President, there's nothing to sacrifice in India to begin with." "Of course!" agreed Nixon.[7]

NIXON AND KISSINGER ASKED NOT JUST WHAT THEY COULD DO FOR China, but what China could do for them. Their new relationship with the People's Republic brought radical possibilities. They could, they realized, use China to scare India out of attacking Pakistan—or, if war came, they could ask China to move its troops to the Indian border, threatening to embroil India in a war against two enemies at once.

This was a daring realpolitik gambit that Metternich himself might have admired. There was an undeniable strategic logic to it—despite the sheer audacity of one democracy trying to pit the People's Liberation Army against another democracy. This would be a complete turnaround from the U.S. position the last time that China went to war against India, back in 1962, when the United States had helped India defend itself.[8]

It would also be a total reversal of Kissinger's own solemn promises to India, made during his Delhi trip in July. Indian officials—whose direst fear was a Chinese attack—had been hugely relieved to get Kissinger's pledges that the United States would back India against any Chinese saber rattling. In Delhi, Kissinger had personally made such assurances to Indira Gandhi herself, as well as to P. N. Haksar, the foreign minister, and the defense minister.[9]

Kissinger gradually warmed up to the idea of unleashing China against India. Impressed by his firsthand experience of Zhou Enlai's hatred for India, he believed that the only way that India could lose a war with Pakistan would be if China joined in. The chairman of the Joint Chiefs of Staff later suggested that India might have to divert five or six divisions to the Chinese border, offsetting India's massive advantage over Pakistan in ground troops. At the White House, Alexander Haig, Kissinger's deputy, planted the seed in Nixon's mind: "Despite all their brave talk about being able to defend against the Chinese and fighting on two fronts against Pakistan, the Indians are still haunted by the 1962 humiliation."[10]

In August, Kissinger warily told Nixon, "At this stage in our China exercise we would be presented with excruciating choices if the Chinese were to attack India following an outbreak of Indo-Pakistani hostilities." Kissinger's aides, without his unfettered ingenuity, were worrying about preventing China from attacking India, rather than *encouraging* it. The State Department, which wanted to offer military help to India if China invaded, was even more in the dark. So was the American public, almost half of whom would have wanted to send supplies or U.S. troops to help India if it was attacked by communists.[11]

India's officials had more paranoid imaginations. They wondered what mysterious understandings Kissinger might have secured behind closed doors in Beijing. Back in January, the R&AW had secretly concluded that China was unlikely to fight for Pakistan, but expected that if India and Pakistan went to war, China would "adopt a threatening posture on the Sino-Indian border and even stage some border incidents and clashes." This, the R&AW warned, could pin down Indian troops, keeping them away from fighting against Pakistan. In June, Swaran Singh, the foreign minister, had feared that China might fight India directly or "keep us busy on the borders and tie up our troops."[12]

So as war loomed, and China spat rhetorical venom at India, India's ambassador raced to Kissinger to find out where he really stood. Kissinger, retreating somewhat from his Delhi promises, now said that if it was not clear who started a war, with Indian irregulars in East Pakistan and Pakistani troops in Kashmir, the United States would not help India against China. But Kissinger declared that, as the ambassador wrote, "in a 1962 type of situation"—meaning a Chinese invasion of India— the United States would give "all-out help to India against China." If Pakistan attacked India, with China supporting Pakistan, then the United States "would not hesitate to help us with arms, although not with men."[13]

Even after this latest, more conditional pledge, the prospect churned in Kissinger's prodigious mind. By September, he decided that China's enduring animosity toward India would make a useful tool of U.S. diplomacy. Despite his own promises to India, he concluded that the United States should avoid making any pledges to defend India against a Chinese attack, since it might encourage India. A few days later, he told the Indian ambassador that if India attacked Pakistan, and that sparked a Chinese invasion of India, it would be hard for the United States to help out.[14]

Kissinger had much more in mind than that. If China provoked border incidents, he directed the White House and State Department staffs to leave India to its fate. In the Oval Office, Kissinger told Nixon that "if we could shock the Indians we would—because our judgment is that Chinese almost certainly come in at the Indians." The president immediately took to the idea. Nixon told Josip Broz Tito of Yugoslavia that China could not stand by if Pakistan was attacked.[15]

India put its trust in two frozen friends: the Soviet Union and the coming winter. First, China might be scared off by India's treaty with the Soviet Union. Even with war on the horizon, the Indian embassy in Beijing reported a surprising lack of public Chinese support for Pakistan. Major General Jacob-Farj-Rafael Jacob, chief of staff of the Indian army's Eastern Command, remembers India's friendship treaty with the Soviet Union as crucial, allowing his troops to operate.[16]

Second, ever since Indira Gandhi had first asked her generals for war plans, they had told her to wait for winter, when the Chinese army would be blocked off from an attack by the coming of the winter snows in the Himalayas. General Jacob says that his superior, General Sam Manekshaw, the chief of the army staff, was obsessed with Chinese intervention. Vice Admiral Mihir Roy, the director of India's naval intelligence, remembers, "That's why Manekshaw said, let's choose the season—where there's no rain, and there's snow on the Himalayas."[17]

IN LATE OCTOBER, KISSINGER MADE A SECOND CHINA TRIP, HAMMERing out the details for Nixon's own upcoming visit to Beijing. The city was in the grip of one of the worst leadership crises in the People's Republic's history. China was under martial law, with armed troops on the streets and banners at the airport denouncing "running dog" capitalists. But meeting with Zhou Enlai in the cavernous Great Hall of the People, communists and capitalists at least found common ground in excoriating India.[18]

"We from the East and you from the West have the most to do with East Pakistan," said Zhou. Kissinger reminded the Chinese premier that the United States, despite pro-Indian sentiment in Congress, was the only major Western country that had not condemned Pakistan.

Kissinger said that he had read a book that Zhou had recommended, which blamed the 1962 China-India war on Indian provocations and aggression, and said that the White House believed that now "the Indians are applying essentially the same tactics." "That is their tradition," said Zhou. India, said Kissinger, saw the crisis as a chance to smash Pakistan once and for all. Zhou agreed: India "doesn't believe in the existence of Pakistan." Kissinger said, "We believe she will try to destroy East Pakistan." He expected India either to attack in the next month or so, or to provoke Pakistan into attacking. Kissinger reassured Zhou that the United States was completely opposed to Indian military strikes against Pakistan.[19]

After returning to Washington, Kissinger privately confided that he preferred working with China to India. Fresh back from the violent convulsions of China in the Cultural Revolution, he still showed no fondness for Indian democracy. Nixon said, "Recently with the Chinese—goddamn it, they talk directly." Kissinger heartily agreed: "Oh, the Chinese are a joy to deal with compared to the Indians."[20]

"THE BRITISH GOT OUT TOO SOON"

In Washington, the first brisk nights of autumn brought more than a seasonal chill. Kissinger's staff at the White House—using the exact same reasoning as the generals in India—warned that mid-October or November could bring an Indian attack: "The monsoon will be over, and weather in the Himalayas will begin to close in for the winter and make Chinese operations more difficult."[21]

The Indian and Pakistani militaries were bracing for confrontation, with the Indian army in intensive training for war, while the Mukti Bahini intensified its guerrilla campaign. The rebels, more aggressive and popular than ever, fought with automatic weapons and mortars, and had grown skilled at blowing up bridges and mining ships. There was so much Pakistani artillery fire at the rebels that the Indian army was, as General Jacob later wrote, "officially authorized to occupy areas across the border to prevent Pakistani shelling." The Bangladeshi exile government claimed it now had some seventy thousand trained guerrillas, and privately admitted that the Indian army was giving indispensable artillery cover for the rebels.[22]

Pakistan complained of frequent shellings from Indian troops along the border, in defense of the Bengali insurgents. The Indian mission in Islamabad reported anxiously that "a 'Crush India' campaign was whipped up all over West Pakistan to produce an artificial war hysteria." Yahya, indignant at India's "open hostility and her unabashed support and aid to the miscreants"—his word of choice still for rebellious Bengalis—asked Nixon to dissuade India.[23]

Although the United States warned both sides not to attack, Kissinger and his team gloomily wondered not whether war would break out, but how. The CIA director warned that Pakistan might launch a preemptive attack on India in a few weeks.[24]

If war came, the Nixon administration knew that Pakistan would be trounced. The U.S. military and the State Department's intelligence bureau agreed that Pakistan's defeat was all but inevitable. The chairman of the Joint Chiefs of Staff said that the crucial factor in a war would be India's four-to-one advantage in ground forces. He expected a short war, before both sides began running out of supplies in four to six weeks: "India will prevail because of superior numbers."[25]

THERE WAS ONE REMAINING BIG DIPLOMATIC CHANCE FOR THE UNITED States to try to prevent a war: Indira Gandhi's upcoming trip to Washington. Kissinger's aides told him that this summit, which had been put on Nixon's schedule several months earlier, would be their last opportunity to restrain India.[26]

Nixon dreaded her visit. When Kissinger reminded him that it was on the calendar, he exhaled softly, "Jesus Christ." The president suspiciously wanted to be sure that "she doesn't come in here and, frankly, pull our legs."[27]

Kissinger stoked Nixon's wrath. Declaring that the Indians were plotting to undo Partition by destroying Pakistan, he pushed a stereotype of wily Indian brains: "In their convoluted minds they really believe they can give Pakistan a powerful blow from which it won't recover and solve everything at once." Nixon told the British foreign secretary, "All that I can say is that I think the British got out too soon."[28]

In the Oval Office, Nixon angrily told Kissinger, "Well, you let the Indians know, they get their aid stopped when a war starts. They aren't going to get any aid." This was a tough threat. The United States gave substantial foreign aid to India—about $220 million annually, plus another $220 million worth of development loans and $65 million in food aid. The State Department recoiled at slashing off India's aid, noting the "hyper-sensitivity" of Indians to a "neo-colonialist attitude," and warning of a "new level of bitterness" that would long poison U.S.-Indian relations. Still, Kissinger told a Situation Room meeting, Nixon was deadly serious about cutting off aid if India went to war: "The Indians must understand that we mean it. The President has said so. In fact, he tells me every day."[29]

INDIA NEEDED TO FIRM UP SOVIET SUPPORT FOR A LIKELY WAR. SO Indira Gandhi flew to Moscow, arriving in the coolness of late September. She was treated to all the baleful tributes that the Soviet state could muster: a military honor guard at the airport, crowds unspontaneously lining the wide avenues, forced accolades in the captive press, lodgings at the Kremlin. She met with Soviet political and military leaders, driving home to them the social pressures that the refugees were causing in India. Afterward, the Soviets unleashed at full blast an official press campaign against Pakistan, led by *Pravda,* demanding Mujib's release and an end to the killings. Still, Gandhi could not quite extract a Soviet endorsement for a war. The Soviets emphasized the benefits of peace, arguing that war would only make India's burdens worse. (While Gandhi was finishing up her rounds at the Kremlin, Nixon and Kissinger were in the Oval Office working over Andrei Gromyko, the Soviet foreign minister, who said that the Soviet Union had urged her not to pick a fight and that she had assured them should would not.) The best that Gandhi could get was a firm statement from Aleksei Kosygin, the Soviet premier, calling for a swift political settlement in Pakistan and for the safe return of the refugees.[30]

Next, on October 24, Gandhi and Haksar, her top adviser, left India for a three-week Western tour, including stops in Britain, France, and West Germany, with the most important encounter scheduled for Washington on November 4 and 5. As on her prior trips, Gandhi got rhetorical commiseration and some humanitarian aid, but not much more. "Mrs. Gandhi went around the world saying this is a genocide," says Admiral Mihir Roy of the Indian navy. "Nobody listened to her." Austria was promoting Kurt Waldheim, a diplomat hiding his Nazi past, to be the next secretary-general of the United Nations, and did not want to alienate the Muslim bloc. Britain still wanted to keep Pakistan united. Gandhi fared better in France, where President Georges Pompidou's government urged the release of Mujib, the Awami League leader, and saw the independence of Bangladesh as inevitable. (André Malraux, the French novelist who had fought in the Spanish Civil War, now offered to take up arms again with the Mukti Bahini—which might have been somewhat more intimidating to Yahya if he had not been seventy years old.) In West Germany, Chancellor Willy Brandt proved refreshingly sympathetic. But none of this would be enough to prevent war.[31]

In London, exhausted, Gandhi seemed close to breaking under the strain. She once again went clangingly heavy on the Nazi analogies, saying that she could no more meet with Yahya before the woes of the Bengali refugees were addressed than Winston Churchill could have met with Adolf Hitler before the end of World War II. When a British reporter challenged her for supporting the Mukti Bahini, for a moment she seemed almost overcome with anger and grief, blinking rapidly and swallowing hard, but not faltering. Did quieting the situation "mean we support the genocide?" she shot back with steely fury. "When Hitler was on the rampage, why didn't you tell us keep quiet and let's have peace in Germany and let the Jews die, or let Belgium die, let France die?"[32]

SMALL STEPS

As Gandhi's visit approached, Nixon and Kissinger tried to explain what they had done to forestall war. It was not a long list, but there were some achievements on it. In the late summer and fall, the Nixon administration had belatedly begun to urge Yahya to take some actions to undermine India's reasons for war. Even the most bullish U.S. officials admitted that these steps only made a grim situation somewhat less grim, while Archer Blood later said they were "all too little and too late, as well as completely out of touch with reality in East Pakistan." All of them were aimed at mitigating the consequences of worse decisions already made by Pakistani leaders.[33]

One success came when Joseph Farland, the U.S. ambassador to Pakistan, urged Yahya to get rid of the reviled Lieutenant General Tikka Khan and appoint a civilian Bengali as governor of East Pakistan. At first Yahya refused, but later he installed a docile Bengali loyalist as governor and replaced the hated Tikka Khan with the somewhat less hated Lieutenant General A. A. K. Niazi, the army commander in East Pakistan. For once, even the Indian government was briefly impressed, but Haksar soon realized that the new regime—still under the military's thumb—was little different from before. The ostensible civilian administration was, a senior Pakistani official later admitted, "merely to hoodwink public opinion at home and abroad. . . . Real decisions in all important matters still lay with the army." As the Pakistan army's Major General Rao Farman Ali—who worked alongside General Niazi—testified later, "The army virtually continued to control civil administration."[34]

Also, the Nixon administration privately rebuked Yahya when he launched a secret treason trial for Mujib, which seemed likely to end with his execution—and an explosion of Indian outrage, possibly even war. This trial iced any hopes of political reconciliation with the Bengali nationalists. Even Nixon was shocked. "Why did he do that?" he asked Kissinger in amazement. "He's a big, honorable, stupid man," said Kissinger. "For Christ sakes," Nixon said. "He can't do that." The next day, Kissinger was more sanguine: "If he won't shoot him, I think we can survive it." Nixon asked, "Did you tell him not to shoot him?" Kissinger replied, "I tell you, the Pakistanis are fine people"—at this point the tape is bleeped out on purported grounds of national security.[35]

So the U.S. ambassador to Pakistan told Yahya "as a friend" that while this was "completely an internal affair," executing Mujib could "definitely and decisively affect virtually all assistance, humanitarian and economic." Yahya, while still putting Mujib on trial and leaving the political process in tatters, replied that "you can stop worrying because I am not going to execute the man even though he is a traitor."[36]

Perhaps the most important U.S. pressure came in response to reports that East Pakistan, ravaged by civil war, was facing a risk of famine. The Dacca consulate warned of a latter-day version of the notorious 1943 Bengal famine, in which millions of people died, while the CIA director said, "This will make Biafra look like a cocktail party." Kissinger worried that famine would produce a new wave of refugees, which could be the last straw for India. Thus he explained to Nixon that by preventing a famine they would deprive India of an excuse to attack Pakistan.[37]

This time, the United States acted. "I'm talking about Pakistan," Kissinger told a Situation Room meeting. "We're not so eager to do things for India. We want to make a demonstrable case to prevent famine in East Pakistan." Nixon wrote to Yahya, asking him to make a big effort to avert famine, thereby undercutting India's "pretext for interference."[38]

But the White House staff, the State Department, and the U.S. embassy in Islamabad all warned that Pakistan's government—indifferent, incompetent, and corrupt—was botching the relief efforts. The Nixon administration urged Yahya to get his act together, and donated almost $10 million in food and $3 million in vessels for inland transportation, helping United Nations relief workers. The United States single-handedly spent slightly more for Pakistan than the rest of the world. The distribution of food, Kissinger told Nixon, "has been handicapped again by the goddamned Indians because most of the roads run parallel to the frontier and very close to the frontier, and they're blowing them up every night." Nixon said, "Let's stay out of this damn thing and just help refugees, stay out of the fight between the two."[39]

The threat of famine receded. The food situation there was still dire, and would require more aid, but should hold until the spring. The United States and the United Nations could claim true lifesaving credit, although there was another, uglier factor in this success, as the White House staff noted: nine million people had already fled from East Pakistan into India. Still, Kissinger correctly told Nixon, this was a big U.S. contribution to regional peace, preventing "many millions more" Bengali refugees from rushing into India. "It is hard to prove, but the situation could have been a great deal worse by now."[40]

BUT WHILE ALLEVIATING SOME SYMPTOMS, BELATED U.S. PRESSURE DID little to end the fundamental crisis. These were all partial retreats from calamitous decisions by Yahya: while good not to have a famine, it would have been better still not to have created the conditions for one; while preferable to be rid of Tikka Khan, better not to have installed him to terrorize the Bengalis in the first place; and while it was a relief that Mujib was not executed, the winner of a democratic election might have been at a negotiating table rather than in a secret military jail. These were all faint hints of a better future that could have been—without civil war, fierce military rule, or the quashing of democratic leadership.[41]

The inadequacy was perfectly plain from Washington. Both Nixon and Kissinger were informed that huge numbers of refugees were still fleeing, and almost none returning. As U.S. officials in Dacca explained, the Pakistani government's efforts to win over the Bengalis had failed. Some middle-class Bengalis in the cities wanted peace no matter what, but younger Bengalis, especially in the countryside, were fixed in their bitterness against Pakistan's government and army. This loathing was intensified by persistent reports of atrocities, convincing even many conservative Bengalis that the Pakistan army had to be forced out.[42]

A top U.S. development official, after visiting Pakistan, wrote, "Elections, political accommodation, welcoming the return of all refugees, amnesty—these are fine policy pronouncements, but their implementation is in the hands of the Army commanders who govern the Eastern Province, and these Army commanders do not as yet appear subject to foreign influences." When Yahya made showy policy statements, it was an illusory "public relations diplomacy."[43]

Nixon did write to Yahya that it would be "helpful" for him to enlist the elected Bengali politicians for national reconciliation, and later added that he was sure that Yahya wanted "maximum" participation of the Bengalis' elected representatives. Yahya, having done his worst, had seemingly moved into the mopping-up phase of the crackdown, and professed a greater willingness to consider political accommodation. But Kissinger's own aides called Yahya's political efforts inadequate and "vacuous." Yahya moved frustratingly slowly in planning for a new East Pakistan government, while refusing to lift the ban on the Awami League or to make serious efforts to deal with the victors of the election. The White House staff noted that "the army will try 45% of its elected representatives." Kissinger still hoped to hold Pakistan together with autonomy for East Pakistan, but without a deal with legitimate Bengali leaders, there was little chance of any lasting peace there.[44]

Yahya said that he would welcome a secret meeting between Pakistani officials and Bengali politicians who accepted a unified Pakistan. The White House searched in vain for influential Awami League representatives who would settle for less than independence, but went no further than that, not wanting to mediate. The U.S. consul in Calcutta was authorized to tell the Bangladeshi exile government based there that Yahya was interested in talks. But the Bangladeshi leadership insisted that only Mujib could speak for them, and Kissinger complained that they wanted unconditional independence, which put an end to any possible negotiations. As for Yahya freeing Mujib and negotiating with him, Kissinger said, "I think that's inconceivable! Unless Yahya's personality has changed 100% since I saw him in July."[45]

With no political deal in sight, U.S. diplomats in Pakistan painted a bleak picture. Few Bengalis believed in the declared amnesty, as arrests continued and few prominent people were released. The civilian governor seemed obviously a cat's paw of the martial law authorities. Whatever good had been done by removing Tikka Khan, argued the second-ranked U.S. official in Islamabad, it was undercut by continuing army reprisals against the population. As the CIA noted, martial law continued: "Any civilian government established in East Pakistan under the army's aegis is likely to be more shadow than substance."[46]

Yahya's steps were welcome, but from the viewpoint of skeptical U.S. officials in Washington and Delhi, the White House's successes gave a small but tantalizing preview of what might have been possible if the United States had tried harder to use its leverage in a serious way from the start. From India's perspective, Yahya was trimming his sails out of fear of an Indian attack. As much as Nixon and Kissinger would later brag about these achievements, at this late date they unfortunately mattered little.

Trapped in a desk job in the State Department bureaucracy, Archer Blood was doing his best to endure his ouster from the Dacca consulate with a stiff upper lip. While he was usually in no position to remind his bosses that he had told them so, the ex-consul's prognostications in his cables were being confirmed by events. He once managed to get a half-hour meeting with the second-ranked official at the State Department, and declared confidently that the Bengalis, helped by Indian intervention, would eventually win their struggle. Their escalating guerrilla campaign, he said, was bleeding Pakistan white. The independent Bangladesh that he had predicted was well on the way to becoming a reality. "My husband had a different, long view," remembers Meg Blood. "He could see it was not going to simmer down or go away."[47]

AS INDIRA GANDHI'S TRIP TO WASHINGTON APPROACHED, NIXON'S policy seemed to the Indians to be almost completely one-sided. As an Indian diplomat scornfully noted, the Nixon administration's real policy was to treat the issue as an internal matter for Pakistan, give as much diplomatic and economic aid to Pakistan as possible, try to keep up arms supplies to Pakistan, and not condemn Pakistan's atrocities. This was leavened only by relief assistance to India for the refugees, which had been "played up out of all proportion to its quantum."[48]

India, dismissing Yahya as "looking for quislings," argued that Pakistan had to negotiate with Mujib himself. Haksar did not see how there could be any viable political deal without the overwhelming democratic choice of the Bengalis. When William Rogers, the secretary of state, said that the Americans could not force Yahya to talk to a man he saw as a traitor, Haksar retorted, "Churchill said worse things about Gandhi." Haksar told Rogers, "The British talked to Gandhi and Nehru, . . . but Yahya Khan is not willing to talk with Mujibur Rahman."[49]

Nor was India especially impressed with U.S. aid to the refugees—even before the Nixon administration started threatening to cut off foreign aid, a blow that would more than cancel out prior U.S. donations for the refugees. India saw the refugees as a symptom, not the disease, and anyway thought that the symptom was going almost entirely untreated.

It was true that, as the White House privately reckoned, the United States had provided a substantial $89 million, and other foreign governments had scraped together $95 million. While the Nixon administration had asked for more funding—$150 million more for India, as well as $100 million more for Pakistan—the foreign aid bill had stalled in Congress. Even if the White House's motive was to deny Gandhi a pretext for war, this U.S. assistance unquestionably saved many lives, and Nixon and Kissinger deserve real credit for that.

But this U.S. aid was overshadowed by something approaching ten million refugees. India was buckling under that burden, which cost far more than anything on offer from the United States, or any outside power. By a White House account, the expense of the refugees was by now roughly between $700 million and $1 billion annually—at least a sixth of India's normal spending on development for its own people. To date, the United States had met perhaps a tenth of the cost of looking after the refugees for this year only, and the rest of the world had covered another tenth—leaving roughly 80 percent of the expense on poverty-stricken India. And this was at the peak of international concern for the refugees, before the world's attention inevitably moved on to other matters, leaving India to cope alone.[50]

BEFORE GANDHI'S ARRIVAL, THE NIXON ADMINISTRATION MADE ONE last push to get concessions out of Yahya—something that could put Gandhi on the spot when she showed up in Washington. Nixon wrote to Kissinger that there should be no pressure on Pakistan, only on India: "The main justification for some action on the part of Yahya, and I believe there is some, is that then we will be able to hit Madame Gandhi very hard when she comes here for her visit."[51]

In mid-October, India's complaints had reached a new crescendo after Pakistan started "a massive build-up" of troops, armor, and artillery on the western front, including Kashmir. India responded with its own deployment, leaving the two armies facing off. So the United States proposed a mutual withdrawal of Indian and Pakistani troops from the borders. Yahya gamely said he was willing to pull his troops and armor back. (The State Department noted with some jaundice that it was he who had first moved his troops to confront India.) As the summit approached, Yahya said that he would move first in withdrawing some of his troops, although wanting a promise from Gandhi to Nixon that she would soon follow suit.[52]

Gandhi shrugged this off. Indian officials protested that Yahya was trying to seem reasonable by undoing his own deployment, while Gandhi dismissed Yahya's gesture as meaningless, complaining that he would withdraw on the West Pakistan front but not in East Pakistan, where the real danger was. More to the point, India knew just as well as the Americans how the military balance stood, and was not about to let Yahya off the hook. So India took a hard line, backing the Mukti Bahini and keeping the pressure building on Pakistan.[53]

WASHINGTON

Before Washington, Indira Gandhi stopped in New York, where she daz-zled Hannah Arendt, herself a longtime critic of British rule in India. The political theorist breathlessly described Gandhi as "*very* good-looking, almost beautiful, very charming, flirting with every man in the room, without chichi, and entirely calm—she must have known already that she was going to make war and probably enjoyed it even in a perverse way. The toughness of these women once they have got what they wanted is really something!"[54]

The Indian government was expecting a frosty summit. Kissinger warned Nixon that Gandhi was trying to set the president up, to claim that the Americans had driven her to war. The United States would help the refugees, Kissinger said, but would not help India wreck Pakistan's political structure.[55]

"You know they are the aggressors," Kissinger told the president, about the Indians. Briefing Nixon for Gandhi's arrival, he assured him that Pakistan's record was impressive. "I have a list for you of what the Pakistanis have done," he said, "and really short of surrendering they've done everything." (When he said that the United States had "stopped the military pipeline" to Pakistan, it came as a surprise to Nixon: "We have?") Kissinger said that Yahya was willing to grant autonomy for East Pakistan, but blasted India for insisting that Yahya negotiate that with Mujib: "no West Pakistan leader can do that without overthrow-ing themselves." By demanding Mujib's participation, Kissinger said, the Indians were "in effect asking for a total surrender of the Pakistanis and that would mean to me that they want the war."[56]

ON NOVEMBER 4, INDIRA GANDHI ARRIVED AT THE WHITE HOUSE. FROM the welcoming ceremony onward, it was a disaster. Despite Kis-singer's reminders to Nixon to be on his best behavior in public, the two leaders, standing at attention on the South Lawn on a bright, crisp morn-ing, were a portrait in sullen antipathy. They were visibly uncomfortable to be physically so close together. Gandhi, wrapped in a light orange overcoat against the autumn chill, glowered fixedly out from underneath her towering white-streaked coif. Nixon, his belly straining against his dark suit jacket, sported a particularly heartfelt version of his trademark scowl.[57]

Kissinger later wrote that Gandhi's "dislike of Nixon" showed in her "icy formality." Samuel Hoskinson, Kissinger's aide, was struck by the tension and mutual loathing. "This was now between the heads of state who are deeply suspicious of each other," he remembers. "He was the antithesis for her." He says, "Shit, she thought this was the moment she was going to make history, destroy Pakistan entirely."[58]

The state dinner went off miserably. There was an attempt at good cheer: a performance by the New York City Ballet; Pat Nixon draped in a floor-length gown of blinding 1970s cotton-candy pink; Gandhi only slightly less loud in a crimson sari with gold trim; and Nixon rather dashing in a tuxedo. But the president never enjoyed these functions at the best of times. He privately complained about the lack of patriotic spirit in the U.S. officials, with "only the shit-asses in the government" left unmoved by things like the Marine Corps Band. "The Congress, they sit there like a bunch of blasé bastards. They really do. The State Department people are horrible." His main consolation was giving a genuinely delightful toast to Gandhi—composed, he said, without using anything prepared by the State Department, and delivered without notes, to dazzle the press corps with his grasp of foreign policy. He boasted, "I can do toasts and arrival statements better than anybody in the world. I have traveled all over the world."[59]

But Gandhi and Haksar were left cold. The Indians were amazed that the president avoided mentioning the Bengali crisis in his toast. In hers, Gandhi made no attempt to charm. "Can you imagine the entire population of Michigan State suddenly converging onto New York State?" she asked. "Has not your own society been built of people who have fled from social and economic injustices? Have not your doors always been open?"[60]

Kissinger had more fun at the dinner. ("I liked the ballerina," he told the president afterward.) But, chewing it over in the Oval Office the next morning, Nixon and Kissinger were both appalled by Gandhi's toast. She "had gone on forever last night," grumbled H. R. Haldeman, the White House chief of staff. Kissinger said, "The president made really one of the best toasts I've heard him make since we came here. Very subtle, very thoughtful, and very warm-hearted. Very, very personal. And she got up and—almost no reference to the president, somewhat friendly reference to Mrs. Nixon, launched into a diatribe against Pakistan, which, you know, it's never done at a state dinner, that you attack another government." (She had managed to avoid mentioning Pakistan by name, but had decried "medieval tyranny.") Kissinger was put off by Gandhi's mention of her democratic mandate: "Then she started praising herself, she said in effect that yes, this praise was well deserved, that I ran an election campaign. . . . And she said it was wrong to treat them the same way as the Pakistanis. Oh, it was really revolting, God."[61]

On November 5, just before the Indian prime minister arrived at the Oval Office, Kissinger stopped by to give the president a final pep talk. He found Nixon already furious. The president said that the United States had given more relief aid to India than the rest of the world combined, and immediately exploded with rage, hollering, "Goddamn, why don't they give us any credit for that?" Kissinger kept him boiling. "I wouldn't be too defensive, Mr. President," he replied. "Because these bastards have played an absolutely brutal, ruthless game with us."

Kissinger laid out their actions that might mollify Gandhi: "famine relief, international relief presence, civilian governor, amnesty, unilateral withdrawal." He said that the arms supply had dried up, while Nixon added that the Pakistanis had agreed not to execute Mujib, the Awami League's popular leader. (Nixon asked, "what's his name? Mujib? How do you pronounce?") Kissinger said, "And also Yahya has said that he would agree to meet with a Bangladesh leader," although not Mujib. "No," said Kissinger. "No, no, no." Meeting Mujib "would be political suicide for Yahya." Nixon, aiming for a high tone, suggested telling Gandhi that while the Americans had no treaty with India, they were "bound by a moral commitment" to promote peace—and then snarled at Gandhi, calling her "the old bitch."[62]

Kissinger urged Nixon to be tough on her. "I think publicly you should be extremely nice," said the national security advisor—and at this point the tape is bleeped out, to hide whatever words he used to urge being rougher in private. Kissinger recommended sternly telling her that her Soviet treaty had cast doubt on India's ostensible nonalignment, and that "a war with Pakistan simply would not be understood."

Kissinger's briefing set Nixon at ease. The president was impressed with what they had gotten the Pakistanis to do. Stumbling on the name, he said, "They've agreed not to execute Muju—Muju—however it is you say his name—" "Mujib," said Kissinger. Nixon fluently rattled off Kissinger's list of Pakistani concessions, such as a civilian governor and the unilateral troop withdrawal. The only options, the president concluded, were "accommodation or war," and war would benefit no one. He was ready.

"I'm going to be extremely tough," said Nixon.[63]

AT LAST, AWAY FROM THE TRAPPINGS AND DISTRACTIONS OF A STATE visit, Richard Nixon and Indira Gandhi faced off in the Oval Office. In an angry and protracted meeting, they grappled one-on-one, with only Kissinger and Haksar attending their chiefs. It was explosive. He thought she was a warmonger; she thought he was helping along a genocide. Summits are often pretty placid affairs, but this was a cathartic brawl, propelled not just by totally opposite views of a brewing war, but by the hearty personal contempt that the president and prime minister had for each other.

Nixon first emphasized U.S. aid to the refugees, but then sharply warned that launching a war was unacceptable. He said that the United States needed to maintain some influence with Pakistan, which explained a "most limited" continuation of military supply. Hitting his talking points, he recited the ways that the United States had ameliorated Pakistan's positions: preventing a famine in East Pakistan, naming a civilian governor of East Pakistan, welcoming back refugees, talking to acceptable Awami League leaders, not executing Mujib, and now withdrawing some troops from India's border. The United States could go no further. Gandhi listened, Kissinger later wrote, with "aloof indifference." Nixon, refusing to push for negotiations with Mujib, said that he "could not urge policies which would be tantamount to overthrowing President Yahya."

India would win on the battlefield, Nixon said, but a war would be "incalculably dangerous." With the superpowers involved on opposite sides, it would threaten world peace. Hinting broadly at a possible Chinese attack on India, he told the prime minister that a war might not be limited to only India and Pakistan.

Gandhi was blunter—if anything, less tactful than Nixon. Kissinger later wrote that her tone was that of "a professor praising a slightly backward student," which Nixon received with the "glassy-eyed politeness" that he showed when trying to muscle down his resentment. She ripped into U.S. arms shipments to Pakistan, which had outraged the Indian people, despite her efforts to restrain her public.

She hammered away at Pakistan's "persistent 'hate India' campaign," which she blamed for the two previous India-Pakistan wars. Then she gave an expansive denunciation of Pakistan. Since its creation, it had jailed or exiled rival politicians. Many of its regions, like Baluchistan and the North-West Frontier Province, sought autonomy. (India, she claimed, had always shown some forbearance toward its own separatists—something that might have come as news to the Nagas and Mizos.) She blasted Pakistan's "treacherous and deceitful" mistreatment of the Bengali people, and told detailed atrocity stories. She said that it was unrealistic to expect East and West Pakistan to remain united; the pressures for autonomy were too strong.

The prime minister turned to the huge numbers of refugees still streaming into India. (There were, by India's count, over nine and a half million on that autumn day.) Nixon, trying to undercut what he and Kissinger saw as India's pretext for war, said he would keep pressing Congress for a large relief effort. He wanted the refugees to go home. But Gandhi said that the refugees were from a different background and religion from Indians in the border states, leaving her government hard pressed to prevent bloody communal riots.

Nixon denounced the Bengali insurgents for interfering with relief supplies on ships near Chittagong harbor. This kind of guerrilla warfare, the president said, had to rely on sophisticated training and equipment. Gandhi dodged the accusation, foggily saying that "India had been accused of supporting guerrilla activity but that the situation was not that clear." Nobody sitting in the Oval Office believed that, least of all Gandhi and Haksar. She perplexingly compared the insurgency to Cuban exiles in Florida striking against Cuba.

The two leaders sparred fiercely. It was, Kissinger later wrote, "a classic dialogue of the deaf." Gandhi complained bitterly of Yahya's talk of "Holy War," and said that the vital issue was Mujib, who was a symbol of the autonomy movement. She raised Nixon's and Kissinger's hackles by mentioning her Soviet friendship treaty. Nixon, claiming that the United States had put "great pressure on Pakistan," brought up again Yahya's offer to unilaterally pull back his troops. Haksar dodged that, for which Nixon slapped him down.

Nixon ended with a steely warning. He said that the U.S. government would continue to help with humanitarian relief, urge restraint on Yahya, and try to find a political solution. But he declared that the disintegration of Pakistan would do no good for anyone, and rumbled, "The initiation of hostilities by India would be almost impossible to understand." He warned, "It would be impossible to calculate with precision the steps which other great powers might take if India were to initiate hostilities"—hinting not just at the reaction of the United

States but also the possibility of Chinese intervention. This implicit threat hung in the Oval Office as the final ugly moment.[64]

NIXON AND KISSINGER WERE STUNNED BY THE SHOWDOWN. THEY HAD been sorely taxed by the sustained need to be civil to Gandhi. The next morning, in the Oval Office, alone except for Haldeman, they vented their frustrations. "This is just the point when she is a bitch," said the president. Kissinger replied, "Well, the Indians are bastards anyway. They are starting a war there."

The two men stripped the bark off the Indians. Kissinger, struck by Gandhi's unyielding condemnation of Pakistan, suspected that she was out not just to free East Pakistan but to smash West Pakistan. He lavished praise on Nixon's performance: "While she was a bitch, we got what we wanted too."

Nixon was revolted by the politesse shown to Gandhi. "We really slobbered over the old witch," he said. Kissinger, doing a little slobbering of his own, reassured the president: "How you slobbered over her in things that did not matter, but in the things that did matter, you didn't give her an inch." Kissinger flattered Nixon's toughness and skill, while Nixon gloated, "You should have heard, Bob, the way we worked her around. I dropped stilettos all over her."

Kissinger said, "Mr. President, even though she was a bitch, we shouldn't overlook the fact that we got what we wanted, which was we kept her from going out of here saying that the United States kicked her in the teeth." He added, "You didn't give her a goddamn thing." Although it would have been "emotionally more satisfying" to rip into her, Kissinger said "it would have hurt us. . . . I mean if you had been rough with her then she'd be crying, going back crying to India." Thanks to the president, Kissinger said, Gandhi could not say that the United States had been cold to her and therefore she had to attack Pakistan.

Kissinger understandably winced at Gandhi's protestations that she knew nothing about the guerrillas in East Pakistan. He was also incensed by India's relationship with the Soviet Union: "They have the closest diplomatic ties now with Russia. They leak everything right back to them." And Nixon cheered Kissinger, who had "stuck it to her on that book"—the one recommended to Kissinger by Zhou Enlai, which, in Kissinger's words, "proves that India started the '62 War" against China. Kissinger sarcastically said, "It was done with an enormous politeness and courtesy and warmth." Nixon added that "she knew goddamn well that I knew what happened."

Nixon and Kissinger were bitter at India for winning support in the U.S. media and Congress. "You stuck it to her about the press," said Kissinger. "On that I hit it hard," Nixon agreed. "I raised my voice a little."

Kissinger had also met with Haksar, whom Nixon called "that clown." Kissinger said that he had been just as rough on Haksar. He had complained to the senior Indian official that India gave visiting Democratic politicians "a royal reception, tremendous publicity, personal meetings. And then after you do all of this you come over here and ask us to solve all your problems." Nixon said, "Good for you." Kissinger continued, "I said look at the record the last 3 months. You've had a press campaign against us. You put out the word that our relations are the worst ever. You get Kennedy over. . . . You make a treaty with the Russians. And then you come here and say we have to solve your problems for you."

Nixon decided to make that day's meeting "cool." Kissinger suggested giving Gandhi a rougher day, as the conversation turned to Vietnam and other international issues: "even though she is a bitch, I'd be a shade cooler today."[65]

SAMUEL HOSKINSON, KISSINGER'S AIDE, HAD THE JOYLESS DUTY OF MEETing Gandhi and Haksar at the White House diplomatic entrance and escorting them up to see the president again. From the alcove in the diplomatic entrance, he remembers, he telephoned Nixon's secretary, Rose Mary Woods. Woods told him to delay. After an interminable half hour, he says, Gandhi was "getting frosty as hell." He called upstairs again. Woods told him not yet. "It's clear to me what's happening," recalls Hoskinson. "They're standing her up a little bit. You wait for the president of the United States, lady."

After something like forty-five minutes, Hoskinson got the call to take her upstairs. "Then Rose Mary says, 'Would you please take Madame Gandhi to the Roosevelt Room?' I wait another ten or fifteen minutes. She is totally pissed. They're whispering back and forth. It was the most excruciating scene you can imagine." Finally, Hoskinson says, Nixon burst in, turning on the charm, and saying he did not know she had been kept waiting. "She was flabbergasted," says Hoskinson. "It was a kind of one-upmanship. Nixon felt he had to show her he was in control."[66]

With that, the exasperated president squared off against the offended prime minister in their final Oval Office session. "Mrs. Gandhi didn't indicate much interest in anything in her conversations with the President," Kissinger recalled a few days later. "When he asked her about military withdrawal, she said she would let him know the next day, and she didn't even have the courtesy to mention it again."[67]

To Nixon's and Kissinger's annoyance, Gandhi had asked that their second meeting cover issues beyond South Asia. With less at stake in this encounter, there was less to raise the temperature. This time, Nixon explained his opening to China, while Gandhi blandly said she supported it—not mentioning his implicit warning the day before that great powers might intervene against India. The prime minister asked about Vietnam, where India remained bitterly critical of the U.S. war effort. Haksar warily asked about China. The two leaders were able to wrap up on somewhat better form and be rid of each other. With not much to do, Haksar spent his Oval Office time mesmerized by the two Americans. He fought a strong urge to touch Nixon's "mask-like" face, which seemed "unreal." The president's only sign of emotion, Haksar thought, was his sweat.[68]

No wonder Kissinger later declared that these were undoubtedly the worst meetings Nixon held with any foreign leader. Pakistan's unilateral withdrawal plan was a dead letter. The Indians saw no shift in the White House's attitude, with Yahya still seen as irreplaceable. With nothing in hand, with no plan to defuse the confrontation, Gandhi and her retinue departed Washington. "My visit to Nixon did anything but avert the war," she later said.[69]

The main discernible outcome of the summit was that the two leaders of these massive democracies now hated each other rather more. The last big chance to prevent a war had slipped away.

Chapter 17

The Guns of November

HENRY KISSINGER DESPAIRINGLY TOLD RICHARD NIXON, "PAKS are up the creek." The president replied, "The Indians have screwed us." After the failure of the Washington summit, the Nixon administration fully expected war.[1]

Indira Gandhi, despairing of any political deal in Pakistan, reportedly ordered a military solution. Indian troops stepped up their border skirmishes with the Pakistanis, often sparked by India's sponsorship of the Bengali insurgents. When the Mukti Bahini fought against Pakistani troops, the Pakistani soldiers would sometimes wind up in hot pursuit back across the Indian border—resulting in clashes with the Indian troops at the frontier. India, increasingly open about crossing onto Pakistani soil, sent troops into Pakistani territory in strength on two separate occasions. India complained that Pakistan was firing shells and bullets into Indian territory.[2]

Although these clashes were too big to hide, Gandhi's government was prickly about its troops being caught on the wrong side of the border. On November 7, Sydney Schanberg of the *New York Times* trekked out to the Indian border with East Pakistan. The next day, he filed a front-page story reporting that Indian troops had ventured into East Pakistan to take out Pakistani guns that had been lobbing artillery into a town in India. Schanberg's article flew in the face of India's official line that its troops had "strict orders" not to cross the border, even when provoked. When they read the *Times* story, both Haksar and Gandhi hit the roof. Haksar reprimanded the defense ministry, saying that Gandhi wanted a thorough investigation into leaks to Schanberg.[3]

India's defense secretary hauled Schanberg in to protest a story that seemed perfectly accurate. Schanberg politely stood his ground and, according to an Indian account, deployed a traditional dodge of the foreign correspondent: blaming nitwit editors back home for slanting the story. He effectively boxed in the Indians by purporting not to see the harm in what they were doing. But he said that he could not believe the official claim that Indian troops were under instructions not to cross the border. The prime minister gave Indian officials fresh orders to hold their tongues.[4]

Worried that the State Department was sending mixed signals, Nixon ordered Kissinger to swiftly get word to China that the United States was unfaltering in support of Pakistan. Kissinger promised to do so, planning to use the Paris channel.[5]

But if the United States' commitment to Pakistan was unwavering, China's seemed wobbly. When Pakistan sent Zulfiqar Ali Bhutto to Beijing to firm up Chinese support, Indian intelligence suggested that Bhutto had gotten a "frosty" reception in Beijing, with the Chinese urging him to avoid war. Despite Bhutto's public claims that China had promised its support if India attacked, this at best seemed to mean arms and ammunition, not the kind of direct intervention that Nixon and Kissinger were hoping for. The CIA reckoned that there was little chance that China would do much to bail Pakistan out in a war.[6]

After the face-off with Gandhi at the White House, Kissinger was freshly energized in his anger against India. Her fierce Oval Office condemnations of Pakistan had stuck with him, and he repeatedly brought them up: "She spent most of her time telling him [Nixon] that Baluchistan should never have been made a part of Pakistan." Thus he expected India to rip away East Pakistan, driving West Pakistan to collapse, in order to "settle the Pakistan problem once and for all." Although he thought India would attack, he also saw the desperate logic of a Pakistani first strike: "If they will lose East Pakistan politically anyhow, why not lose in a war?"[7]

Gandhi was under tremendous public pressure, which only intensified as the Indian Parliament reconvened for its winter session—"thirsting for blood," as Kissinger later wrote. Returning from Washington, she denounced "the thinly disguised legalistic formulation that it was merely an internal affair of Pakistan," and cheered on the Mukti Bahini's "heroic struggle . . . in defence of the most elementary democratic rights and liberties." Although she urged Nixon to commit "the vast prestige of the United States" to finding a political deal with Mujib, there was no hope that any such thing was going to happen.[8]

"I wish we could do more!" Nixon told Pakistan's foreign secretary in an Oval Office meeting. "I wish we could do more, believe me." Here Nixon, for the first time in eight months of killing, personally beseeched a Pakistani official to find "political solutions" rather than solve a problem by force. But it was unclear if the president meant Pakistan cutting a deal with the Bengali nationalists, or defusing the military standoff between India and Pakistan.[9]

Soon after the failure of the summit, the Nixon administration began preparations for some U.S. military saber rattling—a customary part of their playbook. Admiral John McCain Jr., the commander in chief of the Pacific Command, drew up plans to pull an aircraft carrier task group away from providing tactical air support in Vietnam and sail it into the Bay of Bengal. The Joint Chiefs of Staff quickly agreed, as the White House staff briefed Kissinger about the military's secret planning.[10]

Nixon and Kissinger had bet everything on Yahya, but they realized that he was being swept away by events. Back in August, while planning the White House's calendar of upcoming summits for December, H. R. Haldeman had asked if Yahya was still on the schedule. "No," said Nixon, after an awkward pause. Kissinger added softly, after another painful interval, "I don't think he'll be in office by then."[11]

Soon after the Gandhi summit, the White House staff warned Kissinger that an isolated Yahya was no longer calling the shots with his own military. He had no real idea what was happening in East Pakistan, where the army had nearly complete control. Yahya might listen to U.S. suggestions, but the army did not implement them. Although Nixon was still loyally calling Yahya "a good friend to me," Kissinger starkly warned the president that the Pakistani leader was on his way out. At the same time, Kissinger told Nixon of ongoing "terror raids" and noted, "Reprisal operations continue to focus against Hindus."[12]

Much of this grim news to Nixon should have been familiar from the reporting by U.S. officials in Dacca. It had long been clear that there was no real civilian government in East Pakistan; that the civil war was raging out of control; that Yahya's political concessions were too little to matter; that Hindus were still being singled out for persecution; that the Bengalis were only getting angrier at their overlords in West Pakistan; and that the refugees would not go home. Now these unpleasant facts were sinking in for Nixon and Kissinger. It was too late.

"PAKISTAN WILL GET RAPED"

Indian troops were allowed to go ten miles into East Pakistan—instructions that Indian officers quickly used to bolster their offensive posture, capturing substantial areas and wiping out Pakistan army posts. On the night of November 21–22, there was a frightening escalation, culminating in the first air battle of the crisis.[13]

India and Pakistan accused each other of starting this border clash, though Major General Jacob-Farj-Rafael Jacob later conceded that India had moved first. He recalled that on November 20 an Indian infantry division launched a preliminary attack around Boyra, in East Pakistan near the Indian border. Then the Pakistan Air Force struck back, losing three Sabre jets in the process. The Pakistan army's U.S.-made M-24 Chaffee light tanks made a disastrous thrust over open ground—it reminded Jacob of the charge of the Light Brigade—into concentrated fire from Indian tanks and recoilless guns. In the combat, Pakistan lost thirteen or fourteen tanks and many men. Then the Pakistani troops crossed into India and struck at several Indian villages. India claimed that Pakistani shelling wounded several Indians.[14]

But in public, India stuck to a version blaming Pakistan for attacking. In this less embarrassing account, the trouble began when a Pakistani infantry brigade, fortified by tanks, artillery, and air support, attacked a Mukti Bahini base in the Boyra area, in East Pakistan, about five miles from the Indian border. India, admitting that it had crossed into Pakistan's territory, claimed it had no choice. Haksar argued that India had remained restrained despite Pakistan's repeated violations of Indian airspace and shelling of Indian territory bordering East Pakistan. In Haksar's retelling, India then struck at Boyra to take out Pakistani tanks and guns; the next day, three Pakistani Sabre jets crossed into Indian airspace and were shot down. India captured two pilots who had bailed out over Indian soil.[15]

The battle suited India's strategic purposes. General Jacob later confessed that the air battle had been controlled from his command at Fort William in Calcutta. D. P. Dhar, one of the most bellicose officials in India's ruling circles, welcomed war but wanted to be sure that, when it came, it detonated out of the civil war in East Pakistan. India, he wrote, would need to be "able to furnish the elaborate pretext" that India was helping with a Bengali "war of liberation."[16]

Just as important, this clash was right on schedule for India. According to Jacob, when Indira Gandhi first asked the army to march into East Pakistan back in April, he had told her that the earliest they would be ready for war was November 15. General Sam Manekshaw, on his own account, had wanted six months to prepare. When November 15 came, Jacob privately wrote to another general, "In the East conditions are ripe for a swift offensive." It was the season for war: the monsoons were over; the army had had time to train; and wintry weather in the Himalayas would foil any Chinese troops.[17]

THAT MORNING AT THE WHITE HOUSE, KISSINGER BURST INTO HALDE-man's office saying that India had attacked Pakistan. Relying only on Pakistani radio broadcasts, unsure of what was really going on, Kis-singer sounded the alarm to Nixon. There was, he told the president by telephone, a big encroachment taking place, "heavily backed by the Indi-ans." Nixon stormed that he wanted Kissinger to "lay it out hard" that all aid would be stopped to both India and Pakistan, which would "hurt the Indians more."[18]

The Pakistanis, Kissinger said, were "saying it's war." Nixon said, "And the Indians say it isn't." Kissinger, still without the facts, insisted, "It's a naked case of aggression, Mr. President." Nixon sulkily pointed out that John Connally, the Treasury secretary, had told him that "the Indians have been kicking us in the ass for twenty-five years." Kissinger said that they did not want an Indian assault that made Pakistan disin-tegrate. He suggested that if there were debates at the United Nations Security Council, the United States did not have to go as far as China—whose delegation spoke in wild Cultural Revolution polemics—in con-demning India. Nixon exploded: "I want to go damn near as far! You understand? I don't like the Indians."[19]

The next day, Kissinger said, "India is outrageous." India's actions, he asserted, were part of a Soviet plan to humiliate the United States. While calling the Indians "those sons of bitches," Kissinger prepared a high-minded stance against aggression for a press briefing: "'It is against the Charter of the United Nations, it's against the principles of this country,' and make them attack us on that ground." But when privately told that a discussion at the United Nations was the only way forward, Kissinger snapped, "Let's not kid ourselves—that means Pakistan will get raped."[20]

After the battle at Boyra, General Manekshaw quietly ordered the Indian army to launch new and increasingly brazen attacks into Paki-stani territory. Although the CIA argued that this was a limited operation, the chairman of the Joint Chiefs was convinced that Indian troops were involved. "There is no way guerrillas could get tanks and aircraft and be operating in brigade formation," Kissinger said. "We can play this charade only so long. What kind of a world is it where countries can claim these are guerrilla actions?" Without evidence, he was sure that India had attacked with regular units inside East Pakistan's borders. Kissinger decided that India had long been planning this attack. He seemed to compare India's actions to Nazi Germany's invasion of Lithuania in 1941: "You have 12 planes against 200. It's the Germans claiming they were attacked by the Lithuanians."[21]

Pakistan declared a state of emergency, and Yahya drunkenly told a *New Yorker* reporter that he expected to be at war within ten days. When a State Department official suggested that this might be a good time for Yahya to cut a deal with Mujib before it was too late, Kissinger—although indifferent to the thought of an independent Bangladesh ("We don't give a damn")—shot back, "So, India having attacked Pakistan, the logical conclusion is that we should squeeze Yahya to talk to Mujib. What Indian troops can't achieve, we should achieve for them." He fumed, "If the situation were reversed and Pakistani troops were moving into India, the *New York Times, Washington Post* and the Senate Foreign Relations Committee would be committing mass hara-kari, and there would be marches on Washington."[22]

By chance, Kissinger was scheduled for his first secret meeting in New York with Chinese diplomats the day after the Boyra battle. Late at night, Kissinger—along with George Bush, Alexander Haig, and Winston Lord—snuck into a seedy CIA safe house in an old brownstone on Manhattan's East Side to meet a Chinese delegation led by Huang Hua, the new ambassador at the United Nations. "For these purposes, Mr. Bush works directly for me," Kissinger conspiratorially told the Chinese. "No one else in the Government except the people in this room knew about this channel." Kissinger and Haig gave a military briefing, accusing Indian troops of attacking near Jessore and Chittagong—and tantalizingly suggesting that India had left its northern border with China exposed. "This violates every security rule," said Kissinger, about his sharing of U.S. intelligence. They coordinated the Chinese and U.S. positions for United Nations Security Council debates. Demonstrating U.S. support for Pakistan, Kissinger told Huang that India had no right to use military force to relieve the pressure caused by the refugees. Soon after, Kissinger fretted about what China would think "if the friend of the United States and China in the subcontinent gets raped without any resistance."[23]

The battle at Boyra was still something less than war. Indira Gandhi had full-scale invasion plans, but she did not launch them. Nor did Pakistan, which dithered in its response. While Kissinger was convinced this was clear Indian aggression, Nixon was at first skeptical about whether the clash really meant the start of war: a jet fight, he said, "doesn't mean that there's a damn war going on."[24]

But Kissinger pressed him: "the guerrillas have been operating with brigade strength with artillery support and air support and tanks." Won over, Nixon said, "It's like North Vietnam still denying they are in South Vietnam." He added, "They want Pakistan to disintegrate." Thus he instructed Kissinger to tilt their policy toward Pakistan wherever they could. Kissinger, ratcheting up, said that India aimed at regional domination.

Although Nixon knew that India would win a war, his support for Yahya did not waver. "He'll be demolished," the president said. "Pakistan eventually will disintegrate." Even now, at the eleventh hour, he never faltered in his sentimental attachment to Yahya. Rather than merely defending the Pakistani strongman as a tainted but necessary partner, Nixon repeatedly vouched for his friend's integrity. "Yahya is a thoroughly decent and reasonable man," he said. "Not always smart politically, but he's a decent man."

Nixon insisted that he bore no responsibility for the situation that he had allowed Yahya to unleash back in March. He did not want to "take the heat for a miserable war that we had nothing do with." Kissinger bucked him up, saying that if they had made any mistake, it was being too hard on Pakistan. Nixon said, "We just got to get it across to the American people that we cannot be responsible for every goddamn war in the world. . . . We are not responsible for this war." This battle, the refugees, Pakistan's convulsions: "we couldn't avoid that, could we?"[25]

SYDNEY SCHANBERG SET OUT FROM CALCUTTA TO PROVE THAT INDIA was forging into Pakistani territory in several places. "The Indian army was making interventions that none of us are allowed to see," he remembers. India was still officially denying that any of its troops had crossed the border; it had closed off the frontline areas to the press, and he was definitely not allowed to go to Boyra. But the *New York Times* reporter found a way. Each time he came to a checkpoint, he bluffed his way past by telling the Indian soldiers that he did not want to go to the border, he just wanted to talk to their lieutenant. This ruse got him to a staging area a few miles from the border, which was buzzing with military activity. In under two hours, he saw hundreds of troops stream past, heading for the border, on truck convoys that kicked up red dust. The soldiers had automatic weapons and full ammunition packs. There were trucks massing, covered with camouflage netting and loaded with ammunition. "They had everything from tanks and desks, office supplies," he says. "You knew they were going inside."

In the distance, he could hear artillery fire. The Indians stopped him. Schanberg found a group of officers drinking beer, and tried an old reporter's trick. Rather than asking if they were inside East Pakistan, he simply assumed that they were. He told a major, "You must be kicking the bejesus out of the Pakistan army." The Indian officer said yes, they were all the way to Jessore. Schanberg wrote it all down. He got his scoop plastered on the front page of the *New York Times*.[26]

Gandhi was finally forced to admit for the first time that Indian troops had gone into East Pakistan, although India claimed it was self-defense. At a raucous rally in Calcutta, India's defense minister announced that its troops had permission to go as far into Pakistan as the range of Pakistani artillery, meaning several miles. At that event, a Congress party speaker cried, "India will break Pakistan to pieces." Another declared, "We will make shoes out of Yahya's skin." In retaliation for Schanberg's story, the West Bengal government canceled his border permit. Schanberg says that an Indian cabinet minister told him years later that they had debated throwing him out of the country.[27]

Nixon and Kissinger both wanted to slash all military aid to India. But Kissinger soon decided it was better to block the most crucial 70 percent of U.S. arms deals, saving the remainder in case of further misdeeds. As Kissinger told Nixon, they would cut off some $17 million of military supply, grounding India's C-119 military transport planes, and stopping all ammunition.[28]

Kenneth Keating, the U.S. ambassador in Delhi, was sent over to the Indian foreign ministry to break the bad news on December 2. ("He may start weeping all over them," Kissinger said.) The Indian defense ministry privately pointed out that it could have been worse, but the Indian government was angered, and the public was shocked. Nixon also ended funding for a food program and stopped a loan, amounting to roughly $100 million.[29]

Gandhi was coldly determined. Shrugging off United Nations

mediation, she denounced the ongoing "military repression and denial of basic human rights in East Bengal." Keating found her more grim than he had ever seen her. She bluntly refused to pull back her troops to ease the pressure on Yahya: "we are not in a position to make this easier for him." She did not see how she could tell Indians to keep waiting: "I can't hold it."[30]

On December 2, Pakistan's ambassador told Kissinger that Yahya "wants to take further actions."[31]

Chapter 18

The Fourteen-Day War

MAJOR GENERAL JACOB-FARJ-RAFAEL JACOB, THE CHIEF OF STAFF of the Indian army's Eastern Command, had been preparing for war for months, and a bit longer too. The son of a prominent Sephardic Jewish family from West Bengal, he had learned how to box and shoot as a schoolboy in Calcutta. He liked it.

Jake Jacob was a stocky, robust bull of a man with heavy-lidded eyes. When Nazi Germany stepped up its persecution of European Jews, with Jacob's family sheltering refugees who had fled as far as Calcutta, he decided there was an enemy that had to be defeated. So in 1941 he enrolled in the British army, he says, "to fight the Nazis." His regiment got cut to pieces fighting off German troops in Libya, and Jacob was wounded in hellish swamp conditions in Burma, but he survived to enlist in an independent India's army. After serving in the 1965 war against Pakistan, he rocketed up through the senior ranks. Jacob is the rare person who speaks fondly of Indira Gandhi, who charmed him with kindly questions about India's Jews (her favorite musical, he says, was *Fiddler on the Roof*) and stories about her children. "I liked her very much," he says. "I don't care what other people say."[1]

Jacob savors the fact that three of the Indian generals fighting against Pakistan were a Parsi, a Sikh, and a Jew. General Sam Manekshaw, India's topmost army commander—a dashing and jovial Parsi veteran of World War II who sported an outsized bristling mustache—was, like Jacob, confident of victory.[2]

The Indian generals knew they had an overwhelming military advantage in East Pakistan. The CIA estimated that India's army had 1.1 million soldiers overall, dwarfing Pakistan's three hundred thousand. India had built up and modernized its war machine, and had planned coordinated efforts from its army, air force, and navy. In East

Pakistan, the Indians had the enthusiastic support of much of the Bengali populace, as well as a local fighting partner in the Mukti Bahini, which pinned down the Pakistan army and offered deep knowledge of the terrain. Pakistan's eastern troops were outnumbered, demoralized, and exhausted from trying to quash the Bengali citizenry and rebels. Archer Blood had always known East Pakistan was a military liability: "They could never defend it against India because it is surrounded virtually by India and separated by over a thousand miles."[3]

India's war plans bore this out. In the east, the Indians seem to have chosen a daring strategy, which Jacob says he proposed: "You go straight for Dacca. Ignore the subsidiary towns." Several other generals hashed out the plan of attack, but they agreed on the core concept. As Jacob explains, "Dacca is the center of gravity, the geopolitical heart of East Pakistan. Unless you take Dacca, the war cannot be completed."

It is a measure of how well the war went that India's generals have squabbled about credit ever since. According to Jacob, when they discussed the plan back in August, Manekshaw and other generals had wanted to take the other two main cities, Chittagong and Khulna, which would make Dacca fall. Jacob says, "I said, 'No way. Chittagong is peripheral. It has no bearing on the war.' He said, 'Sweetie, don't'"—the endearment being Manekshaw's way of prefacing a rebuke.[4]

PAKISTAN STRIKES

December 3, 1971, was a quiet political day in Delhi. Indira Gandhi was off in Calcutta, and her senior cabinet was scattered. A little before 6 p.m., air-raid sirens howled in the capital.[5]

"We were going to attack on December 4," says Vice Admiral Mihir Roy, India's director of naval intelligence. "They guessed it, I suppose." Gandhi had reportedly approved General Manekshaw's plans to attack on December 4, taking advantage of a full moon. According to K. F. Rustamji of the Border Security Force, he had instructions from the army for when war came. Their task was to force the Pakistani troops out of their bases and scatter them, and to fight skirmishes at the border. The rest would be handled by the army.[6]

But Pakistan struck first. At 5:30 p.m. on December 3, Pakistan's air force launched coordinated surprise attacks on India's major airfields in the north, in cities in Punjab, Rajasthan, and Uttar Pradesh. Soon after, the Pakistan army began heavily shelling Indian army positions all along the western border, opening up a wide front in Punjab and Kashmir. In Kashmir, United Nations military observers reported an attack by Pakistani troops at Poonch. According to a Pakistani post-war judicial commission, Yahya had on November 29 decided on the assault, without knowing about India's own plans to strike.[7]

In Calcutta, Gandhi—who had been addressing an immense rally of as many as a million people—privately said, "Thank God, they've attacked us." She had wanted Pakistan to get the blame. Now it would. The prime minister showed no visible emotion when she got the news, but later that night as she winged back to Delhi, she was nervous that Pakistan's air force might try to blow her airplane out of the sky. She met with her chiefs of staff, raced to the map room to take stock of the military situation, and then consulted with parliamentary leaders. She was in a gloweringly bad mood. One of her top aides remembered her "almighty rage" at an underwhelming speech her staff had hastily written for her. Atal Bihari Vajpayee, the hawkish Jana Sangh politi-cian, remembered her as "a picture of worry and concern."[8]

The prime minister directed India's armed forces to fight back. Gen-eral Manekshaw later said that, with the prime minister and defense minister away, he had to decide to retaliate, and to have that decision approved later by the cabinet. After midnight on the night of December 3–4, Gandhi told Indians by radio, in a slow and grave voice, "Today the war in Bangla Desh has become a war on India." On December 4, Yahya—having made his last big mistake—declared that Pakistan was at war with India.[9]

Yahya's attack gave India the high moral ground. "We meet as a fighting Parliament," Gandhi stormed before the Lok Sabha. "A war has been forced upon us, a war we did not seek and did our utmost to prevent." She justified the war not merely as self-defense, but invoked liberty and human rights in Bangladesh. Writing to Richard Nixon, she condemned Pakistan's aggression as well as its "repressive, brutal and colonial policy," which "culminated in genocide."[10]

Arundhati Ghose, the Indian diplomat posted in Calcutta, remem-bers, "We thought, now they're going to hit Calcutta. It's jammed with people. Even a firecracker would kill people." In Delhi, people jumped at air-raid alarms in the dead of night and the sounds of jet aircraft overhead. But the country rallied behind the war. For all the theatrics— the government imposed a nightly blackout and encouraged civilians to dig trenches—the fighting was far away from the population centers, leaving most civilians feeling safe enough to enjoy the government's reports of uninterrupted martial triumph. Despite his past criticisms, even Jayaprakash Narayan proclaimed his full support for Gandhi, arguing that there was no time for factionalism in this national emergency. One Indian activist wrote, "I wish to thank God, in whom I do not believe, that a strong, determined and fearless person like Indira Gandhi is our Prime Minister at this time of crisis." P. N. Haksar worked hard at using the government's pronouncements to drive home "the why and wherefore" of the war to India's citizenry.[11]

Sydney Schanberg of the *New York Times* recalls, "Jacob was delighted that night. Now we'll show you what an army is." Jacob's superior was just as confident. "Don't look so scared, sweetie," General Manekshaw told the anxious officer who informed him of Pakistan's attack. "Do I look worried?"[12]

IN WASHINGTON, RICHARD NIXON AND HENRY KISSINGER, WITHOUT the facts, were immediately convinced that India had started the war. The outbreak of war distilled all of Nixon's and Kissinger's resentments of India down to their essence. They would brook no dissent. They snapped into a state of self-righteousness, suddenly convinced that they and Pakistan had made herculean efforts, while India had done everything wrong.[13]

Kissinger, nobody's fool, realized correctly that India had been waiting for the opportune moment for war: "they moved as early as they were able to. The rains were over; the passes from China were closed with snow; the Bangla Desh had now been trained and the Indians had moved their own forces." But even if the Pakistanis had actually struck first, Kissinger forgivingly said, the U.S. line should be that they had been provoked into aggression: "it's like Finland attacking Russia."[14]

Nixon told Kissinger, "by God, I can't emphasize too strongly how I feel." The president was lost in bitter rage. "[W]e are not going to roll over after they have done this horrible thing," he ordered Kissinger. "[W]e will cut the gizzard out." Kissinger passed this presidential fire on down through the ranks. Nixon, he pointedly informed underlings, was "raging" or "raving." He told a Situation Room meeting, "I've been catching unshirted hell every half-hour from the President who says we're not tough enough."[15]

Nixon immediately ordered a stop to military and economic aid to India. He ordered Kissinger to scour every option to punish that country. As Kissinger told Alexander Haig, his deputy, "He wants to cut off all aid; he thinks I'm too soft"—a thought that made Kissinger burst out laughing. Nixon aimed to do lasting economic damage by cutting off aid to India for a long time.[16]

Both Nixon and Kissinger only regretted not tilting more toward Pakistan. On arms shipments to Pakistan, Nixon—unconcerned that Pakistan had used U.S. weapons for domestic repression rather than foreign defense—wished that he had given more. He thought that cutting off U.S. military assistance to Pakistan might have encouraged India to attack its weakened enemy. Kissinger wished that the administration had boldly cut off military and economic aid to India earlier, which might have held India back.[17]

For Kissinger, this was no mere local clash, but a Cold War contest of wills against the Soviet Union: "here we have Indian-Soviet collusion, raping a friend of ours." He told the president, "if we collapse now, the Soviets won't respect us for it; the Chinese will despise us"— which, he said, would wreck their opening to China. He argued that all their foreign achievements were coming undone: "The Russians are playing for big stakes here." If the White House backed down, "this will then be the Suez '56 episode of our Administration."[18]

Kissinger expected that the war would lead to Yahya's overthrow. Nixon was cut to the quick at the thought. "It's such a shame," he said mournfully. "So sad. So sad."[19]

Nixon and Kissinger reviled Indira Gandhi. Nixon intoned, "she says she is not going to be threatened by a country of whites 3 or 4 thousand miles away. Well, she didn't object to the color of our money." The president worried "whether or not I was too easy on the goddamn woman when she was here." Kissinger thought he probably should have "recommended to you to brutalize her privately." Nixon vowed that "she's going to pay. She's going to pay."[20]

Nixon's and Kissinger's wrath also encompassed the Indian people. When Nixon noted that some people might not want to alienate millions of Indians, Kissinger cut him off: "Well, but we haven't got them anyway, Mr. President." Nixon agreed: "We've got their enmity anyway. That's what she's shown in this goddamn thing, hasn't she?" Kissinger asked, "when have these bastards ever supported us?" "Never," said Nixon. Early in the war, the president said, "The arguments from the *New York Times* and others will be 'we will buy ourselves a century or decades of hatred and suspicion from the Indian people.' Bullshit!" Decades of U.S. foreign aid had only bought "hatred and suspicion from the Indian people." "Exactly," said Kissinger. "Tell me one friend we've got in India, do you know any?" "Exactly," said Kissinger.[21]

The Democrats, Nixon said, would "probably say we're losing India forever. All right, who's going to care about losing India forever?" Kissinger said, "We've got to keep the heat on them now. They have to know they paid a price. Hell, if we could reestablish relations with Communist China, we can always get the Indians back whenever we want to later—a year or two from now." He did not seem to grasp how winning back hundreds of millions of angry Indian citizens might be different from winning over Zhou Enlai. "I don't give a damn about the Indians," Nixon later said. Soon after that, he scorned elites who worried that "we'll lose six hundred million Indians." With withering sarcasm, he said, "Great loss."[22]

KISSINGER IN CRISIS

Henry Kissinger has burnished the image of himself as supremely coolheaded in a crisis—the real person you want to get that phone call at three o'clock in the morning. But to Nixon and his senior team, Kissinger, already worn out from the strain of handling the China opening and the Vietnam War, appeared to be coming frighteningly unglued. After months dedicating himself to preventing a major war, he had failed. His voice was shot, which Nixon thought was due to tension. He seemed exhausted and irrational.[23]

Alone in the Oval Office with H. R. Haldeman, the president suggested—in an empathetic, almost fatherly tone—that Kissinger's problem was "maybe deep down recognizing his own failure. Now that's what my guess is." Haldeman agreed it was "a self-guilt thing." Nixon said, "I think he's gotten emotional. He sounded awfully fatigued to me." Haldeman agreed that the "overexcited" Kissinger got "overdepressed about his failures."[24]

Nixon, fatalistically convinced that nothing could have been done to prevent the war, said Kissinger "feels very badly about this thing, because he always has a feeling that something we have done could have avoided it." After yet another tiff with the State Department, Kissinger stormed into Haldeman's office to say he would have to resign. "He's mixed up," said an exasperated Nixon. "He's tormented internally," agreed Haldeman. A few weeks later, after press criticism about anti-Indian policies set Kissinger off again, the president's aide John Ehrlichman noted, "Nixon wondered aloud if Henry needed psychiatric care."[25]

Enervated and humiliated, out of favor with the president, Kissinger became erratic in his behavior. In his fury, he turned apocalyptic, invoking the 1930s in ways that spooked even the most rock-ribbed White House officials. Haldeman warned Nixon that a "raging" Kissinger "talks about Chamberlain, and how this is our Rhineland." Even Haldeman, no squish, recoiled at Kissinger's "doomsday" talk of World War II. He dismissed the analogy of "Germany taking the Rhineland or something like that, but I mean there's a little difference there. India doesn't have a plan for world conquest."[26]

Nixon pointed out that Kissinger, scapegoating the bureaucracy, "really has the inability to see that . . . he himself is ever wrong." George H. W. Bush found Kissinger paranoid and out of control. "Henry is very excitable, very emotional almost," he wrote privately. While admiring Kissinger's intelligence and wit, he noted that he "is absolutely brutal on these [State Department] guys, insisting that they don't know anything and asking why they are screwing up policy etc. I went through that, and . . . had a little bit of a battle myself."[27]

So the war arrived with Kissinger seeking vindication, needing a win to bolster his standing with the president. For all his commitment to dispassionate realpolitik, he seemed propelled almost as much by emotion as by calculation. He would not admit that the United States had missed opportunities to avoid war by pressuring Pakistan. Despite having spent months denying that the United States bore responsibility for Pakistan's actions, he now wholeheartedly blamed the Soviet Union for India's. Nixon, despite his visceral hatred of India, saw the bigger picture: this was just one crisis in just one part of the world, where the United States was playing a losing hand. But Kissinger, in his despondency and rage, kept trying to escalate. He wanted to force the Soviet Union to back down.[28]

ONE WAR ON TWO FRONTS

India waged starkly different campaigns in the east and west, with goals as dissimilar as the terrain. In the east, Indian troops fought a blazingly rapid war for the independence of Bangladesh, racing across swampland toward a decisive victory in Dacca, needing to get there before the United Nations Security Council stopped them in their tracks. Before the war, D. P. Dhar wrote to Haksar that they needed to finish up completely within eight days before foreign intervention halted them.[29]

Thus, as Indian generals argued, charging to Dacca itself was a fast way to secure Bangladesh. While blocking the territory's ports and airfields from any help from the West Pakistanis, the Indian army launched a devastating assault of several different forces of infantry and armor.[30]

No such feats were possible on the western front. There Pakistan meant to punish India and gain land in Kashmir to compensate for eastern losses; as Pakistan's generals used to say, the defense of East Pakistan was in the west. West Pakistan itself was a tough redoubt, with invaders facing highly motivated Pakistani troops in bunkers and pillboxes, defenses such as antitank ditches, and, as Jacob noted respectfully, a "well equipped force strong in armour." Indian forces were only somewhat stronger than Pakistan's there, without the kind of decisive superiority required for a successful offensive. So India and Pakistan became locked in a bloody but inconclusive stalemate, with tanks dustily clashing in the desert or in the mountains of Kashmir. General Manekshaw later said that his troops kept a "mainly defensive posture" against West Pakistan, only launching "limited offensives" meant to defend communications and bases and to improve their positions in Kashmir.[31]

Pakistan, encouraged by long months of White House support, hoped for foreign succor and perhaps intervention. As the CIA noted before the war, Pakistan's "prideful, honor-conscious generals" might suddenly assault India, knowing defeat was likely, but hoping for good luck or a timely intervention by the great powers. Manekshaw would later speculate that Pakistan had attacked in the hope of grabbing large parts of Kashmir to compensate for the amputation of Bangladesh, and "to internationalise the whole issue and rouse World opinion, especially the USA in the hope of preventing INDIA from striking back. They were also perhaps expecting much more help from CHINA."[32]

When Yahya attacked on December 3, he obviously had in mind something like the Israeli air force's preemptive strike on Egyptian airfields in the Six-Day War in 1967, to be followed by devastating advances on the western front. He failed. India had dispersed and protected its air force in anticipation, and the Pakistani attack proved surprisingly ineffectual.[33]

Indian MiG-21 fighter-bombers pounded Dacca's airport. Thousands of people watched thunderstruck from the crowded city's streets and rooftops as Pakistani F-86 Sabre jet fighters fought them in quicksilver dogfights. The air was thick with flak, appearing as red tracers at night and puffy white smoke in daylight. In the U.S. consulate in Dacca, some of Archer Blood's remaining dissenters cheered the Indians on.

"It's hard to describe this without seeming callous," says Desaix Myers, the rebellious junior development officer, "but we were taking sides at this point. We didn't think that Pakistan was going to be able to put it back together, we thought that what Pakistan was doing was wrong, we thought they needed to be controlled, we thought that Indira had to take action, we wanted the army to reach Dacca as soon as possible and to end the war." Holed up at the Intercontinental Hotel, with blackout curtains on the windows, they could watch Indian warplanes flying in to bomb the airport, coming out of the sun to make themselves a harder target.[34]

The Indian air force—which had a three-to-one advantage in aircraft—quickly established mastery of the eastern skies, pulverizing the Dacca airfield into uselessness, and wiping out most of Pakistan's small collection of warplanes in the east. With this air superiority, India's air force provided cover for its advancing troops below, and pummeled Pakistan's remaining warplanes and airfields, radar units, fuel dumps, and armored columns.[35]

Lieutenant General Jagjit Singh Aurora, the general officer commanding-in-chief of the Indian army's Eastern Command—a tough and brainy Sikh soldier, with sharp eyes and upturned mustache—would later call the fight for Bangladesh "the battle of obstacles." He and Jacob, his chief of staff, raced their troops across terrain unforgivingly sliced by fast-flowing rivers and streams, improvising as they went, relying on engineers, bridging equipment, and rivercraft to get the troops across. Adding to the challenge, the Mukti Bahini guerrillas had already blown up many of the bridges.[36]

But the Mukti Bahini—who would later in the war be brought under General Aurora's command—more than compensated by establishing bridgeheads and organizing local transport for the Indian troops. These Bengali rebels, relying on the support of local civilians, sped the Indians' advance with riverboats, rickshaws, and bullock carts. Bengali villagers carried guns and ammunition across their familiar countryside for the Indian troops. At one point, twenty locals pushed a 5.5-inch medium gun through a boggy rice field, with other Bengalis carrying its ammunition.[37]

India's air superiority left the Indian columns free to advance without fear of strafing from enemy warplanes, without having to disperse or take cover. India used helicopters to drop battalions of paratroopers deep inside East Pakistan, to link up with the Mukti Bahini and, eventually, the Indian army. To General Jacob's satisfaction, they went ahead with a big paratrooper drop precisely on schedule with the war plan—confident enough of their air supremacy to land the paratroopers in daylight. The helicopters became, in an Indian general's words, an "air bridge."[38]

With Pakistani soldiers dug into bunkers and fortified positions, the Indians preferred to bypass them rather than attack them directly, leaving behind enough Indian troops—or in many cases a Mukti Bahini force—to keep the Pakistanis stuck there. "We went around the towns and went straight for Dacca," recalls Admiral Roy. There was no time to capture cities. Bent on reaching Dacca, Indian troops wound up taking only two major towns, Jessore and Comilla. Rather than taking the highways, which were sure targets, the Indians tried to go on dirt roads or through fields, helped along by the Mukti Bahini's peerless knowledge of the local riverine terrain. In a bombed-out school, an Indian officer told Sydney Schanberg of the New York Times, "We are kicking the shit out of them."[39]

In many places, like Jamalpur, the Indians faced pitched resistance from the Pakistan army. "Give my love to the Muktis," wrote one Pakistani colonel in reply to an Indian demand for surrender, enclosing a Chinese-made bullet in his letter. At another village, Schanberg, who accompanied an Indian tank unit, remembers staring in horror at charred Pakistani soldiers in a trench that had been blown up by tank fire. In a field, he counted twenty-two dead Pakistani soldiers in their bunkers, some of them seemingly peaceful, but others mangled or torn apart by Indian artillery bursts. One bunker had collapsed completely, with two booted feet sticking up from what had become a grave.[40]

The Mukti Bahini fought alongside the Indians. As a Bangladeshi commander later bragged, "Once again we demonstrated to the world that the Bengalis are a fighting martial race." After an Indian pilot got shot down, the rebels sheltered him. When the insurgents attacked Pakistani soldiers, terrified villagers fled, sometimes getting cut down in the crossfire. Wading knee deep through the muddy water, one rebel incongruously remembered small fish "friskily moving around . . . playing their own games in their own world." This guerrilla recalled his jubilation while watching the "beautiful" sight of three Indian Gnat fighter planes swooping down out of a clear sky toward Pakistani gunboats on a river, followed by blasts and dense smoke.[41]

The euphoric Indian troops were greeted with cheers and hugs from the local Bengalis. As the Indian army advanced, Schanberg noticed that nervous Bengali civilians followed about a mile or two behind

them, hoping to return to their homes. Some, the victims of final spiteful attacks by the retreating Pakistanis, would not make it. The *New
York Times* reporter saw two dead Bengali civilians left in a field to be
gnawed by dogs, and another with his left arm sliced off and his chest
torn open. For their part, some of the Mukti Bahini and Bengalis took
cruel revenge on Pakistani troops and collaborators. Despite Indian
army orders against reprisal executions, an Indian army captain saw
the mutilated corpses of Pakistani soldiers, their fingers and nipples
slashed off and their throats cut.[42]

On both sides, as even partisans had to admit, soldiers fought with
extraordinary courage. Still, with the Pakistan army crumbling in the
east, India urged the enemy troops to surrender rather than die for no
reason. Manekshaw broadcast repeated appeals emphasizing that prisoners of war would be treated honorably under the Geneva Conventions. There was another, nastier incentive for the Pakistanis to yield to
the Indians: as senior Indian officials surmised, Pakistani troops would
probably fare better if they surrendered to Indian soldiers rather than
to the Mukti Bahini.[43]

India's victories were not just the product of the bravery of its
soldiers, but also the quality of their equipment and weapons—the
fruit of India's own defense industry and Soviet support. Manekshaw
thanked the Soviet Union for its camouflaged PT-76 amphibious light
tanks, which could handle mud and marsh in Bangladesh, and its Mi-4
transport helicopters, which got Indian troops across streams and rivers, and evacuated wounded soldiers. India's sturdy Soviet-made T-55
medium tanks could take out Pakistan's U.S.-made M-54 Chaffee
light tanks. Soviet commanders, proud as Indian troops redeemed the
iffy reputation of their armaments, praised India's armed forces with
their highest compliment: comparing them to Soviet fighters in World
War II.[44]

AS INDIAN TROOPS AND BENGALI GUERRILLAS CLOSED IN ON DACCA,
the non-Bengali minority in Bangladesh—the Urdu-speaking Biharis,
many of whom had supported Pakistan—were at terrible risk of vengeful atrocities by the Mukti Bahini. Yahya told Joseph Farland, the U.S.
ambassador, that India would kill "not thousands but millions." Farland, echoing that, alerted the State Department to the "potential . . .
for one of the greatest blood lettings" of the century, with Bengalis
mercilessly taking revenge upon Biharis who had helped the West Pakistanis. Bihari men, women, and children would be butchered, he wrote,

unless the Indian army prevented it. A senior United Nations official in Dacca warned that Biharis had gathered there, "armed to the teeth," gripped by "animal fear" exacerbated by "threats of reprisals" on All India Radio.[45]

Kissinger responded well. He swiftly wanted to call on all parties to prevent massacres. So the United States urged India to prevent retaliation against Biharis and—as India had already pledged to do—treat Pakistani troops humanely under the Geneva Conventions. Of course, Kissinger had shown no such alacrity when the Bengalis were slaughtered; since the Biharis were, in his eyes, Pakistani citizens facing peril from other Pakistani citizens, their protection should not have been an international concern; and the White House was plainly seeking to puncture India's pretense of moral superiority. He told Nixon that "in six months the liberals are going to look like jerks because the Indian occupation of East Pakistan is going to make the Pakistani one look like child's play." Nixon was eager for signs of Indian atrocities: "Here they are raping and murdering, and they talk about West Pakistan, these Indians are pretty vicious in there, aren't they? Aren't they killing a lot of people?" Even when his own officials denied him such evidence, he persisted, at one point furiously saying, "Henry, I just want the Indians to look bad. I want them to look bad for bombing that orphanage"—an incident that the U.S. consulate and the UN representative in Dacca believed had actually been done by a Pakistani airplane, in order to discredit India's air force. But such hypocrisies are beside the point. The United States was asking for decent behavior, which could save innocent lives. It was right to do so.[46]

India, keenly aware of world public opinion, pledged that it was not out for vengeance. It promised to protect Biharis and surrendered Pakistani soldiers from retribution, following the Geneva Conventions. Haksar ordered Indian diplomats to pound home to Bangladeshi leaders the need for mercy: "they should say that they have been victims of such bloodshed and would not wish to spill any blood and deal with their opponents with humanity as a civilised State. Bangla Desh is emerging as a State in the family of nations. Their representatives have everything to gain by appearing dignified, calm, and self-possessed." After reading the warning from that UN official in Dacca, Haksar instructed General Manekshaw, the defense ministry, and other outlets to declare "that Indian Armed Forces will not resort to the barbarism of Pakistan Armed Forces, that everybody who peacefully surrenders will be treated with respect and his life safeguarded."[47]

There were still many horrible revenge killings. The most that can be said is that Indian influence meant there were fewer than there otherwise might have been. This is cold comfort. Under Indian pressure, the Bangladesh government pledged to respect the Geneva Conventions, promising humane treatment for prisoners of war and civilians—a declaration that Haksar had broadcast on All India Radio and read out at a government press conference. On December 9, the CIA reported, "The Indians appear to be making good on their promise to try to protect these people from vengeance-seeking Bengalis."[48]

THROUGHOUT THE CONFLICT, THE INDIAN NAVY WAS EAGER TO SHOW its mettle. By severing maritime outlets to West Pakistan, it cut off the Pakistani troops in the east from reinforcement or resupply. And by choking the ports of Chittagong and Khulna, the navy relieved the army of the need to capture them on land.[49]

To blockade the key eastern port of Chittagong, India deployed its sole aircraft carrier, the British-built INS *Vikrant,* backed up with supporting ships and submarines. From the carrier, India could launch Sea Hawk fighter-bombers into battle. But only if it worked. Even in India's motley navy, the creaky *Vikrant*—in constant need of repair— was the butt of countless jokes. Three months before the war, the navy deemed it inoperable, with a crack in its boiler. "What's the bloody point of having an aircraft carrier if it cannot be used during a war?" spat Admiral S. M. Nanda, India's top navy man. The Indians patched it up as best they could and deployed it, dreading attacks by Pakistan's biggest and mightiest submarine, PNS *Ghazi,* which had been provided to the Pakistan navy by the United States.[50]

Yahya himself hoped his navy would sink the *Vikrant.* But the unlucky *Ghazi* suffered an underwater explosion so loud that it broke windows on dry land: the result of plowing into Indian depth charges, according to Indian naval officers, or of hitting one of its own mines, according to the Pakistan navy. The great submarine sank to the bottom. The *Vikrant,* freed from its fear of the *Ghazi,* led attacks on Chittagong and Cox's Bazar, paralyzing these vital harbors, and setting Chittagong's main oil refinery alight. India's eastern naval commander signaled his sailors, "MOTTO FOR EASTERN FLEET IS—'ATTACK— ATTACK—ATTACK.' " East Pakistan was blocked off from any sea outlet to West Pakistan.[51]

At the same time, in West Pakistan, where Pakistani warplanes still challenged them for the skies, the Indian air force launched frightening strikes on airports and military installations in Rawalpindi and—again and again—Karachi. In Lahore, the Indian warplanes mostly hit military targets, although they did buzz the U.S. consul's residence. When Nixon heard that the Indians had blown up a U.S. plane at the Islamabad airport—which actually belonged to the famous test pilot Chuck Yeager—he flew into a wild, screaming rage, berating his staff: "Now goddamn it, *what the hell is the shit-ass State Department* doing about objecting with those planes?"[52]

The Indian air force and navy had planned a daring surprise assault on the heavily defended port of Karachi, to destroy Pakistan's crucial oil storage facilities, which held four-fifths of Pakistan's supply, vital to keeping Pakistan's armor moving. Late at night on December 4, Indian warplanes struck, while India's navy surreptitiously crept up the coast and unleashed missiles on the city's oil depots. The massive blaze turned the sky a bizarre, unearthly pink.[53]

Off Karachi, Indian warships blasted in half and sank a massive Pakistani destroyer, PNS *Khyber,* and badly damaged a second, PNS *Shahjehan.* In a second big raid on December 8, the Indian navy fired another barrage on the Karachi area, blowing up fuel tanks and tankers. The next day, as the city weathered its thirteenth air raid, the fires spread, leaving half of the city's oil storage up in flames. For seven terrifying days, Karachi burned.[54]

THE BATTLE OF CHHAMB

Although understandably nobody who lived through Karachi's oily inferno could see it this way, India actually had to fight a relatively cautious land war against a thoroughly formidable West Pakistan. While India hoped to pummel Pakistan's offensive war machine and to improve its position in Kashmir, there was no chance of the kind of decisive victories that it was scoring in the east.[55]

These military facts were well understood in Washington. The CIA, based on a source purportedly with access to Indian cabinet deliberations, explained that India planned a "defensive posture" in the west, preventing Pakistan from lunging deeper into Kashmir. Kissinger informed Nixon of this defensive Indian stance. The president thought India would face "real rough going up through those mountains" in West Pakistan. It would be, he said, "a good trade" if Pakistan grabbed Kashmir while India took East Pakistan.[56]

The combat in the west was sharp and devastating. Death came at every moment: in the dead of night, when a bright moon gave away Pakistani tanks moving in the desert; in daylight, when a twenty-two-year-old Indian lieutenant was killed instantly by a direct hit on his tank's turret; or in a hurried breakfast, as a Border Security Force officer was eating chapatis when a Pakistani shell came out of nowhere to slice open his windpipe. Indian and Pakistani troops screamed back and forth with the filthiest Punjabi curses they knew.[57]

Pakistan launched massive thrusts in Kashmir and Rajasthan. In the Poonch sector in Kashmir, Indian troops struggled to hold fast against Pakistani artillery and machine guns. It was only after five days of hard fighting, with heavy casualties, that India thought Poonch was secure. Indian troops made a bold thrust into Sindh, as well as pressing hard into Pakistan's Punjab. But the western front cast a shadow over the breakfast meetings where Indira Gandhi and General Manekshaw nervously updated each other. When the fighting bogged down on the sixth day of the war, she tried to buck him up: "But Sam, you can't win every day."[58]

In Kashmir, Pakistan attacked fiercely in the Chhamb sector. The combat there was the worst of the war. Pakistan had massed terrifying firepower: some two hundred heavy guns as well as medium ones, which rained down sixty thousand rounds on the Indians in under two days. Soon the hillsides were burned black. The Pakistanis would start deafening artillery barrages late in the afternoon and keep firing until long after midnight, eerily lighting up the night. The ground shook. The Indian soldiers had a sick sense of doom. The incoming shells cratered the battlefield, propelling solid rock and soil high into the air. They smashed sandbagged concrete bunkers. When they hit a trench, they blasted up a grotesque rain of mud and human limbs. A nearby shallow river reddened.[59]

The Pakistanis endured punishing attacks from Indian fighter-bombers, while the Indians faced a hellish combination of Pakistani airstrikes, artillery, and charges by infantry and tanks. On December 5, the battle reached a smoky, gory climax, with Pakistan's notorious Lieutenant General Tikka Khan redoubling his troops' attack. One Indian Sikh regiment used rocket launchers against the tanks, thrilling the troops at the sight of four of the metal behemoths immobilized by their own tank killers. The Indians' machine guns jammed from overuse. After that, the Pakistanis took advantage of their superior numbers with an infantry charge, which the Indians tried to force back with gruesome hand-to-hand fighting with bayonets. "Let them know they are fighting a Sikh regiment," bellowed the Indian major in command, who was himself a Hindu.[60]

The base camp hospitals were overrun with the shrieking wounded, ripped apart by shrapnel and bullets, bleeding out. Against their terror, the troops carried photographs of their wives and children, or a deity. One Indian soldier, firing in a frenzy at charging Pakistani columns, was blasted by a bomb, suffering horrible internal injuries. "Lord, save me for the sake of my one-month-old son and my wife," he prayed. An officer, on the verge of death, kept shouting at the surgeons to let him return to the front to avenge his brother. Another soldier, who had kept on shooting because it was the only chance of surviving, was vomiting blood. Others had lost hands, feet, and legs.[61]

On December 6, ground down by combined barrages of airstrikes and artillery, the Indians had to fall back. They fought on afterward, but had been bested by the Pakistanis. The battlefield was left strewn with burned-out tanks, jeeps, and trucks, as well as abandoned guns. It reeked of human corpses rotting in the sun. With minefields in place, troops on both sides did not dare recover their dead.[62]

THE UNITED NATIONS AT WORK

Indira Gandhi had a mystical, hallucinatory experience of wartime leadership. She had "an extended vision I had known at times in my youth," she told a startled friend. "The color red suffused me throughout the war."[63]

More prosaically, the outbreak of war finally allowed her to recognize Bangladesh, on December 6. This was, the Indians hoped, the birth of a new democracy that respected human rights. Baiting Nixon, Gandhi invoked America's own independence struggle, justifying Bangladesh's statehood by misusing words from Thomas Jefferson: "the Government of Bangla Desh is supported by the 'will of the nation, substantially expressed.'"[64]

India's recognition of Bangladesh was not just about preventing chaos or a power vacuum, or enshrining the Awami League in power. It meant to prove that this was not a war of conquest. "The act of recognition shows a voluntary restraint which we have imposed upon ourselves," Haksar instructed Indian officials. "It signifies our desire not to annex or occupy any territory." To underline Bangladesh's independence, Indian officials scrambled to find photographs and film of Bengali guerrillas fighting for their own country, or of Bengalis welcoming the Indian army as liberators. Gandhi publicly declared, "We do not want anybody's territory."[65]

In Washington, Nixon and Kissinger were usually contemptuously dismissive of the United Nations. But once the war started, they suddenly discovered the usefulness of the world organization—as a cudgel against India. By getting the United Nations Security Council to demand pulling back all troops, they could deny India its battlefield victory. As Nixon said, "the Indians are susceptible to this world public opinion crap."[66]

So India's war effort became reliant on Soviet diplomats in New York, temporizing or vetoing, buying enough time for General Manekshaw's troops to win in Bangladesh. (This was particularly awkward since the Soviet Union had long warned India against a war in the subcontinent.) Kissinger bluntly explained to Nixon, "At the Security Council, the Indians and Soviets are going to delay long enough so a resolution cannot be passed. If it was, the Soviets would veto. UN will be impotent. So the Security Council is just a paper exercise—it will get the *Post* and *Times* off our backs. And the Libs will be happy that we turned it over to the UN. . . . [T]his proves that countries can get away with brutality."[67]

For three exasperating days, while Indian troops battled toward Dacca, the Security Council debated and delayed. Confirming India's worst fears of the United Nations, the Nixon administration secretly worked with China to poleax India. On December 4, George H. W. Bush, the U.S. ambassador to the United Nations, offered a resolution for an immediate cease-fire and the withdrawal of troops—which would undo the Indian campaign for Bangladesh. Nixon laid out their party line to Bush: "if you want to put it, we're not pro-Pakistan or pro-Indian, but we are pro-peace."[68]

Bush, while assiduously dodging any direct reference to Pakistani atrocities, condemned India for attacking "in violation of the United Nations Charter." Brushing aside any discussion of the origins of the conflict, he said, "This has been a full-scale invasion in East Pakistan and it must stop." The Indian foreign ministry, stung at being labeled an aggressor by a superpower at war in Vietnam, privately groused that the United States had encouraged Pakistan's "unprovoked and naked aggression" and "genocide in East Pakistan." When Pakistan decried India's interference in its internal affairs as a brazen transgression of the United Nations Charter, Indian diplomats countered far and wide that "genocide in Bangla Desh . . . is not an internal matter of Pakistan and is the concern of the international community, under the Genocide Convention and other international instruments."[69]

The Indian foreign ministry secretly slammed Bush as "completely pro-Pakistan," ignoring the Bangladeshis' plight. For his part, Bush took showy offense at Indian advocacy. He boasted to Nixon that when one of India's diplomats had dared to mention the president by name, Bush had "climbed on him." He was having fun. He told Nixon, "it's been fantastic."[70]

Nixon and Kissinger relished the absurdity of the pinstriped show in New York. The U.S. resolution overpoweringly carried the day, winning eleven votes, with only the Soviet Union—which cast a veto—and its satellite Poland defending India. If there was an anti-Indian resolution, Kissinger explained, "the Russians will veto it," and if "it's anti-Pakistan, the Chinese will veto it." Nixon burst out laughing. Standing firm, they had Bush introduce another similar resolution, daring the Soviet Union to veto again. As draft resolutions piled up, the Soviet Union made a second veto for India, despite another embarrassing vote of eleven to two. Kissinger told Nixon, about the Soviets, "They are having a good time."[71]

Kissinger warned the Soviet Union that "we are at a watershed in our relationship," while Nixon sent Leonid Brezhnev a letter harshly complaining that he was supporting Indian force against Pakistan's independence and integrity. Kissinger urged Nixon to confront the Soviets: "Every time we've been tough with them they've backed off."[72]

By the night of December 6, the hopelessly deadlocked Security Council gave up, punting the whole mess to the General Assembly. Bush neatly elided the difference between the atrocities against Bengali civilians and his own accusations of Indian aggression: "Stopping the slaughter, stopping the invasion somehow seems to our people to be desperately important." He eagerly told Nixon that "there was a *strong* groundswell. The minute we made our resolution, in that first resolution, the U.S. resolution, that got beat eleven to two, many ambassadors, not on the Security Council, that had never voted with us, Zambia, Tanzania, Morocco, came up and said we ought to go to the General Assembly. This is an *excellent* position. We don't sometimes vote with the U.S. but you're absolutely right."[73]

THE NEXT DAY, DECEMBER 7, INDIA FACED A GLOBAL VERDICT ON THE war. In a crushingly lopsided tally, fully 104 countries voted for a resolution calling for a cease-fire and withdrawal.[74]

This was a worldwide repudiation of India's case for liberating Bangladesh. Indians fumed that these same governments had been desultory in preventing carnage or providing for the refugees. Despite plangent appeals from Indira Gandhi and her team, India only won backing from the Soviet Union, a few Soviet satrapies and satellites, and neighboring little Bhutan (Nixon snapped, "Bhutan isn't a country, for Christ's sake")—just eleven votes, a tenth of what the United States and China together mustered. Bush told Nixon that "we got strong support through Africa and through the Arab countries." India was abandoned by the Non-Aligned Movement, including Yugoslavia, Egypt, Ghana, and Indonesia. This vote had no binding authority, but it was tremendously humiliating.[75]

Nixon and Kissinger were jubilant. "Hoh, Christ!" laughed Nixon. He told Kissinger, "The Indian lovers are a breed apart. But by God they don't rule in the UN, do they?" The president gloated at the slap to India's supporters in the United States, particularly Ted Kennedy. Kissinger concurred: "these damn liberals, what can they say? Security Council eleven to two? And the General Assembly 104 to eleven?"[76]

The most ebullient American was George Bush, who sounded like he had just won the war himself. When Nixon telephoned to congratulate him, he could hardly contain his joy. "We felt *very, very* good about it," Bush told Nixon, who sounded like he could not get off the phone fast enough. Despite strong Soviet and Indian lobbying, Bush said, "all they got was their Iron Curtain." He explained that "there was *total* agreement on the principle of ceasefire and withdrawal, which we had—you made fundamental to what was—and the fact also that India, in spite of its sanctimony, was really the *aggressor*."

This set off Nixon, who fumed, "the Indians put on this sanctimonious peace Gandhi-like Christ-like attitude, and they're the greatest, the world's biggest democracy, and Pakistan is one of the most horrible dictatorships." Bush followed Nixon's lead, saying he had told the United Nations, "look, we're talking about war and peace. We're talking about *invasion*. We're talking about 150,000 troops in the other guy's country." This was the early voice of the future president who would two decades later go to war to undo Iraq's invasion of Kuwait.

Still, showing a bit of bad conscience over the Pakistani atrocities that they were not mentioning, Bush said, "that's the point where the United States is *right*. We're trying to stop that. We're not whitewashing Yahya." Nixon pointed to the administration's success in using its influence on Yahya over the refugees, United Nations observers, and talks with, as he put it, "Mujib deal and all that jazz." Nixon admitted that much of the criticism of Yahya's government was "justified," but ringingly said that "it does *not* justify resort to invasion of another country. If we ever allow the internal problems of one country to be justification for the right of another country, bigger, more powerful, to invade it, then international order is finished in the world. That's really the principle, isn't it?" Bush agreed enthusiastically: "That's the fundamental. And that's why they lost the vote."

Nixon warmed to the principle that a sovereign government could do whatever it wanted inside its own borders. He conceded that "as far as Yahya is concerned, there's no clean hands there either. I mean, they handled this very clumsily, very badly." But he and Bush reserved their anger for the Indians. The president growled, "They're caught in a bloody bit of aggression." He gave Bush his marching orders: "the main thing, as I say, all this yak, if you can constantly emphasize that *world opinion,* world opinion, it isn't a question of being pro-democracy or against—anti-democracy, it's not a question of being for six hundred million as against sixty million. Aggression is *wrong.* And the difference in size between countries does not justify it. The difference in systems of governments does not justify it. Aggression on the part of a democracy, if it is not justified, is just as wrong as aggression on the part of a dictatorship." He concluded, "It is aggression that is wrong. That's what the UN is built upon, after all. Those goddamn communist countries are all, if they engage in it, it's wrong on their part, but if a democracy engages in aggression, it's wrong."

Bush had much more to say, but Nixon cut him off, said, "Knock 'em dead," and hung up without saying goodbye.[77]

"I WANT TO PISS ON THEM"

At home, Nixon and Kissinger unleashed the full power of the White House to brand the war to Americans as flagrant Indian aggression. Any way they could—from Kissinger's background briefings, Vice President Spiro Agnew, White House flacks, cabinet secretaries, State Department officials, and surrogates in Congress such as Gerald Ford—they got the word out. "Let the Indians squeal," said Nixon. "Let the liberals squeal."[78]

"I want a public relations program developed to piss on the Indians," Nixon told Kissinger. "I want to piss on them for their responsibility." He fumed, "I want the Indians blamed for this, you know what

I mean? We can't let these goddamn, sanctimonious Indians get away with this. They've pissed on us on Vietnam for 5 years, Henry."[79]

The White House skillfully took advantage of Americans' distaste for the Vietnam War. "Let's let our opponents side with India at this time, with this aggression," said Nixon. "People don't like war. They'll turn against it."[80]

Kissinger set out to make the case against the Indians to the White House press corps. He contemptuously said that "of course, they are bleeding about the refugees. But it's beginning to tilt against India." In a press background briefing, he kept a straight face while saying that he was unaware if Nixon preferred Pakistan's leaders over India's. While deploring to the reporters the American public's "love affair with India," he privately grew confident that American support for India was shallow. He told Nixon, "The sons-of-bitches in this country can piss on you as much as they want." He explained that "our liberal establishment" is "morally corrupt, but it's also intellectually so totally corrupt. What they're telling you is, in effect, to preside over the rape of an ally." He added, "I don't know which American likes India." "Nobody," said Nixon. "Except those intellectuals who are against you," Kissinger added.[81]

Once the war started, Ted Kennedy and his fellow Democrats could not compete with the president's bully pulpit. Nixon and Kissinger lashed back at their Democratic critics, encouraging Republican allies in Congress to decry India. After the United Nations General Assembly's vote, Nixon gloated to Kissinger, "God damn, I must say, these Churches, Henry, and these Kennedys, and the *New York Times,* and the rest, and *Time,* they'll look at that vote." Kissinger urged him to go on the attack against Kennedy.[82]

Nixon thought of himself as a man of ideals, and justified his policies as a necessary moral stand against aggression. He insisted that something "that State needs to get pounded into its goddamned head" was that U.S. policy was not determined by "whether a country is a democracy or whether it is not a democracy." He told Kissinger, "By God, we just don't do it that way. . . . [A]n evil deed is not made good by the form of government that executes the deed, Henry. I mean, as I've often said, the most horrible wars in history have been fought between the Christian nations of Western Europe." Aggression, he argued, was worse when committed by a democracy, because democracies should have higher moral standards. With satisfaction, he added, "I really think that puts the issue to these sons-of-bitches."[83]

Driven by the White House's campaigning, the American mood swung against India. Despite unease about Nixon's own handling of the subcontinent's war, Americans came to sympathize somewhat more with Pakistan than India. Many more Americans simply tuned out, not caring about either side or not being sure what was going on. As the president told Kissinger, "People don't give a shit whether we're to blame—not to blame—because they don't care if the whole goddamn thing goes down the cesspool." Nixon, while regretting that public opinion did not allow him to do more to help Pakistan, was reassured. "[T]hey're not going to touch us with this thing," he said. "Because, by God, the country doesn't give a shit."[84]

Kissinger was relieved. As the Pakistan army faced defeat in the east, he said, with his voice dripping contempt, "That means no one can bleed anymore about the dying Bengalis."[85]

Chapter 19

"I Consider This Our Rhineland"

ON DECEMBER 7, LIEUTENANT GENERAL A. A. K. NIAZI, THE COMmander of Pakistan's Eastern Command, was haggard and exhausted. According to another general, he wept loudly in a meeting. After only a few days of combat, the Pakistan army was being routed in Bangladesh. Richard Nixon and Henry Kissinger became sincerely convinced that ripping Pakistan in half would not be enough for India. India could next redeploy its eastern forces for a crushing assault against West Pakistan.[1]

What was India fighting for: the liberation of Bangladesh or something more? "The destruction of Pakistan, which seemed to be the ultimate war aim at the time," answers Samuel Hoskinson, Kissinger's aide, without hesitation. "Indeed, she was ready to do it. We had pretty good information that this was under serious consideration in the war cabinet." Once Bangladesh was secured, the White House staffer says, "Her intention was to move troops across northern India and attack in the west, to finish off this problem." He says, "I know that it was being discussed actively with her generals and her top people." This was intolerable for the White House. "This would be a mighty strategic defeat for the U.S.," says Hoskinson. "She had taken on an ally and destroyed it. Nixon and Kissinger were always aware of national prestige. . . . This would be a total victory for the Soviets."

Although the most sensitive wartime records are still secret, it is not clear that India was seriously trying to break apart West Pakistan. As Kissinger briefed Nixon, "the Indians still seem to be essentially on the defensive" in the west. Even if India could smartly finish up its eastern campaign, it would take more time to redeploy its troops westward than the Soviet Union, stalling a cease-fire at the United Nations, could accept: the CIA reckoned that it would take five or six days for India's

290 ~ The Blood Telegram

airborne division to move to the western front, and much longer for their infantry and armor fighting in the east. U.S. intelligence analysts argued that in order to hack apart West Pakistan, India would have to not just defeat the Pakistan army, but completely wipe it out—something probably beyond India's capacities, even if it wanted to do so.[2]

Hoskinson's verdict, echoing that of Nixon and Kissinger, depended heavily on raw intelligence from a CIA mole with access to Indira Gandhi's cabinet. Based on this one source, the CIA reported that Gandhi meant to keep fighting until Bangladesh was liberated, India had seized a contested area of Kashmir currently controlled by Pakistan, and Pakistan's armor and air force were "destroyed so that Pakistan will never again be in a position to plan another invasion of India."[3]

It is still not certain who the mole was, nor how reliable he was. Many intelligence analysts doubted the report. For a start, the real debates and decisions happened in the prime minister's secretariat, sometimes widening to include a small political affairs committee of key ministers, but certainly not the whole unwieldy cabinet of blabbermouths. It is true that Indian diplomats were evasive when asked about that contested area of Kashmir, and Indian officials later admitted wanting to gain some other small, strategic bits of territory in Kashmir—but they emphasized that Gandhi had overruled her hawks and insisted on waging a basically defensive war in the west. Whether the informant was worth much, the U.S. government relied overwhelmingly on this information.[4]

Kissinger, whose emotions were already running high, was jolted. He did not question the intelligence, which confirmed his preconceived view of India. He did not ask how India would manage such a major campaign against West Pakistan, nor about how it could extricate itself afterward. Instead, he decided that the United States needed to get much tougher on India. On December 8, he told Nixon, "the Indian plan is now clear. They're going to move their forces from East Pakistan to the west." They would then "smash" Pakistan's army and air force and annex some of Kashmir. This, he argued—going beyond the CIA intelligence—could well mean "the complete dismemberment" of West Pakistan, with secessionism in Baluchistan and the North-West Frontier Province. "All of this would have been achieved by Soviet support, Soviet arms, and Indian military force." So Soviet client states in the Middle East and elsewhere would feel free to attack with impunity, while China would think the Americans were "just too weak." The crisis was, he told Nixon, "a big watershed."[5]

Nixon was hit hard too. Like Kissinger, he swiftly accepted the intelligence, without wondering whether this was bluster or if India would really be so reckless, or asking skeptical questions about India's military difficulties besieging West Pakistan. Both Nixon and Kissinger might have seen this one source as revealing hostile but standard Indian war aims in the west: some gains in Kashmir, substantial damage to Pakistan's war machine, all of it limited by West Pakistan's own formidable resistance. Instead, they foresaw the imminent annihilation of West Pakistan. Extrapolating beyond the CIA mole's information, Nixon spoke of a U.S. intelligence "report on Mrs. Gandhi's Cabinet meeting where she said that, she said deliberately that they were going to try to conquer West Pakistan, they were going to move their forces from the East to the West."[6]

KISSINGER'S SECRET ONSLAUGHT

Yahya's only hope was outside help from China and the United States. Pakistan's General Niazi says that he was told to hold out for help from "Yellows from the North and Whites from the South"—the Chinese and the Americans. Kissinger urged Nixon to "scare them"—the Indians—"off an attack on West Pakistan as much as we possibly can. And therefore we've got to get another tough warning to the Russians."[7]

Kissinger now proposed three dangerous initiatives. The United States would illegally allow Iran and Jordan to send squadrons of U.S. aircraft to Pakistan, secretly ask China to mass its troops on the Indian border, and deploy a U.S. aircraft carrier group to the Bay of Bengal to threaten India. He urged Nixon to stun India with all three moves simultaneously.

Kissinger knew that the American public would be shocked by this gunboat diplomacy. "I'm sure all hell will break loose here," he said. Still, Nixon quickly agreed to all three steps: "let's do the carrier thing. Let's get assurances to the Jordanians. Let's send a message to the Chinese. Let's send a message to the Russians. And I would tell the people in the State Department not a goddamn thing they don't need to know."[8]

NIXON AND KISSINGER'S MOST PERILOUS COVERT GAMBIT WAS THE OVERture to Mao's China—already on poisonous terms with India. Kissinger believed that Zhou Enlai was somewhat unhinged when it came to India, and the deployment of Chinese soldiers could easily have sparked border clashes. Such a movement of Chinese troops would have made an effective threat precisely because of the danger of escalation out of control. At worst, this could have ignited a wider war.[9]

That, in turn, risked expanding into a nuclear superpower confrontation. If China was moving troops to help Pakistan, India would surely want the Soviet Union to do likewise. According to the CIA's mole in Delhi, Indira Gandhi claimed that the Soviet Union had promised to counterbalance any Chinese military actions against India. Just two years before, China had set off hydrogen bombs in its western desert to threaten the Soviet Union. Would the Soviets dare to confront the Chinese? And if the Soviets got dragged in, how could the Americans stay out?[10]

Back on November 23, Kissinger had enticingly suggested to a Chinese delegation in New York that India's northern border might be vulnerable. Now, on December 6, Nixon told Kissinger that he "strongly" wanted to tell China that some troop movements toward India's border could be very important. "[D]amnit, I am convinced that if the Chinese start moving the Indians will be petrified," the president said. "They will be petrified." He shrugged off the obvious problem of winter snows in the Himalayas, admiringly recalling China's bravery in the Korean War: "The Chinese, you know, when they came across the Yalu, we thought they were a bunch of goddamn fools in the heart of the winter, but they did it."[11]

Kissinger had personally and repeatedly promised Indian leaders at the highest levels—including Haksar and Gandhi herself—that the United States would stand with India *against* threats of Chinese aggression. Now the Nixon administration was secretly doing the opposite.[12]

Kissinger was heartened at U.S. intelligence reports of truckloads of military supplies flowing from China into West Pakistan. But the CIA insisted that China was "keeping its head down," neither prepared for nor capable of a full-scale war against India. In harsh mountainous terrain, it would be tremendously hard to move forces fast enough to matter. The CIA argued that it would take at least two months for China to get ready for a moderate amount of combat with India. Still, the CIA noted, with India's "traumatic" memory of the last war with China, Chinese saber rattling and harassing attacks could cause real trouble for India, even without a war. India would have to divert large numbers of troops to guard its northern flank. As Kissinger wrote to Nixon, the CIA did think that China could launch smaller but still substantial military efforts, from "overt troop movements" to a "limited diversionary attack."[13]

Kissinger linked the China gambit to the United States secretly providing aircraft from Iran and Jordan to Pakistan. On December 8, in the private office that Nixon kept in the ornate Executive Office Building, next door to the White House, Kissinger told the president that "we could give a note to the Chinese and say, 'If you are ever going to move this is the time.'" Nixon immediately agreed. Kissinger did not think it would be so simple to scare off the Soviet Union. He admitted that if the administration's bluff was called, they would lose, but added that if they did not act now, they would definitely lose. Nixon was resolute, saying they had to "calmly and cold-bloodedly make the decision."

The president argued that "we can't do this without the Chinese helping us. As I look at this thing, the Chinese have got to move to that damn border. The Indians have got to get a little scared." Kissinger agreed, proposing that they notify the Chinese about what Nixon was secretly doing, and tell them of the advantages of China moving some of its soldiers to India's frontier. Nixon bluntly instructed Kissinger to go to New York, to the Chinese mission at the United Nations, with a message directly from him to Zhou Enlai. Kissinger, who wanted to impress the Chinese leadership by showing the administration's toughness, guessed that China might start a small diversion—enough to prevent India from moving too many of its troops west.[14]

Nixon was tantalized by the prospect that the Chinese would move if they thought that the White House would act too. Although Kissinger cautioned that China had "just had a semi-revolt in the military" and had "a million Russians on their border," the president said, "Boy, I tell you, a movement of even some Chinese toward that border could scare those goddamn Indians to death."[15]

"IS IT REALLY SO MUCH AGAINST OUR LAW?"

Kissinger told Nixon, "We are the ones who have been operating against our public opinion, against our bureaucracy, at the very edge of legality." That understates it. In fact, to help Pakistan, Nixon and Kissinger knowingly broke U.S. law—and did so with the full awareness of George H. W. Bush, H. R. Haldeman, Alexander Haig, and others.[16]

Yahya desperately needed U.S. military supplies, particularly aircraft. On the second day of the war, he begged for U.S. help, adding, "for God's sake don't hinder or impede the delivery of equipment from friendly third countries." That day, Kissinger told Nixon that they had received a desperate appeal from Yahya, saying that his military supplies had been cut off, leaving him acutely vulnerable. Could the Americans help him through Iran, one of Pakistan's most reliable friends? Nixon and Kissinger swiftly agreed to this, without considering any legal issues. Kissinger was concerned only that the United States would have to replace whatever Iranian weaponry was lost in the fighting. Nixon agreed: "If it is leaking we can have it denied. Have it done one step away." Kissinger told the president, "If war does continue, give aid via Iran." Nixon was relieved: "Good, at least Pakistan will be kept from being paral[y]zed."[17]

They determinedly kept their actions in the shadows, circumventing normal State Department communications by using a back channel between Nixon and the shah of Iran, Muhammad Reza Pahlavi. Nixon, reassured that the U.S. ambassador in Tehran was oblivious, was delighted: "Good, well we'll have some fun with this yet. God, you know what would really be poetic justice here is if some way the Paks could really give the Indians a bloody nose for a couple of days." The next day, the shah agreed to a U.S. request to send Iranian military equipment to Pakistan, with the United States replacing whatever Iran sent.[18]

Jordan also got a request from Yahya, for eight to ten sophisticated U.S.-made F-104 Starfighter fighter-interceptors. King Hussein seemed keen to move his squadrons, but, fearing congressional wrath, did not want to act without express approval. When he nervously asked the U.S. embassy in Amman for advice, the diplomats balked. Kissinger noted with exasperation that these U.S. officials were lecturing the king of Jordan that it would be immoral to get involved in a faraway war; these diplomats had not conceived of the last-ditch possibility of using Iran and Jordan to provide U.S. weapons to the tottering Pakistani military.[19]

THIS WAS ILLEGAL. THAT FACT WAS DRIVEN HOME TO KISSINGER BY lawyers at the State Department and Pentagon, as well as by the White House staff.

On December 6, in the war's early days, Kissinger for the first time proposed the operation in a Situation Room meeting—not mentioning that the president had already made up his mind, and that the Iranians were already acting. But a State Department official immediately warned Kissinger that transferring Jordanian weapons to Pakistan "is prohibited on the basis of present legal authority." Kissinger countered, "My instinct is that the President will want to do it"—his way of saying that Nixon had already decided. "He is not inclined to let the Paks be defeated if he can help it."[20]

After this Situation Room meeting, Kissinger walked upstairs to the Oval Office, where Nixon was waiting for the press. Before the cameras arrived, Kissinger told the president that "this military aid to Iran that Iran might be giving to West Pakistan. The only way we can really do it—it's not legal, strictly speaking, the only way we can do it is to tell the shah to go ahead through a back channel, to go ahead." Nixon did not flinch at breaking the law. Kissinger continued, "He'd sent you a message saying that he's eager to do it as long as we don't—the damn press doesn't know about it and we keep our mouths shut." Nixon's only concern was that the shah did not inform the U.S. ambassador in Tehran: "I don't want that son of a bitch to know." "Oh no, no, no, no," Kissinger assured him.

Nixon and Kissinger then plotted to conceal what they were doing. "We'll have to say we didn't know about it," Kissinger said, "but we'll cover it as soon as we can." "Shit, how do we cover it?" Nixon asked. Kissinger explained, "By giving him"—the shah—"some extra aid next year." "Do it," said Nixon. He gave his official line: "I don't know anything about it." Then he laid out how they could publicly justify increasing military aid to compensate Iran, without mentioning the real reason. "Let's put it this way: if I go to the Mideast, I think we need a stronger anchor in that area, and I determine, at this moment, that aid to Iran should substantially be increased next year." Kissinger agreed.[21]

The State Department, sensing the impending scandal, quickly drew up a legal memorandum to stop Kissinger. Pakistan was still formally under a U.S. arms embargo. So, the State Department's lawyers explained, the president could only consent to the transfer of U.S. weapons to Pakistan from another country if the United States declared it would be willing to directly provide the stuff itself. Nixon and Kissinger knew that that kind of presidential declaration was politically impossible—an overt step that would never be tolerated by the infuriated Congress. Such a White House action would also, as the State Department noted, be in conflict with the ban on military assistance and arms sales to Pakistan in pending foreign aid legislation that had been approved by both the Senate and the House of Representatives. After quoting from the relevant public law, the State Department emphatically warned, "Under the present U.S. policy of suspending all arms transfers to Pakistan, the U[nited] S[tates] G[overnment] could not consent to such a transfer."[22]

The Pentagon's lawyers agreed. They repeated all of the State Department's legal analysis, chapter and verse, and helpfully sent along copies of each of the laws to the White House. As the Pentagon's legal experts pointed out, the law "prohibits 'third-country transfers' to eligible recipients where simple direct transfers would not be permitted for policy reasons." Leery of White House skullduggery, they warned that "if simple subterfuge is the only reason for preferring a 'third-country transfer,' then that is the type of 'abuse' which the Congress intended to prohibit."[23]

Harold Saunders, Kissinger's staffer at the White House, echoed these legal alarms. He had actually floated the idea of looking away while Iran and Jordan snuck weapons into Pakistan, but soon after prominently highlighted the legal "serious problem" for Kissinger—leaving his adventurous boss in no doubt that any U.S. weapons that found their way from Iran or Jordan to Pakistan would stand as a stark violation of U.S. law.[24]

UNDERSTANDING CLEARLY THAT WHAT THEY WERE DOING WAS ILLE-gal, Nixon and Kissinger did it anyway.

In the Oval Office, Nixon explained to Haldeman that they had told "the Iranians we're going to provide arms through third countries and so forth and so on." He casually added, "We're trying to do something where it's a violation of law and all that." The White House chief of staff did not object—or even comment—when the president said that he and Kissinger were planning to break U.S. law.[25]

On December 8, in a Situation Room meeting, Kissinger laced into State Department officials for trying to stop him. "I have reviewed the cables to Jordan which enthusiastically tell Hussein he can't furnish planes to the Paks," he said. "We shouldn't decide this on such doctrinaire grounds"—that is, obeying U.S. law. "The question is, when an American ally is being raped, whether or not the U.S. should participate in enforcing a blockade of our ally, when the other side is getting Soviet aid." After a Pentagon official reminded him about the law, Kissinger blew up at the group: "We have a country, supported and equipped by the Soviet Union, turning one half of another country into a satellite state and the other half into an impotent vassal. Leaving aside any American interest in the subcontinent, what conclusions will other countries draw from this in their dealings with the Soviets?"[26]

Kissinger urged the president, "I would encourage the Jordanians to move their squadrons into West Pakistan and the Iranians to move their squadrons." When Nixon asked what effect these squadrons would have, Kissinger replied, "Enough. Militarily in Pakistan we have only one hope now. To convince the Indians that the thing is going to escalate. And to convince the Russians that they're going to pay an enormous price." Nixon wanted to "immediately" tell the Jordanians to act. Kissinger said, "I'd let the Jordanians move another squadron to Pakistan simply to show them some exclamation and let the Iranians move their two squadrons to Jordan if they want to." Nixon agreed. Kissinger pressed him: "right now we're in the position where we are telling allies not to assist another ally that is in mortal danger."[27]

Nixon and Kissinger worried about getting caught. The president warned that if Kissinger raised these weapons transfers in a Situation Room meeting, "the whole damn thing will get out in the papers." When Kissinger doubted that the Jordanians could move squadrons of planes without reporters finding out, Nixon said they would pretend that the Jordanians had acted on their own. Kissinger told Pakistan's ambassador to "stop all cable traffic with respect to help on ammunition and so forth. We are doing what we can and we will send a coded message. It's getting too dangerous for you to send it." Kissinger cautioned him that "we are working very actively on getting military equipment to you—but for God's sake don't say anything to anybody!"[28]

Even Kissinger's own White House staffers, who suspected something was up, were kept in the dark. Samuel Hoskinson denies knowing about the operation. "This would have been in a channel outside of us," he says. "Covert action was in a separate vein." Later, Kissinger grew sufficiently nervous about this illegality that he had Alexander Haig, his deputy, gather evidence fixing the blame on Nixon. Haig wrote to Kissinger, "Here are three telcons [telephone conversations] all of which confirm the President's knowledge of, approval for and, if you will, directive to provide aircraft to Iran and Jordan."[29]

Nixon and Kissinger made no appeal to theories of executive power, and drew up no legal briefs supporting their actions; they simply acted. For their crucial meeting on the Iranian and Jordanian arms transfers, on December 8, they were joined in the president's hideaway office in the Executive Office Building by John Mitchell, the attorney general, who proved as unconcerned about violating the law as they were. (The crucial parts of this meeting are bleeped out on the White House tapes, but the State Department has released a declassified transcript.)

Kissinger candidly said, "it's illegal for them to move them." A little later, Nixon said, "You say it's illegal for us to do, also for the Jordanians." Kissinger explained that "the way we can make it legal is to resume arms sales through—if we, if you announce that Pakistan is now eligible for the purchase of arms." That would be a massive policy shift, and Nixon balked: "That would be tough, Henry, to go that way." Kissinger concurred: "you would do more if it were not for this goddamn Senate."

Instead, Kissinger, unfazed by the presence of the attorney general, said, "the way you get the Jordanian planes in there is to tell the King we cannot give you legal permission. On the other hand, we'd have to figure out a message, which says, 'We'll just close our eyes. Get the goddamned planes in there.'" Similarly, Kissinger said, the shah of Iran did not dare to act without a "formal commitment from us." To safeguard their secret, Nixon and Kissinger agreed to covertly send a "special emissary"—probably either the CIA director or an Israeli—bearing that message to King Hussein. "We'd have to do it that way," said Kissinger. "We cannot authorize it."

None of this elicited protest from the chief law enforcement officer of the United States. Mitchell waited patiently through the meeting, occasionally jumping into the conversation to disparage "the goddamn Indians" and to slam Ted Kennedy as "stupid." When Nixon wanted to keep the State Department in the dark, Mitchell immediately concurred. When Kissinger pointed out that the State Department had to know about the movement of the Jordanian planes, Mitchell proposed a cover-up: "Well, you've got to give them the party line on that or all a sudden the Secretary of State will say that's illegal." Kissinger insisted that the Jordanians had to be told that they would not be punished "if they move them against our law." Nixon agreed.

The president said, "All right, that's an order. You're goddamn right." In front of the attorney general, Nixon asked, "Is it really so much against our law?" Kissinger admitted that it was. Referring to the Iranians and the Jordanians, he explained again, "What's against our law is not what they do, but our giving them permission." Nixon said, "Henry, we give the permission privately." "That's right," agreed Kissinger.

"Hell," said the president, "we've done worse."[30]

"WE GO BALLS OUT"

This was a radical set of steps. They could ignite a border war between China and India, set up a confrontation with the Soviet Union, cause a domestic firestorm, and get the administration dragged through U.S. courts. If Nixon stood his ground, the crisis could escalate out of control; if he did not, then the United States would lose credibility—always a big concern for Nixon's team.

Nixon momentarily got cold feet. "The partition of Pakistan is a fact," he told Kissinger, who conceded as much. Nixon said, "You see those people welcoming the Indian troops when they come in. Now the point is, why is then, Henry, are we going through all this agony?" Kissinger stiffened the president's resolve. "We're going through this agony to prevent the West Pakistan army from being destroyed," he crisply replied, after a pause to consider the question. "Secondly, to maintain our Chinese arm. Thirdly, to prevent a complete collapse of the world's psychological balance of power, which will be produced if a combination of the Soviet Union and the Soviet armed client state can tackle a not so insignificant country without anybody doing anything."

Kissinger then went apocalyptic. "I would keep open the possibility that we'll pour in arms into Pakistan," he said angrily. "I don't understand the psychology by which the Russians can pour arms into India but we cannot give arms to Pakistan. I don't understand the theory of non-involvement. I don't see where we will be as a country. I have to tell you honestly, I consider this our Rhineland."

Kissinger direly warned that "the rape" of Pakistan, an ally of the United States, would have terrible consequences in Iran, Indonesia, and the Middle East. When this did not sway Nixon, he added that if the Soviet Union grew too confident after an Indian victory, there could be a Middle East war in the spring. Nixon nervously said, "We have to know what we're jeopardizing and know that once we go balls out we never look back." Kissinger agreed that the president was gambling his relationship with the Soviets, but hoped that the very willingness to bet such big stakes would scare them.

This doomsday argument persuaded Nixon. He went forward on all the interlocking parts of Kissinger's plan: moving a U.S. aircraft carrier and asking China to deploy its troops toward India's border. And the president again approved the illegal movement of Jordanian warplanes. Kissinger said, "I'd let the Jordanians move some of their planes in," and added, "And then we would tell State to shut up." Nixon

agreed to that. Kissinger continued, "we would have to tell him"—
King Hussein—"it's illegal, but if he does it we'll keep things under
control." Once again, neither Nixon nor Kissinger flinched at breaking
the law. Nixon said, "with regard to the Jordanians, no sweat." Soon
after, he ordered, "Get the planes over."[31]

NIXON AND KISSINGER LAID THEIR RELATIONSHIP WITH THE SOVIET
Union on the line, deliberately risking the cancellation of an upcoming
summit of the two superpowers. That afternoon, Nixon hauled the visiting Soviet agriculture minister into the Oval Office for a beating. The
startled minister was said to be a close personal friend of Brezhnev, but
he was beyond his brief and out of his depth. Nixon—sending a message to Brezhnev—warned that the war could "poison" his relationship with the Soviet Union and cause "a confrontation."[32]

Afterward, Nixon said, "I really stuck it to him." "Well, but you did
it so beautifully," Kissinger replied. He predicted that the war would
end now, with the United States coming out damaged but not as badly
as it could have been, and with India thwarted from launching an
onslaught against West Pakistan.[33]

Kissinger told a Soviet diplomat that the United States was moving some of its military forces: as he explained to Nixon, "in effect it
was giving him sort of a veiled ultimatum." Nixon sternly wrote to
Brezhnev, urging him to use his influence to restrain India, and telling
him that he shared responsibility for India's actions.[34]

Soon after, Kissinger told the Soviets that they had until noon on
December 12, or "we will proceed unilaterally." With vague menace,
he said that "we may take certain other steps." Nixon privately said
that the Soviet Union was abetting Indian aggression. Kissinger, who
called the situation "heartbreaking," agreed: "now that East Pakistan
has practically fallen there can no longer be any doubt that we are dealing with naked aggression supported by Soviet power."[35]

MEANWHILE, THE ILLEGAL TRANSFERS OF U.S. WEAPONRY TO PAKISTAN
went ahead. As Kissinger frankly told Nixon, "Four Jordanian planes
have already moved to Pakistan, 22 more are coming. We're talking to
the Saudis, the Turks we've now found are willing to give five. So we're
going to keep that moving until there's a settlement."[36]

Kissinger pressed a Situation Room meeting: "What if Jordan
should send planes to Pakistan? Why would this be such a horrible
event?" A senior State Department official again explained the legal

problem. Kissinger's insistence sparked suspicions. Harold Saunders, the White House staffer, warily wrote that Jordan might have already delivered F-104s.[37]

The CIA spotted the covert operation, reporting that a squadron of Jordanian F-104s had gone to Pakistan, totaling twelve warplanes. En route the planes stopped in Saudi Arabia, with some of them flown by Jordanian pilots and others allegedly guarded by Pakistanis. The State Department, too, observed eleven of these Jordanian F-104s in Saudi Arabia, and surmised they were bound for Pakistan. While the U.S. embassy in Amman was never notified, its staffers did notice a conspicuous absence of Jordanian fighter pilots at their favorite bars.[38]

Haig secretly told a Chinese delegation that Jordan had sent six fighter aircraft to Pakistan and would send eight more soon; Iran was replacing Jordan's lost airplanes; and Turkey might be sending as many as twenty-two planes. Kissinger assured the Chinese, "Jordan has now sent fourteen aircraft to Pakistan and is considering sending three more." Nixon later asked, "Did the Jordan[ian]s send planes[?]" Kissinger replied, "17."[39]

NOW KISSINGER COULD ASK CHINA TO MOVE ITS TROOPS TOWARD INDIA'S border. Nixon, keen for the People's Liberation Army to deploy its soldiers, was convinced India would back down: "these Indians are cowards." About the Chinese, he said, "All they've got to do is move something. Move their, move a division. You know, move some trucks. Fly some planes. You know, some symbolic act. We're not doing a god-damn thing, Henry, you know that."[40]

So Kissinger raced up to New York on December 10, bringing with him Haig and Winston Lord, his special assistant and China aide. George H. W. Bush got a call from the White House, telling him to come to an Upper East Side address, which was a CIA safe house. Bush arrived first, then Kissinger and Haig, followed by China's tough ambassador to the United Nations, Huang Hua. It was an extraordinarily secret gathering. Kissinger assured the Chinese, "George Bush is the only person outside the White House who knows I come here." Although Kissinger cringed at the apartment's mirrored walls and tacky paintings, the place was chosen because it had no doorman and few occupants, so that gossipy New Yorkers would not see Chinese officials in Mao suits entering a building, soon followed by someone looking a lot like Henry Kissinger.[41]

With candor verging on gusto, Kissinger told the Chinese that the

Americans were breaking U.S. law: "We are barred by law from giving equipment to Pakistan in this situation. And we also are barred by law from permitting friendly countries which have American equipment to give their equipment to Pakistan." Making a show of being untroubled by the illegality, he explained that they had told Jordan, Iran, and Saudi Arabia—and would tell Turkey too—that if they shipped U.S. arms to Pakistan, the Americans would understand. The administration would only feign mild protest, and would make up the Jordanian and Iranian losses in the next year's budget.

This operation, he said, was under way: "On this basis, four planes are leaving Jordan today and 22 over the weekend. Ammunition and other equipment is going from Iran." And there would be "six planes from Turkey in the near future." Kissinger reminded the Chinese how sensitive this information was.

While Kissinger spoke, Lord, Haig, and Bush—a future assistant secretary of state, a future secretary of state, and a future president of the United States—all kept quiet. George Bush was well aware of the illegal acts: after the meeting, he wrote, "Kissinger talked about the fact that we would be moving some ships into the area, talked about military supplies being sent from Jordan, Turkey and Iran"—prudently leaving out Kissinger's admissions of lawbreaking. Winston Lord, who took the official notes, says, "How they were handling it, whether they were stretching or breaking limits, I don't remember precisely. Clearly it was to help Pakistan and to impress the Chinese. In terms of the legality or morality of it, I can't untangle that in my own memory."

Next, as Bush noted, "Henry unfolded our whole policy on India-Pakistan, saying that we were very parallel with the Chinese." Kissinger said that the Americans had cut off aid to India, including military supplies, pointedly mentioning that they had canceled all radar equipment for India's northern defense—an invitation for China to strike one day. And he said that they were moving an aircraft carrier and several destroyers toward the Indian Ocean, in an armada that far outmatched the Soviet fleet there.

Kissinger then turned to his main goal: getting the Chinese to move troops against India. He said, "the President wants you to know" that "if the People's Republic were to consider the situation on the Indian subcontinent a threat to its security, and if it took measures to protect its security, the US would oppose efforts of others to interfere with the People's Republic." In case all that diplomatic verbiage was unclear, he later bluntly said, "When I asked for this meeting, I did so to suggest Chinese military help, to be quite honest. That's what I had in mind."

Kissinger laid out all of the administration's innermost secrets to the Chinese. One of the documents he showed them was, a Chinese translator pointed out, classified as "exclusively eyes only." Kissinger joked, "There's a better one that says 'burn before reading.'" Turning to Bush, he said, "Don't you discuss diplomacy this way."

Huang denounced Indian aggression and the dismemberment of a sovereign Pakistan, harshly comparing India to Imperial Japan. Kissinger, trying to match the Chinese venom at India, said, "I may look weak to you, Mr. Ambassador, but my colleagues in Washington think I'm a raving maniac."[42]

Returning to Washington, Kissinger hopefully noted that China was calling up reserve troops for its mountain divisions. He told Nixon that he was pretty sure that the Chinese would do something. Nixon was optimistically inclined to believe that if China moved troops, it would not "stiffen the Russians" to back up India. Kissinger was confident that China would move.[43]

Bush—whom Kissinger mostly used for comic relief—was frightened by Kissinger's behavior and startled by how much information he unveiled to the Chinese. After the meeting, Bush privately wrote that he was uncomfortable to be "in close cahoots with China," and would have preferred to "keep a fairly low profile, let Red China do what they had do to counteract the Russian threat." He distrusted Huang, who was "a one-way street. We are supplying him with a great deal of information, he is doing nothing." About Kissinger, Bush noted, "I think he goes too far in some of these things," especially when Kissinger said he would support any Chinese resolution at the United Nations: "That is going very far indeed, it's going too far." But Bush, a team player on his way up, kept his misgivings to himself.[44]

"ARMAGEDDON TERMS"

With the Indian army closing in on Dacca, the crisis built to a crescendo. Nixon privately wrote off East Pakistan, and concentrated on safeguarding West Pakistan. Kissinger warned the president on December 10 that "the east is down the drain. The major problem now has to be to protect the west. . . . Their army is ground down. And 2 more weeks of war and they're finished in the west as much as they are in the east."[45]

Nixon's and Kissinger's efforts to back Pakistan seemingly wound up encouraging its military rulers to fight on in the east. Although a quick surrender would have saved soldiers' lives, the Pakistani junta still hoped for rescue by the great powers. Even though Yahya seemed to realize that he could not hold East Pakistan, he vowed that his troops there would fight "to the last Muslim" for Pakistan and Islam. On December 10, a senior Pakistani general desperately offered an eastern cease-fire through the United Nations—but Yahya quickly withdrew the proposals. These cease-fire terms were also scorned by Zulfiqar Ali Bhutto, appointed by Yahya as deputy prime minister and foreign minister in a new wartime civilian Pakistani government. In Delhi, Haksar was shocked at the military junta's willingness to allow continued wasteful bloodshed.[46]

On December 11, the Pakistan army's chief of staff exaggeratedly wrote to General Niazi, the commander of Pakistan's Eastern Command, that the United States' Seventh Fleet would soon be in position and that China had activated a front. With India under strong Soviet and U.S. pressure, the chief of staff instructed Niazi to hold out, following Yahya's wishes.[47]

With Niazi's troops still battling on, Indian officials needed more time to win in the east. So a frenetic Haksar insisted that a cease-fire must address "the basic causes of the conflict"—an effective way of stalling. Indira Gandhi, despite the staggering rebuke from the United Nations General Assembly, told foreign governments that a cease-fire without firm commitments to get the Bengali refugees home would merely "cover up the annihilation of an entire nation."[48]

Still, Haksar briefed Indian officials that they had no territorial claims in either Bangladesh or West Pakistan. He urged them to avoid saying or doing anything that would help those who were trying to label India the aggressor. India was, he wrote, "fighting a purely defensive battle" against West Pakistan.[49]

Trying to mollify the Nixon administration even as Indian soldiers fought on, Haksar instructed the embassy in Washington to explain that India wanted no West Pakistani soil, and that India's recognition of Bangladesh was a "self-imposed restraint" proving it had absolutely no territorial ambitions there. By way of contrast, he reminded the U.S. government that Pakistan was attacking in Kashmir and elsewhere on the western front. The Indians were clumsy about explaining their goals in one particular area of Kashmir, called Azad Kashmir, under Pakistan's control but claimed by India; but even there, Haksar said that India would not wrest that land from Pakistani rule by force. Swaran Singh, India's foreign minister, told George Bush that India had "no major ambitions" there, leaving open the possibility of what Bush called "minor rectifications." The Indians assured Bush they did not want to prolong the war. Haksar soothingly wrote that "we have no desire to aggravate the situation and shall exercise self-restraint consistent with the needs of self-defence."[50]

The State Department's analysts confirmed that—at least for the moment—India's troops matched Haksar's words. Kissinger told Nixon that Indian troops were still in a holding posture on the western front, despite Indian airstrikes at military sites across West Pakistan. At the same time, Pakistan was on the offensive in Punjab and especially in Kashmir; as the CIA reported, Pakistan's troops had driven the Indians out of Chhamb and were still advancing. India and Pakistan were, the CIA reckoned, roughly equally matched in Kashmir and the northwest. But the CIA had some signals intelligence to suggest that India might be preparing to shift some troops from the eastern front to the western.[51]

Fearing the worst from China, India shored up its Soviet support. Gandhi's government sent D. P. Dhar racing back to Moscow on December 11, carrying a personal message for the Soviet premier. The Soviet leadership stood by India, but cautiously; they were not willing to recognize Bangladesh yet. Still, the Soviet ambassador in Delhi secretly pledged that if China intervened against India, the Soviet Union would open its own border diversionary action against China. Indira Gandhi warned a long list of world leaders that the intervention of outside powers would "lead to a wider conflagration with incalculable consequences"—a reminder of Soviet backing for India.[52]

ON THE MORNING OF DECEMBER 12, IN THE OVAL OFFICE, NIXON AND Kissinger reached a peak of Cold War brinksmanship. They had warned the Soviet Union to restrain India by noon that day, or face unilateral U.S. retaliatory measures. Believing that China was about to move its troops toward the Indian border, they braced themselves to stand behind China in deadly confrontations against both India and the Soviet Union—with the terrible potential of superpower conflict and, at worst, even nuclear war. Kissinger seemed ready to order bombing in support of China. As he later put it, he and Nixon made their "first decision to risk war in the triangular Soviet-Chinese-American relationship."[53]

306   The Blood Telegram

Despite the reassuring signals coming from Indian diplomats, Kissinger wanted China to move some troops. Until the Chinese had acted, he did not want to hear any more of their bombast against India. The opening to China rested on U.S. toughness now, he argued: "If the Chinese feel we are nice people, well-meaning, but totally irrelevant to their part of the world, they lose whatever slight, whatever incentives they have for that opening to us."

Nixon wanted to "hit in there hard and tough," publicly accusing India of Soviet-supported "naked aggression." Calling Gandhi "that bitch," Kissinger said they needed "to impress the Russians, to scare the Indians, to take a position with the Chinese." The president resolved to press the Soviet Union. "It's a typical Nixon plan," Kissinger told him. "I mean it's bold. You're putting your chips into the pot again." Without acting, he said, they faced certain disaster; with brinksmanship, they confronted a high possibility of disaster, "but at least we're coming off like men. And that helps us with the Chinese."

Urging the president on, Kissinger blasted critics who said they were alienating the Indians: "We are to blame for driving 500 million people. Why are we to blame? Because we're not letting 500 million people rape 100 million people." Nixon compared India to Nazi Germany: "Everybody worried about Danzig and Czechoslovakia and all those other places."[54]

THEN ALEXANDER HAIG STRODE INTO THE OVAL OFFICE WITH A MESsage from China. "The Chinese want to meet on an urgent basis," Kissinger said. "That's totally unprecedented," he said. "They're going to move. No question, they're going to move." Nixon asked if the Chinese were really going to send their troops. "No question," replied Kissinger.

Kissinger now fully expected a standoff between Chinese and Indian soldiers, with obvious potential for skirmishing or worse. Although Kissinger often bragged around Washington that he was the only thing standing between a madman president and atomic annihilation ("If the President had his way, we'd have a nuclear war every week"), here he played the instigator. In this nerve-racking session, he repeatedly pressed the president to escalate the crisis to maximum danger. Now that the United States had seemingly unleashed China against India, India would have to beg the Soviet Union for help. If that caused a confrontation between the Soviet Union and China, Kissinger insisted that Nixon had to back China: "If the Soviets move against them, and then we don't do anything, we'll be finished."[55]

Nixon balked. "So what do we do if the Soviets move against them?" he grilled Kissinger. "Start lobbing nuclear weapons in, is that what you mean?" But Kissinger, rather than backing off at that dire prospect, held fast: "Well, if the Soviets move against them in these conditions and succeed, that will be the final showdown. We have to—and if they succeed, we'll be finished. We'll be through."

Nixon was not swayed. "Then we better call them off," said Kissinger, about the Chinese. Then he realized, "I think we can't call them off, frankly." Haig said that the Chinese could only be dissuaded now at a terrible price. Kissinger said that "if we call them off, I think our China initiative is pretty well down the drain." Nixon saw the logic there: "our China initiative is down the drain. And also our stroke with the Russians is very, very seriously jeopardized."

Kissinger goaded Nixon to confront the Soviet Union, despite the peril: "If the Russians get away with facing down the Chinese, and if the Indians get away with licking the Pakistanis, what we are now having is the final, we may be looking right down the gun barrel." Bucking Nixon up, he said, "I think the Soviets will back off if we face them." But he did not give any suggestions about what to do if they did not.

Nixon yielded to Kissinger's pressure, hoping that the Soviet Union would be satisfied with its gains from India's battlefield victories and in no mood for further confrontation. Kissinger said that "we've got to trigger this quickly."

The president rounded on Kissinger: "The way you put it, Henry, the way you put it is very different as I understand. You said, look, we're doing all these things, why don't you threaten them. Remember I said, threaten, move a couple of people. . . . Look, we have to scare these bastards." In a frightening analogy, Kissinger compared this moment to China's entry into the Korean War: "They are acting for the same reason they jumped us when we approached the Chinese border in Korea."

Kissinger demanded that Nixon stand firm. He ratcheted up the geopolitical stakes: "if the outcome of this is that Pakistan is swallowed by India, China is destroyed, defeated, humiliated by the Soviet Union, it will be a change in the world balance of power of such magnitude" that the United States' security would be damaged for decades and maybe forever.

This induced in Nixon a doomsday vision of a solitary United States isolated against a Soviet-dominated world. "Now, we can really get into the numbers game," he said darkly. "You've got the Soviet Union with 800 million Chinese, 600 million Indians, the balance of Southeast Asia terrorized, the Japanese immobile, the Europeans, of course, will suck after them, and the United States the only one, we have maybe parts of Latin America and who knows." Kissinger replied, "This is why, Mr. President, you'll be alone." "That's fine," said Nixon, standing tough against his own phantasm. "We've been alone before."

After that, Nixon tried to take a step back from the brink: "I'd put [it] in more Armageddon terms than reserves when I say that the Chinese move and the Soviets threaten and then we start lobbing nuclear weapons. That isn't what happens. That isn't what happens." Instead, he said, they would use the hotline to the Soviets and talk to them.

"We don't have to lob nuclear weapons," agreed Kissinger. "We have to go on alert." But now he wanted to get the United States to join the war. "We have to put forces in," he said bluntly. "We may have to give them bombing assistance."

Nixon added, "we clean up Vietnam at about that point." Kissinger agreed: "at that point, we give an ultimatum to Hanoi. Blockade Haiphong." (He would make good on this in May 1972 with the mining of Haiphong harbor.)

Trying again to cool off, the president said, "we're talking about a lot of ifs. Russia and China aren't going to go to war." But Kissinger disagreed: "I wouldn't bet on that, Mr. President." The Soviets "are not rational on China," he said, and if they could "wipe out China," then Nixon's upcoming visit there would be pointless. Despite believing that a war—possibly a nuclear war—was possible between the Soviet Union and China, Kissinger still insisted on backing China in a spiraling crisis.

Haig—who would become Ronald Reagan's secretary of state—concurred, suggesting that the United States might tacitly support a Chinese invasion of India: "they feel they know that if the United States moves on the Soviets that will provide the cover they need to invade India. And we've got to neutralize the Soviet Union." The president asked, "suppose the Chinese move and the Soviets threaten, then what do we do?" They planned to tell the Soviet Union that war would be "unacceptable" once China began moving troops.

They all agreed. The White House was ready to escalate.[56]

NIXON AND KISSINGER, HAVING SET INFERNAL MACHINERY IN MOTION, were rewarded by the more fearful judgments of the Soviet Union and

China. A few minutes after that supercharged Oval Office session, the Soviets, having checked with Indira Gandhi, soothingly reassured Kissinger that India's government "has no intention to take any military actions against West Pakistan."[57]

Kissinger rushed into the Oval Office to tell Nixon that the Soviets, making the noon deadline he had set, had extracted an assurance from Gandhi that she would not attack West Pakistan. That was what they had been looking for. Kissinger did not disguise his relief: "goddamn it, we made it and we didn't deserve it." But he was proud of their brinksmanship earlier that day: "What you did this morning, Mr. President, was a heroic act." "I had to do it," said Nixon. "Yes," Kissinger replied. "But I know no other man in the country, no other man who would have done what you did."

Nixon reveled in his victory. Taking a historical turn, he said that in World War II and the Korean War, the right path was toughness. Kissinger concurred, saying that the Soviets had backed down because they "knew they were looking down the gun barrel."[58]

The two men congratulated themselves. "Mr. President, your behavior in the last 2 weeks has been heroic in this," Kissinger said. "You were shooting—your whole goddamn political future for next year. . . . Against your bureaucracy. . . . [A]gainst the Congress, against public opinion. All alone, like everything else. Without flinching, and I must say, I may yell and scream but this hour this morning is worth 4 years here." Nixon gamely accepted the praise: "It wasn't easy. . . . [T]he reason the hour this morning was that I had a chance to reflect a little and to see where it was going. The world is just going down the goddamn drain."[59]

CHINA WAS NOT ACTUALLY GOING TO MOVE ITS TROOPS. THE CHINESE leadership knew that picking a fight with the Soviet Union's friend meant exposing themselves to a million Soviet soldiers on their border. After that dramatic Oval Office meeting, Alexander Haig and Winston Lord bolted up to New York for another secret session with the Chinese delegation. But Huang Hua said nothing to them about deploying Chinese troops to confront India.[60]

General Sam Manekshaw would later say that despite noticeable Chinese military activity along India's northern border, China avoided any significant provocations. Although China hurled mephitic revolutionary propaganda against India, the Indian embassy noticed that the People's Daily refrained from promising any direct action. Indian spies in the R&AW did think that China was stirring up insurgencies among India's restless Nagas and Mizos, and cracked down in response—but this was harassment, not the start of a border clash. India was confident enough that China would stand by that it moved most of its Himalayan mountain divisions from the Chinese frontier to face Pakistan instead.[61]

In the end, China would only act immediately after the news that Dacca had fallen. It would not be until December 16, as India was securing a cease-fire, that China issued a protest note accusing seven Indian troops of violating China's border at Sikkim, a small Indian state nestled in the Himalayas—a place where the winter weather would not be such an impediment to Chinese intervention. India would flatly deny the charges. Although Kissinger hopefully told Nixon that this "could be the prelude to limited Chinese military actions along the border with India," it would all come too late to matter. The note was, the Indian embassy in Beijing concluded, "a grudging acceptance of the *fait accompli* in the East accompanied by fears that the existence of West Pakistan could be in jeopardy." When Zhou Enlai delivered a furious banquet speech against India, India's diplomats in Beijing smugly dismissed it as "impotent rage."[62]

Years later, at a summit in Beijing, Kissinger would tell Deng Xiaoping, "President Nixon and I had made the decision—for your information—that if you had moved and the Soviet Union had brought pressure on you, we would have given military support" to China. He added, "We understand why you didn't, but you should know our position, our seriousness of purpose."[63]

IN ENTERPRISE OF MARTIAL KIND

On December 12, after that agitated session in the Oval Office, a top Soviet diplomat in Washington assured Kissinger that they would soon get results from the Indians, and that there was no need for "a fist fight in the Security Council because we are in agreement now." Kissinger soothingly said that the United States would be cooperative. Although a U.S. aircraft carrier group was on its way, he downplayed that, saying that the Americans had to stand by their allies, but had now gone through that exercise.[64]

There was a fistfight anyway. The same day, in New York, the United Nations Security Council reconvened. After the last debacle, Haksar had sent Swaran Singh, India's foreign minister, to confront

George Bush and Zulfiqar Ali Bhutto, who was now leading the Pakistani delegation. Haksar told Gandhi that "the art of diplomacy lies not merely in advocating one's cause, but in reducing one's opponents." That Singh did skillfully. "Is Mr. Bhutto still harbouring dreams of conquering India and coming to Delhi as a visitor?" he caustically asked. When Bush, on Nixon's and Kissinger's instructions, inquired about India's ultimate intentions in the war, Singh asked about U.S. intentions in Vietnam. He denounced Pakistan: "It is not India which has set a record in political persecution, the genocide of a people and the suppression of human rights that inevitably led to the present conflagration."[65]

For the third and last time, the Soviet Union shielded India with its veto, knocking down another Security Council resolution calling for an immediate cease-fire and withdrawal. Kissinger, not checking with Nixon, threatened to scrap the upcoming Soviet summit.[66]

All the while the diplomats traded insults, Nixon and Kissinger had the USS *Enterprise* carrier group sailing fast toward the Bay of Bengal. To use the wholly implausible pretext of evacuating Americans, Kissinger told the chair of the Joint Chiefs of Staff, "Send it where there are Americans—say, Karachi." Kissinger informed Bhutto that U.S. warships would soon cross the chokepoint of the Strait of Malacca, heading for the Bay of Bengal, and be spotted by the Indians. Nixon insisted that it continue toward India unless there was a settlement.[67]

The *Enterprise,* a nuclear aircraft carrier from the U.S. Seventh Fleet, was accompanied by the rest of its formidable task force: the helicopter carrier USS *Tripoli,* seven destroyers, and an oiler. (They were under the Honolulu-based command of Admiral John McCain Jr., the father of John McCain III, the Arizona senator and 2008 Republican presidential candidate.) With alarming symbolism, the carrier group set sail not merely from the Vietnam war zone, but, as the Indian government unhappily claimed, from the Gulf of Tonkin.[68]

Nixon and Kissinger had a schoolboy enthusiasm for moving military units without meaning too much by it. Still, compared with India's ragtag fleet, this was an awfully intimidating force. An Indian official called it "a nuclear-studded armada including the most powerful ship in the world." The *Enterprise* had helped blockade Cuba during the missile crisis there. It was a modern, mammoth warship, almost five times larger than India's own rickety aircraft carrier, INS *Vikrant.* Even one of the *Enterprise*'s escorts, the *Tripoli,* was bigger than the *Vikrant.* The *Enterprise,* powered by atomic reactors, could sail around the world without refueling; the *Vikrant* was lucky if its boiler worked. This U.S. carrier group was, the vice admiral of India's eastern fleet recalled, "a fantastic threat."[69]

Indian troops were simultaneously closing in on Dacca from the north, south, and east. While the news of the Seventh Fleet's deployment broke in the Indian press, Gandhi rallied a gigantic crowd in Delhi, speaking in simple, blunt Hindi. Indian warplanes circled overhead. As one of her top advisers nervously noted, this huge gathering could have made a tempting bombing target.[70]

The wartime prime minister complained that the United States' alliance with Pakistan was supposed to be against communism, not democracy. Although not naming the United States or China, she warned that India would stand firm against "severe threats" of "some other attack." And, in words so inflammatory that her press office cut them from the printed version of her speech, she irately declared that the world was against India because of the color of its people's skin. She led the masses in roaring *"Jai Hind!"*—victory to India.[71]

That victory was almost in hand. Triumphant in Bangladesh and under pressure from both superpowers to leave it at that, India lost whatever appetite it might have had for a wider war. India by now held some pockets of Pakistani territory in the west, and two Soviet diplomats tried to ascertain the country's intentions from Haksar and then from Gandhi herself—hoping to restrain them from reckless steps that might drag the United States into the war. The CIA noted that the Soviet Union had advised India to be satisfied with liberating Bangladesh and not to seize any West Pakistani territory, including that contested area in Kashmir known as Azad Kashmir. As Haksar anxiously wrote to Gandhi, the Soviets believed that the United States was firmly committed to defend West Pakistan's territorial integrity. Thus Indian provocations against West Pakistan could drive the Americans to "enlarge the conflict."[72]

Haksar urged the prime minister to impress upon General Manekshaw that his troops must use "extreme care" on the western front. The United States, Haksar nervously wrote, would react to any military moves that gave the impression that India was trying to grab land in West Pakistan, including Azad Kashmir, or that India was planning to transfer forces from the eastern theater to charge deep into West Pakistan.[73]

With Indian troops racing against the UN's clock, Haksar was grateful for every deferral and adjournment of the byzantine Security

Council. While Haksar eagerly awaited the end of military operations in Bangladesh, he came up with a quibbling series of stalling tactics for the United Nations, meant to be "sufficiently elastic to generate discussion and give time." But the Soviet Union, having endured more than its fill of embarrassments on India's behalf, was, as Haksar told Gandhi, anxious for India to allow it to say something in the Security Council that was not completely negative.[74]

The same CIA intelligence that had so alarmed Nixon and Kissinger now reported that India was almost ready to end its war. According to the CIA's mole in Delhi, India would accept a cease-fire once an Awami League government was set up in Dacca. Although hawkish military leaders and Jagjivan Ram, the defense minister, reportedly wanted to fight on in southern Azad Kashmir and to smash Pakistan's war machine, Gandhi had had enough. She wanted to avoid more trouble with the United States and China. Under Soviet pressure to accept a cease-fire as soon as Bangladesh was a fact, India, according to the CIA, was set to "assure the Soviet Union that India has no plans to annex any West Pakistani territory." Once the war ended, according to this CIA mole, Gandhi was confident that Yahya's military regime would fall and there would be new pressure for autonomy in Baluchistan, the North-West Frontier Province, and other restive areas in West Pakistan. India would dominate South Asia.[75]

GENERAL JACOB REMEMBERS, "BY THIRTEENTH DECEMBER WE DEPLETED strength on the outskirts on Dacca." He and the other generals were closely watching the United Nations, as the Soviet Union kept on vetoing cease-fire resolutions. Then, he recalls, "The Russians say, no more veto. Panic—sorry, 'concern'—in Delhi." That night he prayed. He says that God evidently answered, as he received information that General Niazi, commander of Pakistan's Eastern Command, would be going to a meeting at Government House in Dacca. He bombed the gathering. This terrified the remainder of the local Pakistani government. That evening, Jacob says, Niazi went to Herbert Spivack, the U.S. consul general, with a cease-fire proposal.[76]

General Manekshaw, the Indian chief of army staff, sent a third note asking Pakistan to surrender. Once again, he offered protection under the Geneva Conventions to all surrendering soldiers and paramilitaries, and promised to protect ethnic minorities—meaning the Urdu-speaking Biharis, who were terrified of the Mukti Bahini's vengeance. With the Bangladeshi forces under his command, he promised that Bangladesh's government had also ordered compliance with the Geneva Conventions. "For the sake of your own men I hope you will not compel me to reduce your garrison with the use of force."[77]

General Niazi urged the United States to help get a cease-fire to spare his troops and avoid street fighting in the city. Yahya accused India of inflicting bloodshed on his military and civilian forces of "holocaust" proportions.[78]

In Delhi, Haksar warned India's defense ministry that the dominant interest of the United States and China was preserving West Pakistan. He thus cautioned against any statements or military actions that indicated that India had serious intent to sever parts of West Pakistan or seize Azad Kashmir. To Haksar's annoyance, India's information ministry had been hard at work generating exactly that kind of impression, by preparing propaganda trying to whip up Sindhi irredentism in West Pakistan. He ordered a stop to that, and demanded the withdrawal of all propaganda "fanning Sindhi, Baluchi or Pathan irredentism."[79]

Even with the war lost, the CIA reported that pro-Pakistan forces killed "a large number of Bangla Desh intellectuals" soon before the fall of Dacca. According to the State Department, as many as two hundred people were killed. Later, after an Indian general visited the massacre site, he could not eat. Arundhati Ghose, the Indian diplomat, remembers telling him that he was a soldier, accustomed to seeing dead bodies. Yes, the general replied, but he had found the hand of a woman, with her nails painted. He said, "I can't get that out of my head."[80]

YAHYA BEGGED NIXON TO SEND THE SEVENTH FLEET TO PAKISTAN'S shores to defend Karachi. But Nixon, despite often sounding like he was on the verge of war with India, had no intentions of any naval combat. The USS *Enterprise* carrier group was an atomic-powered bluff, meant to spook the Indians and increase Soviet pressure on India for a cease-fire, but nothing more. Kissinger privately said that "we don't want to get militarily involved and there isn't a chance. Can you imagine the President even listening to that for three seconds." Kissinger worried that the American public would not be able to stomach the mere sight of a U.S. aircraft carrier threatening India—let alone actually opening fire. As for Nixon, he left no doubt: "we're not going to intervene."[81]

Samuel Hoskinson, the White House staffer, who remains convinced that India meant to destroy Pakistan, applauds the deployment of the carrier group. "To my way of thinking, it was a brilliant strategic move," he says. "I know Nixon and Kissinger have been faulted for that. I think more than anything else it stopped Madame Gandhi in her tracks."

But India's military commanders seem to have doubted the Americans would fight them. "I didn't think the Americans were so foolhardy," recalls General Jacob. "We had land-based aircraft." Vice Admiral Mihir Roy, the director of naval intelligence, says he briefed Indira Gandhi about the composition of the task force, and explained it was possible that it could strike India. But with Vietnam going on, he told the prime minister, he did not believe the Americans would attack. He also noted that the Seventh Fleet could try to break India's blockade of Pakistan by coming between India's navy and the land; Vice Admiral N. Krishnan, leading India's eastern fleet, feared that the *Enterprise* task force would do this at Chittagong. Krishnan even considered having an Indian submarine torpedo the U.S. fleet to slow it down. But he told his underlings in the Maritime Operations Room that any direct U.S. attack could cause "the end of the world," or embroil the Americans in "a Vietnam to end all Vietnams." In defiance of the *Enterprise,* India intensified its naval assault on Chittagong and Cox's Bazar.[82]

India's political leaders claim to have been equally skeptical that the *Enterprise* would actually fight them. Thanks to Soviet surveillance, they knew that Dacca was going to fall before the Seventh Fleet could do anything about it. They were well aware how impossible it would be for Nixon, mired in Vietnam, to send U.S. troops into a new Asian war against India. Gandhi later said, "Naturally, if the Americans had fired a shot, if the Seventh Fleet had done something more than sit there in the Bay of Bengal . . . yes, the Third World War would have exploded. But, in all honesty, not even that fear occurred to me."[83]

Still, the Indian government asked the Soviet Union to warn against the dire consequences of this threatening movement of the U.S. Navy. At the same time, Haksar ordered D. P. Dhar, the Indian envoy sent to Moscow, to personally reassure Soviet premier Aleksei Kosygin that India had no territorial ambitions in either Bangladesh or West Pakistan, and that India's western position was entirely defensive. The Soviet ambassador assured India that a Soviet fleet in the Indian Ocean would not allow the United States to intervene.[84]

On December 15, India's R&AW spy agency warned that U.S. warships were moving past Thailand, heading toward India. That day, the *Enterprise* carrier group entered the Bay of Bengal.[85]

This caused some panic among Indian officials, according to General Manekshaw, although Gandhi and Haksar publicly affected nonchalance. Manekshaw claimed that in a cabinet meeting Swaran Singh and other ministers urged an immediate cease-fire to avoid facing U.S. troops or even nuclear weapons. There were some overheated rumors of a shooting war between Americans and Indians. India was tipped off, seemingly by an American source, that the Seventh Fleet might move into action, maybe even landing troops. One senior Indian official in Washington claimed that the task force was ready to establish a beachhead, with three Marine battalions at the ready, and that bombers on the *Enterprise* had been authorized by Nixon to bomb Indian army communications if necessary. When India's ambassador in Washington asked a senior State Department official about the prospect of U.S. troops establishing a beachhead, he got a less than categorical denial, although the official said he had not heard of the possibility. The Indian ambassador fed the story to the press, lashing out against the Nixon administration on American television.[86]

Nixon and Kissinger enjoyed frightening India. Kissinger said that India's ambassador "says he has unmistakable proof that we are planning a landing on the Bay of Bengal. Well, that's okay with me." "Yeah," said Nixon, "that scares them." Kissinger added with satisfaction, "That carrier move is good."[87]

Still, the Pentagon said that the task force never got far into the Bay of Bengal, staying over a thousand miles away from Chittagong. Although admitting there were four or five Soviet ships in the same area, the Pentagon said that the Americans never saw any of them, nor any Indian or Pakistani ships. The Indian ambassador assured the State Department that the Soviet warships were not going to get close to the fighting. In the end, the *Enterprise* carrier group did rather little militarily.[88]

EVEN BEFORE THE *ENTERPRISE* TASK FORCE ENTERED THE BAY OF BENgal, anti-Americanism in India had reached worrisome heights. After Pakistani jets bombed an Indian village in Punjab, the survivors found bombs with U.S. markings. With pieces of dead buffaloes strewn about and the smell of burned human flesh lingering, a college student who had just lost his sister screamed out that he blamed Nixon.[89]

Now the threat from the *Enterprise* drove Indians to a whole new level of wrath. Jaswant Singh, who would later become foreign minister, remembers the hollering of India's newspapers as the carrier group steamed into the Bay of Bengal, becoming a lasting symbol of American hostility. Even he—as worldly as any person could be—seethes at the memory: "It served no purpose. What possible military purpose did it serve? Was it going to launch an attack on Calcutta?"[90]

That possibility was uppermost in the minds of anxious people in Calcutta. Arundhati Ghose, the Indian diplomat there, who is a Bengali Indian, remembers, "When it entered the Bay of Bengal, there's a particular kind of fish called *hilsa,* which Bengalis love. And we said, 'Don't let them touch our *hilsa.*' And a lot of people said, 'They'll bomb Calcutta,' and we said, 'Great, so we can rebuild it properly this time.'" There were "rubbish" rumors in Calcutta that the Americans "were making a nuclear threat on us, basically to stop our progress in West Pakistan, because they didn't care about the Bangladeshis in any case." Then, dropping her jocular tone, she intones, "I couldn't believe it. I couldn't believe that the Americans were threatening us. I just couldn't believe it." She says, "We didn't think the Americans would threaten us. We thought the Chinese might. But the Chinese didn't. It was the *Enterprise* which threatened us."

The Parliament went predictably berserk. Atal Bihari Vajpayee from the Jana Sangh joined a West Bengali legislator from the Communist Party (Marxist) in demanding that Gandhi's government denounce the United States. Beyond Parliament, the perennial critic Jayaprakash Narayan was incandescent with rage at this attempt to "frighten India to submit to Nixon's will." If the Americans actually tried to establish a beachhead, he threatened "the most destructive war that history has yet witnessed."[91]

Kissinger did not care about such Indian emotions. When a reporter asked if the deployment of the carrier group was meant to influence the outcome of the war, Kissinger said, "What the Indians are mad at is irrelevant."[92]

But many Americans were appalled too. Harold Saunders, Kissinger's senior aide for South Asia, says the Indians were right to be furious. In Delhi, Kenneth Keating, the U.S. ambassador who had confronted Nixon and Kissinger in the Oval Office, had spent the war marinating in Indian grievances. At the start of the fighting, he had decried the hasty U.S. accusations that India was the aggressor, blaming Pakistan's airstrikes. After Kissinger gave a press briefing, Keating cabled that much of it was misleading or outright false.[93]

Amid roiling rumors of possible U.S. direct intervention to help Pakistan, Keating cabled that if people in Washington were seriously considering doing so, or directly providing U.S. weapons to Pakistan, he wanted to evacuate American families and nonessential American personnel from India. When the *Enterprise* entered the Bay of Bengal, Keating—fearing that Yahya would be encouraged to fight on—objected that he could no longer defend U.S. policy.[94]

Sydney Schanberg, the *New York Times* reporter, was in Calcutta when he heard the news about the *Enterprise*. "I had a sinking feeling," he says bitterly. "I'm an American, I'm standing in Calcutta, and my country is sailing up, and now I'm the enemy of my country? Because I'm living in India and thinking they're on the right side? It was the worst feeling, to this day, one of the worst feelings in my life. You don't want to hate your government. Somehow someone's tipped the world upside down."

THE *ENTERPRISE* TASK FORCE COULD HAVE REACHED EAST PAKISTAN by the early hours of December 16. But the day before, Pakistan's General Niazi sent a message to General Manekshaw saying he wanted a cease-fire, passed along through the U.S. embassy in Delhi. In reply, Manekshaw repeated his promises to safeguard the surrendering Pakistanis and the minority Biharis. As a goodwill gesture, Manekshaw ordered a pause in air action over Dacca. Despite Bhutto's theatrics at the United Nations, where he ripped up papers and stormed out of the chamber vowing to fight on, the war was all but over.[95]

Niazi's cease-fire letter was delivered to Haksar by Galen Stone, a U.S. diplomat in the Delhi embassy who was possibly even more pro-Indian than Keating. Haksar asked him, "Galen, where are we heading?" Stone, according to Haksar, replied with high emotion, saying that the U.S. relationship with India was being destroyed and wondering if he should resign. Stone said that he—and many people in the State Department—simply did not understand Nixon's policies. According to Stone, Haksar, in tears, asked what kind of relationships Indian and American children would have.[96]

Haksar pounced on this show of pro-Indian sentiment. He drew up a tough letter for the prime minister to send to Nixon, aiming directly at American hearts and minds, as a way of publicly refuting the accusations made against India by George H. W. Bush and other U.S. officials. Haksar took the United States' own Declaration of Independence and repurposed it for Bangladesh. Thus Gandhi wrote to Nixon, "That Declaration stated whenever any form of Government becomes destructive of man's inalienable rights to life, liberty and pursuit of happiness, it was the right of the people to alter or abolish it." This gave her a way to write off Pakistan's sovereignty, like British rule of

America: "while Pakistan's integrity was certainly sacrosanct, human rights, liberty were no less so." Professing grief at the downward spiral in relations with the United States, she bitterly blamed Nixon for not using U.S. influence over Yahya. But she did assure him, "We do not want any territory of what was East Pakistan and now constitutes Bangla Desh. We do not want any territory of West Pakistan."[97]

Kissinger dismissed the letter as "defensive and plaintive," but he told Nixon that a cease-fire was imminent: "we are home, now it's done." The Soviet Union had promised that India would not annex any West Pakistani territory. "It's an absolute miracle, Mr. President," Kissinger said, praising him for having "put it right on the line." Although the cease-fire was a foregone conclusion, Nixon said, "I'd like to do it in a certain way that pisses on the Indians."[98]

In private, Kissinger, still relying on the CIA mole in Delhi, remained convinced that India had meant "to knock over West Pakistan." Nixon said, "Most people were ready to stand by and let her do it, bombing [Karachi] and all." Kissinger agreed, "They really are bastards."[99]

"Look, these people are savages," said Nixon. Kissinger usually spoke of India raping Pakistan, but Nixon now had a better verb in mind. He wanted to put out the spin that "we cannot have a stable world if we allow one member of the United Nations to cannibalize another. Cannibalize, that's the word. I should have thought of it earlier. You see, that really puts it to the Indians. It has, the connotation is savages. To cannibalize . . . that's what the sons of bitches are up to."[100]

SURRENDER

An exhausted group of Mukti Bahini fighters were ecstatic—and relieved—to hear that Pakistan was about to yield. They found abandoned buses and loaded them up with jubilant rebels bound for Dacca. People packed the streets and rooftops, chanting, *"Joi Bangla!"* Coming into the city, hearing the crowds, a rebel later wrote, "We felt liberated at last." With the first column of Indian troops about to enter Dacca, the chumminess of elite South Asian officers was not to be disturbed by the minor matter of a war. An Indian commander sent a note to General Niazi, whom he knew personally: "My dear Abdullah, I am here. The game is up. I suggest you give yourself up to me, and I will look after you."[101]

On December 16, Niazi, emphasizing the "paramount considerations of saving human lives," offered his surrender on the eastern front. Manekshaw dispatched General Jacob, the chief of staff of the Eastern Command, by helicopter to Dacca, to negotiate a swift capitulation.[102]

Jacob remembers that India actually had only three thousand troops outside of Dacca, while Pakistan still had over twenty-six thousand in the city. "Just go and get a surrender," Manekshaw told Jacob. He rushed onto a helicopter, joined by the wife of his superior, Lieutenant General Jagjit Singh Aurora, the general officer commanding-in-chief of the Eastern Command, who said that her place was with her husband. When they landed in Dacca, Jacob remembers, there was still fighting going on between the Mukti Bahini and Pakistani troops. As insurgents shot at his car, he jumped up to show them his olive green Indian army uniform, which stopped their firing. Once he got to Pakistani headquarters, Jacob remembers, General Niazi said, "Who said I'm surrendering? I only came here for a cease-fire." Alone and acutely aware of how outnumbered the Indians really were at the moment, he took Niazi aside. Jacob recalls, "I said, 'You surrender, we take care of you, your families, and ethnic minorities. If you don't, what can I do? I wash my hands.' He said I blackmailed him, to have him bayoneted. I said, 'I'll give you thirty minutes, and if you don't agree, I'll order the resumption of hostilities and the bombing of Dacca.'" As Jacob walked out, "I thought, my God, I have nothing in my hand." But Niazi, surely knowing how many more Indian troops were following the tip of the spear outside Dacca, yielded.

With battalions of the Indian army and Mukti Bahini guerrillas crowding into the city, the short eastern war came to an abrupt end. On the afternoon of December 16, General Niazi tearfully surrendered to General Aurora at the Dacca Race Course, surrounded by Hindu neighborhoods that had been destroyed by some of the Pakistan army back in the spring. Preserving the Pakistanis' dignity, Jacob says, they set up solemn ceremonies at the Race Course. Niazi handed a pistol to Aurora. When Sydney Schanberg, covering it for the *New York Times*, told Jacob that the surrender of a Pakistani general to a Jewish Indian general made one hell of a story, Jacob indignantly told him not to write it. General Aurora, beaming, was hoisted aloft by crowds of leaping, cheering Bengalis. While street skirmishes continued, crowds thronged into the streets shouting *"Joi Bangla!"* and shooting bullets into the skies.[103]

General Manekshaw telephoned Indira Gandhi with the welcome tidings. She ran into the Lok Sabha, exuberant. She informed the Parliament of the unconditional surrender of Pakistan's forces in the east. "Dacca is now the free capital of a free country," she declared with satisfaction. "We hail the people of Bangla Desh in their hour of triumph."[104]

Gandhi got big cheers when she praised India's military and the Mukti Bahini, and when she said that Indian forces were under orders to treat Pakistani prisoners of war according to the Geneva Conventions, and that the Bangladesh government would do the same. "Our objectives were limited—to assist the gallant people of Bangla Desh and their Mukti Bahini to liberate their country from a reign of terror and to resist aggression on our own land." There was exuberant jubilation throughout the chamber, with lawmakers giving her thunderous standing ovations and throwing papers and hats into the air.[105]

Yet there was also an uglier side to the surrender. General Aurora was bound by India's promise of protection for West Pakistanis and ethnic minorities. "If we don't protect the Pakistanis and their collaborators," an Indian officer told Schanberg, "the Mukti Bahini will butcher them nicely and properly." Indian soldiers kept surrendering Pakistanis off the roads lest they be attacked. Aurora even allowed thousands of Pakistani troops who had surrendered to keep their weapons for protection against vengeful Bengalis.[106]

But the Indian army could not stop an awful wave of revenge killings. Gandhi admitted that her generals—although officially in command of the Bangladeshi forces—could not meaningfully promise that there would be no reprisals against loyalists. In Dacca, a *Los Angeles Times* reporter saw five civilians lying dead in the street, executed as collaborators. The CIA noted "blood-chilling reports of atrocities being perpetrated by revenge-seeking Bengalis in Dacca." Still, India worked to disarm guerrillas roaming Dacca, and detained one Mukti Bahini leader who whipped up a crowd to torture and murder four men at a public rally. After a few horrific days of bloodshed, the CIA reported that the situation had calmed down.[107]

MEANWHILE IN THE WEST, THERE WERE STILL TANK BATTLES GOING on. This was the moment of truth for India's war goals. India could declare victory in Bangladesh and go home, or launch a new and more aggressive phase, trying to capture land and cities in West Pakistan.

The hawks were in full cry. Pakistan was in chaos and vulnerable, and there were some indications that Indian troops were gaining the upper hand in the west. But Manekshaw, as he later claimed, told the prime minister that a unilateral cease-fire in the west was "the right thing to do." Haksar agreed. "I must order a cease-fire on the western front also," Gandhi told an aide, wary of the country's euphoric mood. "If I don't do it today, I shall not be able to do it tomorrow." According to her closest friend, Gandhi heard discussions from the army's chief and her top advisers about the feasibility of seizing one of Pakistan's cities. The military said that such a battle against Pakistan's well-trained soldiers would cost roughly thirty thousand casualties. She sat silently for a while. She knew that the United States and China would have to react. She decided it was time to end the war.[108]

The same day that Pakistan surrendered in the east, Gandhi declared, "India has no territorial ambitions. Now that the Pakistani Armed Forces have surrendered in Bangla Desh and Bangla Desh is free, it is pointless in our view to continue the present conflict." She unilaterally ordered India's armed forces to cease fire all along the western front as of 8 p.m. on December 17.[109]

The guns fell silent. India said that 2,307 of its warfighters had been killed, 6,163 wounded, and 2,163 were missing. The death toll was slightly higher in the west, where 1,206 Indians had been killed, against 1,021 in the east. And Pakistan's losses were presumably worse.[110]

These were terrible human losses. Even so, vastly more Bangladeshi civilians died than Indian and Pakistani soldiers combined. A senior Indian official put the Bengali death toll at three hundred thousand, while Sydney Schanberg, who had excellent sources, noted in the New York Times that diplomats in Dacca thought that hundreds of thousands of Bengalis—maybe even a million or more—had been killed since the crackdown started on March 25. Even the lowest credible Pakistani estimates are in the tens of thousands, while India sought vindication with bigger numbers: Swaran Singh quickly claimed that a million people had been killed in Bangladesh. A few days before the end of the war, Gita Mehta, an Indian journalist working for NBC, showed Indira Gandhi a film on the Bengali refugees. The prime minister, watching with her son Rajiv Gandhi, wept as she saw the images of young and old refugees.[111]

General Jacob, when asked about violating Pakistan's sovereignty, explodes in anger. "If you knew what was happening there," he thunders. "You know the rape and massacres that were taking place there? When we get ten million refugees, what do we do with them?" In Bangladesh, he had picked up a diary and read about Bengalis being bayoneted. He is convinced it was an "awful genocide," although "I didn't think it was like what the Nazis did." His fury unabated, Jacob continues hotly, "They had raped, they had killed, several hundred thousand. I was listening to Dacca University on the twenty-fifth–twenty-sixth March night. They slaughtered the students. So we should keep quiet? So I have no problem." Finally cooling down, he finishes, "I have no second thoughts on it. I'm proud of it."

Soon after the surrender, Schanberg took a trip across the traumatized new country of Bangladesh. Everywhere the *New York Times* reporter went, people showed him "all the killing grounds" where people were lined up and shot. "You could see the bones in the river, because it was a killing place." In Dacca, he went to a hillside burial place. "There were shrubs and bushes, and there was a little boy, maybe twelve or thirteen, he was on his hands and knees, scratching the earth, looking for things. He looked disturbed. He was looking for his father, who he said was buried there. If you scratched enough there—it was shallow graves—you'd find a skull or bones. There were cemeteries everywhere. There was no doubt in my mind, evil was done."

KISSINGER, H. R. HALDEMAN NOTED, WAS "PRACTICALLY ECSTATIC" AT the imminent cease-fire. Nixon was not. "Dacca has surrendered," the president told Kissinger glumly.[112]

Sharing none of Kissinger's ebullience, Nixon was sunk in bitterness at Pakistan's defeat. He was, he said, "outraged" at India's media advocacy, and "really teed off" that Kissinger had not adequately publicized their accusations of an Indian plan to destroy Pakistan. With Kissinger's assent, he wanted to move toward a conflict with India: "If the Indians continue the course they are on we have even got to break diplomatic relations with them."

The president took some comfort in the fact, relayed by Kissinger, that Jordan had illegally sent warplanes to help Pakistan. But Nixon complained that "when the chips are down India has shown that it is a Russian satellite." He fumed, "I know the bigger game is the Russian game, but the Indians also have played us for squares here. They have done this once and when this is over they will come to us ask us to forgive and forget. This we must not do."[113]

Soon after, Kissinger telephoned the president to report the cease-fire in the west. Kissinger saw this as an enduring achievement for himself. Jolly once again, he tried to cheer Nixon up: "Congratulations, Mr. President. You saved W[est] Pakistan." Nixon brooded, not wanting Indira Gandhi to gloat in victory. "She shouldn't get credit for starting the fire and then calling in the fire department," he said. "It's back to Hitler."[114]

Kissinger savored a victory lap. He separately told Haldeman and George Shultz, "We have turned disaster into defeat," and thanked John Connally, the anti-Indian Treasury secretary, for giving him "the moral courage to do it." He spent the rest of the day calling reporters to claim credit and working the phones to try to cobble together a feeble United Nations Security Council resolution. About the Indians, he told the British ambassador, "I don't know how you tolerated them for those years." Kissinger joked to Bush, "don't screw it up the way you usually do."

"I want a transfer when this is over," replied George Bush. "I want a nice quiet place like Rwanda."[115]

Aftermaths

THE COLD WAR EXPIRED WITHOUT A FORMAL RECKONING OF THE superpowers' different crimes: no international war crimes tribunal, no truth commission. There was nothing like a Nuremberg after the glorious democratic revolutions of 1989. Americans and Russians have been able to walk away without serious afterthought.

But if Americans have been able to forget the legacy of 1971, the peoples of the subcontinent have not. The atrocities remain Bangladesh's defining national trauma, leaving enduring scars on the country's politics and economy. Economic development was always going to be difficult there, but the challenges were made much worse by the loss of so many people, the disruption of families and rural communities, the decimation of the ranks of the educated, the devastation of infrastructure, the radicalization of political life, the widespread availability of leftover weapons from the insurgency, and the burden of getting the refugees back home.[1]

Nor could Bangladesh depend on India, as Richard Nixon and Henry Kissinger feared it would. Although India, proving as good as its wartime word, quickly agreed to withdraw its troops from the new country, relations between the two neighbors rapidly soured. P. N. Haksar told Indira Gandhi, "Bangla Desh at present is, politically speaking, a primordial slime. Out of this chaos, cosmos has to be created." The Bangladeshi government found the embrace of their Indian liberators stifling, with politicians making prickly complaints about the gargantuan shadow that India cast.[2]

Sheikh Mujib-ur-Rahman, freed from a West Pakistani jail, set up a new democracy, but it did not endure long. As Haksar and other Indians had warned, Bangladesh's underdevelopment and poverty proved overwhelming. Mujib's government quickly sank into corruption. As the Indian foreign ministry noted nervously, the rural poor were hungry, while the middle class were disillusioned as their living standards declined. In December 1974, Mujib seized emergency powers for himself, gutting the democratic constitution that he had helped fashion. Then in August 1975, army officers launched a violent coup, storming Mujib's Dacca house and shooting him dead, as well as his wife, brother, sons, and daughters-in-law. (Today, the house is a gruesomely preserved museum, displaying bloodstains on the steps and brain matter that splashed up onto the ceiling.) Bangladesh plunged into unrest and instability, with a brief flickering period of civilian rule followed by another coup, and then another. Haksar asked what was next: "Another night of the long knife?"[3]

Today, India stands aloof from Bangladesh. The two countries squabble about border enclaves, bizarre leftovers from Partition: tiny bits of Bangladeshi territory that are inside India, and little blobs of Indian territory located inside Bangladesh. India has separated itself from its neighbor with armed guards at a massive fence with barbed wire, running along most of the border. Since 2000, Indian forces have killed almost a thousand Bangladeshis trying to get across the border.[4]

Yet in recent years, Bangladesh's investments in education have paid off, with reduced poverty and a nascent middle class. Even with crumbling infrastructure and awful—sometimes lethal—working conditions in the vital garment industry, even though millions of people still have no hope of anything more lucrative than subsistence farming, Bangladesh has managed impressive and sustained economic growth. But the country still suffers from broken politics. Mujib's daughter, Sheikh Hasina, is currently prime minister, and a rather awful one. There are unexplained disappearances and killings; Muhammad Yunus, the Nobel laureate who broke new ground in microcredit, is hassled by the authorities; corruption is endemic; and opposition politicians face arrest or harassment. There are angry street protests.

While there is a new war crimes tribunal charged with the atrocities of 1971, it is only pursuing Bangladeshis accused of collaborating with Yahya's regime—which conveniently implicates members of the country's biggest Islamist party, opponents of Sheikh Hasina. True justice for the horrors is vital, but the slanted trials so far have failed to live up to both Bangladeshi and international standards of due process. Showing how deeply Bangladeshis still feel the wounds of 1971, when a defendant got a life sentence rather than the death penalty, that was enough to spark the largest mass demonstrations in Dacca in the past two decades.[5]

It will be up to Bangladeshis to fix their own politics, but Americans should realize that this distant people's task has been made harder from the outset by the U.S.-backed horrors of 1971. If an apology from Henry Kissinger is too much to expect, it would be an act of decency for the U.S. government to recognize a special American responsibility to make amends to the Bangladeshi people.

PAKISTAN

Pakistan was stunned by its military defeat. The population was in shock, dazed and resentful. During the war, the state-controlled press had falsely told Pakistanis that their army was winning; when the government abruptly lifted censorship, Pakistanis were unprepared for the hard slap of reality. They suddenly learned about the army's atrocities and military defeats, leaving people disillusioned and disgusted.[6]

This second partition was devastating for Pakistan. "They know that India was the midwife of Bangladesh," says Scott Butcher, the junior political officer in the U.S. consulate in Dacca back in 1971. "They [India] defeated the military, which is proud. That was a real sock in the gut for Pakistani dignity. They lost half their country and more than half their population."

Yahya himself was so much in denial that he defiantly vowed to keep fighting for the east. But in the city streets of what had been West Pakistan and was now simply a truncated Pakistan, crowds screamed for Yahya and his cronies to be put on trial as traitors. Infuriated by Yahya's drinking, mobs in Karachi burned liquor stores. The CIA reported that some of the military and the public thought he should commit suicide. Days after Dacca fell, Nixon's friend reluctantly announced that he was resigning, swept aside by Zulfiqar Ali Bhutto. Despite his electoral success back in 1970, Bhutto came to Pakistan's presidency under a cloud: some Pakistanis blamed him for an aggressive obduracy in the constitutional negotiations that had helped lead to the current catastrophe.[7]

Piling on the humiliation, India worked energetically to frame the defeat as a foundational challenge to Pakistan's ideal of itself as an Islamic nation. Indian thinkers rejected Pakistan's "two-nation theory," the belief that Hindus and Muslims comprised two distinct nations—which Haksar called "the purest fiction ever invented by the human mind." The creation of Bangladesh "has sounded a death knell to the so-called two-nation theory," gloated a senior Indian diplomat, rub-bishing the "concept of Pakistan as an Islamic State." Although Indians underestimated Pakistan's reliance on other ideals such as nationalist modernization, Pakistanis still grapple with this breakdown. More than a decade after the war, the journalist Tariq Ali wrote, "The 'two-nations' theory, formulated in the middle-class living rooms of Uttar Pradesh, was buried in the Bengali countryside."[8]

Nor did Pakistani leaders believe that India was done hammering them. In June 1971, Swaran Singh, India's foreign minister, had secretly told his diplomats about other ways to crack up West Pakistan itself, by stirring up rebellion in restive areas such as Baluchistan and the North-West Frontier Province—hoping to get those places to follow Bangladesh's lead. After the success of Indian intelligence in covertly sponsoring the Mukti Bahini, Indian officials pushed to expand the use of the spy agencies more widely. Disastrously, this came to include R&AW sponsorship of the Liberation Tigers of Tamil Eelam, who went on to assassinate Rajiv Gandhi.[9]

Among the mandarins in India's ruling circles, Jaswant Singh is one of the most sympathetic to Pakistani fears. He says, "Now when you say, 'Come on, it's over. Why do you sink yourself into this hellhole of state-sponsored terrorism? Why do you try to kill India with a thou-sand cuts?' Friends in Pakistan tell me, 'Well, we can't forget '71.' It simmers." Arundhati Ghose, Haksar's protégée at the Indian foreign ministry, says, "We haven't yet absorbed that the Pakistanis today are not thinking about Partition anymore. It's '71 that they agonize about. That's what they hold against India. That we split their country. It was already difficult, but it's a very powerful thing from the Pakistani side of it. There's terrible resentment. We don't seem to be aware of it."

This trauma could have been an opportunity for self-examination in Pakistan. As one of Yahya's ministers later wrote, "The Pakistan Army's brutal actions . . . can never be condoned or justified in any way. The Army's murderous campaign in which many thousands of inno-cent people including women, the old and sick, and even children, were brutally murdered while millions fled from their homes to take shelter either in remote places or in India, constituted a measureless tragedy." Days after the shooting stopped, Bhutto set up a judicial commission to investigate the battlefield defeat in East Pakistan. Led by Pakistan's chief justice as well as two other eminent judges, it produced a scathing official record condemning the military for corruption, turpitude, and brutality, and demanding courts-martial for Yahya, Niazi, and other disgraced military leaders. While the report concentrates on military defeats, it includes frank testimony on the atrocities from senior army officers and civilian officials. This judicial commission, convinced that "there can be no doubt that a very large number of unprovoked and vindictive atrocities did in fact take place," urged Pakistan's government to set up a "high-powered court or commission of inquiry" to "hold trials of those who indulged in these atrocities, brought a bad name to the Pakistan Army and alienated the sympathies of the local population by their acts of wanton cruelty and immorality against our own people."[10]

But nothing happened. The report was so harsh on the military that it was suppressed, and only came to light in an Indian magazine in 2000 and in Karachi's intrepid *Dawn* newspaper in 2001. While Bhutto was keen to discredit the likes of Yahya and Niazi, he—far from facing up to the horrors—refused to accept losing Bangladesh and insisted on the necessity of the crackdown. "I would have done it with more intelligence, more scientifically, less brutally," Bhutto told an interviewer, heaping all blame on "Yahya Khan and his gang of illiterate psychopaths." Bhutto put the notorious General Tikka Khan in charge of the army, insisting that during the massacres "he was a soldier doing a soldier's job." (Tikka Khan later became a leader of the Pakistan People's Party.) He denied not just the inflated Bangladeshi statistic of three million dead, but also the number of ten million refugees, insisting that Indira Gandhi had sent people from West Bengal. As for the women who were raped and killed, he flatly said, "I don't believe it." While saying that "such brutality" against the people was unnecessary, Bhutto defended the use of force at home: "You can't build without destroying. To build a country, Stalin was obliged to use force and kill. Mao Tse-tung was obliged to use force and kill."[11]

For liberal Pakistanis today, the year 1971 marks a failure to fashion a workable constitutional order. In Lahore's *Friday Times,* Najam Sethi, an outspoken liberal journalist, recently criticized Pakistan's effort to centralize its control in both the west and east wings, resulting in the "exploitation and repression" of the Bengalis: "The consequence of this false start was disintegration of the country in 1971 and the rise of dangerous sub-nationalisms and separatisms in what remains of Pakistan." After all, the loss of East Pakistan, as grievous as that was, was always a rather likely event. Anatol Lieven, an eminent Pakistan expert with deep sympathy for the country, has thoughtfully argued that the real catastrophe was the "terrible circumstances" in which Bangladesh left—more like Yugoslavia than Czechoslovakia—not the fact that it did. The separation, he believes, was all but inevitable.[12]

But Pakistani remembrances of 1971 usually omit the military's own atrocities. The army, the big political parties, and many newspapers would all prefer to forget their responsibilities. Even someone as sophisticated as Benazir Bhutto remembered that, as a Harvard College student in 1971, she initially "refused to believe" American newspapers, and "found security in the official jingoistic line in our part of the world that the reports in the Western press were 'exaggerated' and a 'Zionist plot' against an Islamic state." As she later forthrightly wrote, "How many times since have I asked God to forgive me for my ignorance?"[13]

To this day, the country's memories about its treatment of its former east wing remain, as one leading Pakistani publication put it, shrouded in "a fog of confusion" or lost in "collective amnesia." Although upper-level textbooks can be much better, many of Pakistan's textbooks have whitewashed out the atrocities against Bengalis and falsely claimed that the United States wanted Pakistan divided. In the big cities, there is more awareness; in cosmopolitan Lahore, a recent poll found that 79 percent of youthful respondents remember that East Pakistan was treated unfairly. But overall, just 38 percent of young Pakistanis say that East Pakistan was dealt with unfairly, while 19 percent say it was treated fairly, and 40 percent simply do not know.[14]

THIS WAS THE RUBBLE OUT OF WHICH BHUTTO HAD TO REBUILD HIS country. He sought out a new national identity and new foreign friends. Perhaps the most bizarre outcome of Nixon's and Kissinger's hell-bent support of Pakistan was that its new president and many of his fellow citizens felt *betrayed* by the United States.[15]

Bhutto had long been anti-American, but Pakistan's dismemberment redoubled his suspicions. During the civil war, many Pakistani elites and army officers had seen the United States as fickle at best, or secretly scheming to rip Pakistan apart. Lieutenant General A. A. K. Niazi, who surrendered to the Indian generals, bitterly claimed that his troops could have held out if not betrayed by conspiracies, and wrote that his humiliation suited the Americans. Other Pakistanis discerned a shadowy American plot—sometimes blamed in part on American Jews—to dismember their country.[16]

This is perplexing and unfair. Whatever else might be said of them,

Nixon and Kissinger cannot be faulted for any lack of commitment to Pakistan. "In everything we do with Yahya," Kissinger directed the U.S. ambassador in Pakistan, "we cannot have it said that we stabbed Pakistan in the back. This must be your guiding principle." Kissinger instructed George H. W. Bush that Nixon "[d]oesn't want anyone to say we pushed Pakistan over the edge." During the war, Bhutto told Kissinger that "we are completely satisfied" with U.S. backing, and promised a lavish show of appreciation when peace came.[17]

But Nixon's and Kissinger's kind of support was not likely to win over ordinary Pakistanis. Their most enthusiastic acts on behalf of Pakistan—encouraging Chinese military mobilization and illegal arms transfers through Iran and Jordan—were so secret that hardly anyone in Pakistan could have known about them. And the most conspicuous U.S. support went to the junta, not the public, even when Yahya showed contempt for democratic election results in both wings of the country. This was fundamentally an alliance with Yahya and his generals; when they were ousted and discredited, it left little popular goodwill.[18]

Instead, Bhutto's Pakistan cooled toward the United States and turned to other countries for succor. In 1972, China used its first United Nations Security Council veto to block the United Nations from admitting Bangladesh, which China saw as a breakaway province no better than Taiwan. (The United States, yielding to reality, would not go so far.) At the same time, Bhutto cast his lot with friendly Muslim countries, culminating in a gala Islamic summit in Lahore in 1974 for leaders such as Hafez al-Assad of Syria, Anwar al-Sadat of Egypt, King Faisal of Saudi Arabia, and Muammar al-Qaddafi of Libya, who declared that Pakistan was the "citadel of Islam in Asia." In 1973, Pakistan got a new constitution including some distinctly Islamic inflections, which grew more extreme during the ideological dictatorship of Muhammad Zia-ul-Haq, the general who overthrew Bhutto in a military coup in July 1977.[19]

Today the loss of Bangladesh is widely remembered in Pakistan as an early American betrayal, presaging a long series of them: a tepid U.S. response to India's nuclear test in 1974, U.S. support for Zia's authoritarianism, sanctions against Pakistan's nuclear program, backing for Pervez Musharraf's military regime in the aftermath of the September 2001 terrorist attacks on New York and Washington, and ongoing drone strikes. From the standard Pakistani nationalist viewpoint, in 1971, despite all of Pakistan's help with Nixon's opening to China, the United States was at best useless in preventing the loss of half the country.[20]

. . .

SOME INDIAN STRATEGISTS HAD HOPED THAT A DISMEMBERED AND defeated Pakistan would be finished as a threat. But despite Pakistan's losses—and some ninety-three thousand Pakistani prisoners of war—it rearmed and girded for future confrontation. Although Indira Gandhi's government had to insincerely welcome Bhutto as a democratically elected president, his fear and hostility toward India were radically increased. Under Bhutto, defense spending rocketed up. Just over two months after the war, the Indian army saw that Pakistan was replacing its losses, modernizing its tank units, and bolstering its infantry. "A defeated army will naturally seek revenge to restore its image in the country," General Sam Manekshaw said. "They will therefore want another round of hostilities for which we should be fully prepared."[21]

Gandhi, bargaining from strength, met Bhutto in a summit at Simla in June 1972. (He brought along his daughter, Benazir Bhutto.) Although they sparred over Kashmir, she gave him generous terms: the return of some five thousand square miles of Pakistani territory seized by Indian troops, and the repatriation of ninety-three thousand Pakistani prisoners of war, with the approval of Mujib's government in Bangladesh. Many Indians were startled by Bhutto's success at Simla, with the opposition arguing that Gandhi had lost at the negotiating table what the army had won in war. But the Indian foreign ministry hailed the Simla agreement as a generous peace, not imposed on the defeated, the diametrical opposite of the punitive Treaty of Versailles. Bhutto assured her that he would get his people to accept the upgrading of the line of control in Kashmir into an actual border, but then gave a hard-line speech about Kashmir.[22]

Pervez Musharraf, a young Pakistani commando officer during the 1971 war, flung his jacket on the floor in disgust at the humiliating defeat. He wanted revenge against India—something still on his mind in 1999 when he seized power in a military coup to become Pakistan's military dictator. The old vendetta between Pakistan and India, freshly intensified after 1971, has had terrible consequences far beyond the region. The rout of Pakistan's army drove home as never before to Pakistan's leadership the need for alternative ways of fighting India. It did this in three ways, all of them tragic.[23]

First, the army, always strong, has become an overweening force in Pakistan's political life. After the humiliating skunking of Pakistan's military, Bhutto at first sought to limit the generals' power. But confronted with an insurrection in Baluchistan in 1973, Bhutto showed hardly more imagination than the far less intelligent Yahya, sending in some eighty thousand troops. Once again, Pakistan went to war with its own people. In recent years, the generals have pushed aside civilian control and weakened the prospects for deepening democracy. "We are almost a failed state," Musharraf recently said. "This is what democracy brings Pakistan."[24]

Second, Pakistan has turned to guerrillas and terrorists to carry on the struggle against India for Kashmir. Zia, who sought to install a politicized Islam at the core of Pakistan's politics, turned to young Islamist fighters as his beleaguered country's last hope against Indian and Soviet armies. After guerrillas proved successful against Soviet troops in Afghanistan, Pakistani intelligence deployed similar means against India in Kashmir. In the 1990s, Pakistan's powerful Inter-Services Intelligence secretly backed and armed the Taliban, with the undeclared support of the Pakistan army and much of the civilian leadership. By 1999, the Pakistan army's chiefs were convinced that jihadists were the only reliable way to challenge the Indian army—even indulging Osama bin Laden. Until 2001, the ISI nurtured Lashkar-e-Taiba, a terrorist group aiming against India but today with a much wider reach. (Of course, this kind of covert sponsorship was out of India's playbook for the Mukti Bahini.) Still, such support has proved to be a catastrophic strategy for Pakistan. Both inside and outside Pakistan's borders, terrorist attacks have become a grimly regular part of life, often from groups that have been the secret beneficiaries of the Pakistani state. Untold Pakistani civilians have been murdered.[25]

In Afghanistan today, Pakistan's fear of India drives some of the policies that are most dangerous to the United States. Pakistani politicians and generals worry that a rising India will dominate Afghanistan, leaving it with another hostile state on its border. To offset that, Pakistan's ISI has kept up its ties with the Taliban, which serves as a way of balancing India's influence in Afghanistan. Scott Butcher says, "You look at Afghanistan, it's all colored by Pakistan's fear of India."[26]

Third, there is Pakistan's nuclear arsenal. Bhutto had long argued that Pakistan needed its own atomic bomb, even if its people had to go hungry. Soon after losing the Bangladesh war, he decided to produce one. This was the genesis of the burgeoning nuclear program that has grown into one of the biggest nightmares of U.S. national security officials. Pakistan nurtures a growing arsenal of nuclear weapons and short-range missiles to deliver them, and is reckoned to have between seventy and 120 nuclear devices. When Benazir Bhutto was asked why nuclear weapons are popular among Pakistanis, she replied, "In 1971, our country was disintegrated." A. Q. Khan, the chief of Pakistan's nuclear weapons program—who remains a nationalist hero even though his smuggling network evidently sold nuclear technology to North Korea, Libya, and Iran—recently invoked the Bangladesh war as an apology for his dangerous brand of nuclear proliferation: "Had Iraq and Libya been nuclear powers, they wouldn't have been destroyed in the way we have seen recently. If we had had nuclear capability before 1971, we would not have lost half of our country—present-day Bangladesh—after disgraceful defeat."[27]

INDIA

India, accustomed to military humiliations, largely remembers the war as a famous victory—unlike the two previous wars against Pakistan and the 1962 drubbing by China. India's euphoric government hailed its 1971 victory as decisive, and for at least a little while it loomed as the dominant power in the subcontinent. To this day, Indians recall the Bangladesh war with a rare triumphalism. In a country that often dwells on its failures, this heady moment stands out. Commemorating the fortieth anniversary of the war, the *Hindustan Times* ran the proud headline 1971 WAR: INDIA'S GREATEST TRIUMPH.[28]

Indians see the war as a moral triumph too, a victory for democracy and human rights. As the leading Indian scholar and analyst Pratap Bhanu Mehta wrote, "India's 1971 armed intervention in East Pakistan—undertaken for a mixture of reasons—is widely and fairly regarded as one of the world's most successful cases of humanitarian intervention against genocide. Indeed, India in effect applied what we would now call the 'responsibility to protect' (R2P) principle, and applied it well."[29]

Some of the best political thinkers outside of India agree. Michael Walzer, probably the most distinguished philosopher of justice in war, repeatedly points to India's Bangladesh war as a canonical example of a justifiable humanitarian intervention, in a radical emergency when there was no other plausible way to save innocent human lives. In recent years, when dictators quashed opposition movements—in Haiti in 1994, in Syria since 2011—and sent refugees fleeing for their lives into neighboring countries, it looks like a small-scale version of what India faced. Turkey's prime minister, Recep Tayyip Erdoğan, recently echoed Indira Gandhi's argument that Pakistan's internal problem had become India's: "We do not see the Syria issue as an external one. It is an internal issue for us."[30]

Still, this was at best a war of mixed motives. As Arundhati Ghose astutely asks, "Yes, Mrs. Gandhi got the support of the people because of the atrocities, but was the decision taken because of the atrocities?" It is impossible to see Indira Gandhi as much of a guardian of human rights. Her own record—in Mizoram, Nagaland, Kashmir, and West Bengal; in a bloody crackdown in Punjab in 1984; and nationwide in her suspension of Indian democracy in the Emergency—shows scant commitment to such ideals. At the same time, as both Walzer and Mehta rightly note, she certainly saw the chance to smash Pakistan. Indian officials were sincere in their outrage at the slaughter of the Bengalis, but also keenly aware of the strategic opportunity handed to them. The Indian government wanted to hurt Pakistan, to resist China, to heighten its dominance over South Asia, to shore up its border states from Naxalite revolutionary violence, to avert communal tension between Hindus and Muslims, and, above all, to shuck off the crushing permanent burden of ten million refugees. But at the same time, India's democratic society—including its ruling elites—was moved by a remarkably unanimous humanitarianism, with real solidarity with the Bengalis.[31]

THE END OF THE WAR MARKED THE LOW POINT FOR INDIA'S RELATIONship with the United States. Beginning a protracted sulk, Nixon wrote to Gandhi, in a baldly undiplomatic tone, "If there is a strain in our relations, and there is, it is because your government spurned these proposals and without any warning whatever chose war instead."[32]

The Indian embassy in Washington despairingly reported that Nixon's policies had sent "Indo-US relations plunging to their lowest ebb." Before the crisis, fully two-thirds of Indians had held a good opinion of the United States, with only 9 percent with a bad or very bad opinion of the country. After the war, over half of Indians had a bad or very bad opinion of the United States, with just over a quarter having a good or very good opinion. The sourness lasted for decades. Jaswant Singh says that Indian bitterness at the deployment of the USS *Enterprise* carrier group did not begin to dissipate until Bill Clinton's presidency.[33]

More pointedly, one of Gandhi's top advisers has argued that the bullying of the *Enterprise* prodded India to accelerate its nuclear program—leading to the detonation of a nuclear device at Pokhran,

in the vast Rajasthan desert, in May 1974. To this day, Indian nationalists often argue that the *Enterprise* proves why India needs nuclear
weapons. "India had that experience in 1971, when the USS *Enterprise*
entered the Bay of Bengal," Arundhati Ghose once told a reporter. "I
have always felt that this was what prompted Indira Gandhi to explode
the nuclear device in 1974."[34]

This is more a reflection of Indian resentment than of historical fact.
After all, even Nixon—more hostile to India than any U.S. president—
was obviously deterred from anything more than a symbolic gesture
by India's *conventional* military strength. So, evidently, was a bellicose
China, which had menacingly tested its own bomb back in 1964. True,
it seems that Gandhi authorized the building of a nuclear device in
1972, after the war, having publicly rejected an Indian bomb as recently
as June 1971. But it is not clear when she decided to authorize building
the device, with some accounts placing that before the *Enterprise*'s visit
to the Bay of Bengal. India was certainly debating its nuclear options
before the Bangladesh crisis, and the idea of a peaceful nuclear explosion was gaining ground in the summer of 1971, before Nixon's gunboat diplomacy.[35]

Rather than being driven by fear of the United States, India in its
decision to detonate a nuclear bomb seems to have been motivated in
large part by Gandhi's desire for domestic popularity. Many Indians
cheered the blast. And the *Enterprise* definitely wounded the pride of
India's leaders, as well as reminding them of their relative weakness.
They were shocked by this expression of American contempt. As the
scholar George Perkovich argued, India was mostly driven to develop
nuclear capacity not by any urgent new threat, but by the wish for
major-power status.[36]

WITH THIS GREAT VICTORY, INDIRA GANDHI STOOD AT THE APEX OF
her power. Her former critics sang her praises, as her favorability rating
in the polls soared to an astonishing 93 percent. In March 1972, state
elections were called for thirteen states, and her Congress party easily
rode her coattails to win all of them. Even in West Bengal, the Congress came out well, although it had to ally itself with the Communist
Party of India, and use shocking measures of terror and voter fraud.
She had stood up to the cruel Pakistanis, the fanatical Chinese, and the
arrogant Americans. People hailed her as Durga, the invincible Hindu
warrior goddess.[37]

Gandhi was intoxicated by her battlefield success. "I am no longer the same person," she euphorically told her closest friend. That friend was worried: adrift in all the adulation, the prime minister seemed to be losing the ability to doubt herself. The war had fostered something close to a cult of personality around Gandhi. The Congress—which tellingly eventually came to be known as the Congress (I), for "Indira"—was more than ever her instrument. She weakened the restraints of India's democratic institutions, installing loyalists to run key states, packing the civil service, and even trying to hold sway over the judiciary.[38]

But Durga still had a poor country to run. India's coffers were drained by waging war, sheltering refugees, and sponsoring an insurgency. India had also lost U.S. economic aid. As the monsoons failed, the economy was in a shambles, battered by high oil prices and inflation. The country fell into labor strikes, with factories shuttered and people in misery. She turned away from Haksar, relying increasingly on her corrupt and callow second son, Sanjay Gandhi, who pressed her toward autocracy. "The Prime Minister had become very arrogant," recalled one of her aides. "She loved being called Durga. The Bangladesh victory was the turning point."[39]

History does not march so directly, but Gandhi certainly grew less tolerant after her war. Throughout the Bangladesh crisis, the activist Jayaprakash Narayan had pressed her to confront Pakistan. Rather than embracing him as part of the war effort, Gandhi spoke of him with vehement contempt. "Jayaprakash has never taken me seriously," she told her friend. "One has to be really ruthless if the need arises." To her fury, Narayan launched a new and radicalized protest movement, capitalizing on the country's economic woes. Her popularity sank steadily, while he alarmingly called for "total revolution." Escalating the confrontation, she unleashed the police on Narayan and his followers in Bihar. Gandhi became prey to conspiratorial claims that Narayan's movement was secretly backed by the United States as payback for the Bangladesh humiliation. The prime minister, knowing how much Nixon loathed her, worried about "the foreign hand."[40]

In June 1975, after a high court handed down a startling ruling that threw the prime minister out of Parliament and barred her from office for six years, Gandhi launched her Emergency. Indians were devastated at this nightmare betrayal of their freedom. Egged on by Sanjay, Indira Gandhi rounded up and jailed hundreds of opposition politicians, including Narayan. She imprisoned unionists, students, and politicians who had anything to do with rival parties like the Jana Sangh and the Congress (O). She imposed humorless censorship and cut electricity to newspapers. India's famously rambunctious press—which had done so much to bring to light the atrocities against Bengalis back in 1971—was forced to kill stories about strikes and demonstrations, cut out the political jokes, and instead run official drivel from South Block.[41]

This kind of rupture was something that Haksar—now shoved aside—had long dreaded. With a bitter awareness of the fragility of democracy, he had once written, "If our Parliament goes berserk and becomes an instrument of oppression, our democracy would have failed and something else would take its place. If such turbulence were to take place in our country, waving of the Constitution against the flood waters of dark reaction or revolution will not stem the tide." But it was his own prime minister who had now gone berserk.[42]

Throughout the darkest days of the Bangladesh crisis, Indians had taken pride in their own democratic system as a sign of moral superiority over Pakistan's junta. Now—until Gandhi held new elections in March 1977—India had an autocrat of its own. Some Indians painfully heard echoes of Pakistani dictatorship in the Emergency. After all, Yahya had subordinated freedom to stability too; the Pakistani military had also taken power to rescue their country from itself. The Bengalis of East Pakistan had accused Pakistan's generals of cementing West Pakistan's domination over them; now southern Indians complained that Gandhi was enshrining northern preeminence through her Emergency powers.[43]

Less than two months after the Emergency began, Mujib was assassinated in Dacca. India, for all its wartime rhetoric about Bangladeshi democracy, kept up normal ties, readily accepting a new military president to replace the dead Mujib. The Indian foreign secretary, in no position to lecture about the abnegation of democracy, told the Bangladeshi high commissioner, "It is for the Bangladesh nation to decide what is best for them." Gandhi, horrified, was convinced that she would be next. The army officers in Bangladesh had shot dead Mujib's nine-year-old son; her grandson, Rahul Gandhi, was about the same age. She spent the rest of her life in dread of assassination, until the day in October 1984 when she was gunned down at her home by two of her Sikh bodyguards.[44]

Indira Gandhi left behind a family dynasty that still looms over Indian politics. Her daughter-in-law Sonia Gandhi is a monumental political force, and her grandson Rahul Gandhi is trying his level best. He has even tried to kick-start his spluttering political career by capitalizing on his grandmother's breakup of Pakistan. "I belong to the family which has never moved backwards, which has never gone back on its words," he said at a rally in Uttar Pradesh in 2007. "You know that when any member of my family had decided to do anything, he does it. Be it the freedom struggle, the division of Pakistan or taking India to the 21st century." This was met with derision by Indian politicos and fury by Pakistan, but the Nehru-Gandhi dynasty still dominates the country, jealously guarding Indira Gandhi's legacy.[45]

THE UNITED STATES

On March 1, 1973, in the Oval Office, Nixon and Kissinger were talking about Soviet Jews. Kissinger, who had at least thirteen close relatives murdered in the Holocaust, showed his lack of interest in the starkest possible terms: "if they put Jews into gas chambers in the Soviet Union, it is not an American concern. Maybe a humanitarian concern." Nixon agreed: "I know. We can't blow up the world because of it."[46]

When this tape recording was made public some thirty-seven years later, an embarrassed Kissinger apologized and tried to explain his remark as having been taken out of context. But the torment of Bangladesh suggests a simpler truth: he meant what he said. In the spring of 1971, he and Nixon were faced with mass atrocities on a scale that, at least for Nixon, called to mind Hitler's extermination of German Jews. To be sure, Pakistan had no gas chambers; Yahya was not Hitler; this was not the Holocaust. Still, although Nixon and Kissinger stood behind many dictatorships—in Brazil, Greece, Portugal, Indonesia, Iran, Spain, South Korea—this was an enormity that went beyond the workaday cruelties of statecraft, as Nixon himself understood. And yet in that dire circumstance, Nixon and Kissinger, in word and in deed, stood resolutely behind Pakistan's murderous generals.[47]

During the grueling year of 1971, Nixon and Kissinger were often outraged. Nixon saw Indira Gandhi's aggressiveness as morally wrong, not just strategically inconvenient. Kissinger was indignant at William Rogers, exasperated with Kenneth Keating, and appalled by Archer Blood. But when it came to mass murder, he was oddly diffident. The worst he would say about Yahya was that he thought the man was stupid, and Kissinger thought that almost everyone was stupid.

No country, not even the United States, can prevent massacres everywhere in the world. But these atrocities were carried out by a close U.S. ally, which prized its warm relationship with the United States, and used U.S. weapons and military supplies against its own people. Surely there was some U.S. responsibility here. And yet Nixon and Kissinger, for all their clout with Pakistan, despite all the warnings from Blood and others, continued to support this military dictatorship while it committed grievous crimes against humanity.

NIXON AND KISSINGER HAVE BEEN IMPRESSIVELY SUCCESSFUL IN POL-ishing the grit off their own reputations. At night on August 7, 1974, facing impeachment and conviction over Watergate, Nixon finally decided to resign. He summoned Kissinger to his side in the residence at the White House, and asked how history would view his foreign policy. As Nixon boozily sobbed, Kissinger recited the president's achievements, assuring the shattered man that history would remember him as a great peacemaker. Just in case, the next day, Nixon, in his final televised address from the Oval Office, rattled off his successes with Vietnam, China, the Middle East, and the Soviet Union—and, unsurprisingly, made no mention of India or Bangladesh.[48]

"We have taken . . . shit ever since," Nixon said soon before his death. After resigning, he spent the rest of his days seeking rehabilitation. Bob Woodward aptly writes that Nixon waged a "war against history," churning out ten books, trying to salvage his historical reputation by touting his achievements in foreign policy. Nixon's self-exculpatory books show his old fondness for Pakistan's helpful generals, but he limits his references to their role in smoothing his way to China—and certainly never considers the Bengali lives lost in exchange for Yahya's assistance. While Nixon's and Kissinger's massive tomes try to elevate them into the redemptive company of titans like Charles de Gaulle and Konrad Adenauer, they are more properly remembered alongside a rampaging Yahya.[49]

Nixon and Kissinger largely failed at sanitizing their record on Watergate, Vietnam, and Cambodia—but on Bangladesh they proved to be remarkably deft at ducking public judgment. Just two years later, when Kissinger became secretary of state, a Gallup poll found that he was the most admired person in the United States. Far from ending up a pariah, he remains a superstar, glistening as the single most famous and revered American foreign policy practitioner. Bangladesh ought to rank with Vietnam and Cambodia among the darkest incidents in Nixon's presidency and the entire Cold War. But few Americans today remember anything about these atrocities, let alone about Nixon's and Kissinger's support for the government that was committing them. In this forgetting, Americans have absorbed some of Nixon's and Kissinger's contempt for Bangladesh. Faraway, poor, brown—the place is all too easily ignored or mocked.[50]

For those primarily concerned with the health of the United States, Nixon's and Kissinger's actions back in 1971 deserve scrutiny for their contempt for the rule of law. As Bob Woodward and Carl Bernstein have rightly pointed out, Nixon was trampling the law long before June 1972, when the burglars were arrested while breaking into Democratic Party headquarters at the Watergate. In December 1971, Nixon and Kissinger were already abusing government power by unlawfully transferring weapons to Pakistan from Iran and Jordan. They took no notice of legal warnings from the State Department, the Pentagon, and the White House staff; in the Nixon White House, it already went without saying that the president was above the law. And unlike with Watergate, Nixon and Kissinger largely got away with this illegal covert operation, never facing anything like the Iran-contra investigation.[51]

Kissinger did take some knocks in the press over India, which sent him into a frenzy. Some of the records of his Situation Room meetings were leaked to the muckraking columnist Jack Anderson, who even found out that Kissinger had toyed with the idea of illegally sending Jordanian F-104s to Pakistan, although he did not realize that Nixon and Kissinger had actually done it. "We cannot survive the kind of internal weaknesses we are seeing," Kissinger raged to Nixon. John Ehrlichman noted that Kissinger was lashing back with a forceful press campaign, "trying to change the fact that during his . . . [Situation Room] meetings Henry had lost his objectivity and he'd been exceedingly intemperate in his attacks on India." Nixon, seeing how Kissinger "ranted and raved," briefly considered firing him. "He's personalizing this India thing," the president told Alexander Haig. "[H]e just starts to wear himself out and crack up." Still, Nixon shared Kissinger's desire for revenge against Anderson. A year after Yahya started his slaughter, E. Howard Hunt and G. Gordon Liddy were drawing up far-fetched possible plans to kill Anderson—by poisoning his drink, or putting LSD on his car's steering wheel so he would hallucinate and crash.[52]

Today, Nixon's and Kissinger's fog of self-justification, pumped out by the White House's publicity machine, has thickened into fact. In the weeks after the Bangladesh war ended, Nixon and Kissinger became fortified in their wartime conviction that they had done it all right. "God almighty!" Nixon said. "We did everything that we could possibly do." They had, he said, "a hell of a record." Kissinger con-

342 ~ The Blood Telegram

curred: "We are infinitely better off in China, and we're somewhat better off in Pakistan. So on balance, it was a cold-blooded calculation." He assured Nixon, "By next July, Mr. President, we'll look damn good on it." Kissinger—in a tirade against liberals, intellectuals, and Democrats—angrily told Nixon, "Not one has yet understood what we did in India-Pakistan and how it saved the China option which we need for the bloody Russians. Why would we give a damn about Bangladesh?" "We don't," agreed Nixon.[53]

Later, when Kissinger wrote a gargantuan eight-hundred-page history of diplomacy, Pakistan pops up only as a plucky Cold War ally, with no mention of the atrocities. In his memoirs, Nixon cannot even bring himself to mention the slaughter in East Pakistan or the stolen election, instead blaming the trouble on a Bengali rebellion and Indian aggression. Blurring events into haze, he writes in passing of the "almost unbelievable cruelty of the fighting on both sides" in East Pakistan. His other books brush past Yahya's massacres, while denouncing Indira Gandhi for seeking to wipe out Pakistan. While both Nixon and Kissinger understandably gloried in the opening to China, they worked hard to forget how horribly Bengalis suffered in order to secure the Pakistani junta's goodwill.[54]

Kissinger's memoirs are a lengthy masterpiece of omission. Although he devotes a long chapter to glossing up his record in South Asia, he says almost nothing about the slaughter of Bengalis, while still insisting that Pakistan's atrocities were "clearly under its domestic jurisdiction." (The suffering of the Bengalis does show up when he stands on the principle of nonintervention, fearing the loss of "all restraints" in the world if "shortsighted and repressive domestic policies are used to justify foreign military intervention"—a solicitude for sovereignty that did not quite apply to, say, Chile or Cambodia.) He lays blame for some of the most controversial decisions on Nixon and even the steamrollered William Rogers, who on most days in this crisis might as well have stayed in bed. He leaves out his encouraging China to move troops against India and the illegal Iranian and Jordanian arms transfers, while praising the bravery of Nixon's reckless decision to back China against India. He dismisses the administration's critics as driven by "fluctuating emotions" and an ignorance of the White House's own "essentially geopolitical point of view." He sanitizes out Nixon's racial animus toward Indians. No book has done more to bury the memory of the Bengalis.[55]

THE DISSENTERS

On April 4, 1972, the United States recognized Bangladesh as a sovereign state, formalizing the reality that Archer Blood and his staff had seen coming long before. The recognition came almost exactly a year after Blood's dissent cable, and one of Blood's own staffers managed to get in the last word.[56]

Scott Butcher—who had drafted the Blood telegram as a junior political officer in the Dacca consulate—rode out Nixon's and Kissinger's wave of reprisal firings, although not without some jitters. When he returned to Washington on home leave a few months after the dissent telegram was sent, he got a call from an official at the State Department's personnel office. "I thought, 'Oh man, I'm being assigned to Timbuktu.' He said, 'A number of us are very supportive.'" To his relief, Butcher wound up as a desk officer for Pakistan at the State Department.

As such, he was responsible for all things Bangladeshi. That included drafting the words with which Richard Nixon would grudgingly accept the reality of the new country. Nixon's genuine sentiments would have been unprintable; the president who normalized relations with Mao's China had repeatedly vowed to never, ever recognize Bangladesh, pounding his desk for emphasis. But writing up Nixon's letter of recognition for Bangladesh, Butcher worked in some genuinely heartfelt words of his own: "The United States has maintained an official mission in Dacca since 1949 and over the years many Americans, both in private and official capacities, have derived great satisfaction from the opportunity to work side by side with the Bengalee people in a variety of enterprises aimed at combatting disease, illiteracy, poverty, hunger and the impact of natural disaster."[57]

Coming from Nixon, this would pass as so much presidential pabulum. Not so from Butcher, who always fondly remembered his time in Dacca: "Here we are in this little godforsaken part of the world, with this really appealing, dynamic people, having a certain amount of progress." From him, it reads as a final, wistful commemoration of the kind of work that Blood's consulate was happily doing before the shooting started. "It was very satisfying for me," Butcher says quietly.

ARCHER BLOOD LATER BITTERLY RECALLED THE "PAINFUL REPERCUSsions" of his dissent. "Nixon ordered my transfer from Dacca and for

344 The Blood Telegram

the next six years, while Kissinger was still in power, I was in professional exile, excluded from any work having to do with foreign policy."[58]

Blood morosely departed Dacca on June 5, 1971. "He left quite suddenly," says Eric Griffel, the chief U.S. development officer working there. "I knew he was disturbed. We all knew why he was leaving." In Washington, Blood wound up in the State Department's personnel office—a hard fall for someone who had been in the thick of the action overseas. He was given a State Department award for courage, but the Islamabad embassy hamstrung his future career prospects with a performance evaluation that claimed he had whipped up the Americans in Dacca against Pakistan. He whiled away his time in this internal exile. Although he tried to make the best of it, and was not the type to complain, he lost about two and a half stagnant years there. By then, Kissinger was secretary of state. Blood met him once, and told him his name, but Kissinger did not react.[59]

There was worse to come. Nixon's rage over disloyalty in the ranks had ratcheted up after the publication of the Pentagon Papers in the *New York Times* and other newspapers, and Kissinger evidently nursed his old grudge. When Blood's immediate superior at the State Department asked the ousted former consul what he wanted to do, Blood replied crisply that, of course, he wanted to run an embassy somewhere. But, he added, "I've always felt that since, you know, Dacca and particularly Mr. Kissinger as Secretary, my chances were nil." To check if he was still on Kissinger's bad side, he said, he floated his name for the embassy in Upper Volta (now Burkina Faso). That was swiftly shot down.[60]

Then Kissinger somehow got word that Blood had dared to show his face at a conference in India. When he returned from the trip, Blood got a telephone call at home from his direct boss. As Blood later recalled, this diplomat told him, "When the Secretary recognized who that was, he hit the roof, and he said, 'Get that guy out of Washington.' So you have got to get out of Washington. Where do you want to go? I mean, fast." Blood fled the State Department to a post at the Army War College. He had been shoved out of Dacca and now out of Washington. He recalled, "I spent three and a half years there waiting out Dr. Kissinger's departure from the State Department."[61]

With his upward path blocked, he watched as his prime years passed him by. His colleagues became ambassadors. Those who sailed through

1971 with more biddable consciences moved up in the world—George H. W. Bush and Gerald Ford most spectacularly. When Blood could have been an ambassador or in a senior policy job in Washington, he was stuck. "There was no chance that he would ever represent the feelings of the people in Washington," says Meg Blood. "It was a change in his life's goals." After Nixon resigned, Kissinger remained ensconced as Ford's secretary of state. It was only in the Carter administration that Archer Blood could try to launch a late restart of his career. In 1979, at last, he went back to Delhi as deputy chief of mission. "It was serious," says Scott Butcher, "but far beneath what he would have otherwise aspired to. He had the adulation of his peers but not the success he would have had had he not stuck his neck out." Blood returned to Washington in 1981. He was discouraged by his job options. The only assignment he was offered was a hardship post as chargé d'affaires in Kabul. He started learning Dari, but the communist government refused to give him a visa. They would, he was sure, take anyone except him.[62]

Despondent, Blood decided to retire from the Foreign Service in May 1982. He became a diplomat-in-residence at Allegheny College, which was certainly a pleasant life. After his death in 2004 at the age of eighty-one, the U.S. embassy in Dacca named its library for him. Meg Blood says, "He wasn't robbed of everything, as they would have liked." But her sense of grievance is undimmed after all these years. "My Arch," she says sadly. "He was giving up the career he had wanted. It had been so definite." She thought he was worthy to be an ambassador or an assistant secretary of state, or more, despite Nixon and Kissinger. "For some reason they thought it could be kept quiet! All of those killings!"[63]

Notes

NOTE ON SOURCES

This book is based on three different kinds of primary sources: White House tapes of the conversations of Richard Nixon and Henry Kissinger, interviews with Americans and Indians who witnessed or participated in these events, and recently declassified documents from archives in the United States and India.

Starting in February 1971, and continuing throughout the Bangladesh crisis, Nixon secretly taped his talks in the Oval Office and elsewhere in the West Wing and the Executive Office Building. These audiotapes, thousands of hours of them, are an invaluable trove of evidence about the unfeigned thinking of Nixon and Kissinger, often far more revealing than the paper trail. But the tapes remain a surprisingly untapped resource, in part because they are so difficult to use: enormous, frustratingly organized, often bleeped, laborious to transcribe, and hard to understand. Working with a team of researchers, we made about a hundred new transcriptions, bringing unheard discussions to light.

In the United States, India, and Bangladesh, I did long interviews with Margaret Millward Blood, Scott Butcher, Arundhati Ghose, Eric Griffel, Shahudul Haque, Samuel Hoskinson, Jacob-Farj-Rafael Jacob, Winston Lord, Jagat Mehta, Desaix Myers, K. C. Pant, Mihir Roy, Harold Saunders, Sydney Schanberg, Nevin Scrimshaw, and Jaswant Singh. Some of them were interviewed several times. Myers also gave me his letters and draft cables, and Scrimshaw provided a chapter from his forthcoming memoirs. For subjects who have died, I have had to rely on memoirs and interviews conducted by others, although using them as sparingly as possible, since it was impossible to do follow-ups or to press these people on the particular topics of this book. To screen out self-serving hindsight, the interviews were based on the documents, and wherever possible, I have checked the recollections of interviewees against the archival record and other accounts.

The documentary record, while voluminous beyond belief, is nevertheless incomplete. Over four decades later, the U.S. government still has not declassified many of the relevant papers. There are still documents withheld from public view at the Nixon Presidential Library and the National Archives, on grounds of national security. Kissinger's papers at the Library of Congress are not available to researchers, at his own request. But the State Department's historians have done an exceptional job of declassifying sensitive papers and White House tapes for their *Foreign Relations of the United States* series, which is a peerless resource. The National Security Archive at George Washington University, which skillfully and tenaciously uses the Freedom of Information Act and other legal tools to shine light on the workings of the U.S. government, has gotten a great amount of valuable material declassified, including some of Kissinger's records—most notably the transcripts of many of his own secretly taped telephone conversations. Other researchers have made excellent use of the Freedom of Information Act. With the help of the National Security Archive, I have made my own requests for a mandatory declassification review under the terms of an executive order, but I am still waiting for the results.

Official opacity is far worse in India, despite the passage in 2005 of the landmark Right to Information Act. Indira Gandhi's own papers as prime minister are still guarded jealously by the Gandhi dynasty. The best source on her foreign policy is P. N. Haksar's papers, at the Nehru Memorial Museum and Library in Delhi, as well as those of T. N. Kaul, also there. The Nehru Memorial Museum and Library has been extraordinarily successful in building up its archival collections, and— despite some spectacular fights over access in recent years—generously makes them available to Indian and foreign scholars. The National Archives of India, too, provides access to an important collection of documents from the foreign ministry and the prime minister's secretariat. But at all these Indian archives, the material is nowhere near as comprehensive as what has been released by the U.S. government, and often leaves out the most significant and controversial papers.

I have spelled out the dizzying plethora of abbreviations and acronyms used in U.S. and Indian cables. It is a diplomatic convention that cables to Washington are usually addressed to the secretary of state (SECSTATE WASHDC), and they are cited as such (e.g., Keating to Rogers). Where possible, I have identified the primary drafter or approver of a cable from Washington. Outgoing cables are routinely "signed" by the secretary of state, even when written by someone else; but unless I specifically cite William Rogers in the main text as the author of a cable, those are not his own words.

For the sake of simplicity, I have spelled the names of cities the same way that they were spelled in 1971, not the way they are spelled today: Dacca instead of Dhaka, and Calcutta instead of Kolkata.

Key to Citations

Richard Nixon Presidential Library and Museum, Yorba Linda, California
   NSC Files: National Security Council Files
   White House tapes
      Oval Office
      White House telephone
      Executive Office Building (EOB)
United States National Archives II, College Park, Maryland
   R.G. (Record Group) 59: State Department papers
      POL: Political affairs
      REF: Refugee affairs
   FRUS: the State Department's official *Foreign Relations of the United States* series
United States Library of Congress, Washington, D.C.
   Foreign Affairs Oral History Collection
National Security Archive, George Washington University, Washington, D.C.
   NSA: online at www.gwu.edu/~nsarchiv/, and nsarchive.chadwyck.com/home.do
Nehru Memorial Museum and Library, Teen Murti Bhavan, New Delhi
   NMML, P. N. Haksar Papers, III Installment
      Indo-Pakistan and Indo-Bangladesh Relations
      Prime Minister's Secretariat Files
      India's Relations with USSR, other countries, and United Nations
   NMML, T. N. Kaul Papers, I–III Installment
      Ministry of External Affairs papers
National Archives of India, Janpath, New Delhi

PMS: Prime Minister's Secretariat papers
MEA: Ministry of External Affairs papers

Other Abbreviations in Notes

memcon: memorandum of conversation
telcon: telephone conversation
WSAG: Washington Special Actions Group
SRG: Senior Review Group

PREFACE

1. POL 23-9 PAK, Box 2530, Blood to Rogers, 7 April 1971, Dacca 1168. POL 23-9 PAK, Box 2530, Blood to Rogers, 30 March 1971, Dacca 986.
2. POL 23-9 PAK, Box 2530, Blood to Rogers, 30 March 1971, Dacca 986. POL 23-9 PAK, Box 2530, Blood to Rogers, 31 March 1971, Dacca 1010. POL 23-9 PAK, Box 2530, Bell to Shakespeare, 9 April 1971, Dacca 1211. POL 23-9 PAK, Box 2530, Blood to Rogers, 30 March 1971, Dacca 986.
3. Archer K. Blood, *The Cruel Birth of Bangladesh: Memoirs of an American Diplomat* (Dacca: University Press of Bangladesh, 2002), p. 213. POL 23-9 PAK, Box 2530, Blood to Rogers, 28 March 1971, Dacca 959. POL 1 PAK-US, Box 2535, Blood to Rogers, 6 April 1971, Dacca 1138; NSC Files, Box 138, Kissinger Office Files, Country Files—Middle East, Blood to Rogers, 6 April 1971, Dacca 1138.
4. MEA, WII/109/31/71, vol. I, Singh statement to UN Security Council, 12 December 1971.
5. David S. Wyman, *The Abandonment of the Jews: America and the Holocaust, 1941–1945* (New York: Pantheon, 1984). Samantha Power, *"A Problem from Hell": America and the Age of Genocide* (New York: Basic Books, 2002). The United States was aligned with Iraq during the 1987–88 genocidal campaign against the Iraqi Kurds (Power, *"A Problem from Hell,"* p. 174), and turned a blind eye to Saddam Hussein's atrocities. While this is probably the example that comes closest to the Pakistani case, the United States and Pakistan were treaty allies with an enduring relationship—closer ties than those between the United States and Iraq (Power, *"A Problem from Hell,"* pp. 172–245).
6. NSC Files, Box 574, Indo-Pak War, South Asian Congressional, Kennedy speech, 23 September 1971. NSC Files, Box 570, Indo-Pak Crisis, South Asia, CIA Office of National Estimates, "The Indo-Pakistani Crisis," 22 September 1971. Tad Szulc, "U.S. Military Goods Sent to Pakistan Despite Ban," *New York Times,* 22 June 1971, pp. A1, A11. Indian officials spoke of a million dead, and Bangladeshis of three million, which are inflated numbers. Richard Sisson and Leo Rose interviewed a senior Indian official who stated the death toll at three hundred thousand (*War and Secession: Pakistan, India, and the Creation of Bangladesh* [Berkeley: University of California Press, 1990], p. 306n24). The *New York Times* reporter Sydney Schanberg wrote that diplomats in Dacca believed that hundreds of thousands of Bengalis, perhaps as many as a million or more, had been killed (Sydney H. Schanberg, "Long Occupation of East Pakistan Foreseen in India," *New*

York Times, 26 December 1971, pp. A1, A13). A more recent study based on world health surveys came up with roughly 269,000 deaths (Ziad Obermeyer, Christopher J. L. Murray, and Emmanuela Gakidou, "Fifty Years of Violent War Deaths from Vietnam to Bosnia," *British Medical Journal*, vol. 336 [28 June 2008], pp. 1482–86). Robert Dallek estimates that as many as five hundred thousand people were killed by Yahya's troops (*Nixon and Kissinger: Partners in Power* [New York: HarperCollins, 2007], p. 335); so does Walter Isaacson (*Kissinger: A Biography* [New York: Simon & Schuster, 1992], p. 372). On the low side, Pakistan's postwar judicial inquiry—working from the army's Eastern Command situation reports—estimated that the military had killed in action roughly twenty-six thousand people, while admitting that local commanders "tried to minimise the result of their own actions" (Government of Pakistan, *The Report of the Hamoodur Rehman Commission of Inquiry into the 1971 War* [Lahore: Vanguard, 2001], pp. 317, 340, 513; for a somewhat higher estimate in a book that is critical of Bangladeshi nationalism, see Sarmila Bose, *Dead Reckoning: Memories of the 1971 Bangladesh War* [New York: Columbia University Press, 2011], p. 181). In South Asia, the tolls of death and dispossession are only rivaled by Partition, in which half a million or a million people died, and twelve million people were displaced (Yasmin Khan, *The Great Partition: The Making of India and Pakistan* [New Haven, Conn.: Yale University Press, 2007], p. 6).

7. U.S. Department of State, *Foreign Relations of the United States: South Asia Crisis, 1971* (Washington, D.C.: U.S. Government Printing Office, 2005), vol. 11, Louis J. Smith, ed., 40 Committee meeting, 9 April 1971, pp. 63–65. Hereafter cited as *FRUS*.

8. See, for instance, NSA, SRG meeting, 17 January 1972, 3:09–4:05 p.m., and NSC Files, Box 626, Country Files—Middle East, Pakistan, vol. VII, Hoskinson to Kissinger, 13 August 1971. Samuel Hoskinson wrote that an account of a talk with a senior Pakistani general was "phrased and sanitized so that it could be released to State and Defense without causing any problems." Daun van Ee letter to author, Manuscript Division, Library of Congress, 30 September 2010, on file with author.

9. Dom Moraes, *Mrs Gandhi* (London: Jonathan Cape, 1980), p. 188. For a mixed verdict, see Inder Malhotra, *Indira Gandhi: A Personal and Political Biography* (London: Hodder & Stoughton 1989), pp. 133, 188. MEA, HI/121/13/71, vol. II, Sen statement to UN Security Council, 4 December 1971. Michael Walzer, *Just and Unjust Wars: A Moral Argument with Historical Illustrations* (New York: Basic Books, 1977), pp. 90, 101–8; Michael Walzer, "On Humanitarianism," *Foreign Affairs*, vol. 90, no. 4 (July–August 2011), pp. 77–79; Pratap Bhanu Mehta, "Reluctant India," *Journal of Democracy*, vol. 22, no. 4 (October 2001), p. 100; Nicholas J. Wheeler, *Saving Strangers: Humanitarian Intervention in International Society* (Oxford: Oxford University Press, 2000); Michael W. Doyle, "A Few Words on Mill, Walzer, and Nonintervention," *Ethics and International Affairs*, vol. 23, no. 4 (2010), p. 363; Thomas M. Franck, *Recourse to Force: State Action Against Threats and Armed Attacks* (Cambridge: Cambridge University Press, 2002), pp. 139–43; Subrata Roy Chowdhury, *The Genesis of Bangladesh: A Study in International Legal Norms and Permissive Conscience* (New York: Asia Publishing House, 1972); John Salzberg, "UN Prevention of Human Rights Violations," *International Organization*, vol. 27, no. 1 (winter 1973),

pp. 115–27; Richard Lillich, "The International Protection of Human Rights by General International Law," in *Report of the International Committee on Human Rights of the International Law Association,* vol. 38 (1972), p. 54. For a cogent critique, see Thomas M. Franck and Nigel S. Rodley, "After Bangladesh," *American Journal of International Law,* vol. 67 (1973), pp. 275–305. See Ramachandra Guha, "The Challenge of Contemporary History," *Economic and Political Weekly,* vol. 43, no. 26–27 (28 June 2008), pp. 192–200.

10. This book extends my argument that liberal states can be driven toward humanitarian intervention (*Freedom's Battle: The Origins of Humanitarian Intervention* [New York: Alfred A. Knopf, 2008], pp. 11–38), expanding its scope from Europe to Asia, adding India as a least likely case: a liberal state, but one with a potent postcolonial doctrine against violating national sovereignty, unusually divided domestic politics, and a prime minister without a deep commitment to human rights. India was driven by an impure mix of humanitarian and strategic motives, but the presence of such humanitarian impulses in Indian domestic debates lends support to my argument about the impact of liberal norms and institutions. (Gary King, Robert O. Keohane, and Sidney Verba, *Designing Social Inquiry: Scientific Inference in Qualitative Research* [Princeton: Princeton University Press, 1994], pp. 44–46, 209–12; see also Harry Eckstein, "Case Study and Theory in Political Science," in Fred I. Greenstein and Nelson W. Polsby, eds., *Handbook of Political Science* [Reading, Mass.: Addison-Wesley, 1975], vol. 7, pp. 79–137; Stephen Van Evera, *Guide to Methods for Students of Political Science* [Ithaca, N.Y.: Cornell University Press, 1997], pp. 49–88; and Robert H. Bates et al., *Analytic Narratives* [Princeton: Princeton University Press, 1998], pp. 3–18.) While India certainly wanted to harm Pakistan, that was always true, and does not explain why war came in 1971 rather than in previous years. Although India had particular solidarities with Bengalis and Hindus, that had less impact than might be expected, as will be discussed. The case studies in this book, of the United States and India, are also meant to fill out a wider collective empirical project of process-tracing about the decision making in massive human rights crises, including Martha Finnemore, *The Purpose of Intervention: Changing Beliefs About the Use of Force* (Ithaca, N.Y.: Cornell University Press, 2003); J. L. Holzgrefe and Robert O. Keohane, eds., *Humanitarian Intervention: Ethical, Legal, and Political Dilemmas* (Cambridge: Cambridge University Press, 2003); Brendan Simms and D. J. B. Trim, *Humanitarian Intervention: A History* (Cambridge: Cambridge University Press, 2011); Jennifer Welsh, ed., *Humanitarian Intervention and International Relations* (Oxford: Oxford University Press, 2004); Adam Hochschild, *Bury the Chains: Prophets and Rebels in the Fight to Free an Empire's Slaves* (Boston: Houghton Mifflin, 2005); Adam Hochschild, *King Leopold's Ghost: A Story of Greed, Terror, and Heroism in Colonial Africa* (Boston: Houghton Mifflin, 1998); Martin Gilbert, *Auschwitz and the Allies* (New York: Holt, 1981); David S. Wyman, ed., *The World Reacts to the Holocaust* (Baltimore: Johns Hopkins University Press, 1996); Richard Breitman, *Official Secrets: What the Nazis Planned, What the British and Americans Knew* (New York: Hill & Wang, 1998); Power, *"A Problem from Hell"*; Bernard Kouchner, *Le malheur des autres* (Paris: Éditions Odile Jacob, 1991); Norman Naimark, *Fires of Hatred: Ethnic Cleansing in Twentieth-Century*

Europe (Cambridge, Mass.: Harvard University Press, 2001); Wheeler, *Saving Strangers*; Philip Gourevitch, *We Wish to Inform You That Tomorrow We Will Be Killed with Our Families: Stories from Rwanda* (New York: Farrar, Straus & Giroux, 1999); and Geoffrey Robinson, *"If You Leave Us Here, We Will Die": How Genocide Was Stopped in East Timor* (Princeton: Princeton University Press, 2010). Archer Blood could be remembered in the company of other Americans who tried to stop genocide, whose stories are recounted magnificently in Power, *"A Problem from Hell"* (see pp. 514–16).

11. *FRUS: Documents on South Asia, 1969–1972*, vol. E-7 (online at http://history.state.gov/historicaldocuments/frus1969-76ve07), White House tapes, Oval Office 637-3, 12 December 1971, 8:45–9:42 a.m. Hereafter cited as *FRUS*, vol. E-7.

12. For a range of intelligent skepticism, left and right, see Alan Wolfe, *Political Evil: What It Is and How to Combat It* (New York: Alfred A. Knopf, 2011); Mahmood Mamdani, *Saviors and Survivors: Darfur, Politics, and the War on Terror* (New York: Pantheon, 2009); Jonathan Rauch, "When Moralism Isn't Moral," *New York Times Book Review*, 7 October 2011; "A Solution from Hell," *n+1*, no. 12, August 2011.

13. Sunil Khilnani, *The Idea of India* (New York: Farrar, Straus & Giroux, 1999), p. 4. See Amartya Sen, *The Argumentative Indian: Writings on Indian History, Culture and Identity* (New York: Farrar, Straus & Giroux, 2005); Pratap Bhanu Mehta, *The Burden of Democracy* (New York: Penguin, 2003); and Perry Anderson, "Gandhi Centre Stage," *London Review of Books*, 5 July 2012, pp. 3–11. See Steve Coll, *On the Grand Trunk Road: A Journey into South Asia* (New York: Times Books, 1994), pp. 33–52, 118–23, 262–63; Atul Kohli, ed., *The Success of India's Democracy* (Cambridge: Cambridge University Press, 2001); Jean Drèze and Amartya Sen, "Putting Growth in Its Place," *Outlook India*, 14 November 2011; Ashutosh Varshney, "Is India Becoming More Democratic?" *Journal of Asian Studies*, vol. 59, no. 1 (February 2000), pp. 3–25; Pradeep Chhibber and Ken Kollman, "Party Aggregation and the Number of Parties in India and the United States," *American Political Science Review*, vol. 92, no. 2 (June 1998), pp. 329–42; Granville Austin, *Working a Democratic Constitution: The Indian Experience* (New Delhi: Oxford University Press, 1999); Judith M. Brown, *Modern India: The Origins of an Asian Democracy* (New Delhi: Oxford University Press, 1985). For poverty numbers, see Nikhila Gill and Vivek Dehejia, "What Does India's Poverty Line Actually Measure?" *India Ink* blog, *New York Times*, 4 April 2012. On inequality, see Pratap Bhanu Mehta, "Breaking the Silence," *The Caravan*, 1 October 2012, and Atul Kohli, *Poverty amid Plenty in the New India* (Cambridge: Cambridge University Press, 2012). For a brilliant portrait of the real lives of poor Indians, see Katherine Boo, *Behind the Beautiful Forevers: Life, Death, and Hope in a Mumbai Undercity* (New York: Random House, 2012).

14. For thoughtful skepticism, see Ramachandra Guha, "Will India Become a Superpower?" *Outlook*, 30 June 2008, and Coll, *Grand Trunk Road*, pp. 274–82, 88–91. For outstanding literary reflections of these events, see Salman Rushdie, *Midnight's Children* (New York: Alfred A. Knopf, 1981), pp. 419–55, and Tahmima Anam, *A Golden Age* (New York: Harper, 2008).

15. Tad Szulc, *The Illusion of Peace: Foreign Policy in the Nixon Years* (New York: Viking, 1977), p. v. The entire India-Pakistan crisis warrants just five

cursory pages in Stephen Ambrose's monumental three-volume biography
of Nixon, which totals 1,933 pages of writing (not counting notes and bib-
liography). See Stephen E. Ambrose, *Nixon,* 3 vols. (New York: Simon &
Schuster, 1988–91). There are good sections about Bangladesh in three excellent works—Isaacson's *Kissinger,* Dallek's *Nixon and Kissinger,* and Seymour M. Hersh's *The Price of Power: Kissinger in the Nixon White House*
(New York: Summit, 1983)—although my project gives the crisis a more central place and tries to offer a more comprehensively detailed account of it
than would be practical for those already-long books. For a first-rate short
account of U.S. policy, see Robert J. McMahon, "The Danger of Geopolitical Fantasies," in Fredrik Logevall and Andrew Preston, eds., *Nixon in the
World: American Foreign Relations, 1969–1977* (New York: Oxford University Press, 2008). For an outstanding book on Indian and Pakistani decision
making, based on interviews with almost all the senior participants, see Sisson and Rose, *War and Secession.* See A. M. A. Muhith, *American Response
to Bangladesh Liberation War* (Dacca: University Press, 1996). For a bracing and sophisticated castigation, which does not condemn Bangladesh to
the usual amnesia, see Christopher Hitchens, *The Trial of Henry Kissinger*
(London: Verso, 2001).

CHAPTER 1: THE TILT

1. Richard Reeves, *President Nixon: Alone in the White House* (New York:
   Simon & Schuster, 2007), p. 278. On Nixon's moralism, see Garry Wills,
   Nixon Agonistes: The Crisis of the Self-Made Man (Boston: Houghton
   Mifflin, 1970), pp. 427–33.
2. White House tapes, Oval Office 520-6, 15 June 1971, 11:02 a.m.–12:34 p.m.
   Richard M. Nixon, *RN: The Memoirs of Richard Nixon* (New York: Simon
   & Schuster, 1990), pp. 134, 137.
3. Robert J. McMahon, *The Cold War on the Periphery: The United States,
   India, and Pakistan* (New York: Columbia University Press, 1994), p. 2.
   Nixon, *RN,* pp. 131–32. See Robert J. McMahon, "The Danger of Geopolitical Fantasies," in Fredrik Logevall and Andrew Preston, eds., *Nixon in
   the World: American Foreign Relations, 1969–1977* (New York: Oxford University Press, 2008), pp. 250–51; and White House tapes, Oval Office 505-4,
   26 May 1971, 10:03–11:35 a.m. On Nehru and nonalignment, see Srinath
   Raghavan, *War and Peace in Modern India* (New York: Palgrave Macmillan,
   2010); Sunil Khilnani, "Nehru's Judgement," in Richard Bourke and Raymond Geuss, eds., *Political Judgement: Essays for John Dunn* (Cambridge:
   Cambridge University Press, 2009); Sarvepalli Gopal, *Jawaharlal Nehru:
   A Biography,* 3 vols. (London: Jonathan Cape, 1975–84); Shashi Tharoor,
   Nehru: The Invention of India (New York: Arcade, 2003). For lucid analy-
   ses of U.S.-Indian relations, see W. Norman Brown, *The United States and
   India, Pakistan, Bangladesh,* 3rd ed. (Cambridge, Mass.: Harvard University
   Press, 1972); Selig S. Harrison, *India: The Most Dangerous Decades* (Princ-
   eton: Princeton University Press, 1960); G. W. Choudhury, *India, Pakistan,
   Bangladesh, and the Major Powers: Politics of a Divided Subcontinent* (New
   York: Free Press, 1975); Norman D. Palmer, *The United States and India:
   The Dimensions of Influence* (New York: Praeger, 1984); Dennis Merrill,
   Bread and the Ballot: The United States and India's Economic Development
   (Chapel Hill: University of North Carolina Press, 1990); and Andrew J. Rot-

ter, *Comrades at Odds: The United States and India, 1947–1964* (Ithaca, N.Y.: Cornell University Press, 2000). Richard Nixon, *Leaders* (New York: Warner Books, 1982), p. 271.

4. McMahon, "Geopolitical Fantasies," p. 251. Nixon, *RN*, p. 133. Richard Nixon, *In the Arena: A Memoir of Victory, Defeat, and Renewal* (New York: Simon & Schuster, 1990), p. 71.

5. Stephen P. Cohen, *The Pakistan Army* (Karachi: Oxford University Press, 1998), pp. 137–39. Henry Kissinger, *Diplomacy* (New York: Simon & Schuster, 1994), pp. 527, 548–49, 636–37. Dennis Kux, *Estranged Democracies: India and the United States, 1941–1991* (New Delhi: Sage, 1993), pp. 105–15. H. W. Brands, *India and the United States: The Cold Peace* (Boston: Twayne, 1990), pp. 73–77. M. Srinivas Chary, *The Eagle and the Peacock: U.S. Foreign Policy Toward India Since Independence* (Westport, Conn.: Greenwood Press, 1995), pp. 93–104. Michael R. Beschloss, *Mayday: Eisenhower, Khrushchev and the U-2 Affair* (New York: Harper & Row, 1988). Mussarat Jabeen and Muhammad Saleem Mazhar, "Security Game," *Pakistan Economic and Social Review*, vol. 49, no. 1 (summer 2011), pp. 115–22.

6. NMML, Haksar Papers, Subject File 170, Gandhi to Nixon, 7 August 1971. NMML, Haksar Papers, Subject File 170, Haksar to Jha, 7 August 1971.

7. The State Department had a lower official reckoning of U.S. support for Pakistan: since 1950, Pakistan had received a total of $779.9 million in foreign military sales and military assistance (NSC Files, Box 574, Indo-Pak War, South Asian Congressional, Van Hollen to Keating, 28 July 1971, State 137256). MEA, WII/125/112/71, "Supply of Arms by USA to Pakistan," Kaul to Singh, 2 December 1971. For the lower sum of $1.5 billion, see MEA, WII/121/54/71, vol. II, "Supply of Arms by USA to Pakistan," 3 July 1971.

8. Brands, *India and the United States*, pp. 76, 90–96. See K. Subrahmanyam, "Military Aid to Pakistan and Its Repercussions on Bangla Desh," in Ranjit Gupta and Radhakrishna, eds., *World Meet on Bangla Desh* (New Delhi: Impex, 1971), pp. 110–13. Vojtech Mastny, "The Soviet Union's Partnership with India," *Journal of Cold War Studies*, vol. 12, no. 3 (summer 2010), pp. 55–59, 62–63. Kux, *Estranged Democracies*, pp. 118–20, 140–60. T. N. Kaul, *The Kissinger Years: Indo-American Relations* (New Delhi: Arnold-Heinemann, 1980), pp. 30–36. Chary, *Eagle and the Peacock*, pp. 105–7.

9. John Kenneth Galbraith, *Ambassador's Journal* (Boston: Houghton Mifflin, 1969), pp. 487–93. Raghavan, *War and Peace in Modern India*, pp. 307–10. Brands, *India and the United States*, pp. 99–101. For a splendid short account of the war, see Srinath Raghavan, "A Bad Knock," in Daniel Marston and Chandar Sundaram, eds., *A Military History of India and South Asia* (Westport, Conn.: Praeger, 2006). MEA, WII/125/112/71, Kholsa to Menon, 2 December 1971. By 1965, this totaled some $77.6 million (MEA, WII/125/112/71, Subramanian memorandum, 3 July 1971). Another account puts it at $76 million (MEA, WII/125/112/71, Kholsa to Menon, 2 December 1971). Kux, *Estranged Democracies*, pp. 181–83, 186–218. Chary, *Eagle and the Peacock*, pp. 113–24.

10. NMML, Haksar Papers, Subject File 170, Gandhi to Nixon, 7 August 1971. NMML, Haksar Papers, Subject File 170, Haksar to Jha, 7 August 1971. Henry Kissinger, *White House Years* (Boston: Little, Brown, 1979), p. 846. Sumit Ganguly, "Of Great Expectations and Bitter Disappointments," *Asian Affairs*, vol. 15, no. 4 (winter 1988–89), pp. 212–19. Subrahmanyam, "Mili-

tary Aid to Pakistan and Its Repercussions on Bangla Desh," p. 114. Kux, *Estranged Democracies,* pp. 235–40. Brands, *India and the United States,* pp. 110–11.

11. MEA, WII/125/112/71, Subramanian memorandum, 3 July 1971. See MEA, WII/125/112/71, Kholsa to Menon, 2 December 1971. For the whole period, India reckoned it got $85.4 million in grants and arms sales (MEA, WII/125/112/71, Subramanian memorandum, 3 July 1971; see MEA, WII/125/112/71, Kholsa to Menon, 2 December 1971). According to the U.S. government, since 1950, India had received $173.3 million in foreign military sales and military assistance from the United States (NSC Files, Box 574, Indo-Pak War, South Asian Congressional, Van Hollen to Keating, 28 July 1971, State 137256). Ganguly, "Great Expectations," pp. 212–19. T. N. Kaul, *Reminiscences Discreet and Indiscreet* (New Delhi: Lancers Publishers, 1982), pp. 277–90. James W. Bjorkman, "Public Law 480 and the Policies of Self-Help and Short Tether," in Lloyd I. Rudolph and Susanne Hoeber Rudolph, eds., *The Regional Imperative* (New Delhi: Concept, 1980), pp. 201–62. Kux, *Estranged Democracies,* pp. 240–47, 264–68. Brands, *India and the United States,* pp. 116–18, 121–22. Chary, *Eagle and the Peacock,* pp. 124–27.

12. White House tapes, Oval Office 622-1, 22 November 1971, 3:51–3:58 p.m. For a sketch of his foreign policy orientation, see Richard M. Nixon, *Richard Nixon: Speeches, Writings, Documents,* ed. Rick Perlstein (Princeton: Princeton University Press, 2008), pp. 191–99. For classic overviews of the man and the era, see Wills, *Nixon Agonistes;* Tom Wicker, *One of Us: Richard Nixon and the American Dream* (New York: Random House, 1991); Walter Isaacson, *Kissinger: A Biography* (New York: Simon & Schuster, 1992); Robert Dallek, *Nixon and Kissinger: Partners in Power* (New York: HarperCollins, 2007); Rick Perlstein, *Nixonland: The Rise of a President and the Fracturing of America* (New York: Scribner, 2008); and David Greenberg, *Nixon's Shadow: The History of an Image* (New York: Norton, 2003). On the global context, see Odd Arne Westad, *The Global Cold War: Third World Interventions and the Making of Our Times* (Cambridge: Cambridge University Press, 2006), and Daniel Sargent, "From Internationalism to Globalism: The United States and the Transformation of International Politics in the 1970s," PhD diss., Harvard University, 2009. Brands, *India and the United States,* pp. 60–67. Chary, *Eagle and the Peacock,* pp. 57–69. POL 23-9 PAK, Box 2530, Keating to Rogers, 8 April 1971, New Delhi 5243; MEA, HI/1012/78/71, Jha to Kaul, 7 April 1971; MEA, WII/109/31/71, vol. I, Singh statement to UN Security Council, 13 December 1971.

13. Nixon, *In the Arena,* pp. 328–29.

14. White House tapes, Oval Office 461-10, 2 March 1971, 12:07–12:44 p.m. *FRUS,* vol. E-7, Nixon-Yahya memcon, 25 October 1970, 10:49–11:45 a.m. Kissinger, *White House Years,* p. 848.

15. White House tapes, Oval Office 617-17, 15 November 1971, 4:31–4:39 p.m. White House tapes, White House telephone 16-48, 8 December 1971, 11:06–11:14 a.m.

16. Kissinger, *White House Years,* p. 848. Shashi Tharoor, *Reasons of State: Political Development and India's Foreign Policy Under Indira Gandhi, 1966–1977* (New Delhi: Vikas, 1982), pp. 112–13. Nixon, *RN,* pp. 131–32. Krishan Bhatia, *Indira: A Biography of Prime Minister Gandhi* (New York:

Praeger, 1974), p. 250. Nixon, *In the Arena*, pp. 48–49. Tad Szulc, *The Illusion of Peace: Foreign Policy in the Nixon Years* (New York: Viking, 1977), pp. 4–5, 16. NSA, Nixon-Kissinger telcon, 26 November 1971, 10:42 a.m. See Nixon, *Leaders*, pp. 273–74. Kux, *Estranged Democracies*, p. 280.

17. White House tapes, Oval Office 462-5, 5 March 1971, 8:30–10:15 a.m.; White House tapes, Oval Office 505-4, 26 May 1971, 10:03–11:35 a.m.

18. Oriana Fallaci, *Interviews with History and Conversations with Power* (New York: Rizzoli, 2011), p. 43. Wicker, *One of Us*, pp. 651–53. See Kissinger, *White House Years*, p. 760; Wills, *Nixon Agonistes*, p. 409; Dallek, *Nixon and Kissinger*, p. 91. For Nixon's reflections on friendship, including the Chinese leadership, see his *In the Arena*, pp. 238–44.

19. MEA, WII/121/54/71, Kissinger-Singh meeting, 7 July 1971. Kissinger, *White House Years*, pp. 848–49. Government of Pakistan, *The Report of the Hamoodur Rehman Commission of Inquiry into the 1971 War* (Lahore: Vanguard, 2001), p. 67. *FRUS*, vol. E-7, Nixon-Yahya memcon, 25 October 1970, 10:49–11:45 a.m.

20. Owen Bennett Jones, *Pakistan: Eye of the Storm* (New Haven, Conn.: Yale University Press, 2009), insert after p. 160. *Hamoodur Rehman Commission Report*, pp. 122–23, 289. Archer K. Blood, *The Cruel Birth of Bangladesh: Memoirs of an American Diplomat* (Dacca: University Press of Bangladesh, 2002), p. 41.

21. White House tapes, Oval Office 610-1, 1 November 1971, 4:04–5:08 p.m. NSA, Nixon-Kissinger telcon, 5 December 1971. White House tapes, Oval Office 558-10, 9 August 1971, 5:44–6:18 p.m. See Bob Woodward and Carl Bernstein, *The Final Days* (New York: Simon & Schuster, 1976), pp. 185–96; Dallek, *Nixon and Kissinger*, p. 93; Isaacson, *Kissinger*, pp. 139–51.

22. Henry A. Kissinger, *A World Restored: Metternich, Castlereagh, and the Problems of Peace, 1812–22* (Boston: Houghton Mifflin, 1973), p. 328. For a provocative argument on how Kissinger's past and thought shaped his foreign policy in office, see Jeremi Suri, *Henry Kissinger and the American Century* (Cambridge, Mass.: Belknap Press of Harvard University Press, 2007); see also Isaacson, *Kissinger*, pp. 21–67. Wicker, *One of Us*, pp. 655–63. See Jeremi Suri, "Henry Kissinger and American Grand Strategy," and Fredrik Logevall and Andrew Preston, "The Adventurous Journey of Nixon in the World," both in Logevall and Preston, eds., *Nixon in the World*; and David Rothkopf, *Running the World: The Inside Story of the National Security Council and the Architects of American Foreign Policy* (New York: PublicAffairs, 2004), pp. 111–12.

23. White House tapes, Oval Office 561-4, 11 August 1971, 9:10–11:40 a.m. See Dallek, *Nixon and Kissinger*, pp. 78–103.

24. H. R. Haldeman, *The Haldeman Diaries: Inside the Nixon White House* (New York: G. P. Putnam's Sons, 1994), 3 March 1971, pp. 253–54; 22 February 1971, pp. 249–50; 2 March 1971, p. 253. See Isaacson, *Kissinger*, pp. 195–98. Haldeman, *Haldeman Diaries*, 9 March 1971, p. 255. White House tapes, Oval Office 519-1, 14 June 1971, 8:49 a.m. See John Ehrlichman, *Witness to Power: The Nixon Years* (New York: Simon & Schuster, 1982), pp. 296–300; H. R. Haldeman with Joseph DiMona, *The Ends of Power* (New York: Times Books, 1978), pp. 94–95; Isaacson, *Kissinger*, pp. 209–11.

25. Henry A. Kissinger, "Reflections on American Diplomacy," *Foreign Affairs*, October 1956. See Henry A. Kissinger, "Domestic Structure and Foreign

Policy" (1966), *American Foreign Policy: Three Essays* (New York: Norton, 1969), p. 19; Kissinger, *World Restored*, p. 326. NSA, Zhou-Kissinger memcon, 9 July 1971, 4:35 p.m.

26. Haldeman, *Haldeman Diaries,* 29 June 1971, p. 309, and 19 February 1971, p. 248. See Isaacson, *Kissinger,* p. 136. Kissinger would have the FBI wiretap many of his own staffers (Isaacson, *Kissinger,* pp. 212–27).

27. NMML, Haksar Papers, Subject File 171, Jha to Kaul, 9 August 1971. NMML, Haksar Papers, Subject File 277, Jha to Kaul, 18 April 1971.

28. Kissinger, *White House Years,* pp. 847, 842. Library of Congress, Association for Diplomatic Studies and Training, Foreign Affairs Oral History Project, Winston Lord interview, 28 April 1998.

29. Library of Congress, Association for Diplomatic Studies and Training, Foreign Affairs Oral History Project, Winston Lord interview, 28 April 1998 and subsequent. Szulc, *Illusion of Peace,* pp. 20–21. NSA, Kissinger talk to White House interns, 11 August 1971. See Isaacson, *Kissinger,* pp. 188–95.

30. Kissinger, *Diplomacy,* p. 564.

31. NSA, Kissinger-Sisco telcon, 27 July 1971, 10:13 a.m.

32. In 1967, under Lyndon Johnson, the United States began to supply spare parts and nonlethal equipment to both India and Pakistan. Because Pakistan already had such a large stock of U.S. weapons, this fresh provision of spare parts had been far more of a boon to Pakistan than to India (MEA, WII/125/112/71, Kholsa to Menon, 2 December 1971). U.S. arms sales to Pakistan crept back, with a total of almost $65 million by 1970 (NSC Files, Box 574, Indo-Pak War, South Asian Congressional, Van Hollen to Keating, 28 July 1971, State 137256). NSC Files, Box 624, Country Files—Middle East, Pakistan, vol. III, Nutter to Laird, 22 October 1970. POL 23-9 PAK, Box 2531, Keating to Rogers, 16 April 1971, New Delhi 5734. The State Department publicly admitted that U.S. support was running to about $10 million a year, but the *New York Times* reported that U.S. Air Force sales alone from 1967 to 1970 came to almost $48 million (Tad Szulc, "U.S. Military Goods Sent to Pakistan Despite Ban," *New York Times,* 22 June 1971, pp. A1, 11).

33. NMML, Haksar Papers, Subject File 220, Heath-Gandhi conversation, 24 October 1971. See Subrahmanyam, "Military Aid to Pakistan," p. 114. NMML, Haksar Papers, Subject File 235, Manekshaw-Kulikov talks, 24–25 February 1972.

34. NSC Files, Box 624, Country Files—Middle East, Pakistan, vol. III, Nixon-Yahya memcon, 25 October 1970, 10:45 a.m. *FRUS,* vol. E-7, Nixon-Yahya memcon, 25 October 1970.

CHAPTER 2: CYCLONE PAKISTAN

1. Archer K. Blood, *The Cruel Birth of Bangladesh: Memoirs of an American Diplomat* (Dacca: University Press of Bangladesh, 2002), p. xvii.

2. Ibid., p. 15.

3. Library of Congress, Association for Diplomatic Studies and Training, Foreign Affairs Oral History Project, Archer Blood interview, 27 June 1989.

4. Blood, *Cruel Birth,* pp. 1–2, 5.

5. They had two daughters, Shireen, eleven years old, and Barbara, ten, and a son, Peter, eight. They later had a second son, Archer Lloyd. (Ibid., pp. 22–23.)

6. Ibid., pp. 5, 12–13, 9, 16.
7. Library of Congress, Association for Diplomatic Studies and Training, Foreign Affairs Oral History Project, Archer Blood interview, 27 June 1989. Blood, *Cruel Birth,* p. 23.
8. Library of Congress, Association for Diplomatic Studies and Training, Foreign Affairs Oral History Project, Archer Blood interview, 27 June 1989. Blood, *Cruel Birth,* pp. 25–31.
9. Blood, *Cruel Birth,* p. 35.
10. The phrase "basket case" is usually attributed to Kissinger, who did use it, but it actually seems to have been first coined by U. Alexis Johnson. "They'll be an international basket case," he said. "But not necessarily our basket case," Kissinger replied. (*FRUS,* WSAG meeting, 6 December 1971, 11:07–11:56 a.m., p. 666.) This was published by the columnist Jack Anderson ("U.S. Moves Give Soviets Hold on India," *Washington Post,* 16 December 1971). To this day, Bangladeshis understandably resent the slap. Its recent economic growth belies the label (Sadanand Dhume, "Bangladesh, 'Basket Case' No More," *Wall Street Journal,* 29 September 2010); for a nuanced discussion, see Mohammad Rezaul Bari, "The Basket Case," *Forum* (Dacca), vol. 3, no. 3 (March 2008). Azizur Rahman Khan, "The Comilla Model and the Integrated Rural Development Programme of Bangladesh," *World Development,* vol. 7, nos. 4–5 (1979), pp. 397–422. Nasim Yousaf, "A Tribute to Dr. Akhter Hameed Khan," *Statesman,* 17 October 2006.
11. Blood, *Cruel Birth,* p. 36.
12. See Sydney H. Schanberg, *Beyond the Killing Fields: War Writings* (Washington, D.C.: Potomac Books, 2010).
13. Owen Bennett Jones, *Pakistan: Eye of the Storm* (New Haven, Conn.: Yale University Press, 2009), pp. 143–45. Ayesha Jalal, *The Sole Spokesman: Jinnah, the Muslim League and the Demand for Pakistan* (Cambridge: Cambridge University Press, 1985). POL 23-9 PAK, Box 2530, Keating to Rogers, 8 April 1971, New Delhi 5243. Blood, *Cruel Birth,* p. 2. On Partition, see Yasmin Khan, *The Great Partition: The Making of India and Pakistan* (New Haven, Conn.: Yale University Press, 2007); Patrick French, *Liberty or Death: India's Journey to Independence and Division* (London: HarperCollins, 1997); Ian Talbot and Gurharpal Singh, *The Partition of India* (Cambridge: Cambridge University Press, 2009).
14. Blood, *Cruel Birth,* p. 2. P. N. Dhar, *Indira Gandhi, the "Emergency," and Indian Democracy* (Oxford: Oxford University Press, 2000), p. 149. Joseph Lelyveld, "Divided Pakistan Was Born from Shaky Abstraction," *New York Times,* 7 April 1971.
15. Dhar, *Indira Gandhi, the "Emergency," and Indian Democracy,* p. 152. Tariq Ali, *Can Pakistan Survive? The Death of a State* (London: Penguin, 1983), p. 91. Sydney H. Schanberg, "Hours of Terror for a Trapped Bengali Officer," *New York Times,* 17 April 1971. Dom Moraes, *Mrs Gandhi* (London: Jonathan Cape, 1980), p. 189. NSC Files, Box H-052, SRG Meetings, Hoskinson to Kissinger, 5 March 1971. Jones, *Pakistan,* pp. 145–48. See G. W. Choudhury, *The Last Days of United Pakistan* (Bloomington: Indiana University Press, 1974), pp. 1–12.
16. Blood, *Cruel Birth,* pp. 2–3. Jones, *Pakistan,* pp. 146-53.
17. Khawaja Alqama, *Bengali Elite Perceptions of Pakistan* (Karachi: Royal Book Co., 1997), pp. 264–85. NSC Files, Box H-052, SRG Meetings, NSSM-

118, 3 March 1971; NSC Files, Box H-081, WSAG Meetings, NSSM-118, 3 March 1971. See MEA, HI/121/13/71, vol. I, Singh statement to United Nations General Assembly, 27 September 1971. Blood, *Cruel Birth*, p. 3. For a superb analysis, see Ayesha Jalal, *Democracy and Authoritarianism in South Asia: A Comparative and Historical Perspective* (Cambridge: Cambridge University Press, 1995), pp. 48–63.

18. Library of Congress, Association for Diplomatic Studies and Training, Foreign Affairs Oral History Project, Archer Blood interview, 27 June 1989. Blood, *Cruel Birth*, pp. 31–32.

19. MEA, HI/1012/30/71, Chib to Kaul, 4 March 1971. MEA, HI/1012/32/71, Sen Gupta to Acharya, 5 February 1971. Blood, *Cruel Birth*, pp. 33, 37. *FRUS*, vol. E-7, Nixon-Yahya memcon, 25 October 1970.

20. NSC Files, Box 624, Country Files—Middle East, Pakistan, vol. III, Sober to Rogers, 5 October 1970, Rawalpindi 7809. See Blood, *Cruel Birth*, p. 64.

21. POL 23-9 PAK, Box 2531, Bell to Shakespeare, 21 April 1971, Dacca 1440. Blood, *Cruel Birth*, pp. 74, 98–99, 107, 113. See NSC Files, Box 624, Country Files—Middle East, Pakistan, vol. III, Inter-Departmental Working Group on East Pakistan Disaster Relief, Daily Status Report, 20 November 1970; and NSC Files, Box 624, Country Files—Middle East, Pakistan, vol. III, Holly to Farland, 15 November 1970, State 187185.

22. POL 23-9 PAK, Box 2531, Bell to Shakespeare, 21 April 1971, Dacca 1440. See NSC Files, Box 624, Country Files—Middle East, Pakistan, vol. III, Inter-Departmental Working Group on East Pakistan Disaster Relief, Daily Status Report, 20 November 1970; and NSC Files, Box 624, Country Files— Middle East, Pakistan, vol. III, Holly to Farland, 15 November 1970, State 187185. Blood, *Cruel Birth*, p. 97. Library of Congress, Association for Diplomatic Studies and Training, Foreign Affairs Oral History Project, Archer Blood interview, 27 June 1989.

23. Library of Congress, Association for Diplomatic Studies and Training, Foreign Affairs Oral History Project, Archer Blood interview, 27 June 1989. Blood, *Cruel Birth*, pp. 79–85, 98–101, 110–14, 120–21.

24. The United States donated some $9 million in emergency relief aid, and U.S. military helicopters airlifted over a million pounds of supplies into the disaster zone (NSC Files, Box 624, Country Files—Middle East, Pakistan, vol. III, Kissinger to Nixon, 4 January 1971). Nixon committed an extra 150,000 tons of grain to help people left hungry from the cyclone, worth some $16 million. (NSC Files, Box 624, Country Files—Middle East, Pakistan, vol. III, Williams to Nixon, n.d. January 1971. See NSC Files, Box 624, Country Files—Middle East, Pakistan, vol. III, Kissinger to Nixon, 23 November 1970; NSC Files, Box H-054, SRG Meeting, Pakistan and Ceylon, 19 April 1971, Saunders to Kissinger, 16 April 1971.) NSC Files, Box 624, Country Files—Middle East, Pakistan, vol. III, Spengler to Farland, 19 November 1970. See NSC Files, Box 624, Country Files—Middle East, Pakistan, vol. III, Kissinger to Nixon, 21 November 1970. POL 23-9 PAK, Box 2531, Bell to Shakespeare, 21 April 1971, Dacca 1440.

25. NSC Files, Box 624, Country Files—Middle East, Pakistan, vol. III, Kissinger to Nixon, 23 November 1970. See Blood, *Cruel Birth*, p. 91. NSC Files, Box 624, Country Files—Middle East, Pakistan, vol. III, Inter-Departmental Working Group on East Pakistan Disaster Relief, Daily Status Report, 25 November 1970. Library of Congress, Association for Diplomatic Studies

and Training, Foreign Affairs Oral History Project, Archer Blood interview, 27 June 1989. Blood, *Cruel Birth,* pp. 77, 100. India was actually preoccupied with refugees fleeing the disaster zone into India. (PMS, 7/371/71, vol. I, Gandhi to Shukla, 3 January 1971. PMS, 7/371/71, vol. I, Gandhi to Sukhadia, 3 January 1971. PMS, 7/371/71, vol. I, Gandhi to Naik, 3 January 1971. PMS, 7/371/71, vol. I, Patil to Gandhi, 13 January 1971. PMS, 7/371/71, vol. I, Naik to Gandhi, 19 April 1971. PMS, 7/411/70, Satpathy to Gandhi, 27 November 1970. PMS, 7/411/70, Kaul to Sanpathy, 28 November 1970.)

26. NSC Files, Box 624, Country Files—Middle East, Pakistan, vol. III, Kissinger to Nixon, 19 November 1970. NSC Files, Box 624, Country Files—Middle East, Pakistan, vol. III, Kissinger to Nixon, 20 November 1970.

27. MEA, HI/1012/32/71, Sen Gupta to Acharya, 5 February 1971. Blood, *Cruel Birth,* pp. 114–15.

28. Ved Mehta, *The New India* (New York: Viking, 1978), p. 131. For a laudatory biography, see Yatindra Bhatnagar, *Mujib: The Architect of Bangla Desh* (New Delhi: Indian School Supply Depot, 1971). Blood, *Cruel Birth,* pp. 46–48.

29. NSC Files, Box 625, Country Files—Middle East, Pakistan, vol. IV, Saunders to Kissinger, 1 March 1971. See MEA, HI/1012/30/71, Chib to Kaul, 4 March 1971, and Peggy Durdin, "The Political Tidal Wave That Struck East Pakistan," *New York Times Magazine,* 2 May 1971. Library of Congress, Association for Diplomatic Studies and Training, Foreign Affairs Oral History Project, Archer Blood interview, 27 June 1989. Blood, *Cruel Birth,* pp. 115–18, 69–70, 125–28. NSC Files, Box 624, Country Files—Middle East, Pakistan, vol. III, INR note, 23 November 1970.

30. NSC Files, Box H-112, SRG Minutes, SRG meeting, 6 March 1971, 11:40 a.m. NSC Files, Box 624, Country Files—Middle East, Pakistan, vol. III, INR note, 23 November 1970. Library of Congress, Association for Diplomatic Studies and Training, Foreign Affairs Oral History Project, Archer Blood interview, 27 June 1989. Blood, *Cruel Birth,* pp. 125, 132.

31. NSC Files, Box 624, Country Files—Middle East, Pakistan, vol. III, INR note, 23 November 1970. Choudhury, *Last Days of United Pakistan,* pp. 106–26. Blood, *Cruel Birth,* pp. 128, 115–19. NMML, Kaul Papers, Subject File 19, part II, Singh briefing in London, n.d. June 1971. Jones, *Pakistan,* pp. 153–54. For a harsh verdict on Yahya, see Government of Pakistan, *The Report of the Hamoodur Rehman Commission of Inquiry into the 1971 War* (Lahore: Vanguard, 2001), p. 336.

32. NMML, Kaul Papers, Subject File 19, part II, Singh briefing in London, n.d. June 1971. Choudhury, *Last Days of United Pakistan,* p. 85. Jones, *Pakistan,* pp. 151, 155.

33. *FRUS,* vol. E-7, White House tapes, Oval Office 624-21, 24 November 1971, 12:27 p.m. Ramachandra Guha, *India After Gandhi: The History of the World's Largest Democracy* (New York: Ecco, 2003), p. 449. NSC Files, Box 624, Country Files—Middle East, Pakistan, vol. III, INR note, 23 November 1970. Blood, *Cruel Birth,* pp. 44–45. Zulfikar Ali Bhutto, *Politics of the People: A Collection of Articles, Statements and Speeches,* vol. 3, ed. Hamid Jalal and Khalid Hasan (Rawalpindi: Pakistan Publications, n.d.), pp. 1–179. See Salmaan Taseer, *Bhutto: A Political Biography* (New Delhi: Vikas, 1980).

34. Blood, *Cruel Birth,* pp. 123–24.

35. Blood, *Cruel Birth,* p. 33. NSC Files, Box H-052, SRG Meetings, Hoskinson

to Kissinger, 5 March 1971. Choudhury, *Last Days of United Pakistan,* pp. 52–66, 73–104. Blood, *Cruel Birth,* pp. 128–29.

36. MEA, HI/121/13/71, vol. I, Singh statement to United Nations General Assembly, 27 September 1971. The National Assembly had 313 seats. See MEA, HI/1012/32/71, Sen Gupta to Acharya, 5 February 1971. The Awami League won 160 directly elected seats out of 162 (Dhar, *Indira Gandhi, the "Emergency," and Indian Democracy,* p. 147).

37. See Samuel P. Huntington, *The Third Wave: Democratization in the Late Twentieth Century* (Norman: University of Oklahoma Press, 1991), pp. 174–92. POL 23-9 PAK, Box 2530, INR note, 27 February 1970.

38. Jones, *Pakistan,* pp. 156–59. See MEA, HI/1012/30/71, Chib to Kaul, 4 March 1971; Blood, *Cruel Birth,* pp. 128–29. POL 23-9 PAK, Box 2531, Farland to Rogers, 19 April 1971, Islamabad 3523.

39. POL 23-9 PAK, Box 2530, Blood to Rogers, 2 April 1971, Dacca 1067. Blood, *Cruel Birth,* pp. 129–34, 146–49.

40. Blood, *Cruel Birth,* pp. 136–37. NSC Files, Box 624, Country Files—Middle East, Pakistan, vol. III, Sisco to Farland, 26 February 1971, State 33384. See NSC Files, Box 625, Country Files—Middle East, Pakistan, vol. IV, Saunders to Kissinger, 1 March 1971. See MEA, HI/1012/30/71, Chib to Kaul, 4 March 1971. Library of Congress, Association for Diplomatic Studies and Training, Foreign Affairs Oral History Project, Archer Blood interview, 27 June 1989.

41. Pakistan's Lieutenant General A. A. K. Niazi argued that respect for the democratic process could have held Pakistan together (Niazi, *The Betrayal of East Pakistan* [Karachi: Oxford University Press, 1998], p. 220). Pakistan's own Hamoodur Rehman commission later wrote that Yahya "was fully determined not to hand over power to the people at this or any other stage." (*Hamoodur Rehman Commission Report,* p. 93.)

42. NSC Files, Box H-052, SRG Meetings, Rogers to Nixon, 23 February 1971. NSC Files, Box 624, Country Files—Middle East, Pakistan, vol. III, Saunders and Hoskinson to Kissinger, 24 February 1971. NSC Files, Box 624, Country Files—Middle East, Pakistan, vol. III, Kissinger to Nixon, 22 February 1971. See NSC Files, Box 625, Country Files—Middle East, Pakistan, vol. IV, Pavelle to Laird, 26 March 1971.

43. NSC Files, Box 625, Country Files—Middle East, Pakistan, vol. IV, Saunders to Kissinger, 4 March 1971. NSC Files, Box 625, Country Files—Middle East, Pakistan, vol. IV, Saunders to Kissinger, 1 March 1971.

44. Choudhury, *Last Days of United Pakistan,* p. 149. NSC Files, Box 625, Country Files—Middle East, Pakistan, vol. IV, Saunders to Kissinger, 1 March 1971. See MEA, HI/1012/31/71, Bakshi to Acharya, 18 March 1971; Choudhury, *Last Days of United Pakistan,* pp. 132–79.

45. Library of Congress, Association for Diplomatic Studies and Training, Foreign Affairs Oral History Project, Archer Blood interview, 27 June 1989. Blood, *Cruel Birth,* p. 155. See Peggy Durdin, "The Political Tidal Wave That Struck East Pakistan," *New York Times Magazine,* 2 May 1971.

46. POL 23-9 PAK, Box 2530, Farland to Rogers, 26 March 1971, Islamabad 2756. See MEA, HI/1012/30/71, Chib to Kaul, 8 April 1971. Blood, *Cruel Birth,* pp. 165–66.

47. Blood, *Cruel Birth,* p. 158–59, 167. See Ayesha Jalal, *The State of Martial*

Rule: *The Origins of Pakistan's Political Economy of Defence* (Cambridge: Cambridge University Press, 1992), p. 310. For Pakistani accusations of atrocities by Bengalis, see *Hamoodur Rehman Commission Report*, pp. 507–8; Niazi, *Betrayal of East Pakistan*, pp. 41–43.

48. POL 23-9 PAK, Box 2530, Farland to Rogers, 26 March 1971, Islamabad 2756. NSC Files, Box H-052, SRG Meetings, Yahya broadcast, 6 March 1971.

49. NSC Files, Box 625, Country Files—Middle East, Pakistan, vol. IV, Sisco to Rogers, 2 March 1971; NSC Files, Box 625, Country Files—Middle East, Pakistan, vol. IV, Eliot to Kissinger, 3 March 1971. See NSC Files, Box 624, Country Files—Middle East, Pakistan, vol. III, Sisco to Farland, 26 February 1971, State 33384. White House tapes, Oval Office 461-10, 2 March 1971, 12:07–12:44 p.m. White House tapes, Oval Office 462-5, 5 March 1971, 8:30–10:15 a.m.

50. NSC Files, Box H-052, SRG Meetings, Hoskinson to Kissinger, 5 March 1971.

51. NSC Files, Box H-052, SRG Meetings, NSSM-118, 3 March 1971. NSC Files, Box H-052, SRG Meetings, Saunders to Kissinger, 5 March 1971. His italics. Saunders argued that "the bloodshed would be minimal," since the army would soon be defeated. See NSC Files, Box H-052, SRG Meetings, Saunders and Hoskinson to Kissinger, 4 March 1971; NSC Files, Box H-052, SRG Meetings, Saunders and Hoskinson to Kissinger, 5 March 1971; NSC Files, Box H-052, SRG Meetings, Saunders to Kissinger, 5 March 1971. See NSC Files, Box 625, Country Files—Middle East, Pakistan, vol. IV, Saunders to Kissinger, 5 March 1971; and NSC Files, Box 625, Country Files—Middle East, Pakistan, vol. IV, Hoskinson to Kissinger, 5 March 1971.

52. NSC Files, Box H-112, SRG Minutes, SRG meeting, 6 March 1971, 11:40 a.m.

53. Kissinger later wrote, "For better or worse, the strategy of the Nixon Administration on humanitarian questions was not to lay down a challenge to sovereignty that would surely be rejected, but to exert our influence without public confrontation." (*White House Years* [Boston: Little, Brown, 1979], p. 854.)

54. NSC Files, Box H-112, SRG Minutes, SRG meeting, 6 March 1971, 11:40 a.m. See NSC Files, Box H-052, SRG Meetings, NSSM-118, 3 March 1971. Blood, *Cruel Birth*, pp. 171–72.

55. NSC Files, Box 625, Country Files—Middle East, Pakistan, vol. IV, Saunders and Hoskinson to Kissinger, 8 March 1971, with Kissinger's handwritten notes. NSC Files, Box 625, Country Files—Middle East, Pakistan, vol. IV, Saunders to Haig, 12 March 1971.

56. NSC Files, Box 625, Country Files—Middle East, Pakistan, vol. IV, Kissinger to Nixon, 13 March 1971.

57. *FRUS*, 40 Committee meeting, 9 April 1971, pp. 63–65.

58. MEA, HI/1012/31/71, Bakshi to Acharya, 6 April 1971.

59. MEA, HI/1012/30/71, Chib to Kaul, 8 April 1971. Blood, *Cruel Birth*, p. 173. POL 23-9 PAK, Box 2530, Blood to Rogers, 9 March 1971, Dacca 647.

60. POL 23-9 PAK, Box 2530, Blood to Rogers, 22 March 1971, Dacca 903. Blood, *Cruel Birth*, pp. 179, 159–61. A senior World Bank official later estimated that from the beginning of March, Yahya was building up his forces in East Pakistan with ten to fifteen daily flights of Boeing airplanes loaded with

military personnel. (NMML, Haksar Papers, Subject File 168, B. R. Patel to I. G. Patel, 18 June 1971.) Choudhury, *Last Days of United Pakistan*, p. 155.

61. Blood, *Cruel Birth*, pp. 175–76.

62. In the middle of the crisis, Mujib's birthday fell on St. Patrick's Day, and Blood, riffing on the commonplace joke that the fractious Bengalis were the Irish of South Asia, merrily sent him a copy of John Kennedy's *Profiles in Courage* and a happy birthday message that "drew parallels between Irish and Bengalis (may all sons of old Erin forgive me for this blasphem)." POL 23-9 PAK, Box 2530, Blood to Rogers, 20 March 1971, Dacca 880. POL 23-9 PAK, Box 2530, Blood to Rogers, 19 March 1971, Dacca 866. See POL 23-9 PAK, Box 2530, Blood to Rogers, 18 March 1971, Dacca 853. Blood, *Cruel Birth*, pp. 182, 189–90. POL 23-9 PAK, Box 2530, Blood to Rogers, 2 April 1971, Dacca 1067.

63. NSC Files, Box 625, Country Files—Middle East, Pakistan, vol. IV, Blood to Farland, 11 March 1971, Dacca 726.

64. NSC Files, Box 625, Country Files—Middle East, Pakistan, vol. IV, Blood to Farland, 11 March 1971, Dacca 726. Blood, *Cruel Birth*, pp. 187–88.

65. POL 23-9 PAK, Box 2530, Blood to Rogers, 13 March 1971, Dacca 773. Blood, *Cruel Birth*, pp. 183–84. POL 23-9 PAK, Box 2530, Blood to Rogers, 16 March 1971, Dacca 818. POL 23-9 PAK, Box 2530, Blood to Rogers, 20 March 1971, Dacca 883. POL 23-9 PAK, Box 2530, Blood to Rogers, 24 March 1971, Dacca 911. See POL 23-9 PAK, Box 2530, Farland to Rogers, 25 March 1971, Islamabad 2679; POL 23-9 PAK, Box 2530, Blood to Rogers, 22 March 1971, Dacca 903.

66. Choudhury, *Last Days of United Pakistan*, p. 161. POL 23-9 PAK, Box 2530, Blood to Rogers, 19 March 1971, Dacca 868. Blood, *Cruel Birth*, pp. 189, 193–94. POL 23-9 PAK, Box 2530, Blood to Rogers, 20 March 1971, Dacca 885. POL 23-9 PAK, Box 2530, Blood to Rogers, 20 March 1971, Dacca 880.

67. POL 23-9 PAK, Box 2530, Barrow to Rogers, 2 April 1971, Lahore 515. POL 23-9 PAK, Box 2530, Blood to Rogers, 2 April 1971, Dacca 1067. POL 23-9 PAK, Box 2530, Farland to Rogers, 19 March 197 1, Islamabad 2499. See POL 23-9 PAK, Box 2530, Farland to Rogers, 20 March 1971, Islamabad 2527. POL 23-9 PAK, Box 2530, Blood to Rogers, 23 March 1971, Dacca 906. POL 23-9 PAK, Box 2530, Barrow to Rogers, 2 April 1971, Lahore 515. Blood, *Cruel Birth*, pp. 190–91. POL 23-9 PAK, Box 2530, Farland to Rogers, 20 March 1971, Islamabad 2527.

68. POL 23-9 PAK, Box 2530, Blood to Rogers, 24 March 1971, Dacca 927. POL 23-9 PAK, Box 2530, Sisco to Blood, 24 March 1971, State 49323. See POL 23-9 PAK, Box 2530, Blood to Rogers, 24 March 1971, Dacca 919. See POL 23-9 PAK, Box 2530, Farland to Rogers, 26 March 1971, Islamabad 2752.

69. POL 23-9 PAK, Box 2530, Blood to Rogers, 22 March 1971, Dacca 903.

CHAPTER 3: MRS. GANDHI

1. Pupul Jayakar, *Indira Gandhi: An Intimate Biography* (New York: Pantheon, 1992), pp. 22–47.

2. Amartya Sen, "Tagore and His India," *New York Review of Books,* 26 June 1997. Indira Nehru to Jawaharlal Nehru, 7 July 1934, Sonia Gandhi, ed., *Freedom's Daughter: Letters Between Indira Gandhi and Jawaharlal Nehru, 1922–39* (London: Hodder & Stoughton, 1989), p. 122. Katherine Frank,

Indira: The Life of Indira Nehru Gandhi (New York: HarperCollins, 2001), pp. 86–90.

3. Jawaharlal Nehru to Indira Nehru, 25 January 1934, Sonia Gandhi, ed., *Freedom's Daughter,* p. 110. Indira Nehru to Jawaharlal Nehru, 27 March 1935, Sonia Gandhi, ed., *Freedom's Daughter,* p. 149. Indira Nehru to Jawaharlal Nehru, 7 July 1934, Sonia Gandhi, ed., *Freedom's Daughter,* p. 122. Indira Nehru to Jawaharlal Nehru, 12 January 1935, Sonia Gandhi, ed., *Freedom's Daughter,* p. 136. Jayakar, *Indira Gandhi,* pp. 43–47. Rabindranath Tagore, *A Tagore Reader,* ed. Amiya Chakravarty (Boston: Beacon Press, 1961), p. 27. Ramachandra Guha, ed., *Makers of Modern India* (Cambridge, Mass.: Belknap Press of Harvard University Press, 2011), pp. 171–72. Henry C. Hart, *Indira Gandhi's India* (Boulder, Colo.: Westview, 1976). Amartya Sen, *The Argumentative Indian: Writings on Indian History, Culture and Identity* (New York: Farrar, Straus & Giroux, 2005), pp. 90–91, 113–19. The institution is commonly known as Santiniketan, which refers to the town and grounds, but the school itself is named Viswa-Bharati (India in the World). On Tagore, see Guha, ed., *Makers of Modern India,* pp. 170–86; Sen, *Argumentative Indian,* pp. 89–120; Pankaj Mishra, *From the Ruins of Empire: The Intellectuals Who Remade Asia* (New York: Farrar, Straus & Giroux, 2012); Sugata Bose, *A Hundred Horizons: The Indian Ocean in the Age of Global Empire* (Cambridge, Mass.: Harvard University Press, 2006); and Krishna Dutta and Andrew Robinson, *Rabindranath Tagore: The Myriad-Minded Man* (London: Bloomsbury, 1995).

4. Jayakar, *Indira Gandhi,* pp. 87–89, 101–2.

5. Sen, *Argumentative Indian,* p. 117. Jayakar, *Indira Gandhi,* pp. 106, 111, 114.

6. Janny Scott, "In Tapes, Candid Talk by Young Kennedy Widow," *New York Times,* 12 September 2011, p. A1. See Oriana Fallaci, *Interviews with History and Conversations with Power* (New York: Rizzoli, 2011), p. 262. Jayakar, *Indira Gandhi,* pp. 37, 61. P. N. Dhar, *Indira Gandhi, the "Emergency," and Indian Democracy* (Oxford: Oxford University Press, 2000), p. 120. Shashi Tharoor, *Reasons of State: Political Development and India's Foreign Policy Under Indira Gandhi, 1966–1977* (New Delhi: Vikas, 1982), p. 125.

7. Myron Weiner, *The Indian Paradox: Essays in Indian Politics,* ed. Ashutosh Varshney (New Delhi: Sage, 1989), p. 33. For a brilliant account of India's high democratic ideals and harsh realities, see Sunil Khilnani, *The Idea of India* (New York: Farrar, Straus & Giroux, 1999). For an insightfully selected and introduced sample of Nehru's own thinking, see Guha, ed., *Makers of Modern India,* pp. 299–37. See Jawaharlal Nehru, "The Unity of India," *Foreign Affairs,* vol. 16, no. 2 (January 1938), pp. 231–43; Sunil Khilnani, "Nehru's Faith," *Economic and Political Weekly,* vol. 37, no. 48 (30 November–6 December 2002), pp. 4793–99; Myron Weiner, *Party Politics in India: The Development of a Multi-Party System* (Princeton: Princeton University Press, 1957); Pratap Bhanu Mehta, *The Burden of Democracy* (New York: Penguin, 2003). Dhar, *Indira Gandhi, the "Emergency," and Indian Democracy,* pp. 133, 123. Ramachandra Guha, *India After Gandhi: The History of the World's Largest Democracy* (New York: Ecco, 2003), pp. 433–34. Henry Hart, "Political Leadership in India," in Atul Kohli, ed., *India's Democracy: An Analysis of Changing State-Society Relations* (Prince-

ton: Princeton University Press, 1990), pp. 18–61. Dennis Kux, *Estranged Democracies: India and the United States, 1941–1991* (New Delhi: Sage, 1993), p. 287. As president of the Congress party, she campaigned against the educational overreach of a communist government in the southern state of Kerala, trying to impose the rule of the central government there. Her father, the prime minister, was at first appalled at her efforts to topple a properly elected government, but eventually grudgingly went along with it (Jayakar, *Indira Gandhi*, pp. 112–14). It was arguably the greatest lapse in Nehru's record of encouraging a real political opposition as a core part of India's democracy (Guha, *India After Gandhi*, pp. 515–16).

8. Guha, *India After Gandhi*, pp. 414–15. Jayakar, *Indira Gandhi*, pp. 122–33. For an astute profile of Indira Gandhi, see Patrick French, *India: A Portrait* (New York: Alfred A. Knopf, 2011), pp. 34–46.

9. Jayakar, *Indira Gandhi*, pp. 146–47.

10. NMML, Haksar Papers, Subject File 167, Haksar to Narain, 24 February 1971. On communal worries and foreign policy, see Surjit Mansingh, *India's Search for Power: Indira Gandhi's Foreign Policy, 1966–1982* (New Delhi: Sage, 1984), pp. 205–13. For important work on the dynamics of Hindu-Muslim violence in India, see Ashutosh Varshney, *Ethnic Conflict and Civic Life: Hindus and Muslims in India* (New Haven, Conn.: Yale University Press, 2003); Steven Wilkinson, *Votes and Violence: Electoral Competition and Ethnic Violence in India* (Cambridge: Cambridge University Press, 2004); Martha C. Nussbaum, *The Clash Within: Democracy, Religious Violence, and India's Future* (Cambridge, Mass.: Belknap Press of Harvard University Press, 2007); Sen, *Argumentative Indian*, pp. 207–11; Kanchan Chandra, "Civic Life or Economic Interdependence?" *Commonwealth and Comparative Politics*, vol. 39, no. 1 (2001), pp. 110–18; Paul R. Brass, *The Production of Hindu-Muslim Violence in Contemporary India* (Seattle: University of Washington Press, 2003); and Gopal Krishna, "Communal Violence in India," *Economic and Political Weekly*, vol. 20, no. 3 (19 January 1985), pp. 117–31.

11. Anatol Lieven, *Pakistan: A Hard Country* (New York: PublicAffairs, 2011), p. 21. J. F. R. Jacob, *Surrender at Dacca: Birth of a Nation* (New Delhi: Manohar, 1997), p. 30. The Indian government also redrew the border of Punjab to turn it into a federal state for the Sikhs. (Guha, *India After Gandhi*, pp. 406–9.) India often blamed the insurgencies on Chinese and Pakistani support for the rebels (Dhar, *Indira Gandhi, the "Emergency," and Indian Democracy*, pp. 151, 154). See Ashutosh Varshney, "India, Pakistan, and Kashmir," *Asian Survey*, vol. 31, no. 11 (November 1991), pp. 997–1019; Sumit Ganguly, "Explaining the Kashmir Insurgency," *International Security*, vol. 21, no. 2 (autumn 1996), pp. 76–107; and Paul R. Brass, "The Punjab Crisis and the Unity of India," in Kohli, ed., *India's Democracy*, pp. 169–213.

12. Guha, *India After Gandhi*, pp. 438–40. Jayakar, *Indira Gandhi*, pp. 146–47, 155–59. Ashis Nandy, "Indira Gandhi and the Culture of Indian Politics," *At the Edge of Psychology: Essays in Politics and Culture* (New Delhi: Oxford University Press, 1980), pp. 112–30. Gandhi's Congress was known as Congress (R), while her rivals had Congress (O).

13. Guha, *India After Gandhi*, p. 497, 515. Ved Mehta, *Portrait of India* (New

York: Farrar, Straus & Giroux, 1970), pp. 545–46. She tried to get rid of Soviet atlases that did not show India's borders in accordance with the official Indian view, and endorsed blacking out similarly offending maps in the *Encyclopedia Britannica* (NMML, Haksar Papers, Subject File 227, Gandhi note, "Soviet Maps," n.d. 1970 or 1971). See A. G. Noorani, "Map Fetish," *Frontline*, 14–27 January 2012. Tharoor, *Reasons of State*, pp. 54–56.

14. White House tapes, Oval Office 611-21, 2 November 1971, 12:47–1:13 p.m. Frank, *Indira*, pp. 312–14, 333. Ramachandra Guha, "The Men in Indira's Life," *Times of India*, 13 May 2007. Dhar, *Indira Gandhi, the "Emergency," and Indian Democracy*, pp. 117–19, 124. Guha, *India After Gandhi*, p. 435. Haksar was also remarkably good at keeping documents, which makes his papers one of the preeminent sources on this era (Guha, *India After Gandhi*, pp. 435, 560).

15. P. N. Haksar, *One More Life* (New Delhi: Oxford University Press, 1990), vol. 1, pp. xii, 18.

16. Haksar, *One More Life*, vol. 1, pp. 120, 6, 101, 28–29, 83. P. N. Haksar, *Premonitions* (Bombay: Interpress, 1979), p. 231.

17. Haksar, *Premonitions*, pp. 231–32. Haksar, *One More Life*, vol. 1, p. 30. NMML, Haksar Papers, Subject File 167, Nehru to Kher, 3 July 1952.

18. NMML catalogue, list no. 389. Guha, *India After Gandhi*, p. 435. In a fit of pique at not being given a suitable rank, he once quit the foreign service, and had to be personally cajoled back into government by Nehru (NMML, Haksar Papers, Subject File 167, Nehru to Kher, 23 June 1952). Dhar, *Indira Gandhi, the "Emergency," and Indian Democracy*, p. 143. Frank, *Indira*, pp. 161, 313.

19. Guha, *India After Gandhi*, pp. 433–34. NMML, Haksar Papers, Subject File 171, Haksar notes for constitutional debate, August 1971. See P. N. Haksar, *Contemplations on the Human Condition: Selected Writings, Speeches and Letters*, ed. Subrata Banerjee (Chandigarh, India: Centre for Research and Industrial Development, 2004), vol. 1, pp. 125–34.

20. Tharoor, *Reasons of State*, pp. 141–45.

21. Dhar, *Indira Gandhi, the "Emergency," and Indian Democracy*, pp. 119, 143, 160–61.

22. NMML, Haksar Papers, Subject File 163, Haksar to Gandhi, 10 January 1971; NMML, Haksar Papers, Subject File 163, Gandhi to Bandaranaike, revised draft, n.d. January 1971. *FRUS*, Jha-Kissinger memcon, 25 August 1971, p. 368. Haksar, *Contemplations on the Human Condition*, pp. 224–42, 379–80. Dhar, *Indira Gandhi, the "Emergency," and Indian Democracy*, p. 113. As Ramachandra Guha hilariously puts it, "His political views were those of the left wing of the British Labour Party, c. 1945" (*India After Gandhi*, p. 435). Dhar, *Indira Gandhi, the "Emergency," and Indian Democracy*, p. 160.

23. Dhar, *Indira Gandhi, the "Emergency," and Indian Democracy*, pp. 139–40. Jayakar, *Indira Gandhi*, pp. 138–41, 150–51. Kux, *Estranged Democracies*, pp. 248–61. Vojtech Mastny, "The Soviet Union's Partnership with India," *Journal of Cold War Studies*, vol. 12, no. 3 (summer 2010), pp. 64–67. See Raghunath Ram, "Soviet Policy Towards India from the Tashkent Conference to the Bangladesh War," *International Studies*, vol. 22, no. 4 (1985), pp. 353–68; Ashok Kapur, "Indian Security and Defense Policies

Under Indira Gandhi," *Journal of Asian and African Studies,* vol. 22, nos. 3–4 (1987), pp. 176–93. NMML, Haksar Papers, Subject File 203, Kosygin-Singh conversation, 8 June 1971.

24. NMML, Haksar Papers, Subject File 163, notes for Gandhi speech in Uttar Pradesh, 21 January 1971. NMML, Haksar Papers, Subject File 163, Haksar to Gandhi, 6 January 1971. Haksar later said that Nixon "lacked moral principles," while Kissinger was "an egomaniac who fancied himself another Metternich" (Frank, *Indira*, pp. 336–37).

25. Guha, *India After Gandhi*, pp. 515–16. Tharoor, *Reasons of State*, p. 59. In August 1969, she had a favorable rating of 71 percent, and 64 percent in December 1970–February 1971, although Indian polls in this period are not especially reliable.

26. Election Commission of India, *Statistical Report on General Elections, 1971 to the Fifth Lok Sabha* (New Delhi: Election Commission of India, 1973), vol. 1, p. 4.

27. NSC Files, Box 134, Kissinger Office Files, Country Files—Middle East, Gandhi toast, 4 November 1971. NMML, Haksar Papers, Subject File 163, notes for Gandhi speech in Uttar Pradesh, 21 January 1971. NMML, Haksar Papers, Subject File 163, Haksar to Gandhi, 14 January 1971. Guha, *India After Gandhi*, pp. 445–47. Jayakar, *Indira Gandhi*, pp. 160–61.

28. Dhar, *Indira Gandhi, the "Emergency," and Indian Democracy*, pp. 134, 146, 232–33. Guha, *India After Gandhi*, pp. 446–49. Jayakar, *Indira Gandhi*, pp. 160–61. NMML, Haksar Papers, Subject File 203, Kosygin-Singh conversation, 8 June 1971. See R. L. Gupta, *Politics of Commitment* (New Delhi: Trimurti Publications, 1972); Suresh K. Tameri, *The Wonder Elections 1971* (New Delhi: Vivek Publishing House, 1971). NMML, Haksar Papers, Subject File 229, Schanberg to S. K., n.d. See *FRUS*, vol. E-7, White House tapes, Oval Office 521-13, 15 June 1971, 5:13–5:40 p.m.

29. NMML, Haksar Papers, Subject File 166, Gandhi statement in Lok Sabha, 24 May 1971.

30. NMML, Haksar Papers, Subject File 169, Haksar notes, 15 July 1971. NMML, Haksar Papers, Subject File 165, Haksar to Dhar, 7 April 1971. Guha, *India After Gandhi*, pp. 443–44. NMML, Haksar Papers, Subject File 163, Haksar to Gandhi, 6 January 1971. H. Balakrishnan, "From Naxalbari to Nalgonda," *The Hindu Magazine,* 5 December 2004. See Sukhwant Singh, *India's Wars Since Independence: The Liberation of Bangladesh* (New Delhi: Vikas, 1980), vol. 1, p. 6. Maoist guerrillas are still active in parts of India to this day (see Aman Sethi, "The Bloody Crossroads," *Caravan,* 1 May 2011; Arundhati Roy, *Walking with the Comrades* [New York: Penguin, 2012]).

31. NMML, Haksar Papers, Subject File 169, Haksar notes, 15 July 1971. NMML, Haksar Papers, Subject File 163, Haksar to Gandhi, 27 January 1971. NMML, Haksar Papers, Subject File 167, Gandhi to Giri, Haksar draft, February 1971.

32. NMML, Haksar Papers, Subject File 227, Dhavan to Gandhi, 19 March 1971. His italics. NMML, Haksar Papers, Subject File 227, Jha to Kaul, 12 March 1971.

33. NMML, Haksar Papers, Subject File 167, Jha to Kaul, 22 December 1970.

34. MEA, HI/1012/32/71, Sen Gupta to Acharya, 20 January 1971. NMML, Haksar Papers, Subject File 220, R&AW report, "Threat of a Military Attack or Infiltration Campaign by Pakistan," January 1971. NMML, Hak-

sar Papers, Subject File 203, Kosygin-Singh conversation, 8 June 1971. POL 23-9 PAK, Box 2530, Bush to Rogers, 2 April 1971, airgram A-499, for Sen note verbale to Thant, 30 March 1971.

35. NMML, Haksar Papers, Subject File 163, Haksar to Gandhi, 5 January 1971.
36. Dhar, *Indira Gandhi, the "Emergency," and Indian Democracy*, p. 161. Guha, *India After Gandhi*, p. 452. Tharoor, *Reasons of State*, pp. 147–48. NMML, Haksar Papers, Subject File 220, R&AW to Haksar, 14 January 1971. NMML, Haksar Papers, Subject File 220, R&AW report, "Threat of a Military Attack or Infiltration Campaign by Pakistan," January 1971.
37. NMML, Haksar Papers, Subject File 220, R&AW report, "Threat of a Military Attack or Infiltration Campaign by Pakistan," January 1971. Dhar, *Indira Gandhi, the "Emergency," and Indian Democracy*, p. 149.
38. NMML, Haksar Papers, Subject File 167, Haksar to Dhar, 25 February 1971.
39. MEA, HI/1012/32/71, Sen Gupta to Acharya, 20 January 1971.
40. MEA, HI/1012/32/71, Sen Gupta to Acharya, 20 January 1971. MEA, HI/1012/32/71, Sen Gupta to Acharya, 5 February 1971.
41. MEA, HI/1012/31/71, Bakshi to Acharya, 18 March 1971. NMML, Haksar Papers, Subject File 203, Kosygin-Singh conversation, 8 June 1971. MEA, HI/1012/31/71, Bakshi to Acharya, 19 January 1971. See MEA, HI/1012/31/71, Bakshi to Acharya, 2 February 1971; MEA, HI/1012/31/71, Bakshi to Acharya, 18 March 1971. MEA, HI/1012/30/71, Chib to Kaul, 4 March 1971. MEA, HI/1012/30/71, Chib to Kaul, 5 August 1971. Dhar, *Indira Gandhi, the "Emergency," and Indian Democracy*, p. 152.
42. NMML, Haksar Papers, Subject File 220, Sadiq to Gandhi, 2 February 1971. NMML, Haksar Papers, Subject File 166, Haksar to Kaul, 22 May 1971. NMML, Haksar Papers, Subject File 167, Haksar to Kaul, 15 February 1971. NMML, Haksar Papers, Subject File 167, Haksar to Gandhi, 5 February 1971. "Hashim Qureshi Formally Charged in 1971 Plane Hijacking Case," Press Trust of India, 27 December 2002. "Separatist in 1971 Hijacking Surrenders on Return to India," Associated Press, 30 December 2000. NMML, Haksar Papers, Subject File 167, Gandhi draft statement, 6 February 1971. NMML, Haksar Papers, Subject File 167, Haksar to Gandhi, 24 February 1971. NMML, Haksar Papers, Subject File 167, Yahya to Kosygin, 7 February 1971. NSC Files, Box 625, Country Files—Middle East, Pakistan, vol. V, Yahya to Nixon, 24 May 1971. MEA, HI/1012/30/71, Chib to Kaul, 4 March 1971. MEA, HI/1012/32/71, Sen Gupta to Acharya, 15 February 1971.
43. MEA, HI/1012/31/71, Bakshi to Acharya, 2 March 1971. See MEA, HI/1012/30/71, Chib to Kaul, 4 March 1971.
44. MEA, HI/1012/30/71, Chib to Kaul, 4 March 1971. MEA, HI/1012/30/71, Chib to Kaul, 8 April 1971.
45. MEA, HI/1012/32/71, Sen Gupta to Acharya, 1 March 1971. See MEA, HI/1012/32, vol. II, East Pakistan Weekly Press Review, 20 February 1971. Dhar, *Indira Gandhi, the "Emergency," and Indian Democracy*, p. 151.
46. NMML, Haksar Papers, Subject File 220, R&AW tasking, 2 March 1971.
47. NMML, Haksar Papers, Subject File 227, Jha to Kaul, 12 March 1971.
48. POL 23-9 PAK, Box 2530, Sober to Rogers, 15 March 1971, Islamabad 2277. MEA, HI/1012/30/71, Chib to Kaul, 4 March 1971. NMML, Haksar Papers, Subject File 227, Manekshaw to Swaminathan, 22 March 1971. NMML,

Haksar Papers, Subject File 220, R&AW report, "Threat of a Military Attack or Infiltration Campaign by Pakistan," January 1971.

49. NMML, Haksar Papers, Subject File 164, Haksar to Gandhi, 19 March 1971.

CHAPTER 4: "MUTE AND HORRIFIED WITNESSES"

1. POL 23-9 PAK, Box 2530, Blood to Rogers, 25 March 1971, Dacca 932.
2. POL 23-9 PAK, Box 2530, Blood to Rogers, 25 March 1971, Dacca 942. For a recent similar refusal by South African port workers to unload arms likely to be used against a civilian public, see Celia W. Dugger, "Zimbabwe Arms Shipped by China Spark an Uproar," *New York Times,* 19 April 2008.
3. Archer K. Blood, *The Cruel Birth of Bangladesh: Memoirs of an American Diplomat* (Dacca: University Press of Bangladesh, 2002), pp. 195–96. For corroborating reports from a Ford Foundation official in Dacca, see POL 23-9 PAK, Box 2530, Farland to Rogers, 31 March 1971, Islamabad 2928; POL 23-9 PAK, Box 2530, Farland to Rogers, 1 April 1971, Islamabad 3017.
4. POL 23-9 PAK, Box 2530, McCarthy to Rogers, 27 March 1971, Karachi 646. Simon Dring, "How Dacca Paid for a United Pakistan," *Daily Telegraph,* 30 March 1971. G. W. Choudhury, *The Last Days of United Pakistan* (Bloomington: Indiana University Press, 1974), pp. 184–85.
5. Today this is the Ruposhi Bangla Hotel, at 1 Minto Road in Dacca.
6. POL 23-9 PAK, Box 2530, Blood to Rogers, 27 March 1971, Dacca 949. Blood, *Cruel Birth,* p. 199. See POL 23-9 PAK, Box 2530, Blood to Rogers, 27 March 1971, Dacca 949. Pakistan formally protested "highly malicious, exaggerated and provocative reports" by All India Radio (POL 23-9 PAK, Box 2530, Farland to Rogers, 28 March 1971, Islamabad 2788).
7. Sydney H. Schanberg, "Sheik Mujib Calls Strike," *New York Times,* 26 March 1971. POL 23-9 PAK, Box 2530, Blood to Rogers, 27 March 1971, Dacca 950. POL 23-9 PAK, Box 2530, McCarthy to Rogers, 27 March 1971, Karachi 646. Blood, *Cruel Birth,* p. 199. See POL 23-9 PAK, Box 2530, Smith to Farland, 29 March 1971, State 52825.
8. Blood, *Cruel Birth,* p. 199. Library of Congress, Association for Diplomatic Studies and Training, Foreign Affairs Oral History Project, Archer Blood interview, 27 June 1989. See POL 23-9 PAK, Box 2530, Farland to Rogers, Islamabad 2824; POL 23-9 PAK, Box 2530, Van Hollen to Farland, 28 March 1971, State 52028; POL 23-9 PAK, Box 2530, Blood to Rogers, 31 March 1971, Dacca 999.
9. Sydney H. Schanberg, " 'All Part of a Game'—a Grim and Deadly One," *New York Times,* 4 April 1971.
10. POL 23-9 PAK, Box 2530, Farland to Rogers, 26 March 1971, Islamabad 2706. POL 23-9 PAK, Box 2530, Farland to Rogers, 26 March 1971, Islamabad 2756. See POL 23-9 PAK, Box 2530, Farland to Rogers, 26 March 1971, Islamabad 2757; POL 23-9 PAK, Box 2530, Farland to Rogers, 29 March 1971, Islamabad 2830. POL 23-9 PAK, Box 2530, Farland to Rogers, 27 March 1971, Islamabad 2766. POL 23-9 PAK, Box 2530, Luppi to Farland, 27 March 1971, Karachi 640. See POL 23-9 PAK, Box 2530, Luppi to Farland, 31 March 1971, Karachi 673; POL 23-9 PAK, Box 2530, Vance to Farland, 31 March 1971, Karachi 673. For Bhutto's version, see Oriana Fallaci, *Interviews with History and Conversations with Power* (New York: Rizzoli, 2011), pp. 290–93. POL 23-9 PAK, Box 2530, Farland to Rogers,

27 March 1971, Islamabad 2765. POL 23-9 PAK, Box 2530, Farland to Rogers, 26 March 1971, Islamabad 2724. See POL 23-9 PAK, Box 2530, Luppi to Farland, 26 March 1971, Karachi 633. POL 23-9 PAK, Box 2530, Gordon to Rogers, 26 March 1971, Calcutta 459. POL 23-9 PAK, Box 2530, Farland to Rogers, 26 March 1971, Islamabad 2724. Government of Pakistan, *The Report of the Hamoodur Rehman Commission of Inquiry into the 1971 War* (Lahore: Vanguard, 2001), p. 510.

11. Blood, *Cruel Birth,* p. 198.
12. POL 23-9 PAK, Box 2530, Blood to Rogers, 30 March 1971, Dacca 986. *Hamoodur Rehman Commission Report,* p. 509. POL 23-9 PAK, Box 2530, Blood to Rogers, 27 March 1971, Dacca 949. On continuing persecution at Dacca University, see POL 23-9 PAK, Box 2531, Blood to Rogers, 10 April 1971, Dacca 1246. See POL 23-9 PAK, Box 2531, "India and 'Bangla Desh,'" INR note, 26 April 1971; POL 23-9 PAK, Box 2531, Greene to Rogers, London 3222.
13. POL 23-9 PAK, Box 2530, Blood to Farland, 4 April 1971, Dacca 1107. See Simon Dring, "How Dacca Paid for a United Pakistan," *Daily Telegraph,* 30 March 1971. Blood, *Cruel Birth,* pp. 201–2.
14. POL 23-9 PAK, Box 2530, Blood to Rogers, 29 March 1971, Dacca 978. Blood, *Cruel Birth,* p. 203. See POL 23-9 PAK, Box 2530, Blood to Rogers, 29 March 1971, Dacca 973.
15. POL 23-9 PAK, Box 2530, Farland to Rogers, 27 March 1971, Islamabad 2778; POL 23-9 PAK, Box 2530, Sisco to Farland, 26 March 1971, State 51571; POL 23-9 PAK, Box 2530, Sisco to Farland and Keating, 28 March 1971, State 51992. POL 23-9 PAK, Box 2530, Bell to Shakespeare, 5 April 1971, Dacca 1126. Blood, *Cruel Birth,* p. xvi.
16. POL 23-9 PAK, Box 2530, Blood to Rogers, 27 March 1971, Dacca 956. POL 23-9 PAK, Box 2530, Farland to Rogers, 28 March 1971, Islamabad 2790.
17. POL 23-9 PAK, Box 2530, Farland to Rogers, 29 March 1971, Islamabad 2797. For the State Department's defensive reply, see POL 23-9 PAK, Box 2530, Sisco to Farland, 29 March 1971, State 52804. See MEA, HI/1012/78/71, Jha to Kaul, 7 April 1971.
18. POL 23-9 PAK, Box 2530, Farland to Rogers, 29 March 1971, Islamabad 2827. POL 23-9 PAK, Box 2530, Farland to Rogers, 29 March 1971, Islamabad 2831. See POL 23-9 PAK, Box 2530, Austin to Shakespeare, 30 March 1971, Islamabad 2852. See also POL 23-9 PAK, Box 2530, Keating to Rogers, 1 April 1971, New Delhi 4743; POL 23-9 PAK, Box 2530, Farland to Rogers, 30 March 1971, Islamabad 2883; POL 23-9 PAK, Box 2530, Sisco to Greene, 27 March 1971, State 51949. POL 23-9 PAK, Box 2530, Farland to Rogers, 27 March 1971, Islamabad 2759. POL 23-9 PAK, Box 2530, Blood to Rogers, 27 March 1971, Dacca 955. See POL 23-9 PAK, Box 2530, Van Hollen to Farland, 27 March 1971, State 51990. POL 23-9 PAK, Box 2530, Loomis to Rogers, 28 March 1971, USIA 4843. POL 23-9 PAK, Box 2530, Bell to Shakespeare, 4 April 1971, Dacca 1095. NSC Files, Box H-112, SRG Minutes, SRG meeting, 31 March 1971.
19. NSC Files, Box H-081, WSAG Meetings, Kissinger to Nixon, 26 March 1971; NSC Files, Box 625, Country Files—Middle East, Pakistan, vol. IV, Kissinger to Nixon, 26 March 1971.
20. Philip Gourevitch, "Alms Dealers," *The New Yorker,* 11 October 2010. *FRUS,* vol. E-5, Kissinger to Nixon, 28 January 1969; *FRUS,* vol. E-5, Morris

to Kissinger, 12 February 1969. John de St. Jorre, *The Nigerian Civil War* (London: Hodder & Stoughton, 1972). John J. Stremlau, *The International Politics of the Nigerian Civil War, 1967–1970* (Princeton: Princeton University Press, 1977), pp. 62–81, 215–52, 255–308, 320–87. George A. Obiozor, *The United States and the Nigerian Civil War: An American Dilemma in Africa, 1966–1970* (Lagos: Nigerian Institute of International Affairs, 1993), pp. 14–21. See Samantha Power, *"A Problem from Hell": America and the Age of Genocide* (New York: Basic Books, 2002), pp. 81–82; Jean Buhler, *Tuez-les tous! Guerre de sécession au Biafra* (Paris: Flammarion, 1968). White House tapes, Oval Office 784-21, 21 September 1972, 12:25–2:01 p.m. Late in the Biafran crisis, Nixon wrote, "I hope the Biafrans survive!" (*FRUS*, vol. E-5, Kissinger to Nixon, 15 May 1969). Nixon was fitful in his sympathies for the Biafrans, although far more generous to them than he ever was to the Bengalis. Despite pro-Biafra campaign rhetoric, as president, he saw a Nigerian victory as best for U.S. interests, and sought to avoid political involvement (*FRUS*, vol. E-5, Kissinger to Nixon, 22 February 1969). In April 1969, Nixon briefly decided it was wrong to support the Nigeria federal government (*FRUS*, vol. E-5, Kissinger to Nixon, 8 April 1969). But after that, the United States stayed neutral, with William Rogers and Alexander Haig backing Nigeria (*FRUS*, vol. E-5, Haig to Kissinger, 16 February 1970), and Nixon reluctantly hoping for a Nigerian victory (*FRUS*, vol. E-5, Morris to Kissinger, 13 June 1969). Nixon later began an effort to resolve the civil war (*FRUS*, vol. E-5, Butterfield to Kissinger, 14 July 1969; *FRUS*, vol. E-5, Kissinger to Nixon, 11 August 1969; *FRUS*, vol. E-5, Kissinger to Nixon, 20 September 1969; *FRUS*, vol. E-5, Haig to Kissinger, 9 January 1970; *FRUS*, vol. E-5, Morris to Kissinger, 10 January 1970), which stalled in the face of State Department obstruction (*FRUS*, vol. E-5, Morris to Newsom, 6 October 1969; *FRUS*, vol. E-5, Morris to Kissinger, 24 October 1969; *FRUS*, vol. E-5, Morris to Lake, 7 November 1969; *FRUS*, vol. E-5, Kissinger to Nixon, 10 December 1969) soon before Nigerian forces conquered Biafra in January 1970.

21. POL 23-9 PAK, Box 2530, Farland to Rogers, 27 March 1971, Islamabad 2766. POL 23-9 PAK, Box 2530, Farland to Rogers, 27 March 1971, Islamabad 2780. POL 23-9 PAK, Box 2530, Van Hollen to Farland, 28 March 1971, State 52028. POL 23-9 PAK, Box 2530, Farland to Rogers, 29 March 1971, Islamabad 2830. MEA, HI/1012/30/71, Chib to Kaul, 4 March 1971. Tillman Durdin, "In Pakistan, United States Is Villain," *New York Times,* 26 March 1971. *FRUS,* WSAG meeting, 26 March 1971, 3:03–3:32 p.m., pp. 23–29.

22. NSC Files, Box H-081, WSAG Meetings, Saunders et al. to Kissinger, 26 March 1971. NSC Files, Box 625, Country Files—Middle East, Pakistan, vol. IV, Pavelle to Laird, 26 March 1971. *FRUS,* WSAG meeting, 26 March 1971, 3:03–3:32 p.m., pp. 23–29.

23. NSA, Nixon-Kissinger telcon, 27 March 1971, 2:05 p.m.

24. Blood, *Cruel Birth,* pp. 153, xv.

25. Blood, *Cruel Birth,* p. 209. POL 23-9 PAK, Box 2530, Blood to Rogers, 27 March 1971, Dacca 950.

26. POL 23-9 PAK, Box 2530, Blood to Rogers, 28 March 1971, Dacca 960.

27. Blood, *Cruel Birth,* p. 213.

28. The Genocide Convention defines genocide as killings or persecutions done "with an intent to destroy, in whole or in part, a national, ethnical, racial or

religious group." It would thus cover what Blood called "selective genocide" as genocide.

29. POL 23-9 PAK, Box 2530, Blood to Rogers, 28 March 1971, Dacca 959.
30. Ibid.
31. Ibid.
32. Blood interview, 27 June 1989, Foreign Affairs Oral History Collection of the Association for Diplomatic Studies and Training, Library of Congress. There is no extant documentary evidence of the State Department asking Americans in Dacca to stop sheltering Bengalis, as Blood himself admitted, although he insisted that it happened (Blood, *Cruel Birth,* p. 214). The consul in Karachi did later warn Blood that if reporters spread word about these Americans who had protected Bengalis, Pakistani troops might enter and loot abandoned American homes. (POL 23-9 PAK, Box 2530, Luppi to Blood, 8 April 1971, Karachi 805.)
33. Blood, *Cruel Birth,* p. 280.
34. Ibid., pp. 215–16.
35. John Lewis Gaddis, *We Now Know: Rethinking Cold War History* (Oxford: Clarendon, 1997), pp. 268–69. Max Holland, "A Luce Connection," *Journal of Cold War Studies,* vol. 1, no. 3 (fall 1999), pp. 139-67. Thomas G. Paterson, "The Historian as Detective," *Diplomatic History,* vol. 11, no. 1 (winter 1987), pp. 67–70. Dino A. Brugioni, *Eyeball to Eyeball: The Inside Story of the Cuban Missile Crisis* (New York: Random House, 1990), pp. 167–72. Kenneth Keating, "My Advance View of the Cuban Crisis," *Look,* 3 November 1964. Richard Reeves, *President Kennedy: Profile of Power* (New York: Simon & Schuster, 1993), p. 370. William V. Shannon, *The Heir Apparent: Robert Kennedy and the Struggle for Power* (New York: Macmillan, 1967), pp. 31–33. Robert J. Samuelson, "Embittered Incumbent Fights Back," *Harvard Crimson,* 30 October 1964. Kenneth B. Keating, *Government of the People* (Cleveland: World Publishing, 1964).
36. POL 23-9 PAK, Box 2530, Keating to Rogers, 27 March 1971, New Delhi 4416. For a view of Keating's good relationship with Indian officials, see NMML, Kaul Papers, Subject File 19, part I, Keating-Singh meeting, 22 December 1970.
37. POL 23-9 PAK, Box 2530, Keating to Rogers, 29 March 1971, Delhi 4494. For a United Nations official calling the situation a "genocide," see POL 23-9 PAK, Box 2530, Wolff to Bergstrom, 31 March 1971, Dacca 1002.
38. POL 23-9 PAK, Box 2530, Keating to Rogers, 1 April 1971, New Delhi 4743. See POL 23-9 PAK, Box 2530, Keating to Rogers, 1 April 1971, New Delhi 4750. POL 23-9 PAK, Box 2530, Farland to Rogers, 2 April 1971, Islamabad 3069. POL 23-9 PAK, Box 2530, Keating to Rogers, 1 April 1971, New Delhi 4743. See POL 23-9 PAK, Box 2530, Sisco to Keating, 31 March 1971, State 53954. Schanberg confirmed to me that Keating fed him the story. Sydney H. Schanberg, "Heavy Killing Reported," *New York Times,* 30 March 1971.
39. POL 23-9 PAK, Box 2530, Keating to Rogers, 2 April 1971, New Delhi 4861. POL 23-9 PAK, Box 2530, Rogers to Keating, 5 April 1971, State 56694. This cable, drafted by Van Hollen, was approved by Sisco and Rogers. See POL 23-9 PAK, Box 2530, Keating to Rogers, 3 April 1971, New Delhi 4877; POL 23-9 PAK, Box 2530, Sisco to Keating, 3 April 1971, State 56552; POL 23-9 PAK, Box 2530, Keating to Sisco, 4 April 1971, Calcutta 542. See also POL 23-9 PAK, Box 2531, Keating to Rogers, 16 April 1971, New Delhi 5734; POL

23-9 PAK, Box 2531, Johnson to Keating, 16 April 1971; POL 23-9 PAK, Box 2531, Irwin to Keating, 15 April 1971, State 63807; POL 23-9 PAK, Box 2531, Greene to Rogers, 16 April 1971, London 3434; POL 23-9 PAK, Box 2531, Schneider to Keating, 19 April 1971, State 66510; POL 23-9 PAK, Box 2531, Farland to Rogers, 20 April 1971, Islamabad 3573.

40. NSC Files, Box 625, Country Files—Middle East, Pakistan, vol. V, Kissinger to Nixon, 27 July 1971. Library of Congress, Association for Diplomatic Studies and Training, Foreign Affairs Oral History Project, Farland interview, 31 January 2000. FRUS, vol. E-7, White House tapes, Oval Office 549-25, 28 July 1971, 4:21 p.m.

41. Blood, Cruel Birth, pp. 41–42. Library of Congress, Association for Diplomatic Studies and Training, Foreign Affairs Oral History Project, Farland interview, 31 January 2000. Library of Congress, Association for Diplomatic Studies and Training, Foreign Affairs Oral History Project, Archer Blood interview, 27 June 1989. Blood, as a consul general, was entitled to send his cables directly to Washington, rather than have his views filtered through the embassy in Islamabad.

42. NSC Files, Box 759, Presidential Correspondence File, Yahya to Nixon, 31 March 1971. See POL 23-9 PAK, Box 2530, Keating to Rogers, 5 April 1971, New Delhi 4968. POL 23-9 PAK, Box 2530, Farland to Rogers, 26 March 1971, Islamabad 2705. See POL 23-9 PAK, Box 2530, Farland to Rogers, 27 March 1971, Islamabad 2766; POL 23-9 PAK, Box 2530, Farland to Rogers, 28 March 1971, Islamabad 2787; POL 23-9 PAK, Box 2530, Barrow to Rogers, 29 March 1971, Lahore 505. POL 23-9 PAK, Box 2530, Farland to Rogers, 7 April 1971, Islamabad 3180. POL 23-9 PAK, Box 2531, Farland to Rogers, 19 April 1971, Islamabad 3523. NMML, Kaul Papers, Subject File 19, part II, Singh briefing in London, n.d. June 1971. MEA, HI/1012/31/71, Bakshi to Acharya, 6 April 1971.

43. FRUS, vol. E-7, Farland to Rogers, 31 March 1971, Islamabad 2954. POL 23-9 PAK, Box 2530, Farland to Rogers, 26 March 1971, Islamabad 2754. For risks of unrest in Karachi, see POL 23-9 PAK, Box 2530, Farland to Rogers, 26 March 1971, Islamabad 2732. POL 23-9 PAK, Box 2530, Farland to Rogers, 30 March 1971, Islamabad 2891.

44. POL 23-9 PAK, Box 2530, Barrow to Rogers, 30 March 1971, Lahore 521. POL 23-9 PAK, Box 2530, Farland to Luppi, 29 March 1971, Islamabad 2814. FRUS, vol. E-7, Farland to Rogers, 31 March 1971, Islamabad 2954. Farland later said that he probably would have acted the same way that Blood did if he had been in Dacca (Library of Congress, Association for Diplomatic Studies and Training, Foreign Affairs Oral History Project, Farland interview, 31 January 2000).

45. POL 23-9 PAK, Box 2530, Farland to Blood, 29 March 1971, Islamabad 2813. FRUS, vol. E-7, Blood to Rogers, 10 April 1971, Dacca 1249.

46. NSC Files, Box 625, Country Files—Middle East, Pakistan, vol. IV, Hoskinson to Kissinger, 28 March 1971. See NSC Files, Box H-112, SRG Minutes, SRG meeting, 31 March 1971.

47. FRUS, Nixon-Kissinger telcon, 28 March 1971, p. 34.

48. NMML, Haksar Papers, Subject File 277, Jha to Kaul, 18 April 1971.

49. FRUS, Nixon-Kissinger telcon, 29 March 1971, pp. 35–36.

50. FRUS, 40 Committee meeting, 9 April 1971, pp. 63–65. NMML, Haksar Papers, Subject File 277, Jha to Kaul, 18 April 1971.

51. POL 23-9 PAK, Box 2531, Helms to Irwin, 5 April 1971. See POL 23-9 PAK, Box 2531, Irwin to Helms, 10 April 1971.
52. NSC Files, Box 625, Country Files—Middle East, Pakistan, vol. IV, Hoskinson and Kennedy to Kissinger, 30 March 1971.
53. FRUS, Nixon-Kissinger telcon, 30 March 1971, p. 37 (punctuation corrected).
54. FRUS, Nixon-Kissinger telcon, 30 March 1971, p. 37. See NSA, Popanak-Kissinger telcon, 30 March 1971, 10:50 a.m.
55. NSC Files, Box H-112, SRG Minutes, SRG meeting, 31 March 1971. The scholar Sarmila Bose claims that this student was not in fact killed, contrary to what Kissinger was told ("Anatomy of Violence," Economic and Political Weekly, vol. 40, no. 41 [8–14 October 2005], p. 4471n16; Dead Reckoning: Memories of the 1971 Bangladesh War [New York: Columbia University Press, 2011], p. 60).

CHAPTER 5: THE BLOOD TELEGRAM

1. NMML, Haksar Papers, Subject File 166, Haksar to Gandhi, briefing for opposition leaders, before 7 May 1971.
2. POL 23-9 PAK, Box 2530, Gordon to Rogers, 25 March 1971, Calcutta 453. POL 23-9 PAK, Box 2530, Van Hollen to Keating, 29 March 1971, State 52767. See POL 23-9 PAK, Box 2530, Eaves to Farland, 30 March 1971, State 53691.
3. NSC Files, Box H-112, SRG Minutes, SRG meeting, 6 March 1971, 11:40 a.m. POL 23-9 PAK, Box 2530, Blood to Rogers, 30 March 1971, Dacca 979. POL 23-9 PAK, Box 2530, Blood to Rogers, 1 April 1971, Dacca 1040; POL 23-9 PAK, Box 2530, Blood to Bennett, 2 April 1971, Dacca 1064.
4. POL 23-9 PAK, Box 2530, Blood to Rogers, 30 March 1971, Dacca 979. POL 23-9 PAK, Box 2530, Blood to Rogers, 1 April 1971, Dacca 1040; POL 23-9 PAK, Box 2530, Blood to Bennett, 2 April 1971, Dacca 1064. POL 23-9 PAK, Box 2530, Blood to Rogers, 31 March 1971, Dacca 1010. N. C. Menon, "Sabres Strafe Natore," Hindustan Times, 14 April 1971. See POL 23-9 PAK, Box 2530, Gordon to Rogers, 31 March 1971, Calcutta 513; POL 23-9 PAK, Box 2530, Gordon to Rogers, 1 April 1971, Calcutta 519; POL 23-9 PAK, Box 2530, Spengler to Farland, 9 April 1971, State 61066. POL 23-9 PAK, Box 2531, Blood to Rogers, 10 April 1971, Dacca 1237; POL 23-9 PAK, Box 2531, Blood to Rogers, 17 April 1971, Dacca 1365.
5. POL 23-9 PAK, Box 2531, Blood to Rogers, 15 April 1971, Dacca 1321. POL 23-9 PAK, Box 2530, Blood to Rogers, 1 April 1971, Dacca 1040; POL 23-9 PAK, Box 2530, Blood to Bennett, 2 April 1971, Dacca 1064. See Steven J. Zaloga, M24 Chaffee Light Tank, 1943–85 (Oxford: Osprey, 2003), pp. 23, 32, 47. POL 23-9 PAK, Box 2531, Blood to Rogers, 15 April 1971, Dacca 1321.
6. NSC Files, Box 625, Country Files—Middle East, Pakistan, vol. IV, Saunders and Hoskinson, 1 April 1971. POL 23-9 PAK, Box 2530, Keating to Rogers, 31 March 1971, New Delhi 4639. See POL 23-9 PAK, Box 2530, Van Hollen to Farland, 31 March 1971, State 54508; POL 23-9 PAK, Box 2530, Smith to Farland, 2 April 1971, State 56469; POL 23-9 PAK, Box 2530, Keating to Rogers, 1 April 1971, New Delhi 4756; and POL 23-9 PAK, Box 2530, Keating to Rogers, 2 April 1971, New Delhi 4864.
7. NSA, Nixon-Kissinger-Suharto memcon, 26 May 1970, 10:45 a.m. POL 23-9 PAK, Box 2530, Farland to Rogers, 9 April 1971, Islamabad 3261.

8. POL 23-9 PAK, Box 2530, Blood to Rogers, 29 March 1971, Dacca 969. See POL 23-9 PAK, Box 2530, Bush to Blood, 29 March 1971, USUN 804; POL 23-9 PAK, Box 2530, Blood to Rogers, 30 March 1971, Dacca 989; POL 23-9 PAK, Box 2530, Blood to Rogers, 30 March 1971, Dacca 987. *FRUS*, vol. E-7, Blood to Rogers, 10 April 1971, Dacca 1249.

9. POL 23-9 PAK, Box 2530, Rogers to Nixon, 3 April 1971. POL 23-9 PAK, Box 2530, Spengler to posts, 5 April 1971, State 57352. See NSC Files, Box 138, Kissinger Office Files, Country Files—Middle East, Farland to Sisco, 6 April 1971, Islamabad 3196; NSC Files, Box 625, Country Files—Middle East, Pakistan, vol. IV, Farland to Sisco, 6 April 1971, Islamabad 3196; POL 23-9 PAK, Box 2530, Smith to Farland, 6 April 1971, State 57970. On April 7, the State Department spokesman announced that the evacuation of Americans was complete, with some five hundred flown out. Benjamin Welles, "U.S. Urges Pakistan Seek Peaceful Accommodation," *New York Times*, 8 April 1971, p. A3. Sydney H. Schanberg, "Consul Urges U.S. Start Evacuation in East Pakistan," *New York Times*, 31 March 1971, pp. A1–A2. NSC Files, Box 759, Presidential Correspondence File, Nixon to Yahya, 17 April 1971. On the importance of rescuing the Americans, see NSC Files, Box 625, Country Files—Middle East, Pakistan, vol. IV, Kissinger to Nixon, 26 March 1971; NSC Files, Box H-081, WSAG Meetings, Saunders et al. to Kissinger, 26 March 1971; *FRUS*, WSAG meeting, 26 March 1971, 3:03–3:32 p.m., pp. 23–29; NSC Files, Box 138, Kissinger Office Files, Country Files—Middle East, Rogers to Blood, 6 April 1971, State 58039; POL 23-9 PAK, Box 2530, Rogers to Blood, 6 April 1971, State 58039; and POL 23-9 PAK, Box 2530, Rogers to Nixon, 3 April 1971. POL 23-9 PAK, Box 2530, Farland to Blood, 1 April 1971, Islamabad 2969. See POL 23-9 PAK, Box 2530, Blood to Rogers, 3 April 1971, Dacca 1078. On Americans in Chittagong, see POL 23-9 PAK, Box 2530, Schneider to Farland, 5 April 1971, State 56709.

10. POL 23-9 PAK, Box 2530, Blood to Rogers, 27 March 1971, Dacca 953. POL 23-9 PAK, Box 2530, Blood to Rogers, 1 April 1971, Dacca 1040; POL 23-9 PAK, Box 2530, Blood to Bennett, 2 April 1971, Dacca 1064; POL 23-9 PAK, Box 2530, Blood to Rogers, 5 April 1971, Dacca 1118; POL 23-9 PAK, Box 2530, Blood to Rogers, 6 April 1971, Dacca 1149. See POL 23-9 PAK, Box 2530, Luppi to Farland, 1 April 1971, Karachi 685. *FRUS*, vol. E-7, Blood to Rogers, 10 April 1971, Dacca 1249.

11. See Archer K. Blood, *The Cruel Birth of Bangladesh: Memoirs of an American Diplomat* (Dacca: University Press of Bangladesh, 2002), p. 239.

12. Ibid., p. xvi.

13. POL 23-9 PAK, Box 2530, Blood to Rogers, 2 April 1971, Dacca 1067. POL 23-9 PAK, Box 2530, Blood to Rogers, 2 April 1971, Dacca 1052.

14. G. W. Choudhury, *The Last Days of United Pakistan* (Bloomington: Indiana University Press, 1974), p. 190. A. A. K. Niazi, *The Betrayal of East Pakistan* (Karachi: Oxford University Press, 1998), pp. 45–46.

15. Government of Pakistan, *The Report of the Hamoodur Rehman Commission of Inquiry into the 1971 War* (Lahore: Vanguard, 2001), p. 317. On rape in Bangladesh, see Susan Brownmiller, *Against Our Will: Men, Women, and Rape* (New York: Simon & Schuster, 1975), pp. 78–86, and Bina D'Costa, *Nationbuilding, Gender, and War Crimes in South Asia* (New York: Routledge, 2011). See also Elisabeth Jean Wood, "Variation in Sexual Violence

During War," *Politics and Society,* vol. 34, no. 3 (September 2006), pp. 307–42; Elisabeth Jean Wood, "Armed Groups and Sexual Violence," *Politics and Society,* vol. 37, no. 1 (March 2009), pp. 131–61. *Report of the Hamoodur Rehman Commission,* pp. 509–10 (punctuation corrected).

16. POL 23-9 PAK, Box 2530, Blood to Rogers, 29 March 1971, Dacca 978. See POL 23-9 PAK, Box 2530, Blood to Rogers, 29 March 1971, Dacca 973. On the difficulties of documenting genocide, see Samantha Power, *"A Problem from Hell": America and the Age of Genocide* (New York: Basic Books, 2002), p. 504. POL 23-9 PAK, Box 2530, Bell to Shakespeare, 8 April 1971, Dacca 1183. POL 23-9 PAK, Box 2530, Blood to Rogers, 29 March 1981, Dacca 964. POL 23-9 PAK, Box 2530, Blood to Rogers, 29 March 1971, Dacca 978. See POL 23-9 PAK, Box 2530, Blood to Rogers, 29 March 1971, Dacca 973.

17. POL 23-9 PAK, Box 2530, Blood to Rogers, 31 March 1971, Dacca 1010.

18. POL 23-9 PAK, Box 2530, Blood to Rogers, 2 April 1971, Dacca 1066. POL 23-9 PAK, Box 2531, Bell to Shakespeare, 12 April 1971, Dacca 1271. POL 23-9 PAK, Box 2530, Blood to Rogers, 2 April 1971, Dacca 1066. POL 23-9 PAK, Box 2530, Bell to Shakespeare, 2 April 1971, Dacca 1058.

19. POL 23-9 PAK, Box 2530, Bell to Shakespeare, 1 April 1971, Dacca 1037. See POL 23-9 PAK, Box 2530, Keating to Rogers, 2 April 1971, New Delhi 4864.

20. POL 23-9 PAK, Box 2530, Blood to Rogers, 3 April 1971, Dacca 1087. See POL 23-9 PAK, Box 2530, Blood to Rogers, 3 April 1971, Dacca 1088, and POL 23-9 PAK, Box 2530, Blood to Rogers, 6 April 1971, Dacca 1144. POL 23-9 PAK, Box 2530, Blood to Rogers, 5 April 1971, Dacca 1128. POL 23-9 PAK, Box 2530, Bell to Shakespeare, 5 April 1971, Dacca 1126. POL 23-9 PAK, Box 2530, Blood to Farland, 4 April 1971, Dacca 1107. See POL 23-9 PAK, Box 2530, Gordon to Rogers, 8 April 1971, Calcutta 596; POL 23-9 PAK, Box 2531, Bell to Shakespeare, 10 April 1971, Dacca 1236; POL 23-9 PAK, Box 2531, Blood to Rogers, 10 April 1971, Dacca 1246; POL 23-9 PAK, Box 2531, Greene to Rogers, London 3222.

21. Desaix Myers, "Ki Korbo?" n.d. 1971, on file with author.

22. POL 23-9 PAK, Box 2530, Blood to Rogers, 31 March 1971, Dacca 1007. See POL 23-9 PAK, Box 2530, Rogers to Nixon, 3 April 1971, and POL 23-9 PAK, Box 2530, Sisco to Rogers, 2 April 1971. For a dismissive account, see POL 23-9 PAK, Box 2530, Spengler to Strausz-Hupé, 31 March 1971, State 53712. This death toll was roughly the same number murdered at Srebrenica, in Bosnia, in July 1995, although Dacca had a population of 1.5 million, far more than Srebrenica. (David Rohde, *Endgame: The Betrayal and Fall of Srebrenica, Europe's Worst Massacre Since World War II* [New York: Farrar, Straus & Giroux, 1997].)

23. NSC Files, Box 625, Country Files—Middle East, Pakistan, vol. IV, Saunders and Hoskinson to Kissinger, 1 April 1971 (emphasis removed).

24. POL 23-9 PAK, Box 2530, Blood to Rogers, 28 March 1971, Dacca 959. POL 23-9 PAK, Box 2530, Smith to Farland, 2 April 1971, State 56154; Blood, *Cruel Birth,* pp. 214–15. NSC Files, Box 574, Indo-Pak War, South Asian Military Supply, Kennedy statement, 1 April 1971. Reuters story, 1 April 1971, in POL 23-9 PAK, Box 2530, Fuller to Blood, 2 April 1971, State 55459; POL 23-9 PAK, Box 2530, Spengler to Blood, 2 April 1971, State 56532.

25. Blood, *Cruel Birth,* p. 215. POL 23-9 PAK, Box 2530, Farland to Keating,

31 March 1971, Islamabad 2906. POL 23-9 PAK, Box 2530, Keating to Far-land, 31 March 1971, New Delhi 4687.

26. NSA, Kissinger to Nixon, 7 May 1971. Farland blamed Keating too (POL 23-9 PAK, Box 2530, Farland to Rogers, 4 April 1971, Islamabad 3133).

27. Myers, "Ki Korbo?"

28. Hannah Gurman, *The Dissent Papers: The Voices of Diplomats in the Cold War and Beyond* (New York: Columbia University Press, 2012), pp. 169–98. Hannah Gurman, "The Other Plumbers Unit," *Diplomatic History,* vol. 35, no. 2 (April 2011), pp. 321–49.

29. In April 1970, twenty Foreign Service officers had written to Rogers to pro-test Nixon's decision to invade Cambodia (Gurman, *Dissent Papers,* p. 171). Blood was not the only person to suffer retribution for a dissent cable. In 1977, H. Allen Harris was blocked for promotion after speaking up over Argentine human rights abuses (Gurman, "Other Plumbers Unit," p. 341). In the 1990s, diplomats protested U.S. policy toward Bosnia, and some resigned (Power, *"A Problem from Hell,"* pp. 296–304, 312–18).

30. David Halberstam, *The Best and the Brightest* (New York: Ballantine, 1993), p. 281; and see pp. 132, 175, 179–80, 187–88, 258, 581, 596.

31. Blood, *Cruel Birth,* pp. 243–44.

32. POL 1 PAK-US, Box 2535, Blood to Rogers, 6 April 1971, Dacca 1138; NSC Files, Box 138, Kissinger Office Files, Country Files—Middle East, Blood to Rogers, 6 April 1971, Dacca 1138. Blood, *Cruel Birth,* p. 243.

33. POL 1 PAK-US, Box 2535, Blood to Rogers, 6 April 1971, Dacca 1138. The signatories were Brian Bell, Robert L. Bourquein, W. Scott Butcher, Eric Griffel, Zachary M. Hahn, Jake Harshbarger, Robert A. Jackson, Lawrence Koegel, Joseph A. Malpeli, Willard D. McCleary, Desaix Myers, John L. Nesvig, William Grant Parr, Robert Carle (misspelled as Carce), Rich-ard L. Simpson, Robert C. Simpson, Richard E. Suttor, Wayne A. Sweden-burg, Richard L. Wilson, and Shannon W. Wilson.

34. Blood, *Cruel Birth,* pp. 243–44. Later Blood would only regret the line about insufficient effort at protecting American civilians. POL 1 PAK-US, Box 2535, Blood to Rogers, 6 April 1971, Dacca 1138.

35. POL 1 PAK-US, Box 2535, Baxter et al. to Rogers, 6 April 1971, State 7105326. These signatories were Craig Baxter (see his *Bangladesh: From a Nation to a State* [Boulder, Colo.: Westview, 1997]), A. Peter Burleigh, Townsend S. Swayze, Joel M. Woldman, Anthony C. E. Quainton, How-ard B. Schaffer, Douglas M. Cochran, John Eaves Jr., and Robert A. Flaten. Blood, *Cruel Birth,* p. 248.

36. Blood, *Cruel Birth,* p. 244. NSA, Rogers-Kissinger telcon, 6 April 1971, 9:35 a.m.

37. NSA, Rogers-Kissinger telcon, 6 April 1971, 9:35 a.m. Kissinger referred to a photograph of a Bengali holding a severed head—a gruesome image that the *New York Times* had run over a story that actually described a West Pakistani "surprise attack with tanks, artillery and heavy machine guns against a virtually unarmed population" (Sydney H. Schanberg, "'All Part of a Game'—a Grim and Deadly One," *New York Times,* 4 April 1971).

38. Roger Morris, *Uncertain Greatness: Henry Kissinger and American Foreign Policy* (New York: Harper & Row, 1977), pp. 219–20. Blood, *Cruel Birth,* p. 248.

39. POL 1 PAK-US, Box 2535, Blood to Rogers, 6 April 1971, Dacca 1138. Henry

Kissinger, *White House Years* (Boston: Little, Brown, 1979), p. 853. NSC Files, Box 138, Kissinger Office Files, Country Files—Middle East, Rogers to Blood, 7 April 1971, State 58039; NSC Files, Box 625, Country Files—Middle East, Pakistan, vol. IV, Rogers to Blood, 7 April 1971, State 58039; POL 23-9 PAK, Box 2530, Rogers to Blood, 7 April 1971, State 58039. NSC Files, Box 138, Kissinger Office Files, Country Files—Middle East, Farland to Sisco, 6 April 1971, Islamabad 3196. NSC Files, Box 625, Country Files—Middle East, Pakistan, vol. IV, Farland to Sisco, 6 April 1971, Islamabad 3196.

40. POL 23-9 PAK, Box 2530, Van Hollen to Farland, 6 April 1971, State 58038. POL 23-9 PAK, Box 2530, Sisco to Farland, 7 April 1971, State 59106. Benjamin Welles, "U.S. Urges Pakistan Seek Peaceful Accommodation," *New York Times,* 8 April 1971, p. A3. See POL 23-9 PAK, Box 2531, Blood to Rogers, 10 April 1971, Dacca 1232; POL 23-9 PAK, Box 2530, Spengler to Farland, 8 April 1971, State 60070.

41. Govinda Chandra Dev, *Buddha, the Humanist* (Dacca: Paramount, 1969). Blood, *Cruel Birth,* pp. 207, 223. Blood said, "I think he was killed solely because he was a Hindu" (Library of Congress, Association for Diplomatic Studies and Training, Foreign Affairs Oral History Project, Archer Blood interview, 27 June 1989).

42. *FRUS,* vol. E-7, Blood to Rogers, 10 April 1971, Dacca 1249. The Genocide Convention covers the "intent to destroy, in whole or in part, a national, ethnical, racial or religious group, as such." The Awami League, as a political movement, would not seem to qualify, unless perhaps one tried to claim it was a part of the national or ethnical group of Bengalis. William Schabas, "Genocide Law in a Time of Transition," *Rutgers Law Review,* vol. 61, no. 1 (2008); William Schabas, "Genocide and the International Court of Justice," *Genocide Studies and Prevention,* vol. 2, no. 2 (2007), pp. 101–22; William Schabas, *Genocide in International Law* (Cambridge: Cambridge University Press, 2009); Paola Greta, ed., *The UN Genocide Convention: A Commentary* (Oxford: Oxford University Press, 2009); Scott Straus, "Contested Meanings and Conflicting Imperatives," *Journal of Genocide Research,* vol. 3, no. 3 (2001), pp. 349–75; A. Dirk Moses, "Raphael Lemkin, Culture, and the Concept of Genocide," in Donald Bloxham and A. Dirk Moses, eds., *The Oxford Handbook of Genocide Studies* (New York: Oxford University Press, 2010), pp. 19–41. For recent important precedents, see *Prosecutor v. Akayesu,* International Criminal Tribunal for Rwanda, 1998; *Prosecutor v. Nahimana, Barayagwiza, and Ngeze,* International Criminal Tribunal for Rwanda, 2003; *Prosecutor v. Krstić,* International Criminal Tribunal for the Former Yugoslavia, 2004; and *Bosnia and Herzegovina v. Serbia and Montenegro,* International Court of Justice, 2007.

43. Ian Talbot, *Pakistan: A Modern History* (New York: Palgrave Macmillan, 2009), p. 208. Guha, *India After Gandhi,* p. 450. Choudhury, *Last Days of United Pakistan,* p. 103. Sydney H. Schanberg, "Hours of Terror for a Trapped Bengali Officer," *New York Times,* 17 April 1971. The Punjabis were powerful in West Pakistan, but West Pakistan of course also included Baluchis, Pashtuns, and Sindhis.

44. Blood, *Cruel Birth,* p. 205.

45. NSC Files, Box H-082, WSAG Meetings, Williams to Rogers, 3 September 1971. POL 23-9 PAK, Box 2530, Blood to Rogers, 8 April 1971, Dacca 1193.

Blood, *Cruel Birth,* pp. 222–23. POL 23-9 PAK, Box 2531, Bell to Shake-speare, 19 April 1971, Dacca 1386. Lieutenant General A. A. K. Niazi replaced Lieutenant General Tikka Khan as commander of the Eastern Command in early April, but Tikka Khan was installed as governor and martial law administrator (Niazi, *Betrayal of East Pakistan,* pp. 48–49).

46. Myers, "Ki Korbo?"
47. Ibid.
48. *Hamoodur Rehman Commission Report,* pp. 415, 509–10.
49. Blood, *Cruel Birth,* p. 216. POL 23-9 PAK, Box 2530, Blood to Rogers, 8 April 1971, Dacca 1193. Blood also wrote, "Hindu genocide should increase prospect of India's aid" (POL 23-9 PAK, Box 2530, Blood to Rogers, 2 April 1971, Dacca 1067).
50. POL 23-9 PAK, Box 2530, Bell to Shakespeare, 9 April 1971, Dacca 1211. POL 23-9 PAK, Box 2530, Blood to Rogers, 8 April 1971, Dacca 1193.
51. POL 23-9 PAK, Box 2530, Blood to Rogers, 8 April 1971, Dacca 1193. POL 23-9 PAK, Box 2530, Bell to Shakespeare, 9 April 1971, Dacca 1211. POL 23-9 PAK, Box 2530, Blood to Rogers, 9 April 1971, Dacca 1214. POL 23-9 PAK, Box 2531, Bell to Shakespeare, 16 April 1971, Dacca 1338. Blood, *Cruel Birth,* pp. 217–18. *FRUS,* vol. E-7, Blood to Rogers, 10 April 1971, Dacca 1249. Blood could only point to "international moral obligations" rather than legal ones, since the United States would not ratify the Genocide Convention until 1988.
52. *FRUS,* vol. E-5, Allen to Kissinger, 13 February 1969, enclosing composite Nixon statements, 17 July and 10 September 1968. Nixon said that "geno-cide is what is taking place right now—and starvation is the grim reaper." See John J. Stremlau, *The International Politics of the Nigerian Civil War, 1967–1970* (Princeton: Princeton University Press, 1977), pp. 112–27, 289–94; John de St. Jorre, *The Nigerian Civil War* (London: Hodder & Stoughton, 1972), pp. 272–73; George A. Obiozor, *The United States and the Nigerian Civil War: An American Dilemma in Africa, 1966–1970* (Lagos: Nigerian Institute of International Affairs, 1993), pp. 22–96. For a CIA argument that the Nigerian government did not have genocidal aims against the Ibos, see *FRUS,* vol. E-5, CIA memorandum, 5 August 1969. But as Biafra's resistance collapsed, Roger Morris, Kissinger's aide, warned him, "Anything short of a strong approach to Lagos will be de facto acquiescence in some degree of genocide." (*FRUS,* vol. E-5, Morris to Kissinger, 10 January 1970.) NSA, Kissinger-Mitchell telcon, 9 February 1970, 3:35 a.m. The subject index of the Nixon White House tapes shows no other mention of genocide in this period. Power, *"A Problem from Hell,"* pp. 61–85, 151–69.
53. POL 23-9 PAK, Box 2530, Keating to Rogers, 7 April 1971, New Delhi 5091. See POL 23-9 PAK, Box 2530, Sisco to Farland, 7 April 1971, State 58813; POL 23-9 PAK, Box 2530, Keating to Rogers, 8 April 1971, New Delhi 5241. POL 23-9 PAK, Box 2530, Farland to Rogers, 8 April 1971, Islamabad 3228. POL 23-9 PAK, Box 2530, Blood to Farland, 9 April 1971, Dacca 1221. See POL 23-9 PAK, Box 2530, Blood to Rogers, 9 April 1971, Dacca 1212. POL 23-9 PAK, Box 2530, Blood to Rogers, 9 April 1971, Dacca 1209.
54. NSA, Rogers-Kissinger telcon, 6 April 1971, 9:35 a.m. See *FRUS,* WSAG meeting, 8 September 1971, pp. 395–96.
55. POL 23-9 PAK, Box 2530, Blood to Rogers, 8 April 1971, Dacca 1193.

NMML, Haksar Papers, Subject File 235, Omega report, 30 January 1972. POL 23-9 PAK, Box 2531, Bush to Rogers, 16 April 1971, USUN 970.

56. POL 23-9 PAK, Box 2530, Bell to Shakespeare, 1 April 1971, Dacca 1038. NMML, Haksar Papers, Subject File 235, Omega report, 30 January 1972. Srinath Raghavan, "A Dhaka Debacle," *Indian Express*, 30 July 2011. POL 23-9 PAK, Box 2530, Blood to Rogers, 9 April 1971, Dacca 1214. See POL 23-9 PAK, Box 2531, Luppi to Rogers, 16 April 1971. POL 23-9 PAK, Box 2530, Blood to Rogers, 9 April 1971, Dacca 1217. See POL 23-9 PAK, Box 2531, Blood to Rogers, 27 April 1971; POL 23-9 PAK, Box 2531, Blood to Rogers, 27 April 1971, Dacca 1503. See also POL 23-9 PAK, Box 2531, Bell to Shakespeare, 28 April 1971, Dacca 1515; POL 23-9 PAK, Box 2531, Carle to Rogers, 28 April 1971, Dacca 1521.

57. Blood, *Cruel Birth*, p. 250. *FRUS*, WSAG meeting, 8 September 1971, pp. 395–96. For detailed accounts of the awful suffering of the Biharis, see Sarmila Bose, *Dead Reckoning: Memories of the 1971 Bangladesh War* (New York: Columbia University Press, 2011), and Sarmila Bose, "The Question of Genocide and the Quest for Justice in the 1971 War," *Journal of Genocide Research*, vol. 13, no. 4 (2011), pp. 393–419. Bose praises Nixon for not rushing to moralistically condemn the West Pakistan side (*Dead Reckoning*, p. 72). For convincing critiques of Bose for playing down the Pakistan army's killing of Bengalis, see Srinath Raghavan, "A Dhaka Debacle," *Indian Express*, 30 July 2011, and Naeem Mohaiemen, "Flying Blind," *Economic and Political Weekly*, vol. 46, no. 36 (3 September 2011), pp. 40–52. For an exchange between Bose and Mohaiemen, see *Economic and Political Weekly*, vol. 46, no. 53 (31 December 2011), pp. 76–80.

58. White House tapes, Oval Office 477-1, 12 April 1971, 10:24–10:33 a.m. For a partial transcript, see *FRUS*, pp. 65–66.

CHAPTER 6: THE INFERNO NEXT DOOR

1. MEA, HI/1012/30/71, Chib to Kaul, 8 April 1971.

2. P. N. Dhar, *Indira Gandhi, the "Emergency," and Indian Democracy* (Oxford: Oxford University Press, 2000), p. 151.

3. MEA, HI/1012/30/71, Chib to Kaul, 6 May 1971. Dhar, *Indira Gandhi, the "Emergency," and Indian Democracy*, p. 152. NMML, Haksar Papers, Subject File 164, Haksar notes for Gandhi meeting with opposition, March 1971. See NMML, Haksar Papers, Subject File 164, Haksar, draft parliamentary statement, 27 March 1971; MEA, HI/1012/30/71, Chib to Kaul, 8 April 1971.

4. POL 23-9 PAK, Box 2530, Keating to Rogers, 27 March 1971, New Delhi 4414. See MEA, HI/1012/30/71, Chib to Kaul, 8 April 1971; POL 23-9 PAK, Box 2531, "India and 'Bangla Desh,'" INR note, 26 April 1971. POL 23-9 PAK, Box 2530, Keating to Rogers, 27 March 1971, New Delhi 4416. See Dhar, *Indira Gandhi, the "Emergency," and Indian Democracy*, p. 152.

5. POL 23-9 PAK, Box 2530, Gordon to Rogers, 3 April 1971, Calcutta 540. POL 23-9 PAK, Box 2530, Keating to Rogers, 1 April 1971, New Delhi 4756. POL 23-9 PAK, Box 2530, Keating to Rogers, 2 April 1971, New Delhi 4864.

6. NMML, Haksar Papers, Subject File 89, Dhar letter, 18 April 1971. NMML, Haksar Papers, Subject File 164, Haksar to Gandhi, 29 March 1971;

NMML, Haksar Papers, Subject File 164, Working Committee of the Indian National Congress draft resolution, 29 March 1971. Sydney H. Schanberg, "Parliament in India Condemns Pakistani 'Massacre' in East," *New York Times,* 1 April 1971, pp. A1, A6. See POL 23-9 PAK, Box 2530, Keating to Rogers, 30 March 1971, New Delhi 4591. POL 23-9 PAK, Box 2530, Keating to Rogers, 29 March 1971, New Delhi 4503. See MEA, HI/1012/30/71, Chib to Kaul, 8 April 1971; NSC Files, Box H-112, SRG Minutes, SRG meeting, 31 March 1971; POL 23-9 PAK, Box 2530, Bush to Rogers, 29 March 1971, USUN 803. See Benjamin N. Schoenfeld, "The Birth of India's Samyukta Socialist Party," *Pacific Affairs,* vol. 38, no. 3–4 (fall 1965–winter 1966), pp. 245–68; Lewis P. Fickett Jr., "The Major Socialist Parties of India in the 1967 Election," *Asian Survey,* vol. 8, no. 6 (June 1968), pp. 489–98. Peter Popham, "The Orator Who Finds Himself Miscast as a Warmonger," *Independent,* 25 May 2002. "Delhi Urged to Give Open Support to Bangla Desh," *Times of India,* 29 March 1971, p. 3. See NMML, Haksar Papers, Subject File 280, Dhar-Gromyko meeting, 4 August 1971; POL 23-9 PAK, Box 2531, Keating to Rogers, 15 April 1971, New Delhi 5646. On the Jana Sangh, see Martha C. Nussbaum, *The Clash Within: Democracy, Religious Violence, and India's Future* (Cambridge, Mass.: Belknap Press of Harvard University Press, 2007), pp. 152–85; on its successors, see Steve Coll, *On the Grand Trunk Road: A Journey into South Asia* (New York: Times Books, 1994), pp. 198–210.

7. POL 23-9 PAK, Box 2530, Gordon to Rogers, 28 March 1971, Calcutta 475; POL 23-9 PAK, Box 2530, Gordon to Rogers, 28 March 1971, Calcutta 476; POL 23-9 PAK, Box 2530, Gordon to Rogers, 30 March 1971, Calcutta 503; POL 23-9 PAK, Box 2530, Gordon to Rogers, 1 April 1971, Calcutta 519.
8. See NMML, Haksar Papers, Subject File 164, draft Lok Sabha resolution, 30 March 1971. Indira Gandhi, *India and Bangla Desh: Selected Speeches and Statements, March to December 1971* (New Delhi: Orient Longman, 1972), pp. 13–14. See POL 23-9 PAK, Box 2530, Keating to Rogers, 31 March 1971, New Delhi 4677; POL 23-9 PAK, Box 2530, Keating to Rogers, 1 April 1971, New Delhi 4755; POL 23-9 PAK, Box 2530, Farland to Rogers, 3 April 1971, Islamabad 3116.
9. MEA, HI/1012/30/71, Chib to Kaul, 8 April 1971. See MEA, HI/1012/31/71, Bakshi to Acharya, 6 April 1971; MEA, HI/1012/30/71, Chib to Kaul, 8 April 1971; POL 23-9 PAK, Box 2531, Shahi to Thant, 7 April 1971, attached to POL 23-9 PAK, Box 2531, Bush to Rogers, 19 April 1971. Pakistan's Hamoodur Rehman commission noted, "The need for protecting their independence and sovereignty is felt more keenly by the small states than by the big powers who are strong enough to safeguard their own interests." (Government of Pakistan, *The Report of the Hamoodur Rehman Commission of Inquiry into the 1971 War* [Lahore: Vanguard, 2001], p. 129.) NMML, Haksar Papers, Subject File 276, Subrahmanyam, "Bangla Desh and Our Policy Options," 4 April 1971.
10. See, for instance, NMML, Haksar Papers, Subject File 166, Haksar to Khadilkar, 17 May 1971. POL 23-9 PAK, Box 2530, Keating to Rogers, 5 April 1971, New Delhi 4952. See POL 23-9 PAK, Box 2531, "India and 'Bangla Desh,'" INR note, 26 April 1971; POL 23-9 PAK, Box 2530, Keating to Rogers, 2 April 1971, New Delhi 4861; POL 23-9 PAK, Box 2530, Bush to Rogers, 2 April 1971, airgram A-499; POL 23-9 PAK, Box 2530, Keating to

Rogers, 3 April 1971, New Delhi 4878. NMML, Haksar Papers, Subject File 165, Haksar to Gandhi, 5 April 1971.

11. MEA, HI/1012/30/71, Chib to Kaul, 8 April 1971. NMML, Haksar Papers, Subject File 164, Haksar notes for Gandhi meeting with opposition, March 1971. See NMML, Haksar Papers, Subject File 164, Haksar draft parliamentary statement, 27 March 1971; POL 23-9 PAK, Box 2530, Keating to Rogers, 1 April 1971, New Delhi 4755; NMML, Haksar Papers, Subject File 165, Haksar to Acharya, 7 April 1971; NMML, Haksar Papers, Subject File 166, Haksar notes, 20 May 1971; NMML, Haksar Papers, Subject File 203, Kosygin-Singh conversation, 8 June 1971.

12. POL 23-9 PAK, Box 2531, Keating to Rogers, 10 April 1971, New Delhi 5280. POL 23-9 PAK, Box 2530, Keating to Rogers, 30 March 1971, New Delhi 4568. POL 23-9 PAK, Box 2530, Gordon to Rogers, 5 April 1971, Calcutta 551. See POL 23-9 PAK, Box 2531, Gordon to Rogers, 23 April 1971, Calcutta 725. POL 23-9 PAK, Box 2530, Keating to Rogers, 6 April 1971, New Delhi 5030. POL 23-9 PAK, Box 2530, Keating to Rogers, 5 April 1971, New Delhi 4891. POL 23-9 PAK, Box 2530, Keating to Rogers, 5 April 1971, New Delhi 4952. POL 23-9 PAK, Box 2530, Keating to Rogers, 7 April 1971, New Delhi 5133.

13. NMML, Haksar Papers, Subject File 165, Haksar to Dhar, 7 April 1971. See NMML, Haksar Papers, Subject File 165, Haksar to Acharya, 7 April 1971.

14. Desaix Myers, "Ki Korbo?" n.d. 1971, on file with author.

15. Dhar, Indira Gandhi, the "Emergency," and Indian Democracy, pp. 154–55. POL 23-9 PAK, Box 2530, Keating to Rogers, 1 April 1971, New Delhi 4755. POL 23-9 PAK, Box 2531, Gordon to Rogers, 13 April 1971, Calcutta 638. Guha, India After Gandhi, p. 452. Shashi Tharoor, Reasons of State: Political Development and India's Foreign Policy Under Indira Gandhi, 1966–1977 (New Delhi: Vikas, 1982), p. 125.

16. PMS, 7/371/71, vol. I, "Influx from East Pakistan," 27 March 1971. NMML, Haksar Papers, Subject File 227, Dias to Gandhi, 27 April 1971. See POL 23-9 PAK, Box 2531, Bush to Rogers, 16 April 1971, USUN 970. Dhar, Indira Gandhi, the "Emergency," and Indian Democracy, pp. 152–53.

17. NMML, Haksar Papers, Subject File 164, Haksar to Gandhi, 31 March 1971. NMML, Haksar Papers, Subject File 164, Congress draft resolution, 29 March 1971. POL 23-9 PAK, Box 2531, Gordon to Rogers, 16 April 1971, Calcutta 671. India estimated twenty-five thousand refugees in West Bengal, and ten thousand more in Assam and Tripura. Independently, the Times of India put the total at 175,000. (POL 23-9 PAK, Box 2531, Keating to Rogers, 20 April 1971, New Delhi 5900.) MEA, HI/1012/30/71, Chib to Kaul, 6 May 1971. POL 23-9 PAK, Box 2531, Gordon to Rogers, 13 April 1971, Calcutta 638.

18. POL 23-9 PAK, Box 2531, Keating to Rogers, 26 April 1971, New Delhi 6254. Sukhwant Singh, India's Wars Since Independence: The Liberation of Bangladesh (New Delhi: Vikas, 1980), vol. 1, p. 9.

19. See NMML, Haksar Papers, Subject File 227, Kao to Gandhi, 13 April 1971. Tharoor, Reasons of State, p. 125. MEA, HI/1012/30/71, Chib to Kaul, 6 May 1971. NMML, Haksar Papers, Subject File 235, Manekshaw-Kulikov talks, 24–25 February 1972. Dhar, Indira Gandhi, the "Emergency," and Indian Democracy, p. 157. POL 23-9 PAK, Box 2531, Keating to Rogers, 15 April 1971, New Delhi 5646. NMML, Haksar Papers, Subject File 227, unsigned top secret note, 1 May 1971.

20. NMML, Haksar Papers, Subject File 276, Subrahmanyam to Haksar, 4 April 1971. POL 23-9 PAK, Box 2530, Keating to Rogers, 5 April 1971, New Delhi 4952. NSC Files, Box 625, Country Files—Middle East, Pakistan, vol. V, Hilaly to Kissinger, 14 June 1971. Subrahmanyam argued that India's national security would depend on the fortunes of a new Bangladesh, and that India must act decisively to safeguard the infant state's survival. See K. Subrahmanymam, "U.S. Policy Towards India," *China Report*, January–April 1972, pp. 36–53; P. R. Kumaraswamy, ed., *Security Beyond Survival: Essays for K. Subrahmanymam* (New Delhi: Sage, 2004); Rory Metcalf, "A Farewell to India's Henry Kissinger," *Foreign Policy* online, 3 February 2011; B. G. Verghese, "The Legend That Is K Subrahmanyam," Rediff.com, 5 October 2004.

21. NMML, Haksar Papers, Subject File 276, Subrahmanyam, "Bangla Desh and Our Policy Options," 4 April 1971. See Inder Malhotra, *Indira Gandhi: A Personal and Political Biography* (London: Hodder & Stoughton, 1989), p. 133.

22. Pupul Jayakar, *Indira Gandhi: An Intimate Biography* (New York: Pantheon, 1992), p. 184.

23. See J. F. R. Jacob, *Surrender at Dacca: Birth of a Nation* (New Delhi: Manohar, 1997), p. 36.

24. *FRUS*, WSAG meeting, 26 May 1971, 4:35 p.m., pp. 149–56. V. K. Singh, *Leadership in the Indian Army: Biographies of Twelve Soldiers* (New Delhi: Sage, 2005), pp. 204–5. For another version, see Jacob, *Surrender at Dacca*, pp. 181–83. Manekshaw told a similar but less grandiose version to Pupul Jayakar (*Indira Gandhi*, pp. 166–67). She puts this meeting on April 25, but she sometimes gets dates wrong by as much as a month.

25. Jayakar, *Indira Gandhi*, p. 167. Singh, *Leadership in the Indian Army*, pp. 204–5. See K. F. Rustamji, *The British, the Bandits and the Bordermen: From the Diaries of K. F. Rustamji*, ed. P. V. Rajgopal (New Delhi: Wisdom Tree, 2009), p. 317; Malhotra, *Indira Gandhi*, pp. 134–35; Singh, *Liberation of Bangladesh*, pp. 18–29. P. N. Dhar, seeking to disprove the claim that India had a plan to dismember Pakistan, has claimed that Gandhi only asked Manekshaw for his opinion, knowing what his answer would be, as a way of cooling off her hawks (Dhar, *Indira Gandhi, the "Emergency," and Indian Democracy*, p. 157). But in both Manekshaw's and Jayakar's versions, Gandhi was advocating war herself.

26. POL 23-9 PAK, Box 2530, Keating to Rogers, 2 April 1971, New Delhi 4806. NMML, Haksar Papers, Subject File 227, "Situational Report of Bangladesh Army," 5 July 1971. POL 23-9 PAK, Box 2530, Farland to Rogers, 8 April 1971, Islamabad 3228; POL 23-9 PAK, Box 2531, Gordon to Rogers, 27 April 1971, Calcutta 744; NSC Files, Box 625, Country Files—Middle East, Pakistan, vol. IV, Pavelle to Laird, 26 March 1971; NMML, Haksar Papers, Subject File 169, Haksar minutes of Kissinger meeting, 6 July 1971; NMML, Haksar Papers, Subject File 171, "Political Prospective," 18 August 1971; A. T. M. Abdul Wahab, *Mukti Bahini Wins Victory* (Dacca: Columbia Prokashani, 2004), pp. 131–33. Pakistan later tried to lure these dangerously trained men back, with a hedged offer from General Tikka Khan, East Pakistan's military governor, that those who returned to their posts would be "treated compassionately" (POL 23-9 PAK, Box 2531, Bell to Shakespeare, 19 April 1971, Dacca 1386). Library of Congress, Association for Diplo-

matic Studies and Training, Foreign Affairs Oral History Project, Archer Blood interview, 27 June 1989. NMML, Haksar Papers, Subject File 227, "Situational Report of Bangladesh Army," 5 July 1971. See POL 23-9 PAK, Box 2531, Blood to Rogers, 19 April 1971, Dacca 1388; POL 23-9 PAK, Box 2531, Farland to Rogers, 24 April 1971, Islamabad 3779. Pakistan's own Lieutenant General A. A. K. Niazi writes that "the Bengali troops had not yet mutinied" when Pakistan began its crackdown (*The Betrayal of East Pakistan* [Karachi: Oxford University Press, 1998], p. 45). POL 23-9 PAK, Box 2531, Farland to Rogers, 24 April 1971, Islamabad 3779.

27. MEA, HI/1012/30/71, Chib to Kaul, 6 May 1971. Sydney H. Schanberg, "Bengalis Form a Cabinet as the Bloodshed Goes On," *New York Times,* 14 April 1971, pp. A1, A12.

28. NMML, Haksar Papers, Subject File 89, Dhar to Haksar, n.d. 1971. NMML, Haksar Papers, Subject File 227, Dhar to Haksar, 4 April 1971 (his italics).

29. Rustamji, *The British, the Bandits and the Bordermen,* pp. 298–99. See K. F. Rustamji, *I Was Nehru's Shadow: From the Diaries of K. F. Rustamji,* ed. P. V. Rajgopal (New Delhi: Wisdom Tree, 2006).

30. Rustamji, *The British, the Bandits and the Bordermen,* p. 302. NMML, Haksar Papers, Subject File 227, "Special Assistance," 1 April 1971. The paper is unsigned, but it could well be written by Haksar.

31. NMML, Haksar Papers, Subject File 165, Haksar to Swaminathan, 17 April 1971. See B. Raman, *The Kaoboys of R&AW: Down Memory Lane* (New Delhi: Lancer, 2007), p. 9. On the R&AW and the functioning of India's intelligence agencies, see NMML, Haksar Papers, Subject File 170, "Rationalisation of the intelligence and Security set-up," August 1971.

32. NSC Files, Box 625, Country Files—Middle East, Pakistan, vol. V, Hilaly to Kissinger, 14 June 1971. NMML, Haksar Papers, Subject File 166, Haksar to Gandhi, 6 May 1971. NMML, Haksar Papers, Subject File 227, Rustamji to Narain, 14 April 1971. Rustamji, *The British, the Bandits and the Bordermen,* p. 315. See Abdul Wahab, *Mukti Bahini Wins Victory,* p. 152. Jacob, *Surrender at Dacca,* pp. 37–39.

33. NMML, Haksar Papers, Subject File 227, Kao to Gandhi, 13 April 1971. NMML, Haksar Papers, Subject File 166, Haksar to Gandhi, briefing for opposition leaders, before 7 May 1971. She gave the sum of 600 million rupees, and India in August 1971 announced a continuation of an official exchange rate of 7.5 rupees to the dollar.

34. Jacob, *Surrender at Dacca,* p. 41. POL 23-9 PAK, Box 2531, Keating to Rogers, 19 April 1971, New Delhi 5827. See POL 23-9 PAK, Box 2531, Keating to Rogers, 23 April 1971, New Delhi 6149; POL 23-9 PAK, Box 2531, Gordon to Rogers, 19 April 1971, Calcutta 688; POL 23-9 PAK, Box 2531, Gordon to Rogers, 23 April 1971, Calcutta 726. The proclamation was made on April 10, and asserted that Mujib had declared Bangladesh's independence on March 26. (H. Rahman, ed., *History of the Bangladesh War of Independence: Documents* [Dacca: Bangladesh Ministry of Information, 1982], vol. 3, pp. 4–6.) NMML, Haksar Papers, Subject File 227, "Points for the Meeting," 6 May 1971. This was probably written by Haksar. See POL 23-9 PAK, Box 2531, "India and 'Bangla Desh,'" INR note, 26 April 1971.

35. NMML, Haksar Papers, Subject File 166, Haksar to Gandhi, briefing for opposition leaders, before 7 May 1971. See NMML, Haksar Papers, Subject File 166, Haksar to Gandhi, 6 May 1971; Muyeedul Hasan, "1971:

PNH in Bridging the Security Gap," Subrata Banerjee, ed., *Contributions in Remembrance: Homage to P. N. Haksar* (Chandigarh, India: Centre for Research and Industrial Development, 2004), vol. 2, pp. 21–28. See also M. Rashiduzzaman, "The National Awami Party of Pakistan," *Pacific Affairs,* vol. 43, no. 3 (fall 1970), pp. 394–409.

36. Rustamji, *The British, the Bandits and the Bordermen,* p. 315.

37. Ibid., pp. 303–5. Jacob, *Surrender at Dacca,* pp. 41–43. NMML, Haksar Papers, Subject File 227, Rustamji to Narain, 14 April 1971. See NMML, Haksar Papers, Subject File 227, "Situational Report of Bangladesh Army," 5 July 1971. On Tajuddin Ahmad, see NMML, Haksar Papers, Subject File 227, Rustamji to Narain, 14 April 1971; Rustamji, *The British, the Bandits and the Bordermen,* pp. 300–301.

38. Singh, *Leadership in the Indian Army,* p. 206. NMML, Haksar Papers, Subject File 235, Manekshaw-Kulikov talks, 24–25 February 1972.

39. NMML, Haksar Papers, Subject File 258, Rustamji to Manekshaw, 23 April 1971. Rustamji says that the army took charge on April 30 in West Bengal, and sixteen days later in Assam and Tripura (Rustamji, *The British, the Bandits and the Bordermen,* p. 318). Jacob says he got his orders to train the rebels on or about April 22, which matches when Manekshaw made to take control of the Border Security Force.

40. NMML, Haksar Papers, Subject File 227, Kao report, "Bangla Desh," 3 July 1971.

41. Dhar, *Indira Gandhi, the "Emergency," and Indian Democracy,* p. 164. POL 23-9 PAK, Box 2531, Keating to Rogers, 16 April 1971, New Delhi 5738.

42. POL 23-9 PAK, Box 2531, Gordon to Rogers, 24 April 1971, Calcutta 729. POL 23-9 PAK, Box 2531, Gordon to Rogers, 28 April 1971, Calcutta 750. POL 23-9 PAK, Box 2531, Gordon to Rogers, 21 April 1971, Calcutta 699.

43. Sydney H. Schanberg, "Bengalis Form a Cabinet as the Bloodshed Goes On," *New York Times,* 14 April 1971, pp. A1, A12. In my interview, he said "Assam" instead of "Tripura." See Sydney H. Schanberg, "Bengalis Seeking to Regroup Their Forces for Guerrilla Action," *New York Times,* 22 April 1971.

44. POL 23-9 PAK, Box 2530, Farland to Rogers, 8 April 1971, Islamabad 3228; POL 23-9 PAK, Box 2531, Keating to Rogers, 12 April 1971, New Delhi 5311; POL 23-9 PAK, Box 2531, Gordon to Rogers, 16 April 1971, Calcutta 671; POL 23-9 PAK, Box 2531, Davies to Farland, 20 April 1971, State 67455. POL 23-9 PAK, Box 2531, Gordon to Rogers, 27 April 1971, Calcutta 744. POL 23-9 PAK, Box 2531, Gordon to Rogers, 24 April 1971, Calcutta 729. *FRUS,* SRG meeting, 19 April 1971, 3:10–4:10 p.m., pp. 76-84. See NSC Files, Box 570, Indo-Pak Crisis, South Asia, CIA Office of National Estimates, "The Indo-Pakistani Crisis," 22 September 1971. NSC Files, Box 625, Country Files—Middle East, Pakistan, vol. IV, Kissinger to Nixon, 28 April 1971. POL 23-9 PAK, Box 2531, Keating to Rogers, 12 April 1971, New Delhi 5311.

45. POL 23-9 PAK, Box 2531, Keating to Rogers, 25 April 1971, New Delhi 6171; NSC Files, Box 625, Country Files—Middle East, Pakistan, vol. V, Farland to Rogers, 22 May 1971, Karachi 1186; NSC Files, Box 625, Country Files—Middle East, Pakistan, vol. V, Hilaly to Kissinger, 14 June 1971. POL 23-9 PAK, Box 2531, Stone to Rogers, 4 May 1971, New Delhi 6741. MEA,

HI/121/13/71, vol. II, Dixit to heads of mission, 4 December 1971. NMML, Haksar Papers, Subject File 227, unsigned top secret note, 1 May 1971.

46. NMML, Haksar Papers, Subject File 166, Haksar to Gandhi, 6 May 1971.

47. NMML, Haksar Papers, Subject File 227, Haksar to Gandhi, 6 May 1971; NMML, Haksar Papers, Subject File 166, Haksar to Gandhi, 6 May 1971.

48. NMML, Haksar Papers, Subject File 166, Haksar to Gandhi, briefing for opposition leaders, before 7 May 1971.

49. Sen notes, 27 October 1971, Jayaprakash Narayan, *Selected Works,* ed. Bimal Prasad (New Delhi: Manohar, 2008), vol. 9, pp. 862–69. NMML, Haksar Papers, Subject File 89, Dhar letter, 18 April 1971.

50. NMML, Haksar Papers, Subject File 227, Kao to Gandhi, 13 April 1971. For similar assessments, see POL 23-9 PAK, Box 2531, Blood to Rogers, 19 April 1971, Dacca 1399; POL 23-9 PAK, Box 2531, Gordon to Rogers, 10 April 1971, Calcutta 618; POL 23-9 PAK, Box 2531, Gordon to Rogers, 13 April 1971, Calcutta 638; POL 23-9 PAK, Box 2531, Gordon to Rogers, 16 April 1971, Calcutta 671.

51. Archer K. Blood, *The Cruel Birth of Bangladesh: Memoirs of an American Diplomat* (Dacca: University Press of Bangladesh, 2002), pp. 271–78. NMML, Haksar Papers, Subject File 227, Dias to Gandhi, 27 April 1971. See POL 23-9 PAK, Box 2531, Gordon to Rogers, 19 April 1971, Calcutta 687.

52. POL 23-9 PAK, Box 2531, Gordon to Rogers, 19 April 1971, Calcutta 688. NMML, Kaul Papers, Subject File 19, part II, Singh briefing in London, n.d. June 1971. NMML, Haksar Papers, Subject File 166, Haksar to Gandhi, briefing for opposition leaders, before 7 May 1971.

53. NMML, Haksar Papers, Subject File 276, Subrahmanyam, "Bangla Desh and Our Policy Options," 4 April 1971. NMML, Haksar Papers, Subject File 89, Dhar to Haksar, n.d. 1971.

54. NMML, Haksar Papers, Subject File 227, Kao report, "Bangla Desh," 3 July 1971.

55. NMML, Haksar Papers, Subject File 166, Haksar to Gandhi, briefing for opposition leaders, before 7 May 1971.

CHAPTER 7: "DON'T SQUEEZE YAHYA"

1. James Mann, *About Face: A History of America's Curious Relationship with China, from Nixon to Clinton* (New York: Alfred A. Knopf, 1998), pp. 3–4. Library of Congress, Association for Diplomatic Studies and Training, Foreign Affairs Oral History Project, Winston Lord interview, 28 April 1998.

2. White House tapes, Oval Office 626-10, 30 November 1971, 11:23 a.m.– 12:03 p.m. NSA, Kissinger to Nixon, circa 12 September 1970. NSA, Kissinger-Sainteny memcon, 27 September 1970; NSA, Smyser to Kissinger, 7 November 1970; NSA, Smyser to Kissinger, 18 January 1971. NSA, Ceauşescu-Kissinger memcon, 27 October 1970. See Huang Hua, *Memoirs* (Beijing: Foreign Languages Press, 2008), pp. 222–23; John H. Holdridge, *Crossing the Divide: An Insider's Account of Normalization of U.S.-China Relations* (Lanham, Md.: Rowman & Littlefield, 1997), pp. 32–37, 39–43.

3. *FRUS,* vol. E-7, Nixon-Yahya memcon, 25 October 1970. See NSC Files, Box 624, Country Files—Middle East, Pakistan, vol. III, Nixon-Yahya memcon, 25 October 1970, 10:45 a.m. On Yahya's impressions of China, see White House tapes, Oval Office 603-1, 27 October 1971, 9:40 a.m.–12:22 p.m.

NSA, Hilaly-Kissinger memcon, 9 December 1970, 6:05 p.m. See Ji Chaozu, *The Man on Mao's Right: From Harvard Yard to Tiananmen Square, My Life Inside China's Foreign Ministry* (New York: Random House, 2008), pp. 244–45; Patrick E. Tyler, *A Great Wall: Six Presidents and China* (New York: PublicAffairs, 1999), p. 87. NSA, Kissinger-Hilaly memcon, 16 December 1970.
4. Henry Kissinger, *White House Years* (Boston: Little, Brown, 1979), p. 913.
5. NSA, Kissinger-Bogdan memcon, 11 January 1971. See NSA, Bogdan-Kissinger memcon, 29 January 1971, 12:30 p.m. Tyler, *Great Wall,* p. 88. H. R. Haldeman, *The Haldeman Diaries: Inside the Nixon White House* (New York: G. P. Putnam's Sons, 1994), 14 April 1971, p. 272. White House tapes, Oval Office 479-1, 14 April 1971, 9–9:45 a.m. See White House tapes, Oval Office 477-1, 12 April 1971, 10:24–10:33 a.m. On the Sainteny channel, see Kissinger, *White House Years,* p. 703. Haldeman, *Haldeman Diaries,* 20 April 1971, p. 275. On the Warsaw channel, see Kissinger, *White House Years,* pp. 688–93. NSA, Haig to Walters, 27 April 1971. White House tapes, Oval Office 486-1, 22 April 1971, 9:41–10:41 a.m. On the Romanian channel, see Kissinger, *White House Years,* pp. 699, 703–4. See Walter Isaacson, *Kissinger: A Biography* (New York: Simon & Schuster, 1992), pp. 333–39.
6. Kissinger, *White House Years,* p. 855. Library of Congress, Association for Diplomatic Studies and Training, Foreign Affairs Oral History Project, Winston Lord interview, 28 April 1998 and subsequent.
7. POL 23-9 PAK, Box 2531, Bell to Shakespeare, 10 April 1971, Dacca 1234.
8. Archer K. Blood, *The Cruel Birth of Bangladesh: Memoirs of an American Diplomat* (Dacca: University Press of Bangladesh, 2002), p. 278. Desaix Myers, "Ki Korbo?" n.d. 1971, on file with author.
9. POL 23-9 PAK, Box 2530, Spengler to Farland, 30 March 1971, State 53692. POL 23-9 PAK, Box 2530, Smith to Farland, 29 March 1971, State 52825. POL 23-9 PAK, Box 2530, Gordon to Rogers, 1 April 1971, Calcutta 521. See POL 23-9 PAK, Box 2530, Gordon to Rogers, 3 April 1971, Calcutta 539; POL 23-9 PAK, Box 2530, Sisco to Farland, 1 April 1971, State 55431. See James Fearon, "Domestic Political Audiences and the Escalation of International Disputes," *American Political Science Review,* vol. 88, no. 3 (September 1994), p. 581. POL 23-9 PAK, Box 2531, Keating to Rogers, 21 April 1971, New Delhi 5974. MEA, HI/1012/78/71, Jha to Kaul, 7 May 1971.
10. NSC Files, Box H–053, SRG Meetings, Rogers to Nixon, 7 April 1971. POL 23-9 PAK, Box 2531, Sisco to Farland, 12 April 1971, State 61721. POL 23-9 PAK, Box 2531, Farland to Rogers, 13 April 1971, Islamabad 3337. For another copy, see POL 23-9 PAK, Box 2531, Irwin to Bush, 13 April 1971, State 62172.
11. *FRUS,* vol. E-7, Blood to Rogers, 10 April 1971, Dacca 1249. NSC Files, Box 625, Country Files—Middle East, Pakistan, vol. IV, Blood to Rogers, 12 April 1971. There are some garbles in the cable, which I have corrected. POL 23-9 PAK, Box 2531, Blood to Rogers, 16 April 1971, Dacca 1337. NSC Files, Box 625, Country Files—Middle East, Pakistan, vol. IV, Blood to Rogers, 16 April 1971, Dacca 1337. See NSC Files, Box 625, Country Files—Middle East, Pakistan, vol. IV, Nixon-Ahmad memcon, 10 May 1971.
12. POL 23-9 PAK, Box 2531, Keating to Rogers, 12 April 1971, New Delhi 5311.

13. NSA, Kissinger-Rogers telcon, 21 April 1971, 5:45 p.m. NSC Files, Box H-053, SRG Meetings, Saunders and Hoskinson to Kissinger, 8 April 1971. Italics removed.
14. FRUS, Farland to Kissinger, 21 April 1971, pp. 87–90.
15. FRUS, vol. E-7, Blood to Rogers, 10 April 1971, Dacca 1249.
16. POL 23-9 PAK, Box 2531, Farland to Rogers, 20 April 1971, Islamabad 3570. Blood, Cruel Birth, pp. 286–89.
17. White House tapes, Oval Office 478-2, 13 April 1971, 9:30–11:13 a.m.
18. POL 23-9 PAK, Box 2531, Blood to Rogers, 15 April 1971, Dacca 1321. See POL 23-9 PAK, Box 2531, Van Hollen to Blood, 13 April 1971, State 62716; Blood, Cruel Birth, pp. 283–86.
19. NSC Files, Box H-053, SRG Meetings, Saunders and Hoskinson to Kissinger, 7 April 1971. See POL 23-9 PAK, Box 2531, Keating to Rogers, 15 April 1971, New Delhi 5646.
20. U.S. Senate, Subcommittee on Refugees, Relief Problems in East Pakistan and India (Washington, D.C.: U.S. Government Printing Office, 1971), 28 June 1971 hearing, pp. 28–29.
21. NSC Files, Box H-054, SRG Meetings, SRG meeting, Pakistan and Ceylon, 19 April 1971, Saunders to Kissinger, 16 April 1971. For 1971, Saunders explained to Kissinger, the president had already signed off on a credit of $13 million for purchasing spares, ammunition, and other equipment. See NSC Files, Box H-053, SRG Meetings, Saunders and Hoskinson to Kissinger, 7 April 1971. NSC Files, Box 574, Indo-Pak War, South Asian Military Supply, Saunders and Hoskinson to Kissinger, 17 May 1971. NSC Files, Box 574, Indo-Pak War, South Asian Military Supply, Kissinger to Nixon, 25 June 1971.
22. POL 23-9 PAK, Box 2531, Smith to Farland, 12 April 1971, State 61940. See POL 23-9 PAK, Box 2531, Van Hollen to Farland, 15 April 1971, State 64521. NSC Files, Box 574, Indo-Pak War, South Asian Military Supply, Kissinger to Nixon, 25 June 1971. NSC Files, Box 574, Indo-Pak War, South Asian Military Supply, Saunders and Hoskinson to Kissinger, 17 May 1971. NSC Files, Box 574, Indo-Pak War, South Asian Military Supply, Kissinger to Nixon, 25 June 1971.
23. Christopher Van Hollen, "The Tilt Policy Revisited," Asian Survey, vol. 20, no. 4 (April 1980), pp. 343–44. FRUS, SRG meeting, 9 April 1971, 11:15 a.m.–12:15 p.m., pp. 56–62.
24. NSC Files, Box 574, Indo-Pak War, South Asian Military Supply, Kissinger to Nixon, 25 June 1971. NSA, Kissinger-Bundy telcon, 27 April 1971, 9:05 a.m.
25. FRUS, SRG meeting, 19 April 1971, 3:10–4:10 p.m., pp. 76–84.
26. POL 23-9 PAK, Box 2531, Blood to Rogers, 17 April 1971, Dacca 1360; POL 23-9 PAK, Box 2531, Blood to Rogers, 21 April 1971, Dacca 1437; POL 23-9 PAK, Box 2531, Bell to Shakespeare, 24 April 1971, Dacca 1483; POL 23-9 PAK, Box 2531, Blood to Rogers, 19 April 1971, Dacca 1388. POL 23-9 PAK, Box 2531, Farland to Rogers, 13 April 1971, Islamabad 3362. POL 23-9 PAK, Box 2531, Blood to Rogers, 12 April 1971, Dacca 1276. See POL 23-9 PAK, Box 2531, Bell to Shakespeare, 13 April 1971, Dacca 1296. POL 23-9 PAK, Box 2531, Blood to Rogers, 16 April 1971, Dacca 1337. See POL 23-9 PAK, Box 2531, Blood to Rogers, 19 April 1971, Dacca 1399.
27. James D. Fearon and David D. Laitin, "Ethnicity, Insurgency, and Civil War,"

American Political Science Review, vol. 97, no. 1 (February 2003), pp. 75–90; James D. Fearon, "Why Do Some Civil Wars Last So Much Longer than Others?" *Journal of Peace Research,* vol. 41, no. 3 (May 2004), pp. 275–302; Stathis N. Kalyvas, *The Logic of Violence in Civil War* (Cambridge: Cambridge University Press, 2006); Virginia Page Fortna, "Does Peacekeeping Keep Peace?" *International Studies Quarterly,* vol. 48, no. 2 (2004). POL 23-9 PAK, Box 2531, Blood to Rogers, 20 April 1971, Dacca 1403. POL 23-9 PAK, Box 2531, Bell to Shakespeare, 19 April 1971, Dacca 1386. See POL 23-9 PAK, Box 2531, Bell to Shakespeare, 28 April 1971, Dacca 1515. See A. A. K. Niazi, *The Betrayal of East Pakistan* (Karachi: Oxford University Press, 1998), pp. 50–55.

28. Chuck Yeager and Leo Janos, *Yeager: An Autobiography* (New York: Bantam, 1985), pp. 306–7, 311–12.

29. Blood, *Cruel Birth,* pp. 287–89.

30. *FRUS,* Nixon-Haig telcon, 29 April 1971, p. 99. *FRUS,* SRG meeting, 19 April 1971, 3:10–4:10 p.m., pp. 76–84. See NSA, Kissinger-Bundy telcon, 27 April 1971, 9:05 a.m.

31. NSC Files, Box 759, Presidential Correspondence File, Yahya to Nixon, 17 April 1971; POL INDIA-US, Box 2369, Yahya to Nixon, 17 April 1971.

32. *FRUS,* SRG meeting, 19 April 1971, 3:10–4:10 p.m., pp. 76–84. *FRUS,* SRG meeting, 9 April 1971, 11:15 a.m.–12:15 p.m., pp. 56–62. Kissinger makes the comparison to the American Civil War in *White House Years,* p. 852.

33. For a transcript of Keating's interview, see POL 23-9 PAK, Box 2531, Keating to Rogers, 16 April 1971, New Delhi 5734. His exact quote is "We have expressed concern publicly and privately about the possible use of US arms by the military in what is going on in East Pakistan so that the phrase 'internal affair' should [not] be overdone so far as our government's statements are concerned." (His transcript leaves out "not," but it is clear from the context.) See POL 23-9 PAK, Box 2531, Irwin to Keating, 15 April 1971, State 63807; POL 23-9 PAK, Box 2531, Greene to Rogers, 16 April 1971, London 3434. POL 23-9 PAK, Box 2531, Johnson to Keating, 16 April 1971. POL 23-9 PAK, Box 2531, Van Hollen to Farland, 17 April 1971, State 65745. *FRUS,* vol. E-7, Blood to Rogers, 10 April 1971, Dacca 1249.

34. POL 23-9 PAK, Box 2531, Bush to Rogers, 20 April 1971, USUN 990. POL 23-9 PAK, Box 2531, Bush to Rogers, 26 April 1971, USUN 1066. POL 23-9 PAK, Box 2531, Bush to Rogers, 16 April 1971, USUN 970. POL 23-9 PAK, Box 2531, Armitage to Bush, 27 April 1971, State 72610.

35. Briefing Kissinger, Saunders was more circumspect, calling Farland's analysis "fairly sound" but also including Keating's "familiar views." NSC Files, Box H-054, SRG Meetings, SRG meeting, Pakistan and Ceylon, 19 April 1971, Saunders and Hoskinson to Kissinger, 16 April 1971.

36. NSC Files, Box H-053, SRG Meetings, Saunders and Hoskinson to Kissinger, 7 April 1971. NSC Files, Box H-054, SRG Meetings, SRG meeting, Pakistan and Ceylon, 19 April 1971, Saunders to Kissinger, 16 April 1971. See NSC Files, Box H-054, SRG Meetings, SRG meeting, Pakistan and Ceylon, 19 April 1971, Sisco to Kissinger, 16 April 1971. *FRUS,* SRG meeting, 19 April 1971, 3:10–4:10 p.m., pp. 76–84.

37. NSC Files, Box H-054, SRG Meetings, SRG meeting, Pakistan and Ceylon, 19 April 1971, Sisco to Kissinger, 16 April 1971. NSC Files, Box 625, Country Files—Middle East, Pakistan, vol. IV, Saunders to Kissinger, 19 April

1971. His italics. NSC Files, Box H-054, SRG Meetings, SRG meeting, Pakistan and Ceylon, 19 April 1971, Kennedy, Saunders, and Hoskinson to Kissinger, 16 April 1971.
38. *FRUS,* SRG meeting, 9 April 1971, 11:15 a.m.–12:15 p.m., pp. 56–62. *FRUS,* SRG meeting, 19 April 1971, 3:10–4:10 p.m., pp. 76–84.
39. NSC Files, Kissinger Office Files, Country Files—Middle East, Box 138, Nixon note, passed by Kissinger to Hilaly, 10 May 1971. NSA, Zhou to Nixon, 21 April 1971. See Tyler, *Great Wall,* p. 92.
40. NSA, Haig to Walters, 27 April 1971.
41. White House tapes, Oval Office 486-1, 22 April 1971, 9:41–10:41 a.m. NSA, Nixon-Kissinger telcon, 27 April 1971, 8:18 p.m.
42. NSC Files, Box 625, Country Files—Middle East, Pakistan, vol. IV, Lord to Kissinger, 21 April 1971.
43. NSC Files, Box 625, Country Files—Middle East, Pakistan, vol. IV, Kissinger to Nixon, 28 April 1971. White House tapes, Oval Office 486-1, 22 April 1971, 9:41–10:41 a.m. Richard Nixon, *In the Arena: A Memoir of Victory, Defeat, and Renewal* (New York: Simon & Schuster, 1990), p. 16.
44. Robert Jackson, *South Asian Crisis: India, Pakistan and Bangla Desh; A Political and Historical Analysis of the 1971 War* (New York: Praeger, 1975), pp. 47–48. White House tapes, Oval Office 568-12, 9 September 1971, 4:05–6 p.m. NSC Files, Box 625, Country Files—Middle East, Pakistan, vol. IV, Kissinger to Nixon, 28 April 1971.
45. *FRUS,* p. 98n2. NSC Files, Box 625, Country Files—Middle East, Pakistan, vol. IV, Kissinger to Nixon, 28 April 1971.
46. Stanley I. Kutler, *The Wars of Watergate: The Last Crisis of Richard Nixon* (New York: Alfred A. Knopf, 1990), pp. 94–96. J. Anthony Lukas, *Nightmare: The Underside of the Nixon Years* (New York: Viking, 1976), p. 18. Haldeman, *Haldeman Diaries,* 28 June 1971, p. 308. See NSA, Nixon-Kissinger telcon, 23 May 1971, 2:30 p.m.
47. Haldeman, *Haldeman Diaries,* 20 June 1971, p. 303. See MEA, HI/1012/78/71, Jha to Kaul, 14 July 1971; Sam Tanenhaus, *Whittaker Chambers: A Biography* (New York: Random House, 1997), pp. 230–45, 254–73, 297–322, 438–39. Haldeman, *Haldeman Diaries,* 29 June 1971, p. 311.
48. Richard Reeves, *President Nixon: Alone in the White House* (New York: Simon & Schuster, 2007), pp. 333, 339, 349. Bob Woodward and Carl Bernstein, "40 Years After Watergate, Nixon Was Far Worse than We Thought," *Washington Post,* 8 June 2012. See Reeves, *President Nixon,* pp. 330–39, 368–69; H. R. Haldeman with Joseph DiMona, *The Ends of Power* (New York: Times Books, 1978), pp. 111–12; Isaacson, *Kissinger,* pp. 327–31.
49. NSA, Huang-Kissinger memcon, 23 November 1971, 10–11:55 p.m. NSA, Kissinger-Sisco telcon, 22 November 1971, 5:47 p.m.
50. NSA, Kissinger-Bundy telcon, 27 April 1971, 9:05 a.m. *FRUS,* vol. E-7, White House tapes, Oval Office 521-13, 15 June 1971, 5:13–5:40 p.m.
51. Farland pointedly told Washington how the British government had yanked one of its senior diplomats out of Dacca. (POL 23-9 PAK, Box 2531, Farland to Van Hollen, 16 April 1971, Islamabad 3337. Blood, *Cruel Birth,* p. 323.)
52. Blood, *Cruel Birth,* p. 289.
53. Ibid., p. 271.
54. See Kissinger, *White House Years,* p. 854.
55. POL 23-9 PAK, Box 2531, Carle to Rogers, 26 April 1971, Dacca 1492. POL

23-9 PAK, Box 2531, Carle to Rogers, 27 April 1971, Dacca 1501. Blood, *Cruel Birth,* pp. 292–93.

CHAPTER 8: EXODUS

1. See Stanley Wolpert, *India* (Berkeley: University of California Press, 1999), p. 236. Since Partition, Indian officials had complained that Pakistan was driving minority refugees from East Pakistan into India (MEA, WII/109/31/71, vol. I, Singh statement to UN Security Council, 12 December 1971). And Indian officials remembered that the communists had tried to mobilize Partition refugees in West Bengal after 1947. (Ian Talbot and Gurharpal Singh, *Region and Partition: Bengal, Punjab and the Partition of the Subcontinent* [New York: Oxford University Press, 1999], pp. 329–44; Joya Chatterji, *The Spoils of Partition: Bengal and India, 1947–1967* [Cambridge: Cambridge University Press, 2007].) There was also an eerie echo of a near war. Back in 1950, in the aftermath of Partition, a far smaller Pakistani crackdown had sent a far smaller but still large number of refugees—almost fifty thousand in Calcutta alone—streaming into India. Hindu chauvinists in India lashed out at Indian Muslims in West Bengal, many of whom fled into East Pakistan. Hindu nationalists and much of the ruling Congress party demanded war. Jawaharlal Nehru, fearing escalation and the loss of domestic progress, worked hard to defuse a possible war. He successfully resolved the crisis through a combination of showily mobilizing Indian troops while offering a pact with Pakistan to safeguard minority rights. (Srinath Raghavan, *War and Peace in Modern India* [New York: Palgrave Macmillan, 2010], pp. 150–87.)
2. NMML, Haksar Papers, Subject File 166, Haksar to Gandhi, 12 May 1971. NMML, Haksar Papers, Subject File 227, "Points for the Meeting," 6 May 1971. This report estimates one and a half million refugees. NMML, Haksar Papers, Subject File 166, Haksar to Sikri, 13 May 1971. On April 24, India reckoned there were half a million refugees (POL 23-9 PAK, Box 2531, Keating to Rogers, 25 April 1971, New Delhi 6171).
3. NMML, Haksar Papers, Subject File 227, Dias to Gandhi, 27 April 1971. See PMS, 7/371/71, vol. II, Afzalpurkar to Gandhi, 12 August 1971.
4. Manojit Mitra, "Flight from Butchery," *Statesman,* 23 May 1971.
5. NMML, Kaul Papers, Subject File 19, part II, Singh briefing in London, n.d. June 1971. NMML, Haksar Papers, Subject File 166, Haksar to Sikri, 13 May 1971. See NMML, Haksar Papers, Subject File 166, Haksar notes, 20 May 1971.
6. P. N. Dhar, *Indira Gandhi, the "Emergency," and Indian Democracy* (Oxford: Oxford University Press, 2000), p. 154. NMML, Haksar Papers, Subject File 166, Haksar to Sikri, 13 May 1971. See NMML, Haksar Papers, Subject File 227, Dhar to Haksar, 4 April 1971.
7. NMML, Haksar Papers, Subject File 169, Haksar minutes of Kissinger meeting, 6 July 1971. There had been a slow trickle of Bengali Hindus into India since Partition, with about five million coming between 1949 and 1971 (NSC Files, Box 570, Indo-Pak Crisis, South Asia, CIA Office of National Estimates, "The Indo-Pakistani Crisis," 22 September 1971). But this sudden rush would exceed that number in a matter of months. The first wave of refugees had been Muslims, but that had quickly changed. (MEA, WII/121/54/71, vol. II, East Bengal memorandum, n.d. 1971.) See also MEA, HI/1012/30/71, Chib to Kaul, 9 June 1971.

8. Narayan-Islam meeting, 8–9 July 1971, Jayaprakash Narayan, *Selected Works,* ed. Bimal Prasad (New Delhi: Manohar, 2008), vol. 9, p. 847. MEA, WII/121/54/71, vol. II, refugee statistics, 3 July 1971. NMML, Kaul Papers, Subject File 19, part II, Singh briefing in London, n.d. June 1971.

9. Dhar, *Indira Gandhi, the "Emergency," and Indian Democracy,* pp. 152–54. See NMML, Haksar Papers, Subject File 227, Dias to Gandhi, 27 April 1971.

10. POL 23-9 PAK, Box 2530, Keating to Rogers, 24 April 1971, New Delhi 6163. See POL 23-9 PAK, Box 2531, Keating to Rogers, 4 May 1971, New Delhi 6741; and PMS, 7/371/71, vol. II, Afzalpurkar to Gandhi, 12 August 1971. NMML, Kaul Papers, Subject File 19, part II, Singh briefing in London, n.d. June 1971. Sydney H. Schanberg, "The Only Way to Describe It Is 'Hell,'" *New York Times,* 20 June 1971; Sydney H. Schanberg, "West Pakistan Pursues Subjugation of Bengalis," *New York Times,* 14 July 1971. John Kenneth Galbraith, "The Unbelievable Happens in Bengal," *New York Times Magazine,* 31 October 1971. NMML, Kaul Papers, Subject File 19, part II, Singh briefing in London, n.d. June 1971. NMML, Haksar Papers, Subject File 166, Gandhi statement in Lok Sabha, 24 May 1971. Pupul Jayakar repeats this as fact (*Indira Gandhi: An Intimate Biography* [New York: Pantheon, 1992], p. 167). See also NMML, Haksar Papers, Subject File 170, Haksar to Gandhi, 8 August 1971.

11. See POL 23-9 PAK, Box 2530, Bell to Shakespeare, 1 April 1971, Dacca 1037; POL 23-9 PAK, Box 2530, Keating to Rogers, 2 April 1971, New Delhi 4864. NMML, Kaul Papers, Subject File 19, part II, Singh briefing in London, n.d. June 1971. See NMML, Haksar Papers, Subject File 280, Dhar-Gromyko meeting, 4 August 1971; MEA, WII/109/31/71, vol. I, Singh statement to UN Security Council, 12 December 1971. NMML, Haksar Papers, Subject File 227, Dhar to Kaul, 28 April 1971.

12. MEA, HI/1012/30/71, Chib to Kaul, 9 June 1971. MEA, HI/1012/57/71, Dhar to Kaul, 13 May 1971. Dhar also wrote of "the holocaust in East Bengal" (NMML, Haksar Papers, Subject File 227, Dhar to Haksar, 29 April 1971). See Shashi Tharoor, *Reasons of State: Political Development and India's Foreign Policy Under Indira Gandhi, 1966–1977* (New Delhi: Vikas, 1982), pp. 145–46. MEA, WII/121/54/71, vol. II, East Bengal memorandum, n.d. 1971. The foreign ministry also wrote that Yahya's regime was engaged in a "purge of non-Muslims from East Bengal." In a May 1971 interview with *Blitz,* Gandhi said, "Formerly it was the Pakistan Army against the Bangla Desh people—Hindus and Muslims alike. Now Hindus seem to be the target." (R. K. Karanjia and K. A. Abbas, *Face to Face with Indira Gandhi* [New Delhi: Chetana Publications, 1974], p. 66.)

13. NMML, Haksar Papers, Subject File 163, Haksar to Gandhi, 10 January 1971. NMML, Haksar Papers, Subject File 163, Haksar to Gandhi, 10 January 1971. On Vietnam, see NMML, Haksar Papers, Subject File 163, Haksar to Gandhi, Trudeau briefing, 11 January 1971. India's shifting views of sovereignty confirm the argument of Stephen D. Krasner, *Sovereignty: Organized Hypocrisy* (Princeton: Princeton University Press, 1999), especially pp. 3–42, 73–90, 105–26. See Louis Henkin, "That 'S' Word," *Fordham Law Review,* vol. 68, no. 1 (October 1999), pp. 1–14; Louis Henkin, *International Law: Politics, Values and Functions* (Norwell, Mass.: Kluwer Academic Publishers, 1995), pp. 23–44; Louis Henkin, "The Mythology of

Sovereignty," *American Society of International Law Newsletter,* March–May 1993.

14. NMML, Haksar Papers, Subject File 164, Haksar notes for Gandhi meeting with opposition, March 1971. See NMML, Haksar Papers, Subject File 164, Haksar draft parliamentary statement, 27 March 1971; POL 23-9 PAK, Box 2530, Bush to Rogers, 2 April 1971, airgram A-499, for Sen note verbale to Thant, 30 March 1971; P. N. Haksar, *Premonitions* (Bombay: Interpress, 1979), pp. 42–43; G. W. Choudhury, *The Last Days of United Pakistan* (Bloomington: Indiana University Press, 1974), p. 187.

15. NMML, Haksar Papers, Subject File 220, R&AW report, "Threat of a Military Attack or Infiltration Campaign by Pakistan," January 1971. NMML, Haksar Papers, Subject File 164, Haksar to Gandhi, 31 March 1971. NMML, Haksar Papers, Subject File 164, Haksar notes for Gandhi meeting with opposition, March 1971. See NMML, Haksar Papers, Subject File 164, Haksar draft parliamentary statement, 27 March 1971; NMML, Haksar Papers, Subject File 227, Jha to Kaul, 12 March 1971; NMML, Haksar Papers, Subject File 170, Kashmir memorandum, August 1971; MEA, HI/121/13/71, vol. II, Dixit to heads of mission, 4 December 1971. NMML, Haksar Papers, Subject File 227, Dhar to Haksar, 4 April 1971.

16. Narayan statement, 27 March 1971, Narayan, *Selected Works,* pp. 610–11. See POL 23-9 PAK, Box 2531, Bell to Rogers, 22 April 1971, Dacca 1456. POL 23-9 PAK, Box 2530, Bush to Rogers, 2 April 1971, airgram A-499, for Sen note verbale to Thant, 30 March 1971. POL 23-9 PAK, Box 2531, Bush to Rogers, 20 April 1971, USUN 990; POL 23-9 PAK, Box 2531, Bush to Rogers, 26 April 1971, USUN 1066.

17. Haksar tried and failed to persuade Gandhi to say that "the Rulers of Pakistan ought to know that the civil laws of every State calling itself civilised clearly provide that the right to do what you may wish within the four corners of your own house does not confer a right to commit nuisance or negligence affecting one's neighbour" (NMML, Haksar Papers, Subject File 166, Haksar to Gandhi, 23 May 1971). NMML, Haksar Papers, Subject File 166, Haksar to Gandhi, 12 May 1971. See NMML, Haksar Papers, Subject File 227, Dhar to Kaul, 28 April 1971. Narayan statement, 2 April 1971, Narayan, *Selected Works,* pp. 612–13.

18. Joseph Lelyveld, *Great Soul: Mahatma Gandhi and His Struggle with India* (New York: Alfred A. Knopf, 2011), pp. 33–131. Mark Mazower, *No Enchanted Palace: The End of Empire and the Ideological Origins of the United Nations* (Princeton: Princeton University Press, 2009), pp. 152–89. Nehru declared that the United Nations proved itself "a guardian of human rights" (Mazower, *No Enchanted Palace,* p. 179). NMML, Haksar Papers, Subject File 220, Heath-Gandhi meeting, 24 October 1971. NMML, Haksar Papers, Subject File 163, Haksar to Gandhi, Trudeau briefing, 11 January 1971. MEA, HI/121/13/71, vol. II, "Implications of the General Assembly Resolution," n.d. December 1971. See NMML, Haksar Papers, Subject File 171, Haksar revised draft speech, August 1971. In 1968, the Indian government pushed a draft UN Security Council resolution condemning the execution of political prisoners as a "threat to international peace and security"—the standard for justifiable intervention. India urged a reluctant Britain "to take urgently all necessary measures including the use of force" (UN Security Council draft resolution by India et al., S/8545,

16 April 1968). India, joined by Pakistan, invoked Chapter VII of the UN Charter. In 1966, for the first time, the UN Security Council invoked Chapter VII to impose mandatory economic sanctions. See J. Leo Cefkin, "The Rhodesian Question at the United Nations," *International Organization*, vol. 22, no. 3 (1968), pp. 649–69; Walter Darnell Jacobs, "Rhodesia," *World Affairs*, vol. 130, no. 1 (April–June 1967), pp. 34–44; "Danger of Using Force in Rhodesia," *Guardian*, 28 March 1968; Philip Murphy, "'An Intricate and Distasteful Subject,'" *English Historical Review*, vol. 121, no. 492 (2006), pp. 746–77; and Carl Watts, "'Moments of Tension and Drama,'" *Journal of Colonialism and Colonial History*, vol. 8, no. 1 (spring 2007). Britain and the white Rhodesian regime disputed whether Rhodesia really counted as independent of Britain (Richard M. Cummings, "Rhodesian Unilateral Declaration of Independence and the Position of the International Community," *New York University Journal of International Law and Politics*, vol. 6 [1973], pp. 57–84). NMML, Haksar Papers, Subject File 276, Subrahmanyam, "Bangla Desh and Our Policy Options," 4 April 1971. MEA, WII/121/54/71, vol. II, East Bengal memorandum, n.d. 1971.

19. NMML, Haksar Papers, Subject File 166, Haksar notes, 20 May 1971.
20. MEA, WII/125/59/71, Singh statement in Lok Sabha, 20 July 1971. NMML, Kaul Papers, Subject File 19, part II, Singh briefing in London, n.d. June 1971.
21. See, for instance, Jayakar, *Indira Gandhi*, p. 166.
22. Dhar, *Indira Gandhi, the "Emergency," and Indian Democracy*, p. 158. Tharoor, *Reasons of State*, p. 125. Surjit Mansingh, *India's Search for Power: Indira Gandhi's Foreign Policy, 1966–1982* (New Delhi: Sage, 1984), pp. 216–17.
23. NMML, Haksar Papers, Subject File 229, Haksar to Dhar, 22 May 1971.
24. Dhar, *Indira Gandhi, the "Emergency," and Indian Democracy*, p. 156.
25. NMML, Haksar Papers, Subject File 166, Gandhi statement in Lok Sabha, 24 May 1971. Dhar, *Indira Gandhi, the "Emergency," and Indian Democracy*, pp. 156–58.
26. Ibid., p. 158. NMML, Haksar Papers, Subject File 166, Haksar to Gandhi, 23 May 1971.
27. NMML, Haksar Papers, Subject File 166, Gandhi statement in Lok Sabha, 24 May 1971. See NMML, Haksar Papers, Subject File 166, Haksar to Gandhi, 23 May 1971. MEA, HI/121/13/71, vol. I, Ranganathan to heads of mission, 17 June 1971.
28. NMML, Haksar Papers, Subject File 166, Gandhi statement in Lok Sabha, 24 May 1971. Using language that hearkened back to the United Nations Charter, she said, "They are threatening the peace and stability of the vast segment of humanity represented by India." Although India had no hope that the United States or China would allow such a thing, Chapter VII of the United Nations Charter empowers the Security Council to determine if a situation constitutes "any threat to the peace" and to take steps "to maintain or restore international peace and security." On refugees as a reason for war, see Jack Snyder, "Realism, Refugees, and Strategies of Humanitarianism," Andrew Hurrell, "Refugees, International Society, and Global Order," and Adam Roberts, "Refugees and Military Intervention," all in Alexander Betts and Gil Loescher, eds., *Refugees in International Relations* (Oxford: Oxford University Press, 2011); Martha Finnemore, *The Purpose of Intervention:*

Changing Beliefs About the Use of Force (Ithaca, N.Y.: Cornell University Press, 2003); Kelly M. Greenhill, *Weapons of Mass Migration: Forced Displacement, Coercion, and Foreign Policy* (Ithaca, N.Y.: Cornell University Press, 2010).

29. NMML, Kaul Papers, Subject File 19, part II, Singh briefing in London, n.d. June 1971.

30. Ajit Bhattacharjea, *Jayaprakash Narayan: A Political Biography* (New Delhi: Vikas, 1975), pp. 7–8, 66–67, 78, 130–37, 163. Ratan Das, *Jayaprakash Narayan: His Life and Mission* (New Delhi: Sarup & Sons, 2007), p. 56. Ramachandra Guha, *India After Gandhi: The History of the World's Largest Democracy* (New York: Ecco, 2003), p. 494. For a fascinating selection of Narayan's writings, see Ramachandra Guha, ed., *Makers of Modern India* (Cambridge, Mass.: Belknap Press of Harvard University Press, 2011), pp. 368–93. See Allan and Wendy Scarfe, *J.P.: His Biography* (New Delhi: Orient Longman, 1977, 1998).

31. NMML, Kaul Papers, Subject File 19, part II, Rogers-Gandhi talk, n.d. October 1971. See POL 23-9 PAK, Box 2531, Keating to Rogers, 4 May 1971, New Delhi 6741; Dhar, *Indira Gandhi, the "Emergency," and Indian Democracy*, p. 157. NMML, Haksar Papers, Subject File 170, Haksar to Gandhi, 8 August 1971. See Narayan statement, 2 April 1971, Narayan, *Selected Works,* pp. 612–13; Narayan to Moraes, 4 April 1971, Narayan, *Selected Works,* pp. 614–15; Narayan statement, 29 July 1971, Narayan, *Selected Works,* p. 632. Bhattacharjea, *Jayaprakash Narayan,* p. 78. See Narayan statement, 16 March 1971, Narayan, *Selected Works,* pp. 608–9. Jayakar, *Indira Gandhi,* pp. 169–70.

32. Narayan statement, 18 September 1971, Narayan, *Selected Works,* pp. 648–55. Narayan-Islam meeting, 8–9 July 1971, Narayan, *Selected Works,* pp. 840–49. Narayan–Mukti Fouj meeting, 9 July 1971, Narayan, *Selected Works,* pp. 849–52. See Narayan to Kaul, 15 July 1971, Narayan, *Selected Works,* p. 628, and Narayan to Gandhi, 15 July 1971, Narayan, *Selected Works,* p. 629. See also Rahman to Narayan, 13 July 1971, Narayan, *Selected Works,* p. 853. Sen notes, 27 October 1971, Narayan, *Selected Works,* pp. 862–69. Narayan to participants, 3 September 1971, Narayan, *Selected Works,* pp. 640–41. Narayan statement, 18 September 1971, Narayan, *Selected Works,* pp. 648–55. Narayan to Radhakrishna, 24 May 1971, Narayan, *Selected Works,* pp. 620–21. Nagorski to Narayan, 11 June 1971, *Selected Works,* pp. 839–40. MEA, HI/1012/5/71, Bahadur Singh to Kaul, 14 June 1971. Sen notes, 27 October 1971, Narayan, *Selected Works,* p. 863. NSC Files, Box 596, Country Files—Middle East, India, vol. III, Saunders and Hoskinson to Kissinger, 9 June 1971. MEA, HI/1012/78/71, Jha to Kaul, 14 July 1971. NSC Files, Box 596, Country Files—Middle East, India, vol. III, Sisco to Keating, 8 June 1971, State 100740. See NMML, Haksar Papers, Subject File 225, Sen to Patel, 9 June 1971; NSC Files, Box 759, Presidential Correspondence File, Yahya to Nixon, 18 June 1971, "Excerpts from Latest Statements of Indian Leaders on the East Pakistan Situation."

33. Narayan to Gandhi, 15 September 1971, Narayan, *Selected Works,* pp. 642–48. See Ranjit Gupta and Radhakrishna, eds., *World Meet on Bangla Desh* (New Delhi: Impex, 1971); Bangladesh conference resolutions, 18–20 September 1971, Narayan, *Selected Works,* pp. 858–61; Dandavate to

Narayan, 21 September 1971, Narayan, *Selected Works,* pp. 861–62. Jayakar, *Indira Gandhi,* pp. 169–70.

34. Habib Tanvir, "The Rebel Poets of Bangla Desh," *Times of India,* 6 June 1971.

35. Joya Chatterji, *Bengal Divided: Hindu Communalism and Partition, 1932–1947* (Cambridge: Cambridge University Press, 1994), pp. 1–17. Britain had tried an earlier administrative partition in 1905. See John R. McLane, "The Decision to Partition Bengal in 1905," *Indian Economic and Social History Review,* vol. 2, no. 3 (July 1965); Yasmin Khan, *The Great Partition: The Making of India and Pakistan* (New Haven, Conn.: Yale University Press, 2007), pp. 63–80. POL 23-9 PAK, Box 2530, Bush to Rogers, 2 April 1971, airgram A-499, for Sen note verbale to Thant, 30 March 1971. Sukhwant Singh, *India's Wars Since Independence: The Liberation of Bangladesh* (New Delhi: Vikas, 1980), vol. 1, p. 16. Kissinger argued that India was "scared to death of their own Bengalis. Deep down the Indians don't really want an independent East Pakistan, because within ten years of that the West Bengalis are going to start bringing pressure on them for autonomy" (*FRUS,* 40 Committee meeting, 9 April 1971, pp. 63–65). See *FRUS,* Nixon-Kissinger telcon, 29 March 1971, pp. 35–36; NSC Files, Box H-112, SRG Minutes, SRG meeting, 31 March 1971; White House tapes, Oval Office 477-1, 12 April 1971, 10:24–10:33 a.m.

36. See NMML, Haksar Papers, Subject File 175, Haksar to Gandhi, 13 January 1972. Amberish K. Diwanji, "Arundhati Ghose," Rediff.com, 6 July 1998.

37. NMML, Haksar Papers, Subject File 165, Haksar to Dhar, 7 April 1971. NMML, Haksar Papers, Subject File 227, Sen to Gandhi, 30 March 1971.

38. NMML, Haksar Papers, Subject File 164, Haksar to Gandhi, 31 March 1971; NMML, Haksar Papers, Subject File 227, Haksar to Gandhi, 31 March 1971.

39. NMML, Haksar Papers, Subject File 165, Haksar to Gandhi, 5 April 1971. The official was Ashok K. Ray, formerly India's deputy high commissioner in Dacca. NMML, Haksar Papers, Subject File 175, Haksar to Gandhi, 13 January 1972.

40. John Saar, "Faces Emptied of All Hope," *Life,* 18 June 1971, pp. 22–29.

41. Sydney H. Schanberg, "Bengalis Ride a Refugee Train of Despair," *New York Times,* 17 June 1971. Sydney H. Schanberg, "Disease, Hunger and Death Stalk Refugees Along India's Border," *New York Times,* 9 June 1971.

42. NMML, Haksar Papers, Subject File 171, Dutt to Haksar, 23 June 1971. NMML, Haksar Papers, Subject File 171, Dutt to Haksar, 23 June 1971.

43. MEA, WII/121/54/71, vol. II, refugee statistics, 3 July 1971. See NMML, Haksar Papers, Subject File 168, Gandhi to Franjieh, draft, June 1971. MEA, HI/1012/30/71, Chib to Kaul, 9 June 1971. Dhar, *Indira Gandhi, the "Emergency," and Indian Democracy,* p. 158.

44. Dhar, *Indira Gandhi, the "Emergency," and Indian Democracy,* p. 154.

45. REF PAK, Box 3008, Farland to Rogers, 28 June 1971, Islamabad 6487. Joseph Sisco noted, "The Pakistanis don't seriously question the figures" (*FRUS,* SRG meeting, 23 July 1971, pp. 270–83). See Choudhury, *Last Days of United Pakistan,* p. 190; NMML, Haksar Papers, Subject File 166, Haksar to Kaul, 22 May 1971; NMML, Haksar Papers, Subject File 227, Dhar to Kaul, 28 April 1971; MEA, HI/1012/30/71, Chib to Kaul, 9 June 1971.

46. NMML, Haksar Papers, Subject File 171, Patel to Haksar, 20 July 1971; NMML, Haksar Papers, Subject File 171, World Bank report, 8 July 1971. There is another copy in U.S. Senate, Subcommittee on Refugees, *Relief Problems in East Pakistan and India* (Washington, D.C.: U.S. Government Printing Office, 1971), pp. 211–26. The World Bank team spent twelve days in East Pakistan in early June. See NMML, Haksar Papers, Subject File 225, Sen to Patel, 9 June 1971; NMML, Haksar Papers, Subject File 168, B. R. Patel to I. G. Patel, 18 June 1971.

47. NMML, Haksar Papers, Subject File 169, "Report on the visit of Border Areas of Assam, Meghalaya and Tripura," 7 July 1971. See PMS, 7/371/71, vol. II, Afzalpurkar to Gandhi, 12 August 1971.

48. Robert McNamara, at the World Bank, once suggested that India was deliberately making the conditions bad in order to stem the tide of refugees (NSA, Kissinger-McNamara telcon, 13 August 1971, 8:40 a.m.). I found no Indian documentary evidence to back this up, although given the state of Indian archives, this does not definitively refute the allegation. Perhaps more to the point, even if India had done everything it could, the camps would still have been miserable. PMS, 7/371/71, vol. II, Gandhi note, 16 June 1971. See PMS, 7/371/71, vol. II, Mishra to Gandhi, n.d. June 1971. PMS, 7/371/71, vol. II, National Federation of Indian Women to Gandhi, 14 July 1971. NMML, Haksar Papers, Subject File 169, "Report on the visit of Border Areas of Assam, Meghalaya and Tripura," 7 July 1971.

49. PMS, 7/371/71, vol. II, National Federation of Indian Women to Gandhi, 14 July 1971. NMML, Haksar Papers, Subject File 169, "Report on the visit of Border Areas of Assam, Meghalaya and Tripura," 7 July 1971. See Dhar, *Indira Gandhi, the "Emergency," and Indian Democracy,* p. 156.

50. Richard Sisson and Leo E. Rose, *War and Secession: Pakistan, India, and the Creation of Bangladesh* (Berkeley: University of California Press, 1990), p. 153. See PMS, 7/371/71, vol. II, National Federation of Indian Women to Gandhi, 14 July 1971. NMML, Haksar Papers, Subject File 169, "Report on the visit of Border Areas of Assam, Meghalaya and Tripura," 7 July 1971. See NMML, Haksar Papers, Subject File 168, Action Committee for the People's Republic of Bangla Desh appeal, 24 June 1971.

CHAPTER 9: INDIA ALONE

1. Roderick MacFarquhar and Michael Schoenhals, *Mao's Last Revolution* (Cambridge, Mass.: Belknap Press of Harvard University Press, 2006), pp. 222–23. For a superb history of Nehru's diplomacy in this period, see Srinath Raghavan, *War and Peace in Modern India: A Strategic History of the Nehru Years* (New York: Palgrave Macmillan, 2010). See John W. Garver, *Protracted Contest: Sino-Indian Rivalry in the Twentieth Century* (Seattle: University of Washington Press, 2001). MEA, HI/1012/14/71, Mishra to Kaul, 7 May 1971.

2. NMML, Haksar Papers, Subject File 220, Heath-Gandhi conversation, 24 October 1971. See NMML, Haksar Papers, Subject File 165, Haksar to Dhar, 7 April 1971. NMML, Haksar Papers, Subject File 220, R&AW report, "Threat of a Military Attack or Infiltration Campaign by Pakistan," January 1971. See POL 23-9 PAK, Box 2530, Keating to Rogers, 8 April 1971, New Delhi 5242; POL 23-9 PAK, Box 2531, Farland to Rogers, 19 April 1971, Islamabad 3523. NMML, Haksar Papers, Subject File 220, R&AW report,

"Threat of a Military Attack or Infiltration Campaign by Pakistan," January 1971. NMML, Haksar Papers, Subject File 170, "Rationalisation of the intelligence and Security set-up," August 1971.

3. NMML, Haksar Papers, Subject File 227, Dhar to Kaul, 4 April 1971. POL 23-9 PAK, Box 2531, Zhou to Yahya, 12 April 1971, in Farland to Rogers, 13 April 1971, Islamabad 3360. See MEA, HI/1012/30/71, Chib to Kaul, 6 May 1971; MEA, HI/1012/14/71, Mishra to Kaul, 7 May 1971; POL 23-9 PAK, Box 2531, Osborn to Rogers, 12 April 1971, Hong Kong 2241; POL 23-9 PAK, Box 2531, Farland to Rogers, 13 April 1971, Islamabad 3311; POL 23-9 PAK, Box 2530, Keating to Rogers, 8 April 1971, New Delhi 5242; POL 23-9 PAK, Box 2530, Farland to Rogers, 8 April 1971, Islamabad 3237.

4. NMML, Haksar Papers, Subject File 203, Singh-Gromyko conversation, 7 June 1971. NMML, Haksar Papers, Subject File 165, Haksar to Dhar, 7 April 1971. See also note from "Shri K"—perhaps R. N. Kao of the R&AW—in NMML, Haksar Papers, Subject File 220, n.d. Kaul shared the same concerns (POL 23-9 PAK, Box 2530, Keating to Rogers, 8 April 1971, New Delhi 5242), as did a leading Bengali journalist (POL 23-9 PAK, Box 2530, Gordon to Rogers, 8 April 1971, Calcutta 598). POL 23-9 PAK, Box 2530, Gordon to Rogers, 8 April 1971, Calcutta 590.

5. NMML, Haksar Papers, Subject File 220, R&AW report, "Threat of a Military Attack or Infiltration Campaign by Pakistan," January 1971. Patrick E. Tyler, *A Great Wall: Six Presidents and China* (New York: PublicAffairs, 1999), pp. 71–73. Thomas J. Christensen, *Worse than a Monolith: Alliance Politics and Problems of Coercive Diplomacy in Asia* (Princeton: Princeton University Press, 2011), pp. 146–259. Odd Arne Westad, *Brothers in Arms: The Rise and Fall of the Sino-Soviet Alliance, 1945–1963* (Stanford, Calif.: Stanford University Press, 1998). NMML, Haksar Papers, Subject File 229, Dhar-Grechko discussions, 5 June 1971.

6. NSC Files, Box 596, Country Files—Middle East, India, vol. III, Keating-Kissinger memcon, 3 June 1971. Gandhi told this to Keating, who passed it along to Kissinger. MEA, HI/1012/30/71, Chib to Kaul, 9 June 1971. NMML, Haksar Papers, Subject File 165, Haksar to Dhar, 7 April 1971.

7. NMML, Haksar Papers, Subject File 276, Dhar to Kaul, 25 March 1971. See, for instance, MEA, HI/1012/57/71, Dhar to Kaul, 8 April 1971; NMML, Haksar Papers, Subject File 227, Dhar to Kaul, 29 April 1971; NMML, Haksar Papers, Subject File 227, Dhar to Kaul, 28 April 1971. NMML, Haksar Papers, Subject File 227, Dhar to Kaul, 4 April 1971.

8. NMML, Haksar Papers, Subject File 203, Dhar to Kaul, 3 March 1971. NMML, Haksar Papers, Subject File 227, Dhar to Kaul, 29 April 1971. NMML, Haksar Papers, Subject File 229, Dhar-Grechko discussions, 5 June 1971. NMML, Haksar Papers, Subject File 89, Kaul memorandum, 15 June 1971. NMML, Haksar Papers, Subject File 280, Kosygin-Dhar meeting, 5 August 1971. P. N. Dhar, *Indira Gandhi, the "Emergency," and Indian Democracy* (Oxford: Oxford University Press, 2000), p. 170. Shashi Tharoor, *Reasons of State: Political Development and India's Foreign Policy Under Indira Gandhi, 1966–1977* (New Delhi: Vikas, 1982), p. 106.

9. POL 23-9 PAK, Box 2530, Spengler to Farland, 3 April 1971, State 56617. See MEA, HI/1012/57/71, Dhar to Kaul, 8 April 1971; MEA, HI/1012/57/71, Dhar to Kaul, 13 May 1971; MEA, HI/1012/30/71, Chib to Kaul, 6 May 1971; POL 23-9 PAK, Box 2530, Farland to Rogers, 4 April 1971, Islam-

abad 3126; and POL 23-9 PAK, Box 2530, Keating to Rogers, 6 April 1971, New Delhi 5053. NMML, Haksar Papers, Subject File 227, Dhar to Kaul, 4 April 1971. See NMML, Haksar Papers, Subject File 89, Dhar letter, 18 April 1971; NMML, Haksar Papers, Subject File 227, Dhar to Haksar, 29 April 1971; NMML, Haksar Papers, Subject File 227, Dhar to Kaul, 28 April 1971; MEA, HI/1012/57/71, Dhar to Kaul, 13 May 1971; MEA, HI/1012/57/71, Dhar to Kaul, 15 June 1971. For unhappy U.S. responses, see POL 23-9 PAK, Box 2530, Blood to Rogers, 5 April 1971, Dacca 1118; and POL 23-9 PAK, Box 2530, Keating to Sisco, 5 April 1971, Calcutta 553.

10. NMML, Haksar Papers, Subject File 165, Haksar to Dhar, 7 April 1971. NMML, Haksar Papers, Subject File 89, Dhar letter, 18 April 1971. NMML, Haksar Papers, Subject File 165, Kosygin to Gandhi, 14 April 1971, in NMML, Haksar Papers, Subject File 165, Haksar to Dhar, 15 April 1971. See POL 23-9 PAK, Box 2531, Beam to Rogers, 14 April 1971, Moscow 2348. MEA, HI/1012/57/71, Dhar to Kaul, 13 May 1971. NMML, Haksar Papers, Subject File 89, Dhar letter, 18 April 1971. NMML, Haksar Papers, Subject File 165, Haksar to Dhar, 15 April 1971.

11. The Indians had requested 110 T-55 battle tanks. The Soviets put up fifty-five, half of them coming only by the end of the year. (NMML, Haksar Papers, Subject File 276, Dhar-Sidorovich meeting, 22 March 1971. NMML, Haksar Papers, Subject File 276, Dhar to Kaul, 25 March 1971.) The Soviet Union had already pledged fifty armored personnel carriers to be delivered to India by mid-September, as well as forty thousand artillery rounds; Dhar requested thirty-five more armored personnel carriers and fifty thousand more artillery rounds. (NMML, Haksar Papers, Subject File 229, Dhar-Grechko discussions, 5 June 1971. NMML, Haksar Papers, Subject File 89, Kaul memorandum, 15 June 1971.) NMML, Haksar Papers, Subject File 227, Dhar to Haksar, 29 April 1971. NMML, Haksar Papers, Subject File 165, Gandhi to Kosygin, 27 April 1971. NMML, Haksar Papers, Subject File 165, Haksar to Gandhi, 27 April 1971. The Soviet Union, while pledging to sell India much of the requested weaponry, was still holding back on bombers, maritime reconnaissance aircraft, and aircraft that could do vertical takeoff and landing from INS *Vikrant*, India's sole aircraft carrier—although the Soviet brass was not sure these marquee jets were of any particular military value. See NMML, Haksar Papers, Subject File 165, Haksar to Dhar, 28 April 1971; NMML, Haksar Papers, Subject File 227, Dhar to Kaul, 30 April 1971; Yefim Gordon, *Yakoklev Yak-36, Yak-38 & Yak-41* (Hinckley, U.K.: Midland Publishing, 2008). NMML, Haksar Papers, Subject File 227, Dhar to Kaul, 29 April 1971. See NMML, Haksar Papers, Subject File 235, Manekshaw-Kulikov talks, 24–25 February 1972. NMML, Haksar Papers, Subject File 229, Dhar to Haksar, 30 May 1971. Haksar showed this letter to Gandhi on June 1. See NMML, Haksar Papers, Subject File 227, Dhar to Kaul, 29 April 1971. On India's ability to build a nuclear weapon, see NSC Files, Box 572, Indo-Pak War, Saunders to Kissinger, 9 December 1971. NMML, Haksar Papers, Subject File 227, Dhar to Kaul, 29 April 1971. See NMML, Haksar Papers, Subject File 227, Dhar to Kaul, 28 April 1971. NMML, Haksar Papers, Subject File 166, Haksar to Khadilkar, 17 May 1971. NMML, Haksar Papers, Subject File 203, Kosygin-Singh conversation, 8 June 1971. See NMML, Haksar Papers, Subject File 166,

Stoph to Gandhi, 21 May 1971; MEA, HI/1012/57/71, Dhar to Kaul, 15 June 1971.

12. NMML, Haksar Papers, Subject File 165, Haksar to Kaul, 5 April 1971. NMML, Haksar Papers, Subject File 165, Dhar to Kaul, 4 April 1971.

13. POL 23-9 PAK, Box 2530, Bush to Rogers, 9 April 1971, USUN 902. POL 23-9 PAK, Box 2530, Bush to Rogers, 1 April 1971, USUN 835. POL 23-9 PAK, Box 2531, Bush to Rogers, 20 April 1971, USUN 984. POL 23-9 PAK, Box 2531, Davies to Farland, 20 April 1971, State 67455. POL 23-9 PAK, Van Hollen to Farland, 24 April 1971, State 70700. POL 23-9 PAK, Box 2531, Farland to Rogers, 16 April 1971, Islamabad 3509. POL 23-9 PAK, Box 2530, Farland to Rogers, 3 April 1971, Islamabad 3112. POL 23-9 PAK, Box 2531, Bush to Rogers, 16 April 1971, USUN 970. NSC Files, Box H-058, SRG Meetings, Eliot to Kissinger, "Humanitarian Relief Measures in East Pakistan," 5 August 1971. NSC Files, Box 627, Country Files—Middle East, Pakistan, vol. VIII, Nixon-Sadruddin memcon, 16 November 1971. POL 23-9 PAK, Box 2531, Davies to Farland, 20 April 1971, State 67455. POL 23-9 PAK, Box 2530, Bush to Rogers, 1 April 1971, USUN 837. Bush indelicately blamed this in part on Sadruddin being "associated with Ismaili sect" (POL 23-9 PAK, Box 2530, Bush to Rogers, 5 April 1971, USUN 864).

14. NMML, Haksar Papers, Subject File 166, Haksar to Gandhi, 12 May 1971. NMML, Haksar Papers, Subject File 166, Gandhi to world leaders, 14 May 1971. POL INDIA-US, Box 2369, Gandhi to Nixon, 13 May 1971.

15. NMML, Haksar Papers, Subject File 166, Haksar to Prasad et al., 14 May 1971; NMML, Haksar Papers, Subject File 169, list of heads of state, 4 June 1971. NMML, Haksar Papers, Subject File 166, Haksar to Jha, 15 May 1971. POL INDIA-US, Box 2369, Gandhi to Nixon, 13 May 1971. White House tapes, Oval Office 475-21, 8 April 1971, 1:12–2 p.m. POL INDIA-US, Box 2369, Gandhi to Nixon, 13 May 1971.

16. NMML, Haksar Papers, Subject File 166, Haksar to Gandhi, briefing for opposition leaders, before 7 May 1971.

17. Indian envoys were sent to Bucharest, Warsaw, Cyprus, Oslo, The Hague, Tokyo, Kuala Lumpur, Canberra, Manila, Cairo, Damascus, Baghdad, Kabul, Tehran, Helsinki, and Luxembourg. (NMML, Haksar Papers, Subject File 169, Gandhi to Maurer, 3 July 1971; Gandhi to Jaroszewiez, 3 July 1971; Gandhi to Gokhale, July 1971; Gandhi to Borten, 15 July 1971; NMML, Haksar Papers, Subject File 168, Gandhi to de Jong, 3 June 1971; Gandhi to Sato, 4 June 1971; Gandhi to McMahon, 4 June 1971; Gandhi to Marcos, 4 June 1971; Gandhi to Sadat, draft, n.d. June 1971; Gandhi to Assad, draft, n.d. June 1971; Gandhi to Bakr, draft, n.d. June 1971; Gandhi to Zahir, draft, 24 June 1971; Gandhi to Pahlavi, draft, 24 June 1971; NMML, Haksar Papers, Subject File 169, Gandhi draft, 15 July 1971.) By the eve of the war, India had sent missions to the United States, the Soviet Union, West Germany, Britain, France, Canada, Indonesia, Nepal, Ceylon, Lebanon, Syria, Egypt, Yugoslavia, Czechoslovakia, Bulgaria, East Germany, Japan, Australia, Malaysia, Thailand, Sweden, Hungary, Austria, Italy, Afghanistan, Iran, Poland, Romania, Sudan, Libya, Tunisia, Morocco, Algeria, Switzerland, Denmark, Kuwait, Saudi Arabia, both Yemens, Jordan, Zambia, Tanzania, Kenya, Ethiopia, Burundi, Somalia, Uganda, Sierra Leone, Ghana, Congo, Senegal, Guinea, Nigeria, Brazil, Ecuador, Argentina, Chile, Peru, Venezu-

ela, Nicaragua, Mexico, Cuba, Guyana, Trinidad, Jamaica, and Panama. (MEA, HI/121/13/71, vol. I, Dixit to heads of mission, 29 October 1971.) See NMML, Haksar Papers, Subject File 166, Gandhi to Kreisky (draft), May 1971. NMML, Haksar Papers, Subject File 168, Haksar to Singh, 29 June 1971. NMML, Haksar Papers, Subject File 168, Haksar to Singh, 3 June 1971. See NMML, Haksar Papers, Subject File 168, Haksar to Singh, 3 June 1971; NMML, Haksar Papers, Subject File 168, Haksar to Mani, 1 June 1971; NMML, Haksar Papers, Subject File 168, Haksar to Singh, 29 June 1971; NMML, Haksar Papers, Subject File 168, Haksar to Mani, 1 June 1971.

18. NMML, Haksar Papers, Subject File 227, Dhar to Haksar, 4 April 1971. MEA, HI/121/13/71, vol. I, Singh to heads of mission, 15 May 1971. NMML, Kaul Papers, Subject File 19, part II, Singh briefing in London, n.d. June 1971. NMML, Haksar Papers, Subject File 229, Choudhury to Syed Nazrul Islam, July 1971. For more Indian publicity, see MEA, HI/121/13/71, vol. I, Ranganathan to heads of mission, 17 June 1971. NMML, Haksar Papers, Subject File 169, "Report on the visit of Border Areas of Assam, Meghalaya and Tripura," 7 July 1971. See NMML, Haksar Papers, Subject File 168, Action Committee for the People's Republic of Bangla Desh appeal, 24 June 1971.

19. NMML, Kaul Papers, Subject File 19, part II, Singh briefing in London, n.d. June 1971.

20. NMML, Haksar Papers, Subject File 203, Singh-Gromyko conversation, 7 June 1971. NMML, Haksar Papers, Subject File 203, Gromyko-Singh conversation, 8 June 1971. See NMML, Haksar Papers, Subject File 229, Dhar-Grechko discussions, 5 June 1971; NMML, Haksar Papers, Subject File 89, Kaul memorandum, 15 June 1971. NMML, Kaul Papers, Subject File 19, part II, Singh briefing in London, n.d. June 1971. NMML, Haksar Papers, Subject File 203, Kosygin-Singh conversation, 8 June 1971. See NMML, Haksar Papers, Subject File 89, Kaul memorandum, 15 June 1971. NMML, Haksar Papers, Subject File 203, Dhar to Kaul, 8 June 1971. See MEA, HI/1012/57/71, Purushottam to Kaul, 9 July 1971. India had been worried that the Soviet Union was warming up to Pakistan (Richard Sisson and Leo E. Rose, *War and Secession: Pakistan, India, and the Creation of Bangladesh* [Berkeley: University of California Press, 1990], pp. 196–98), but this was now overtaken by events.

21. NMML, Haksar Papers, Subject File 168, Haksar to Ministry of External Affairs, 25 June 1971. The education minister, Siddhartha Shankar Ray, became chief minister of West Bengal and later wound up as India's ambassador in Washington. ("Ray, Bengal's Last Aristocrat Politician, Departs," *Times of India,* 7 November 2010.)

22. MEA, HI/121/13/71, vol. I, Dixit to heads of mission, 26 October 1971. Pant's tour took him to Guyana, Trinidad and Tobago, Jamaica, Panama, Nicaragua, Cuba, and Mexico, from September 6 to 21.

23. NMML, Kaul Papers, Subject File 19, part II, Singh briefing in London, n.d. June 1971. NMML, Haksar Papers, Subject File 168, Heath to Gandhi, 27 May 1971. NMML, Haksar Papers, Subject File 171, Chatterjee to Narendra Singh, 6 July 1971.

24. MEA, HI/1012/30/71, Chib to Kaul, 10 November 1971. See MEA, HI/121/13/71, vol. I, Gandhi press conference, 19 October 1971; NMML,

Haksar Papers, Subject File 172, Gandhi to Tito, Haksar draft, 4 September 1971. Despite this, Tito was clearly worried by India's turn to the Soviet Union (White House tapes, Oval Office 605-9, 28 October 1971, 11:23 a.m.– 12:45 p.m.). P. N. Haksar, *Premonitions* (Bombay: Interpress, 1979), pp. 95– 113. NMML, Haksar Papers, Subject File 89, Dhar letter, 18 April 1971. MEA, HI/1012/30/71, Chib to Kaul, 9 July 1971. Sen notes, 27 October 1971, Jayaprakash Narayan, *Selected Works,* ed. Bimal Prasad (New Delhi: Manohar, 2008), vol. 9, pp. 862–69. NMML, Haksar Papers, Subject File 164, Haksar to Gandhi, 31 March 1971.

25. POL 23-9 PAK, Box 2531, Thacher to Rogers, 27 April 1971, Jidda 1343. The U.S. ambassador was baffled, noting that the U.S. government "has in fact done nothing which could possibly be interpreted as interfering in Pak affairs, and in fact has resisted strongly pressures for public statements critical of Pak actions in East Bengal." NMML, Kaul Papers, Subject File 19, part II, Singh briefing in London, n.d. June 1971.

26. NMML, Haksar Papers, Subject File 220, Bahadur Singh to Arora, 19 January 1972. The Egyptian press ran some foreign news agencies' accounts of the early days of the crackdown (MEA, HI/1012/5/71, Bahadur Singh to Kaul, 4 April 1971), but by April it was downplaying the atrocities (MEA, HI/1012/5/71, Bahadur Singh to Kaul, 6 May 1971; MEA, HI/1012/5/71, Bahadur Singh to Kaul, 14 June 1971; MEA, HI/1012/5/71, Bahadur Singh to Kaul, 12 July 1971; Narayan note, 29 June 1971, Narayan, *Selected Works,* p. 625). See NMML, Haksar Papers, Subject File 89, Dhar letter, 18 April 1971; MEA, HI/1012/5/71, Shunker to Siddharthacharry, 6 August 1971. MEA, HI/121/13/71, vol. II, Dixit to heads of mission, 3 December 1971. NMML, Haksar Papers, Subject File 220, Bahadur Singh to Arora, 19 January 1972.

27. NMML, Haksar Papers, Subject File 220, Bahadur Singh to Arora, 19 January 1972. One Indian diplomat argued, with casual antisemitism, that "[t]he state of Israel is small (though energetic) but the Israeli 'nation' spreads all over the world and is powerful out of all proportion to its numbers," and would be invaluable for "propaganda" and "finance" (NMML, Haksar Papers, Subject File 171, Chatterjee to Singh, 6 July 1971). Ora Cohen, "Soltam Heirs Near End of Feud over Father's $200–300m Fortune," *Ha'aretz,* 10 December 2004. NMML, Haksar Papers, Subject File 220, Prakash Kaul to Haksar, 3 August 1971; NMML, Haksar Papers, Subject File 220, Meir to Zabludowicz, 23 August 1971. The arms maker was Shlomo Zabludowicz. Israel also reportedly funneled aid to the Mukti Bahini through an Israeli government official in Bombay (Sen notes, 27 October 1971, Narayan, *Selected Works,* pp. 862–69).

28. MEA, HI/1012/14/71, Mishra to Kaul, 17 December 1971. MEA, HI/1012/14/71, Mishra to Kaul, 7 January 1972. MEA, HI/1012/14/71, Mishra to Kaul, 4 June 1971. MEA, HI/1012/14/71, Mishra to Kaul, 9 July 1971. MEA, HI/1012/14/71, Mishra to Kaul, 3 September 1971. MEA, HI/1012/14/71, Mishra to Kaul, 8 October 1971.

29. NMML, Haksar Papers, Subject File 169, Haksar to Gandhi, 16 July 1971. See NMML, Haksar Papers, Subject File 227, Dhar to Haksar, 4 April 1971. NMML, Haksar Papers, Subject File 169, Gandhi to Zhou, Haksar draft, 16 July 1971. NMML, Haksar Papers, Subject File 170, Haksar to Gandhi, 8 August 1971.

30. See NMML, Haksar Papers, Subject File 169, Haksar to Kaul, 9 July 1971.

NMML, Haksar Papers, Subject File 171, "Political Prospective" and "A Note on How the [sic] Help the Mukti Fouj Win the Bangla Desh Liberation War?" 18 August 1971. Haksar evidently saw the report on August 18, but it was written earlier. There were hints of a possible arms supply from Yugoslavia (where the Non-Aligned Movement had been founded) and South Yemen. The shah of Iran secretly suggested a face-to-face meeting between Yahya and Gandhi, which Gandhi rejected as "quite an extraordinary suggestion divorced from any sense of reality" (NMML, Haksar Papers, Subject File 168, Haksar to Kaul, 25 June 1971). See NMML, Haksar Papers, Subject File 220, Sultan Khan to Dehlavi, 2 October 1971; POL INDIA-US, Box 2369, Sultan-Kissinger memcon, 8 July 1971. NMML, Haksar Papers, Subject File 170, Haksar to Gandhi, 8 August 1971.

31. NMML, Kaul Papers, Subject File 19, part II, Singh briefing in London, n.d. June 1971. See Sham Lal, "The Realpolitik of Charity," *Times of India,* 11 June 1971.

32. NMML, Haksar Papers, Subject File 170, Haksar to Gandhi, 8 August 1971. See NMML, Haksar Papers, Subject File 89, Dhar to Haksar, n.d. 1971. MEA, WII/121/54/71, vol. II, refugee statistics, 3 July 1971. The White House estimated that India would need more than $400 million for a whole year (NSC Files, Box 596, Country Files—Middle East, India, vol. III, Saunders and Hoskinson to Kissinger, 14 June 1971). NSC Files, Box 596, Country Files—Middle East, India, vol. III, Saunders and Hoskinson to Kissinger, 14 June 1971. A few weeks later, India said it had gotten promises of help that totaled $149 million, including $93 million from the United States, $10 million from the Soviet Union, and over $4 million from United Nations agencies (MEA, WII/121/54/71, vol. II, refugee statistics, 3 July 1971). White House tapes, Oval Office 605-9, 28 October 1971, 11:23 a.m.–12:45 p.m. NMML, Haksar Papers, Subject File 168, McMahon to Gandhi, 3 June 1971.

33. *FRUS,* Nixon-Haig telcon, 29 April 1971, p. 99.

34. NSC Files, Box 625, Country Files—Middle East, Pakistan, vol. IV, Kissinger to Nixon, n.d. April 1971. NSC Files, Box 625, Country Files—Middle East, Pakistan, vol. IV, Haig to Nixon, 29 April 1971. *FRUS,* WSAG meeting, 26 May 1971, 4:35–5 p.m., pp. 149–56. NSC Files, Box 625, Country Files—Middle East, Pakistan, vol. V, Van Hollen to Farland, 17 May 1971. NSC Files, Box 625, Country Files—Middle East, Pakistan, vol. V, Farland to Rogers, 22 May 1971, Karachi 1186.

35. NSC Files, Box 625, Country Files—Middle East, Pakistan, vol. V, Hoskinson to Kissinger, 22 May 1971. *FRUS,* Nixon-Kissinger telcon, 23 May 1971, 2:30 p.m., p. 140. POL 23-9 PAK, Box 2531, Sisco to Rogers, 18 May 1971 (forwarded in POL 23-9 PAK, Box 2531, Eliot to Kissinger, 20 May 1971). NSC Files, Box 625, Country Files—Middle East, Pakistan, vol. V, Van Hollen to Farland, 17 May 1971. NSC Files, Box 596, Country Files—Middle East, India, vol. III, Saunders and Hoskinson to Kissinger, 14 June 1971.

36. NSC Files, Box H-082, WSAG Meetings, Hoskinson and Kennedy to Kissinger, 25 May 1971. Spelling not corrected. NSC Files, Box 625, Country Files—Middle East, Pakistan, vol. V, Hoskinson to Kissinger, 22 May 1971. See Government of Pakistan, *The Report of the Hamoodur Rehman Commission of Inquiry into the 1971 War* (Lahore: Vanguard, 2001), pp. 135–36, 194–95. *FRUS,* WSAG meeting, 26 May 1971, 4:35–5 p.m., pp. 149–56.

37. NSC Files, Box 596, Country Files—Middle East, India, vol. III, Kissinger-Jha memcon, 21 May 1971. *FRUS*, Nixon-Kissinger telcon, 23 May 1971, 2:30 p.m., p. 140. Nixon, preparing wartime spin, would later say, "We are anti-aggression, as a means of solving an internal, a very difficult internal problem." (*FRUS*, vol. E-7, White House tapes, Oval Office 631-4, 7 December 1971, 3:55–4:29 p.m.)

38. NSC Files, Box 596, Country Files—Middle East, India, vol. III, Saunders and Hoskinson to Kissinger, 14 June 1971.

39. NSC Files, Box 625, Country Files—Middle East, Pakistan, vol. V, Hoskinson to Kissinger, 20 May 1971. NSC Files, Box 625, Country Files—Middle East, Pakistan, vol. V, Hoskinson to Kissinger, 20 May 1971. *FRUS*, WSAG meeting, 26 May 1971, 4:35–5 p.m., pp. 149–56; *FRUS*, Kissinger to Nixon, 7 June 1971, pp. 170–72. NMML, Haksar Papers, Subject File 168, Nixon to Gandhi, 28 May 1971; NSC Files, Box 755, Presidential Correspondence File, Nixon to Gandhi, 28 May 1971; POL INDIA-US, Box 2369, Nixon to Gandhi, 28 May 1971. NSC Files, Box H-058, SRG Meetings, Eliot to Kissinger, 21 July 1971. Sydney H. Schanberg, "Pakistani Airlift Plan Causing Concern," *New York Times*, 12 June 1971. *FRUS*, pp. 116–17.

40. NSC Files, Box 596, Country Files—Middle East, India, vol. III, Saunders and Hoskinson to Kissinger, 14 June 1971. NMML, Haksar Papers, Subject File 168, Nixon to Gandhi, 28 May 1971; NSC Files, Box 755, Presidential Correspondence File, Nixon to Gandhi, 28 May 1971; POL INDIA-US, Box 2369, Nixon to Gandhi, 28 May 1971. NSC Files, Box 596, Country Files—Middle East, India, vol. III, Saunders and Hoskinson to Kissinger, 14 June 1971. The Soviet Union gave $12 million. NMML, Haksar Papers, Subject File 168, Haksar to Gandhi, 1 June 1971. He noted that Nixon's phrasing sounded suspiciously like Heath's.

41. *FRUS*, vol. E-7, White House tapes, Oval Office 505-4, 26 May 1971, 10:38 a.m. India, because of its democratic governance and free press, had not had any mass famines since independence (Jean Drèze and Amartya Sen, *Hunger and Public Action* [Oxford: Clarendon, 1989], pp. 122, 126, 211–15, 221–25).

CHAPTER 10: THE CHINA CHANNEL

1. White House tapes, Oval Office 478-2, 13 April 1971, 9:30–11:13 a.m.

2. See Kissinger, *White House Years*, p. 849; NSC Files, Box 138, Kissinger Office Files, Country Files—Middle East, Kissinger to Yahya, 29 October 1971. See also Rick Perlstein, *Nixonland: The Rise of a President and the Fracturing of America* (New York: Scribner, 2008), p. 570.

3. Kenneth N. Waltz, *Theory of International Politics* (New York: McGraw-Hill, 1979), pp. 116–28, 166. Hans J. Morgenthau, *Politics Among Nations: The Struggle for Power and Peace*, 3d ed. (New York: Alfred A. Knopf, 1964), p. 184. Kissinger, *On China* (New York: Penguin, 2011), p. 215. See Henry A. Kissinger, *Diplomacy* (New York: Simon & Schuster, 1994), p. 729.

4. NSC Files, Box H-058, SRG Meetings, Saunders to Kissinger, "Analytical Summary," 10 August 1971.

5. NSC Files, Box 759, Presidential Correspondence File, Haig to Nixon, 7 May 1971. NSC Files, Box 759, Presidential Correspondence File, Nixon to Yahya, 7 May 1971.

6. NSC Files, Box 138, Kissinger Office Files, Country Files—Middle East, Hilaly conversation, 5 May 1971. NSA, Haig to Nixon, 5 May 1971.

7. NSC Files, Box 138, Kissinger Office Files, Country Files—Middle East, Kissinger to Farland, 14 May 1971. NSA, Kissinger to Farland, 20 May 1971. Library of Congress, Association for Diplomatic Studies and Training, Foreign Affairs Oral History Project, Farland interview, 31 January 2000. See White House tapes, Oval Office 502-12, 20 May 1971. See NSC Files, Box 138, Kissinger Office Files, Country Files—Middle East, Kissinger to Farland, 14 May 1971. Henry Kissinger, *White House Years* (Boston: Little, Brown, 1979), p. 722. *FRUS,* Kissinger-Farland conversation, 7 May 1971, pp. 106–9. See NSA, Kissinger to Nixon, 7 May 1971. On a personal note, Farland groused about living conditions in Pakistan and hoped that he could get a new posting if the China meeting went well.

8. NSC Files, Box 138, Kissinger Office Files, Country Files—Middle East, Nixon note, passed by Kissinger to Hilaly, 10 May 1971. See White House tapes, Oval Office 504-13, 27 May 1971, 2:42–4:26 p.m.; White House tapes, Oval Office 496-9, 19 May 1971, 12:57–1:30 p.m.; White House tapes, Oval Office 501-16, 19 May 1971, 1:50 p.m.; and F. S. Aijazuddin, *From a Head, Through a Head, to a Head: The Secret Channel Between the US and China Through Pakistan* (Karachi: Oxford University Press, 2000).

9. *FRUS,* Kissinger-Farland memcon, 7 May 1971, pp. 106–9. NSA, Kissinger-McNamara telcon, 15 May 1971, 10:04 a.m. NSA, Kissinger-McNamara telcon, 21 June 1971, 6:40 p.m. NSA, Kissinger-Connally telcon, 15 May 1971, 10 a.m. See *FRUS,* Jha-Kissinger memcon, 11 June 1971, 1:03 p.m., pp. 174–75.

10. *FRUS,* Nixon-Kissinger telcon, 23 May 1971, 2:30 p.m., p. 140.

11. Tad Szulc, "U.S. Military Goods Sent to Pakistan Despite Ban," *New York Times,* 22 June 1971, pp. A1, 11. Sydney H. Schanberg, "Kennedy, in India, Terms Pakistan Drive Genocide," *New York Times,* 17 August 1971.

12. NSC Files, Box 625, Country Files—Middle East, Pakistan, vol. IV, Haig to Nixon, 10 May 1971. White House tapes, Oval Office 558-10, 9 August 1971, 5:44–6:18 p.m. NSC Files, Box 759, Presidential Correspondence File, Kissinger to Nixon, 2 July 1971. NSC Files, Box 759, Presidential Correspondence File, Saunders to Kissinger, 24 June 1971. *FRUS,* Irwin to Nixon, 9 June 1971, pp. 172–74.

13. NSA, Saunders to Kissinger, 18 May 1971. *FRUS,* SRG meeting, 23 July 1971, pp. 270–83. *FRUS,* WSAG meeting, 26 May 1971, 4:35–5 p.m., pp. 149–56. See NSC Files, Box 625, Country Files—Middle East, Pakistan, vol. V, Van Hollen to Farland, 17 May 1971; NSC Files, Box 626, Country Files—Middle East, Pakistan, vol. VI, Williams to Rogers, 20 August 1971, Islamabad 8534 (the cable is signed Farland, following protocol, but is actually from Williams); NSC Files, Box 626, Country Files—Middle East, Pakistan, vol. VI, Saunders to Kissinger, 13 August 1971.

14. POL 23-9 PAK, Box 2531, Farland to Rogers, 14 May 1971, Islamabad 4655.

15. White House tapes, Oval Office 520-6, 15 June 1971, 11:02 a.m.–12:34 p.m.

16. NSC Files, Box 625, Country Files—Middle East, Pakistan, vol. IV, Nixon-Ahmad memcon, 10 May 1971. See NSC Files, Box 625, Country Files—Middle East, Pakistan, vol. IV, Ahmad-Kissinger memcon, 10 May 1971.

17. *FRUS,* Farland to Rogers, 22 May 1971, Karachi 1184, pp. 132–36. NSC Files, Box 625, Country Files—Middle East, Pakistan, vol. V, Farland to Rogers, 22 May 1971, Karachi 1187. This two cables are signed Luppi, as a matter of protocol, since they were sent from Karachi, but they were written by Farland.

18. NSC Files, Box 625, Country Files—Middle East, Pakistan, vol. V, Farland to Rogers, 5 June 1971, Islamabad 5590. See NMML, Haksar Papers, Subject File 170, Yahya to Kosygin, 6 August 1971. The bigger problem may have been the exclusion from the amnesty of those who had committed murder, rape, arson, or looting—a category big enough to be readily abused by Pakistani authorities. MEA, HI/1012/30/71, Chib to Kaul, 9 July 1971.

19. NSC Files, Box 759, Presidential Correspondence File, Nixon to Yahya, 28 May 1971, in Rogers to Farland, 28 May 1971, State 95111.

20. FRUS, Yahya to Nixon, 28 June 1971, pp. 208–9. NSC Files, Box 759, Presidential Correspondence File, Yahya to Nixon, 18 June 1971. He added, "There is no justification whatsoever for exploiting human misery for political gains." (NSC Files, Box 625, Country Files—Middle East, Pakistan, vol. V, Yahya to Nixon, 24 May 1971. See MEA, HI/1012/30/71, Chib to Kaul, 9 July 1971.) NSC Files, Box H-058, SRG Meetings, Eliot to Kissinger, 21 July 1971.

21. FRUS, Sisco to Rogers, 30 June 1971, pp. 211–12. FRUS, Irwin to Nixon, 9 June 1971, pp. 172–74. FRUS, Kissinger-Sisco telcon, 29 June 1971, 10:40 a.m., pp. 209–11. See FRUS, Sisco to Rogers, 30 June 1971, pp. 211–12. NSC Files, Box H-058, SRG Meetings, Saunders and Kennedy to Kissinger, "Analytical Summary," 12 July 1971. REF PAK, Box 3008, Stone to Rogers, 11 June 1971, New Delhi 9162. This note was from Galen Stone, the chargé d'affaires.

22. NSC Files, Box 138, Kissinger Office Files, Country Files—Middle East, Zhou to Nixon, 29 May 1971. H. R. Haldeman, The Haldeman Diaries: Inside the Nixon White House (New York: G. P. Putnam's Sons, 1994), 2 June 1971, p. 295.

23. Haldeman, Haldeman Diaries, 3 June 1971, p. 295. NSA, Nixon to Zhou, 4 June 1971. See NSA, Lord to Kissinger, 21 June 1971. White House tapes, Oval Office 505-4, 26 May 1971, 10:03–11:35 a.m.

24. See NSC Files, Box 625, Country Files—Middle East, Pakistan, vol. V, Saunders to Kissinger, 2 June 1971.

25. FRUS, Keating-Kissinger memcon, 3 June 1971, pp. 163–67.

26. FRUS, vol. E-7, White House tapes, Oval Office 512-4, 4 June 1971, 9:42–9:51 a.m.

27. FRUS, vol. E-7, White House tapes, Oval Office 521-13, 15 June 1971, 5:13–5:40 p.m.

28. Ibid.

29. White House tapes, Oval Office 611-21, 2 November 1971, 12:47–1:13 p.m. FRUS, vol. E-7, White House tapes, Oval Office 523-2, 16 June 1971, 2:58–3:41 p.m. See NSC Files, Box 596, Country Files—Middle East, India, vol. III, Kissinger to Nixon, 16 June 1971.

30. FRUS, vol. E-7, White House tapes, Oval Office 523-2, 16 June 1971, 2:58–3:41 p.m. See NSC Files, Box 596, Country Files—Middle East, India, vol. III, Kissinger to Rogers, 18 June 1971. NMML, Kaul Papers, Subject File 19, part II, Singh briefing in London, n.d. June 1971. See MEA, HI/1012/78/71, Jha to Kaul, 14 July 1971.

31. Tad Szulc, "U.S. Military Goods Sent to Pakistan Despite Ban," New York Times, 22 June 1971, pp. A1, A11.

32. MEA, HI/1012/78/71, Jha to Kaul, 14 July 1971. MEA, WII/109/13/71, vol. II, "Supply of Arms by USA to Pakistan," n.d. November 1971. See MEA,

HI/1012/78/71, Jha to Kaul, 7 September 1971. The Indian government considered options for intercepting Pakistani shipments, but ruled them out. (MEA, WII/109/13/71, vol. IV, Jagota memorandum, 26 June 1971.) MEA, WII/125/27/71, M.P.'s notices, 23 June 1971. See NMML, Kaul Papers, Subject File 19, part I, Singh-Kissinger meeting, 7 July 1971. MEA, HI/121/13/71, vol. I, Singh statement in Lok Sabha and Rajya Sabha, 24 June 1971. MEA, WII/125/112/71, Singh statement to Lok Sabha, 12 July 1971.

33. NSC Files, Box H-058, SRG Meetings, Davis to Irwin, "Military Supply Policy for Pakistan," 29 July 1971. NSC Files, Box 574, Indo-Pak War, South Asian Military Supply, Saunders and Hoskinson to Kissinger, 17 May 1971. NSC Files, Box H-058, SRG Meetings, Saunders and Kennedy to Kissinger, "Military Assistance," 21 July 1971. FRUS, WSAG meeting, 26 May 1971, 4:35–5 p.m., pp. 149–56.

34. NSC Files, Box H-058, SRG Meetings, Davis to Irwin, "Military Supply Policy for Pakistan," 29 July 1971. Since April, Pakistan had applied for licenses for military equipment worth almost $25 million, of which about $21 million was Pentagon arms sales. NSC Files, Box 570, Indo-Pak War, South Asia, Kissinger to Nixon, 3 August 1971.

35. NSC Files, Box H-058, SRG Meetings, Eliot to Kissinger, 12 July 1971. Over $18 million of that was from Pentagon foreign military sales to Pakistan, and the remaining $11 million was commercial sales, of spare parts for tanks and armored vehicles, military telephone sets, electronic spares, and aiming devices for fire control systems. One of the Pentagon licenses was for almost $3 million worth of military ammunition, although that had not shipped yet, so it could be held back. That left about $318,000 worth of ammunition. NSC Files, Box 627, Country Files—Middle East, Pakistan, vol. VIII, Kissinger to Nixon, "Military Supply to Pakistan," n.d. November 1971. NSC Files, Box H-058, SRG Meetings, Eliot to Kissinger, 12 July 1971. Of that $15 million, some $13 million was from Pentagon arms sales, and the rest from commercial arms sales. See MEA, WII/121/60/71, McCloskey statement, 27 August 1971. The export licenses were good for one year, so with every passing day there was less equipment that could go to Pakistan (NSC Files, Box 570, Indo-Pak War, South Asia, Kissinger to Nixon, 3 August 1971; FRUS, SRG meeting, 23 July 1971, p. 281).

36. NSC Files, Box 625, Country Files—Middle East, Pakistan, vol. V, Haig to Kissinger, 27 May 1971. Tim Weiner, "Alexander M. Haig Jr. Dies at 85; Was Forceful Aide to 2 Presidents," New York Times, 20 February 2010, p. A1. NSC Files, Box 574, Indo-Pak War, South Asian Military Supply, Saunders and Hoskinson to Kissinger, 17 May 1971.

37. NSC Files, Box H-058, SRG Meetings, Saunders and Kennedy to Kissinger, "Military Assistance," 21 July 1971. NSC Files, Box 626, Country Files—Middle East, Pakistan, vol. VII, Saunders to Kissinger, 1 September 1971.

38. NSC Files, Box 574, Indo-Pak War, South Asian Military Supply, Rogers to Nixon, 23 June 1971. NSC Files, Box 574, Indo-Pak War, South Asian Military Supply, Haig to Nixon, 25 June 1971. NSC Files, Box 574, Indo-Pak War, South Asian Military Supply, Kissinger to Nixon, 25 June 1971. Kissinger noted that the administration had never tried to hold up U.S. weapons already on its way to Pakistan. See also NSC Files, Box 625, Country Files—Middle East, Pakistan, vol. V, Farland to Rogers, 25 June 1971, Islamabad

6402; NSC Files, Box 627, Country Files—Middle East, Pakistan, vol. VIII, Kissinger to Nixon, "Military Supply to Pakistan," n.d. November 1971.
39. NSA, Kissinger to Farland, n.d. June 1971. NSA, Hilaly to Kissinger, 19 June 1971.
40. NSA, Kissinger to Farland, n.d. June 1971.
41. White House tapes, Oval Office 529-20, 28 June 1971, 10:23–10:51 a.m. Haldeman, *Haldeman Diaries,* 28 June 1971, p. 307. See NSA, Nixon-Kissinger memcon, 1 July 1971. Richard Nixon, *In the Arena: A Memoir of Victory, Defeat, and Renewal* (New York: Simon & Schuster, 1990), p. 16. Haldeman, *Haldeman Diaries,* 10 July 1971, p. 317; 8 July 1971, p. 316.
42. NSC Files, Box 138, Kissinger Office Files, Country Files—Middle East, Farland to Kissinger, 19 May 1971. NSA, Farland to Kissinger, 22 May 1971.

CHAPTER 11: THE EAST IS RED

1. MEA, WII/121/54/71, vol. I, Viets to Sutendra, 2 July 1971. MEA, WII/121/54/71, vol. I, Stone to Menon, 2 July 1971. Henry Kissinger, *White House Years* (Boston: Little, Brown, 1979), pp. 729, 732. Conrad Black, *Richard M. Nixon: A Life in Full* (New York: PublicAffairs, 2007), p. 725.
2. Leo J. Daugherty III, *The Marine Corps and the State Department: Enduring Partners in United States Foreign Policy, 1798–2007* (Jefferson, N.C.: McFarland, 2009), pp. 211–14.
3. MEA, WII/121/54/71, vol. I, Menon memorandum, 1 July 1971.
4. *FRUS,* Kissinger-Haksar memcon, 6 July 1971, pp. 220–21.
5. MEA, WII/109/13/71, vol. II, "Supply of Arms by USA to Pakistan," n.d. November 1971. NMML, Haksar Papers, Subject File 169, Haksar minutes of Kissinger meeting, 6 July 1971. There are two more copies in NMML, Haksar Papers, Subject File 229. Haksar jotted down his notes after the meeting, although they are not verbatim.
6. *FRUS,* Kissinger-Haksar memcon, 6 July 1971, pp. 220–21.
7. NMML, Haksar Papers, Subject File 169, Haksar minutes of Kissinger meeting, 6 July 1971. The transcript actually says "whole Roman Empire." See NMML, Haksar Papers, Subject File 170, Haksar to Gandhi, 8 August 1971.
8. NMML, Haksar Papers, Subject File 169, Haksar minutes of Kissinger meeting, 6 July 1971. *FRUS,* Kissinger-Haksar memcon, 6 July 1971, pp. 220–21.
9. NMML, Haksar Papers, Subject File 169, Haksar minutes of Kissinger meeting, 6 July 1971.
10. *FRUS,* Kissinger-Haksar memcon, 6 July 1971, pp. 220–21.
11. NMML, Haksar Papers, Subject File 169, Haksar minutes of Kissinger meeting, 6 July 1971.
12. NMML, Haksar Papers, Subject File 169, Haksar to Gandhi, 7 July 1971. *FRUS,* Kissinger-Haksar memcon, 6 July 1971, pp. 220–21.
13. MEA, WII/121/54/71, vol. II, Kissinger's visit schedule, n.d. July 1971. MEA, WII/125/59/71, Kissinger's visit to India, n.d. July 1971. MEA, WII/121/54/71, Menon to Singh, 17 July 1971, covering Kissinger minutes, 12:30 p.m., 7 July 1971. NMML, Haksar Papers, Subject File 229, Kissinger-Subramaniam memcon, 7 July 1971. POL INDIA-US, Box 2369, Kissinger-Subramaniam memcon, 7 July 1971. Kissinger, *White House Years,* pp. 738–39.

14. MEA, WII/121/54/71, vol. II, Menon to Kaul, 5 July 1971. POL 7 US-KISSINGER, Box 2693, Kissinger memorandum, n.d. July 1971. MEA, WII/121/54/71, vol. I, Girilal Jain, "Mr. Kissinger's Visit," *Times of India,* 6 July 1971. MEA, WII/121/54/71, vol. I, Patel to Gandhi, 8 July 1971.

15. POL INDIA-US, Box 2369, Kissinger-academics memcon, 7 July 1971.

16. NSC Files, Box 1025, Presidential/HAK MemCons, Haksar-Kissinger memcon, 7 July 1971, 1:10 p.m. Jagjivan Ram, *Four Decades of Jagjivan Ram's Parliamentary Career* (New Delhi: S. Chand, 1977). MEA, WII/121/54/71, Kissinger-Ram meeting, 7 July 1971 (attached to Menon to Singh, 13 July 1971). NMML, Haksar Papers, Subject File 229, Kissinger-Ram meeting, 7 July 1971.

17. See MEA, HI/121/13/71, vol. I, Singh statement in Lok Sabha and Rajya Sabha, 24 June 1971. POL INDIA-US, Box 2369, Singh-Kissinger memcon, 7 July 1971. MEA, WII/121/54/71, Kissinger-Singh meeting, 7 July 1971. NMML, Kaul Papers, Subject File 19, part I, Singh-Kissinger memcon, 7 July 1971. See T. N. Kaul, *The Kissinger Years: Indo-American Relations* (New Delhi: Arnold-Heinemann, 1980), pp. 37–51, 58–60.

18. NSC Files, Box 1025, Presidential/HAK MemCons, Haksar-Kissinger memcon, 7 July 1971, 1:10 p.m.

19. POL 7 US-KISSINGER, Box 2693, Kissinger memorandum, n.d. July 1971. See NMML, Kaul Papers, Subject File 19, part I, Singh-Kissinger memcon, 7 July 1971.

20. MEA, WII/121/54/71, Kissinger-Ram meeting, 7 July 1971 (attached to Menon to Singh, 13 July 1971). NMML, Haksar Papers, Subject File 229, Kissinger-Ram meeting, 7 July 1971.

21. For Haksar's talking points for Gandhi, see NMML, Haksar Papers, Subject File 169, Haksar to Gandhi, 7 July 1971.

22. NMML, Haksar Papers, Subject File 169, Nixon to Gandhi, 1 July 1971. See NMML, Haksar Papers, Subject File 169, Haksar to Kaul, 8 July 1971. Keating was upset at not being told what was in Nixon's letter to Gandhi (POL 15-1 US-NIXON, Box 2708, Keating to Rogers, 12 July 1971, New Delhi 11090).

23. NMML, Haksar Papers, Subject File 225, Gandhi-Kissinger conversation, 7 July 1971. The American notes have Gandhi going further, saying the arms did "not make much practical difference" (POL INDIA-US, Box 2369, Gandhi-Kissinger memcon, 7 July 1971), but the Indian notes do not.

24. POL INDIA-US, Box 2369, Gandhi-Kissinger memcon, 7 July 1971. NMML, Haksar Papers, Subject File 225, Gandhi-Kissinger conversation, 7 July 1971.

25. NSC Files, Box H-052, SRG Meetings, Saunders to Kissinger, 5 March 1971. Kissinger was also personally warned of imminent Pakistani violence by the State Department officials U. Alexis Johnson and Christopher Van Hollen (NSC Files, Box H-112, SRG Minutes, SRG meeting, 6 March 1971, 11:40 a.m.). POL INDIA-US, Box 2369, Gandhi-Kissinger memcon, 7 July 1971.

26. NMML, Haksar Papers, Subject File 225, Gandhi-Kissinger conversation, 7 July 1971.

27. MEA, WII/121/54/71, "Salient Points Mentioned by Dr. Kissinger," n.d. July 1971.

28. POL INDIA-US, Box 2369, Gandhi-Kissinger memcon, 7 July 1971. The

Indian notes omit this embarrassment (NMML, Haksar Papers, Subject File 225, Gandhi-Kissinger conversation, 7 July 1971).

29. NMML, Haksar Papers, Subject File 169, Haksar to Jha, 21 July 1971. See P. N. Dhar, *Indira Gandhi, the "Emergency," and Indian Democracy* (Oxford: Oxford University Press, 2000), p. 163.

30. POL INDIA-US, Box 2369, Sultan-Kissinger memcon, 8 July 1971. See NMML, Haksar Papers, Subject File 169, Haksar to Jha, 17 July 1971. *FRUS,* SRG meeting, 23 July 1971, pp. 270-83. *FRUS,* vol. E-7, White House tapes, Oval Office 549-25, 28 July 1971, 4:21–4:54 p.m.

31. POL 7 US-KISSINGER, Box 2693, Kissinger memorandum, n.d. July 1971. See *FRUS,* Haig to Nixon, n.d. July 1971, p. 235.

32. See Library of Congress, Foreign Affairs Oral History Collection, Joseph Wheeler interview, 17 June 1998, and Robert Mark Ward interview, 27 May 1998.

33. POL INDIA-US, Box 2369, Farland-Kissinger memcon, 8 July 1971.

34. Chuck Yeager and Leo Janos, *Yeager: An Autobiography* (New York: Bantam, 1985), pp. 306–7, 311–12. POL INDIA-US, Box 2369, Farland-Kissinger memcon, 8 July 1971. NSC Files, Box 571, Indo-Pak War, State Department working group situation report, 5 December 1971.

35. POL INDIA-US, Box 2369, Sultan-Kissinger memcon, 8 July 1971.

36. *FRUS,* Nixon to Yahya, 1 July 1971, pp. 213–14.

37. For preparations, see NSC Files, Box 625, Country Files—Middle East, Pakistan, vol. V, Saunders to Kissinger, 11 July 1971. *FRUS,* Kissinger to Haig, 9 July 1971, pp. 242–43. Kissinger, *White House Years,* p. 861.

38. White House tapes, Oval Office 558-10, 9 August 1971, 5:44–6:18 p.m. *FRUS,* SRG meeting, 23 July 1971, pp. 270–83. Kissinger, *White House Years,* p. 861.

39. Kissinger, *White House Years,* p. 862.

40. Ibid., p. 739. See John H. Holdridge, *Crossing the Divide: An Insider's Account of Normalization of U.S.-China Relations* (Lanham, Md.: Rowman & Littlefield, 1997), pp. 52–55.

41. NSC Files, Box 625, Country Files—Middle East, Pakistan, vol. V, Saunders to Kissinger, 11 July 1971. His italics.

42. Library of Congress, Association for Diplomatic Studies and Training, Foreign Affairs Oral History Project, Winston Lord interview, 28 April 1998. Lord sometimes claims that he ran to the front of the plane (James Mann, *About Face: A History of America's Curious Relationship with China, from Nixon to Clinton* [New York: Alfred A. Knopf, 1998], pp. 3–4), but admits here that that is an exaggeration. NSA, Kissinger to Nixon, 14 July 1971. Kissinger, *White House Years,* pp. 740–42. See Huang Hua, *Memoirs* (Beijing: Foreign Languages Press, 2008), pp. 224–26; Ji Chaozu, *The Man on Mao's Right: From Harvard Yard to Tiananmen Square, My Life Inside China's Foreign Ministry* (New York: Random House, 2008), pp. 245–48; Walter Isaacson, *Kissinger: A Biography* (New York: Simon & Schuster, 1992), pp. 343–49.

43. NSA, Kissinger to Haig, 11 July 1971. NSA, Kissinger to Nixon, 14 July 1971. For a beautiful analysis of Nixon's and Kissinger's trips to Beijing in the context of other Western encounters, see Jonathan D. Spence, *The Chan's Great Continent: China in Western Minds* (New York: Norton, 1998), pp. 218–23.

44. Library of Congress, Association for Diplomatic Studies and Training, For-

eign Affairs Oral History Project, Winston Lord interview, 28 April 1998
and subsequent.

45. Kissinger, *White House Years,* pp. 750–51. Tyler, *Great Wall,* p. 100. NSA, Kissinger to Nixon, 14 July 1971. NSA, Zhou-Kissinger memcon, 10 July 1971, 11:20–11:50 p.m. Kissinger, *White House Years,* p. 862. For a balanced evaluation of Chinese and India claims, see Srinath Raghavan, *War and Peace in Modern India* (New York: Palgrave Macmillan, 2010), pp. 227–310.

46. NSA, Zhou-Kissinger memcon, 10 July 1971, 12:10 p.m. In fact, as recently as the Kennedy administration, the CIA had been secretly supporting guerrillas fighting Chinese rule in Tibet, a project that Chinese officials presumed had Indian backing. (John B. Roberts and Elizabeth A. Roberts, *Freeing Tibet* [Saranac Lake, N.Y.: Amacom, 2009], pp. 91–103.)

47. NSA, Zhou-Kissinger memcon, 10 July 1971, 12:10 p.m.

48. NSA, Zhou-Kissinger memcon, 11 July 1971, 10:35–11:55 a.m. NSA, Kissinger to Nixon, 14 July 1971.

49. NSA, Kissinger to Nixon, 14 July 1971. NSA, Zhou-Kissinger memcon, 11 July 1971, 10:35–11:55 a.m.

50. NSA, Kissinger-Huang memcon, 16 August 1971, 9:05–10:45 a.m.

51. NSA, Zhou-Kissinger memcon, 11 July 1971, 10:35–11:55 a.m. Kissinger told Nixon that Zhou wanted to make "sure that we would continue to use the Yahya channel occasionally because 'one should not burn bridges that have been useful.'" (NSA, Kissinger to Nixon, 14 July 1971.)

52. NSA, Kissinger to Nixon, 14 July 1971. See Evelyn Goh, "Nixon, Kissinger, and the 'Soviet Card' in the U.S. Opening to China, 1971–1974," *Diplomatic History,* vol. 29, no. 3 (June 2005), pp. 481–82.

53. NSA, Kissinger-McNamara telcon, 13 August 1971, 8:40 a.m. Nixon noted, "The Chinese have been exterminating people for years." (White House tapes, Oval Office 784–21, 21 September 1972, 12:25–2:01 p.m.) See Yang Jisheng, *Tombstone: The Great Chinese Famine, 1958–1962,* trans. Stacy Mosher and Guo Jian (New York: Farrar, Straus & Giroux, 2012); Frank Dikötter, *Mao's Great Famine: The History of China's Most Devastating Catastrophe, 1958–1962* (New York: Walker, 2011); Roderick MacFarquhar, *The Origins of the Cultural Revolution,* 3 vols. (New York: Oxford University Press, 1974–97).

54. Kissinger, *White House Years,* p. 755. See White House tapes, Oval Office 549-25, 28 July 1971, 4:21–4:54 p.m.

55. H. R. Haldeman, *The Haldeman Diaries: Inside the Nixon White House* (New York: G. P. Putnam's Sons, 1994), 10 July 1971, p. 317; 13 July 1971, pp. 318–19.

56. NSC Files, Box 1025, Presidential/HAK MemCons, Farland-Kissinger memcon, 30 July 1971. See Huang, *Memoirs,* p. 232.

57. NSC Files, Box 138, Kissinger Office Files, Country Files—Middle East, Nixon to Yahya, 26 July 1971. See NSC Files, Box 138, Kissinger Office Files, Country Files—Middle East, Nixon to Yahya, 7 August 1971. NSC Files, Box 138, Kissinger Office Files, Country Files—Middle East, Kissinger to Yahya, 26 July 1971. White House tapes, Oval Office 549-25, 28 July 1971, 4:21–4:54 p.m. See White House tapes, Oval Office 551-6, 29 July 1971, 11:52 a.m.–12:20 p.m. Kissinger, *White House Years,* p. 739. Haldeman, *Haldeman Diaries,* 17 July 1971, p. 322.

58. MEA, HI/1012/30/71, Chib to Kaul, 5 August 1971. MEA, HI/1012/78/71, Jha to Kaul, 7 September 1971. MEA, HI/1012/14/71, Mishra to Paranjpe, 20 August 1971.
59. MEA, HI/1012/30/71, Chib to Kaul, 5 August 1971. See MEA, WII/125/59/71, Singh statement in Lok Sabha, 20 July 1971.
60. Archer K. Blood, *The Cruel Birth of Bangladesh: Memoirs of an American Diplomat* (Dacca: University Press of Bangladesh, 2002), p. 257.
61. *FRUS,* NSC meeting, 16 July 1971, pp. 264–67.
62. NSA, Nixon and Kissinger talk to White House staff, 19 July 1971, 11:40 a.m.

CHAPTER 12: THE MUKTI BAHINI

1. For his reported version, see Sydney H. Schanberg, "Bengalis Form a Cabinet as the Bloodshed Goes On," *New York Times,* 14 April 1971, pp. A1, A12.
2. MEA, HI/121/13/71, vol. I, Gandhi press conference, 19 October 1971.
3. J. F. R. Jacob, *Surrender at Dacca: Birth of a Nation* (New Delhi: Manohar, 1997), pp. 90–94. NMML, Haksar Papers, Subject File 89, Dhar to Haksar, n.d. 1971. NMML, Haksar Papers, Subject File 169, Sen to Gandhi, 30 June 1971. The exiles had raised £100,000 worth of arms.
4. Oriana Fallaci, *Interviews with History and Conversations with Power* (New York: Rizzoli, 2011), p. 264. NMML, Haksar Papers, Subject File 89, Dhar to Haksar, n.d. 1971.
5. NMML, Haksar Papers, Subject File 171, "Political Prospective" and "A Note on How the [*sic*] Help the Mukti Fouj Win the Bangla Desh Liberation War?" 18 August 1971. Haksar evidently saw the report on August 18, but it was written earlier. See A. T. M. Abdul Wahab, *Mukti Bahini Wins Victory* (Dacca: Columbia Prokashani, 2004), pp. 171–97.
6. NMML, Haksar Papers, Subject File 229, Choudhury to Syed Nazrul Islam, July 1971. NMML, Haksar Papers, Subject File 171, "Political Prospective" and "A Note on How the [*sic*] Help the Mukti Fouj Win the Bangla Desh Liberation War?" 18 August 1971.
7. NMML, Haksar Papers, Subject File 229, Choudhury to Syed Nazrul Islam, July 1971; NMML, Haksar Papers, Subject File 169, Choudhury to Syed Nazrul Islam, July 1971. NMML, Haksar Papers, Subject File 220, "SSB and Bangladesh," 3 February 1972.
8. NMML, Haksar Papers, Subject File 227, Narayan to Haksar, 4 July 1971. NMML, Haksar Papers, Subject File 89, Dhar to Haksar, n.d. 1971. NMML, Haksar Papers, Subject File 169, "Report on the visit of Border Areas of Assam, Meghalaya and Tripura," 7 July 1971. Narayan-Mukti Fouj meeting, 9 July 1971, Jayaprakash Narayan, *Selected Works,* ed. Bimal Prasad (New Delhi: Manohar, 2008), vol. 9, pp. 849–52. NMML, Haksar Papers, Subject File 171, "Political Prospective" and "A Note on How the [*sic*] Help the Mukti Fouj Win the Bangla Desh Liberation War?" 18 August 1971.
9. NMML, Haksar Papers, Subject File 169, "Report on the visit of Border Areas of Assam, Meghalaya and Tripura," 7 July 1971. According to Jayaprakash Narayan, one special unit was mustered "directly under the command of Gen. Manekshaw," although under orders from D. P. Dhar to work under the Bengali sector commanders (Sen notes, 27 October 1971,

414 Notes to Pages 181–184

Narayan, *Selected Works*, pp. 862–69). Narayan based this on information from Tajuddin Ahmad. See P. N. Dhar, *Indira Gandhi, the "Emergency," and Indian Democracy* (Oxford: Oxford University Press, 2000), p. 168.

10. NMML, Haksar Papers, Subject File 170, "Rationalisation of the intelligence and Security set-up," August 1971. NMML, Haksar Papers, Subject File 227, Kao report, Bangla Desh, 3 July 1971. NMML, Haksar Papers, Subject File 220, "SSB and Bangladesh," 3 February 1972.

11. White House tapes, White House telephone 10-116, 7 October 1971, 10:32–10:58 a.m. See Abdul Wahab, *Mukti Bahini Wins Victory*, pp. 203–12.

12. MEA, WII/109/31/71, vol. I, Indian government press information bureau, Gandhi speech, 12 December 1971. MEA, WII/109/31/71, vol. I, Gandhi statement to Parliament, 16 December 1971.

13. NMML, Haksar Papers, Subject File 169, "Report on the visit of Border Areas of Assam, Meghalaya and Tripura," 7 July 1971. See Habibul Alam, *Brave of Heart: The Urban Guerilla Warfare of Sector-2, During the Liberation War of Bangladesh* (Dacca: Academic Press and Publishers Library, 2006), p. 288.

14. NMML, Haksar Papers, Subject File 169, "Report on the visit of Border Areas of Assam, Meghalaya and Tripura," 7 July 1971. NMML, Haksar Papers, Subject File 229, Choudhury to Syed Nazrul Islam, July 1971; NMML, Haksar Papers, Subject File 169, Choudhury to Syed Nazrul Islam, July 1971.

15. NMML, Haksar Papers, Subject File 169, "Report on the visit of Border Areas of Assam, Meghalaya and Tripura," 7 July 1971. See Sen notes, 27 October 1971, Narayan, *Selected Works*, pp. 862–69. NMML, Haksar Papers, Subject File 229, Choudhury to Syed Nazrul Islam, July 1971; NMML, Haksar Papers, Subject File 169, Choudhury to Syed Nazrul Islam, July 1971.

16. Dom Moraes, *Mrs Gandhi* (London: Jonathan Cape, 1980), p. 188.

17. NMML, Haksar Papers, Subject File 169, "Report on the visit of Border Areas of Assam, Meghalaya and Tripura," 7 July 1971. For an estimate of twenty-five thousand, see Narayan-Mukti Fouj meeting, 9 July 1971, Narayan, *Selected Works*, pp. 849–52. MEA, HI/1012/30/71, Chib to Kaul, 5 August 1971. MEA, HI/1012/30/71, Chib to Kaul, 4 September 1971. MEA, HI/121/13/71, vol. I, Gandhi press conference, 19 October 1971. Her words are an inadvertent and unpoetic version of Byron: "For Freedom's battle once begun, / Bequeath'd by bleeding sire to son, / Though baffled oft is ever won." (Timothy Garton Ash, *The Polish Revolution: Solidarity* [New Haven, Conn.: Yale University Press, 2002], p. 49.)

18. NMML, Haksar Papers, Subject File 168, Haksar to Gandhi, 4 June 1971. See Narayan to Kaul, 15 July 1971, Narayan, *Selected Works*, p. 628; NMML, Haksar Papers, Subject File 171, "Political Prospective" and "A Note on How the [*sic*] Help the Mukti Fouj Win the Bangla Desh Liberation War?" 18 August 1971. NMML, Haksar Papers, Subject File 227, "Situational Report of Bangladesh Army," 5 July 1971. See Sukhwant Singh, *India's Wars Since Independence: The Liberation of Bangladesh* (New Delhi: Vikas, 1980), vol. 1, pp. 30–31.

19. Narayan to Kaul, 15 July 1971, Narayan, *Selected Works*, p. 628. See Muyeedul Hasan, "1971: PNH in Bridging the Security Gap," in Subrata Banerjee, ed., *Contributions in Remembrance: Homage to P. N. Haksar* (Chandigarh,

India: Centre for Research and Industrial Development, 2004), vol. 2, pp. 21–28. NMML, Haksar Papers, Subject File 169, Narain to Swaminathan, 13 July 1971. Narayan to Gandhi, 20 July 1971, Narayan, *Selected Works,* p. 630. Italics added. Narayan to Gandhi, 1 August 1971, Narayan, *Selected Works,* p. 634. See NMML, Haksar Papers, Subject File 89, Dhar to Haksar, n.d. 1971.

20. Singh, *Liberation of Bangladesh,* pp. 38–39. A. A. K. Niazi, *The Betrayal of East Pakistan* (Karachi: Oxford University Press, 1998), pp. 62–68. By one count, there were about six thousand Bengali irregulars trained for war, with five thousand more being trained monthly by the Indians and Bengalis (Narayan-Mukti Fouj meeting, 9 July 1971, Narayan, *Selected Works,* pp. 849–52). They faced roughly eighty thousand Pakistani soldiers and irregulars (NMML, Haksar Papers, Subject File 171, "Political Prospective" and "A Note on How the [*sic*] Help the Mukti Fouj Win the Bangla Desh Liberation War?" 18 August 1971; Haksar evidently saw the report on August 18, but it was written earlier). By late September, the CIA estimated there were eighty thousand Pakistan troops against perhaps fifty thousand Bengalis in some way associated with the resistance (NSC Files, Box 570, Indo-Pak Crisis, CIA Office of National Estimates, "The Indo-Pakistani Crisis," 22 September 1971). Narayan-Islam meeting, 8–9 July 1971, Narayan, *Selected Works,* pp. 840–49. Narayan-Mukti Fouj meeting, 9 July 1971, Narayan, *Selected Works,* pp. 849–52. NMML, Haksar Papers, Subject File 171, "Political Prospective" and "A Note on How the [*sic*] Help the Mukti Fouj Win the Bangla Desh Liberation War?" 18 August 1971. Jayaprakash Narayan, "Bangladesh and India's Future," *Indian Express,* 27–28 October 1971, Narayan, *Selected Works,* pp. 660–66.

21. NMML, Haksar Papers, Subject File 169, "Report on the visit of Border Areas of Assam, Meghalaya and Tripura," 7 July 1971.

22. Mahfuzul H. Chowdhury, *Democratization in South Asia* (London: Ashgate, 2003), pp. 50, 121. NMML, Haksar Papers, III Installment, Subject File 229, Choudhury to Syed Nazrul Islam, July 1971.

23. NMML, Haksar Papers, Subject File 169, "Report on the visit of Border Areas of Assam, Meghalaya and Tripura," 7 July 1971.

24. Jacob, *Surrender at Dacca,* pp. 60–70, 78–83. Singh, *Liberation of Bangladesh,* pp. 65–79. For Indian navy plans in July, see N. Krishnan, *No Way but Surrender: An Account of the Indo-Pakistan War in the Bay of Bengal, 1971* (New Delhi: Vikas, 1980), pp. 19–29. NMML, Haksar Papers, Subject File 220, "SSB and Bangladesh," 3 February 1972.

25. Richard Sisson and Leo E. Rose, *War and Secession: Pakistan, India, and the Creation of Bangladesh* (Berkeley: University of California Press, 1990), pp. 206, 209–10. NMML, Haksar Papers, Subject File 89, Dhar to Haksar, n.d. 1971.

26. Mao Zedong, "On Guerrilla Warfare," in Richard K. Betts, ed., *Conflict After the Cold War* (New York: Pearson-Longman, 2005), p. 457. NMML, Haksar Papers, Subject File 229, Choudhury to Syed Nazrul Islam, July 1971; NMML, Haksar Papers, Subject File 169, Choudhury to Syed Nazrul Islam, July 1971.

27. Narayan-Mukti Fouj meeting, 9 July 1971, Narayan, *Selected Works,* pp. 849–52. NMML, Haksar Papers, Subject File 227, "Situational Report of Bangladesh Army," 5 July 1971. Dhar, *Indira Gandhi, the "Emergency,"*

and Indian Democracy, p. 165. Jacob, *Surrender at Dacca,* pp. 43-44. Abdul Wahab, *Mukti Bahini Wins Victory,* pp. 215–41. NMML, Haksar Papers, Subject File 89, Dhar to Haksar, n.d. 1971. See MEA, WII/121/54/71, vol. II, Menon to Kaul, 5 July 1971. See James D. Fearon and David D. Laitin, "Ethnicity, Insurgency, and Civil War," *American Political Science Review,* vol. 97, no. 1 (February 2003), pp. 75–90. Bangladesh was a likely case for an insurgency: a weak government that ran a brutal counterinsurgency campaign, alienating the people; and rough terrain, foreign base camps, and foreign support to help the rebels. There were other risk factors: a regime that included democratic elements, as in the 1970 elections; instability in the government; foreign diasporas, as in West Bengal; and a large population. Fearon and Laitin use Bangladesh as their key example of a state that is geographically hard to control. The only factor that was missing was the government's loss of foreign support, which did not happen: both the United States and China stood by Yahya.

28. In the 1977 Additional Protocol I to the Geneva Conventions of 1949, Article 37 prohibits the "resort to perfidy" in combat, including "the feigning of civilian, non-combatant status." NMML, Haksar Papers, Subject File 227, Bangla Desh Forces, "Guerillas," n.d. July 1971.

29. Alam, *Brave of Heart,* pp. 17, 23–24. NMML, Haksar Papers, Subject File 227, Bangla Desh Forces, "Guerillas," n.d. July 1971. NMML, Haksar Papers, Subject File 227, "Situational Report of Bangladesh Army," 5 July 1971. For the authorship of the report, see NMML, Haksar Papers, Subject File 227, Roy to Gandhi, 5 July 1971.

30. NMML, Haksar Papers, Subject File 227, "Situational Report of Bangladesh Army," 5 July 1971.

31. Narayan to Gandhi, 20 July 1971, Narayan, *Selected Works,* p. 630. NMML, Haksar Papers, Subject File 227, Kao report, Bangla Desh, 3 July 1971.

32. NMML, Haksar Papers, Subject File 227, Kao report, Bangla Desh, 3 July 1971. See NMML, Haksar Papers, Subject File 220, Kao to Haksar, 9 July 1971.

33. PMS, 7/371/71, vol. II, Gandhi to Kirpal, 2 August 1971. See NSC Files, Box 574, Indo-Pak War, South Asian Congressional, Kennedy report, 1 November 1971.

34. MEA, WII/121/54/71, vol. II, refugee statistics, 3 July 1971. MEA, HI/1012/30/71, refugee statistics, 3 July 1971. MEA, WII/121/54/71, vol. II, East Bengal memorandum, n.d. 1971. Pupul Jayakar, *Indira Gandhi: An Intimate Biography* (New York: Pantheon, 1992), pp. 171–72.

35. NMML, Haksar Papers, Subject File 168, Mukherjee to Dhavan, June 1971. See NMML, Haksar Papers, Subject File 169, Gandhi to Swaminathan, 1 April 1970.

36. NMML, Haksar Papers, Subject File 169, Haksar notes, 15 July 1971.

37. NMML, Haksar Papers, Subject File 169, Haksar notes, 15 July 1971. On West Bengal's political evolution to the present day, see Ashok Malik, "Didi's Long March," *Tehelka Magazine,* vol. 8, no. 20 (21 May 2011).

38. NSC Files, Box 574, Indo-Pak War, South Asian Congressional, Kennedy speech, 26 August 1971.

39. For the ongoing flow of refugees, see MEA, WII/121/54/71, vol. II, refugee statistics, 3 July 1971; MEA, HI/1012/30/71, Kumar memorandum, refugee statistics, 7 September 1971; MEA, HI/1012/30/71, Kumar memorandum,

refugee statistics, 19 September 1971; MEA, HI/1012/30/71, Kumar memorandum, refugee statistics, 22 September 1971. NSC Files, Box 570, Indo-Pak Crisis, South Asia, CIA Office of National Estimates, "The Indo-Pakistani Crisis," 22 September 1971. East Pakistan's population was seventy-six million. NMML, Haksar Papers, Subject File 171, Bhashani to Haksar, 29 July 1971. MEA, WII/121/60/71, Kennedy-Khadilkar conversation, 14 August 1971. NSC Files, Box 574, Indo-Pak War, South Asian Congressional, Kennedy report, 1 November 1971. This report represents the professional judgment of Nevin Scrimshaw and John Lewis, two of the best development and nutrition experts in the United States. NMML, Haksar Papers, Subject File 169, Haksar to Gandhi, 24 July 1971. This would have had more impact if it was not in a draft note to Kosygin.

40. NSC Files, Box 574, Indo-Pak War, South Asian Congressional, Kennedy report, 1 November 1971. Sydney H. Schanberg, "Bengali Refugees Stirring Strife in India," *New York Times,* 6 October 1971. Sisson and Rose, *War and Secession,* p. 181. MEA, WII/121/54/71, vol. II, East Bengal memorandum, n.d. 1971. MEA, HI/1012/30/71, Kumar memorandum, refugee statistics, 7 September 1971. More precisely, by this count, there were 8,386,000 refugees in total, of which 7,120,000 were Hindus and 1,034,000 were Muslims.

41. MEA, WII/121/54/71, vol. II, UN memorandum, n.d. July 1971. NMML, Haksar Papers, Subject File 89, Shriman Narayan to Gandhi, 5 August 1971; Gandhi note in margin, 6 August 1971.

42. NMML, Kaul Papers, Subject File 19, part II, Singh briefing in London, n.d. June 1971. MEA, HI/121/13/71, vol. II, Dixit to heads of mission, 4 December 1971. NMML, Haksar Papers, Subject File 89, Shriman Narayan to Gandhi, 5 August 1971; Gandhi note in margin, 6 August 1971.

43. MEA, HI/121/13/71, vol. II, Dixit to heads of mission, 4 December 1971. MEA, WII/121/60/71, Kennedy-Kaul discussion, 14 August 1971.

44. NMML, Kaul Papers, Subject File 19, part II, Singh briefing in London, n.d. June 1971.

45. MEA, WII/121/60/71, Kennedy-Kaul discussion, 14 August 1971; NMML, Kaul Papers, Subject File 19, part I, "Possible Questions and Answers on the Simla Agreement," n.d. 1972; MEA, HI/121/13/71, vol. II, Dixit to ambassadors, 6 December 1971. NMML, Haksar Papers, Subject File 171, Chatterjee to Haksar, 6 July 1971.

46. Richard Reeves, *President Nixon: Alone in the White House* (New York: Simon & Schuster, 2007), p. 386. See MEA, WII/161/1/71, Dixit to ambassadors, 4 March 1971; MEA, WII/161/1/71, Menon to Dixit, 25 May 1971; MEA, WII/161/1/71, Sen to Dixit, n.d. 1971; MEA, WII/161/1/71, Chadha to ambassadors, 18 August 1971; MEA, WII/161/1/71, Dixit to ambassadors, 23 July 1971. MEA, HI/121/13/71, vol. II, Fu speech, 19 November 1971. MEA, HI/121/13/71, vol. II, Dixit to heads of mission, 6 December 1971. NMML, Haksar Papers, Subject File 171, Chatterjee to Narendra Singh, 6 July 1971. The ambassador wanted to use the Economic and Social Council (ECOSOC), which held talks on July 16. (NMML, Haksar Papers, Subject File 220, Mirza to Pakistani ambassadors, 1 October 1971.)

47. MEA, WII/121/54/71, Singh to Kaul, 3 July 1971. MEA, HI/121/13/71, vol. I, Dixit to heads of mission, 29 October 1971. NMML, Haksar Papers, Subject File 171, Chatterjee to Narendra Singh, 6 July 1971. MEA, HI/121/13/71, vol. I, Ali statement to UN General Assembly, 27 September 1971. MEA,

HI/121/13/71, vol. I, Singh statement to UN General Assembly, 27 September 1971. See MEA, HI/121/13/71, vol. I, Singh statement to UN General Assembly, 28 September 1971.

48. NMML, Haksar Papers, Subject File 171, Chatterjee to Narendra Singh, 6 July 1971. Thant did this on July 20 (MEA, HI/121/13/71, vol. II, Dixit to heads of mission, 4 December 1971). PMS, 7/371/71, vol. II, Gandhi to Kirpal, 2 August 1971.

49. NMML, Haksar Papers, Subject File 220, Mirza to Pakistani ambassadors, 1 October 1971. See White House tapes, EOB 272-17, 11 August 1971, 4:56–6:31 p.m. MEA, HI/121/13/71, vol. II, Dixit to heads of mission, 4 December 1971. See NMML, Kaul Papers, Subject File 19, part II, Singh briefing in London, n.d. June 1971, and MEA, HI/1012/78/71, Jha to Kaul, 7 September 1971. NMML, Haksar Papers, Subject File 169, Haksar to Kaul, 12 July 1971.

50. NMML, Haksar Papers, Subject File 169, Haksar to Gandhi, 26 July 1971. MEA, HI/121/13/71, vol. II, Dixit note, 25 November 1971. NMML, Haksar Papers, Subject File 168, Haksar to Gandhi, 21 June 1971. MEA, WII/121/54/71, vol. I, Rasgotra to Menon, 30 June 1971. See Samantha Power, *Chasing the Flame: Sergio Vieira de Mello and the Fight to Save the World* (New York: Penguin, 2008), pp. 25–26; MEA, HI/121/13/71, vol. II, Sadruddin speech, 18 November 1971; MEA, HI/121/13/71, vol. II, Sen speech, 18 November 1971. REF PAK, Box 3008, Van Hollen to Keating, 26 June 1971, State 115314. See White House tapes, Oval Office 619-13, 16 November 1971, 11:38 a.m.–12:05 p.m.; *FRUS,* Kissinger-Sisco telcon, 29 June 1971, 10:40 a.m., pp. 209–11. NMML, Haksar Papers, Subject File 169, Haksar to Gandhi, 26 July 1971.

51. NSC Files, Box H-058, SRG Meetings, Saunders to Kissinger, 22 July 1971. NSC Files, Box H-058, SRG Meetings, Eliot to Kissinger, 21 July 1971. White House tapes, Oval Office 605-9, 28 October 1971, 11:23 a.m.–12:45 p.m. Pakistan also supported it (NMML, Haksar Papers, Subject File 220, Ahmad to European ambassadors, 8 October 1971; NMML, Haksar Papers, Subject File 220, Sultan Khan to Dehlavi, 2 October 1971; MEA, HI/1012/30/71, Chib to Kaul, 5 August 1971). MEA, UI/251/33/71, vol. III, Rasgotra to Kaul, 14 July 1971. See MEA, UI/251/33/71, vol. III, Narendra Singh to Jha, 14 July 1971; MEA, UI/251/33/71, vol. III, Krishnan to Kaul, 14 July 1971. NMML, Haksar Papers, Subject File 169, Haksar to Gandhi, 26 July 1971. For Gandhi's public denials that India was hiding anything, see MEA, HI/121/13/71, vol. I, Gandhi press conference, 19 October 1971. See MEA, HI/121/13/71, vol. II, Dixit to heads of mission, 4 December 1971.

52. NMML, Haksar Papers, Subject File 169, Haksar to Gandhi, 24 July 1971. NMML, Haksar Papers, Subject File 170, Haksar to Gandhi, 14 August 1971. MEA, HI/121/13/71, vol. II, Dixit to heads of mission, 4 December 1971. NSC Files, Box H-082, WSAG Meetings, Eliot to Kissinger, 1 September 1971.

53. MEA, UI/251/33/71, vol. III, Rasgotra to Kaul, 14 July 1971. MEA, HI/121/13/71, vol. II, Dixit to heads of mission, 4 December 1971. NMML, Kaul Papers, Subject File 19, part II, Singh briefing in London, n.d. June 1971.

54. Shashi Tharoor, *Reasons of State: Political Development and India's Foreign Policy Under Indira Gandhi, 1966–1977* (New Delhi: Vikas, 1982), pp.

324–41. MEA, HI/121/13/71, vol. I, Gandhi press conference, 19 October 1971. MEA, UI/251/33/71, vol. III, Rasgotra to Kaul, 14 July 1971. Due to a cable garble, Schanberg was identified as DISNEY SCHANBERG.

55. Ajit Bhattacharjea, "A Day in Liberated Territory," *Times of India,* 8 April 1971; Ajit Bhattacharjea, "A Trickle Becomes a Stream," *Times of India,* 9 April 1971; Sudhir Thapliyal, "Operation Navaran," *Statesman,* 23 April 1971; Frank Moraes, "Waiting for the Monsoon," *Indian Express,* 1 May 1971; F. Chakravarty, "Ten Days with the Mukti Fauj," *Indian Express,* 10 May 1971; Manash Ghose, "War Scars of Jessore," *Statesman,* 3 April 1971; Chand Joshi, "The Lull," *Hindustan Times,* 7 April 1971. On the Indian press, see Robin Jeffrey, *India's Newspaper Revolution: Capitalism, Politics and the Indian-Language Press, 1977–1999* (New York: Palgrave Macmillian, 2000). NMML, Haksar Papers, Subject File 89, Dhar to Haksar, n.d. 1971. MEA, HI/121/13/71, vol. II, Dixit to heads of mission, 4 December 1971.

56. NMML, Haksar Papers, Subject File 89, Dhar letter, 18 April 1971. NMML, Haksar Papers, Subject File 168, Haksar to Gandhi, 10 June 1971. This was Romesh Thapar (see Bernard Weinraub, "The Kitty Kelley of Delhi Scandalizes the Nabobs," *New York Times,* 9 July 1991).

57. NMML, Haksar Papers, Subject File 170, Haksar to Gandhi, 8 August 1971. See NMML, Kaul Papers, Subject File 19, part II, Rogers-Gandhi talk, n.d. October 1971; NMML, Kaul Papers, Subject File 19, part I, Singh-Kissinger memcon, 7 July 1971; MEA, HI/121/13/71, vol. I, Singh statement in Lok Sabha and Rajya Sabha, 24 June 1971. MEA, WII/109/13/71, vol. I, "MPs Angry over Arms Sale to Pakistan," *Indian Express,* 25 June 1971. MEA, WII/109/13/71, vol. IV, Menon to Rasgotra, 25 June 1971. See MEA, WII/109/13/71, vol. IV, Jha to Singh, 22 June 1971, and MEA, HI/121/13/71, vol. I, Singh statement in Lok Sabha and Rajya Sabha, 24 June 1971.

58. Communist Party of India pamphlet, *Case for Bangla Desh,* May 1971. Dhar, *Indira Gandhi, the "Emergency," and Indian Democracy,* p. 166. For an overview of Parliament's abilities and limits, see Tharoor, *Reasons of State,* pp. 215–81. NMML, Haksar Papers, Subject File 169, Haksar to Gandhi, 24 July 1971. NMML, Haksar Papers, Subject File 169, Gandhi to Madhok, Haksar draft, July 1971. See NMML, Haksar Papers, Subject File 89, Narayan to Gandhi, 5 August 1971. On Hindu nationalism, see Ashutosh Varshney, *Contested Meanings: India's National Identity, Hindu Nationalism, and the Politics of Anxiety* (Cambridge, Mass.: Harvard Center for International Affairs, 1993); and Atul Kohli, "Can Democracies Accommodate Ethnic Nationalism?" *Journal of Asian Studies,* vol. 56, no. 2 (May 1997), pp. 323–44. On Indian ethnic parties, see Kanchan Chandra, *Why Ethnic Parties Succeed: Patronage and Ethnic Headcounts in India* (Cambridge: Cambridge University Press, 2004).

59. NMML, Haksar Papers, Subject File 89, Dhar to Haksar, n.d. 1971. See Gandhi speech, 15 August 1971, *The Years of Endeavour: Selected Speeches of Indira Gandhi, August 1969–August 1972* (New Delhi: Indian Ministry of Information and Broadcasting, 1975), vol. 2, pp. 117–21. On the popular dissatisfaction that often arises in democracies in long wars, see Donald Kagan, *Pericles of Athens and the Birth of Democracy* (New York: Simon & Schuster, 1991), pp. 230–31.

60. NMML, Haksar Papers, Subject File 89, Dhar to Haksar, n.d. 1971. See

420 Notes to Pages 196–198

NSC Files, Box 570, Indo-Pak War, Sisco to Keating, 10 June 1971, State 102568.

61. Jayaprakash Narayan, "Bangladesh and India's Future," *Indian Express,* 27–28 October 1971, Narayan, *Selected Works,* pp. 660–66. See Narayan note, 29 June 1971, Narayan, *Selected Works,* p. 627. NMML, Haksar Papers, Subject File 89, Gandhi-Kennedy conversation, Malhoutra notes, 16 August 1971. Ramachandra Guha, *India After Gandhi: The History of the World's Largest Democracy* (New York: Ecco, 2003), pp. 462–63, 515–16.

62. Tharoor, *Reasons of State,* p. 59. Gandhi had a favorable rating of 68 percent in August 1971, actually up four percentage points since her election victory. Tharoor, *Reasons of State*, pp. 282–92, 304–24. See Devesh Kapur and Pratap Bhanu Mehta, *The Indian Parliament as an Institution of Accountability* (Geneva: United Nations Research Institute for Social Development, 2006). Tharoor, *Reasons of State,* p. 291–96, 299. The exact numbers were 57 percent for recognizing Bangladesh to 24 percent against. This poll was in October 1971. See PMS, 7/371/71, vol. II, Afzalpurkar to Gandhi, 12 August 1971.

63. NMML, Haksar Papers, Subject File 169, Haksar to Gandhi, 14 July 1971. Dhar, *Indira Gandhi, the "Emergency," and Indian Democracy,* pp. 168–69. NMML, Haksar Papers, Subject File 168, Haksar to Mitra, 26 June 1971. NMML, Haksar Papers, Subject File 169, Narain to Swaminathan, 1 July 1971; NMML, Haksar Papers, Subject File 229, Narain to Swaminathan, 1 July 1971 (Haksar showed this letter to Gandhi on July 14); NMML, Haksar Papers, Subject File 169, Swaminathan to Haksar, 3 July 1971; NMML, Haksar Papers, Subject File 169, Swaminathan to Narain, 3 July 1971. NMML, Haksar Papers, Subject File 229, Haksar to Dhar, 22 May 1971.

64. NMML, Haksar Papers, Subject File 89, Dhar to Haksar, n.d. 1971.

CHAPTER 13: "THE HELL WITH THE DAMN CONGRESS"

1. For the famous stories breaking the news of My Lai, see Seymour Hersh, "Lieutenant Accused of Murdering 109 Civilians," *St. Louis Post-Dispatch,* 13 November 1969; Seymour Hersh, "Hamlet Attack Called 'Point-Blank Murder,'" *St. Louis Post-Dispatch*, 20 November 1969; and Seymour Hersh, "Ex-GI Tells of Killing Civilians at Pinkville," *St. Louis Post-Dispatch,* 25 November 1969, all in *Reporting Vietnam: American Journalism, 1969–1975* (New York: Library of America, 1998), vol. 2, pp. 13–27. See Telford Taylor, "Judging Calley Is Not Enough," *Life,* 9 April 1971, pp. 20–23. Richard Reeves, *President Nixon: Alone in the White House* (New York: Simon & Schuster, 2007), pp. 306–8. Calley was sentenced to life imprisonment, doing hard labor. Nixon quickly had Calley released to his apartment, telling H. R. Haldeman with satisfaction that "at least a P[resident] can do something once in a while." Haldeman wrote that the "general public reaction has been stupendous" in support of Calley (H. R. Haldeman, *The Haldeman Diaries: Inside the Nixon White House* [New York: G. P. Putnam's Sons, 1994], 1 April 1971, p. 265). Some 79 percent of Americans disapproved of the Calley verdict, although 50 percent thought that the My Lai massacre was a common incident. (George H. Gallup, *The Gallup Poll: Public Opinion, 1935–1971* [New York: Random House, 1972], vol. 3, 7 April 1971 poll, p. 2296.) Nixon—backed by Gerald Ford, then the House minority leader, and Jimmy Carter, then the governor of Georgia—freed Calley from the

stockade, and his sentence was later reduced to ten years. After Nixon's resignation, his army secretary would parole Calley. (Richard M. Nixon, *RN: The Memoirs of Richard Nixon* [New York: Simon & Schuster, 1990], pp. 499–500.)

2. *Gallup Poll,* vol. 3, 18 March 1971 poll, p. 2292. Some 28 percent named Vietnam as the most important problem for the country, ahead of 24 percent for the economy, 12 percent for other world issues, 7 percent for crime, and 7 percent for race relations. Stephen E. Ambrose, *Nixon: The Triumph of a Politician, 1969–1972* (New York: Simon & Schuster, 1989), vol. 2, p. 417; David Greenberg, "Nixon as Statesman," and Lien-Hang T. Nguyen, "Waging War on All Fronts," both in Fredrik Logevall and Andrew Preston, eds., *Nixon in the World: American Foreign Relations, 1969–1977* (New York: Oxford University Press, 2008). For an excellent analysis of the domestic scene, see Rick Perlstein, *Nixonland: The Rise of a President and the Fracturing of America* (New York: Scribner, 2008).

3. Walter Isaacson, *Kissinger: A Biography* (New York: Simon & Schuster, 1992), pp. 159–68, 171–79, 234–55. Stanley I. Kutler, *The Wars of Watergate: The Last Crisis of Richard Nixon* (New York: Alfred A. Knopf, 1990), pp. 21–31, 69–74. MEA, HI/1012/78/71, Jha to Kaul, 7 May 1971. Reeves, *President Nixon,* pp. 318–21. See Garry Wills, *Nixon Agonistes: The Crisis of the Self-Made Man* (Boston: Houghton Mifflin, 1970), pp. 388–402. MEA, HI/1012/78/71, Jha to Kaul, 7 April 1971. MEA, HI/1012/78/71, Jha to Kaul, 14 July 1971. *Gallup Poll,* vol. 3, 9 May 1971 poll, p. 2305. *Gallup Poll,* vol. 3, 11 July 1971 poll, pp. 2314–15.

4. Tom Wicker, *One of Us: Richard Nixon and the American Dream* (New York: Random House, 1991), p. 591. *Gallup Poll,* vol. 3, 31 January 1971 poll, p. 2285. The number favoring withdrawal was 73 percent. *Gallup Poll,* vol. 3, 7 March 1971 poll, p. 2291. Forty-six percent approved of Nixon's handling of Vietnam, while 41 percent disapproved; 65 percent thought Nixon's team was not telling enough.

5. Henry Kissinger, *White House Years* (Boston: Little, Brown, 1979), p. 854. In the *New York Times,* Anthony Lewis wrote that Nixon claimed that the United States could not pull all its troops out of Vietnam yet because "there might be a 'bloodbath' in South Vietnam. Well, there has just been a bloodbath in East Pakistan, one of the largest and most blatant in a very long time, and the sounds of protest from Washington have not been audible." ("America and the World," *New York Times,* 12 June 1971.) John Kenneth Galbraith, "The Unbelievable Happens in Bengal," *New York Times Magazine,* 31 October 1971. Desaix Myers, "Ki Korbo?" n.d. 1971, on file with author.

6. White House tapes, White House telephone 16-76, 9 December 1971, 7:42–8:10 p.m. White House tapes, Oval Office 477-1, 12 April 1971, 10:24–10:33 a.m. Nixon made a similar point in his Oval Office face-off with Kenneth Keating, when the ambassador brought up Congress: "Hell, they had us involved in a civil war in Biafra, and now they want us out of Pakistan." (*FRUS,* vol. E-7, White House tapes, Oval Office 521-13, 15 June 1971, 5:13–5:40 p.m.) White House tapes, Oval Office 658-31, 27 January 1972, 3:13–3:46 p.m.

7. Jean Drèze and Amartya Sen, *Hunger and Public Action* (Oxford: Clarendon Press, 1989), pp. 122, 126, 212–15, 221–25. Jean Drèze and Amartya Sen, *India: Economic Development and Social Opportunity* (Oxford: Oxford

University Press, 1995), pp. 57–86, 87–92. Naeem Mohaiemen, "Accelerated Media and 1971 Genocide," *Forum* (Dacca) 5, no. 12 (December 2011).

8. MEA, HI/1012/78/71, Jha to Kaul, 7 April 1971. See "Bloodbath in Bengal," *New York Times,* 7 April 1971. MEA, HI/1012/78/71, Jha to Kaul, 7 May 1971. See MEA, HI/1012/78/71, Jha to Kaul, 7 September 1971. See R. Narayan, "American Response," in Mohammed Ayoob et al., *Bangla Desh: A Struggle for Nationhood* (New Delhi: Vikas, 1971), pp. 133–67. MEA, WII/109/31/71, vol. II, "Attitudes in the US Congress," n.d. December 1971. POL 23-9 PAK, Box 2530, Keating to Rogers, 8 April 1971, New Delhi 5243. Indira Gandhi was somewhat more popular among Americans than Nixon, with 41 percent admiring her greatly and 24 percent admiring her somewhat (Harris Survey, October 1971).

9. MEA, WII/109/31/71, vol. II, "Attitudes in the US Congress," n.d. December 1971.

10. NMML, Haksar Papers, Subject File 167, Jha to Kaul, 22 December 1970.

11. White House tapes, Oval Office 505-18, 28 May 1971, 9:08 a.m. Haldeman, *Haldeman Diaries,* 9 June 1971, p. 297. *Gallup Poll,* vol. 3, 11 March 1971, p. 2291. Kennedy got 25 percent, Muskie 26 percent, and Hubert Humphrey 21 percent. In direct contests, he beat out both Muskie and Hubert Humphrey (*Gallup Poll,* vol. 3, 28 March 1971 poll, pp. 2294-95). Among Democrats, Kennedy beat Humphrey 47 percent to 42 percent, and Muskie 45 percent to 43 percent. In another poll, Kennedy got 29 percent of Democrats, to Muskie's 21 percent (*Gallup Poll,* vol. 3, 16 May 1971, p. 2306). In January, 38 percent of respondents said they would vote for Kennedy, while 47 percent preferred Nixon (*Gallup Poll,* vol. 3, 22 January 1971 poll, p. 2284). Peter S. Canellos, ed., *Last Lion: The Fall and Rise of Ted Kennedy* (New York: Simon & Schuster, 2009), pp. 145–73, 184–86.

12. POL 23-9 PAK, Box 2531, Kennedy to Rogers, 6 April 1971. NSC Files, Box 574, Indo-Pak War, South Asian Congressional, Hilaly to Kissinger, n.d. August 1971. NSC Files, Box 574, Indo-Pak War, South Asian Congressional, Hilaly to Kennedy, 4 June 1971. POL 23-9 PAK, Box 2531, Abshire to Kennedy, 20 April 1971. NSC Files, Box 626, Country Files—Middle East, Pakistan, vol. VI, Eliot to Kissinger, 17 August 1971. See POL 23-9 PAK, Box 2530, Keating to Rogers, 3 April 1971, New Delhi 4878; POL 23-9 PAK, Box 2530, Keating to Rogers, 5 April 1971, New Delhi 4952. POL 23-9 PAK, Box 2531, Keating to Rogers, 10 April 1971, New Delhi 5280.

13. NSC Files, Box 574, Indo-Pak War, South Asian Congressional, Kennedy statement, 18 June 1971. See NSC Files, Box 574, Indo-Pak War, South Asian Congressional, Kennedy speech, 2 June 1971. Kennedy's subcommittee was part of the Senate Judiciary Committee. POL 23-9 PAK, Box 2530, Gordon to Rogers, 8 April 1971, Calcutta 589. NSC Files, Box 574, Indo-Pak War, South Asian Congressional, Hilaly to Kennedy, 3 June 1971. NSC Files, Box 626, Country Files—Middle East, Pakistan, vol. VI, Haig to Kissinger, 3 August 1971. *Gallup Poll,* vol. 3, 4 June 1971 poll, p. 2309. Nixon got 42 percent, Kennedy 41 percent, George Wallace 10 percent, and 7 percent were undecided. On Vietnam, see *Gallup Poll,* vol. 3, 6 June 1971 poll, p. 2309.

14. POL 23-9 PAK, Box 2530, Spengler to Farland, 9 April 1971, State 61066. NMML, Haksar Papers, Subject File 166, Rasgotra to Kaul, 15 May 1971. NSC Files, Box 574, Indo-Pak War, South Asian Congressional, Muskie

speech, 4 November 1971. POL 23-9 PAK, Box 2531, Keating to Rogers, 12 April 1971, New Delhi 5379. Archer K. Blood, *The Cruel Birth of Bangladesh: Memoirs of an American Diplomat* (Dacca: University Press of Bangladesh, 2002), pp. 254–56.

15. Blood, *Cruel Birth,* pp. 325–30. The records of the meeting have been lost, but Blood left a series of written answers. The State Department sent them along with a note that his views did not necessarily reflect official policy. REF PAK, Box 3008, Farland to Rogers, 28 June 1971, Islamabad 6487.

16. Isaacson, *Kissinger,* pp. 275–77. On the moral responsibilities of government officials, see Michael Walzer, *Just and Unjust Wars: A Moral Argument with Historical Illustrations* (New York: Basic Books, 1992), pp. 287–96.

17. U.S. Senate, Subcommittee on Refugees, *Relief Problems in East Pakistan and India* (Washington, D.C.: U.S. Government Printing Office, 1971), 28 June 1971 hearing, pp. 40–51, 27. Blood, *Cruel Birth,* pp. 330–31.

18. J. F. R. Jacob, *Surrender at Dacca: Birth of a Nation* (New Delhi: Manohar, 1997), pp. 45–46.

19. Lee Lescaze, "U.S. Arms Aid to Pakistan Bewilders Fearful Bengalis," *Washington Post,* 24 July 1971.

20. Anthony Mascarenhas, "Genocide," *Sunday Times* (London), 13 June 1971. "Bengal: The Murder of a People," *Newsweek,* 2 August 1971. See Anthony Mascarenhas, *The Rape of Bangla Desh* (New Delhi: Vikas, 1971).

21. See NMML, Haksar Papers, Subject File 220, Pakistan ambassadors meeting, 24–25 August 1971; NMML, Haksar Papers, Subject File 220, Muhammad Khan to Dehlavi, 2 October 1971

22. Sydney H. Schanberg, "Hindus Are Targets of Army Terror in an East Pakistan Town," *New York Times,* 4 July 1971. Sydney H. Schanberg, "West Pakistan Pursues Subjugation of Bengalis," *New York Times,* 14 July 1971.

23. See Kissinger, *White House Years,* pp. 854, 858–59.

24. *FRUS,* vol. E-7, White House tapes, Oval Office 549-25, 28 July 1971, 4:21–4:54 p.m. *FRUS,* Kissinger-Farland memcon, 7 May 1971, pp. 106–9. White House tapes, Oval Office 561-4, 11 August 1971, 9:10–11:40 a.m. *FRUS,* WSAG meeting, 8 September 1971, pp. 393–404. NMML, Haksar Papers, Subject File 277, Jha to Kaul, 18 April 1971. NSA, Huang-Kissinger memcon, 23 November 1971, 10–11:55 p.m. NSC Files, Box 625, Country Files—Middle East, Pakistan, vol. IV, Kissinger to Nixon, 14 May 1971.

25. NSC Files, Box H-053, SRG Meetings, Saunders and Kennedy to Kissinger, 7 April 1971. *FRUS,* Hilaly-Kissinger memcon, 23 July 1971, pp. 267–70. *FRUS,* vol. E-7, White House tapes, Oval Office 549-25, 28 July 1971, 4:21–4:54 p.m.

26. NSA, Government Accountability Office memorandum for Kennedy, declassified 3 February 1972. NSC Files, Box H-058, SRG Meetings, Saunders and Kennedy to Kissinger, "Military Assistance," 21 July 1971. NSA, Nixon-Kissinger telcon, 27 July 1971, 7:20 p.m. NSA, Nixon-Kissinger telcon, 1 October 1971, 10:15 a.m. NSA, Nixon-Kissinger telcon, 6 October 1971, 12:50 p.m. *FRUS,* WSAG minutes, 12 November 1971, 11:09 a.m., pp. 505–14.

27. NSC Files, Box H-053, SRG Meetings, Saunders and Kennedy to Kissinger, 7 April 1971. NSC Files, Box 574, Indo-Pak War, South Asian Military Supply, Saunders and Hoskinson to Kissinger, 17 May 1971. NSC Files, Box 574, Indo-Pak War, South Asian Military Supply, Kissinger to Nixon,

25 June 1971. MEA, HI/1012/78/71, Jha to Kaul, 14 July 1971. NSA, Nixon-Kissinger telcon, 11 December 1971, 7:30 p.m. NSC Files, Box H-058, SRG Meetings, Davis to Irwin, "Military Supply Policy for Pakistan," 29 July 1971. For a contrary view, see NSC Files, Box H-058, SRG Meetings, Saunders and Kennedy to Kissinger, 21 July 1971.

28. NSC Files, Box 574, Indo-Pak War, South Asian Congressional, Church to Nixon, 22 June 1971. See NSC Files, Box 574, Indo-Pak War, South Asian Congressional, Church speech, 22 June 1971; NSC Files, Box 574, Indo-Pak War, South Asian Congressional, Saunders to Kissinger, 21 July 1971; NSC Files, Box 574, Indo-Pak War, South Asian Congressional, Schiff to Farland, 18 June 1971, State 108854. NSC Files, Box 574, Indo-Pak War, South Asian Congressional, Kennedy speech, 22 June 1971. Lewis M. Simons, "Kennedy, U.S. Aide Clash on Pakistan," *Washington Post,* 29 June 1971, p. A3. See NSC Files, Box 574, Indo-Pak War, South Asian Congressional, Symington speech, 23 July 1971. NSC Files, Box 574, Indo-Pak War, South Asian Military Supply, Rogers to Nixon, 23 June 1971. NSC Files, Box 574, Indo-Pak War, South Asian Military Supply, Haig to Nixon, 25 June 1971. NSC Files, Box 574, Indo-Pak War, South Asian Military Supply, Kissinger to Nixon, 25 June 1971.

29. NSC Files, Box H-058, SRG Meetings, Eliot to Kissinger, 21 July 1971. NSC Files, Box 574, Indo-Pak War, South Asian Congressional, Saunders to Kissinger, 23 July 1971. NSC Files, Box 574, Indo-Pak War, South Asian Congressional, Van Hollen to Farland, 16 July 1971, State 129207. NSC Files, Box 574, Indo-Pak War, South Asian Congressional, Schiff to Farland, 18 June 1971, State 108854. See NSC Files, Box 574, Indo-Pak War, South Asian Congressional, Gallagher speech, 17 June 1971; NSC Files, Box 574, Indo-Pak War, South Asian Congressional, Muskie speech, 4 November 1971; NSC Files, Box 574, Indo-Pak War, South Asian Congressional, Saunders to Kissinger, 23 July 1971. NSC Files, Box 574, Indo-Pak War, South Asian Congressional, Church statement, 4 August 1971. NSC Files, Box 574, Indo-Pak War, South Asian Congressional, Proxmire statement, 29 July 1971. On Proxmire, see Samantha Power, *"A Problem from Hell": America and the Age of Genocide* (New York: Basic Books, 2002), pp. 61–85, 151–69. Proxmire later said, "Thirty years separate the atrocities of Nazi Germany and the Asian sub-continent, but the body counts are not so far apart. Those who felt that genocide was a crime of the past had a rude awakening during the Pakistani occupation of Bangladesh." (Power, *"A Problem from Hell,"* p. 82.) NSC Files, Box 574, Indo-Pak War, South Asian Congressional, McGovern speech, 8 July 1971. See NSC Files, Box 574, Indo-Pak War, South Asian Congressional, McGovern speech, 23 July 1971. See NSC Files, Box 574, Indo-Pak War, South Asian Congressional, Mondale speech, 6 May 1971; NSC Files, Box H-058, SRG Meetings, Saunders and Kennedy to Kissinger, "Congressional Strategy," 22 July 1971.

30. NSA, Kissinger-Rogers telcon, 6 August 1971, 1:30 p.m. See NSA, Kissinger-Rogers telcon, 18 August 1971, 10:07 a.m. NSC Files, Box H-058, SRG Meetings, Saunders and Kennedy to Kissinger, "Military Assistance," 21 July 1971. NSC Files, Box H-058, SRG Meetings, Saunders and Kennedy to Kissinger, "Congressional Strategy," 22 July 1971. NSA, Government Accountability Office memorandum for Kennedy, declassified 3 February 1972.

31. *FRUS,* SRG meeting, 23 July 1971, pp. 270–83.

32. NSC Files, Box 627, Country Files—Middle East, Pakistan, vol. VIII, Kissinger to Nixon, "Military Supply Policy," 3 November 1971. NSC Files, Box 570, Indo-Pak War, South Asia, Kissinger to Nixon, 3 August 1971. In June, Pakistan might have still gotten up to $34 million of military supply; by mid-July, a new estimate put it at $15 million or less; and by mid-August, it would be under $5 million. See NSC Files, Box 627, Country Files—Middle East, Pakistan, vol. VIII, Kissinger to Nixon, "Military Supply Policy," 3 November 1971; NSC Files, Box H-058, SRG Meetings, Kennedy and Saunders to Kissinger, 30 July 1971.

33. NSA, Nixon-Kissinger telcon, 3 August 1971, 5:25 p.m. NSC Files, Box 570, Indo-Pak War, South Asia, Kissinger to Nixon, 3 August 1971. See NSC Files, Box H-058, SRG Meetings, Eliot to Kissinger, 5 August 1971.

34. NSA, Nixon-Kissinger telcon, 3 August 1971, 5:25 p.m. See NSA, Nixon-Kissinger telcon, 8 November 1971, 7:50 p.m.; NSA, Kissinger-Rogers telcon, 6 August 1971, 1:30 p.m.; NSC Files, Box 574, Indo-Pak War, South Asian Congressional, Church statement, 4 August 1971; NSC Files, Box 574, Indo-Pak War, South Asian Congressional, Saxbe statement, 27 July 1971.

35. FRUS, Saunders and Hoskinson to Kissinger, 29 October 1971, pp. 479–82. See NSC Files, Box 626, Country Files—Middle East, Pakistan, vol. VII, Hoskinson to Kissinger, 13 September 1971. NSC Files, Box 626, Country Files—Middle East, Pakistan, vol. VII, Kissinger-Haq memcon, 10 September 1971. Hoskinson wrote that his notes were "sanitized" so that the State and Defense Departments could see it. (NSC Files, Box 626, Country Files—Middle East, Pakistan, vol. VII, Hoskinson to Kissinger, 13 September 1971.)

36. NSA, Nixon-Kissinger telcon, 27 July 1971, 7:20 p.m. See Kissinger, White House Years, pp. 865, 875. See FRUS, SRG meeting, 30 July 1971, 3:20 p.m., pp. 292–302.

37. FRUS, SRG meeting, 23 July 1971, pp. 270–83.

38. Ibid. See NSC Files, Box H-058, SRG Meetings, Saunders and Kennedy to Kissinger, "Analytical Summary," 12 July 1971.

39. NSC Files, Box H-058, SRG Meetings, Saunders and Kennedy to Kissinger, "Analytical Summary," 12 July 1971. NSC Files, Box H-058, SRG Meetings, Saunders and Kennedy to Kissinger, 21 July 1971. NSC Files, Box H-058, SRG Meetings, Saunders to Kissinger, 10 August 1971. NSC Files, Box H-058, SRG Meetings, Saunders and Kennedy to Kissinger, 21 July 1971. See NSC Files, Box H-058, SRG Meetings, Saunders and Kennedy to Kissinger, "Analytical Summary," 12 July 1971; NSC Files, Box H-058, SRG Meetings, Saunders to Kissinger, 10 August 1971; NSC Files, Box H-058, SRG Meetings, draft memorandum for Kissinger to Nixon, 11 August 1971.

40. FRUS, SRG meeting, 23 July 1971, pp. 270–83.

41. NSC Files, Box 625, Country Files—Middle East, Pakistan, vol. V, Saunders to Kissinger, 30 July 1971. NSC Files, Box 626, Country Files—Middle East, Pakistan, vol. VI, Hoskinson to Kissinger, 25 August 1971. FRUS, SRG meeting, 30 July 1971, 3:20 p.m., pp. 292–302.

42. FRUS, SRG meeting, 23 July 1971, pp. 270–83. See FRUS, SRG meeting, 30 July 1971, 3:20 p.m., pp. 292–302.

43. FRUS, SRG meeting, 30 July 1971, 3:20 p.m., pp. 292–302. NSC Files, Box 1025, Presidential/HAK MemCons, Farland-Kissinger memcon, 30 July 1971. NSA, Nixon-Kissinger telcon, received 3 August 1971.

44. NSA, Kissinger-Sisco telcon, 27 July 1971, 10:13 a.m. *FRUS,* SRG meeting, 23 July 1971, pp. 270–83. NSC Files, Box H-058, SRG Meetings, Davis to Irwin, "Scenario for Action in Indo-Pakistan Crisis," 29 July 1971.

45. *FRUS,* vol. E-7, White House tapes, Oval Office 549-25, 28 July 1971, 4:21–4:54 p.m.

46. NSA, Kissinger-McNamara telcon, 13 August 1971, 8:40 a.m. *FRUS,* WSAG meeting, 8 September 1971, pp. 393–404. White House tapes, Oval Office 558-10, 9 August 1971, 5:44–6:18 p.m.

47. *FRUS,* SRG meeting, 30 July 1971, 3:20 p.m., pp. 292–302.

48. Kissinger, *White House Years,* pp. 863–64. NSC Files, Box 1025, Presidential/HAK MemCons, Farland-Kissinger memcon, 30 July 1971. See NSC Files, Box 625, Country Files—Middle East, Pakistan, vol. V, Saunders to Kissinger, 30 July 1971. White House tapes, Oval Office 553-3, 2 August 1971, 9:45 a.m. These were, respectively, Christopher Van Hollen and Joseph Sisco. See NSA, Kissinger-McNamara telcon, 13 August 1971, 8:40 a.m. For a subsequent showdown between Kissinger and Sisco over arms shipments, see NSC Files, Box 626, Country Files—Middle East, Pakistan, vol. VII, Saunders and Hoskinson to Kissinger, 1 September 1971. NSC Files, Box 626, Country Files—Middle East, Pakistan, vol. VII, Haig to Kissinger, 1 September 1971. NSC Files, Box H-082, WSAG Meetings, Saunders and Hoskinson to Kissinger, 3 September 1971.

49. POL 23-9 PAK, Box 2533, Keating to Rogers, 10 August 1971, New Delhi 12722.

50. White House tapes, Oval Office 553-3, 2 August 1971, 9:45 a.m. *FRUS,* vol. E-7, White House tapes, Oval Office 624-21, 24 November 1971, 12:27 p.m.

51. POL INDIA-US, Box 2369, Gandhi-Kissinger memcon, 7 July 1971.

52. NSA, Nixon-Kissinger telcon, 27 July 1971, 7:20 p.m.

53. *FRUS,* vol. E-7, White House tapes, Oval Office 549-25, 28 July 1971, 4:21–4:54 p.m. See White House tapes, Oval Office 547-6, 27 July 1971, 11:05–11:32 a.m. NSC Files, Box 625, Country Files—Middle East, Pakistan, vol. V, Kissinger to Nixon, 27 July 1971. For an impressively sanitized official record of their talk, see NSC Files, Box 626, Country Files—Middle East, Pakistan, vol. VI, Nixon-Farland memcon, 28 August 1971, 3:30 p.m.

54. Yvonne Shinhoster Lamb, "Brian Bell; Athlete, Journalist and Diplomat," *Washington Post,* 13 October 2006, p. B7. "Brian Bell," *Kentucky New Era,* 19 October 2006, p. A2. *FRUS,* vol. E-7, White House tapes, Oval Office 549-25, 28 July 1971, 4:21–4:54 p.m. Farland said, "Shakespeare got him out"—meaning Frank Shakespeare, the anti-Soviet ideologue whom Nixon had appointed as USIS chief (Richard T. Arndt, *The First Resort of Kings: American Cultural Diplomacy in the Twentieth Century* [Dulles, Va.: Potomac Books, 2005], pp. 438–43).

55. *FRUS,* vol. E-7, White House tapes, Oval Office 549-25, 28 July 1971, 4:21–4:54 p.m.

56. Philip Glass, "George Harrison, World-Music Catalyst and Great-Souled Man," *New York Times,* 9 December 2001.

57. Harrison interview, *The Concert for Bangladesh* DVD (1991).

58. Don Heckman, "The Event Wound Up as a Love Feast," *Village Voice,* 5 August 1971.

59. Ibid. Maureen Orth, "Dylan—Rolling Again," *Newsweek,* 14 January 1974, pp. 46–49. Grace Lichtenstein, "40,000 Cheer 2 Beatles in Dual Benefit

for Pakistanis," *New York Times,* 2 August 1971, pp. A1, A14. Tom Zito, "George, Ringo, Help from a Friend," *Washington Post,* 2 August 1971, pp. B1, B3.

60. NMML, Haksar Papers, Subject File 220, Natwar Singh to Kaul, 12 October 1971. Kamila Shamsie, "Pop Idols," *Granta,* no. 112 (fall 2010). NMML, Haksar Papers, Subject File 220, Hussaini to Pakistani ambassadors, 30 September 1971.

61. White House tapes, Oval Office 553-3, 2 August 1971, 9:45 a.m.

62. *FRUS,* vol. E-7, White House tapes, Oval Office 549-25, 28 July 1971, 4:21–4:54 p.m. White House tapes, Oval Office 553-3, 2 August 1971, 9:45 a.m. See NSC Files, Box H-058, SRG Meetings, Saunders and Kennedy to Kissinger, Analytical Summary, 10 August 1971. White House tapes, Oval Office 561-4, 11 August 1971, 9:10–11:40 a.m. See Kissinger, *White House Years,* p. 869. See also NSC Files, Box H-058, SRG Meetings, Kissinger to Nixon, "Talking Points," 11 August 1971. NSC Files, Box H-058, SRG Meetings, Nixon and SRG memcon, 11 August 1971.

63. On Keating, see NSC Files, Box H-058, SRG Meetings, Saunders to Kissinger, 12 August 1971; NSC Files, Box H-058, SRG Meetings, Davis to Eliot, 2 September 1971; NSC Files, Box H-058, SRG Meetings, Nixon and SRG memcon (sanitized version), 11 August 1971.

64. NSC Files, Box H-058, SRG Meetings, Nixon and SRG memcon, 11 August 1971.

65. *FRUS,* SRG meeting, 11 August 1971, pp. 320–23. See NSC Files, Box H-058, SRG Meetings, Saunders to Kissinger, 10 August 1971.

66. *FRUS,* WSAG meeting, 22 November 1971, 2:39–3:14 p.m., pp. 529–36. *FRUS,* WSAG meeting, 8 September 1971, pp. 393–404. See NSC Files, Box H-082, WSAG Meetings, Saunders and Hoskinson to Kissinger, 3 September 1971; NSA, Kissinger-Johnson telcon, 7 October 1971, 11:37 a.m.; NSA, Kissinger-Johnson telcon, 8 October 1971, 11:30 a.m.; Kissinger, *White House Years,* pp. 863–54.

67. White House tapes, Oval Office 553-3, 2 August 1971, 9:45 a.m.

68. "President Nixon's News Conference," *New York Times,* 5 August 1971.

69. White House tapes, Oval Office 561-4, 11 August 1971, 9:10–11:40 a.m. See White House tapes, Oval Office 784-21, 21 September 1972, 12:25–2:01 p.m. As Samantha Power astutely writes, "It is in the realm of domestic politics that the battle to stop genocide is lost." (*"A Problem from Hell,"* p. xviii.)

CHAPTER 14: SOVIET FRIENDS

1. Singh to Narayan, 10 December 1971, Jayaprakash Narayan, *Selected Works,* ed. Bimal Prasad (New Delhi: Manohar, 2008), vol. 9, p. 878. Sham Lal, "The Realpolitik of Charity," *Times of India,* 11 June 1971. Jayaprakash Narayan, "Bangladesh and India's Future," *Indian Express,* 27–28 October 1971, Narayan, *Selected Works,* pp. 660–66.

2. K. Subrahmanyam, "Military Aid to Pakistan and Its Repercussions on Bangla Desh," in Ranjit Gupta and Radhakrishna, eds., *World Meet on Bangla Desh* (New Delhi: Impex, 1971), pp. 116–18. MEA, WII/121/54/71, vol. II, Menon to Kaul, 5 July 1971. MEA, WII/121/54/71, Gonsalves to Kaul, 6 July 1971. Shashi Tharoor, *Reasons of State: Political Development and India's Foreign Policy Under Indira Gandhi, 1966–1977* (New Delhi: Vikas, 1982), p. 301. In 1970, 66 percent of Indians had a good or very good opinion of the

United States, against 9 percent with a bad or very bad opinion. In 1971, it was 49 percent good or very good, and 28 percent bad or very bad.
3. MEA, HI/121/13/71, vol. I, Singh statement in Lok Sabha and Rajya Sabha, 24 June 1971. MEA, WII/109/15/71, Verma to Menon, 20 August 1971. MEA, WII/109/15/71, Lamabah to Jha, 20 July 1971. Lewis M. Simons, "Pakistan Using U.S. Jetliners to Help Move Men to Bengal," *Washington Post,* 19 August 1971, p. A22. NSC Files, Box H-058, SRG Meetings, Eliot to Kissinger, 5 August 1971. PIA had only seven of its own 707s, in addition to these two leased ones; even if the leased U.S. planes were not carrying troops, they freed up the other 707s to do so. NSC Files, Box H-082, WSAG Meetings, Eliot to Kissinger, "Situation Report: India/Pakistan," 1 September 1971. See Sydney H. Schanberg, "U.S.-India Relations: A New Low," *New York Times,* 27 July 1971; Sydney H. Schanberg, "A Bitter New Delhi Not Likely to Be Easily Soothed," *New York Times,* 6 September 1971.
4. NSC Files, Box 627, Country Files—Middle East, Pakistan, vol. VIII, Kissinger to Nixon, "Military Supply Policy," 3 November 1971. MEA, WII/109/13/71, vol. II, "Supply of Arms by USA to Pakistan," n.d. November 1971. MEA, WII/125/112/71, Singh statement, 12 July 1971.
5. POL INDIA-US, Box 2369, Keating to Rogers, 25 September 1971, New Delhi 15268. "Indians are emotional people who frequently over-react in ways Westerners consider immature," Keating condescendingly wrote.
6. NMML, Haksar Papers, Subject File 171, Haksar to Gandhi, 4 August 1971. Kosygin had visited India several times, but Gandhi had not paid a state visit to the Soviet Union since 1966. NMML, Haksar Papers, Subject File 171, Haksar to Gandhi, 4 August 1971. MEA, HI/1012/57/71, Purushottam to Kaul, 26 August 1971. See NMML, Haksar Papers, Subject File 170, Haksar to Singh and Kaul, 6 August 1971; NMML, Haksar Papers, Subject File 280, Kosygin-Dhar meeting, 5 August 1971
7. NMML, Haksar Papers, Subject File 280, Gromyko-Dhar meeting, 3 August 1971. P. N. Dhar, *Indira Gandhi, the "Emergency," and Indian Democracy* (Oxford: Oxford University Press, 2000), pp. 170–71. The treaty was based on a similar one signed between the Soviet Union and Egypt in May 1971 (MEA, HI/1012/5/71, UAR-USSR treaty, 27 May 1971).
8. NMML, Haksar Papers, Subject File 280, Dhar-Gromyko meeting, 4 August 1971. See NMML, Haksar Papers, Subject File 280, Kosygin-Dhar meeting, 5 August 1971.
9. MEA, HI/1012/57/71, Purushottam to Kaul, 26 August 1971. NMML, Haksar Papers, Subject File 280, Kosygin-Dhar meeting, 5 August 1971.
10. See Anne Applebaum, *Gulag: A History* (New York: Random House, 2003). On Soviet oppression of eastern and central Europe, see Václav Havel, *Open Letters: Selected Writings, 1965–1990,* ed. Paul Wilson (New York: Random House, 1992); Adam Michnik, *Letters from Prison and Other Essays,* trans. Maya Latynski (Berkeley: University of California Press, 1985); Timothy Garton Ash, *The Uses of Adversity: Essays on the Fate of Central Europe* (New York: Random House, 1989); Anne Applebaum, *Iron Curtain: The Crushing of Eastern Europe, 1944–1956* (New York: Doubleday, 2012). NMML, Haksar Papers, Subject File 170, Haksar to Gandhi, 8 August 1971.
11. NMML, Haksar Papers, Subject File 227, Gandhi-Gromyko conversation, Malhoutra notes, 9 August 1971. This meeting was held on August 8. NMML, Haksar Papers, Subject File 170, Haksar to Gandhi, 8 August 1971.

12. NSC Files, Box H-082, WSAG Meetings, Eliot to Kissinger, 1 September 1971. NMML, Haksar Papers, Subject File 227, Gandhi-Gromyko conversation, Malhoutra notes, 9 August 1971.
13. NMML, Haksar Papers, Subject File 220, Treaty of Peace, Friendship and Cooperation Between the Republic of India and the Union of Soviet Socialist Republics, 9 August 1971. MEA, HI/1012/57/71, Damodaran to Kaul, 22 October 1971. See Vojtech Mastny, "The Soviet Union's Partnership with India," *Journal of Cold War Studies,* vol. 12, no. 3 (summer 2010), pp. 68–72; Raymond L. Garthoff, *Détente and Confrontation: American-Soviet Relations from Nixon to Reagan* (Washington, D.C.: Brookings Institution, 1985), pp. 266–69; Robert H. Donaldson, *Soviet Policy Toward India: Ideology and Strategy* (Cambridge, Mass.: Harvard University Press, 1974).
14. NMML, Haksar Papers, Subject File 170, Haksar to Gandhi, 10 August 1971. MEA, HI/1012/30/71, Chib to Kaul, 4 September 1971. NMML, Haksar Papers, Subject File 171, Jha to Kaul, 9 August 1971. NMML, Haksar Papers, Subject File 170, Haksar to Gandhi, 14 August 1971. NMML, Haksar Papers, Subject File 170, Haksar to Gandhi, 10 August 1971.
15. MEA, HI/1012/57/71, Damodaran to Kaul, 22 October 1971. Dhar, *Indira Gandhi, the "Emergency," and Indian Democracy,* p. 170. NMML, Haksar Papers, Subject File 171, Congress draft resolution, 23 August 1971. NMML, Haksar Papers, Subject File 170, Haksar to Gandhi, 10 August 1971. See P. N. Haksar, "India's Sovereignty and Indo-Soviet Relations," and T. N. Kaul, "Indo-Soviet Friendship," in V. D. Chopra, ed., *Studies in Indo-Soviet Relations* (New Delhi: Indian Centre for Regional Affairs, 1986), pp. 13–21, 22–28; T. N. Kaul, *Reminiscences Discreet and Indiscreet* (New Delhi: Lancers Publishers, 1982), pp. 243–67; POL INDIA-US, Box 2369, Keating to Rogers, 25 September 1971, New Delhi 15268. The Soviet Union's popularity did not shift much from 1970 to 1971, but it is not clear when the polls were taken. It did skyrocket after the war, in 1972 (Tharoor, *Reasons of State,* p. 301). Narayan statement, 9 August 1971, *Selected Works,* p. 637. NMML, Haksar Papers, Subject File 171, Congress draft resolution, 23 August 1971. MEA, HI/121/13/71, vol. I, Gandhi press conference, 19 October 1971. NMML, Haksar Papers, Subject File 227, Gandhi-Gromyko conversation, Malhoutra notes, 9 August 1971. MEA, WII/121/60/71.
16. NMML, Haksar Papers, Subject File 170, Kaul to Singh, 7 August 1971. See Oriana Fallaci, *Interviews with History and Conversations with Power* (New York: Rizzoli, 2011), pp. 269–70; NMML, Haksar Papers, Subject File 171, Congress draft resolution, 23 August 1971; MEA, WII/121/60/71, Anthony statement, n.d. 1971; Tharoor, *Reasons of State,* pp. 260–64; T. N. Kaul, *The Kissinger Years: Indo-American Relations* (New Delhi: Arnold-Heinemann, 1980), pp. 60–62; K. P. S. Menon, *The Indo-Soviet Treaty: Setting and Sequel* (New Delhi: Vikas, 1971); Pran Chopra, *Before and After the Indo-Soviet Treaty* (New Delhi: S. Chand & Co., 1971); N. M. Ghatate, ed., *Indo-Soviet Treaty: Reactions and Reflections* (New Delhi: Deendayal Research Institute, 1972). See Christopher Andrew and Vasili Mitrokhin, *The World Was Going Our Way: The KGB and the Battle for the Third World* (New York: Basic Books, 2005), pp. 319–26.
17. White House tapes, Oval Office 558-10, 9 August 1971, 5:44–6:18 p.m. NSC Files, Box H-058, SRG Meetings, Nixon and SRG memcon, 11 August 1971.
18. Henry Kissinger, *White House Years* (Boston: Little, Brown, 1979), p. 867.

See ibid., p. 767. For a sophisticated view of the Cold War's real importance for the subcontinent, see Steve Coll, *On the Grand Trunk Road: A Journey into South Asia* (New York: Times Books, 1994), pp. 257, 259–60. NSC Files, Box 597, Country Files—Middle East, India, vol. IV, Kissinger to Nixon, 24 August 1971. See NSC Files, Box 597, Country Files—Middle East, India, vol. IV, Sonnenfeldt to Kissinger, 18 August 1971; MEA, HI/1012/78/71, Jha to Kaul, 7 September 1971. White House tapes, Oval Office 626-14, 30 November 1971, 5:21–6:09 p.m.

19. *FRUS,* Dobrynin-Kissinger memcon, 17 August 1971, pp. 332–33. NSA, Kissinger-Rockefeller telcon, 3 November 1971, 7 p.m. See Kissinger, *White House Years,* p. 916.

20. NMML, Haksar Papers, Subject File 171, Haksar revised draft speech, August 1971.

21. NMML, Haksar Papers, Subject File 89, Kaul memorandum, 15 June 1971. NMML, Haksar Papers, Subject File 171, Haksar to Jha, 7 August 1971. *FRUS,* Irwin to Nixon, 9 August 1971, pp. 313–15.

22. NSA, Huang-Kissinger memcon, 16 August 1971, Lord to Kissinger, 19 August 1971. *FRUS,* WSAG meeting, 17 August 1971, 4:35 p.m., pp. 339–44. See NSC Files, Box 627, Country Files—Middle East, Pakistan, vol. VIII, Rogers to Nixon, 28 October 1971. NSA, Kissinger-Rockefeller telcon, 3 November 1971, 7 p.m.

23. NSC Files, Box 643, Country Files—Middle East, India/Pakistan, Jha-Kissinger memcon, 9 August 1971. *FRUS,* Jha-Kissinger memcon, 25 August 1971, p. 368. *FRUS,* Jha-Kissinger memcon, 9 August 1971, pp. 315–17.

24. *FRUS,* Kissinger to Nixon, 19 August 1971, pp. 348–51. NMML, Haksar Papers, Subject File 170, Gandhi to Nixon, 7 August 1971. NMML, Haksar Papers, Subject File 170, Haksar to Jha, 7 August 1971.

25. Narayan statement, 18 September 1971, Narayan, *Selected Works,* pp. 648–55. NMML, Haksar Papers, Subject File 165, Haksar to Dhar, 7 April 1971. NMML, Haksar Papers, Subject File 165, Haksar to Dhar, 7 April 1971. For Haksar's draft, see Haksar to Gandhi, 5 August 1971.

26. K. F. Rustamji, *The British, the Bandits and the Bordermen: From the Diaries of K. F. Rustamji,* ed. P. V. Rajgopal (New Delhi: Wisdom Tree, 2009), pp. 321–23.

CHAPTER 15: KENNEDY

1. Lee Lescaze, "U.S. Arms Aid to Pakistan Bewilders Fearful Bengalis," *Washington Post,* 24 July 1971.

2. NSC Files, Box 574, Indo-Pak War, South Asian Congressional, Kennedy speech, 22 July 1971. NSC Files, Box 574, Indo-Pak War, South Asian Congressional, Hilaly to Kissinger, n.d. August 1971. Kennedy gave speeches on April 1, May 12, June 2, June 18, and June 22, and held hearings on June 28 and July 22. NSC Files, Box 574, Indo-Pak War, South Asian Congressional, Kennedy speech, 1 November 1971. Kennedy had previously pressed the White House to help in Biafra (*FRUS,* vol. E-5, Kennedy-Kissinger telcon, 22 January 1970, 8:05 p.m.). NSC Files, Box 574, Indo-Pak War, South Asian Congressional, Van Hollen to Farland, 24 July 1971, State 134519. Lewis M. Simons, "Secret Cables See Famine in E. Pakistan," *Washington Post,* 23 July 1971, p. A7.

3. NSC Files, Box 574, Indo-Pak War, South Asian Congressional, Hilaly to

Kennedy, 2 August 1971. NSC Files, Box H-058, SRG Meetings, Eliot to Kissinger, 5 August 1971. The two aides were Dale de Haan and Jerry Tinker. On de Haan, see Thomas Oliphant, "The Lion at Rest," *Democracy*, winter 2010, p. 100. NSC Files, Box 574, Indo-Pak War, South Asian Congressional, Hilaly to Kennedy, 23 July 1971.

4. MEA, WII/121/60/71, Rasgotra to Menon, 23 July 1971. See MEA, WII/121/60/71, Singh to Kennedy, 26 July 1971. MEA, WII/121/60/71, Kennedy memorials, n.d. August 1971. MEA, WII/121/60/71, Rasgotra to Menon, 27 July 1971. MEA, WII/121/60/71, Luthra to Haksar, 9 August 1971. MEA, WII/121/60/71, Rasgotra to Menon, 31 July 1971. See MEA, WII/121/60/71, Lambah to Menon, 2 August 1971. MEA, WII/121/60/71, Rasgotra to Menon, 23 July 1971.

5. MEA, WII/121/60/71, Vaz to Luthra, 3 August 1971. See MEA, WII/121/60/71, Rasgotra to Menon, 30 July 1971.

6. White House tapes, EOB 267-22, 30 July 1971, 4:46–5:43 p.m.

7. NSC Files, Box 1025, Presidential/HAK MemCons, Farland-Kissinger memcon, 30 July 1971. See White House tapes, EOB 267-22, 30 July 1971, 4:46–5:43 p.m. NSC Files, Box 1025, Presidential/HAK MemCons, Farland-Kissinger memcon, 30 July 1971. NSC Files, Box 626, Country Files— Middle East, Pakistan, vol. VI, Eliot to Kissinger, 17 August 1971. *FRUS*, WSAG meeting, 17 August 1971, 4:35 p.m., pp. 339–44.

8. MEA, WII/121/60/71, Luthra to Haksar, 9 August 1971. Sydney H. Schanberg, "Kennedy, in India, Terms Pakistan Drive Genocide," *New York Times*, 17 August 1971. NSC Files, Box 574, Indo-Pak War, South Asian Congressional, Keating to Rogers, 18 August 1971, New Delhi 13221.

9. MEA, WII/121/60/71, Rasgotra to Menon, 31 July 1971. MEA, WII/121/60/71, Dhavan to Singh, 7 August 1971. MEA, WII/121/60/71, Lambah to Kaul, 9 August 1971. MEA, WII/121/60/71, Rasgotra to Menon, 31 July 1971. The only Americans of interest to Kennedy were Peace Corps volunteers. MEA, WII/121/60/71, Singh to Ray, 4 August 1971. NSC Files, Box 574, Indo-Pak War, South Asian Congressional, Keating to Rogers, 18 August 1971, New Delhi 13221. MEA, WII/121/60/71, *CBS Evening News* report, 11 August 1971. MEA, WII/121/60/71, ABC News report, 11 August 1971.

10. The other expert was John Lewis, the dean of the Woodrow Wilson School at Princeton University and the former USAID chief in India. See MEA, WII/121/60/71, Rasgotra to Menon, 30 July 1971.

11. In addition to an interview, Scrimshaw generously provided me a draft chapter from his forthcoming memoirs, "A Trip to India with Senator Ted Kennedy," 21 February 2012, on file with author.

12. MEA, WII/121/60/71, Menon to Rasgotra, 17 August 1971. NSC Files, Box 574, Indo-Pak War, South Asian Congressional, Kennedy speech, 1 November 1971. NSC Files, Box 574, Indo-Pak War, South Asian Congressional, Kennedy speech, 26 August 1971. NSC Files, Box 574, Indo-Pak War, South Asian Congressional, Keating to Rogers, 18 August 1971, New Delhi 13221.

13. NSC Files, Box 574, Indo-Pak War, South Asian Congressional, Kennedy speech, 1 November 1971. NSC Files, Box 574, Indo-Pak War, South Asian Congressional, Kennedy speech, 26 August 1971. NSC Files, Box 574, Indo-Pak War, South Asian Congressional, Keating to Rogers, 18 August 1971, New Delhi 13221.

14. MEA, WII/121/60/71, Menon to Rasgotra, 17 August 1971. MEA,

WII/121/60/71, Rasgotra to Menon, 31 July 1971. MEA, WII/121/60/71, ABC News report, 11 August 1971. NSC Files, Box 574, Indo-Pak War, South Asian Congressional, Keating to Rogers, 18 August 1971, New Delhi 13221.

15. MEA, WII/121/60/71, Kennedy-Giri talk, 14 August 1971.

16. MEA, WII/121/60/71, Lambah to Luthra, 11 August 1971. MEA, WII/121/60/71, Menon to Rasgotra, 17 August 1971. See NSC Files, Box 574, Indo-Pak War, South Asian Congressional, Keating to Rogers, 18 August 1971, New Delhi 13221. MEA, WII/121/60/71, reception invitees, n.d. August 1971; MEA, WII/121/60/71, Menon to Singh, 2 August 1971. MEA, WII/121/60/71, Menon to Rasgotra, 17 August 1971. U.S. Senate, Subcommittee on Refugees, *Relief Problems in East Pakistan and India, Part II* (Washington, D.C.: U.S. Government Printing Office, 1971), John Lewis statement, p. 288. NSC Files, Box 574, Indo-Pak War, South Asian Congressional, Keating to Rogers, 18 August 1971, New Delhi 13221.

17. MEA, WII/121/60/71, Rasgotra to Menon, 31 July 1971. MEA, WII/121/60/71, Luthra to Haksar, 9 August 1971. NSC Files, Box 574, Indo-Pak War, South Asian Congressional, Keating to Rogers, 18 August 1971, New Delhi 13221. MEA, WII/121/60/71, Kennedy-Kaul discussion, 14 August 1971. See MEA, WII/121/60/71, Kennedy-Khadilkar conversation, 14 August 1971; MEA, WII/121/60/71, Lambah to Singh, 9 August 1971.

18. See Senate Subcommittee on Refugees, *Relief Problems in East Pakistan and India, Part II*, Lewis statement, p. 282.

19. NMML, Haksar Papers, Subject File 89, Gandhi-Kennedy conversation, Malhoutra notes, 16 August 1971.

20. NSC Files, Box 574, Indo-Pak War, South Asian Congressional, Keating to Rogers, 18 August 1971, New Delhi 13221. See MEA, WII/121/60/71, Singh to Ray, 4 August 1971; MEA, WII/121/60/71, Lambah to Singh, 9 August 1971. MEA, WII/121/60/71, Kennedy press conference, 16 August 1971. Sydney H. Schanberg, "Kennedy, in India, Terms Pakistan Drive Genocide," *New York Times,* 17 August 1971.

21. NSC Files, Box 574, Indo-Pak War, South Asian Congressional, Keating to Rogers, 18 August 1971, New Delhi 13221. MEA, WII/121/60/71, Menon to Rasgotra, 17 August 1971. See MEA, WII/121/60/71, Kennedy to Singh, 30 August 1971.

22. MEA, WII/121/60/71, Kennedy press conference, 16 August 1971.

23. MEA, WII/121/60/71, Kennedy-Khadilkar conversation, 14 August 1971. MEA, WII/121/60/71, Menon to Rasgotra, 17 August 1971.

24. White House tapes, Oval Office 563-6, 13 August 1971, 12:29–1:45 p.m. MEA, WII/121/60/71, Tinker to Lambah, 15 September 1971. Senate Subcommittee on Refugees, *Relief Problems in East Pakistan and India, Part II,* 30 September 1971 hearing, pp. 227–61.

25. NSC Files, Box 574, Indo-Pak War, South Asian Congressional, Kennedy speech, 26 August 1971. MEA, WII/121/60/71, Kennedy speech, 26 August 1971.

26. MEA, WII/109/13/71, vol. IV, "America's Conscience," *Indian Express,* 28 August 1971. See MEA, WII/121/60/71, Jha to Menon, 27 August 1971, and MEA, HI/1012/78/71, Jha to Kaul, 7 September 1971.

27. MEA, WII/121/60/71, McCloskey statement, 27 August 1971. *FRUS,* Kissinger to Nixon, 30 September 1971, pp. 427–28. NSC Files, Box H-082,

WSAG Meetings, Saunders to Kissinger, 9 September 1971. Saunders estimated that the United States would shoulder 75 percent of Pakistan's cost, and 40 percent of India's. NSA, Shultz-Kissinger telcon, 29 September 1971.

28. NSC Files, Box 574, Indo-Pak War, South Asian Congressional, Saunders to Kissinger, 8 September 1971. FRUS, WSAG meeting, 8 September 1971, p. 394.

29. NSC Files, Box 574, Indo-Pak War, South Asian Congressional, Saunders to Haig, 30 September 1971. NSC Files, Box 570, Indo-Pak War, Saunders to Haig, "Draft Speech on South Asia," 30 September 1971. See White House tapes, Oval Office 599-12, 22 October 1971, 12:16–12:45 p.m.; White House tapes, Oval Office 626-10, 30 November 1971, 11:23 a.m.–12:03 p.m. NSC Files, Box 574, Indo-Pak War, South Asian Congressional, Saunders to Haig, "Talking Points for Gerald Ford," 29 November 1971. NSC Files, Box 574, Indo-Pak War, South Asian Congressional, Dole speech, 6 October 1971.

30. NSC Files, Box 597, Country Files—Middle East, India, vol. IV, Keating to Finch, 3 September 1971. White House tapes, Oval Office 617-17, 15 November 1971, 4:31–4:39 p.m.

31. NSC Files, Box 574, Indo-Pak War, South Asian Congressional, Kennedy speech, 23 September 1971.

32. NSC Files, Box 574, Indo-Pak War, South Asian Congressional, Van Hollen to Farland, 16 July 1971, State 129207. See NSC Files, Box 574, Indo-Pak War, South Asian Congressional, Van Hollen to Keating, 28 July 1971, State 137256. NSC Files, Box 626, Country Files—Middle East, Pakistan, vol. VII, Saunders and Hoskinson to Kissinger, 29 October 1971.

33. NSC Files, Box 626, Country Files—Middle East, Pakistan, vol. VII, Saunders and Hoskinson to Kissinger, 29 October 1971.

34. NSC Files, Box 574, Indo-Pak War, South Asian Congressional, Muskie speech, 4 November 1971. MEA, HI/1012/30/71, Deb memorandum, weekly refugee statistics, 29 November 1971. The number was 1,766,000. NSC Files, Box 574, Indo-Pak War, South Asian Congressional, Kennedy report, 1 November 1971.

35. NSC Files, Box 574, Indo-Pak War, South Asian Congressional, Kennedy speech, 1 November 1971.

CHAPTER 16: "WE REALLY SLOBBERED OVER THE OLD WITCH"

1. NSC Files, Box 570, Indo-Pak Crisis, CIA Office of National Estimates, "The Indo-Pakistani Crisis," 22 September 1971.

2. FRUS, vol. E-7, Sober to Rogers, 4 October 1971, Islamabad 10043. NSC Files, Box 570, Indo-Pak War, Spivack to Rogers, 13 September 1971, Dacca 3777. Sydney H. Schanberg, "Bengali Refugees Say Soldiers Continue to Kill, Loot and Burn," New York Times, 22 September 1971.

3. NSC Files, Box H-082, WSAG Meetings, Williams to Rogers, 5 November 1971.

4. White House tapes, Oval Office 553-3, 2 August 1971, 9:45 a.m. See NSC Files, Box 574, Indo-Pak War, South Asian Congressional, Haig to Parker, n.d. October 1971. White House tapes, Oval Office 561-4, 11 August 1971, 9:10–11:40 a.m. See FRUS, WSAG meeting, 8 September 1971, pp. 393–404.

5. NSC Files, Box 597, Country Files—Middle East, India, vol. IV, Kissinger to Nixon, 24 August 1971. White House tapes, Oval Office 561-4, 11 August 1971, 9:10–11:40 a.m.

434 ~~ Notes to Pages 237–239

6. NSA, Huang-Kissinger memcon, 16 August 1971, Lord to Kissinger, 19 August 1971. NSA, Kissinger to Nixon, 16 August 1971.

7. NSC Files, Box 597, Country Files—Middle East, India, vol. IV, Kissinger to Nixon, 24 August 1971. See NSC Files, Box 570, Indo-Pak War, South Asia, Kissinger to Nixon, 18 August 1971. The line came from Hoskinson. (*FRUS*, WSAG meeting, 17 August 1971, 4:35 p.m., pp. 339–44. NSC Files, Box H-082, WSAG Meetings, Hoskinson and Kennedy to Kissinger, "Talking Points," 17 August 1971. The White House staffers wrote, *"We must find a way, if at all possible, of not being forced to choose between 700 million Chinese and 600 million Indians and Bengalis."*) White House tapes, Oval Office 626-14, 30 November 1971, 5:21–6:09 p.m.

8. NSC Files, Box 627, Country Files—Middle East, Pakistan, vol. VIII, Rogers to Nixon, 28 October 1971. This included a small but significant secret program of intelligence cooperation that was important to India in monitoring Chinese military moves in Tibet, as well as Chinese nuclear testing.

9. MEA, WII/121/54/71, Jha to Kaul, 27 August 1971. MEA, WII/125/59/71, "Note for Supplementaries," n.d. July 1971. NMML, Haksar Papers, Subject File 225, Gandhi-Kissinger conversation, 7 July 1971. NSC Files, Box 1025, Presidential/HAK MemCons, Haksar-Kissinger memcon, 7 July 1971, 1:10 p.m. See NMML, Haksar Papers, Subject File 169, Haksar minutes of Kissinger meeting, 6 July 1971. POL 7 US-KISSINGER, Box 2693, Kissinger memorandum, n.d. July 1971. See NMML, Kaul Papers, Subject File 19, part I, Singh-Kissinger memcon, 7 July 1971. MEA, WII/121/54/71, Kissinger-Ram meeting, 7 July 1971 (attached to Menon to Singh, 13 July 1971). NMML, Haksar Papers, Subject File 229, Kissinger-Ram meeting, 7 July 1971.

10. *FRUS*, WSAG meeting, 26 May 1971, 4:35–5 p.m., pp. 149–56. *FRUS*, WSAG meeting, 7 October 1971, pp. 436–45. NSC Files, Box 570, Indo-Pak War, Hoskinson to Haig, 7 July 1971. NSC Files, Box 570, Indo-Pak War, Haig to Nixon, n.d. 1971. See *FRUS*, vol. E-7, White House tapes, Oval Office 549-25, 28 July 1971, 4:21–4:54 p.m.

11. NSC Files, Box 570, Indo-Pak War, South Asia, Kissinger to Nixon, 18 August 1971. NSC Files, Box H-082, WSAG Meetings, Saunders and Hoskinson to Kissinger, "Contingency Planning—Indo-Pak Hostilities," 3 September 1971. See NSC Files, Box H-082, WSAG Meetings, Saunders and Hoskinson to Kissinger, 3 September 1971. See also NSC Files, Box H-082, WSAG Meetings, Hoskinson and Kennedy to Kissinger, 25 May 1971; NSC Files, Box H-082, WSAG Meetings, "Analytical Summary of Contingency Paper," 17 August 1971; NSC Files, Box H-082, WSAG Meetings, Hoskinson and Kennedy to Kissinger, "WSAG Meeting on South Asia," 17 August 1971. Henry Kissinger, *White House Years* (Boston: Little, Brown, 1979), p. 865. NSC Files, Box H-058, SRG Meetings, Saunders and Kennedy to Kissinger, "Analytical Summary," 12 July 1971. See NSC Files, Box H-082, WSAG Meetings, "China, the Soviet Union, and UN," Eliot to Kissinger, 1 September 1971. See also NSC Files, Box H-082, WSAG Meetings, Eliot to Kissinger, "Contacts with the Chinese on the South Asian Crisis," 27 August 1971. See NSC Files, Box H-082, WSAG Meetings, "Contingency Paper—Indo-Pakistan Hostilities," Hoskinson and Kennedy to Kissinger, 11 November 1971, attached State Department paper, "Contingency Paper—Indo-Pakistan Hostilities," probably August 1971. Gallup

Organization, Hopes and Fears poll, 2–5 April 1971. Forty percent wanted to send supplies, 8 percent wanted to send troops, 38 percent would refuse to get involved, and 14 percent did not know. They were not asked about supporting the invasion.

12. NMML, Haksar Papers, Subject File 220, R&AW report, "Threat of a Military Attack or Infiltration Campaign by Pakistan," January 1971. NMML, Haksar Papers, Subject File 203, Kosygin-Singh conversation, 8 June 1971.
13. NSC Files, Box 597, Country Files—Middle East, India, vol. IV, Saunders to Kissinger, 7 September 1971. MEA, WII/121/54/71, Jha to Kaul, 27 August 1971. See P. N. Dhar, *Indira Gandhi, the "Emergency," and Indian Democracy* (Oxford: Oxford University Press, 2000), pp. 163, 171.
14. NSC Files, Box 597, Country Files—Middle East, India, vol. IV, Kissinger to Nixon, 24 August 1971. *FRUS*, WSAG meeting, 8 September 1971, pp. 393–404. *FRUS*, Jha-Kissinger memcon, 11 September 1971, pp. 407–8.
15. NSC Files, Box H-082, WSAG Meetings, Hoskinson and Kennedy to Kissinger, "Talking Points," 7 October 1971. NSC Files, Box H-082, WSAG Meetings, Hoskinson and Kennedy to Kissinger, "Possible US Responses to Chinese Military Actions in South Asia," 7 October 1971. *FRUS*, WSAG meeting, 7 October 1971, pp. 443–45. *FRUS*, vol. E-7, White House tapes, Oval Office 582-9, 30 September 1971, 4:10–5:31 p.m. NSA, Nixon-Kissinger telcon, 1 October 1971, 10:15 a.m. White House tapes, Oval Office 605-9, 28 October 1971, 11:23 a.m.–12:45 p.m.
16. MEA, HI/121/13/71, vol. II, Radio Peking broadcast, 5 December 1971. See *FRUS*, notes for Kissinger, 2 July 1971, p. 216; *FRUS*, Haig to Nixon, 9 July 1971, pp. 244–45. MEA, HI/1012/14/71, Mishra to Kaul, 5 November 1971.
17. *FRUS*, WSAG meeting, 7 October 1971, pp. 436–45.
18. H. R. Haldeman, *The Haldeman Diaries: Inside the Nixon White House* (New York: G. P. Putnam's Sons, 1994), 18, 26 and 27 October 1971, pp. 365–66, 368–69. Kissinger, *White House Years*, pp. 776–77. Patrick E. Tyler, *A Great Wall: Six Presidents and China* (New York: PublicAffairs, 1999), p. 114. On the Lin Biao affair, see Gao Wenqian, *Zhou Enlai: The Last Perfect Revolutionary*, trans. Peter Rand and Lawrence R. Sullivan (New York: PublicAffairs, 2007) pp. 201–27; Ji Chaozu, *The Man on Mao's Right: From Harvard Yard to Tiananmen Square, My Life Inside China's Foreign Ministry* (New York: Random House, 2008), p. 249.
19. Neville Maxwell, *India's China War* (London: Jonathan Cape, 1970). NSA, Zhou-Kissinger memcon, 22 October 1971, 4:15–8:28 p.m.
20. White House tapes, Oval Office 613-12, 4 November 1971, 9:40 a.m.
21. NSC Files, Box H-058, SRG Meetings, Saunders talking points for Kissinger, 21 July 1971. See NSC Files, Box H-082, WSAG Meetings, INR assessment, 6 October 1971; and Narayan to Bhattacharya, 1 November 1971, Jayaprakash Narayan, *Selected Works*, ed. Bimal Prasad (New Delhi: Manohar, 2008), vol. 9, p. 677.
22. NMML, Haksar Papers, Subject File 220, Muhammad Khan to Dehlavi, 2 October 1971. NSC Files, Box H-082, WSAG Meetings, INR assessment, 6 October 1971. J. F. R. Jacob, *Surrender at Dacca: Birth of a Nation* (New Delhi: Manohar, 1997), pp. 86–88. POL 23–9 PAK, Box 2533, Spivack to Rogers, 20 October 1971, Dacca 4498. NSC Files, Box 570, Indo-Pak War, Spivack to Rogers, 13 September 1971, Dacca 3777. *FRUS*, WSAG meeting, 7 October 1971, pp. 436–45. *FRUS*, vol. E-7, Sober to Rogers, 4 October

1971, Islamabad 10043. Sen notes, 27 October 1971, Narayan, *Selected Works,* pp. 862–69.

23. *FRUS,* vol. E-7, Sober to Rogers, 4 October 1971, Islamabad 10043. MEA, HI/1012/30/71, Chib to Kaul, 10 November 1971. NSC Files, Box 759, Presidential Correspondence File, Yahya to Nixon, 26 September 1971.

24. *FRUS,* Irwin to Nixon, 22 October 1971, pp. 476–78. *FRUS,* WSAG meeting, 7 October 1971, pp. 440–41. *FRUS,* WSAG meeting, 7 October 1971, pp. 436–45. See NSC Files, Box H-082, WSAG Meetings, Hoskinson and Kennedy to Kissinger, 7 October 1971.

25. NSA, Nixon-Kissinger telcon, 13 November 1971, 10:38 a.m. NSC Files, Box H-082, WSAG Meetings, INR assessment, 6 October 1971. *FRUS,* WSAG meeting, 7 October 1971, pp. 436–45.

26. NSA, Nixon-Kissinger telcon, 1 October 1971, 10:15 a.m. *FRUS,* Saunders and Hoskinson to Kissinger, 16 September 1971, pp. 413–15.

27. White House tapes, Oval Office 561-4, 11 August 1971, 9:10–11:40 a.m. *FRUS,* vol. E-7, White House tapes, Oval Office 582-9, 30 September 1971, 4:10–5:31 p.m.

28. *FRUS,* vol. E-7, White House tapes, Oval Office 582-9, 30 September 1971, 4:10–5:31 p.m. *FRUS,* WSAG meeting, 7 October 1971, pp. 436–45.

29. White House tapes, Oval Office 553-3, 2 August 1971, 9:45 a.m. NSC Files, Box H-082, WSAG Meetings, Saunders and Hoskinson to Kissinger, "Contingency Planning—Indo-Pak Hostilities," 3 September 1971; NSC Files, Box H-082, WSAG Meetings, Eliot to Kissinger, "Contact with the Chinese on the South Asian Crisis," 27 August 1971. NSC Files, Box H-082, WSAG Meetings, Eliot to Kissinger, 3 September 1971. NSC Files, Box H-082, WSAG Meetings, Saunders and Hoskinson to Kissinger, "Cut-Off of Aid to India," 3 September 1971. NSC Files, Box H-082, WSAG Meetings, Eliot to Kissinger, "Cut-Off of Aid to India," 3 September 1971. See NSC Files, Box 627, Country Files—Middle East, Pakistan, vol. VIII, Kissinger to Nixon, "Relief and Economic Assistance," 3 November 1971; NSC Files, Box 627, Country Files—Middle East, Pakistan, vol. VIII, Kissinger to Nixon, 3 November 1971. This added up to over $9 billion over the past fifteen years (NSC Files, Box 627, Country Files—Middle East, Pakistan, vol. VIII, Rogers to Nixon, 28 October 1971). NSC Files, Box H-082, WSAG Meetings, Eliot to Kissinger, 3 September 1971. NSC Files, Box H-082, WSAG Meetings, Saunders and Hoskinson to Kissinger, "Cut-Off of Aid to India," 3 September 1971. NSC Files, Box H-082, WSAG Meetings, Eliot to Kissinger, "Cut-Off of Aid to India," 3 September 1971. *FRUS,* WSAG meeting, 7 October 1971, pp. 436–45.

30. MEA, HI/1012/30/71, Chib to Kaul, 6 October 1971. Gandhi visited Moscow on September 27–29. White House tapes, Oval Office 580-20, 29 September 1971, 3:03–5 p.m. See *FRUS,* Nixon-Gromyko memcon, 29 September 1971, pp. 424–25. MEA, HI/1012/57/71, Sethi to army staff, monthly military digest, 5 October 1971. HI/1012/57/71, Damodaran to Kaul, 22 October 1971. HI/1012/57/71, Damodaran to Kaul, 15 November 1971.

31. *FRUS,* Irwin to Nixon, 22 October 1971, pp. 476–78. NSC Files, Box 627, Country Files—Middle East, Pakistan, vol. VIII, Kissinger to Nixon, 3 November 1971. Katherine Frank, *Indira: The Life of Indira Nehru Gandhi* (New York: HarperCollins, 2001), p. 335. Jonathan Kandell, "Kurt Waldheim Dies at 88; Ex-UN Chief Hid Nazi Past," *New York Times,*

14 June 2007. Pupul Jayakar, *Indira Gandhi: An Intimate Biography* (New York: Pantheon, 1992), p. 169. For a skeptical biography of Malraux, see Olivier Todd, *André Malraux: Une vie* (Paris: Gallimard, 2001). MEA, HI/121/13/71, vol. II, Dixit to ambassadors, 22 November 1971. Oriana Fallaci, *Interviews with History and Conversations with Power* (New York: Rizzoli, 2011), p. 265.

32. MEA, HI/121/13/71, vol. II, Dixit to ambassadors, 22 November 1971. See Gandhi speeches, 24 and 29 October 1971, *The Years of Endeavour: Selected Speeches of Indira Gandhi, August 1969–August 1972* (New Delhi: Indian Ministry of Information and Broadcasting, 1975), vol. 2, pp. 134–36, 140–44. http://www.youtube.com/watch?v=8X_Ex5CCxsk. The interviewer was the BBC's Michael Charlton, on November 1. (See Jayakar, *Indira Gandhi*, p. 174, although her quotes are paraphrases.)

33. *FRUS*, vol. E-7, Farland to Rogers, 28 September 1971, Islamabad 9833. Archer K. Blood, *The Cruel Birth of Bangladesh: Memoirs of an American Diplomat* (Dacca: University Press of Bangladesh, 2002), p. 333.

34. *FRUS*, Farland to Rogers, 15 July 1971, Islamabad 7172, p. 263. See NSC Files, Box H-058, SRG Meetings, Davis to Irwin, "Scenario for Action in Indo-Pakistan Crisis," 29 July 1971. NSC Files, Box H-082, WSAG Meetings, Eliot to Kissinger, "Situation Report: India/Pakistan," 1 September 1971. MEA, HI/1012/30/71, Chib to Kaul, 4 September 1971. NMML, Kaul Papers, Subject File 19, part II, Rogers-Gandhi talk, n.d. October 1971. MEA, HI/1012/30/71, Chib to Kaul, 6 October 1971. Government of Pakistan, *The Report of the Hamoodur Rehman Commission of Inquiry into the 1971 War* (Lahore: Vanguard, 2001), p. 502; see p. 262.

35. *FRUS*, Gandhi to Nixon, 11 August 1971, p. 319. See *FRUS*, WSAG meeting, 7 October 1971, pp. 436–45; NSC Files, Box 626, Country Files—Middle East, Pakistan, vol. VI, Kissinger to Nixon, 24 August 1971. White House tapes, Oval Office 558-10, 9 August 1971, 5:44–6:18 p.m. White House tapes, Oval Office 559-3, 10 August 1971, 9:11–10:05 a.m.

36. *FRUS*, Farland to Rogers, 20 August 1971, Islamabad 8501, pp. 357–58. See White House tapes, Oval Office 611-3, 2 November 1971, 12:47–1:13 p.m.; NSC Files, Box 627, Country Files—Middle East, Pakistan, vol. VIII, Nixon-Sadruddin memcon, 16 November 1971.

37. India had successfully warded off famine in the refugee camps (NSC Files, Box 597, Country Files—Middle East, India, vol. IV, Saunders and Hoskinson to Kissinger, 3 July 1971). NSC Files, Box 570, Indo-Pak War, Eliot to Kissinger, 29 July 1971. See Paul R. Greenough, *Prosperity and Misery in Modern Bengal: The Famine of 1943–1944* (New York: Oxford University Press, 1982); Rakesh Batabyal, *Communalism in Bengal: From Famine to Noakhali, 1943–47* (New Delhi: Sage, 2005); Das Tarakchandra, *Bengal Famine (1943) as Revealed in a Survey of the Destitutes in Calcutta* (Calcutta: University of Calcutta, 1949); Karunamoy Mukerji, *Agriculture, Famine and Rehabilitation in South Asia: A Regional Approach* (Santiniketan, India: Viswa-Bharati, 1965); Ela Sen, *Darkening Days, Being a Narrative of Famine-Stricken Bengal* (Calcutta: Susil Gupta, 1944); Madhusree Mukerjee, *Churchill's Secret War: The British Empire and the Ravaging of India During World War II* (New York: Basic, 2010); Thomas Keneally, *Three Famines: Starvation and Politics* (New York: PublicAffairs, 2011); Jean Drèze, Amartya Sen, and Athar Hussain, eds., *The Political Economy of Hunger*

(Oxford: Clarendon, 1994); and Jean Drèze and Amartya Sen, *Hunger and Public Action* (Oxford: Clarendon, 1989). *FRUS,* SRG meeting, 23 July 1971, pp. 270–83. NSA, Kissinger-Rogers telcon, 6 August 1971, 10:22 a.m. White House tapes, Oval Office 553-3, 2 August 1971, 9:45 a.m.

38. *FRUS,* SRG meeting, 11 August 1971, pp. 320–23. See NSC Files, Box H-058, SRG Meetings, Saunders to Kissinger, 10 August 1971. NSC Files, Box 759, Presidential Correspondence File, Nixon to Yahya, 14 August 1971.

39. NSC Files, Box H-058, SRG Meetings, Saunders to Kissinger, 22 July 1971. NSC Files, Box H-058, SRG Meetings, Eliot to Kissinger, 21 July 1971. NSC Files, Box 625, Country Files—Middle East, Pakistan, vol. V, Farland to Rogers, 15 July 1971, Islamabad 7164. NSC Files, Box H-058, SRG Meetings, Davis to Irwin, "East Pakistan Humanitarian Relief," 29 July 1971. NSC Files, Box H-058, SRG Meetings, Eliot to Kissinger, "Humanitarian Relief Measures in East Pakistan," 5 August 1971. NSC Files, Box 626, Country Files—Middle East, Pakistan, vol. VI, Eliot to Kissinger, 17 August 1971. NSC Files, Box 570, Indo-Pak War, South Asia, Kissinger to Nixon, 18 August 1971. Other countries offered only $12 million for the United Nations' efforts in East Pakistan. White House tapes, Oval Office 553-3, 2 August 1971, 9:45 a.m.

40. NSC Files, Box 575, Indo-Pak War, South Asian Relief, Hoskinson and Saunders brief for Nixon, 27 October 1971.

41. NSC Files, Box H-082, WSAG Meetings, Williams to Rogers, 3 September 1971.

42. NSC Files, Box H-058, SRG Meetings, Saunders and Kennedy to Kissinger, Analytical Summary, 10 August 1971. NSC Files, Box 570, Indo-Pak War, South Asia, Kissinger to Nixon, 18 August 1971. *FRUS,* WSAG meeting, 7 October 1971, pp. 436–45. Kissinger suffered some denial here, questioning if there were really nine million refugees now, and telling a surprised Situation Room crowd, "I don't believe that the Pakistanis are generating refugees." But the World Bank found the nine million figure credible. (MEA, HI/121/13/71, vol. II, Sadruddin speech, 18 November 1971. MEA, HI/121/13/71, vol. II, Dixit to heads of mission, 4 December 1971.) POL 23-9 PAK, Box 2533, Spivack to Rogers, 20 October 1971, Dacca 4498.

43. NSC Files, Box H-082, WSAG Meetings, Williams to Rogers, 5 November 1971.

44. NSC Files, Box 759, Presidential Correspondence File, Nixon to Yahya, 14 August 1971. *FRUS,* Nixon to Yahya, 30 October 1971, pp. 483–85. NSC Files, Box H-082, WSAG Meetings, Saunders to Kissinger, 12 November 1971. NSC Files, Box 626, Country Files—Middle East, Pakistan, vol. VI, Williams to Rogers, 20 August 1971, Islamabad 8534. The cable is signed Farland, following protocol. Yahya planned to publish a new constitution on December 20, to convene the National Assembly on December 27, and after that form a new government in which the Bengali majority would hold most of the ministries. That would be followed by new governors for the provinces, and new provincial assemblies. (*FRUS,* Raynolds to Rogers, 11 October 1971, Karachi 2029, pp. 462–63.) NSC Files, Box H-058, SRG Meetings, Saunders and Kennedy to Kissinger, Analytical Summary, 10 August 1971. *FRUS,* vol. E-7, White House tapes, Oval Office 582-9, 30 September 1971, 4:10–5:31 p.m.

45. *FRUS,* Saunders to Kissinger, 13 August 1971, pp. 329–30. *FRUS,* Farland

to Sisco, 24 August 1971, Islamabad 8631, pp. 365–67. NSC Files, Box 626, Country Files—Middle East, Pakistan, vol. VI, Hoskinson to Kissinger, 25 August 1971. NSC Files, Box H-082, WSAG Meetings, Hoskinson and Kennedy to Kissinger, 7 October 1971. See NSC Files, Box 134, Kissinger Office Files, Country Files—Middle East, "USG Contacts with Bangla Desh," 6 December 1971. *FRUS,* Irwin to Gordon, 21 September 1971, State 173942, pp. 417–18. See NSA, Kissinger-Rockefeller telcon, 3 November 1971, 7 p.m.; NSC Files, Box 571, Indo-Pak War, Farland to Rogers, 29 November 1971, Islamabad 11759; NSC Files, Box 571, Indo-Pak War, Van Hollen to Farland, 27 November 1971, State 214960. *FRUS,* Gordon to Rogers, 18 October 1971, Calcutta 2662, p. 457. *FRUS,* WSAG meeting, 7 October 1971, p. 440. *FRUS,* WSAG meeting, 7 October 1971, pp. 436–45.

46. *FRUS,* vol. E-7, POL PAK, Sober to Rogers, 4 October 1971, Islamabad 10043. NSC Files, Box 570, Indo-Pak Crisis, CIA Office of National Estimates, "The Indo-Pakistani Crisis," 22 September 1971.

47. Blood, *Cruel Birth,* p. 332.

48. MEA, WII/109/31/71, vol. I, "U.S. Administration's policy towards Bangla Desh," n.d. 1971 (September or later). MEA, WII/109/31/71, vol. II, "U.S. Administration's policy towards Bangla Desh," n.d. 1971.

49. MEA, WII/109/31/71, vol. I, Singh-Keating discussion, 7 December 1971, 12:15 p.m. MEA, HI/1012/30/71, Chib to Kaul, 6 October 1971. MEA, HI/1012/30/71, Chib to Kaul, 10 November 1971. NMML, Kaul Papers, Subject File 19, part II, Rogers-Gandhi talk, n.d. October 1971. Haksar was set to retire in on September 4, to be replaced by the economist P. N. Dhar (Dhar, *Indira Gandhi, the "Emergency," and Indian Democracy,* p. 174), but he remained her crucial adviser on foreign policy, and seems to have stayed in office until 1973 (Shashi Tharoor, *Reasons of State: Political Development and India's Foreign Policy Under Indira Gandhi, 1966–1977* [New Delhi: Vikas, 1982], p. 145).

50. NSC Files, Box 627, Country Files—Middle East, Pakistan, vol. VIII, Kissinger to Nixon, "Relief and Economic Assistance," 3 November 1971. See NSC Files, Box 134, Kissinger Office Files, Country Files—Middle East, Relief for Refugees in India, 6 December 1971. The World Bank was recommending about $700 million annually for the refugees (MEA, HI/121/13/71, vol. II, Sadruddin speech, 18 November 1971; MEA, HI/121/13/71, vol. II, Dixit to heads of mission, 4 December 1971). See NSC Files, Box 574, Indo-Pak War, South Asian Congressional, Kennedy speech, 1 November 1971.

51. NSC Files, Box 570, Indo-Pak War, Nixon to Kissinger, 25 October 1971.

52. MEA, WII/109/31/71, vol. I, Singh statement to UN Security Council, 12 December 1971. See MEA, HI/1012/30/71, Chib to Kaul, 10 November 1971. *FRUS,* Irwin to Farland, 30 October 1971, State 198660, pp. 485–89. *FRUS,* Farland to Rogers, 2 November 1971, Islamabad 10905, pp. 490–91. NSC Files, Box 627, Country Files—Middle East, Pakistan, vol. VIII, Kissinger to Nixon, 3 November 1971.

53. MEA, HI/121/13/71, vol. I, Gandhi press conference, 19 October 1971. NSC Files, Box 570, Indo-Pak War, Irwin to Farland, 21 October 1971, State 185010. MEA, HI/121/13/71, vol. II, Gandhi to Thant, 16 November 1971. MEA, HI/1012/30/71, Chib to Kaul, 10 November 1971. MEA, HI/121/13/71, vol. II, Dixit to heads of mission, 4 December 1971. MEA, WII/109/31/71, vol. I, Singh statement to UN Security Council, 12 December

1971. NMML, Kaul Papers, Subject File 19, part II, Rogers-Gandhi talk, n.d. October 1971. NSC Files, Box 627, Country Files—Middle East, Pakistan, vol. VIII, Rogers to Nixon, 28 October 1971. Rogers said that India was running some thirty training camps for the Mukti Bahini, barring United Nations observers, snubbing U Thant as a mediator, and dismissing possible negotiations between Yahya and Bangladeshi leaders.

54. Hannah Arendt, *The Origins of Totalitarianism* (New York: Harcourt, 1976), pp. 132-34. Karuna Mantena, "Genealogies of Catastrophe," in Seyla Benhabib, Roy T. Tsao, and Peter Verovsek, eds., *Politics in Dark Times: Encounters with Hannah Arendt* (Cambridge: Cambridge University Press, 2010). Arendt to McCarthy, 8 December 1971, Carold Brightman, ed., *Between Friends: The Correspondence of Hannah Arendt and Mary McCarthy, 1949–1975* (New York: Harcourt Brace, 1995), p. 303. See Indira Gandhi, *Letters to an American Friend, 1950–1984,* ed. Dorothy Norman (New York: Harcourt Brace Jovanovich, 1985), pp. 134–35.

55. *FRUS,* Jha-Kissinger memcon, 25 August 1971, p. 369. *FRUS,* Jha-Kissinger memcon, 11 September 1971, pp. 407–8. NSA, Nixon-Kissinger telcon, 6 October 1971. NSC Files, Box 643, Country Files—Middle East, India/Pakistan, Jha-Kissinger memcon, 8 October 1971. White House tapes, Oval Office 611-3, 2 November 1971, 12:47–1:13 p.m.

56. White House tapes, Oval Office 612-4, conversation G, 3 November 1971, 4:31–5:31 p.m. See NSC Files, Box 627, Country Files—Middle East, Pakistan, vol. VIII, Rogers to Nixon, 28 October 1971.

57. MEA, HI/121/13/71, vol. II, Dixit to ambassadors, 22 November 1971. White House tapes, Oval Office 612-4, conversation G, 3 November 1971, 4:31–5:31 p.m. Nixon Presidential Library and Museum, White House Photo Office, roll 7724, frame 19.

58. Kissinger, *White House Years,* p. 879.

59. Nixon Presidential Library and Museum, White House Photo Office, roll 7736, frames 02A–07A. White House tapes, Oval Office 615-4, 5 November 1971, between 7:50 and 9:10 a.m. See H. R. Haldeman, *The Haldeman Diaries: Inside the Nixon White House* (New York: G. P. Putnam's Sons, 1994), 4 November 1971, p. 370.

60. NSC Files, Box 134, Kissinger Office Files, Country Files—Middle East, Nixon and Gandhi toasts, 4 November 1971. See MEA, HI/121/13/71, vol. II, Dixit to ambassadors, 22 November 1971.

61. The ballerina was Patricia McBride, from the New York City Ballet, a guest at the dinner. NSC Files, Box 134, Kissinger Office Files, Country Files—Middle East, Nixon and Gandhi toasts, 4 November 1971. White House tapes, Oval Office 615-4, 5 November 1971, between 7:50 and 9:10 a.m.

62. White House tapes, Oval Office 613-12, 4 November 1971, 9:40 a.m. For Kissinger's briefing and talking points for Nixon, see NSC Files, Box 627, Country Files—Middle East, Pakistan, vol. VIII, Kissinger to Nixon, 3 November 1971. NSC Files, Box 627, Country Files—Middle East, Pakistan, vol. VIII, Kissinger to Nixon, "Strategy with Prime Minister Gandhi," 3 November 1971. Rogers offered gentler talking points, in NSC Files, Box 627, Country Files—Middle East, Pakistan, vol. VIII, Rogers to Nixon, 28 October 1971. Nixon was presumably reading NSC Files, Box 627, Country Files—Middle East, Pakistan, vol. VIII, Kissinger to Nixon, "Relief and Economic Assistance," 3 November 1971. Nixon drew from NSC Files, Box

627, Country Files—Middle East, Pakistan, vol. VIII, Kissinger to Nixon, "Achievement of US Influence in Pakistan," 3 November 1971. NSC Files, Box 627, Country Files—Middle East, Pakistan, vol. VIII, Kissinger to Nixon, "Military Supply Policy," 3 November 1971. See Haldeman, *Haldeman Diaries,* 4 November 1971, p. 370; NSC Files, Box 570, Indo-Pak War, Van Hollen to Keating, 8 November 1971, State 203187.

63. White House tapes, Oval Office 613-12, 4 November 1971, 9:40 a.m.

64. NSC Files, Box 643, Country Files—Middle East, India/Pakistan, Nixon-Gandhi memcon, 4 November 1971, 10:30 a.m. NMML, Haksar Papers, Subject File 277, Nixon-Gandhi memcon, 4 November 1971, 10:30 a.m. See *FRUS,* Nixon-Gandhi memcon, 4 November 1971, 10:29 a.m.–12:35 p.m., pp. 493–99. It is not clear how Haksar got a copy of this document, which is classified "Top Secret—Sensitive—Eyes Only." Most of the taped conversation is inaudible, and much of it is bleeped out on the grounds of "National Security"—which is sometimes legitimate, and sometimes used (as in White House tapes, Oval Office 615-4, 5 November 1971, 8:51–9 a.m.) to cover up Nixon's and Kissinger's obscenities about Gandhi. Kissinger, *White House Years,* pp. 878, 880–81. MEA, HI/1012/30/71, Kumar memorandum, refugee statistics, 5 November 1971. The total that day was 9,608,901. See MEA, HI/1012/30/71, Kumar memorandum, refugee statistics, 7 October 1971; MEA, HI/1012/30/71, Kumar memorandum, refugee statistics, 15 October 1971; MEA, HI/1012/30/71, Kumar memorandum, refugee statistics, 22 October 1971; MEA, HI/1012/30/71, Kumar memorandum, refugee statistics, 28 October 1971; MEA, HI/1012/30/71, refugee statistics, 15 November 1971. Gandhi's seeming reference to the Bay of Pigs actually undermined India's denials: the United States had supported that ill-starred proxy invasion.

65. *FRUS,* vol. E-7, White House tapes, Oval Office 615-4, 5 November 1971, 8:51–9 a.m. The audio of this tape is still bleeped out on ostensible grounds of national security, even though the State Department has released a transcript. See Kissinger, *White House Years,* p. 882.

66. For a corroborating version of this snub, see Seymour M. Hersh, *The Price of Power: Kissinger in the Nixon White House* (New York: Summit, 1983), p. 456.

67. *FRUS,* WSAG minutes, 12 November 1971, 11:09 a.m., p. 508.

68. NSC Files, Box 643, Country Files—Middle East, India/Pakistan, Nixon-Gandhi memcon, 5 November 1971, 11:20 a.m. Frank, *Indira,* pp. 336–37.

69. Kissinger, *White House Years,* p. 878. *FRUS,* Van Hollen to Keating, 8 November 1971, State 203187, pp. 500–503. MEA, HI/121/13/71, vol. II, Dixit to ambassadors, 22 November 1971. See T. N. Kaul, *The Kissinger Years: Indo-American Relations* (New Delhi: Arnold-Heinemann, 1980), pp. 71–80. Fallaci, *Interviews with History,* p. 265.

CHAPTER 17: THE GUNS OF NOVEMBER

1. NSA, Nixon-Kissinger telcon, 8 November 1971, 7:50 p.m. Soon after, Nixon asked Kissinger, "There certainly was no misunderstanding with the Paks on this, was there?" Kissinger assured him there was not, and then the rest of their conversation is bleeped out (White House tapes, White House telephone 13-156, 8 November 1971, 8:47–8:54 p.m.).

2. Richard Sisson and Leo E. Rose, *War and Secession: Pakistan, India, and*

the Creation of Bangladesh (Berkeley: University of California Press, 1990), p. 209. Inder Malhotra, "Liberation of Bangladesh," in Pranab Mukherjee, ed., *A Centenary History of the Indian National Congress (1964–1984)* (New Delhi: Academic Foundation, 2011), vol. 5, p. 175. NSC Files, Box 627, Country Files—Middle East, Pakistan, vol. VIII, "Talking Points and Issues," 15 November 1971. See NSC Files, Box H-082, WSAG Meetings, Hoskinson and Kennedy to Kissinger, 11 November 1971; *FRUS,* WSAG minutes, 12 November 1971, 11:09 a.m., pp. 505, 511. MEA, HI/121/13/71, vol. II, Sen statement to UN Security Council, 5 December 1971.

3. Sydney H. Schanberg, "New Delhi Sources Admit Troops Entered Pakistan," *New York Times,* 8 November 1971, pp. A1, A11. NMML, Haksar Papers, Subject File 235, Haksar to Lall, 8 November 1971.
4. NMML, Haksar Papers, Subject File 235, Lall to Haksar, 11 November 1971.
5. NSA, Nixon-Kissinger telcon, 8 November 1971, 7:50 p.m.
6. NMML, Haksar Papers, Subject File 220, Prakash Kaul to Kaul, 12 November 1971. NMML, Haksar Papers, Subject File 220, Mishra to Kaul, 9 November 1971. MEA, HI/1012/14/71, Mishra to Kaul, 17 December 1971. This is corroborated by Pakistan's postwar judicial commission (Government of Pakistan, *The Report of the Hamoodur Rehman Commission of Inquiry into the 1971 War* [Lahore: Vanguard, 2001], p. 181). NMML, Haksar Papers, Subject File 220, Mishra to Kaul, 9 November 1971. *FRUS,* WSAG minutes, 12 November 1971, 11:09 a.m., p. 505.
7. *FRUS,* WSAG minutes, 12 November 1971, 11:09 a.m., pp. 508. See *FRUS,* WSAG meeting, 22 November 1971, 2:39–3:14 p.m., p. 553; *FRUS,* WSAG meeting, 29 November 1971, 2:36–3:36 p.m., p. 575; Henry Kissinger, *White House Years* (Boston: Little, Brown, 1979), p. 881. *FRUS,* WSAG minutes, 12 November 1971, 11:09 a.m., pp. 505–14. See *FRUS,* WSAG meeting, 22 November 1971, 2:39–3:14 p.m., pp. 529–36; White House tapes, White House telephone 14-27, 10 November 1971, 8:07-8:20 p.m.
8. NSC Files, Box H-082, WSAG Meetings, Hoskinson and Kennedy to Kissinger, 11 November 1971. See *FRUS,* WSAG meeting, 7 October 1971, pp. 436–45; NSC Files, Box H-082, WSAG Meetings, Hoskinson and Kennedy to Kissinger, 7 October 1971. Kissinger, *White House Years,* p. 879. MEA, HI/121/13/71, vol. II, Gandhi speech to Lok Sabha and Rajya Sabha, 15 November 1971. NSC Files, Box 755, Presidential Correspondence File, Gandhi to Nixon, 16 November 1971.
9. White House tapes, Oval Office 617-17, 15 November 1971, 4:31–4:39 p.m. See NSC Files, Box 643, Country Files—Middle East, India/Pakistan, Sultan Khan-Kissinger memcon, 15 November 1971, 4 p.m., pp. 514–17; NSC Files, Box 627, Country Files—Middle East, Pakistan, vol. VIII, n.d. November 1971.
10. Scott D. Sagan and Jeremi Suri, "The Madman Nuclear Alert," *International Security,* vol. 27, no. 4 (spring 2003), pp. 150-83. Scott D. Sagan, *The Limits of Safety: Organizations, Accidents, and Nuclear Weapons* (Princeton: Princeton University Press, 1993), pp. 212–24. Philip Taubman, *The Partnership: Five Cold Warriors and Their Quest to Ban the Bomb* (New York: Harper, 2012), pp. 165–66. Henry A. Kissinger, *Years of Upheaval* (New York: Little, Brown, 1982), pp. 575–99. Richard Ned Lebow and Janice Gross Stein, *We All Lost the Cold War* (Princeton: Princeton University Press, 1994), pp.

226–88. NSC Files, Box H-082, WSAG Meetings, McCain to Moorer, 12 November 1971. NSC Files, Box 627, Country Files—Middle East, Pakistan, vol. VIII, Welander to Haig, 15 November 1971. NSC Files, Box 570, Indo-Pak War, Welander to Haig, 15 November 1971. NSC Files, Box H-082, WSAG Meetings, Kennedy and Saunders to Kissinger, 12 November 1971.

11. White House tapes, Oval Office 561-4, 11 August 1971, 9:10–11:40 a.m.

12. NSC Files, Box H-082, WSAG Meetings, Saunders to Kissinger, 12 November 1971. NSC Files, Box H-082, WSAG Meetings, Williams to Rogers, 5 November 1971. NSC Files, Box 627, Country Files—Middle East, Pakistan, vol. VIII, Williams to Rogers, 5 November 1971. See NMML, Kaul Papers, Subject File 19, part II, Rogers-Gandhi talk, n.d. October 1971. White House tapes, Oval Office 617-17, 15 November 1971, 4:31–4:39 p.m. NSC Files, Box 627, Country Files—Middle East, Pakistan, vol. VIII, Kissinger to Nixon, 16 November 1971. See NSC Files, Box H-082, WSAG Meetings, Saunders to Kissinger, 12 November 1971.

13. J. F. R. Jacob, *Surrender at Dacca: Birth of a Nation* (New Delhi: Manohar, 1997), pp. 71–77.

14. Jacob, *Surrender at Dacca,* p. 73. Malhotra, "Liberation of Bangladesh," p. 175. MEA, WII/109/31/71, vol. I, Singh statement to UN Security Council, 12 December 1971. NMML, Haksar Papers, Subject File 173, Haksar to Gandhi, 11 December 1971.

15. Malhotra, "Liberation of Bangladesh," p. 175. MEA, WII/109/31/71, vol. I, Singh statement to UN Security Council, 12 December 1971. MEA, HI/121/13/71, vol. II, Sen statement to UN Security Council, 4 December 1971. NMML, Haksar Papers, Subject File 173, Haksar to Gandhi, 11 December 1971. For Gandhi's public version, see NSC Files, Box H-082, WSAG Meetings, Keating to Rogers, 24 November 1971, New Delhi 18187; NSC Files, Box 571, Indo-Pak War, Keating to Rogers, 24 November 1971, New Delhi 18221. See K. F. Rustamji, *The British, the Bandits and the Bordermen: From the Diaries of K. F. Rustamji,* ed. P. V. Rajgopal (New Delhi: Wisdom Tree, 2009), p. 324; and P. N. Dhar, *Indira Gandhi, the "Emergency," and Indian Democracy* (Oxford: Oxford University Press, 2000), pp. 177–78.

16. Jacob, *Surrender at Dacca,* p. 72. NMML, Haksar Papers, Subject File 89, Dhar to Haksar, n.d. 1971. Dhar, *Indira Gandhi, the "Emergency," and Indian Democracy,* pp. 178–79.

17. See NMML, Haksar Papers, Subject File 225, Sen to Gandhi, 9 June 1971. Jacob to Gill, 15 November 1971, Jacob, *Surrender at Dacca,* p. 179.

18. H. R. Haldeman, *The Haldeman Diaries: Inside the Nixon White House* (New York: G. P. Putnam's Sons, 1994), 22 November 1971, p. 377. NSC Files, Box H-082, WSAG Meetings, Kissinger to Nixon, "Indo-Pak Fighting," 22 November 1971. See NSA, Kissinger-Raza telcons, 22 November 1971, 12 p.m. and 3:23 p.m.; NSC Files, Box 570, Indo-Pak War, Saunders to Kissinger, 22 November 1971; NSC Files, Box 570, Indo-Pak War, Farland to Rogers, 22 November 1971, Islamabad 11534. NSA, Nixon-Kissinger telcon, 22 November 1971, 12:45 p.m. See NSA, Kissinger-Bush telcon, 22 November 1971, 3:47 p.m.

19. White House tapes, Oval Office 622-1, 22 November 1971, 3:51–3:58 p.m.

20. NSA, Kissinger-Rogers telcon, 23 November 1971, 10:55 a.m. See NSA, Kissinger-Brandt telcon, 23 November 1971, 9:51 a.m., and NSA, Kissinger-Raza telcon, 27 November 1971, 10:15 a.m. White House tapes, Oval Office

626-10, 30 November 1971, 11:23 a.m.–12:03 p.m. NSA, Kissinger-Rogers
telcon, 23 November 1971, 10:55 a.m. See NSA, Kissinger-Brandt telcon,
23 November 1971, 9:51 a.m., and NSA, Kissinger-Raza telcon, 27 November 1971, 10:15 a.m. See also NSC Files, Box 571, Indo-Pak War, Yahya
to Nixon, 23 November 1971; NSC Files, Box 571, Indo-Pak War, Nixon
to Gandhi, 25 November 1971; White House tapes, Oval Office 624-10,
24 November 1971, 8:49–9:49 a.m.

21. Jacob, *Surrender at Dacca*, p. 73. See A. A. K. Niazi, *The Betrayal of East
Pakistan* (Karachi: Oxford University Press, 1998), pp. 118–31. *FRUS*,
WSAG meeting, 23 November 1971, 9:12–10:10 a.m., pp. 538–47. See NSA,
Kissinger-Chandler telcon, 29 November 1971, 8:05 p.m. *FRUS*, WSAG
meeting, 24 November 1971, 9:29–10:05 a.m., pp. 548–54. *FRUS*, WSAG
meeting, 29 November 1971, 2:36–3:36 p.m., pp. 571–80. Kissinger, *White
House Years*, pp. 891, 893. *FRUS*, WSAG meeting, 23 November 1971, 9:12–
10:10 a.m., pp. 538–47. See NSA, Kissinger-Chandler telcon, 29 November
1971, 8:05 p.m. See Kissinger, *White House Years*, p. 885.

22. NSC Files, Box 571, Indo-Pak War, Keating to Rogers, 4 December 1971,
New Delhi 18739. MEA, WII/109/31/71, vol. I, Singh statement to UN Security Council, 12 December 1971 (India wrongly said it was a *Newsweek*
reporter). See NSC Files, Box H-082, WSAG Meetings, Keating to Rogers,
24 November 1971, New Delhi 18187. Sydney H. Schanberg, "India Admits
an Incursion, Says It Was Self-Defense," *New York Times*, 25 November 1971, pp. A1, A16. *FRUS*, WSAG meeting, 24 November 1971, 9:29–
10:05 a.m., pp. 548–54.

23. NSA, Huang-Kissinger memcon, 23 November 1971, 10–11:55 p.m. See
NSA, Kissinger to Nixon, 26 November 1971. For a sanitized account,
see Kissinger, *White House Years*, p. 889. Kissinger puts the house in the
East Thirties, and later in the East Seventies, but Huang Hua says it was
on Forty-third Street (*Memoirs* [Beijing: Foreign Languages Press, 2008], p.
236). White House tapes, Oval Office 624-10, 24 November 1971, 8:49–9:49
a.m. The same day, Kissinger said, "What will be the effect if, the first time
something like this happens where China is involved, the U.S. doesn't make
some move" (*FRUS*, WSAG meeting, 24 November 1971, 9:29–10:05 a.m.,
pp. 548–54).

24. Walter Isaacson, *Kissinger: A Biography* (New York: Simon & Schuster,
1992), pp. 374–75. See NSC Files, Box 572, Indo-Pak War, Keating to Rogers, 7 December 1971, New Delhi 18877. White House tapes, Oval Office
624-10, 24 November 1971, 8:49–9:49 a.m. *FRUS*, vol. E-7, White House
tapes, Oval Office 624-21, 24 November 1971, 12:27–1:12 p.m. Later, once
full-scale war started, Kissinger said that the reporter Helen Thomas had
told him that the administration should have been making its case three
weeks earlier, after the battle of Boyra but before Pakistan's airstrikes.
Nixon tellingly replied that "we weren't in a position to claim Indian aggression, basically"—suggesting that even he, on some level, thought that India
had not started the war. (White House tapes, White House telephone 16-37,
16-39, 16-40, 7 December 1971, 11:31–11:54 p.m.)

25. *FRUS*, vol. E-7, White House tapes, Oval Office 624-21, 24 November 1971,
12:27–1:12 p.m. Several weeks earlier, Nixon had admitted that Pakistan
would fall apart and Yahya might well launch a "suicidal" attack on India,
but still could not bring himself to fault Yahya for anything worse than

"stupid" behavior. Nixon doggedly stood by his friend: "He's a very decent man, but it's just been handled badly." When Kissinger said, "He's not very bright, but he has tried," Nixon stoutly defended virtues other than intelligence: "He's a decent man, an honorable man." (*FRUS*, vol. E-7, White House tapes, Oval Office 582-9, 30 September 1971, 4:10–5:31 p.m.) When Nixon was not around, Kissinger showed his contempt for Yahya's stupidity, lapsing into stereotyping. "Yahya is a slow learner," he said. "He is very deliberate, but if you force him to make a decision, his Moslem instinct may assert itself, and perhaps he will start taking rapid action." (*FRUS*, WSAG meeting, 7 October 1971, pp. 436–45.)

26. Sydney H. Schanberg, "Big Indian Force Reported Going into East Pakistan," *New York Times*, 24 November 1971, pp. A1, A10.

27. Sydney H. Schanberg, "India Admits an Incursion, Says It Was Self-Defense," *New York Times*, 25 November 1971, pp. A1, A16. Sydney H. Schanberg, "India Sets Range for Retaliations in East Pakistan," *New York Times*, 29 November 1971, pp. A1, A14. NSC Files, Box H-082, WSAG Meetings, Gordon to Rogers, 24 November 1971, Calcutta 2891.

28. NSA, Kissinger-Rogers telcon, 30 November 1971, 6:30 p.m. White House tapes, Oval Office 626-10, 30 November 1971, 11:23 a.m.–12:03 p.m. Specifically, Kissinger wanted to cut off new export licenses but not cancel the old licenses. White House tapes, Oval Office 624-14, 30 November 1971, 5:21–6:09 p.m. See *FRUS*, vol. E-7, White House tapes, Oval Office 624-21, 24 November 1971, 12:27–1:12 p.m.; *FRUS*, WSAG meeting, 23 November 1971, 9:12–10:10 a.m., pp. 538–47; NSC Files, Box H-082, WSAG Meetings, Saunders to Kissinger, 22 November 1971; NSC Files, Box 571, Indo-Pak War, Irwin to Nixon, 25 November 1971. By another accounting, if the United States cut off new export licenses, that would deprive India of about $16 million worth of military supplies; if the United States totally closed off its arms pipeline, that would leave India without a total of about $30 million worth of military supplies from the Pentagon or from U.S. commercial suppliers (*FRUS*, WSAG meeting, 29 November 1971, 2:36–3:36 p.m., pp. 571–80). This included $2.2 million worth of spares directly from the Pentagon, $8.1 million toward communication links that went with India's Star Sapphire radar system aimed at China, a $2.8 million grant for building a highway in Nepal, a $300,000 grant for training in the fiscal year 1972, and some $20 million on order with U.S. commercial suppliers (NSC Files, Box H-082, WSAG Meetings, Saunders and Hoskinson to Kissinger, 25 November 1971; NSC Files, Box H-082, WSAG Meetings, Laird to Kissinger, 24 November 1971; NSC Files, Box H-083, WSAG Meetings, Saunders to Kissinger, 29 November 1971). For India's somewhat different accounting, see MEA, WII/125/112/71, Kholsa to Menon, 2 December 1971.

29. NSA, Kissinger-Rogers telcon, 30 November 1971, 6:30 p.m. MEA, WII/109/19/71, Jain to Menon, 2 December 1971. MEA, WII/125/112/71, Kholsa to Menon, 2 December 1971. See NSC Files, Box 571, Indo-Pak War, Keating to Rogers, 2 December 1971, New Delhi 18595. The defense ministry reckoned that India was actually losing about $1.5 million for ammunition and related materials, not $2 million, as U.S. officials had said. As for military items from U.S. commercial firms, India had $8.2 million on order, as well as an additional $6.7 million for that air defense system aimed at China. MEA, WII/109/31/71, vol. I, Kaul to Singh, 2 December 1971. MEA,

WII/125/112/71, Kaul to Singh, 2 December 1971. MEA, WII/109/19/71, Singh statement to Lok Sabha, 3 December 1971. *FRUS*, WSAG meeting, 1 December 1971, 4:17–4:50 p.m., pp. 585–90. NSC Files, Box H-082, WSAG Meetings, Saunders to Kissinger, 24 November 1971. See NSC Files, Box 134, Kissinger Office Files, Country Files—Middle East, "Economic Assistance to India," 7 January 1972.

30. MEA, HI/121/13/71, vol. II, Gandhi to Thant, 16 November 1971. NSC Files, Box H-083, WSAG Meetings, Kissinger to Nixon, 1 December 1971. NSC Files, Box 571, Indo-Pak War, Kissinger to Nixon, 1 December 1971. See *FRUS*, WSAG meeting, 1 December 1971, 4:17–4:50 p.m., pp. 585–90. See NSC Files, Box 571, Indo-Pak War, Saunders to Kissinger, 29 November 1971; NSC Files, Box 571, Indo-Pak War, Keating to Rogers, 29 November 1971, New Delhi 18383; NSC Files, Box H-083, WSAG Meetings, Saunders to Kissinger, 1 December 1971.

31. NSA, Kissinger-Raza telcon, 2 December 1971, 12:18 p.m. See NSC Files, Box 571, Indo-Pak War, Yahya to Nixon, 2 December 1971.

CHAPTER 18: THE FOURTEEN-DAY WAR

1. See Aimee Ginsburg, "The Sum of His Many Parts," *Open*, 2 June 2012. Jacob retired at the rank of lieutenant general, but in 1971 was a major general.

2. V. K. Singh, *Leadership in the Indian Army: Biographies of Twelve Soldiers* (New Delhi: Sage, 2005), pp. 184–92. On India's multiethnic army, see Stephen Peter Rosen, *Societies and Military Power: India and Its Armies* (Ithaca, N.Y.: Cornell University Press, 1996).

3. For Indian assessments, see NMML, Haksar Papers, Subject File 220, R&AW report, "Threat of a Military Attack or Infiltration Campaign by Pakistan," January 1971; NMML, Haksar Papers, Subject File 173, Haksar to Kaul, 20 December 1971; NMML, Haksar Papers, Subject File 235, Manekshaw-Kulikov talks, 24–25 February 1972. NSC Files, Box 570, Indo-Pak Crisis, CIA Office of National Estimates, "The Indo-Pakistani Crisis," 22 September 1971. Library of Congress, Association for Diplomatic Studies and Training, Foreign Affairs Oral History Project, Archer Blood interview, 27 June 1989.

4. See J. F. R. Jacob, *Surrender at Dacca: Birth of a Nation* (New Delhi: Manohar, 1997), pp. 66–67.

5. MEA, WII/109/31/71, vol. I, Singh statement to UN Security Council, 12 December 1971. NMML, Haksar Papers, Subject File 173, Gandhi to Nixon, 15 December 1971. See NSC Files, Box 755, Presidential Correspondence File, Gandhi to Nixon, 15 December 1971.

6. Katherine Frank, *Indira: The Life of Indira Nehru Gandhi* (New York: HarperCollins, 2001), p. 338; Owen Bennett Jones, *Pakistan: Eye of the Storm* (New Haven, Conn.: Yale University Press, 2009), p. 167; Richard Sisson and Leo Rose say the Indian attack was set for December 6 (*War and Secession: Pakistan, India, and the Creation of Bangladesh* [Berkeley: University of California Press, 1990], pp. 213–14). K. F. Rustamji, *The British, the Bandits and the Bordermen: From the Diaries of K. F. Rustamji*, ed. P. V. Rajgopal (New Delhi: Wisdom Tree, 2009), p. 325.

7. NMML, Haksar Papers, Subject File 173, Gandhi to Nixon, 15 December 1971. See NSC Files, Box 755, Presidential Correspondence File, Gandhi to

Nixon, 15 December 1971. On Pakistani military plans for preventive war, see Scott D. Sagan, in Scott D. Sagan and Kenneth N. Waltz, *The Spread of Nuclear Weapons: A Debate* (New York: Norton, 1995), pp. 62–63. MEA, HI/121/13/71, vol. II, Sen statement to UN Security Council, 4 December 1971. Government of Pakistan, *The Report of the Hamoodur Rehman Commission of Inquiry into the 1971 War* (Lahore: Vanguard, 2001), p. 204. Sisson and Rose put the decision on November 30 (*War and Secession*, p. 230). Niazi seems to have been unaware of an imminent Indian attack (A. A. K. Niazi, *The Betrayal of East Pakistan* [Karachi: Oxford University Press, 1998], pp. 131–33). He would later regret Pakistan's attack, arguing that India could not have unleashed all-out war against his eastern troops without it (*Hamoodur Rehman Commission Report,* p. 532).

8.   MEA, WII/109/31/71, vol. I, Kaul-Keating discussion, 4 December 1971. Frank, *Indira,* p. 338. Sisson and Rose, *War and Secession,* pp. 213–14. P. N. Dhar, *Indira Gandhi, the "Emergency," and Indian Democracy* (Oxford: Oxford University Press, 2000), p. 122. Pupul Jayakar, *Indira Gandhi: An Intimate Biography* (New York: Pantheon, 1992), p. 176.

9.   NMML, Haksar Papers, Subject File 173, Haksar to Gandhi, 7 December 1971; NMML, Haksar Papers, Subject File 173, Haksar to Gandhi, 11 December 1971. NMML, Haksar Papers, Subject File 235, Manekshaw-Kulikov talks, 24–25 February 1972. See Jacob, *Surrender at Dacca,* pp. 101–2. MEA, WII/109/31/71, vol. I, Singh statement to UN Security Council, 12 December 1971. Charles Mohr, "Mrs. Gandhi Vows to Repel the Foe," *New York Times,* 4 December 1971, pp. A1, A10. MEA, WII/109/31/71, vol. I, Singh statement to UN Security Council, 12 December 1971.

10.   MEA, HI/121/25/71, Gandhi statement in Lok Sabha, 4 December 1971. See MEA, HI/121/13/71, vol. II, Dixit to heads of mission, 4 December 1971; MEA, WII/109/31/71, vol. I, Kaul-Keating discussion, 4 December 1971. NMML, Haksar Papers, Subject File 173, Gandhi to Nixon, 15 December 1971. NSC Files, Box 755, Presidential Correspondence File, Gandhi to Nixon, 5 December 1971.

11.   NSC Files, Box 572, Indo-Pak War, Keating to Rogers, 11 December 1971, New Delhi 19110. Narayan statement, 4 December 1971, Jayaprakash Narayan, *Selected Works,* ed. Bimal Prasad (New Delhi: Manohar, 2008), vol. 9, pp. 692–93. See Narayan to Singh, 3 December 1971, Narayan, *Selected Works,* p. 692. Singh to Narayan, 10 December 1971, Narayan, *Selected Works,* p. 877. NMML, Haksar Papers, Subject File 173, Haksar to Gandhi, 7 December 1971.

12.   Sukhwant Singh, *India's Wars Since Independence: The Liberation of Bangladesh* (New Delhi: Vikas, 1980), vol. 1, p. 129.

13.   NSA, Nixon-Kissinger telcon, 3 December 1971, late afternoon. See NSA, Kissinger-Raza telcon, 3 December 1971, 7 p.m.; *FRUS, WSAG* meeting, 3 December 1971, 11:19–11:55 a.m., pp. 596–604; NSA, Nixon-Kissinger telcon, 4 December 1971; White House tapes, Oval Office 630-2, 6 December 1971, 12:02–12:06 p.m. Kissinger said, "If every time we do something to the Indians, we have to do the same thing to Pakistan, we will be participating in the rape of Pakistan." (*FRUS, WSAG* meeting, 8 December 1971, 11:13 a.m.–12:02 p.m., pp. 690–99.) Even when the CIA director told Kissinger that Pakistan had attacked three Indian airfields, Kissinger suspected Indian aggression (*FRUS, WSAG* meeting, 3 December 1971, 11:19–11:55 a.m.,

pp. 596–604). See NSC Files, Box 643, Country Files—Middle East, India/ Pakistan, Kissinger to Nixon, "The Crisis in the Subcontinent: In Retrospect," 6 December 1971; NSC Files, Box 571, Indo-Pak War, Saunders to Kissinger, "Achievements of US Influence in Pakistan," 6 December 1971.

14. *FRUS,* NSC meeting, 6 December 1971, 1:30–3:30 p.m., pp. 669–73. See NSC Files, Box 643, Country Files—Middle East, India/Pakistan, Kissinger to Nixon, "The Crisis in the Subcontinent: In Retrospect," 6 December 1971. NSA, Nixon-Rogers telcon, 3 December 1971, 10:55 a.m. For Nixon using the Finland analogy, see White House tapes, Oval Office 632-2, 8 December 1971, 9:25–10:18 a.m.

15. NSA, Nixon-Kissinger telcon, 4 December 1971. NSA, Nixon-Kissinger telcon, 5 December 1971. See NSA, Kissinger-Connally telcon, 5 December 1971. NSA, Kissinger-Sisco telcon, 4 December 1971, 9:15 a.m. NSA, Kissinger-Haig telcon, 4 December 1971. *FRUS,* WSAG meeting, 3 December 1971, 11:19–11:55 a.m., pp. 596–604. See NSA, Nixon-Rogers telcon, 3 December 1971, 10:55 a.m.; NSA, Nixon-Rogers telcon, 3 December 1971, 3:45 p.m.; NSA, Kissinger-Sisco telcon, 3 December 1971, 3 p.m.

16. NSA, Nixon-Kissinger telcon, 3 December 1971, late afternoon. NSA, Nixon-Kissinger telcon, 4 December 1971. NSA, Kissinger-Haig telcon, 4 December 1971. White House tapes, Oval Office 632-2, 8 December 1971, 9:25–10:18 a.m. Nixon first cut all military aid, worth about $31 million in total, and then quickly froze some $88 million of economic aid to India. He also refused to sign agreements—agreed upon before the war—for $72 million worth of food aid, and held back $75 million of World Bank development loans. (White House tapes, Oval Office 630-2, 6 December 1971, 12:02–12:06 p.m. NSC Files, Box 134, Kissinger Office Files, Country Files—Middle East, Saunders and Hoskinson to Kissinger, 7 December 1971. NSA, Kissinger-Huang memcon, 10 December 1971, 6:07–7:55 p.m.)

17. NSA, Nixon-Kissinger telcon, 4 December 1971. *FRUS,* National Security Council meeting, 6 December 1971, 1:30–3:30 p.m., pp. 669-73. The worst thing that Nixon ever said about Yahya, on the extremely rare occasion that he found fault there at all, was that "Pakistan mishandled the refugee situation in the beginning." (*FRUS,* vol. E-7, White House tapes, Oval Office 637-3, 12 December 1971, 8:45–9:42 a.m.) NSA, Kissinger-Haig telcon, 4 December 1971.

18. NSA, Kissinger-Connally telcon, 5 December 1971. See *FRUS,* vol. E-7, Kissinger-Rogers telcon, 5 December 1971; Henry Kissinger, *White House Years* (Boston: Little, Brown, 1979), p. 897. For a wiser view, see Steve Coll, *On the Grand Trunk Road: A Journey into South Asia* (New York: Times Books, 1994), p. 257. NSA, Nixon-Kissinger telcon, 5 December 1971.

19. *FRUS,* vol. E-7, White House tapes, Oval Office 630-20, 6 December 1971, 6:14–6:38 p.m.

20. *FRUS,* vol. E-7, White House tapes, EOB 307-27, 8 December 1971, 4:20–5:01 p.m. See NSC Files, Box 643, Country Files—Middle East, India/Pakistan, Kissinger to Nixon, "The Crisis in the Subcontinent: In Retrospect," 6 December 1971. NSA, Nixon-Kissinger telcon, 3 December 1971, 2:45 p.m. *FRUS,* vol. E-7, White House tapes, Oval Office 630-20, 6 December 1971, 6:14–6:38 p.m.

21. NSA, Nixon-Kissinger telcon, 4 December 1971. See NSA, Kissinger-Rogers

telcon, 5 December 1971. NSA, Nixon-Kissinger telcon, 5 December 1971. See Kissinger-Connally telcon, 5 December 1971.

22. *FRUS,* vol. E-7, White House tapes, Oval Office 630-20, 6 December 1971, 6:14–6:38 p.m. See James Mann, *The China Fantasy: How Our Leaders Explain Away Chinese Repression* (New York: Viking, 2007), p. 70. *FRUS,* vol. E-7, White House tapes, Oval Office 633-11, 9 December 1971, 12:44– 1:27 p.m. White House tapes, Oval Office 635-6, 10 December 1971, 9:10– 10:31 a.m.

23. NSC Files, Box 643, Country Files—Middle East, India/Pakistan, Kissinger to Nixon, "The Crisis in the Subcontinent: In Retrospect," 6 December 1971. See Kissinger, *White House Years,* p. 900. White House tapes, Oval Office 632-2, 8 December 1971, 9:25–10:18 a.m.

24. White House tapes, Oval Office 632-2, 8 December 1971, 9:25–10:18 a.m. In his diary, Haldeman wrote, "Henry is physically tired, . . . he does real- ize he's at fault in the failure in India-Pakistan to date and doesn't like that feeling." (H. R. Haldeman, *The Haldeman Diaries: Inside the Nixon White House* [New York: G. P. Putnam's Sons, 1994], 9 December 1971, p. 381.) Haldeman also speculated that Kissinger was most bruised by having to can- cel a dinner at Harvard, where he would have been "raked over the coals" about "the poor East Pak refugees." He said, "He may have thought he had finally bought himself back into his own society, and then all of sudden, zap, he's thrown out of it again." (White House tapes, Oval Office 632-2, 8 December 1971, 9:25–10:18 a.m.)

25. White House tapes, Oval Office 631-7, 7 December 1971, 4:33–5:05 p.m. White House tapes, Oval Office 631-11, 7 December 1971, 6:28–7:04 p.m. White House tapes, Oval Office 632-2, 8 December 1971, 9:25–10:18 a.m. Haldeman, *Haldeman Diaries,* 7 December 1971, p. 380. White House tapes, Oval Office 631-1, 7 December 1971, 12:57–1:58 p.m. See White House tapes, Oval Office 631-7, 7 December 1971, 4:33–5:05 p.m. John Ehrlichman, *Wit- ness to Power: The Nixon Years* (New York: Simon & Schuster, 1982), pp. 307–8. See Walter Isaacson, *Kissinger: A Biography* (New York: Simon & Schuster, 1992), pp. 391–92; Mark Feldstein, *Poisoning the Press: Richard Nixon, Jack Anderson, and the Rise of Washington's Scandal Culture* (New York: Farrar, Straus & Giroux, 2010).

26. White House tapes, Oval Office 632-2, 8 December 1971, 9:25–10:18 a.m. On the impact of World War II on Kissinger's thinking about the vulnerabil- ity of democracies—which did not seem to encompass India's democracy— see Jeremi Suri, *Henry Kissinger and the American Century* (Cambridge, Mass.: Belknap Press of Harvard University Press, 2007).

27. White House tapes, Oval Office 632-2, 8 December 1971, 9:25–10:18 a.m. NSA, Bush notes, 10 December 1971.

28. White House tapes, Oval Office 630-2, 6 December 1971, 12:02–12:06 p.m.

29. NMML, Haksar Papers, Subject File 89, Dhar to Haksar, n.d. 1971. See, for instance, Sen notes, 27 October 1971, Narayan, *Selected Works,* pp. 862–69.

30. NMML, Haksar Papers, Subject File 235, Manekshaw-Kulikov talks, 24–25 February 1972. See Singh, *Liberation of Bangladesh,* pp. 68–69; Lachh- man Singh, *Indian Sword Strikes in East Pakistan* (New Delhi: Vikas, 1979), pp. 82–150; Robert Jackson, *South Asian Crisis: India, Pakistan and Bangla Desh: A Political and Historical Analysis of the 1971 War* (New York: Prae-

ger, 1975), pp. 106–45; D. R. Mankekar, *Pakistan Cut to Size* (New Delhi: Indian Book Company, 1972), pp. 53–54.

31. NMML, Haksar Papers, Subject File 220, R&AW report, "Threat of a Military Attack or Infiltration Campaign by Pakistan," January 1971. Jacob to Gill, 15 November 1971, Jacob, *Surrender at Dacca*, pp. 179–80. NMML, Haksar Papers, Subject File 235, Manekshaw-Kulikov talks, 24–25 February 1972. As the State Department noted a few days into the war, India, while swooping down on East Pakistan, largely maintained a "defensive stance in the West." (NSC Files, Box 571, Indo-Pak War, State Department situation report, 6 December 1971.) See MEA, WII/109/31/71, vol. I, Kaul-Keating discussion, 4 December 1971; Rosen, *Societies and Military Power*, pp. 248–50.

32. NSC Files, Box 570, Indo-Pak Crisis, South Asia, CIA Office of National Estimates, "The Indo-Pakistani Crisis," 22 September 1971. NMML, Haksar Papers, Subject File 235, Manekshaw-Kulikov talks, 24–25 February 1972.

33. *Hamoodur Rehman Commission Report*, p. 173. Mankekar, *Pakistan Cut to Size*, pp. 53, 95–96. Pran Chopra, *India's Second Liberation* (Cambridge, Mass.: MIT Press, 1974), pp. 138–39, 161–62.

34. James P. Sterba, "India MIG's in 8 Raids Against Dacca Airport," *New York Times*, 5 December 1971, p. A24.

35. *FRUS*, Pentagon meeting, 6 December 1971, 9:37–10:40 a.m., pp. 652–56. D. K. Palit, *The Lightning Campaign: The Indo-Pakistan War, 1971* (Salisbury, U.K.: Compton Press, 1972), pp. 114–15. Chopra, *India's Second Liberation*, pp. 140–42, 164. Singh, *Liberation of Bangladesh*, p. 215. *Hamoodur Rehman Commission Report*, pp. 233–37. Mankekar, *Pakistan Cut to Size*, pp. 98–99. For an overview, see S. S. Sethi, *The Decisive War: Emergence of a New Nation* (New Delhi: Sagar Publications, 1972), pp. 138–41.

36. NMML, Haksar Papers, Subject File 235, Manekshaw-Kulikov talks, 24–25 February 1972. Singh, *Liberation of Bangladesh*, p. 58.

37. Palit, *Lightning Campaign*, pp. 101–3, 114. Mankekar, *Pakistan Cut to Size*, pp. 51–54, 63. Singh, *Liberation of Bangladesh*, pp. 192–93. See Ahmed Abdullah Jamal, "Mukti Bahini and the Liberation War of Bangladesh," *Asian Affairs*, vol. 30, no. 4 (October–December 2008), pp. 5–17.

38. Jacob, *Surrender at Dacca*, pp. 125–27. Palit, *Lightning Campaign*, pp. 114–15. Lachhman Singh, *Victory in Bangladesh* (New Delhi: Natraj Publishers, 1981), pp. 148–53. Mankekar, *Pakistan Cut to Size*, p. 62. Chopra, *India's Second Liberation*, pp. 180–81.

39. Jacob, *Surrender at Dacca*, p. 130. Singh, *Victory in Bangladesh*, pp. 37–39; Singh, *Liberation of Bangladesh*, pp. 202–21; Mankekar, *Pakistan Cut to Size*, pp. 53–54.

40. Singh, *Victory in Bangladesh*, pp. 143–47; Mankekar, *Pakistan Cut to Size*, p. 63. Sydney H. Schanberg, "A Village Ablaze, a Blown Bridge; Enraptured Jessore Greets Troops," *New York Times*, 21 December 1971.

41. A. T. M. Abdul Wahab, *Mukti Bahini Wins Victory* (Dacca: Columbia Prokashani, 2004), p. 199. Habibul Alam, *Brave of Heart: The Urban Guerilla Warfare of Sector-2, During the Liberation War of Bangladesh* (Dacca: Academic Press and Publishers Library, 2006), pp. 286–88, 290–91, 51, 283.

42. Sydney H. Schanberg, "A Village Ablaze, a Blown Bridge; Enraptured Jessore Greets Troops," *New York Times*, 21 December 1971.

43. NMML, Haksar Papers, Subject File 173, Manekshaw to Farman Ali,

13 December 1971; NMML, Haksar Papers, Subject File 173, Haksar to Kaul, 13 December 1971; NMML, Haksar Papers, Subject File 235, Manekshaw-Kulikov talks, 24–25 February 1972; Singh, *Leadership in the Indian Army,* pp. 207–8. MEA, WII/109/31/71, vol. I, Kaul-Keating discussion, 4 December 1971. See Singh, *Victory in Bangladesh,* pp. 241–42.

44. NMML, Haksar Papers, Subject File 235, Manekshaw-Kulikov talks, 24–25 February 1972. Singh, *Victory in Bangladesh,* p. 72. MEA, HI/1012/57/71, Sethi to army staff, monthly military digest, 5 January 1972.

45. NSC Files, Box 572, Indo-Pak War, Farland to Rogers, 8 December 1971, Islamabad 12215. NSC Files, Box 572, Indo-Pak War, Farland to Rogers, 9 December 1971, Islamabad 12295. NMML, Haksar Papers, Subject File 174, Henri to Thant, 10 December 1971.

46. *FRUS,* WSAG meeting, 6 December 1971, 11:07–11:56 a.m., pp. 656–67. NSC Files, Box 572, Indo-Pak War, Sisco to Keating, 8 December 1971. NSA, Nixon-Kissinger telcon, 4 December 1971. See White House tapes, White House telephone 16-37, 7 December 1971, 11:31–11:54 p.m. *FRUS,* vol. E-7, White House tapes, Oval Office 635-8, 10 December 1971, 10:51–11:12 a.m. NSC Files, Box 643, Country Files—Middle East, India/Pakistan, Spivack to Rogers, 10 December 1971, Dacca 5570. There is another copy in NSC Files, Box 572, Indo-Pak War.

47. NSC Files, Box 572, Indo-Pak War, Keating to Rogers, 7 December 1971, New Delhi 18877. NSC Files, Box 572, Indo-Pak War, Keating to Rogers, 9 December 1971, New Delhi 19015. NMML, Haksar Papers, Subject File 174, Haksar to Sen, 11 December 1971. NMML, Haksar Papers, Subject File 174, Haksar to Dutt, 13 December 1971.

48. NMML, Haksar Papers, Subject File 173, Haksar to Kaul, 15 December 1971. MEA, HI/121/13/71, vol. II, Tajuddin Ahmad statement, 13 December 1971. NMML, Haksar Papers, Subject File 173, Haksar to Dutt, 15 December 1971. NSC Files, Box 572, Indo-Pak War, CIA situation report, 9 December 1971. This report has many redactions.

49. For an insightful overview of joint operations in India's major wars, see Anit Mukherjee, "The Coordination Model of Jointness," unpublished paper, pp. 21–26. See MEA, WII/109/31/71, vol. I, Gandhi speech in Parliament, 7 December 1971. S. S. Shashi, *Defenders of India* (New Delhi: Indian School Supply Depot, 1972), p. 148. Singh, *Liberation of Bangladesh,* p. 70. See *Hamoodur Rehman Commission Report,* pp. 239–42. See also NMML, Haksar Papers, Subject File 235, Manekshaw-Kulikov talks, 24–25 February 1972; K. P. Candeth, *The Western Front: Indo-Pakistan War, 1971* (New Delhi: Allied Publishers, 1984), pp. 157–60; *FRUS,* WSAG meeting, 6 December 1971, 11:07–11:56 a.m., pp. 656–67.

50. N. Krishnan, *No Way but Surrender: An Account of the Indo-Pakistan War in the Bay of Bengal, 1971* (New Delhi: Vikas, 1980), pp. 8–11, 26–27. Ramananda Sengupta, "'Karachi Burned for Seven Days,'" Rediff .com, 13 May 2009. *Hamoodur Rehman Commission Report,* pp. 242–47.

51. NSC Files, Box 572, Indo-Pak War, Farland to Rogers, 8 December 1971, Islamabad 12215. Chopra, *India's Second Liberation,* pp. 163–64. Mankekar, *Pakistan Cut to Size,* pp. 111–13. Krishnan, *No Way but Surrender,* pp. 39–46. Muhammad Adil Mulki, "Warriors of the Waves," *Express Tribune Sunday Magazine,* 27 May 2012. Pakistan did score one major naval success, torpedoing and sinking a frigate, INS *Khukri.*

452 ~ Notes to Pages 280-282

52. NSC Files, Box 571, Indo-Pak War, State Department situation report, 6 December 1971. Malcolm W. Browne, "For the West Pakistanis, War Is Closer to Home," *New York Times,* 10 December 1971, p. A16. NSC Files, Box 573, Indo-Pak War, Barrow to Rogers, 15 December 1971, Lahore 1606. White House tapes, Oval Office 635-6, 10 December 1971, 9:10–10:31 a.m. See Chuck Yeager and Leo Janos, *Yeager: An Autobiography* (New York: Bantam, 1985), pp. 311–12.

53. *FRUS,* WSAG meeting, 6 December 1971, 11:07–11:56 a.m., pp. 656–67. Ramananda Sengupta, "'Karachi Burned for Seven Days,'" Rediff.com, 13 May 2009. See NSA, Nixon-Kissinger telcon, 4 December 1971; White House tapes, White House telephone 16-6, 5 December 1971, 7:56–8:03 p.m. Benazir Bhutto, *Daughter of the East* (London: Hamish Hamilton, 1988), p. 48.

54. NSC Files, Box 572, Indo-Pak War, CIA situation report, 9 December 1971. *Hamoodur Rehman Commission Report,* pp. 244–47. Palit, *Lightning Campaign,* pp. 147–49. Mankekar, *Pakistan Cut to Size,* p. 110. Chopra, *India's Second Liberation,* pp. 166–68. Sethi, *Decisive War,* p. 139. NSC Files, Box 572, Indo-Pak War, CIA situation report, 9 December 1971. See *FRUS,* WSAG meeting, 4 December 1971, 11:13–11:41 a.m., pp. 620–27. Ramananda Sengupta, "'Karachi Burned for Seven Days,'" Rediff.com, 13 May 2009.

55. Chopra, *India's Second Liberation,* pp. 127–37.

56. *FRUS,* WSAG meeting, 6 December 1971, 11:07–11:56 a.m., pp. 656–67. *FRUS,* NSC meeting, 6 December 1971, 1:30–3:30 p.m., pp. 669–73. *FRUS,* Kissinger to Nixon, 6 December 1971, pp. 650–51. See NSA, Nixon-Kissinger telcon, 4 December 1971; White House tapes, White House telephone 16-6, 5 December 1971, 7:56–8:03 p.m. *FRUS,* vol. E-7, White House tapes, White House telephone 16-14, 6 December 1971, 9:19–9:24 a.m.

57. G. S. Bhargava, *Their Finest Hour: Saga of India's December Victory* (New Delhi: Vikas, 1972), pp. 35, 89, 73, 89–90.

58. NSC Files, Box 572, Indo-Pak War, Kissinger to Nixon, 7 December 1971. Mankekar, *Pakistan Cut to Size,* pp. 87–90. Candeth, *Western Front,* pp. 65–71. NSC Files, Box 571, Indo-Pak War, State Department situation report, 5 December 1971. MEA, WII/109/31/71, vol. I, Gandhi speech in Parliament, 7 December 1971. Jayakar, *Indira Gandhi,* p. 177.

59. *Hamoodur Rehman Commission Report,* pp. 213–15. Chopra, *India's Second Liberation,* p. 162. Henry Kamm, "Pakistani Forces Take Ghost Town in Kashmir," *New York Times,* 13 December 1971, p. A16. Janak Singh, "Chhamb: Scene of Bitterest Fighting," *Times of India,* 9 January 1972, p. A4.

60. Palit, *Lightning Campaign,* pp. 84–85. Bhargava, *Finest Hour,* pp. 59–64. See Candeth, *Western Front,* pp. 74–84. Mankekar, *Pakistan Cut to Size,* p. 99. Sethi, *Decisive War,* pp. 138–41.

61. "The Toll of Battle," *Times of India,* 9 January 1972, p. A4. "Loss of Khukri, Not Leg, Upsets Jawan More," *Times of India,* 29 December 1971, p. 6.

62. Jagjit Singh, *Indian Gunners at War: The Western Front, 1971* (New Delhi: Lancer International, 1994), pp. 96–102. NSC Files, Box 572, Indo-Pak War, DIA analysis, 8 December 1971. Fox Butterfield, "Battle at Kashmir River Said to Leave 900 Dead," *New York Times,* 12 December 1971, p. A26.

Janak Singh, "Chhamb: Scene of Bitterest Fighting," *Times of India*, 9 January 1972, p. A4.

63. Jayakar, *Indira Gandhi*, pp. 177, 184–85.
64. MEA, HI/121/13/71, vol. II, Gandhi to Tajuddin Ahmad, 6 December 1971. MEA, WII/109/31/71, vol. II, Gandhi to Tajuddin Ahmad, 6 December 1971. See NMML, Haksar Papers, Subject File 173, Haksar to Gandhi, 6 December 1971; Narayan statement, 6 December 1971, Narayan, *Selected Works*, p. 694; Narayan to Gandhi, 6 December 1971, Narayan, *Selected Works*, p. 694; MEA, WII/109/31/71, vol. I, Kaul to Jha, 6 December 1971. MEA, HI/121/13/71, vol. II, Sinai to ambassadors, 12 December 1971. MEA, WII/109/31/71, vol. II, Sinai to ambassadors, 12 December 1971. MEA, WII/109/31/71, vol. I, Singh-Keating discussion, 7 December 1971, 12:15 p.m. MEA, HI/121/13/71, vol. II, Dixit to heads of mission, 4 December 1971. MEA, WII/109/31/71, vol. I, Kaul to Jha, 6 December 1971. MEA, HI/121/25/71, Gandhi statement in Lok Sabha and Rajya Sabha, 6 December 1971. NSC Files, Box 571, Indo-Pak War, Keating to Rogers, 6 December 1971, New Delhi 18770. For Haksar's argument about international law, see NMML, Haksar Papers, Subject File 173, Haksar to Singh, 11 December 1971; see also Ved P. Nanda, "Self-Determination in International Law," *American Journal of International Law*, vol. 66, no. 2 (April 1972), pp. 321–36, and M. K. Nawaz, "Bangla Desh and International Law," *Indian Journal of International Law*, vol. 11, no. 2 (April 1971), pp. 251–66. Jefferson wrote of "the choice of the people substantially expressed" in a letter to James Madison in January 1797. But this was not justifying American independence from Britain, but something rather more prosaic: Jefferson's contest with John Adams to become the new country's second president, with Jefferson declaring that Adams had won, no matter the technicalities of the vote in Vermont. (Bruce Ackerman and David Fontana, "Thomas Jefferson Counts Himself into the Presidency," *Virginia Law Review*, vol. 90 [2004], p. 577.)
65. MEA, HI/121/25/71, Kaul to Singh, 6 December 1971. MEA, WII/109/31/71, vol. I, Singh-Keating discussion, 7 December 1971, 12:15 p.m. NMML, Haksar Papers, Subject File 173, "A note on India's objectives in the current conflict with Pakistan," 9 December 1971. Swaran Singh emphasized that India sought neither occupation nor Bangladeshi land: "This is a sort of self-restraint on us in Bangla Desh." (MEA, WII/109/31/71, vol. I, Singh-Keating discussion, 7 December 1971, 12:15 p.m.) See MEA, WII/109/31/71, vol. I, Singh statement to UN Security Council, 12 December 1971; MEA, HI/121/25/71, Kaul to Singh, 6 December 1971; MEA, WII/109/31/71, vol. II, Iyer to Singh, 22 December 1971. MEA, WII/109/31/71, vol. I, Shukla to Singh, 6 December 1971. MEA, WII/109/31/71, vol. I, Indian government press information bureau, Gandhi speech, 12 December 1971. China accused India of carrying out "the Indian reactionaries long planned criminal aim to annex East Pakistan" (Xinhua, 7 December 1971, in MEA, HI/121/13/71, vol. II, Iyer to Singh, 9 December 1971).
66. White House tapes, Oval Office 617-17, 15 November 1971, 4:31–4:39 p.m.; *FRUS*, WSAG minutes, 12 November 1971, 11:09 a.m., pp. 509–10; NSA, Nixon-Kissinger telcon, 13 November 1971, 10:38 a.m.; *FRUS*, WSAG meeting, 22 November 1971, 2:39–3:14 p.m., pp. 529–36; *FRUS*, vol. E-7, White

454 ~ Notes to Pages 283–284

House tapes, Oval Office 624–21, 24 November 1971, 12:27 p.m.; *FRUS,* WSAG meeting, 1 December 1971, 4:17–4:50 p.m., pp. 585–90; *FRUS,* vol. E-7, White House tapes, Oval Office 638-4, 15 December 1971, 8:45–11:30 a.m. NSA, Nixon-Kissinger telcon, 3 December, 5:55 p.m. NSA, Kissinger-Raza telcon, 3 December 1971, 10:23 a.m. NSA, Kissinger-Raza telcon, 3 December 1971, 11:04 a.m. NSA, Kissinger-Raza telcon, 3 December 1971, 7 p.m. *FRUS,* vol. E-7, White House tapes, Oval Office 637-3, 12 December 1971, 8:45–9:42 a.m.

67. MEA, WII/109/31/71, vol. I, Kaul to Sen, 4 December 1971. NMML, Haksar Papers, Subject File 173, Gandhi to Kosygin (Haksar draft), 10 December 1971. MEA, HI/121/13/71, vol. II, draft Security Council resolution by Argentina, Belgium, Italy, Japan, Nicaragua, Sierra Leone, and Somalia, 5 December 1971. NSC Files, Box 643, Country Files—Middle East, India/Pakistan, Nixon-Kissinger telcon, 4 December 1971, 12:15 p.m. See NSA, Kissinger-Sisco telcon, 4 December 1971, 9:15 a.m.

68. NSC Files, Box 643, Country Files—Middle East, India/Pakistan, Nixon-Kissinger telcon, 4 December 1971, 10:50 a.m. NSA, Nixon-Kissinger telcon, 4 December 1971. MEA, HI/121/13/71, vol. II, U.S. draft Security Council resolution, 4–6 December 1971. See *FRUS,* WSAG meeting, 4 December 1971, 11:13–11:41 a.m., pp. 620–27; NSC Files, Box 571, Indo-Pak War, draft Bush statement, 4 December 1971; NSC Files, Box 571, Indo-Pak War, Rogers to Bush, 4 December 1971, State 219431. White House tapes, White House telephone 16-48, 8 December 1971, 11:06–11:14 a.m.

69. NSC Files, Box 572, Indo-Pak War, Bush statement to UN Security Council, 5 December 1971. MEA, WII/109/31/71, vol. I, USIS, Bush statement to UN Security Council, 5 December 1971. MEA, HI/121/13/71, vol. II, Bush statement to UN Security Council, 5 December 1971. See Kissinger, *White House Years,* p. 902. MEA, WII/109/31/71, vol. I, Singh-Keating discussion, 7 December 1971, 12:15 p.m. MEA, WII/109/31/71, vol. II, Kaul-Keating discussion, 6 December 1971, 12:30 p.m. MEA, WII/109/31/71, vol. I, Kaul to Jha, 6 December 1971. See MEA, WII/109/31/71, vol. I, Singh-Keating discussion, 7 December 1971, 12:15 p.m.; NSC Files, Box 572, Indo-Pak War, Keating to Rogers, 7 December 1971, New Delhi 18877. MEA, WII/109/31/71, vol. I, Kaul to Sen, 4 December 1971. See MEA, HI/121/13/71, vol. II, Sen statement to UN Security Council, 4 December 1971; MEA, HI/121/13/71, vol. II, Sen statement to UN Security Council, 5 December 1971. MEA, HI/121/13/71, vol. II, Dixit to heads of mission, 4 December 1971.

70. MEA, HI/121/13/71, vol. II, Kapur note, 13 December 1971. See NMML, Haksar Papers, Subject File 173, Haksar to Gandhi, 15 December 1971. White House tapes, White House telephone 16-48, 8 December 1971, 11:06–11:14 a.m. See NSC Files, Box 572, Indo-Pak War, Bush statement to UN Security Council, 5 December 1971; MEA, HI/121/13/71, vol. II, Bush statement to UN Security Council, 5 December 1971. NSA, Nixon-Bush telcon, 6 December 1971.

71. MEA, HI/121/13/71, vol. II, Krishnan to ambassadors, 13 December 1971. MEA, HI/121/13/71, vol. II, Kapur note, 13 December 1971. White House tapes, White House telephone 16-37, 7 December 1971, 11:31–11:54 p.m. See NSA, Nixon-Kissinger telcon, 5 December 1971; NSC Files, Box 571, Indo-Pak War, Kissinger to Nixon, "South Asia in the Security Council," n.d. December 1971; MEA, HI/121/13/71, vol. II, Krishnan to ambassadors,

13 December 1971; MEA, WII/109/31/71, vol. I, USIS, Bush statement to UN Security Council, 5 December 1971; MEA, HI/121/13/71, vol. II, Bush statement to UN Security Council, 5 December 1971; MEA, WII/109/31/71, vol. I, Singh-Keating discussion, 7 December 1971, 12:15 p.m. The non-permanent members of the Security Council were Argentina, Belgium, Burundi, Italy, Japan, Nicaragua, Poland, Sierra Leone, Somalia, and Tunisia. NSA, Nixon-Kissinger telcon, 5 December 1971. MEA, HI/121/13/71, vol. II, Soviet draft Security Council resolution, 4–6 December 1971. MEA, HI/121/13/71, vol. II, Chinese draft Security Council resolution, 4–6 December 1971. MEA, HI/121/13/71, vol. II, draft Security Council resolution by Argentina, Belgium, Italy, Japan, Nicaragua, Sierra Leone, and Somalia, 5 December 1971. See MEA, HI/121/13/71, vol. II, Kapur note, 13 December 1971; MEA, HI/1012/57/71, Shelvankar to Kaul, 30 January 1972. MEA, HI/121/13/71, vol. II, Kapur note, 13 December 1971. MEA, HI/1012/57/71, Shelvankar to Kaul, 30 January 1972. NSC Files, Box 643, Country Files—Middle East, India/Pakistan, Nixon-Kissinger telcon, 4 December 1971, 10:50 a.m.

72. NSA, Kissinger-Vorontsov telcon, 5 December 1971, 4:55 p.m. *FRUS*, Nixon to Brezhnev, 6 December 1971, pp. 667–68. White House tapes, Oval Office 630-2, 6 December 1971, 12:02–12:06 p.m. See White House tapes, White House telephone 16-30, 6 December 1971, 10:58–11:05 p.m.

73. MEA, HI/121/13/71, vol. II, Kapur note, 13 December 1971. UN Security Council resolution 303, 6 December 1971, at http://daccess-dds-ny.un.org/doc/RESOLUTION/GEN/NR0/261/63/IMG/NR026163.pdf?OpenElement. The vote was eleven in favor, with the Soviet Union, Poland, Britain, and France abstaining. MEA, WII/109/31/71, vol. I, Bush second UN Security Council statement, 6 December 1971. Bush made his appeal under the Uniting for Peace resolution, for those times when the Security Council was deadlocked in the face of aggression. White House tapes, White House telephone 16-48, 8 December 1971, 11:06-11:14 a.m. See White House tapes, White House telephone 16-16, 6 December 1971, 9:37–9:42 a.m.; NSC Files, Box 571, Indo-Pak War, Bush to Rogers, 7 December 1971, USUN 4818.

74. UN General Assembly Resolution 2793 (XXVI), 7 December 1971. MEA, HI/121/13/71, vol. II, "Implications of the General Assembly Resolution," n.d. December 1971. Nicholas J. Wheeler astutely writes that "the overwhelming reaction of the society of states was to affirm Pakistan's right to sovereignty and the rule of non-intervention." (*Saving Strangers: Humanitarian Intervention in International Order* [Oxford: Oxford University Press, 2002], pp. 58, 69.)

75. For an Indian critique, see K. P. Misra, *The Role of the United Nations in the Indo-Pakistani Conflict, 1971* (New Delhi: Vikas, 1973). MEA, WII/109/31/71, vol. I, Gandhi to heads of state, 5 December 1971. Swaran Singh lobbied friendly governments that the crisis came from "unprovoked aggression by Pakistan against us and suppression of human rights" in Bangladesh (MEA, HI/121/13/71, vol. II, Singh to Indian ambassadors, 7 December 1971; MEA, WII/109/31/71, vol. II, Singh to Indian ambassadors, 7 December 1971). White House tapes, White House telephone 16-37, 16-39, 16-40, 7 December 1971, 11:31-11:54 p.m. MEA, HI/1012/57/71, Shelvankar to Kaul, 30 January 1972. NSC Files, Box 572, Indo-Pak War,

Dean to Rogers, 10 December 1971, Hong Kong 8205. India got the votes of the Soviet Union; its two constituent republics with UN votes, Belorussia and Ukraine; Cuba, Bulgaria, Hungary, Mongolia, and Poland; and Bhutan. White House tapes, White House telephone 16-48, 8 December 1971, 11:06–11:14 a.m. MEA, HI/121/13/71, vol. II, Sen to Kaul, 7 December 1971. See NSC Files, Box 572, Indo-Pak War, Bush to Rogers, 8 December 1971, USUN 4843. MEA, HI/121/13/71, vol. II, "Implications of the General Assembly Resolution," n.d. December 1971.

76. White House tapes, White House telephone 16-37, 16-39, 16-40, 7 December 1971, 11:31–11:54 p.m.

77. White House tapes, White House telephone 16-48, 8 December 1971, 11:06–11:14 a.m.

78. MEA, WII/109/31/71, vol. II, Kaul-Keating discussion, 6 December 1971, 12:30 p.m. NSA, Nixon-Kissinger telcon, 4 December 1971. On Ford, see NSC Files, Box 571, Indo-Pak War, Haig to Saunders, "Talking Points for Gerald Ford," 29 November 1971. On Agnew, see White House tapes, White House telephone 16-37, 16-39, 16-40, 7 December 1971, 11:31–11:54 p.m. NSC Files, Box 643, Country Files—Middle East, India/Pakistan, Nixon-Kissinger telcon, 4 December 1971, 10:50 a.m.; NSC Files, Box 643, Country Files—Middle East, India/Pakistan, Nixon-Kissinger telcon, 4 December 1971, 12:15 p.m.; NSC Files, Box 643, Country Files—Middle East, India/Pakistan, Scali to Kissinger, 7 December 1971; NSA, Nixon-Kissinger telcon, 4 December 1971; NSA, Nixon-Kissinger telcon, 5 December 1971.

79. FRUS, vol. E-7, White House tapes, Oval Office 635-8, 10 December 1971, 10:51–11:12 a.m. See White House tapes, Oval Office 635-6, 10 December 1971, 9:10–10:31 a.m.

80. FRUS, vol. E-7, White House tapes, Oval Office 637-3, 12 December 1971, 8:45–9:42 a.m. Charles Colson, Nixon's special counsel—the self-described "chief ass-kicker around the White House," who would later spend seven months in jail after pleading guilty to obstruction of justice—shrewdly argued that Kennedy would lose because he was suggesting "an interventionist policy." Colson said, "that's exactly what people don't want." (White House tapes, White House telephone 16-58, 8 December 1971, 3:46–3:55 p.m.) On Colson, see David Greenberg, "In Remembrance of a Lifelong Political Thug," The New Republic, 25 April 2012.

81. FRUS, vol. E-7, White House tapes, Oval Office 631-4, 7 December 1971, 3:55–4:29 p.m. See White House tapes, Oval Office 631-2, 7 December 1971, 2:59–3:02 p.m.; White House tapes, Oval Office 631-11, 7 December 1971, 6:28–7:04 p.m. NSA, Nixon-Kissinger telcon, 4 December 1971. See NSA, Nixon-Kissinger telcon, 5 December 1971. NSC Files, Box 572, Indo-Pak War, Kissinger background briefing, 7 December 1971, 4:40 p.m. FRUS, vol. E-7, White House tapes, Oval Office 634-19, 9 December 1971, 5:57–6:34 p.m.

82. MEA, WII/109/31/71, vol. II, "Attitudes in the US Congress," n.d. December 1971. NSA, Kissinger-Rogers telcon, 3 December 1971, 3:45 p.m. NSA, Nixon-Kissinger telcon, 3 December 1971, 2:45 p.m. NSA, Kissinger-Sisco telcon, 3 December 1971, 3:10 p.m. NSA, Kissinger-Passman telcon, 3 December 1971, 5:05 p.m. NSA, Nixon-Kissinger telcon, 4 December 1971. White House tapes, White House telephone 16-37, 16-39, 16-40, 7 December 1971, 11:31–11:54 p.m. See White House tapes, White House telephone

16-36, 7 December 1971, 6:51–6:55 p.m.; White House tapes, White House telephone 16-58, 8 December 1971, 3:46–3:55 p.m.; *FRUS,* vol. E-7, White House tapes, Oval Office 630-20, 6 December 1971, 6:14–6:38 p.m.

83. Garry Wills, *Nixon Agonistes: The Crisis of the Self-Made Man* (Boston: Houghton Mifflin, 1970), pp. 427–31. *FRUS,* vol. E-7, White House tapes, Oval Office 634-19, 9 December 1971, 5:57–6:34 p.m. *FRUS,* vol. E-7, White House tapes, EOB 307-27, 8 December 1971, 4:20–5:01 p.m.

84. MEA, WII/109/31/71, vol. I, Jha to Kaul, 5 December 1971. MEA, WII/109/31/71, vol. I, Shukla to Singh, 6 December 1971. MEA, WII/109/31/71, vol. I, Singh-Keating discussion, 7 December 1971, 12:15 p.m. Harris Survey, December 1971. By the end of the war, 23 percent of Americans polled said they sympathized with Pakistan, against 14 percent who leaned toward India, while 27 percent did not sympathize with either side, and 32 percent were not sure. The poll also found that Americans were uneasy about Nixon's own handling of the war. Just 5 percent thought he performed excellently, with roughly a quarter of respondents each saying that the president had done pretty good, only fair, or poor, or simply not being sure. *FRUS,* vol. E-7, White House tapes, Oval Office 637-3, 12 December 1971, 8:45–9:42 a.m. See White House tapes, White House telephone 16-76, 9 December 1971, 7:42–8:10 p.m.; MEA, WII/109/31/71, vol. I, Kaul-Keating discussion, 4 December 1971. White House tapes, Oval Office 636-8, 10 December 1971, 4:18–5:11 p.m. *FRUS,* vol. E-7, White House tapes, Oval Office 637-3, 12 December 1971, 8:45–9:42 a.m. See White House tapes, Oval Office 635-6, 10 December 1971, 9:10–10:31 a.m. See also Haldeman, *Haldeman Diaries,* 10 December 1971, p. 382; White House tapes, White House telephone 16-76, 9 December 1971, 7:42–8:10 p.m.; MEA, WII/109/31/71, vol. I, Kaul-Keating discussion, 4 December 1971.

85. White House tapes, Oval Office 635-6, 10 December 1971, 9:10–10:31 a.m.

CHAPTER 19: "I CONSIDER THIS OUR RHINELAND"

1. Government of Pakistan, *The Report of the Hamoodur Rehman Commission of Inquiry into the 1971 War* (Lahore: Vanguard, 2001), p. 468. NSC Files, Box 572, Indo-Pak War, CIA situation report, 8 December 1971. NSC Files, Box 572, Indo-Pak War, Spivack to Rogers, 8 December 1971, Dacca 5542. NSC Files, Box 643, Country Files—Middle East, India/Pakistan, Nixon-Kissinger telcon, 4 December 1971, 12:15 p.m. See Henry Kissinger, *White House Years* (Boston: Little, Brown, 1979), p. 896. See also White House tapes, White House telephone 16-37, 7 December 1971, 11:31–11:54 p.m.

2. NMML, Haksar Papers, Subject File 235, Manekshaw-Kulikov talks, 24–25 February 1972. Shashi Tharoor, *Reasons of State: Political Development and India's Foreign Policy Under Indira Gandhi, 1966–1977* (New Delhi: Vikas, 1982), pp. 67–68. NSC Files, Box 572, Indo-Pak War, Kissinger to Nixon, 8 December 1971. *FRUS,* WSAG meeting, 8 December 1971, 11:13 a.m.–12:02 p.m., pp. 690-99. NSC Files, Box 572, Indo-Pak War, sanitized intelligence analysis, n.d. December 1971.

3. *FRUS,* CIA cable, 7 December 1971, pp. 686–87.

4. A senior aide to Gandhi claims that the mole was later reportedly unveiled as a bitter political rival of Gandhi's who had been shoved out as deputy prime minister two years earlier (P. N. Dhar, *Indira Gandhi, the "Emer-*

gency," and Indian Democracy [Oxford: Oxford University Press, 2000], p. 181). See Kissinger, White House Years, p. 901. Dhar is referring to the work of the great investigative reporter Seymour Hersh. In The Price of Power: Kissinger in the Nixon White House (New York: Summit, 1983), pp. 449–50, Hersh, relying on U.S. intelligence sources, identified Moraji Desai as the mole, despite Indian and American denials (Josy Joseph, "PV Narasimha Rao Misled Parliament on Help to Writer Seymour Hersh Who Called Moraji Desai a CIA Mole," Times of India, 8 November 2011). Inder Malhotra, Indira Gandhi: A Personal and Political Biography (London: Hodder & Stoughton 1989), pp. 140–41. Richard Sisson and Leo E. Rose, War and Secession: Pakistan, India, and the Creation of Bangladesh (Berkeley: University of California Press, 1990), pp. 140–41, 215, 262. Dhar, Indira Gandhi, the "Emergency," and Indian Democracy, p. 181. See B. Raman, The Kaoboys of R&AW: Down Memory Lane (New Delhi: Lancer, 2007), p. 21. William Bundy, A Tangled Web: The Making of Foreign Policy in the Nixon Presidency (New York: Hill & Wang, 1998), pp. 285–86, 580n96.

5. FRUS, vol. E-7, White House tapes, EOB 307-27, 8 December 1971, 4:20–5:01 p.m. See FRUS, WSAG meeting, 9 December 1971, 10:09–11 a.m., pp. 711–21; FRUS, vol. E-7, White House tapes, White House telephone 16-64, 8 December 1971, 8:03–8:12 p.m. This concern with U.S. credibility was a hallmark of Kissinger's thought, particularly in Vietnam (Garry Wills, Nixon Agonistes: The Crisis of the Self-Made Man [Boston: Houghton Mifflin, 1970], pp. 419–20).

6. Hersh, Price of Power, pp. 459–60. FRUS, vol. E-7, White House tapes, Oval Office 637-3, 12 December 1971, 8:45–9:42 a.m. For a denial from Gandhi, see R. K. Karanjia and K. A. Abbas, Face to Face with Indira Gandhi (New Delhi: Chetana Publications, 1974), p. 80.

7. A. A. K. Niazi, The Betrayal of East Pakistan (Karachi: Oxford University Press, 1998), p. 226. K. P. Candeth, The Western Front: Indo-Pakistan War, 1971 (New Delhi: Allied Publishers, 1984), p. 168. FRUS, vol. E-7, White House tapes, EOB 307-27, 8 December 1971, 4:20–5:01 p.m.

8. FRUS, vol. E-7, White House tapes, EOB 307-27, 8 December 1971, 4:20–5:01 p.m. See FRUS, WSAG meeting, 9 December 1971, 10:09–11 a.m., pp. 711–21. FRUS, vol. E-7, White House tapes, EOB 307-27, 8 December 1971, 4:20–5:01 p.m. The same secretiveness evidently applied to the American public. In his memoirs, Kissinger mentions the White House's boldness and Nixon's Bismarck-like courage, but does not mention encouraging Chinese mobilization or the illegal arms shipments. (Kissinger, White House Years, pp. 898–99, 905, 894–918.)

9. Thomas C. Schelling, Arms and Influence (New Haven, Conn.: Yale University Press, 1966). NSC Files, Box 643, Country Files—Middle East, India/Pakistan, China memorandum, n.d. December 1971.

10. FRUS, vol. E-7, White House tapes, Oval Office 582-9, 30 September 1971, 4:10–5:31 p.m. FRUS, CIA cable, 7 December 1971, pp. 686–87. Patrick E. Tyler, A Great Wall: Six Presidents and China (New York: PublicAffairs, 1999), pp. 71–73.

11. NSA, Huang-Kissinger memcon, 23 November 1971, 10–11:55 p.m. FRUS, vol. E-7, White House tapes, Oval Office 630-20, 6 December 1971, 6:14–6:38 p.m. Nixon knew that "those great mountain passes coming down over

the Himalaya mountains are all covered with snow." (White House tapes, White House telephone 16-50, 8 December 1971, 2:15–2:22 p.m.)

12. NSC Files, Box 1025, Presidential/HAK MemCons, Haksar-Kissinger memcon, 7 July 1971, 1:10 p.m. See NMML, Haksar Papers, Subject File 169, Haksar minutes of Kissinger meeting, 6 July 1971. NMML, Haksar Papers, Subject File 225, Gandhi-Kissinger conversation, 7 July 1971. MEA, WII/121/54/71, Kissinger-Ram meeting, 7 July 1971 (attached to Menon to Singh, 13 July 1971). NMML, Haksar Papers, Subject File 229, Kissinger-Ram meeting, 7 July 1971. MEA, WII/121/54/71, "Salient Points Mentioned by Dr. Kissinger," n.d. July 1971. In late August, Kissinger had retreated somewhat from this pledge, but still said that if Pakistan brazenly attacked India, and China backed up Pakistan, then the United States would "give all-out help to India against China." (MEA, WII/121/54/71, Jha to Kaul, 27 August 1971.) In addition, India had some shopworn pledges from the Kennedy administration. U.S. Department of State, *Foreign Relations of the United States, 1961–1963: South Asia*, ed. Louis J. Smith (Washington, D.C.: U.S. Government Printing Office, 1996), vol. 19, Galbraith to Nehru, 9 July 1963, document 307. See NSC Files, Box H-058, SRG Meetings, Saunders and Kennedy to Kissinger, 21 July 1971.

13. NSC Files, Box 572, Indo-Pak War, Kissinger to Nixon, 7 December 1971. NSC Files, Box 572, Indo-Pak War, CIA intelligence memorandum, "China's Military Options and Capabilities Against India's Border Areas," 7 December 1971. NSC Files, Box 572, Indo-Pak War, Kissinger to Nixon, 8 December 1971 (for an unredacted version, see *FRUS*, pp. 688-89). See NSC Files, Box 572, Indo-Pak War, DIA intelligence appraisal, 9 December 1971.

14. *FRUS*, vol. E-7, White House tapes, EOB 307-27, 8 December 1971, 4:20–5:01 p.m.

15. *FRUS*, vol. E-7, White House tapes, White House telephone 16-64, 8 December 1971, 8:03–8:12 p.m.

16. *FRUS*, vol. E-7, White House tapes, Oval Office 637-3, 12 December 1971, 8:45–9:42 a.m.

17. NSC Files, Box H-084, WSAG Meetings, Kennedy and Saunders to Kissinger, 16 December 1971. *FRUS*, Farland to Kissinger, 4 December 1971, p. 610. NSC Files, Box 643, Country Files—Middle East, India/Pakistan, Nixon-Kissinger telcon, 4 December 1971, 10:50 a.m. NSC Files, Box 643, Country Files—Middle East, India/Pakistan, Nixon-Kissinger telcon, 4 December 1971, 12:15 p.m. The transcript says "paralized." See NSC Files, Box 571, Indo-Pak War, Heck to Rogers, 5 December 1971, Tehran 6850. On Iran's support for Pakistan, see MEA, HI/1012/30/71, Chib to Kaul, 10 November 1971; NMML, Kaul Papers, Subject File 19, Singh briefing in London, n.d. June 1971; MEA, WII/125/59/71, "Note for Supplementaries," n.d. July 1971; POL 23-9 PAK, Box 2530, Farland to Rogers, 1 April 1971, Islamabad 3016; POL 23-9 PAK, Box 2531, MacArthur to Rogers, 15 April 1971, Tehran 1946. See Roham Alvandi, "Nixon, Kissinger, and the Shah," *Diplomatic History*, vol. 36, no. 2 (2012), pp. 337–72.

18. NSA, Kissinger-Afshar telcon, 4 December 1971. See NSA, Kissinger-Raza telcon, 6 December 1971, 1:24 p.m. The U.S. embassy in Tehran seems to have been in the dark (NSC Files, Box 572, Indo-Pak War, Heck to Rogers, 8 December 1971, Tehran 6924). NSA, Nixon-Kissinger telcon, 4 December

1971. See NSC Files, Box H-084, WSAG Meetings, Kennedy and Saunders to Kissinger, 16 December 1971.

19. *FRUS,* vol. E-7, White House tapes, EOB 307-27, 8 December 1971, 4:20–5:01 p.m. NSA, Johnson to Brown, 9 December 1971, State 221847. NSC Files, Box 573, Indo-Pak War, Rogers to Brown, 9 December 1971, State 221847. *FRUS,* p. 610. *FRUS,* vol. E-7, White House tapes, EOB 307-27, 8 December 1971, 4:20–5:01 p.m. See John Fricker and Paul Jackson, "Lockheed F-104 Starfighter," *Wings of Fame* (London: Aerospace Publishing, 1996), vol. 2, pp. 38–99. *FRUS,* vol. E-7, White House tapes, EOB 307-27, 8 December 1971, 4:20–5:01 p.m. See NSC Files, Box H-083, WSAG Meetings, Saunders and Kennedy to Kissinger, "WSAG Meeting—South Asia," 6 December 1971; and NSC Files, Box H-083, WSAG Meetings, Sisco to Brown, "Pakistan Request for Jordanian Military Assistance," draft cable, 12 May 1971.

20. *FRUS,* WSAG meeting, 6 December 1971, 11:07–11:56 a.m., pp. 656–67.

21. White House tapes, Oval Office 630-2, 6 December 1971, 12:02–12:06 p.m.

22. Back in July, John Dean, the White House counsel, had written that he had "cause for concern that such shipments be above legal question." (NSC Files, Box 626, Country Files—Middle East, Pakistan, vol. VI, Dean to Haig, 12 July 1971. See NSC Files, Box 626, Country Files—Middle East, Pakistan, vol. VI, Hoskinson to Haig, 18 August 1971.) NSC Files, Box 574, Indo-Pak War, South Asian Military Supply, Haig to Nixon, 25 June 1971. *FRUS,* vol. E-7, White House tapes, Oval Office 635-8, 10 December 1971, 10:51–11:12 a.m. The crucial legal memorandum is NSC Files, Box H-083, WSAG Meetings, Eliot to Kissinger, 7 December 1971; NSC Files, Box H-084, WSAG Meetings, Eliot to Kissinger, 7 December 1971. The State Department cited the Foreign Military Assistance Act of 1961 and the 1971 amendment to the Foreign Military Sales Act. See NSC Files, Box H-083, WSAG Meetings, Sisco to Brown, "Pakistan Request for Jordanian Military Assistance," draft cable, 12 May 1971.

23. NSC Files, Box H-083, WSAG Meetings, Defense Department memorandum, 7 December 1971; NSC Files, Box H-084, WSAG Meetings, Defense Department memorandum, 7 December 1971. See NSC Files, Box H-083, WSAG Meetings, Saunders and Kennedy to Kissinger, "WSAG Meeting—South Asia," 8 December 1971. See NSC Files, Box H-084, WSAG Meetings, Packard to Kissinger, 7 December 1971.

24. NSC Files, Box H-083, WSAG Meetings, Saunders and Kennedy to Kissinger, "WSAG Meeting—South Asia," 6 December 1971. See NSC Files, Box 575, Indo-Pak War, Saunders to Kissinger, "Jordanian Transfer of F-104s to Pakistan," 7 December 1971. NSC Files, Box H-084, WSAG Meetings, Saunders to Kissinger, "Military Supply for Pakistan," 9 December 1971. NSC Files, Box H-083, WSAG Meetings, Saunders and Kennedy to Kissinger, "WSAG Meeting—South Asia," 6 December 1971. See NSC Files, Box H-083, WSAG Meetings, Saunders to Kissinger, "WSAG Meeting—South Asia," 9 December 1971. Richard Reeves, *President Nixon: Alone in the White House* (New York: Simon & Schuster, 2007), p. 400.

25. White House tapes, Oval Office 631-3, 7 December 1971, 3:04–3:11 p.m.

26. *FRUS,* WSAG meeting, 8 December 1971, 11:13 a.m.–12:02 p.m., pp. 690–99.

27. *FRUS,* vol. E-7, White House tapes, EOB 307-27, 8 December 1971, 4:20–5:01

p.m. The Indian government suspected that Iran was sending U.S. airplanes to Pakistan, and complained to Keating about it (MEA, WII/109/31/71, vol. I, Kaul to Jha, 6 December 1971). *FRUS*, vol. E-7, White House tapes, White House telephone 16-64, 8 December 1971, 8:03–8:12 p.m.

28. *FRUS*, vol. E-7, White House tapes, EOB 307-27, 8 December 1971, 4:20–5:01 p.m. NSA, Kissinger-Raza telcon, 8 December 1971, 2:47 p.m. NSA, Kissinger-Raza telcon, 8 December 1971, 7:10 p.m. Still, Nixon wanted India to see the menacing hand of the United States: "I'd like to make sure that the Indians know we are behind it one way or another." (*FRUS*, vol. E-7, White House tapes, EOB 307-27, 8 December 1971, 4:20–5:01 p.m.)

29. NSC Files, Box H-084, WSAG Meetings, Kennedy and Saunders to Kissinger, 16 December 1971. NSC Files, Box 643, Country Files—Middle East, India-Pakistan, Haig to Kissinger, 19 January 1972.

30. *FRUS*, vol. E-7, White House tapes, EOB 307-27, 8 December 1971, 4:20–5:01 p.m.

31. *FRUS*, vol. E-7, White House tapes, Oval Office 633-11, 9 December 1971, 12:44–1:27 p.m. *FRUS*, vol. E-7, White House tapes, Oval Office 634-19, 9 December 1971, 5:57–6:34 p.m.

32. NSA, Kissinger-Connally telcon, 6 December 1971, 11:10 p.m. White House tapes, White House telephone 16-64, 8 December 1971, 8:03–8:12 p.m. See NSC Files, Box 134, Kissinger Office Files, Country Files—Middle East, Nixon to Brezhnev, 6 December 1971; NSC Files, Box 134, Kissinger Office Files, Country Files—Middle East, Brezhnev to Nixon, 8 December 1971. *FRUS*, vol. E-7, White House tapes, Oval Office 634-12, 9 December 1971, 4–4:41 p.m. See NSC Files, Box 134, Kissinger Office Files, Country Files—Middle East, Nixon to Brezhnev, 6 December 1971, Nixon-Matskevich memcon, 9 December 1971, 4 p.m.; H. R. Haldeman, *The Haldeman Diaries: Inside the Nixon White House* (New York: G. P. Putnam's Sons, 1994), 9 December 1971, p. 381; Kissinger, *White House Years*, p. 904.

33. *FRUS*, vol. E-7, White House tapes, Oval Office 634-12, 9 December 1971, 4–4:41 p.m. See Haldeman, *Haldeman Diaries*, 9 December 1971, p. 381.

34. *FRUS*, vol. E-7, White House tapes, Oval Office 635-17, 10 December 1971, 12:47–1:01 p.m. *FRUS*, Nixon to Brezhnev, 10 December 1971, pp. 746–47.

35. NSA, Kissinger-Vorontsov telcon, 11 December 1971, after 7:30 p.m. NSA, Nixon-Kissinger telcon, 11 December 1971, 7:30 p.m.

36. *FRUS*, vol. E-7, White House tapes, Oval Office 635-8, 10 December 1971, 10:51–11:12 a.m. Kissinger's figures on Jordanian planes are from *FRUS*, Haig to Kissinger, 10 December 1971, p. 750. See also White House tapes, Oval Office 635-6, 10 December 1971, 9:10–10:31 a.m.; White House tapes, Oval Office 636-8, 10 December 1971, 4:18–5:11 p.m.

37. *FRUS*, WSAG meeting, 9 December 1971, 10:09–11 a.m., pp. 711-21. NSC Files, Box H-084, WSAG Meetings, Kennedy and Saunders to Kissinger, 16 December 1971.

38. NSC Files, Box 573, Indo-Pak War, State Department situation report, 16 December 1971. NSC Files, Box 573, Indo-Pak War, State Department situation report, 14 December 1971.

39. U.S. Department of State, *Foreign Relations of the United States: China, 1969–1972*, ed. Stephen E. Phillips (Washington, D.C.: U.S. Government Printing Office, 2006), vol. 17, Huang-Haig meeting, 12 December 1971, 3:50–4:20 p.m., pp. 621–24. NSA, unsigned note for Walters to hand to

the Chinese, 17 December 1971. NSC Files, Box 643, Country Files—Middle East, India-Pakistan, Nixon-Kissinger telcon, 16 December 1971, 9:30 a.m. See Jesse W. Lewis Jr., "Jordan Sent Jets to Pakistan Despite Ban, U.S. Confirms," *Washington Post,* 19 April 1972, p. A14.

40. *FRUS,* vol. E-7, White House tapes, Oval Office 635-8, 10 December 1971, 10:51–11:12 a.m. See *FRUS,* vol. E-7, White House tapes, Oval Office 635-17, 10 December 1971, 12:47–1:01 p.m.

41. NSA, Bush notes, 10 December 1971. NSA, Huang-Kissinger memcon, 10 December 1971, 6:05–7:55 p.m. Kissinger, *White House Years,* pp. 906, 889.

42. NSA, Huang-Kissinger memcon, 10 December 1971, 6:05–7:55 p.m. NSA, Bush notes, 10 December 1971.

43. NSA, Nixon-Kissinger telcon, 11 December 1971, 3 p.m. For a U.S. intelligence analysis saying that China was not moving, see NSC Files, Box 572, Indo-Pak War, DIA intelligence appraisal, 9 December 1971. NSA, Nixon-Kissinger telcon, 11 December 1971, 7:30 p.m. See NSA, Kissinger-Bhutto-Raza telcon, 11 December 1971, 7:28 p.m. On Bhutto's appointment, see NSC Files, Box 572, Indo-Pak War, Farland to Rogers, 7 December 1971, Islamabad 11174.

44. NSA, Bush notes, 10 December 1971.

45. *FRUS,* vol. E-7, White House tapes, Oval Office 634-19, 9 December 1971, 5:57–6:34 p.m. *FRUS,* vol. E-7, White House tapes, Oval Office 635-8, 10 December 1971, 10:51–11:12 a.m. See NSA, Kissinger-Laird telcon, 11 December 1971, 3:35 p.m. See also NSA, Kissinger-Irwin telcon, 10 December 1971, 9 a.m.; *FRUS,* WSAG meeting, 10 December 1971, 9:45–10:17 a.m., pp. 735–39.

46. Robert Jackson, *South Asian Crisis: India, Pakistan and Bangla Desh: A Political and Historical Analysis of the 1971 War* (New York: Praeger, 1975), p. 141. NSC Files, Box 572, Indo-Pak War, Farland to Rogers, 8 December 1971, Islamabad 12215. NMML, Haksar Papers, Subject File 174, Farman Ali to Henry, 10 December 1971. NMML, Haksar Papers, Subject File 174, Henry to Thant, 10 December 1971. NSC Files, Box 134, Kissinger Office Files, Country Files—Middle East, Spivack to Rogers, 10 December 1971, Dacca 5573. NSC Files, Box 572, Indo-Pak War, State Department situation report, 10 December 1971. NSC Files, Box 572, Indo-Pak War, State Department situation report, 10 December 1971. *Hamoodur Rehman Commission Report,* pp. 256–57, 143–44. NSC Files, Box 572, Indo-Pak War, Bush to Rogers, 11 December 1971, USUN 4935. For Niazi's claims that he could have held out, see his *Betrayal of East Pakistan,* pp. 174–95. NMML, Haksar Papers, Subject File 174, Haksar to Dutt, 13 December 1971.

47. *Hamoodur Rehman Commission Report,* p. 475.

48. NMML, Haksar Papers, Subject File 173, "A note on India's objectives in the current conflict with Pakistan," 9 December 1971. For Haksar's anxiety, see NMML, Haksar Papers, Subject File 173, Haksar to Gandhi, 11 December 1971; NMML, Haksar Papers, Subject File 173, Haksar to Singh, 11 December 1971. NMML, Haksar Papers, Subject File 173, Haksar to ambassadors, 10 December 1971. NMML, Haksar Papers, Subject File 173, Gandhi to heads of state, 10 December 1971.

49. NMML, Haksar Papers, Subject File 173, "A note on India's objectives in the current conflict with Pakistan," 9 December 1971.

50. NMML, Haksar Papers, Subject File 174, Haksar to Jha, 11 December 1971. NSC Files, Box 572, Indo-Pak War, Bush to Rogers, 12 December 1971, USUN 4965. See NSC Files, Box 572, Indo-Pak War, Irwin to Rogers, 12 December 1971, State 223704. NMML, Haksar Papers, Subject File 174, Haksar to Jha, 11 December 1971.

51. NSC Files, Box 572, Indo-Pak War, State Department situation report, 12 December 1971. See NSC Files, Box 572, Indo-Pak War, Farland to Rogers, 12 December 1971, Islamabad 12414. NSC Files, Box 572, Indo-Pak War, Kissinger to Nixon, 9 December 1971. See NSC Files, Box 572, Indo-Pak War, Keating to Rogers, 8 December 1971, New Delhi 18944. NSC Files, Box 572, Indo-Pak War, CIA situation report, 9 December 1971. This report has substantial redactions. See NSC Files, Box 572, Indo-Pak War, CIA situation report, 8 December 1971; NSC Files, Box 572, Indo-Pak War, CIA situation report, 7 December 1971; NSC Files, Box 572, Indo-Pak War, DIA intelligence appraisal, 7 December 1971; NSC Files, Box 572, Indo-Pak War, State Department situation report, 9 December 1971. NSC Files, Box 572, Indo-Pak War, CIA analysis, "Pakistan's Capability to Capture and Hold Sections of Indian Kashmir," 9 December 1971.

52. NMML, Haksar Papers, Subject File 173, Gandhi to Kosygin (Haksar draft), 10 December 1971. NMML, Haksar Papers, Subject File 173, Haksar to Gandhi, 10 December 1971. MEA, HI/1012/57/71, Shelvankar to Kaul, 30 January 1972. MEA, HI/1012/57/71, Sethi to army staff, monthly military digest, 5 January 1972. NSC Files, Box 573, Indo-Pak War. Jack Anderson, "U.S. Task Force Didn't Frighten India," *Washington Post,* 21 December 1971. NMML, Haksar Papers, Subject File 173, Haksar to ambassadors, 10 December 1971. NMML, Haksar Papers, Subject File 173, Gandhi to heads of state, 10 December 1971.

53. Kissinger, *White House Years,* p. 909. Kissinger admits the likelihood of conflict: "Had things developed as we anticipated, we would have had no choice but to assist China in some manner against the probable opposition of much of the government, the media, and the Congress. And we were still in the middle of the Vietnam war." (*White House Years,* p. 911.)

54. *FRUS,* vol. E-7, White House tapes, Oval Office 637-3, 12 December 1971, 8:45–9:42 a.m. Kissinger offered another harsh analogy: "If South Africa gobbled up Basutoland and we said, 'Well, there are 7 million South Africans. . . .'" Kissinger scorned "these bastards with this high-sounding morality . . . —we don't even pretend high-sounding morality on some of these issues, except in the deepest sense." See NSC Files, Box 572, Indo-Pak War, Kissinger background briefing, 7 December 1971, 4:40 p.m.

55. *FRUS,* vol. E-7, White House tapes, Oval Office 637-3, 12 December 1971, 8:45–9:42 a.m. Bob Woodward and Carl Bernstein, *The Final Days* (New York: Simon & Schuster, 1976), p. 188; see Walter Isaacson, *Kissinger: A Biography* (New York: Simon & Schuster, 1992), p. 145.

56. *FRUS,* vol. E-7, White House tapes, Oval Office 637-3, 12 December 1971, 8:45–9:42 a.m. On Haiphong, see Isaacson, *Kissinger,* pp. 415–24. In his memoirs, Kissinger wrongly claims that the message about Huang Hua came after 11:30 a.m., when the United States sent a tough hotline message to the Soviet Union (*White House Years,* pp. 909–10). Kissinger does not mention that he asked the Chinese to move their troops. And he presents the decision to confront the Soviet Union as if it were Nixon pushing

him, whereas in fact it was often the other way around (*White House Years*, p. 910).

57. NSA, Kissinger-Vorontsov telcon, 12 December 1971, 10:05 a.m.

58. *FRUS*, vol. E-7, White House tapes, Oval Office 637-6, 12 December 1971, 10:27–10:37 a.m. Nixon said, "But World War II, Henry, was a direct result, a direct result—I mean we can talk all we want to about Hitler doing in the Jews and all that. Sure, it caused all that. But it was a direct result of the Allies backing the pusillanimous"—here the tape is garbled.

59. *FRUS*, vol. E-7, White House tapes, Oval Office 637-6, 12 December 1971, 10:27–10:37 a.m. See *FRUS*, vol. E-7, House tapes, Oval Office 637-6, 12 December 1971, 11:04–11:14 a.m. In his memoirs, Kissinger writes that they sent a tough hotline message to the Soviet Union at 11:30 a.m., and had the White House issue a harsh statement, because the Soviets had not given a reassurance about Indian intentions in Kashmir (*White House Years*, pp. 909–11). But the White House tapes show that both Nixon and Kissinger thought that the Soviet Union had already backed down by then. In other words, they seemingly sent the hotline message to press their advantage after what they saw as victory, not, as Kissinger presents it in his memoirs, to forestall defeat.

60. Tyler, *Great Wall*, pp. 123-24. *FRUS: China, 1969–1972*, vol. 17, Huang-Haig memcon, 12 December 1971, 3:50–4:20 p.m., pp. 621–24.

61. NMML, Haksar Papers, Subject File 235, Manekshaw-Kulikov talks, 24–25 February 1972. See Oriana Fallaci, *Interviews with History and Conversations with Power* (New York: Rizzoli, 2011), p. 266. MEA, HI/121/13/71, vol. II, "Most Preposterous Logic, Flagrant Aggression," *People's Daily*, 6 December 1971, in Iyer to Singh, 8 December 1971; MEA, HI/121/13/71, vol. II, Xinhua, 7 December 1971, in Iyer to Singh, 9 December 1971; MEA, HI/121/13/71, vol. II, Radio Peking broadcast, 5 December 1971; NSC Files, Box 571, Indo-Pak War, Dean to Rogers, 6 December 1971, Hong Kong 8102; MEA, WII/109/31/71, vol. II, Iyer to Singh, 22 December 1971; MEA, WII/109/31/71, vol. II, Li speech, 26 December 1971. MEA, HI/1012/14/71, Mishra to Kaul, 7 January 1972. See NMML, Haksar Papers, Subject File 174, Gandhi to Zhou, 11 December 1971; NMML, Haksar Papers, Subject File 173, Haksar to Gandhi, 11 December 1971; NSC Files, Box 571, Indo-Pak War, Ji statement, 4 December 1971. Raman, *Kaoboys of R&AW*, pp. 15–20. Sisson and Rose, *War and Secession*, p. 216. See *FRUS*, vol. E-7, CIA cable, 13 December 1971.

62. Sisson and Rose, *War and Secession*, p. 216. NSC Files, Box 573, Indo-Pak War, Osborn to Rogers, 17 December 1971, Hong Kong 8355. NSC Files, Box 573, Indo-Pak War, CIA situation report, 16 December 1971. NSC Files, Box 573, Indo-Pak War, Kissinger to Nixon, 16 December 1971. MEA, HI/1012/14/71, Mishra to Kaul, 7 January 1972. See MEA, HI/1012/57/71, Sethi to army staff, monthly military digest, 5 January 1972. MEA, HI/1012/14/71, Mishra to Kaul, 7 January 1972.

63. NSA, Ford-Deng memcon, 3 December 1975, 9:25–11:55 a.m. See Pran Chopra, *India's Second Liberation* (Cambridge, Mass.: MIT Press, 1974), pp. 210–12.

64. NSA, Kissinger-Vorontsov telcon, 12 December 1971, 11:45 a.m. See NSA, Kissinger-Vorontsov telcon, 12 December 1971, 12:30 p.m.; NSA, Nixon-Kissinger telcon, 14 December 1971, 8:15 p.m.

65. NMML, Haksar Papers, Subject File 173, Haksar to Gandhi, 7 December 1971. Kissinger, *White House Years,* p. 911. MEA, WII/109/31/71, vol. I, Singh statement to UN Security Council, 13 December 1971. For Bhutto's speeches, see Zulfikar Ali Bhutto, *Politics of the People: A Collection of Articles, Statements and Speeches,* ed. Hamid Jalal and Khalid Hasan (Rawalpindi: Pakistan Publications, n.d.), vol. 3, pp. 231–76. MEA, WII/109/31/71, vol. I, Singh statement to UN Security Council, 12 December 1971. Recycling almost verbatim a line he had used on September 27 before the UN General Assembly, he said, "Pakistan's military action and the snuffing-out of all human rights and the reign of terror which continues, have shocked the conscience of mankind." He also invoked the Universal Declaration of Human Rights and the articles in the UN Charter that promoted human rights.
66. *FRUS,* p. 790n3. Kissinger, *White House Years,* p. 912.
67. *FRUS,* vol. E-7, White House tapes, Oval Office 634-19, 9 December 1971, 5:57-6:34 p.m. *FRUS,* vol. E-7, White House tapes, Oval Office 635-8, 10 December 1971, 10:51–11:12 a.m. *FRUS,* WSAG meeting, 12 December 1971, 11:15 a.m., pp. 789–91. On the evacuation cover story, see NSA, Kissinger-Laird telcon, 11 December 1971, 3:35 p.m.; Kissinger, *White House Years,* p. 905. NSA, Kissinger-Bhutto telcon, 11 December 1971. NSA, Kissinger-Laird telcon, 11 December 1971, 3:35 p.m. NSA, Nixon-Kissinger telcon, 11 December 1971, 5:20 p.m.
68. MEA, WII/109/31/71, vol. I, Verma to Menon, UPI story, 22 December 1971. MEA, WII/109/31/71, vol. II, Banerji to Haksar, 14 December 1971.
69. MEA, WII/125/44/72, Supplementaries for Rajya Sabha question, 7 April 1972. N. Krishnan, *No Way but Surrender: An Account of the Indo-Pakistan War in the Bay of Bengal, 1971* (New Delhi: Vikas, 1980), pp. 52–56.
70. NSC Files, Box 573, Indo-Pak War, Kissinger to Nixon, 14 December 1971. Sukhwant Singh, *India's Wars Since Independence: The Liberation of Bangladesh* (New Delhi: Vikas, 1980), vol. 1, p. 202–21. Malcolm W. Browne, "Military Situation in East Termed 'Grim' by Pakistan," *New York Times,* 12 December 1971, pp. A1, A26. Pupul Jayakar, *Indira Gandhi: An Intimate Biography* (New York: Pantheon, 1992), p. 179. Dhar, *Indira Gandhi, the "Emergency," and Indian Democracy,* p. 183.
71. NSC Files, Box 573, Indo-Pak War, Keating to Rogers, 14 December 1971, New Delhi 19127. MEA, WII/109/31/71, vol. I, Indian government press information bureau, Gandhi speech, 12 December 1971.
72. NSC Files, Box 573, Indo-Pak War, CIA situation report, 17 December 1971. NMML, Haksar Papers, Subject File 174, Haksar to Gandhi, 13 December 1971.
73. NMML, Haksar Papers, Subject File 174, Haksar to Gandhi, 13 December 1971.
74. NMML, Haksar Papers, Subject File 174, Haksar to Gandhi, 13 December 1971. NMML, Haksar Papers, Subject File 174, Haksar to cabinet's political affairs committee, 13 December 1971.
75. *FRUS,* vol. E-7, CIA cable, 13 December 1971. The mole got at least one fact wrong: claiming that P. N. Dhar was in Moscow, when it was actually D. P. Dhar.
76. See V. K. Singh, *Leadership in the Indian Army: Biographies of Twelve Soldiers* (New Delhi: Sage, 2005), pp. 208–9.

77. NMML, Haksar Papers, Subject File 173, Manekshaw to Farman Ali, 13 December 1971; NMML, Haksar Papers, Subject File 173, Haksar to Kaul, 13 December 1971.

78. *FRUS*, Spivack to Rogers, 14 December 1971, Dacca 5637, pp. 808–10. *FRUS*, Farland to Rogers, 14 December 1971, Islamabad 12537, pp. 810–12.

79. NMML, Haksar Papers, Subject File 174, Haksar to Lall and Dutt, 14 December 1971.

80. NSC Files, Box 573, Indo-Pak War, CIA situation report, 20 December 1971. NSC Files, Box 573, Indo-Pak War, State Department situation report, 20 December 1971. For more pro-Pakistan accounts, see White House tapes, White House telephone 17-100, 26 December 1971, 11:45–11:52 a.m.; *Hamoodur Rehman Commission Report*, pp. 511–12; Sarmila Bose, *Dead Reckoning: Memories of the 1971 Bangladesh War* (New York: Columbia University Press, 2011), pp. 149–56.

81. *FRUS*, Yahya to Nixon, 14 December 1971, pp. 806–7. Daniel Patrick Moynihan introduction to Dennis Kux, *Estranged Democracies: India and the United States, 1941–1991* (New Delhi: Sage, 1993), p. xxii. Joseph Farland, the U.S. ambassador in Islamabad, later said, "We were about to go to World War III over this." (Library of Congress, Association for Diplomatic Studies and Training, Foreign Affairs Oral History Project, Farland interview, 31 January 2000.) Kissinger, *White House Years*, p. 912. NSA, Nixon-Kissinger telcon, 6 December 1971, 11:10 p.m. NSC Files, Box 643, Country Files—Middle East, India/Pakistan, Kissinger to Haig, 13 December 1971. *FRUS*, vol. E-7, White House tapes, Oval Office 633-11, 9 December 1971, 12:44–1:27 p.m.

82. Krishnan, *No Way but Surrender*, pp. 56–58, 65.

83. Dhar, *Indira Gandhi, the "Emergency," and Indian Democracy*, pp. 182–83. NMML, Haksar Papers, Subject File 277, Jha to Haksar, 11 September 1972. Fallaci, *Interviews with History*, p. 265.

84. NMML, Haksar Papers, Subject File 174, Haksar to Singh, 14 December 1971. See MEA, HI/1012/57/71, Shelvankar to Kaul, 30 January 1972. MEA, HI/1012/57/71, Sethi to army staff, monthly military digest, 5 January 1972. NSC Files, Box 573, Indo-Pak War, Jack Anderson, "U.S. Task Force Didn't Frighten India," *Washington Post*, 21 December 1971.

85. MEA, WII/109/31/71, vol. II, Saxena to Haksar, 15 December 1971. MEA, WII/125/44/72, supplementaries for Rajya Sabha question, 7 April 1972.

86. MEA, WII/125/44/72, supplementaries for Rajya Sabha question, 7 April 1972. Tharoor, *Reasons of State*, p. 126. See *FRUS*, Sisco to Keating, 14 December 1971, State 224566, pp. 816–17. NMML, Haksar Papers, Subject File 277, Jha to Haksar, 11 September 1972. MEA, WII/125/44/72, supplementaries for Rajya Sabha question, 7 April 1972. NMML, Haksar Papers, Subject File 277, Jha to Haksar, 11 September 1972.

87. *FRUS*, vol. E-7, White House tapes, Oval Office 638-4, 15 December 1971, 8:45–11:30 a.m.

88. MEA, WII/109/31/71, vol. I, Verma to Menon, UPI story, 22 December 1971; NSC Files, Box 572, Indo-Pak War, DIA analysis, 8 December 1971. Four Americans were killed when a helicopter from the *Tripoli* crashed in a routine flight. MEA, WII/125/44/72, supplementaries for Rajya Sabha question, 7 April 1972. See MEA, HI/1012/57/71, Sethi to army staff, monthly military

digest, 5 January 1972; NMML, Haksar Papers, Subject File 173, Gandhi to Kosygin, 17 December 1971.

89. NSC Files, Box 572, Indo-Pak War, CIA situation report, 8 December 1971. NSC Files, Box 572, Indo-Pak War, Keating to Rogers, 11 December 1971, New Delhi 19110. Fox Butterfield, "Pakistani Jets Bring the War and Death to Indian Village," *New York Times,* 10 December 1971, p. A16.

90. NSC Files, Box 643, Country Files—Middle East, India/Pakistan, Spivack to Rogers, 13 December 1971, Dacca 5622. NSC Files, Box 573, Indo-Pak War, Gordon to Rogers, 14 December 1971, Calcutta 3035. NSC Files, Box 573, Indo-Pak War, Sisco to Keating, 14 December 1971, State 224566. MEA, WII/125/44/72, supplementaries for Rajya Sabha question, 7 April 1972.

91. MEA, WII/125/44/72, supplementaries for Rajya Sabha question, 7 April 1972. Narayan statement, 16 December 1971, Jayaprakash Narayan, *Selected Works,* ed. Bimal Prasad (New Delhi: Manohar, 2008), vol. 9, pp. 700–701.

92. NSA, Kissinger-Schecter telcon, 16 December 1971, 2:58 p.m.

93. NSC Files, Box 571, Indo-Pak War, Keating to Rogers, 5 December 1971, New Delhi 18755. NSC Files, Box 572, Indo-Pak War, Keating to Rogers, 8 December 1971, New Delhi 18950. Kissinger called Keating "a bastard," while Nixon called the ambassador a "soft, son-of-a-bitch." (*FRUS*, vol. E-7, White House tapes, Oval Office 630-20, 6 December 1971, 6:14–6:38 p.m.)

94. NSC Files, Box 573, Indo-Pak War, Keating to Irwin, 14 December 1971, New Delhi 19203. NSC Files, Box 573, Indo-Pak War, Keating to Rogers, 15 December 1971, New Delhi 19243. When Kissinger came up with the idea of deploying a carrier group, he said, "Keating will have a heart attack." (*FRUS,* vol. E-7, White House tapes, EOB 307-27, 8 December 1971, 4:20–5:01 p.m. See *FRUS,* WSAG meeting, 9 December 1971, 10:09–11 a.m., pp. 711–21; White House tapes, Oval Office 631-1, 7 December 1971, 12:57–1:58 p.m.)

95. NSC Files, Box 643, Country Files—Middle East, India/Pakistan, U.S. naval forces note, n.d. December 1971. NMML, Haksar Papers, Subject File 173, Gandhi to Pompidou, 15 December 1971. NMML, Haksar Papers, Subject File 173, Manekshaw to Niazi, 15 December 1971. NSA, Kissinger-Bhutto telcon, 15 December 1971, 1:25 p.m. NSC Files, Box 573, Indo-Pak War, Bush to Rogers, 15 December 1971, USUN 5064. This account of war termination relies on Gideon Rose, *How Wars End: Why We Always Fight the Last Battle* (New York: Simon & Schuster, 2010); H. E. Goemans, *War and Punishment: The Causes of War Termination and the First World War* (Princeton: Princeton University Press, 2000); Stephen D. Biddle, *Military Power: Explaining Victory and Defeat in Modern Battle* (Princeton: Princeton University Press, 2004); Elizabeth A. Stanley, *Paths to Peace: Domestic Coalition Shifts, War Termination and the Korean War* (Stanford, Calif.: Stanford University Press, 2009); and Fred Charles Iklé, *Every War Must End* (New York: Columbia University Press, 1971).

96. NMML, Haksar Papers, Subject File 173, Haksar to Gandhi, 15 December 1971. NSC Files, Box 573, Indo-Pak War, Stone to Rogers, 15 December 1971, New Delhi 19254.

97. NMML, Haksar Papers, Subject File 173, Haksar to Gandhi, 15 December 1971. See NMML, Haksar Papers, Subject File 173, Haksar to Jha, 17 December 1971. NMML, Haksar Papers, Subject File 173, Gandhi to

Nixon, 15 December 1971. NSC Files, Box 755, Presidential Correspondence File, Gandhi to Nixon, 15 December 1971. NSC Files, Box H-084, WSAG Meetings, Gandhi to Nixon, 15 December 1971.

98. NSA, Kissinger-Schecter telcon, 16 December 1971, 2:58 p.m. *FRUS*, vol. E-7, White House tapes, Oval Office 638-4, 15 December 1971, 8:45–11:30 a.m. See NSC Files, Box 573, Indo-Pak War, Saunders to Kissinger, 15 December 1971.

99. *FRUS*, vol. E-7, White House tapes, Oval Office 638-4, 15 December 1971, 8:45–11:30 a.m. Nixon actually said Calcutta, but he clearly meant Karachi; Gandhi was not bombing her own city.

100. *FRUS*, vol. E-7, White House tapes, Oval Office 638-4, 15 December 1971, 8:45–11:30 a.m.

101. Habibul Alam, *Brave of Heart: The Urban Guerilla Warfare of Sector-2, During the Liberation War of Bangladesh* (Dacca: Academic Press and Publishers Library, 2006), pp. 293–94. Singh, *Liberation of Bangladesh*, p. 213. Dom Moraes, *Mrs Gandhi* (London: Jonathan Cape, 1980), p. 192.

102. NMML, Haksar Papers, Subject File 173, Niazi to Manekshaw, 16 December 1971. NMML, Haksar Papers, Subject File 173, Manekshaw to Niazi, 16 December 1971.

103. NSC Files, Box 573, Indo-Pak War, State Department situation report, 16 December 1971. Sydney H. Schanberg, "2 Men at a Table," *New York Times*, 17 December 1971, pp. A1, A16. Niazi, *Betrayal of East Pakistan*, p. 235.

104. Jayakar, *Indira Gandhi*, pp. 180–81. MEA, WII/109/31/71, vol. I, Gandhi statement to Parliament, 16 December 1971.

105. MEA, WII/109/31/71, vol. I, Gandhi statement to Parliament, 16 December 1971. NSC Files, Box 573, Indo-Pak War, Keating to Rogers, 16 December 1971, New Delhi 19337. For Haksar's draft speech, see NMML, Haksar Papers, Subject File 173, Haksar to Gandhi, 16 December 1971. Jayakar, *Indira Gandhi*, pp. 180–81. See Narayan statement, 17 December 1971, Narayan, *Selected Works*, pp. 701–2.

106. NSC Files, Box 573, Indo-Pak War, CIA situation report, 16 December 1971. Sydney H. Schanberg, "2 Men at a Table," *New York Times*, 17 December 1971, pp. A1, A16. NSC Files, Box 573, Indo-Pak War, CIA situation report, 17 December 1971.

107. NSC Files, Box 573, Indo-Pak War, CIA situation report, 17 December 1971. NMML, Haksar Papers, Subject File 173, Gandhi to Pompidou, 15 December 1971. William Drummond, "Dacca Scene Stirring, Horrifying," *Los Angeles Times*, 20 December 1971, p. A7. NSC Files, Box 573, Indo-Pak War, CIA situation report, 21 December 1971. NSC Files, Box 573, Indo-Pak War, CIA situation report, 20 December 1971. Kissinger told Nixon, about the Indians, "There are more verified cases of atrocities under their rule than there were under the Pakistan rule" (White House tapes, White House telephone 17-100, 26 December 1971, 11:45–11:52 a.m.).

108. NSC Files, Box 573, Indo-Pak War, CIA situation report, 17 December 1971. NSC Files, Box 573, Indo-Pak War, State Department situation report, 15 December 1971. Some Pakistani officers—as well as U.S. intelligence—grumbled that Pakistan had not fought hard even in the west (NSC Files, Box 573, Indo-Pak War, CIA situation report, 17 December 1971; NSC Files, Box 573, Indo-Pak War, U.S intelligence agency, "Pakistan's War in the West—A

Lacklustre Effort?" 16 December 1971). Malhotra, *Indira Gandhi*, pp. 140–41. See NSC Files, Box 572, Indo-Pak War, Keating to Rogers, 11 December 1971, New Delhi 19110. Jayakar, *Indira Gandhi*, pp. 181–82.

109. NMML, Haksar Papers, Subject File 173, Haksar to embassies, 16 December 1971. NSC Files, Box 573, Indo-Pak War, State Department situation report, 16 December 1971. NSC Files, Box 573, Indo-Pak War, CIA situation report, 16 December 1971. NSC Files, Box 573, Indo-Pak War, Keating to Rogers, 16 December 1971, New Delhi 19340. NSC Files, Box 573, Indo-Pak War, Keating to Rogers, 16 December 1971, New Delhi 19341. NSC Files, Box 573, Indo-Pak War, CIA situation report, 17 December 1971.

110. NSC Files, Box 573, Indo-Pak War, CIA situation report, 17 December 1971. See Malcolm W. Browne, "Rawalpindi Skies Calm as Foreigners Fly Out," *New York Times*, 13 December 1971, p. A17. See Sethi, *Decisive War*, pp. 146–47.

111. Sisson and Rose, *War and Secession*, p. 306n24. Sydney H. Schanberg, "Long Occupation of East Pakistan Foreseen in India," *New York Times*, 26 December 1971, pp. A1, A13. *Hamoodur Rehman Commission Report*, pp. 317, 340, 513. MEA, WII/109/31/71, vol. II, Kaul to Haksar, 23 December 1971. Jayakar, *Indira Gandhi*, p. 185.

112. Haldeman, *Haldeman Diaries*, 15 December 1971, p. 385. NSC Files, Box 643, Country Files—Middle East, India-Pakistan, Nixon-Kissinger telcon, 16 December 1971, 9:30 a.m.

113. NSC Files, Box 643, Country Files—Middle East, India-Pakistan, Nixon-Kissinger telcon, 16 December 1971, 9:30 a.m.

114. Kissinger, *White House Years*, p. 913–18. NSA, Nixon-Kissinger telcon, 16 December 1971, 10:40 a.m. See NSA, Nixon-Kissinger telcon, 16 December 1971, 12:15 p.m. NSA, Nixon-Kissinger telcon, 17 December 1971, 10:43 a.m. See NSC Files, Box 573, Indo-Pak War, Nixon to Gandhi, 18 December 1971.

115. NSA, Kissinger-Haldeman telcon, 16 December 1971, 6:05 p.m.; NSA, Kissinger-Shultz telcon, 16 December 1971, 6:57 p.m. NSA, Kissinger-Connally telcon, 16 December 1971, 11 a.m. NSA, Kissinger-Hubbard telcon, 16 December 1971, 8:25 p.m.; NSA, Kissinger-Evans telcon, 16 December 1971, 5:50 p.m.; NSA, Kissinger-Schecter telcon, 16 December 1971, 2:58 p.m.; NSA, Kissinger-Alsop telcon, 17 December 1971, 3:13 p.m.; Haldeman, *Haldeman Diaries*, 16 December 1971, p. 385. NSA, Kissinger-Bhutto telcon, 11:15 a.m.; NSA, Kissinger-Raza telcon, 16 December 1971, 3:55 p.m.; NSA, Kissinger-Bush telcon, 16 December 1971, 4:45 p.m.; NSA, Kissinger-Bush telcon, 5:45 p.m.; NSA, Kissinger-Vorontsov telcon, 16 December 1971, 4:40 p.m.; NSA, Kissinger-Bush telcon, 17 December 1971, 11:43 a.m. The result was UN Security Council Resolution 307, 21 December 1971. See MEA, WII/109/31/71, vol. II, Kaul to Haksar, 23 December 1971. NSA, Kissinger-Cromer, 16 December 1971, 3:33 p.m. NSA, Kissinger-Bush telcon, 11:23 a.m.

EPILOGUE: AFTERMATHS

1. There is of course no moral equivalence between the United States and the Soviet Union. David Lewis, *Bangladesh: Politics, Economy and Civil Society* (Cambridge: Cambridge University Press, 2011), pp. 12–19, 76–81. Samantha Power, *Chasing the Flame: Sergio Vieira de Mello and the Fight to Save*

the World (New York: Penguin, 2008), pp. 25-26. William B. Milam, *Bangladesh and Pakistan: Flirting with Failure in South Asia* (New York: Columbia University Press, 2009), pp. 29–37. Craig Baxter, *Bangladesh: A New Nation in an Old Setting* (Boulder, Colo.: Westview, 1984), pp. 49–58. Charles Peter O'Donnell, *Bangladesh: Biography of a Muslim Nation* (Boulder, Colo.: Westview, 1984), pp. 105–8, 110–15. Partha N. Mukherji, "The Great Migration of 1971," *Economic and Political Weekly*, vol. 9, no. 11 (16 March 1974), pp. 449–51.

2. NMML, Kaul Papers, Subject File 19, part 1, "Possible Questions and Answers on the Simla Agreement," n.d. 1972; MEA, WII/109/31/71, vol. I, Gandhi statement to Parliament, 16 December 1971; MEA, WII/109/31/71, vol. II, Kaul to Haksar, 23 December 1971. NMML, Kaul Papers, Subject File 19, part 1, "The New Situation in the Sub-Continent," n.d. 1972; NMML, Haksar Papers, Subject File 235, Manekshaw-Kulikov talks, 24–25 February 1972. NMML, Haksar Papers, Subject File 174, Haksar to Gandhi, 18 December 1971. *FRUS*, Saunders to Kissinger, 16 April 1971, pp. 67–69. NMML, Haksar Papers, Subject File 95, Bangladeshi press clippings, 8 July 1973. "They're occupying East Pakistan, and I don't think they're ever going to get out," said Nixon, about the Indians (White House tapes, White House telephone 17-100, 26 December 1971, 11:45–11:52 a.m.). Kathryn Jacques, *Bangladesh, India and Pakistan: International Relations and Regional Tensions in South Asia* (Basingstoke, U.K.: Macmillan, 2000), pp. 25–142.

3. NMML, Haksar Papers, Subject File 217, Boudhayan Chattopadhyey report on "Economic Impact of Bangla Desh," 22–23 January 1972. MEA, WII/104/21/75, vol. I, joint secretary for Bangladesh to ambassadors, 21 August 1975. Ved Mehta, *The New India* (New York: Viking, 1976), pp. 134–36. Anthony Mascarenhas, *Bangladesh: A Legacy of Blood* (London: Hodder & Stoughton, 1986). Lewis, *Bangladesh*, pp. 81–96. Lawrence Ziring, *Bangladesh from Mujib to Ershad: An Interpretive Study* (Karachi: Oxford University Press, 1992). Milam, *Bangladesh and Pakistan*, pp. 51–70, 95–134. S. R. Chakravarty, *Bangladesh Under Mujib, Zia and Ershad: Dilemma of a New Nation* (New Delhi: Har-Anand Publications, 1995), pp. 79–164. P. N. Haksar, *Premonitions* (Bombay: Interpress, 1979), pp. 70, 79.

4. Yasmin Khan, *The Great Partition: The Making of India and Pakistan* (New Haven, Conn.: Yale University Press, 2007), p. 197. Scott Carney, Jason Miklian, and Kristian Hoelscher, "Fortress India," *Foreign Policy*, July–August 2011. Rumi Ahmed, "Felani's Hanging Body over the Road to Connectivity," bdnews24.com, 19 January 2011.

5. Julhas Alam, "Bangladesh Anticipates 7.2 Percent Economic Growth," Associated Press, 7 June 2012; Bettina Wassener, "In Bangladesh, a Quick Evolution from Backwater to Growth Center," *New York Times*, 24 April 2012, p. B6; Abdul Bayes, "The Quality of Bangladesh's Economic Growth," *Daily Star*, 22 March 2010; Nicholas Kristof, "Pakistan and Times Sq.," *New York Times*, 13 May 2010, p. A31; Lewis, *Bangladesh*, pp. 136–66, 197–205, 97–108. Amartya Sen, "Quality of Life," *New York Review of Books*, 12 May 2011; Moudud Ahmed, *Bangladesh: A Study of the Democratic Regimes* (Dacca: University Press, 2012). Jim Yardley, "Fighting for Bangladesh Labor, and Ending Up in Pauper's Grave," *New York Times*, 10 September 2012,

pp. A1, A6. "Hello, Delhi," and "Banged About," *The Economist,* 26 May 2012, pp. 14, 41–42; "Answering for History," *The Economist,* 16 December 2010. On the importance of using due process to restrain demands for punishment, see my *Stay the Hand of Vengeance: The Politics of War Crimes Tribunals* (Princeton: Princeton University Press, 2000), pp. 20–28, 304–10.

6. Benazir Bhutto, *Reconciliation: Islam, Democracy, and the West* (New York: HarperCollins, 2008), pp. 182–83. See, for instance, NMML, Haksar Papers, Subject File 225, Sen to Patel, 2 March 1972; Mohammad Akbar Khan, *The Mystery of Debacle of Pakistan, 1971* (Karachi: Islamic Military Science Association, 1971). See, for instance, NMML, Haksar Papers, Subject File 225, Brown memorandum, 8 February 1972; and Benazir Bhutto, *Daughter of the East* (London: Hamish Hamilton, 1988), pp. 46–48.

7. NSC Files, Box 573, Indo-Pak War, Farland to Rogers, 16 December 1971, Islamabad 12648; NSC Files, Box 573, Indo-Pak War, State Department situation report, 16 December 1971. Ian Talbot, *Pakistan: A Modern History* (New York: Palgrave Macmillan, 2009), pp. 212–13; NSC Files, Box 573, Indo-Pak War, Kissinger to Nixon, 18 December 1971. NSC Files, Box 573, Indo-Pak War, CIA situation report, 20 December 1971. NSC Files, Box 573, Indo-Pak War, CIA situation report, 17 December 1971. Richard Reeves, *President Nixon: Alone in the White House* (New York: Simon & Schuster, 2007), p. 406. See, for instance, NMML, Haksar Papers, Subject File 225, Brown memorandum, 8 February 1972.

8. Haksar, *Premonitions,* p. 88. See MEA, WII/109/31/71, vol. I, Singh statement to UN Security Council, 12 December 1971. NMML, Kaul Papers, Subject File 19, part 1, "The New Situation in the Sub-Continent," n.d. 1972. See P. N. Dhar, *Indira Gandhi, the "Emergency," and Indian Democracy* (Oxford: Oxford University Press, 2000), pp. 151, 189. See Jayaprakash Narayan, "Bangladesh and India's Future," *Indian Express,* 27–28 October 1971, Jayaprakash Narayan, *Selected Works,* ed. Bimal Prasad (New Delhi: Manohar, 2008), vol. 9, pp. 660–66. Anatol Lieven, *Pakistan: A Hard Country* (New York: PublicAffairs, 2011), pp. 51–57, 60–76. See Surjit Mansingh, *India's Search for Power: Indira Gandhi's Foreign Policy, 1966–1982* (New Delhi: Sage, 1984), p. 227; Haksar, *Premonitions,* p. 88. POL 23-9 PAK, Box 2530, Barrow to Rogers, 2 April 1971, Lahore 515. See POL 23-9 PAK, Box 2530, Spengler to Farland, 27 March 1971, State 51982. Tariq Ali, *Can Pakistan Survive? The Death of a State* (Harmondsworth, U.K.: Penguin, 1983), p. 96. See Amartya Sen, *Identity and Violence: The Illusion of Destiny* (New York: Norton, 2006), pp. 15, 162–63, 171–72; Bhutto, *Daughter of the East,* p. 52; Lieven, *Pakistan,* p. 60; "Two-Nation Theory Died with Pakistan's Break-Up, Says Altaf," *Daily Times* (Lahore), 2 November 2004.

9. Stephen P. Cohen, *The Pakistan Army* (Karachi: Oxford University Press, 1998), pp. 158–61. NMML, Kaul Papers, Subject File 19, Singh briefing in London, n.d. June 1971. See *FRUS,* WSAG minutes, 12 November 1971, 11:09 a.m., pp. 508; *FRUS,* WSAG meeting, 22 November 1971, 2:39–3:14 p.m., p. 553; *FRUS,* WSAG meeting, 29 November 1971, 2:36–3:36 p.m., p. 575. See Steve Coll, *On the Grand Trunk Road: A Journey into South Asia* (New York: Times Books, 1994), pp. 184–87. NMML, Haksar Papers, Subject File 220, "SSB and Bangladesh," 3 February 1972.

10. G. W. Choudhury, *The Last Days of United Pakistan* (Bloomington: Indi-

472   ~   Notes to Pages 329–332

ana University Press, 1974), p. 181. Government of Pakistan, *The Report of the Hamoodur Rehman Commission of Inquiry into the 1971 War* (Lahore: Vanguard, 2001), pp. 281, 340, 352, 535–36, 539.

11. *Hamoodur Rehman Commission Report.* Samar Halarnkar, "Behind Pakistan's Defeat," *India Today,* 21 August 2000. Swapan Dasgupta, "History Creates Hell," *India Today,* 28 August 2000, p. 42. Oriana Fallaci, *Interviews with History and Conversations with Power* (New York: Rizzoli, 2011), pp. 286–88.

12. Najam Sethi, "Roads Not Taken," *Friday Times* (Lahore), 12–18 August 2011. Lieven, *Pakistan,* p. 60.

13. Lieven, *Pakistan,* p. 60. Bhutto, *Daughter of the East,* pp. 46–48.

14. Huma Imtiaz, "Fall of East Pakistan," *Dawn,* 16 December 2010. For a more forthright textbook, used in O-level courses in Pakistan Studies, see Farooq Naseem Balwa, *Pakistan: A Historical and Contemporary Look* (Karachi: Oxford University Press, 2002), pp. 168–71. "How Did West Pakistan Treat East Pakistan?" *Herald Annual,* January 2010, p. 101.

15. Elliot L. Tepper, "The New Pakistan," *Pacific Affairs,* vol. 47, no. 1 (spring 1974), pp. 56-68. MEA, WII/109/31/71, vol. II, Kaul to Haksar, 23 December 1971. Bhutto, *Daughter of the East,* pp. 49, 51.

16. Lee Lescaze, "U.S. Arms Aid to Pakistan Bewilders Fearful Bengalis," *Washington Post,* 24 July 1971; Akbar Khan, *Mystery of Debacle of Pakistan, 1971.* A. A. K. Niazi, *The Betrayal of East Pakistan* (Karachi: Oxford University Press, 1998), p. 194. For his blaming of Bhutto and others, see ibid., pp. 220–31. Qutubuddin Aziz, *Mission to Washington: An Exposé of India's Intrigues in the United States of America in 1971 to Dismember Pakistan* (Karachi: United Press of Pakistan, 1973).

17. *FRUS,* Kissinger to Farland, 10 December 1971, p. 740. NSA, Kissinger-Bush telcon, 10 December 1971, 10:30 a.m. NSA, Kissinger-Bhutto telcon, 11 December 1971. See NSA, Kissinger-Bhutto telcon, 15 December 1971, 1:25 p.m.; NSC Files, Box 627, Country Files—Middle East, Pakistan vol. VIII, Nixon-Bhutto memcon, 18 December 1971.

18. See Mohsin Hamid, "Why They Get Pakistan Wrong," *New York Review of Books,* 29 September 2011. See also Syed Hussain Shaheed Soherwordi, "US Foreign Policy Shift Towards Pakistan Between 1965 & 1971 Pak-India Wars," *South Asian Studies,* vol. 25, no. 1 (January–June 2010), pp. 21–37.

19. "China's First Veto," *Time,* 4 September 1972. Steve Coll, *Ghost Wars: The Secret History of the CIA, Afghanistan, and bin Laden, from the Soviet Invasion to September 10, 2001* (New York: Penguin, 2004), pp. 27, 60–62. Lieven, *Pakistan,* pp. 76–79, 125. Cohen, *Pakistan Army,* pp. 139–41. Talbot, *Pakistan,* pp. 229–30, 235–37, 245–54. Vali Nasr, "Military Rule, Islamism and Democracy in Pakistan," *Middle East Journal,* vol. 58, no. 2 (spring 2004), pp. 195–209.

20. Coll, *Grand Trunk Road,* pp. 256–59. Simon Long, "Perilous Journey: Pakistan," *The Economist,* special report, 11 February 2012, p. 7. Shafqat Hussain Naghmi, "Pakistan's Public Attitude Toward the United States," *Journal of Conflict Resolution,* vol. 26, no. 3 (September 1982), pp. 507-23. Husain Haqqani, "Breaking Up Is Not Hard to Do," *Foreign Affairs,* vol. 92, no. 2 (March–April 2013).

21. NMML, Haksar Papers, Subject File 276, Subrahmanyam, "Bangla Desh and Our Policy Options," 4 April 1971; NMML, Haksar Papers, Subject File

235, Manekshaw-Kulikov talks, 24-25 February 1972; Narayan to Masani, 9 December 1971, Narayan, *Selected Works*, p. 695. Ali, *Can Pakistan Survive?* p. 95. NMML, Haksar Papers, Subject File 174, Haksar to Kaul, 18 December 1971. MEA, WII/109/31/71, vol. II, Kaul to Haksar, 23 December 1971. Talbot, *Pakistan*, pp. 223-24. NMML, Haksar Papers, Subject File 235, Manekshaw-Kulikov talks, 24–25 February 1972.

22. Dhar, *Indira Gandhi, the "Emergency," and Indian Democracy*, pp. 184, 200–204, 210–11; Pupul Jayakar, *Indira Gandhi: An Intimate Biography* (New York: Pantheon, 1992), pp. 187–89; Lachhman Singh, *Victory in Bangladesh* (New Delhi: Natraj Publishers, 1981), p. 242; K. P. Candeth, *The Western Front: Indo-Pakistan War, 1971* (New Delhi: Allied Publishers, 1984), p. 166. NMML, Haksar Papers, Subject File 235, unsigned report, 12 January 1973. NMML, Kaul Papers, Subject File 19, part 1, "The New Situation in the Sub-Continent," n.d. 1972. Ramachandra Guha, *India After Gandhi: The History of the World's Largest Democracy* (New York: Ecco, 2003), pp. 463–65.

23. Coll, *Ghost Wars*, p. 475.

24. Talbot, *Pakistan*, pp. 224–27. Musharraf talk at Council on Foreign Relations, New York, 9 November 2010.

25. Coll, *Ghost Wars*, pp. 475, 60–62, 100, 221, 345, 394, 440, 475–76, 547. Ahmed Rashid, *Taliban: Militant Islam, Oil and Fundamentalism in Central Asia* (New Haven, Conn.: Yale University Press, 2001), pp. 26–29, 35, 39, 44–48, 58–59, 72–76, 129, 178–95, 137–38. Steve Coll, "Looking for Mullah Omar," *The New Yorker*, 23 January 2012, pp. 52–53. John R. Schmidt, *The Unraveling: Pakistan in the Age of Jihad* (New York: Farrar, Straus & Giroux, 2011), pp. 78–99. "A Rivalry That Threatens the World," *The Economist*, 21 May 2011, pp. 47–50.

26. Steve Coll, "Looking for Mullah Omar," *The New Yorker*, 23 January 2012, pp. 52–53. Stephen D. Krasner, "Talking Tough to Pakistan," *Foreign Affairs*, vol. 91, no. 1 (January–February 2012). Jane Perlez, "Musharraf Walked a Tightrope," *New York Times*, 18 August 2008. "The World's Most Dangerous Border," *The Economist*, 21 May 2011, pp. 11–12. See Patterson to Clinton, 21 February 2009, WikiLeaks cable on *Guardian* web site, http://www.guardian.co.uk/world/us-embassy-cables-documents/193196. Some of that fear hearkens back to 1971, when Indian officials were tempted to whip up trouble among Pashtuns in Afghanistan—although Pashtun nationalism has many causes unrelated to India. D. P. Dhar hoped Afghanistan's leaders could "help the oppressed East Bengalis materially by reviving [the Afghans'] vocal interest in the Pakhtoon movement." (NMML, Haksar Papers, Subject File 165, Dhar to Kaul, 4 April 1971.) When India's foreign minister, Swaran Singh, was contemplating ways to break apart West Pakistan, he was intrigued that Afghanistan's government invoked "the slogan of Pakhtoonistan"—reaching out to their fellow Pashtuns living in Pakistan's North-West Frontier Province. "I do not see that the Pakhtoon issue is dead," Singh told a meeting of Indian diplomats. "It is an issue which can be activated with some effort on our part." (NMML, Kaul Papers, Subject File 19, Singh briefing in London, n.d. June 1971.)

27. George Perkovich, *India's Nuclear Bomb: The Impact on Global Proliferation* (Berkeley: University of California Press, 2001), p. 165. Talbot, *Pakistan*, pp. 238–40. See Cohen, *Pakistan Army*, pp. 152–58; Zalmay Khalilzad,

"Pakistan and the Bomb," *Survival*, November–December 1979, pp. 244–50. David E. Sanger, *The Inheritance: The World Obama Confronts and the Challenges to American Power* (New York: Harmony, 2009), pp. xxi, 26, 177–78, 207, 416. Philip Taubman, *The Partnership: Five Cold Warriors and Their Quest to Ban the Bomb* (New York: Harper, 2012), p. 47. James Mann, *The Obamians: The Struggle Inside the White House to Redefine American Power* (New York: Vintage, 2012). Jeffrey Goldberg and Marc Ambinder, "The Ally from Hell," *The Atlantic*, December 2011. "Nuclear Profusion," *The Economist*, 25 August 2012, p. 33. "A Rivalry That Threatens the World," *The Economist*, 21 May 2011, pp. 47–50. Scott D. Sagan and Kenneth N. Waltz, *The Spread of Nuclear Weapons: A Debate* (New York: Norton, 1995), p. 41. A. Q. Khan, " 'I Saved My Country from Nuclear Blackmail,' " *Newsweek*, 16 May 2011.

28. NMML, Kaul Papers, Subject File 19, part 1, "Possible Questions and Answers on the Simla Agreement," n.d. 1972. Guha, *India After Gandhi*, pp. 461–62. Stanley Wolpert, *India* (Berkeley: University of California Press, 1999), p. 237. Shashi Tharoor, *Reasons of State: Political Development and India's Foreign Policy Under Indira Gandhi, 1966–1977* (New Delhi: Vikas, 1982), pp. 72–73. Sumeet Kaul and Bhartesh Singh Thakur, "1971 War: India's Greatest Triumph," *Hindustan Times*, 16 December 2011.

29. Pratap Bhanu Mehta, "Reluctant India," *Journal of Democracy*, vol. 22, no. 4 (October 2001), p. 100. See Nicholas J. Wheeler, *Saving Strangers: Humanitarian Intervention in International Order* (Oxford: Oxford University Press, 2002), pp. 74–75.

30. Michael Walzer, *Just and Unjust Wars: A Moral Argument with Historical Illustrations* (New York: Basic Books, 1977), pp. 90, 101–8; Michael Walzer, "On Humanitarianism," *Foreign Affairs*, vol. 90, no. 4 (July–August 2011), pp. 77–79. "America's Least-Wanted," *The Economist*, 16 July 1994, pp. 23–24; "The Nightmare Next Door," *The Economist*, 24 September 1994, pp. 19–21. Sibel Utku Bila, "Erdoğan Sends Turkish FM to Increase Pressure on Syria," *Hürriyet*, 9 August 2011.

31. Mark Tully and Satish Jacob, *Amritsar: Mrs Gandhi's Last Battle* (London: Jonathan Cape, 1985).

32. NSC Files, Box 573, Indo-Pak War, Nixon to Gandhi, 18 December 1971.

33. MEA, HI/1012/78/71, Jha to Kaul, 11 January 1971. See NMML, Haksar Papers, Subject File 277, Jha to Haksar, 11 September 1972; MEA, WII/109/31/71, vol. II, "Attitudes in the US Congress," n.d. December 1971; NMML, Kaul Papers, Subject File 19, part 1, "The New Situation in the Sub-Continent," n.d. 1972; NMML, Haksar Papers, Subject File 217, Boudhayan Chattopadhyey report on "Economic Impact of Bangla Desh," 22–23 January 1972. In 1970, 66 percent of Indians held a good or very good opinion of the United States, with 9 percent having a bad or very bad opinion; by April 1972, it was 27 percent good or very good, against 52 percent bad or very bad (Tharoor, *Reasons of State*, p. 300). Daniel Patrick Moynihan introduction to Dennis Kux, *Estranged Democracies: India and the United States, 1941–1991* (New Delhi: Sage, 1993), pp. xxii–xxiii; Kux, *Estranged Democracies*, pp. 307–8; C. Raja Mohan, *Crossing the Rubicon: The Shaping of India's New Foreign Policy* (New York: Palgrave Macmillan, 2003), pp. 83–115.

34. Dhar, *Indira Gandhi, the "Emergency," and Indian Democracy*, p. 184.

Amberish K. Diwanji, "This Government Talks Big, but Its Knees Are Made of Jelly," Rediff.com, 6 July 1998. Perkovich, *India's Nuclear Bomb*, pp. 165, 170, 372.

35. Perkovich, *India's Nuclear Bomb*, pp. 171–72, 146, 156–89. One of the most forceful advocates of an Indian bomb was K. Subrahmanyam, who had also pressed Gandhi's government to launch a war for Bangladesh, but he was voicing his nuclear ambitions well before Yahya's crackdown started, and he meant to deter China.

36. Scott D. Sagan, "Why Do States Build Nuclear Weapons? Three Models in Search of a Bomb," *International Security*, vol. 21, no. 3 (winter 1996–97), pp. 63, 65–69. Perkovich, *India's Nuclear Bomb*, pp. 164–68, 177. Kux, *Estranged Democracies*, pp. 314–15. For a more skeptical view about domestic support for nuclear testing, as part of a powerful case against nuclearization, see Amartya Sen, *The Argumentative Indian: Writings on Indian History, Culture and Identity* (New York: Farrar, Straus & Giroux, 2005), pp. 253–57. Haksar, *Premonitions*, pp. 90–94. Jayakar, *Indira Gandhi*, pp. 193–94. Sumit Ganguly, "Nuclear Stability in South Asia," *International Security*, vol. 33, no. 2 (fall 2008).

37. Tharoor, *Reasons of State*, p. 59. Guha, *India After Gandhi*, pp. 462–63.

38. Jayakar, *Indira Gandhi*, pp. 177, 184–85. Guha, *India After Gandhi*, pp. 468–69, 470–73, 497, 515–16. Coll, *Grand Trunk Road*, pp. 120–21. See Dhar, *Indira Gandhi, the "Emergency," and Indian Democracy*, pp. 232–33. On the judiciary, see Pratap Bhanu Mehta, "The Rise of Judicial Sovereignty," *Journal of Democracy*, vol. 18, no. 2 (April 2007), pp. 70–83; and Shylashri Shankar, "India's Judiciary," in Paul Brass, ed., *Handbook of South Asian Politics* (New York: Routledge, 2009).

39. T. N. Kaul, *A Diplomat's Diary (1947–99): China, India and USA* (New Delhi: Macmillan India, 2000), p. 111. See Guha, *India After Gandhi*, pp. 506–8, 514. Jayakar, *Indira Gandhi*, pp. 189–90. Dhar, *Indira Gandhi, the "Emergency," and Indian Democracy*, pp. 233.

40. Jayakar, *Indira Gandhi*, pp. 184–85, 192–95. By September 1974, her favorability rating had plummeted to 47 percent—a loss of 46 percentage points since the war (Tharoor, *Reasons of State*, p. 59). Guha, *India After Gandhi*, pp. 478–79. Ajit Bhattacharjea, *Jayaprakash Narayan: A Political Biography* (New Delhi: Vikas, 1975), pp. 140–44. Dhar, *Indira Gandhi, the "Emergency," and Indian Democracy*, pp. 253–54.

41. Dhar, *Indira Gandhi, the "Emergency," and Indian Democracy*, pp. 257–62, 300. She had handily won her seat in the massive state of Uttar Pradesh (Election Commission of India, *Statistical Report on General Elections, 1971 to the Fifth Lok Sabha* [New Delhi: Election Commission of India, 1973], vol. 1, p. 177), but her opponent had petitioned the court that she had spent more money than was legal, and had used government officials to help her campaign. Guha, *India After Gandhi*, pp. 486–87, 491–93, 498–99, 506–8. Dhar, *Indira Gandhi, the "Emergency," and Indian Democracy*, pp. 257–62. Jayakar, *Indira Gandhi*, pp. 200–18. Kaul, *Diplomat's Diary*, pp. 111–12.

42. NMML, Haksar Papers, Subject File 171, Haksar notes for constitutional debate, August 1971. For later and happier outcomes, see Lloyd I. Rudolph and Susanne Hoeber Rudolph, "Congress Learns to Lose," in Edward Friedman and Joseph Wong, eds., *Political Transitions in Dominant Party Sys-*

tems: Learning to Lose (New York: Routledge, 2008), pp. 15–39; Ashutosh Varshney, "Is India Becoming More Democratic?" *Journal of Asian Studies,* vol. 59, no. 1 (February 2000) pp. 3–25; Kanchan Chandra, "The Transformation of Ethnic Politics in India," *Journal of Asian Studies,* vol. 59, no. 1 (February 2000), pp. 26–61.

43. Guha, *India After Gandhi,* pp. 492–93. Mehta, *New India,* p. 131.

44. NMML, Haksar Papers, Subject File 173, Haksar to Gandhi, 17 December 1971; MEA, HI/121/13/71, vol. II, Sinai to ambassadors, 12 December 1971; MEA, HI/121/25/71, Gandhi statement in Lok Sabha and Rajya Sabha, 6 December 1971; Narayan to Mujib, 31 January 1972, Narayan, *Selected Works,* pp. 718–22. MEA, WII/104/21/75, vol. I, Secretary (East) to ambassadors, 21 August 1975. MEA, WII/104/21/75, vol. I, joint secretary for Bangladesh to ambassadors, 21 August 1975. MEA, WII/104/21/75, vol. I, Foreign Ministry to Sen, 20 August 1975. See MEA, WII/104/21/75, vol. I, joint secretary for Bangladesh to ambassadors, 21 August 1975. Jayakar, *Indira Gandhi,* pp. 219–21. Rahul Gandhi was a few years younger.

45. Nirupama Subramanian, "Pakistan Resents Rahul's Remarks," *Hindu,* 16 April 2007. Suresh Nambath, "'After Rahul's Gaffes, Congress Hopes Shifted to Priyanka,'" *Hindu,* 27 March 2011. Subodh Ghildiyal and Rajeev Deshpande, "Unravelling the Man Who Will Be King," *Times of India,* 13 February 2010. On the Nehru-Gandhi dynasty, see Patrick French, *India: A Portrait* (New York: Alfred A. Knopf, 2011), pp. 37–111.

46. Adam Nagourney, "In Tapes, Nixon Rails About Jews and Blacks," *New York Times,* 10 December 2010, p. A13. Walter Isaacson, *Kissinger: A Biography* (New York: Simon & Schuster, 1992), pp. 28–29.

47. Kissinger wrote, "For someone who lost in the Holocaust many members of my immediate family and a large proportion of those with whom I grew up, it is hurtful to see an out-of-context remark being taken so contrary to its intentions and to my convictions, which were profoundly shaped by these events. References to gas chambers have no place in political discourse, and I am sorry I made that remark 37 years ago." (Henry A. Kissinger, "Putting the Nixon Tape in Context," *Washington Post,* 26 December 2010.) For Kissinger's argument for downplaying the White House tapes, see Reeves, *President Nixon,* pp. 16, 664. White House tapes, Oval Office 477-1, 12 April 1971, 9:10–10:33 a.m. Tad Szulc, *The Illusion of Peace: Foreign Policy in the Nixon Years* (New York: Viking, 1977), p. 804. Anthony Lake and Roger Morris, "The Human Reality of Realpolitik," *Foreign Policy,* vol. 4, no. 4 (fall 1971), pp. 1571–62. NSA, Nixon-Kissinger-Suharto memcon, 26 May 1970, 10:45 a.m. NSA, Kissinger to Nixon, 26 May 1970. NSA, Kissinger to Nixon, 18 July 1969. For Gerald Ford's and Kissinger's acceptance of Indonesia's invasion of East Timor, see NSA, Newsom to Kissinger, 6 December 1975, Jakarta 14946. For the background, see Bradley R. Simpson, *Economists with Guns: Authoritarian Development and U.S.-Indonesian Relations, 1960–1968* (Stanford, Calif.: Stanford University Press, 2008). Nixon, *In the Arena: A Memoir of Victory, Defeat, and Renewal* (New York: Simon & Schuster, 1990), p. 71.

48. Bob Woodward and Carl Bernstein, *The Final Days* (New York: Simon & Schuster, 1976), pp. 422–24. Szulc, *Illusion of Peace,* pp. 800–802. Stanley I. Kutler, *The Wars of Watergate: The Last Crisis of Richard Nixon* (New York: Alfred A. Knopf, 1990), pp. 613–17.

49. Robert Dallek, *Nixon and Kissinger: Partners in Power* (New York: HarperCollins, 2007), p. 3. Kutler, *Wars of Watergate*. J. Anthony Lukas, *Nightmare: The Underside of the Nixon Years* (New York: Viking, 1976). Nixon, *In the Arena*, pp. 26–76, 11, 16. James Hohmann, "Watergate's 'Last Chapter,'" *Politico*, 19 April 2011. Reflecting how much China overshadows Bangladesh, in Margaret MacMillan's impressive recent history of the opening to China, she devotes just one sentence to the Bengali atrocities and another to the refugees (*Nixon and Mao: The Week That Changed the World* [New York: Random House, 2007], p. 220). Richard M. Nixon, *Leaders* (New York: Warner Books, 1982). Monica Crowley, *Nixon in Winter* (New York: Random House, 1998), pp. 3–279. For a forceful critique of Nixon's efforts, see David Greenberg, *Nixon's Shadow: The History of an Image* (New York: Norton, 2003), pp. 270–303.

50. Isaacson, *Kissinger*, p. 13.

51. Bob Woodward and Carl Bernstein, "40 Years After Watergate, Nixon Was Far Worse Than We Thought," *Washington Post*, 8 June 2012. See Bob Woodward, *Shadow: Five Presidents and the Legacy of Watergate* (New York: Simon & Schuster, 1999); Kutler, *Wars of Watergate*, pp. 596–98, 603–7. For a portrait of evolving constraints on executive power, see Jack Goldsmith, *Power and Constraint: The Accountable Presidency After 9/11* (New York: Norton, 2012).

52. NSC Files, Box 572, Indo-Pak War, Jack Anderson, "U.S., Soviet Vessels in Bay of Bengal," *Washington Post*, 14 December 1971. On the Jordanian F-104s, see NSC Files, Box 573, Indo-Pak War, Jack Anderson, "U.S. Moves Give Soviets Hold on India," *Washington Post*, 16 December 1971; NSC Files, Box 573, Indo-Pak War, Jack Anderson, "Jungle War Blunders Are Cited," *Washington Post*, 30 December 1971; and, later, Malcolm W. Browne, "Pakistan Said to Have Got U.S.-Built Jets from Arabs," *New York Times*, 29 March 1972, pp. A1, A3; Jesse W. Lewis Jr., "Jordan Sent Jets to Pakistan Despite Ban, U.S. Confirms," *Washington Post*, 19 April 1972, p. A14. John Ehrlichman, *Witness to Power: The Nixon Years* (New York: Simon & Schuster, 1982), pp. 307–8. See Reeves, *President Nixon*, pp. 406, 409–12. Mark Feldstein, *Poisoning the Press: Richard Nixon, Jack Anderson, and the Rise of Washington's Scandal Culture* (New York: Farrar, Straus & Giroux, 2010), pp. 3–4, 155–74, 278–90, 339. Stephen E. Ambrose, *Nixon: The Triumph of a Politician, 1969–1972* (New York: Simon & Schuster, 1989), vol. 2, pp. 489–90. Jack Anderson with George Clifford, *The Anderson Papers* (New York: Ballantine, 1973), pp. 205–69. See White House tapes, Oval Office 655-1, 3 February 1972, 9:18–10:52 a.m.; NSC Files, Box 573, Indo-Pak War, Seelye to Brown, 16 December 1971, State 226297; Nixon, *In the Arena*, p. 327; Nixon-Haldeman conversation, 26 June 1982, Kutler, *Abuse of Power*, pp. 72–74; Kutler, *Wars of Watergate*, pp. 116–19; Reeves, *President Nixon*, pp. 406, 409–12; Isaacson, *Kissinger*, pp. 381–85.

53. See NSA, Kissinger-conservatives memcon, 5 January 1972. White House tapes, Oval Office 642-15, 3 January 1972, 9:25–10:04 a.m. White House tapes, Oval Office 658-31, 27 January 1972, 3:13–3:46 p.m.

54. Henry Kissinger, *Diplomacy* (New York: Simon & Schuster, 1994). Richard M. Nixon, *RN: The Memoirs of Richard Nixon* (New York: Simon & Schuster, 1990), pp. 525–31. Richard Nixon, *Leaders* (New York: Warner Books, 1982), p. 272.

478 ~ Notes to Pages 342–345

55. Henry Kissinger, *White House Years* (Boston: Little, Brown, 1979), pp. 914–15, 911. For a critique, see Kux, *Estranged Democracies,* p. 307.

56. NSC Files, Box 748, Presidential Correspondence File, Mujib to Nixon, 21 July 1972. See NSC Files, Box 748, Presidential Correspondence File, Mujib to Nixon, n.d. July 1974. NSC Files, Box 748, Presidential Correspondence File, Nixon to Mujib, 17 July 1974.

57. White House tapes, Oval Office 642-15, 3 January 1972, 9:25–10:04 a.m. White House tapes, Oval Office 655-1, 3 February 1972, 9:18–10:52 a.m. *FRUS,* vol. E-7, White House tapes, EOB 307-27, 8 December 1971, 4:20–5:01 p.m. *FRUS,* vol. E-7, White House tapes, Oval Office 635-8, 10 December 1971, 10:51–11:12 a.m. NSC Files, Box 748, Presidential Correspondence File, Nixon to Mujib, 4 April 1972.

58. Archer K. Blood, *The Cruel Birth of Bangladesh: Memoirs of an American Diplomat* (Dacca: University Press of Bangladesh, 2002), p. 258.

59. Blood, *Cruel Birth,* pp. 291, 323, 331–32, 258. Library of Congress, Association for Diplomatic Studies and Training, Foreign Affairs Oral History Project, Archer Blood interview, 27 June 1989.

60. H. R. Haldeman, *The Haldeman Diaries: Inside the Nixon White House* (New York: G. P. Putnam's Sons, 1994), 14 June 1971, p. 300. Blood, *Cruel Birth,* p. 345. Library of Congress, Association for Diplomatic Studies and Training, Foreign Affairs Oral History Project, Archer Blood interview, 27 June 1989.

61. Library of Congress, Association for Diplomatic Studies and Training, Foreign Affairs Oral History Project, Archer Blood interview, 27 June 1989.

62. Blood, *Cruel Birth,* p. 348. Library of Congress, Association for Diplomatic Studies and Training, Foreign Affairs Oral History Project, Archer Blood interview, 27 June 1989.

63. Blood, *Cruel Birth,* p. 348. Judith A. Chammas remarks, Archer K. Blood American Center Library Dedication, 13 December 2005, at http://dhaka.usembassy.gov/12.13.05_american_center_library.html. Joe Holley, "Archer K. Blood, Dissenting Diplomat," *Washington Post,* 23 September 2004, p. B4. Library of Congress, Association for Diplomatic Studies and Training, Foreign Affairs Oral History Project, Archer Blood interview, 27 June 1989.

Acknowledgments

This book was made by the generosity of many good people. At William Morris Endeavor, Tina Bennett is simply the perfect agent: a resolute champion for this work, always looking to make it smarter. Her intellect and cheer made this book possible, and her friendship kept me going. Svetlana Katz, as usual, was unfailingly superb.

At Knopf, Andrew Miller led the charge for this book and did a virtuoso job of editing it, elegantly improving its argument, structure, and line. It is an honor that Sonny Mehta believed in this project, as well as enhancing it with his peerless knowledge of South Asia. Mark Chiusano, a real young literary talent, skillfully steered the manuscript to completion. Meru Gokhale at Vintage India expertly refined the narrative, and made sure this book was properly launched in South Asia. Chip Kidd designed a spectacular jacket, while Knopf's editing and production team made a beautiful book. And all of us mourn the loss of the great Ashbel Green, a paragon of his craft.

The manuscript had the benefit of wise advice and close reading by extraordinary writers: Peter Baker, Peter Canellos, Thomas Christensen, Michael Grunwald, Robert Keohane, Atul Kohli, Rahul Sagar, Amy Waldman, and John Fabian Witt.

For help with my research and travels in South Asia, thanks to Kanchan Chandra, Niraja Gopal Jayal, Pratap Bhanu Mehta, Uday Mehta, David Rohde, Madhuri Sondhi, Shivaji Sondhi, Alexander Star, and Sabrina Tavernise. Srinath Raghavan deserves particular praise both for his kindness and exemplary scholarship. And I'm especially grateful to the participants in these events who patiently shared their recollections and double-checked their records.

At the Nehru Memorial Museum and Library, one of India's towering liberal institutions, my thanks to Mridula Mukherjee, Deepa Bhatnagar, Bhashyam Kasturi, Neelam Vatsa, and Sanjeev Gautham. The new director, Mahesh Ranagrajan, was most helpful. At the National Archives of India, another splendid institution, thanks to Mushirhul Hasan, the director general, and to Jaya Ravindran, G. A. Biradar, Jagmohan Singh and his team, and all the staff in the research room.

In California, my gratitude to Timothy Naftali, Paul Wormser, Jon Fletcher, and the other helpful staff at the Nixon Presidential Library. I'm also grateful to the hardworking staff at the U.S. National Archives. Nate Jones at the invaluable National Security Archive helped with continuing adventures in the Freedom of Information Act. And Keri Matthews at the Miller Center of Public Affairs at the University of Virginia assisted in tracking down elusive White House tapes.

Throughout the long writing process, I learned from the wisdom of David Armitage, Michael Doyle, Noah Feldman, Martha Finnemore, Aaron Friedberg, John Lewis Gaddis, Jack Goldsmith, Ryan Goodman, Oona Hathaway, Stanley Hoffmann, John Ikenberry, Stathis Kalyvas, Devesh Kapur, Stephen Krasner, Thomas Laqueur, Andrew Moravcsik, Joseph Nye, Nathaniel Persily, Kal Raustiala, Stephen Peter Rosen, Scott Sagan, Kathryn Sikkink, Anne-Marie Slaughter, Jack Snyder, and Michael Walzer. At the *New York Times,* Katherine Bouton, Barry Gewen, Pamela Paul, Clay Risen, and Sam Tanenhaus graciously let me try out some of these ideas in their pages.

In Beijing, Evan Osnos provided Cultural Revolution biographies, good counsel, and *jiaozi*. Alastair Iain Johnston, Roderick MacFarquhar, and Wang Jisi explained the Chinese parts of the puzzle. Gao Wenqian provided background on Zhou Enlai.

Laura Schiller and Laura Sullivan at the Senate Foreign Relations Committee searched for congressional records. Bill Emmott and the staff at the London Library in St. James's gave a wonderful place for research and writing. Sean Wilentz and David Kinney guided me to lore on the Concert for Bangladesh, and Mark Feldstein kindly offered help to a complete stranger.

I was lucky to have the help of intrepid research assistants. In Delhi, Ravindra Karnena, a gifted scholar, helped to hunt down some wayward files. In Princeton, Anna Schrimpf organized thousands of pages of documents. Princeton's University Committee on Research in the Humanities and Social Sciences gave a welcome grant to hire superb undergraduates to help me through the morass of the White House tapes. Stephanie Jordan, Joie Hand, Eric Levenson, and Shaina Watrous ably made preliminary transcriptions of scratchy tape recordings, as well as interpreting them with astute psychological insights into Nixon and Kissinger.

In Princeton, thanks to Ceci Rouse, Christina Paxson, and Stephen Kotkin, as well as to the university, for generously covering my research expenses. It's an ongoing privilege to work with Rita Alpaugh, whose graceful professionalism keeps everything running smoothly, despite me. Sandra Johnson and Jennifer Widdis in Nassau Hall helped with my travels. And Nancy Pressman Levy and Terry Caton chased down South Asian papers and books.

I would be nowhere without my old friends: Nurith Aizenman, Michael Dorff, Ariela Dubler, Daniel Franklin, Jason Furman, Jesse Furman, Susan Glasser, Jon Gross, Rebecca Musher Gross, Sarah Cahn Handelsman, Jed Kolko, Jack Levy, Alison Wakoff Loren, Rory MacFarquhar, Rebecca Noonan Murray, Samantha Power, and Richard Primus—plus double thanks here to Peter Baker, Peter Canellos, and Michael Grunwald, for unflagging encouragement as well as editing. Mark Wiedman and Dana Kirchman—and my young friends Sam and Ben—provided a serene haven for frenzied writing. My friend Peter David, always bursting with warmth and joy, was taken from us far too young.

Love and thanks, as ever, to my family: grandmother, brother, and all, and the memory of my grandparents. I still can't thank my parents, Arthur and Karen Bass, enough. And my heartfelt thanks to Jon, Suzanne, and Daniel Glenn for welcoming me warmly into our new family.

My brilliant and lovely wife, Katherine Glenn Bass, is my first and last consult on human rights issues and everything else. From Harare to Brooklyn, she provided love, insight, support, and baked goods. With all my love, this book is dedicated to her.

Index

Page numbers in *italics* refer to the map.